THE

Province and the States

A HISTORY OF THE PROVINCE OF LOUISIANA UNDER
FRANCE AND SPAIN, AND OF THE TERRITORIES
AND STATES OF THE UNITED STATES
FORMED THEREFROM

IN SEVEN VOLUMES

ILLUSTRATED WITH NUMEROUS MAPS AND PORTRAITS

Weston Arthur Goodspeed, LL. B.

Editor-in-Chief

VOL. I

MADISON, WIS.
THE WESTERN HISTORICAL ASSOCIATION
1904.

Press of the Democrat Printing Co., Madison, Wis.

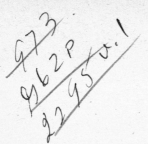
Table of Contents

CHAPTER V.

CHAPTER VI.

CHAPTER VII.

CHAPTER VIII.

CHAPTER XIII.

Illustrations

The Province and the States

CHAPTER I

Spanish Explorations and Discoveries

THE discovery of America by Columbus opened to Spain an opportunity such as never again fell to the lot of that ignorant and expiring nation. She had passed the summit of her glory, had sanctioned the barbarities of innumerable conquests, and had witnessed the moth-like delight of her fawning nobles; but with fatuous blindness had wholly disregarded the call of the scythe and the grateful peans of the plow. Her civilization had sprung from the gospel of the Inquisition, from the creak of the rack, from the expulsion of learning, from the death chants of burning heretics, and from the nightmare of a distorted, brutal and barbarous Christianity. The husbandman and his family were classed with the swine that root in the ground. He was kicked, cowed, cursed and robbed by court and church, by state and supernumerary. The glory of Spain had become the exile and degradation of labor and the enthronement and deification of caste, ignorance and priest-craft. The blasting stupidity of the priests perverted the religion established by the Almighty and proclaimed to all mankind by Jesus of Nazareth. The priestly orders gave their consent to murderous conquest, crime for gold and the unprincipled splendors of church and state. The wealth of the nation in rippling fields of grain, homes of intelligent and happy children, the reign of liberty's beneficent laws, the nobility of labor, and the piety of perpetual peace, was undreamed of and unknown to the swaggering grandees, who thronged the fair

I—2

Spanish cities and jeered at the laborer rooting in the adjacent soil. The nation that took delight in the hideous spectacle of the Spanish bull-fights could not be expected to emblazon "Kindness" on its bloody banner. A people who regarded all persons other than Catholics as heretics fit only for the rack or the stake, found an easy excuse for the deliberate slaughter of the Indian heretics in the New World. In the name of God—Jesus—Mary the glittering Toledo blades of De Soto's grandees and Coronado's cavaliers drank the blood of the natives with the sanction of the priests, just as the Inquisition destroyed other unbelievers in Old Spain. The religion of Castile and Aragon was the murder of heretics; and murderous conquest was the Spanish colonial policy. So the golden opportunity of adding to this miserable civilization a splendid realm of domestic happiness and industrial wealth was wholly unappreciated by the priests and the nobility who dominated the Spanish court. She passed blunderingly by a magnificent empire, which later shone in the West like a star, inviting the wise men of the East to come here to worship at the shrine of domestic happiness and a just Christianity. But her wise men were wanting. They had overridden their camels of conquest and were lost in the desert of their own crimes. She was doomed to decadence from the inherited evil festering in her own cruel and ignorant heart. But listen to the cruel story.*

So far as known Americus Vespucci and his companions were the first persons to view the coast of what is now Louisiana. His numerous business reverses in early life caused him to join the large class of discontented explorers and adventurers then abounding in Spain; and having heard, of course, of the discovery by Columbus of a land to the westward filled with gold and other treasures, he determined to sail at the first opportunity that should offer satisfactory advantages. He accordingly applied to King Ferdinand for service in one of the expeditions destined by the crown for the New World. The Spanish monarchs had previously granted a monopoly of exploration in the west to Columbus; but in April, 1495, this order was revoked and freedom of navigation was opened to all "merchant-adventurers." Four ships were accordingly sent out May 10, 1497, upon one of which stood the man, who, wholly unknown to himself, was thus embarked on the voyage which was destined to perpetuate his name so long as the human race should exist.

It should be said that the monopoly of exploration in the West

---

* Don Bartholomew de las Casas, bishop of Chiapa, states that the Spaniards destroyed forty millions of people in the Americas.

was renewed to Columbus in June, 1497, but too late to stay the sailing of the fleet of Vespucci. It is not known what position in the fleet was assigned to him; but it is known that he possessed a considerable degree of freedom and authority. He was qualified for the duties of astronomer, pilot and navigator and for ship or fleet supercargo, and probably officiated in one of these responsible positions. Although not certainly known, it is presumed on good grounds that Vincente Yañez Pinzon, who had formerly seen service in one of the western expeditions under Columbus, and Juan Diaz de Solis were the chief commanders of the fleet. There is no surviving account of the expedition by either of the above captians, there is but a partial one by Vespucci. Attempts often and even yet made to besmirch the good name of Vecpucci have given place in recent years to the discovery that this expedition passed entirely round the Gulf of Mexico, examining in many places the coast, and occasionally landing where the shore and weather conditions were propitious, instead of passing southward along the coast of South America, as has been so persistently urged by many historians, particularly the Spanish. Varnhagen was the first to show that the expedition of 1497 should not be confounded with any other, and that the whole Gulf coast was traversed and partially explored by this expedition. It cannot be shown that Vespucci was dishonest or that he ever tried to deprive Columbus of any discovery to which he was entitled. On the contrary, his name, which he placed on the maps of the New World made by him, was applied by others to the newly discovered continent. Columbus himself, in a letter to his son Diego Columbus, dated February 5, 1505, said of him: "I spoke with Amerigo Vespucci, the bearer hereof, who is going yonder on business of navigation. He has ever had a desire to do me pleasure; he is a very worthy man; fortune has been adverse to him as to many others; his labors have not profited him so much as justice would require. * * * He goes resolved to do for me everything that shall be possible to him. See yonder in what he can be benefited, and exert yourself for him." Inasmuch as the narratives of Vespucci were already in circulation and had unquestionably been seen by Columbus, it must be admitted that the latter made no complaint, and hence had suffered no wrong by act of the former. The old charge of fraud should, therefore, be withdrawn. The text of the *Lettura* of Vespucci recently published shows all the features of originality—faults of grammar and style, errors of location, the blending of coarse words, the narration of indelicate incidents, which would never have appeared in a letter intentionally prepared to deceive.

There is no doubt that an account of the first voyage of Vespucci was promptly published in Spain, but like thousands of other records of that time it has since disappeared. The positive fact that the account of the first voyage, though circulated both by the participants and by the press, was not disputed with lasting emphasis from a dozen sources, is convincing evidence that the voyage was actually made. Neither Columbus nor his relatives ever denied that the expedition was accomplished in 1497-8. "But upon one point, it is to be observed, there is no difference among them; the voyage of 1501—the first from Portugal—is always the third of the four voyages of Vespucci. This disposes, as Humboldt points out, of the charge that Vespucci waited till after the death of Columbus, in 1506, before he ventured to assert publicly that he had made two voyages by order of the King of Spain prior to entering the service of the King of Portugal."* Thus it is positively known that before the death of Columbus in 1506, Vespucci publicly asserted that he had made four voyages, and that the assertion was not challenged by Columbus, nor after his death by his relatives. Neither was Vespucci such a nonentity as is claimed by some. In 1508 he was appointed major pilot of the kingdom of Spain by King Ferdinand, and probably still occupied the office at the time of his death February 22, 1512.

With the New World and all relating to it on everybody's lip, with the first voyage of Vespucci made public in print, by maps and by the eager tongues of participants, it is preposterous now, in the absence of strong and positive proof, to attempt to show that Vespucci did not make his first voyage substantially as claimed by him at the time and not disputed. If the claim had been false, it would have been known to be so by scores then living; yet there is no record to show that any protest against it was then registered, in face of the fact that the claim was publicly and widely heralded. On the contrary, almost from the start, cartographers, or map-makers, began to apply the name "America" to their representations of the mainland of the New World. There was no cry *then* of the great injustice done Columbus. The strong fact remains that the continent was named America within ten or fifteen years after its discovery and while scores of men were yet living in Spain who were familiar with all the

---

*Narrative and Critical History of America, Vol. II, p. 146.

circumstances of the voyages. If a wrong was done, why did they not publicly proclaim the fact, as they would certainly have done with emphasis? Were there no other facts to sustain the rights of Vespucci, it would be sufficient to state that his claims, though published within ten years after the close of the voyage, remained undisputed and uncontroverted until all the participants were in their graves.

There does not appear any good reason for supposing that from 1492 to 1521 the northern coast of the Gulf was not traversed and partially explored. This was a long period—nearly thirty years.‡ The white inhabitants of the West Indies had become numerous, and were all a sea-faring people. It is more than probable that the coast of Florida and of the country still farther to the west, probably as far as the coast of Louisiana, was explored by clandestine expeditions or others, even though no general attempt was made to penetrate the interior nor to form colonies. That the coast had been traversed prior to the publication of the map of 1521, is pretty conclusively shown by several maps printed at an earlier date, notably that of 1513,* which gives generally the peninsula of Florida, and shows the Gulf coast with a considerable degree of accuracy, and a large river with several mouths farther to the westward, embracing many features of that of the Mississippi.

There no longer can be any doubt that the first white men to explore thoroughly the present coast of Louisiana and the mouth of the mighty Mississippi, were those who accompanied the fleet commanded by Alonso Alvarez de Pineda from Jamaica to the northwest in the year 1519.† This exploration was made under the direction and at the expense of Francisco D'Garay, governor of the island of Jamaica, a man of no little wealth, prestige and ambition, who was mainly influenced to do so by the reports received from Cordova and Grijalva of the immense wealth of what is now Mexico, from which land they had but recently returned, laden with gold ornaments of immense value and with tales of the still greater wonders of the country.** These tales were too alluring for D'Garay to resist; therefore, having secured from the sovereign of Spain permission to prosecute discoveries to the west and northwest or elsewhere, and having

---

‡ Henry Harrisse states that between 1492 and 1504 no less than sixty-six expeditions were made to the New World. See Discovery of North America, 1892. Harrisse.

* The Geography of Ptolomeus, printed at Venice in 1513.

† Peter Martyr.

** They brought back gold to the value of $37,000.

learned all that was possible from discoveries already made in
that section of the world, particularly of the coast in the vicinity
of what is now Panuco, Mexico, where the natives were reported
immensely rich, he fitted out a fleet of four caravels, having on
board two hundred and forty men, including a detachment of
cavalry, and many cross-bowmen and musketeers, and in 1519
set sail in the direction of the Florida coast. The sovereign of
Spain had graciously appointed him adelantado and governor of
the provinces through which ran the river San Pedro and San
Pablo (in Mexico) and of any other lands which he should be so
fortunate as to discover. The supreme command of the fleet was
committed to the distinguished navigator, Alonso Alvarez de
Pineda.* They sailed directly to the coast of Florida (then
called Bimini), which at that time was thought to be an island
by many persons, because they believed that they could more
easily conquer an island than a portion of the mainland of equal
size and strength. In due time they landed on the Florida coast;
but the natives were so savage and such terrible fighters and
wounded so many of them, that they boarded their vessels again
and continued along the coast to the westward, passing the
region called Amichel, the first term applied by Europeans to
Louisiana, landing often, communicating with the natives and
learning all they could concerning the wealth of the country.
They finally came to the river Panuco, about five hundred leagues
to the westward of Florida. At no place had they found the
natives friendly; all had shown the most intense hostility, and had
bitterly opposed any attempt to land, but notwithstanding this
opposition they often went ashore and took possession of the adjacent country in the name of the king of Spain. Many of the
Spaniards were killed at the landing near the mouth of the river
Panuco, on what is now the coast of Mexico. The natives were
cannibals, eating all who fell into their hands and hanging their
skins in their temples to commemorate the victories.‡

"They sailed eight or nine months. * * * Among other
lands low and barren which they discovered, they came across the
country of Florida found by Ponce de Leon; and having sighted
and noticed the same, endeavored to range it, so as to advance
further. But they were unable to do so, on account of the land
which barred the way in extending eastwardly. For that reason,
and owing to constant head winds and strong currents, they were

* Historia verdadera de la conquista de la Nueva Espana: Diaz.
  The memoirs of the conquistador: Lockhart."

‡ Tratado, que compos e nobre & notauel capitao Antonio Galuao.

compelled to alter the course of the ships, and followed the coast towards the west, examining carefully the country, harbours, rivers, inhabitants, and all that which deserved to be noted on the said coast. They thus continued sailing until they met with Fernando Cortes and the Spaniards who were in the same locality. When there, they marked the limit of the country which they had discovered; and wherever they made discoveries and coasted, which extended over more than three hundred leagues, they took possession in our name. They then turned back with the said ships, and entered a river which was found to be very large and deep, at the mouth of which they said they found an extensive town, where they remained forty days and careened their vessels. The natives treated our men in a friendly manner, trading with them, and giving what they possessed. The Spaniards ascended a distance of six leagues up the river, and saw on its banks, right and left, forty villages." * This is the description of the voyage of 1519, written on the letters patent to D'Garay.

"Francisco D'Garay appeared and said that with the authorization of His Majesty, and at his own cost, he sent four ships to discover new countries for the service of the Crown; which were found and discovered by the grace of God our Lord, who showed the way. Nor was a landing effected in any land or part already found or disclosed by any one else at any time. This was from the Rio del Espiritu Santo (Mississippi) over a great extent of country, further below in the direction of the north (sic) towards the river called San Pedro e San Pablo, where the ships arrived."† The authorities unite in locating the San Pedro and

---

* Navarette. The original Spanish of this account is as follows: "Anduvieron ocho ó nueve meses * * entre otra tierra baja esteril que descubrieron toparon la tierra Florida. * * y reconocida y vista quisieron la costear para pasar adelante, è no pudieron, porque le salia la tierra por la proas en derecho donde nace el sol, y por esto y por el viento que res fué siempre contrario, y por la mucha corriente que ansi mismo hallaron, fueles forzado volver costeando la tierra hacia el poniente, por la cual costa fueron muy bien mirando la tierra, puertos, é rios è gente della, è todo lo demas que se debia miror, é tanto andovreron hasta que toparon con Hernando Cortés e los españoles que con el estaban en la misma costa, é llegados allí amojon aron el término hasta donde habian descubierto, é en todo lo que descubieron e costearon, que fueron mas de tres cientas leguas, se tomo posesion ¡en nuestro nomore, é fecho todo esto, se tornaron con los dichos navios hâcias otras, y entraron por un rio que hallaron muy grande y muy caudalosa, á la entrada del cual diz que hallaron un grande pueblo, y estovieron en él mas de cuarenta dias los navios dando carena, e la gente de la tierra muy pacilica con los españoles que en la dicha armada idan, tratando con ellos y cándoles de la que tenian en término de seis leguas que entraron por el dicho rio arriba. Los dichos navios hallaron cuarenta pueblos de una parte y de otra."

† "Parescio Francisco de Garay . . . con licencia de S. M. e a su propria costa, imbio con quatro navios a descobrir tierras nuevas en su Real Servicio, las quales fueron falladas e descobiertas per gracia de Dios Nuestro Señor, que lo encamino, non tocando a Tierra ni en patre alguna que otra persona oblese fallado nin descobiorto en ningund tiempo, que fue dende Rio del Espiritu Santo, e aun mucha parte de tierra mas abaxo hacia el Norte, hacia el rio que discen de San Pedro e San Pablo, donde llegaron los navios." The sworn testimony of Francisco de Garay concerning the discoveries made by himself or under his authority and direction at that date and filed in the Archives of the Indias at Seville.

San Pablo river as far south on the Gulf coast as Tampico, Mexico. The Rio del Espiritu Santo is the Mississippi. According to these statements it seems clear that D'Garay, in 1519, coasted, if he did not actually discover, the shore from the Mississippi southwest to within about three score of miles of Vera Cruz. The sworn statement of D'Garay was necessarily short, and was designed merely to embrace the substance of his discoveries, without particularizing the two trips back and forth along the coast, nor without entering into an account of his discoveries, such detail not being germane to the purposes of the testimony. The affidavit of D'Garay was no doubt intended to be used as an official document to establish the right of Spain to the lands discovered under his patent. In his affidavit he says, "Nor was a landing effected (by the expedition) in any land or part already found or disclosed by any one else at any time." ‡ This is only saying that he made no landing whatever on land that had been discovered before by any one else at any time; or that all the land that this expedition did discover had not previously been discovered by others. The truth of the above description in the letters patent, may be depended upon; because the entry was placed there by the regents, who were acting for Charles V, of Spain, in his absence, and who received it fresh from the expedition and inscribed it in permanent form on the patent itself, a precaution doubtless intended to prevent the separation of the patent and an account of the discovery made under its authorization. At the mouth of the Mississippi they found a large Indian village, but on which side is not stated. Here they remained forty days, beaching their boats, re-caulking them doubtless, securing fresh water, conversing and trading with the friendly natives, ascending the river to the distance of fifteen miles and observing forty other villages on both sides of the river, and taking possession of the whole country in the name of the king of Spain.*

Of course, the large village which D'Garay stated had been found by his expedition at the mouth of the Rio del Espiritu Santo, must not be regarded as one of fixed habitation and other conditions of permanency. Nearly all of the coast Indians were accustomed to go to the interior during the season of ripe fruits; but when these supplies were unripe or exhausted they sought the

---

‡ See Las Casas Lib. II and III; also Herrera; also Navarette.

* It should be borne in mind that D'Garay did not make the voyage himself. De Pineda commanded the expedition, and Camargo was one of the captains under him. These men or their assistants made a full and complete report to D'Garay, who thereupon sent an account of the same to the court of Spain, in accordance with the stipulations of his charter or patent. D'Garay did not witness the events he described.

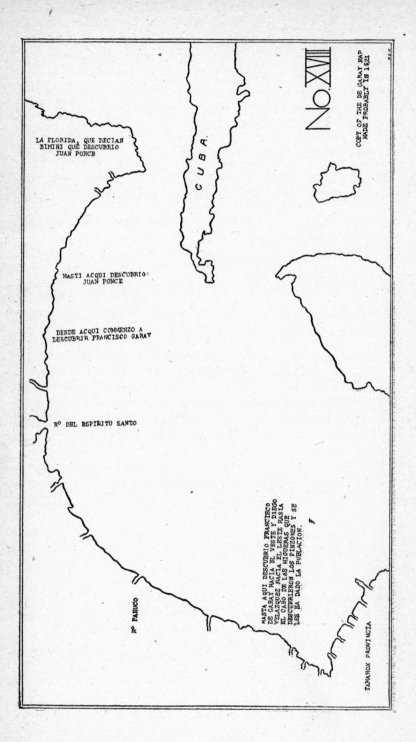

No. XVII

COPY OF THE DE GARAY MAP
MADE PROBABLY IN 1621

CUBA.

LA FLORIDA, QUE DECIAN
BIMINI QUÉ DESCUBRIO
JUAN PONCE

HASTI ACQUI DESCUBRIO:
JUAN PONCE

DESDE ACQUI COMMENZO A
DESCUBRIR FRANCISCO GARAY

Rº DEL ESPIRITU SANTO

Rº PANUCO

HASTA AQUI DESCUBRIO FRANCISCO
DE GARAY HACIA EL VESTE Y DIEGO
VELAZQUEZ HACIA EL LESTE HASTA
EL CABO DE LAS HIGUERAS QUE
DESCUBRIERON LOS PINZONES Y SE
LES HA DADO LA POBLACION.

TAMAHOX PROVINCIA

coast for the shell-fish, etc., cast up by the ocean. Consequently, they lived in temporary huts or wigwams, which could be removed and taken with them on their journeys. They were found here by the Spaniards in July and August, 1519, before the fruits of the interior had become ripe, and before the annual excursion had begun. It would seem at the first glance that forty villages were too great a number to be strung along the Mississippi on both sides for the distance of six leagues or about fifteen miles upward from its mouth; but they were unquestionably small collections of wigwams, probably from ten to thirty, with a half dozen occupants to each wigwam, the representatives, no doubt, of some tribe which then occupied the coast near the mouth of the Mississippi.

On the accompanying map the Spanish statement "La Florida, que decian Bimini, que descubrio Juan Ponce," means "The Florida, called Bimini, discovered by Juan Ponce." "Hasta aqui descubrio Juan Ponce" means, "As far as this was discovered by Juan Ponce." "Desde aqui comenzo a descubrir Francisco Garay." interpreted means "From here Francisco Garay commenced to discover." "Rio del Espiritu Santo" means "River of the Holy Spirit," and is the present Mississippi. "Rio Panuco" is the "River Panuco." "Hasta aqui descubrio Francisco de Garay hacia el uste, y Diego Velazquez hacia el Leste hasta el cabo de las Higueras (figs), que descubrieron los Pinzones, y se les ha dado la poblacion," means, "As far as this place Francisco de Garay discovered toward the west, and Diego Velazquez toward the east, as far as Cabo de las Higueras, which the Pinzons discovered, and the country has given it to them to settle." "Co. y Pa. de las Higueras" means "Cape and Beach of the Figs." Thus, according to this map, D'Garay (or Pineda for him) was the discoverer of the coast from what is now probably Pensacola bay, or possibly Appalachicola bay, westward and then southward along the Gulf coast to the vicinity of Tampico, Mexico. The map was entitled, "Traza de las costas de tierra firme y de las tierras nueves," meaning "Tracing of the coast of the main land and of the new lands."*

Apparently in order to avoid conflict between the explorers of the Gulf coast, their spheres of discovery and conquest seem to have been surveyed and apportioned to them by the patents or commissions under which they acted. Thus it was that Pineda, acting for D'Garay, directed his movements against Panuco instead

---

*Historia verdadera de la conquista de la Nueva Espana: Diaz. Also, see Coleccion de los Viages y Descubrimientos: Navarette.

of some other point of the Gulf coast. Thus, also, the map-makers of Europe became aware of their spheres of action, and marked the same on some of the early charts of discovery. On one of these maps published in 1521,* the Gulf coast is traced and the boundaries of the respective spheres of conquest are fully defined. The four explorers who, at this period, were most active on this coast were Leon, D'Garay, Pineda, Grijalva and Cordova. By reference to the map herewith, it will be observed that the sphere of action for Ponce de Leon was the coast of Florida, probably as far west as Appalachicola bay; thence to the west about as far as Pensacola bay was a vacant or neutral zone of discovery, ready, doubtlessly, for some ambitious discoverer; thence to the west and southwest past Panuco was the field conceded to D'Garay and his representative, De Pineda; and so on to the southeast for the others. Within the field of D'Garay and Pineda will be seen marked Rio del Espirito Santo (River of the Holy Spirit), the only stream named on the map. This was the Mississippi, and was the first term applied to that mighty river. This designation (1521) seems to have been the first unquestionable notice and naming of the Mississippi. Other earlier maps, showing rivers, cannot be said to have definitely and positively located the Mississippi, nor assigned it a name.

The experiences of Alvar Nunez Cabeza de Vaca and his companions, Andres Dorantes, Alonso del Castillo Maldonado and Estevanico, an Arabian, seem to be well authenticated. They accompanied the expedition of Pamphilo de Narvez in 1527 from the West Indies to the Florida coast, were shipwrecked, and afterward sailed westward along the shore in small boats, passing the mouth of the Mississippi, which they noticed poured such a large stream into the Gulf that they took fresh water from the sea. This was in November, 1528. The boat in which was De Vaca was finally cast ashore, either on the western Louisiana or the eastern Texas coast, on an island about thirteen miles long by one and a half miles broad. The island was named Malhado, or Misfortune, by the Spaniards. The Indians at this spot were called Cadoques and Hans. In all, about eighty of the Spaniards reached this island; but at the end of a year they were reduced to about fifteen by death from disease and from the arrows of the savages. The men mentioned above passed five or six years in this vicinity, living like the Indians and with them. During a considerable portion of the time their only food was the prickly

*Coleccion de los Viages y Descubrimientos: Vol. III.—Navarette.

pear, which fact alone proves that they were in Texas. The Ata-
yos referred to by De Vaca were the Adais of later times. The
Huacos were the Wacos, and the Querechos were the Apaches of
the plains, all in modern Texas. The mountains mentioned were
those of central Texas. The Querechos were the same as those
encountered by Coronado a few years later. Having passed northwest through modern Texas, they finally turned southwest and in
due time reached the Spanish settlements of Mexico.

With the explorations of Hernando de Soto, these volumes
have nothing to do save as they relate to the tract of country
embraced within what is now called the "Louisiana Purchase."
His expedition to Florida was for the purpose of finding gold
and jewels. He expected to find the conditions similar to those
of Mexico and Peru, and therefore took with him an army of
about 1,000 soldiers and cavaliers, three hundred and fifty horses,
many fierce bloodhounds, and a large herd of swine. They left
San Lucar in April, 1538, and reached Cuba the latter part of
May, where they remained a year, making thorough preparations
for the conquest of Florida. They landed at Tampa bay, and
afterward marched through Florida, Georgia, Alabama and Mississippi, consuming much time, slaughtering the inhabitants as
they advanced, forcing at the point of the sword provisions from
the hapless natives, and inquiring eagerly for gold and jewels.

They finally came to a small village called Chisca situated near
the banks of the largest river they had ever beheld—no other, in
fact, than the mighty Mississippi. So far as known, this was the
third discovery by white men of this river.* At this spot the
stream was about a mile and a half in width, and the Spaniards
noted that on its vast bosom were borne large quantities of trees
and brush-wood. They were wholly unaware of the importance
of their discovery. Their dreams of riches had fixed wholly in
their minds the thought that every other object than gold was
too base and ignoble to be entertained by the nobility of Spain
in the expedition. It was to them but another difficult stream to
be crossed, only another bar stretched between them and their
gossamer dreams of opulence. They recked not that the navies
of the Old World might ascend the mighty stream, conveying the
commerce of the centuries to millions of civilized beings on its
fertile banks. No such visions lighted their weary marches, vigils
and battles—the only castle in this New Spain was that of GOLD.

Across the wide and rolling river the Spaniards saw a fair and

---

* This spot was probably a short distance below the present city of Helena,
Arkansas, and also below the *old* mouth of the St. Francis river.

fertile land. There, it was hoped, their chances would improve and the expected eldorado be found. The Indians of Chisca had heard nothing of the approach of the Spaniards, but the excesses of the intruders soon roused them to war. Their province was called by them Chucagua, and the same name was applied by them to the great river. The Spaniards had now dwindled to about five hundred men, from whom the dreams of glory, wealth and fame had long since fled. It was now almost a solemn procession of warriors, resigned to their fate in the wilderness under the unconquerable De Soto. With great difficulty, permission was obtained from the chief to remain at the village for six days to nurse his sick and wounded.* Peace must be sought at almost any price, because it was seen by De Soto that about four thousand warriors had been assembled in the space of three hours, and there was no telling how soon as many more might be summoned. At the end of the stay, De Soto warmly thanked the cacique, as the chief was called by his subjects, and the Spaniards marched up the eastern bank of the river. After four days of passage through almost impenetrable thickets, following the windings of the stream, during which time they progressed but twenty-eight miles, they reached a broad opening on elevated ground, covered with rich grass, at which point the river was about a mile and a half wide. During this time they no doubt passed the mouth of the St. Francis river on the opposite shore. From the hills large numbers of Indians could be seen on the opposite bank, apparently drawn up in battle array, with hundreds of canoes lining the shore. Regardless of the hostile array across the river, De Soto resolved to cross at this point. He encamped, and for twenty days was busily engaged in constructing four large flat boats designed to carry his expedition to the other side. The Indians on the eastern bank became quite friendly and supplied the Spaniards with provisions; but those on the west side showed their hostility by coming as near to the shore as possible and firing showers of arrows at the intruders.

One day while thus engaged, the Spaniards saw to their surprise a fleet of fully two hundred large canoes filled with Indians descending the river, decked in the array of war, with gaudy plumes and military paraphernalia, all gleaming in the sun, and greatly impressing the Spaniards with their fighting strength. The latter made friendly overtures, and the boats drew near the

---

* This account is taken mainly from the record of the Inca Garcilasso de la Vega, translated from the French version of Pierre Richelet, which was translated from the original Spanish.

shore. The Indians were armed with bows, arrows, lances and shields of buffalo hide and were powerfully built and athletic. De Soto stood on the shore to greet them, and was thus addressed by the leading cacique or chief: "I am told that you are the leading officer of the most powerful Cacique in the world. I have, therefore, come to tender you my friendship and to aid you so far as I am able." But this fair speech had an immediate set-back. Treacherous intentions were discovered among the whites, hostile movements were made, and the Indians drew off, discharging a flight of arrows as they went, and receiving in return a volley from the cross-bows of the Spaniards, which killed several and wounded others.

From this time forward during the process of construction of the boats, it was necessary to guard them night and day to prevent their being burned by the savages, who seemed determined to prevent the attempt to cross the river. Four boats were finally finished and launched with one hundred and eighty Spaniards, who upon landing found no one to oppose them on the Arkansas side. Rapidly the trips were made until the entire expedition was safe across. They were the second body of Europeans known positively to navigate the Mississippi and to stand upon the soil of what later became the "Louisiana Purchase." After demolishing their boats and saving the iron therefrom, they set off in a northwesterly direction and after four days of arduous travel through an uninhabited region, saw from an eminence which they had ascended an Indian town of about four hundred houses "upon the banks of a river larger than the Guadalquiver which passes by Cordova." Large fields of corn and many fruit trees were seen spread over the valley. This town was undoubtedly on the St. Francis river, probably in what is now either the county of Cross or St. Francis, Arkansas. It was probably not lower, because the distance traveled to reach it—four days—must be accounted for. The inhabitants had learned of their approach and came out to meet and greet them. They placed their property and persons under the protection of the Spaniards and supplied them with provisions. "The capital, the province and the Cacique were called Casquia or Casquin. The Spaniards stopped six days in the town, because of the provisions which they found there. And after two days of marching they arrived at some small villages where the lord of the country held his court, and which were distant four leagues from the capital in ascending the river."* Here the Spaniards were well received and made com-

---

* This was still on the St. Francis river, which the Spaniards had not yet left.

fortable, a decided relief from the incessant war they had encountered on the other side of the Mississippi. Thus the inhabitants
of the Louisiana Purchase from the start have been friendly and
hospitable. The fields of corn, pumpkins, beans, etc., were so
large and numerous, that the Portuguese account speaks of them
as "gardens."

While at Casquin (which was probably in either Cross or St.
Francis county, Arkansas), the cacique came to De Soto, and
after stating that he believed the God of the Spaniards was more
powerful than that of the Indians, begged him to ask for rain, of
which the fields of the natives stood greatly in need. De Soto
agreed, and in order to impress the Indians, directed his carpen-
ters to prepare an immense cross from the tallest pine tree they
could find in the vicinity, which they planted on a very "high
knoll on the borders of the river."* The next day a large procession of Spaniards and Indians, marching side by side, mounted
the knoll and advanced toward the cross, the priests and the
monks chanting their litanies, to which the soldiers responded.
Upon reaching the cross, they fell upon their knees, offering their
prayers to God, imploring for rain and for the success of the
expedition. "On the other side of the river there were about
fifteen or twenty thousand persons of all ages and sexes; they
raised their hands and eyes to heaven, and showed by their pos-
ture that they prayed God to grant to the Christians the favor
which they desired. There was also heard among them cries as
of people who wept, to obtain from heaven as soon as possible
their demand. So that the Spaniards had much joy to see their
Creator acknowledged and the cross adored in a country where
Christianity was unknown. Afterward the clergy sang the 'Te
Deum,' and the Spaniards and the Indians returned to the village in the same order that they had come. This lasted in all
more than four hours. In the meantime our Lord was pleased
to show the subjects of the Cacique Casquin that he heard the
prayers of his servants; for toward the middle of the following
night it began to rain. Some say that it rained during three
entire days and other six; so that the inhabitants of the province,
rejoicing at the favor which God granted them through the means
of the Christians, came with the Cacique to render thanks to the
general (De Soto) for it."* Whether the rain came as a result
of the prayers of these wicked Spaniards, or the prayers of the

*This was no doubt the first formal Christian ceremony in the Louisiana Pur-
chase. It occurred on the banks of the St. Francis river. It has been maintained
by some writers that this ceremony transpired on the banks of the Mississippi,
and in order to meet the description they have been obliged to assume that the

barbarous Indians, has never been satisfactorily explained. But the Spaniards had gained great prestige with the natives, which served them in good stead afterward.

After about ten days, accompanied voluntarily by the cacique and many servants carrying provisions, etc., and by a large troop of armed Indians, who designed to attack their enemies, the inhabitants of the province of Capaha, to which point the Spaniards desired to go, they again set forth in a northerly direction. With five thousand armed Indians and three thousand more carrying provisions and being likewise armed, the advance was made, the Indians leading, but being constantly in communication with the Spaniards. Early in the morning of the fourth day out, they came to a very large swamp, which divided the two provinces, and beyond which the enemy might be expected to be encountered. Having crossed the swamp after great difficulty, and having traveled three more days,* they reached an eminence from which they saw the capital of the province of Capaha. The town stood upon elevated ground, and comprised about five hundred houses, and was distant from the Chucagua or Mississippi river about nine miles. A canal or lagoon extended from the Mississippi to the town and thence completely around it, and was "at least as deep as a pike-staff, and so wide that two large boats abreast could ascend or descend it." This town probably stood in southeast Missouri, near New Madrid. The canal was probably a natural lagoon or bayou, improved somewhat by the Indians. This assumed location meets the requirements of the Portuguese description; no other supposition will. The ditch which surrounded the town was no doubt a loup of the bayou or canal proper, as it is called by the Portuguese writer, because, as it was very broad, deep and extended, it is not probable that the Indians themselves ever dug it. They simply took advantage of the surroundings by building their village on an island which was surrounded by a deep lagoon or bayou, but which they may have improved somewhat. "The ditch which is filled by the canal, surrounds the town, except in a place which is closed by a palisade of large posts fixed in the ground, fastened by other cross-pieces of wood, and plastered with loam and straw. There were,

Mississippi was so narrow that the faces of the natives could be seen and their weeping heard by those at the cross. The river where the cross was erected was the St. Francis, four days' journey northwest from their crossing place on the Mississippi. No other assumption meets the description.

* They thus traveled nine days up the St. Francis river and were now very probably in the vicinity of Kennett or Gayoso, Missouri, or perhaps as high as New Madrid.

besides, in this ditch and in this canal such a quantity of fish
that all the Spaniards and Indians who followed the general (De
Soto) fished from it without it appearing that they had taken a
single fish from it."

The cacique, Capaha,* perceiving the approach of the enemy,
and nearly all his warriors being absent, retreated a considerable
distance and took refuge on an island formed by the high waters
of the Mississippi, or Chucagua river, where he was protected
until the return of his warriors by the inaccessibility and heavy
timber of the position. The subjects of Casquin pillaged the
town, but were prevented from burning it by the efforts of De
Soto. They desecrated the tombs, killed about one hundred and
fifty persons, who were unable to escape, pillaged the "temple,"
and did everything they could to offend and insult their enemies.
But De Soto, by means of messengers, communicated with
Capaha, induced him to return, checked the attack of Casquin,
which he had not authorized, and ended finally by bringing the
two caciques, Casquin and Capaha, together in friendship, or
assumed friendship. But this was not accomplished until after
a battle had been fought, in which the warriors of Casquin and
the Spaniards had emphatically the worst of it. This so alarmed
the former that they fled, leaving the Spaniards to shift for themselves. Thus left to the mercy of probably twenty thousand
fighting warriors, who were far more valiant than any he had
yet encountered, De Soto very prudently and artfully made peace
with Capaha. The wisdom of the latter, who was described as
young and very handsome, contributed to the success of this diplomatic negotiation. The following remarkable occurrence is
narrated, to show the primitive dignity and sense of honor of the
natives, reproduced from the original description by the Portuguese writer, Garcilasso de la Vega:

"Capaha replied to De Soto that the greatest mark he could give
of his obedience was to do what he requested of him, and that he
was ready willingly to unite in friendship with Casquin; and
thereupon the two Caciques embraced each other, but apparently
their caresses were constrained. Nevertheless, they did not omit
to converse ingeniously with the general concerning Spain and
the provinces of Florida. Their conversation lasted until they
came to inform him that it was time to dine, and immediately they
passed into another room, where the table was set for three. The

---

* The Capahas, or Pacahas, were the modern Quapaws, and the Casquins were
the Kaskaskias, who then lived on the St. Francis river.

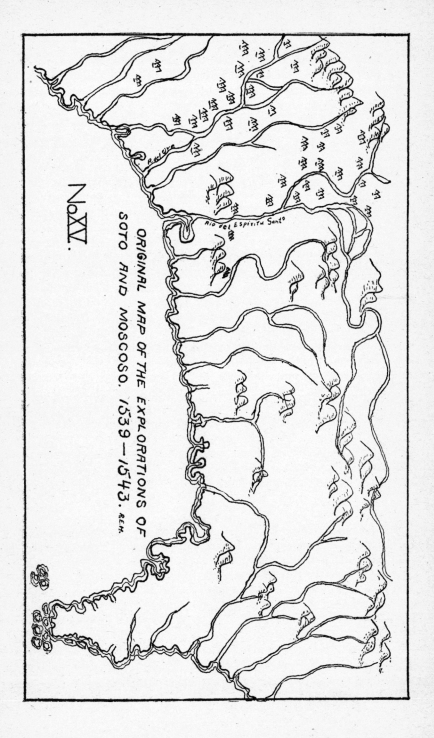

No.XV.

ORIGINAL MAP OF THE EXPLORATIONS OF
SOTO AND MOSCOSO. 1539—1543. R.E.H.

R. del Oro

Rio del Espiritu Santo

general placed himself at the upper end, and Casquin at his right, but Capaha civilly remonstrated with Casquin that as the most distinguished, most powerful and of a more illustrious nobility, that place belonged to him.　De Soto, who saw this contest, wished to know the cause of it, and when he had learned it, he said without regard to the advantages which the one had over the other, Capaha ought to have respect to the white hairs of Casquin, and accord to him the place the most honorable; that it was becoming a young lord, well-bred, to have consideration for the aged.　Capaha replied that if Casquin was his guest he would willingly concede the first place to him without even having regard to his age, but that eating at the table of a third person, he ought not to lose his rank; and that if he were not jealous of his honor, all his subjects would complain of it; that for these considerations, if the general wished that he should eat with him, he should not suffer him to derogate from his rank nor from the glory of his ancestors; that otherwise it would be better for him to go and dine with his soldiers, who knowing his conduct, would love him the more for it. Casquin, who wished to appease Capaha, and who knew that this lord was right, arose and said to De Soto that Capaha demanded nothing but what was very just, and that he begged him to invite him to take his place; that as for him, he esteemed himself so honored to be at his table, that it was of no importance on which side he sat.　As he spoke he passed to the left of the general and calmed Capaha, who during all the time of dining, did not show any resentment.　These circumstances show that even among barbarians, the rank which gives title is something of importance. The Spaniards were astonished at the proceedings of these two chiefs, for they never would have believed that the Indians would have been so sensitive upon the point of honor."

Previous to this time, the Spaniards had suffered greatly from the lack of salt, and having complained to the Indians, were told that "there was some in the mountains at forty leagues from Capaha.　They also said that there was found there the yellow metal of which they had spoken to them.　Our people rejoiced at this news.　Moreno and Silvera, who were careful and wise, offered to go with the (native) merchants and find out the truth of all these things.　The general immediately dispatched them with orders to notice the quality of the land through which they should pass; and Capaha had them escorted by Indians, and gave them pearls, deer-skins and beans with which to purchase gold and salt.　Then they left and at the end of eleven days returned with six loads of fossil salt, clear as crystal, which gave great joy

I—3

to the Spaniards. They also brought back some copper, very
yellow, and said that the country whence they came was sterile
and very poorly populated."*

Soon after this occurrence, De Soto "resumed the route to the
town of Casquin, in order from there to direct his course towards
the West and to explore its lands." After five days spent at
Casquin,‡ resting and recruiting, he "marched four days down
the river (the St. Francis) through a country fertile and populated, and arrived at the province of Quiguate." He was now
probably in the county of Phillips, Arkansas, near the old mouth
of the St. Francis river. He encountered a friendly reception
at the borders of this province, and was requested to continue on
down the river to the capital, which was likewise called Quiguate.
Accordingly, the "general believed what they told him, and continued five days his journey, descending along the Mississippi
river through places abounding in provisions, and on the fifth
arrived at the capital. The town was divided into three quarters. The Spaniards lodged in two, and the Indians in the third,
where was the house of the cacique."**

The inhabitants of Quiguate†† showed themselves to be suspicious, and the Spaniards did not receive at the capital the welcome
they had expected and had been assured they would be accorded.
However, after a few preliminary skirmishes, peace was patched
up, and the Spaniards remained at Quiguate six days. "They
left the seventh, and after marching five days down along the
river, which passes by Casquin,† they arrived at the capital of
the Province of Colima." Here they were not well received,
but the unflinching De Soto again managed to placate or hoodwink the natives. After three days spent here in recruiting and
laying in provisions, "they continued their journey through fertile fields, pleasant forests, easy to pass, and at the end of four

---

*This trip was made, no doubt, to the mountains in the southwestern part of
Missouri, where the natives collected salt from the many salt springs or deposits
in that region. It is probable that they did not have to go the entire distance of
forty leagues and return—240 miles—because they could not have covered the distance in the time mentioned—eleven days. Or perhaps the distance was less.

‡ The Portuguese account says, that "the capital, the province and the cicique
were called Casquin." When, therefore, they "resumed the route to the town of
Casquin," it is to be presumed it was to the capital of Casquin on the St. Francis
river, where they had been so royally entertained before.

** They were now probably on the Mississippi below the mouth of the Arkansas.

†† It will be noticed that the description located Quiguate on the Mississippi
river, and not on the St. Francis, as some writers maintain, because, after leaving
Quiguate, they marched "down and along the river which passes by Casquin"
until they arrived at the capital of Colima. The province of Casquin evidently
lay between the Mississippi and the St. Francis.

† Plainly, the term Casquin here used refers to the province, and not to its chief
town, or capital.

days arrived at the borders of a river where the army encamped."
Here they spent some time and made salt from what De la Vega
calls "sand of an azure color." **

The Elvas Narrative‡ describes the journey down the river
from the province of Capaha in the following language: "The
governor rested forty days in Pacaha (Capaha). From thence
he sent thirty horsemen and fifty footmen to the province of
Caluca to see if he might travel to Chisca,* where the Indians
said there was work of gold and copper. They traveled seven
(eleven?) days' journey through a desert and returned. The
governor, seeing that toward that part of the country was poor
in maize, demanded of the Indians which way it was most inhabited, and they said they had notice of a great province, which was
called Quiguate, and that it was towards the south. The Cacique
of Casquia (afterward the Kaskaskia) commanded the bridge to
be repaired, and the governor returned through his country and
lodged in a field near his town. He gave us a guide and men for
carriers. The governor lodged at a town of his, and the next day
at another near a river (the St. Francis)† whither he caused
canoes to be brought for him to pass over. The governor took
his journey toward Quiguate.§ The fourth of August he came
to the town. The town was the greatest that was seen in Florida." The account given by Luis Fernandez de Biedma, who
likewise accompanied the expedition to the end, was as follows:
"We remained at Pacaha (Capaha) twenty-six or seven days,
anxious to learn if we could take the northern route and cross
to the South Sea. We then marched northeast. We traveled
eight days through swamps, after which we met a troop of
Indians who lived under movable tents. We next came to the
Province of Caluca. Seeing there was no way to reach the South
Sea, we returned toward the north, and afterward in a southwest

---

** Judging by the number of days they had thus marched southward, this stream
could have been no other than Red river.

‡ This narrative was prepared by the "Portuguese gentleman of Elvas," a writer
whose name is unknown, but who accompanied the expedition of De Soto to the
end, and thus participated in the events which he describes.

* This trip was presumably to the mountains of southwest Missouri, as already
narrated from the de la Vega account.

† It will be noticed that the Elvas Narrative cannot escape the conclusion that
another river than the Chucagua (Mississippi) was referred to; and it is amusing
to observe the confusion of subsequent writers in attempting to locate all these
movements on the Mississippi. The St. Francis river is, in many places, but a
short distance from the Mississippi, and as the country is comparatively level,
the communication between the two was easy but slow. By considering the movements to have been on the St. Francis, all confusion is avoided.

§ Quiguate was situated on the Arkansas river near its mouth. The Indians
were afterward called the Akanseas, or Arkansas.

NOTE.—Colima was probably the same as Tanico near the mouth of Red river.

direction to a province called Quiguate, where we found the largest village we had yet seen in all our travels.   It was situated on one of the branches of a great river."*

The Elvas Narrative further says, "As for Quiguate, Casqui and Pacaha, they were plain countries, flat grounds and full of good meadows on the rivers, where the Indians sowed large fields of maize."   It must be admitted that the country was full of corn and other provisions to support four or five hundred Spaniards and their horses for months at a time.   They had now been from two to three months in the provinces of Casquia, Capaha and Quiguate, and had been supported the whole time by the Indians—partly through fear, but as much so from kindly motives, which put to shame the savagery and base intentions of the Spaniards.   The Indians were war-like, and the women were even more savage and courageous in battle than the men.   They did not hesitate to take up the same weapons as the men and join in the desperate struggles against the intruders.   Numerous instances are narrated of their prowess.   The Elvas Narrative says, "From Pacaha (Capaha) to Quiguate may be a hundred leagues."   The actual distance was probably fully that far, counting from near the mouth of the Arkansas upward to about the Missouri state line.   It further says, "The governor asked which way the country was most inhabited.   They said that toward the south, down the river, were great towns and Caciques, which commanded great countries and much people.†   And that toward the northwest there was a province, near to certain mountains, called Coligoa.   From Quiguate to Coligoa may be forty leagues."

The account of de la Vega states, that after leaving Quiguate, they marched *down* the River Mississippi five days and reached the town of Colima, capital of the province of the same name. Leaving here, they seem to have taken a northwesterly direction, continuing for four days, when they arrived "at the borders of a

* Particular attention is called to this description of an eye witness of the scenes which he describes so briefly. He says they marched northeast, but this could not have been so, because they would have had to cross the Mississippi, which they evidently did not do. He says they marched eight days on the trip for gold and salt; the Elvas Narrative says seven and de la Vega eleven. Biedma says they returned toward the north, but, of course it was toward the south. He could hardly have gone northeast and then returned north. They went northwest and returned, and according to Biedma were gone about sixteen days, eight going and presumably the same returning. Upon their return they went in a southwest direction, arriving finally at Quiguate, which he says was situated on a "branch of a great river." This branch could have been no other than the Arkansas. Thus the three accounts of de la Vega, Biedma and the Elvas Narratives fix the St. Francis as the river, upon which these operations were conducted, and where stood the capitals of Capaha and Casquia or Casquin.

† The Elvas Narrative fails to give an account of the journey to Colima, given by de la Vega. This was doubtless because of the absence of exciting or important events; but the details given by the latter are too vivid and definite not to ave been based upon actual observations.

river."* The description shows this to have been a different river from any they had yet seen. Their entire journey during the four days had been through large and well-cultivated fields of corn, pumpkins, beans, etc. The country was very smooth and "easy to pass." The Elvas Narrative continues, "The governor with an Indian, which was his guide, passed through great woods without any way seven days' journey through a desert, where at every lodging they lodged in lakes and pools of very shoal water: there was such store of fish that they killed them with their cudgels. We then crossed vast plains and high mountains, when suddenly we came to Coligoa. The Indians of Coligoa had not known of the Christians, and when they came so near the town that the Indians saw them, they fled up a river which passes near the town and some leaped into it; but the Christians went on both sides of the river and took them. We inquired here for other villages, and they directed us to go south and southwest and we should find them. We traveled five days and came to the province of Palisema.** He found much people, but by reason of the roughness of the country he took none save a few women and children."

From Coligoa De Soto went southwest for five days, at the end of which time he arrived at Tatel Coya, probably on Red river. Thence he marched four days up the river to the province of Cayas, where he stopped at the town called Tanico. In the province of Cayas, the Spaniards made salt and discovered springs of hot water. From Tanico he went to Tulla, a day and a half's journey, but to reach it was obliged to cross high hills. These operations were doubtless along Red river in modern Louisiana.†

The Elvas Narrative says, "We were told that if we were to ascend this river (the Washita) we should find a large province called Cayas. We repaired thither and found it a mountainous country and composed of populous villages. This town was called Tanico (Cayas appears to be Spanish). He pitched his tent in the best part of it, and here, in the province of Cayas, the governor rested a month; in which time the horses fattened, and they drank of very hot water and somewhat brakish. On

---

* It was probably Washita river. The Spanish league is two and one-third miles.
** Probably on the Washita in what is now northern Louisiana.

†It must be admitted that the description of the country over which the expedition passed is so doubtful from the contradictory statements made, that the route cannot be laid down with certainty. It is possible that, instead of being on Red river, these operations were on the Arkansas river, from Little Rock to its mouth. All the latest and best authorities, however, locate these movements along Red river in modern Louisiana.

both sides of the river the country was full of sown fields, and there was a store of maize. * * * The governor asked the Caciques which way the country was best inhabited. He answered that the best country thereabout was a province toward the south a day and a half journey, which was called Tulla." But the Indians there resented the coming of the Spaniards, and De Soto concluded to return to Cayas or Tanico to spend the winter. He carried the cacique (of Tulla) with him; and of all his men there was not one found who understood the speech of Tulla." * * * "The governor informed himself (of) all the country round about, and understood that toward the west was a scattering dwelling, and that toward the southeast were great towns, especially in a province called Autiamque; he traveled five days over rough mountains and came to the town of Guipana, situated at the foot of high hills. Where no Indians could be taken for the roughness of the country, and the town being between hills, there was an ambush laid wherewith they took two Indians, which told them that Autiamque* was six days' journey from thence, and that there was another province towards the south, eight days' journey off, called Guahata. But because Autiamque was nearer, the governor made his journey that way, and in three days he came to a town called Anoixi. Within two days after he came to another town called Catamaya and lodged in the fields of the town. The next day they went to the town and took as much maize as they needed. That day they lodged in a wood and the next day they came to Atiamque. Hard by this town passed a river that came out of the province of Cayas (Tanico) and, above and below, it was very well peopled. They stayed in Atiamque three months (wintered there)."†

"Upon Monday, the 6th of March, 1542, the governor departed from Atiamque to seek Nilco, which the Indians said was near the great river (Red). The governor spent ten days in traveling from Atiamque to a province called Ayays (Adayes in western Louisiana), and came to a town that stood near the river that

---

*They had traveled from Tanico (Cayas), which lay up and near the Red river a considerable distance over high hills. Autiamque was ten days' journey from Tulla, though in a zig-zag course. From Guipana he turned easterly, crossed the high mountains again and descended into a plain, very fertile, where stood Autiamque on the banks of both the Mississippi and the Red rivers. Here he resolved to spend the winter.

†The province of Cayas (Tanico) seems, then, to have been located in the modern parishes of Concordia and Catahoula, Louisiana, bordering on the three rivers, Red, Washita and Mississippi.

passeth by Cayas and Autiamque (the Red).† There he commanded a barge to be made wherewith he crossed the river.
When he had crossed the river, he went three days' journey
through a wilderness and a country so low and so full of lakes
and evil ways that he traveled a whole day in water, sometimes
knee deep, sometimes to the stirrups, and sometimes they swam.
They came to a town called Tutelpinco. There passed by it a
lake that entered unto the river which carried a great stream and
force of water. The governor went a whole day along the lake
seeking a passage but could find none. They made rafts wherewith they crossed the lake;* they traveled three days and came
to a town in the province of Anilco or Nilco called Tianto. They
passed through three or four great towns. In the town where
the Cacique resided, which was two leagues from the place where
the governor remained, they found many Indians who, as soon
as they saw the Christians coming, set fire to the Cacique's house
and fled over a lake that passed near the town, through which the
horses could not pass. The next day being Wednesday, the
29th of March, the governor came to Nilco: he lodged with his
men in the Cacique's town, which stood in a plain field, which was
inhabited for the space of a quarter of a league, and within a
league and a half were other very great towns. This was the
best inhabited country that was seen in Florida, and had most
stores of maize except Coça and Apalache. The river which
passed by Nilco was that which passed by Cayas and Autiamque
and fell into the Rio Grande (the Mississippi), which passed by
Pacaha and Aquixo, and near unto the province of Guachoya, the
lord of which came *up* the river to make war with him of Nilco.
Within a few days the governor determined to go to Guachoya.
As he crossed the river Nilco (Red) there came in canoes the
Indians of Guachoya up the stream, and when they saw him they
returned down the river. The governor (having crossed) sent
a captain with fifty men in six canoes down the river and went
himself by land with the rest. He came to Guachoya‡ upon Sun-
day, the 17th day of April: he lodged in the town of the Cacique,
which was enclosed about (by palisades probably), and seated a
cross-bow shot from the river (Mississippi). That day came an

---

† This ten days' journey was unquestionably westward across the State of Louisiana to the province of Adayes, partly in Louisiana and partly in Texas. The
low country between Natchitoches and Texarkana was where they were obliged
to wade in water.

‡ * This lake seems to have been one of the many bayous situated on Red river.

‡ It is admitted that the town of Guachoya stood on the west bank of the Mississippi, near the mouth of the Red river.

Indian to the governor from the Cacique of Guachoya. The next day they saw many canoes come up the river; and on the other side of the Great River (the Mississippi) they consulted whether they should come or not, and at length concluded to come, and crossed the river. In them came the Cacique of Guachoya. The governor asked him whether he had any notice of the sea. He answered 'no,' nor of any towns down the river on that side, save that at two leagues from thence was a town of a subject of his: and on the other side of the river was the province of Quigalta."** While the army was stationed here, one of the cavaliers—a gentleman of high character and education, Diego de Guzman, by name—voluntarily left the army and took up his abode with the Indians and refused to return. He had fallen in love with an Indian girl and refused to desert her.

Here it was that De Soto, in the words of Biedma, "fell sick and died." The Elvas Narratives are scarcely more explicit, to the following effect: "The 21st of May, 1542, departed out of this life the valorous, virtuous and valiant Captain Don Ferdinand de Soto, Governor of Cuba, and Adelantado of Florida." The death of De Soto was concealed from the Indians, who had been led to believe that the "Christians" were immortal. Having kept his body for three days, his comrades, finally, under cover of darkness, buried him within the walls of the town, near one of the principal gates. The next day the Indians noticed the fresh earth and asked what it meant. The question was evaded, but fearing they might proceed to dig there to satisfy their curiosity, the new commander, Luis de Moscoso de Alvarado, had his body removed in the middle of the night and quietly and secretly taken out into the Mississippi river, where, having been weighted with sand, etc., and no doubt enclosed in a rude wooden coffin, it was consigned forever to the mighty river, the discovery of which, in so definite a way, is destined to perpetuate his name through all the coming centuries.

The subsequent route of the expedition under Moscoso is even more in doubt than that under De Soto. However, it is clear that in July, 1542, he marched northwest or west, and after traversing about one hundred leagues, arrived at a province called Auche or Aguacay. Continuing a westerly direction, they reached Naguatex in six days. They were now west of the province of Tulla (mentioned before) and were doubtless in modern Texas. He passed many Indian villages and crossed

** The Elvas Narrative, by one who participated in the expedition.

many streams, and reached the province of Dacoyo on or near the Trinity river, sending out side expeditions to explore the country through which he passed. Upon his return, he seems to have crossed his route going out, but arrived finally at Guachoya. Near this place, at the villages of Aminoia, or Minioia, or Minoya, they passed the winter of 1542–3, the inducement being 18,000 measures of corn in the possession of the Indians. While here they made brigantines, in which to pass down the Mississippi the following spring on their way to Mexico. They departed on the day of St. John the Baptist, but were pursued and harassed constantly by large bodies of Indians in excellent boats. During the nineteen days required to reach the Gulf, there was scarcely an hour when they were not required to repel an attack. Many of the Spaniards were killed, and every remaining horse was destroyed. In one engagement forty-eight Spaniards were killed, being either drowned, or knocked on the heads with the oars of the savages. The remnant finally reached the Gulf, whereupon, the boats of the Indians not permitting further pursuit being withdrawn the survivors were left in peace. They finally succeeded in reaching Mexico.

The expedition was wholly barren of results. No gold nor precious stones were discovered. It was learned that the country contained no such minerals. But the Spaniards found a land of wonderful fertility, possessing inexhaustible quantities of timber, wild game in great abundance, a splendid climate, and conditions generally which promised every reward to the agriculturalist. But the army of De Soto did not seek the wilderness of Louisiana for the purpose of founding a colony in anything but a land flowing with gold and jewels. They did not see the wonderful possibilities of the soil, the climate, the sun and the velvet savannas. They forced the natives to guide them to their villages that they might despoil them of provisions and of life. For more than a hundred years, while Spain was still in the flower of her somber glory, she had no thought of Louisiana. An empire the fairest the sun ever shone upon went begging so far as miserable Spain was concerned. She was busy thinking how to kill the 40,000,000 savage heretics in the two Americas.

Among the incidents growing out of the journey of De Soto westward of the Mississippi was the detention by the cacique, Anilco, of Roger D'Estrange, who had been sent by De Soto to conciliate that chief after the return of the expedition to the Mississippi. Having finally managed to escape, in company with an Indian friend named Choquo, he wandered around through

eastern Arkansas, his precise route being wholly uncertain, until
at last, through the influence of Choquo, he fell in with a friendly
tribe, among whom there was living Diego de Guzman, who had
voluntarily left or deserted from the army, mainly by reason of
his ardent love for a beautiful Indian girl, Winona, and with
whom he desired to live. He had been made a chief by the
Indians, and was living with them on what is now believed to have
been Washita river in the province called Carguta. In order to
possess the advantage to be derived from the superior knowledge
of the white man, the cacique had adopted De Guzman, and now
for the sam reason, influenced by the latter, D'Estrange was
likewise adopted and made a sub-chief. Both men married
Indian maidens, and made themselves very useful to the Indians,
in improving their military and domestic service. It is claimed
that they succeeded in making rude copper and iron vessels, implements, tools and weapons, having first prepared charcoal. Upon
the return of the army under Moscoso from the west, he encountered the Indians under De Guzman, and tried to induce the latter
to rejoin the Spanish forces; but he refused, whereupon Moscoso
threatened to have him arrested, brought into the Spanish camp,
and punished for desertion. But in the end this course was
found to be wholly impracticable, owing to the deplorable condition of the Spanish army and to the unwisdom of stirring up the
nation of Indians, whom, no doubt, De Guzman could bring to
his assistance. However, D'Estrange, who had long cherished
such a resolution, determined to leave the Indians and the country,
and accordingly did so, taking with him his Indian wife, to whom
he was legally married at the first opportunity. With the army
of Moscoso he sailed down the Mississippi, and thence along the
Gulf of Mexico.*

The "Seven Cities of Cibolo," about which there has been and
doubtless will be a vast degree of conjecture, and the location of
which will always be more or less an uncertainty, seem to have
had once an actual existence. The towns of the Pueblos, with
their many squares, enclosing buildings three hundred and four
hundred feet long and over one hundred fifty feet wide, varying
from two to seven stories high and built of solid walls several
feet thick, had doubtless attained among the natives themselves
distinction and perhaps fame long before Europeans attempted

---

*How much dependence may be placed in this story of D'Estrange is largely a
matter of conjecture. Inasmuch as there seems no good reason to dispute its
main features, the above brief account is therefore here inserted, though not
vouched for.

to reach them. The rich spoils which had fallen to the conquerors of Mexico and Peru, indicated to the Spaniards of the former the probability of finding similar plunder in the region of the "Seven Cities," and still further cast a glamour of splendor over the idea of the conquest that should subject another empire to the kingdom of Spain. The stories of the Indian slave, Tejos, contributed to the belief in the existence of the cities and in the extravagant tales of their magnitude and wealth. His statements were eagerly believed that he had visited the "Cities," and that they were as large and as populous as the City of Mexico. All these reports taken together seemed based upon substantial facts— upon something more real and promising than idle dreams or fantasies. Accordingly, Nuno de Guzman, the master of Tejos, determined to send an expedition to find the "Seven Cities," and reduce them to Spanish authority. He was then at the head of the Royal Audience of Spain, possessed sufficient power in official quarters, and soon succeeded in raising an army of four hundred Spaniards and twenty thousand Indians, and set forth on his journey through an unexplored wilderness of six hundred miles. But his expedition was wholly unprepared for such a journey. The hardships melted his army away, dissipated their dreams, and revealed the impracticability of such a conquest on the lines which he had adopted. It soon came to an abrupt termination followed by a straggling return to Mexico.

But the tales remained unshaken and the dreams undimmed. The arrival of Cabeza de Vaca and his companions revived the idea of conquest. He told of passing through populous lands, where the intelligent and friendly natives lived in fixed habitations in large and flourishing towns. He told of their pursuits, their broad acres of grain, their prodigious wealth, and kindled anew the designs of immediate conquest. The governor of New Gallacia, Francisco Vasquez Coronado, caught the flame and determined to act. He first sent out an expedition of inquiry under Fray Marcos de Nizza, guided by Stephen the Arabian, who had accompanied De Vaca on his journey across the continent. Upon their return after a long time, they told that they had found the "Seven Cities," but had not been permitted to enter therein and that the Arabian had been killed. The stories told surpassed anything yet circulated.

The sentiment of the people would not wait for the return of advices from the crown of Spain. The Spanish blood in the New World was too rapid for such lethargic proceedings, and within a few weeks the people took fire, and began to form themselves into bodies for the exploration of the country. This was a spontaneous movement of the Franciscans, but it was an index of the wishes of the people to be led to the land about which so many golden tales had been told. No doubt, Fray Marcos had much to do in setting the fire raging. Finally, so general became the movement, that the viceroy was obliged to take control of the body of men bent upon making the journey. It now assumed an aristocratic character. Coronado was appointed the commander. At once, courtiers and nobles—the proudest in all Mexico—flocked to his standard, and from them the bravest, richest and most influential were selected—grandees, in whose blood ran the pride of a thousand years. Profiting by the experience of De Guzman, he limited his army and prepared for the hardships of an uncertain and unpropitious future; because battles, continuous and bloody, in the land of the enemy, were expected, and it was realized that many would never return. The forces were rendezvoused at Compostella, the capital of New Gallacia. Late in February, 1540, the army, consisting of about three hundred Spaniards and eight hundred Indians, set out with great pomp and with hopes fluttering far higher than their own high-flown banners. The Viceroy himself accompanied the party for two days, so great was the enthusiasm. But as each man had a heavy load to carry, the labor soon took the gloss from the enthusiasm, as Coronado had intended. When they reached Chiametla they were ready to stop for a few days in order to rest and to secure a fresh supply of provisions. Here their first collision with the natives, an unfortunate affair, occurred, and several Indians were hanged. About this time, also, Melchior Diaz, who had been sent out on a preliminary expedition by Coronado, returned with sad tales of the condition of things to the north. His account differed materially from the gauzy tales of Fray Marcos.

Coronado now left the main body of the Spaniards to the command of Tristan de Arellano, and with fifty horsemen and a few men on foot set out in a northeast direction, leaving instructions for the others to follow him in a fortnight. After traveling for more than a month, he came to a desert, on the border of which was a village. He had thus far met with disappointment everywhere, because the tales told by De Vaca and Fray Marcos were in no respects verified. The natives were poor and had few provisions; but were friendly, doubtless because it would have been folly for them to be otherwise. The village on the border of the desert was called Chichilticalli, or the Red House; and instead of being a populous place not far from the sea, it consisted of a single house, long, ruined, roofless, but bearing the appearance of having been at one time a fortified work of an intelligent people. Continuing in a northeast direction over the desert for two weeks, they came to a turbid river which they called Vermejo. They now learned that they were only eight leagues from Cibola. Early the next day, they barely escaped an ambuscade of the hostile natives, and soon arrived at the famous city of Cibola. What a disappointment! It was a little village of not more than two hundred inhabitants, located on rocky heights and very difficult of access. Coronado renamed it Granada, owing to its rocky situation, and because the name Cibola did not apply to any one village, but to the whole province, which contained seven principal towns. The inhabitants indicated a hostile spirit, and refused the friendly advances of the whites; whereupon, being in sore need of water and provisions, it was resolved to try to carry the place by assault. The attack was accordingly made, but had it not been for the armor of the Spaniards they would doubtless have lost many men, so desperate was the resistance encountered. Clubs, showers of stones, arrows and other missiles met the Spaniard at every turn. Coronado himself was felled to the earth, and came near losing his life. In about an hour's time the place was captured, which strong position gave the Spaniards the command of the entire district or province. But the expected gold was not forthcoming. The turquoises were missing. The dreams of the Spaniards began to dissipate in fleecy clouds along the edges of the Apache desert. Curses and maledictions were heaped on the heads of Fray Marcos and De Vaca. It was soon realized that the great object of the expedition—gold and other riches—would not be realized; whereupon it was determined to make the most of what there was in the way of spoils. No thought was given to the savages by the merciless Spaniards, who prepared to visit their wrath on them for the lies which scores of years had accumulated. The Spaniards did not scruple to take the last in the larder of the poverty-stricken savages. It was done, however, in the name of God and Mary and the cross, amid the prayers of the many priests who accompanied the expedition for the principal purpose of saving the souls of the soldiers who should be wounded, by administering to them extreme unction just before their wicked souls should slip over the divide between the here and the hereafter.

Here Coronado determined to await the arrival of the remainder of his forces, before deliberately ransacking and destroying the villages of the unfortunate natives. In the meantime he sent dispatches containing an account of his expedition thus far to the viceroy under date of August 3, 1540, the year of our Lord. The diabolical designs of these gold-maddened wretches put one in mind of the atrocities of that other historic, Spanish institution— the Holy Inquisition. All was done in the name of God. The zealous priest had before the dying eyes of the murdered native the cross of Christ, thinking to save his heathen spirit, but really to quiet his own consciousness for dastardly wrongdoing and to impress his miserable followers with the glories of the Catholic faith. Nothing could stay the ruthless intentions of the savage Spaniards. Their disappointment must be glutted in the blood of the Indians, in the ruin of their villages, in the desecration of their simple temples, in the ravishment of their homes and the enslavement of the people. What matter if these unknown wretches should be wholly swept from the earth? On these hills would rise the missions of the Catholics and the cross of Christ. It was right that the gold of the heathen should advance the cause of the true God. It was right that the worshippers of the sun and the monstrous idols should give way to the avarice and the sword of the so-called Christians. So it came to pass that not one thought was given the doomed savages by the no less savage and barbarous grandees.

In November, 1540, they reached the province of Tiguex, through which flowed a large river, since called the Rio Grande del Norte. While here, they heard tales of immense quantities of gold farther to the east—always farther away like a will-of-the-wisp. Coronado was assured by a native called "The Turk" that large quantities of gold could be found by traveling toward the rising sun. Here the harsh treatment of the natives by the Spaniards to compel them to tell all they knew in regard to gold kindled the indignation and eventual hostility of all the natives. The nature of the Spaniards was such that they could not treat the natives humanely; they must necessarily abuse and maltreat them beyond the point of forbearance or endurance. The trouble arose over some gold bracelets which "The Turk" said the natives possessed; but which they denied, calling "The Turk" a liar. The leaders were accordingly taken by the Spaniards and kept in chains for six months in order to force them to tell where the bracelets were. It transpired that there were no such bracelets in existence. "The Turk" had really lied. But the punishment fell on the native leaders, and their incarceration set the inhabitants on fire.

It was in Tiguex that the Spaniards saw private houses seven stories in height. It was now December, 1540, and snow fell almost every night. The cold was severe, but there was an abundance of fuel, so that the troops were kept from freezing. But the natives had revolted and were now all hostile, owing to the harsh treatment they had received. · Gold, the root of all evil, had caused the trouble. They demanded a large quantity of cloth of the natives, and, when it was not forthcoming soon enough, proceeded forcibly to strip the clothing from the natives they met. This led to open war, in which the savages acquitted themselves with the greatest courage. An act of base treachery, whereby the Spaniards violated the commonest rules of warfare, still further kindled the wrath of all the natives against them and led to the widening of the fields of combat. One town after another began to fall, but not without severe loss to the Spaniards, from the poisoned arrows of the natives and otherwise. Whole provinces were soon subjugated.

As soon as the ice began to break in the spring of 1541, Coronado made preparations to advance eastward to the country where "The Turk" had declared so much gold existed—Quivira, Arche, Guyas, etc. The army departed from Tiguex on April 23, 1541, taking a southeasterly course; and after five days of travel reached a river so large that they were forced to build a bridge to cross it. This is thought to have been the Pecos. After passing this river, they still pursued a southeast direction over the rich plains, and after many days came upon an immense herd of buffaloes, which was being pursued by a band of Querechos. The latter were friendly and told Coronado that farther to the east were the people who possessed the gold. The Querechos possessed large packs of hunting dogs, and were very strong and skillful with the bow, being able to drive an arrow entirely through a buffalo. They said that to the east was a large river, where a dense population dwelt, and that their nearest village was called Haxa. Ten men under Diego Lopez were sent to find and explore this village; but, after marching twenty leagues, they returned without having found anything of note. The gaudy stories of "The Turk" began to be discredited from this moment. The guides conflicting in their advices, Coronado sent out another expedition of a few men on a scout before advancing with his whole army, but learned nothing, except that an old native told them that he had seen the party of La Vaca which had passed there a few years before. The whole army coming up, they deliberately took possession of all the tanned skins of the natives—a large quantity—greatly to their indignation. Thus the

Spaniards eternally continued to rob, cheat, or hoodwink the friendly natives, changing them to deadly enemies and stultifying themselves. Civil words will never quite wipe out the record of the infamous treatment inflicted on the natives, who, at first, were exceedingly friendly, giving up their last robe and provision to the strangers, but who were then robbed of the remainder of their possessions and shot, if they dared to show resentment, which they invariably did, be it said to their credit. It was coax, cajole, rob, shoot, ravish and devastate, until history should stamp the word "knave" or "murderer" on the name of every Spaniard who had any dealings with the native Americans.

A reconnoitering party sent out came upon a small band of wandering Indians who called themselves Teyas (probably Texas), and who conducted the army for three days to their village called Cona. Here the Spaniards learned that Quivira was distant about thirty days' march in a northerly direction. A little farther on they reached a very large and fine valley, where wild fruits were abundant, and here they rested. It was now evident that the stories of gold were false, that "The Turk" had lied, that many natives had been guilty of the same offense, and that the object of the expedition had dissipated in visions. A council of war was held and it was determined that Coronado should take about thirty of the strongest and bravest horsemen and set out in search of Quivira, while the remainder of the army under Arrellano should return to Tiguex. This decision met with considerable opposition from the soldiers, who did not wish to be separated from Coronado and especially from the search after Quivira. But something must be done and this was regarded as the wisest course. They were now, doubtless, in northern, central Texas.

Coronado set out to find Quivira, taking a northerly direction, and for thirty or forty days traveled over the dry plains of Texas, Indian Territory, and Kansas, until he finally arrived at a large river, which was doubtless, the Arkansas. He must have arrived in the vicinity of the modern Kinsley, Kansas, because, when he continued, he journeyed *down* the river in a *northeasterly* direction, which would have been impossible had he reached any other portion of that river. It could not have been the Missouri, because no where does the Missouri flow northeasterly. The only other river it might have been was the Republican fork of the Kansas in Nebraska, but it is not likely that this branch was the one reached. It could not have been the Red river, because it had required thirty or forty days of travel to reach it after

105°   100°

Louisiana In Possession Of The French.

105°

No.II.

GULF OF MEXICO.
No. 3. 1715
London H. Moll.
Old Maps of America.
Vol. I. No. 13.   R.E.H.

100°

Old Maps Showing the
Extent of Louisiana

No. X

C.DE.FUNDABZ.ILL

23°11'

CANTINO. 1502.

No.XI.

C. DE. FUNDABRIL

RUYSCH 1507.
R.E.H.

Old Maps Showing Florida
and the Gulf

No. VII.   No.VIII.   No. IX.

C. de fim d aabz.ill

CANERIO 1503   STOBNICZA 1512   MAP OF WALDSEEMÜLLER
                                          1513

R.E.H.   R.E.H.   R.E.H.

Old Maps Showing Florida and the Gulf

leaving the main army. The Arkansas is the only river that answers all the conditions. They had been in Texas, where, it was recorded, two crops a year were raised by the Indians. The distance covered—about three hundred sixty miles—in the time mentioned would be about right, because they had to travel in the heat of midsummer and had to cross all the water courses at right angles, which would necessarily make their progress comparatively slow. He named the river Saints Peter and Paul and stopped to rest on its banks. Another much larger river was far ahead, it was reported, and was called Teucarea, no doubt the Missouri or Platte. During the wearisome journey across the plains he and his men had lived almost exclusively on buffalo meat, and had often used the milk of that animal to drink. Learning that there were villages down the river, he crossed the stream and continued down the same along the north bank in a *northeasterly* direction, until finally on a branch of the main river he reached the first of the towns on this water course. Continuing four or five days more he reached in succession six or seven other villages, until finally he arrived at one called Quivira, on one of the northern branches of the Arkansas. But what a sore disappointment! Instead of the six or seven-storied, stone buildings, the spacious squares, a happy people clad in warm, thick cloth, and an abundance of gold and silver ornaments, the infuriated Spaniards beheld only straw-built huts, a savage people who ate their buffalo meat raw, no cloth whatever, but in its place only tanned buffalo skins, and not an ounce of gold or silver in the entire province, if the people were intelligent enough to have such a civic subdivision. The Spaniards had for some time anticipated such a finality, and as a matter of precaution had placed "The Turk" in chains to prevent his possible escape. They now closely questioned him as to his motive in thus so roundly lying to them. He replied that, as his own country lay beyond Quivira, he had done so to prevent the Spaniards from visiting and impoverishing his people; and that the inhabitants of Cibola had begged him to lead the Spaniards astray in the desert in hopes that they would all perish and never again be seen in Cibola. One night, while at Quivira, he endeavored to incite an attack on the Spanish forces, hoping thus to massacre all of them, but the attempt was discovered before any damage had been done. However, his participancy in the attempt was discovered, whereupon the Spaniards in fury fell upon him and strangled him to death. Thus fell a man whose falsehoods were of such gigantic character

I—4

that his name should be placed by the side of those of Ananias and Munchausen; but it may be said that this man lied to save his people and his race, and that, therefore, his falsehoods were justifiable. The statement should be permitted to stand as against the murderous Spaniards.

Coronado fixes Quivira in forty degrees of north latitude; but of course not having suitable instruments he may have missed the correct location by thirty minutes or more. He said the soil was rich and black and watered by many streams and had an abundance of grapes and plums. He remained in the vicinity of these villages, possibly on Republican river, for about twenty-five days, sending out exploring parties in the meantime in hopes of making some discovery of importance. But in this he was doomed to disappointment. The plains of Kansas had no gold for him. But the soil was there offering a bountiful harvest to the husbandman, the streams were there with their never-failing supply of moisture for the grain of the civilized man; the rich pastures, rolling like green silk beneath the stirring breeze and the glowing sun, offered food to thousands of cattle and sheep. But these happy pictures were the last in the minds of the gold-mad Spaniards. Filled with bitterness, they prepared to leave the fabled Quivira enveloped in maledictions, while they pointed doubtless with grim satisfaction to the rude grave of "The Turk," who had lied so well to save his poor people from the Spanish barbarians. The Spaniards collected all the corn they could from the inhabitants, and the latter part of July started to rejoin their comrades at Tiguex. They returned over the route they had come as far as the river Saints Peter and Paul, but then instead of going nearly southward, turned somewhat toward the west and finally came out at the spot where they had first met the Querechos, and had been turned from the direct course to Quivira by the subterfuge of the poor "Turk." Thus they traversed again Kansas, Indian Territory, and Texas. Finally, after forty days of travel on their return, they reached Cicuyé.

The expedition of Don Diego D'Peñalosa, which left Santa Fe in March, 1662, in search of Quivira, consisted of about eighty Spanish dragoons, half a dozen priests, 1,000 Indians on foot, thirty-six carts loaded with supplies, eight hundred horses and three hundred mules. The expedition appears to have reached the same Quivira that was visited by Coronado. Some writers insist that there were several Quiviras. The facts will ever remain in doubt and be the subject of dispute. It seems that

Quivira was more or less mythical. The savages, in order to get rid of the pestiferous Spaniards, who were despoiling them of everything they possessed, promptly and gladly pointed onward, when asked to locate Quivira. It was anywhere that would get rid of the robbers. His precise route is unknown. Other expeditions from New Mexico to what afterward became the Louisiana Purchase were doubtless made. There are records to prove that, in 1599, Juan D'Onate, with a band of adherents, marched eastward in pursuit of riches. Capt. Don Juan Dominguez in 1684 visited Quivira, wherever it may have been.

Doubtless, the extravagant stories of gold in the regions of the west and southwest were founded upon fact. The semi-civilized people of Mexico, for centuries before America was discovered by Europeans, had inhabited all the western country far up along the Pacific coast, and had slowly accumulated from year to year much of the free, surface, or placer gold, worth in the aggregate, no doubt, many millions of dollars, all of which had gradually sought the more populous towns, to be converted into ornaments and vessels for the native rulers. These stories were realities to the natives; but, after the conquest of Mexico and Peru, the bewildered Spaniards greedily drank the golden tales, enlarged from their own desires and vivid imaginations, and in mysterious pictures of fancy they turned the western country, particularly the unknown portions, into populous lands, burdened with the accumulated gold of many centuries. The results of the conquests of Mexico and Peru and the true tales of the Indians, must account for the ready belief of the Spaniards in the existence of large quantities of gold in Arizona and New Mexico; and also account for the fanciful vision of the "Seven Cities of Cibola," and of "Quivira."

When the Spaniards under D'Garay beached their boats at the mouth of the Mississippi for the purpose of cleaning and repairing them, the natives met the new-comers with pleasant words and smiles, accompanied with gifts of all they had to bestow. Here the Spaniards remained for forty days, taking all the natives had in the way of pearls and provisions, and giving in exchange beads, hawk's-bells and other useless trinkets and trifles. But the Indians were satisfied—were, in fact, pleased to be permitted to render any service to the Spaniards in their power, without recompense. While here the Spaniards went in parties up the river to the distance of fifteen miles, observing as many as forty villages on both sides of the river—only temporary villages of

canes, robes, etc.; because the annual overflow of the river prevented the erection of permanent structures. There is no evidence to show that the Spaniards misused the Indians, or that
the latter were displeased with their visitors. It may be set down,
therefore, that the first visit of the Spaniards to the modern Louisiana Purchase was one of peace and friendly barter with the
natives, but through no fault of the Spaniards. They simply
were not given an opportunity of showing the material of which
they were made. But the fact that no unpleasant incident
occurred is worthy of note.

The experiences of Cabeza de Vaca with the natives of what
is now the state of Texas are especially worthy of being
remembered. After suffering incredibly from hardships put upon
him by the natives who had previously been abused by the Spaniards, he finally marched toward the north where no whiteman
had ever been, and a new heaven and a new earth opened before
him. He was everywhere regarded, much to his astonishment,
as a superior being. In other words, when he left the regions
where the cruelties of the Spaniards had alienated the friendship
of the Indians, and reached regions where their barbarities were
unknown and unfelt as yet, he began to be treated more like a
god than a human being. He had no sooner advanced into the
interior, than he was received by the natives with a pomp, ceremony and distinction that surprised yet delighted him beyond
measure. The simple and confiding natives thought him a messenger from God, and deemed it a mark of extreme distinction
to be permitted to touch his garments, to render him menial service, and to lug his contraptions through forests and marshes,
rain and shine, cold and heat, across pleasant valleys and over
barren mountain divides. This was an agreeable change which
De Vaca and his wondering companions were careful not to dis-
courage or restrain. Their journey westward through Texas
was a continual ovation; they were feasted, carried over streams
and fairly worshipped by every nation they met. In return they
modestly posed as special messengers from God, sent to the world
to befriend the humble natives and to bless their belongings and
them. Thus everything they touched was deemed consecrated
and was ever afterward regarded as sacred—until other Spaniards
had dispelled the fantastic vision.

But a change was destined to come over the spirit of their
dreams. The poor Querechos of Kansas or Texas, whose goods
De Vaca and his comrades had blessed in 1536, could scarcely

believe their eyes when the Spaniards under Coronado in 1542 cruelly appropriated not only those robes, but all others they could lay their hands on. During their trip through Texas to the Rio Grande, De Vaca and his companions met with nothing but surprising hospitality and homage, simply because they treated the Indians with a kindness and consideration that completely won their hearts. They used no particular arts to accomplish this result. The instincts of the Indians recognized the apparent superiority of the Spaniards, and in the absence of ill-usage and in the presence of kindly offices, spontaneously raised them to the height of gods. There was no mystery about it. The same causes would produce again the same effects. Kindness and wise offices would again kindle the light of love and homage. Thus runs the way of the human heart. First under D'Garay and second under De Vaca, the mystic chords of benevolent disinterestedness opened a pathway to the willing subserviency of the natives. Was the religion of Christ as exemplified by the Spanish priests equal to the splendid task of rekindling this glorious light of love and homage?

When De Soto crossed the Mississippi, the caciques of Casquin, Capaha and Akansea tendered him their services, houses, provisions and women—shared with his soldiers everything they had; nay, denied themselves that the strangers might be comfortable and happy. The object of the Spaniards was unknown to the natives—their cruel past was a blank, so the greetings were friendly. But the Spaniards began at once to impoverish the country, desecrate the native temples, scorn their simple yet sincere religious and other ceremonies, debauch their women, make slaves of the people; but even yet the natives regarded the newcomers so highly that they continued friendly and subservient. At Capaha the Spaniards encountered war, because they went there to wage war. From this time forward the savages sullenly submitted to the Spaniards rather than rendered them homage and honor. The nobility of the caciques, shown in all their doings, shines in sparkling contrast to the diabolical designs of the Spaniards. In every respect the savage was nobler than the civilized. The savage was more civilized and the civilized more savage. The splendid dignity and magnificent hospitality of Casquin and Capaha were the wonderment of the brazen and treacherous representatives of Aragon and Castile.

The inhabitants of Quiguate received the Spaniards with suspicion, because stories of their abuses had preceded them. They met the same reception at Colima, for the same reason. These towns were all close together. Farther away, at Caligoa and Palisema they were well received; but did not tarry long, because the poor natives had little the visitors required or wanted. At Cayas they found the Indians friendly; but at Tulla they encountered war, because the story of their evil deeds had preceded them. At Guipana, Anoixi and Catamaya they were welcomed and supplied with immense quantities of maize and other provision, for which they gave little or nothing. Where they were unknown, they were invariably received with friendliness and distinction and offered all the natives had; but just as invariably they left the natives their enemy, because of the outrageous wrongs they committed. Think a moment what it meant to the natives to be compelled to support such an army for months at a time, under penalty of being cut to pieces,—five hundred voracious men, several hundred head of horses and as many swine— all swine in fact; fully as many more camp-followers—poor natives impressed at the point of the sword to do menial duty, and deliberately run through their bodies if they shirked or refused.

In the rich province of Atiamque this hungry and merciless army remained all winter, consuming the stores, debauching the people, desecrating every sacred object they possessed, and forcing many of them to do menial duty in the Spanish camp. Recollect, that all these villages were in the modern Louisiana and Arkansas, a land the sun kissed with sunshine, and blessed with shimmering harvests of golden grain, as well as of golden mines. Not finding the latter, the Castillian nobles consumed all they could of the former. In the spring, at Ayayes, Tutelpinco, Tianto, Nilco and Guachoya, the Spaniards were warmly received and given practical possession of the provinces. At the latter place De Soto died. He could have been spared from earth long before and no vigorous complaint been raised. He had left a trail of devastation, cruelty, wickedness and murder which no prayers nor pens can wipe out. But after he had been called hence, the same tale of friendly reception by the natives may be told of his successor, Moscoso, in the wearisome journey to Texas and return, across the central part of modern Louisiana. Kind treatment encountered the friendship and submission of the natives. Kind words and simple gifts brought guides and provisions; swords and bullets brought war clubs and poisoned arrows. Was there ever better ground for the seeds of Christianity? If there was merit in the cross carried by the Spanish priests, here was the opportunity for its glorious exemplification on this miserable little earth. But the cross was in ignorant and unclean hands; the simple beauty of the Nazarene's teachings never glorified the steps of De Soto's army; the beatitudes were forgotten by the grandees who burned for the possession of gold and great riches; the sincere religious ceremonials of the natives that recognized a supreme being, were unfeelingly spurned instead of adroitly turned in the direction of truth and divinity. While the priests were chanting mass, the troopers were cutting throats in the nearest thickets. The butcheries were a poor fulfillment of the boundless promises of the priests. The untutored mind of the savage unbecomingly associated the atrocity with the religion. The good seed had been sown with too many tares. Hence the priests made no proselytes in Akansea of the Louisiana Purchase. The savages preferred the religion of the perpetual sun and of the emerald plains spread out forever.

From the moment the army of De Soto landed on the coast of Florida to that when his whipped and slinking survivors hurriedly reached the mouth of the Mississippi on their way to Mexico, it is probable that not one of the participants gave a solitary glance at that object of the expedition which provided for the establishment of a permanent colony. The army, composed almost wholly of the pride of Spain, gave to colonization not the glimmer of a thought. They were in pursuit of riches and fame—and they received both with a vengeance. The sober and steady life of a colonist—the cultivation of the soil, the harvesting of grain, the rearing of cattle—was beneath the nobles who shone in De Soto's army.

The Spanish ministry realized the great importance of founding colonies to hold the lands discovered; but the army of De Soto was wholly unsuited for this object. What a splendid opportunity Spain had! A magnificent new empire was hers for the price of a few colonies. This pleasing truth was recognized by the Spanish court, be it said to their credit. But the conquest of Mexico had turned every brain to fire and every heart to stone. Unscrupulous adventurers, instead of agriculturalists and artisans, sought the new shores. "Conquest!" was the cry. The ring of gold was the slogan that swept throughout the Moresque corridors of Spain; and by that heartless and bloody battle-call she lost the fairest land the sun ever shone upon. The tremendous effort expended by the army of De Soto would have saved the whole Mississippi valley to Spain, had it been applied properly to the formation of happy colonial homes on the banks of the great river.

If the expedition of De Soto was valueless to Spain, that of Coronado was both valueless and villainous. While both were ostensibly designed for the establishment of colonies in the countries invaded, the real object was the pursuit of gold and other forms of riches. Both were aimed at the heart of the modern Louisiana Purchase—at the gold and silver which had actually been seen by the natives in Colorado, Montana and the Black Hills. The avowed object of the expedition of Coronado was the conquest and subjugation of the famous "Seven Cities of Cibola," in order that the golden stream might be turned into the exhausted coffers of the Spanish crown. The bloody yet golden promises prompted the ready acquiescence of the "Most Catholic Monarch" in the nefarious expedition. But the ministry hoped that the expedition would likewise accomplish the establishment of colonies in the conquered country. Again, as in the case of De Soto's army, the forces of Coronado were composed of court favorites, the self-constituted *dilettante* exquisites, who had sprung up, like mushrooms in a manure heap, from the ashes of the Aztec ruins and from the crimes of unforgivable murders. No thought was given to colonization. The purpose was mostly murder, and the priests were taken along to grant absolution to the butchered natives. Perhaps, also, the confessional might be prostituted to compel the expiring savages to reveal the hiding places of their gold and precious stones. The denial of the chiefs of Tiguex that they had golden bracelets was met by binding them in chains and flinging them into prison. The candor of the Querechos in exhibiting their many valuable robes—their only acquired wealth—was met by the heartless appropriation of the whole lot. Everywhere the Indians were compelled to support the army. If a levy were not forthcoming, murder was committed, and the priests were hurriedly called to dangle the cross before the fading eyes of the bleeding wretches. If ever there was hell upon earth, it followed the swish of the Spanish swords of Coronado's army in the beautiful valley of the Rio Grande. If ever civilized man should flush with shame, he should do so at the mention of the name of Coronado.

No wonder that such a nation went down "to chaos and old night." No wonder the gilt of the cavalier looked pale and poor when compared with the gleaming plow of the hardy and honest colonist. But the sacrifice was made. Spain had not the splendid prevision to claim and possess the land now peopled with millions and golden with the triumphs of man and the glories of God. Her wretched civilization failed to comprehend the wonderful wealth of the sun, the rain, the soil, the forests with their whispering lullabies and the streams with their melodious laughter. So she surrendered without regret a realm, bursting with the blossoms of beauty, an empire of possibilities, which the kind years, through the grace of God, have transformed into castellated homes more substantial than dreams of gold.

CHAPTER II

French Explorations and Discoveries

THE most surprising fact in connection with the formation and growth of the colonies in North America, is the vast extent of time that was permitted to elapse from the discovery of San Salvador by Columbus to the establishment of permanent settlements by the principal European nations. It was more than a hundred years before Jamestown was founded by the English. France did better in the valley of the St. Lawrence; and Spain also did better, or worse, in Florida and in Mexico. It is safe to say that could the statesmen of the sixteenth century have looked ahead to the beginning of the twentieth century and have seen this marvelous country as it is today, they not only would have exhausted every national resource they possessed to colonize the whole country, but from time to time would have taken every means to prevent the colonies from attaining their independence. Even after the wonderful natural resources of this country had become well known to Europeans, attempts at settlement were strangely lukewarm and the wishes of the colonists were unfeelingly disregarded. The ill-treatment of the Atlantic colonies by Great Britain was a piece of stupendous folly, which only the imbecile George III would have been guilty of. The oppression of the Louisiana colonists by the monopolies of Crozat and the Western Company, under sovereign sanction, was no less unwise, nor less destructive of French ascendency in America. For more than a century and a half Spain refused to take Louisiana or Texas as a gift. All three countries—Spain, Great Britain and France—looked first for gold, second for other colonial profits, third for means of outwitting one another, and fourth for an agricultural empire. At all times the colonies must be oppressed for the benefit of the crowns. International jealousy and individual enterprise and adventure had more to do in settling the ownership to North America than any other factors. It will be well to note what France did toward the settlement of the present Louisiana Purchase.

The grant to Sir Robert Heath by the English crown in 1627 embraced the Carolina coast from the thirty-first to the thirty-sixth parallels of latitude and extended westward to the South Sea. Later this patent was sold to Lord Maltravers and by him to Doctor Daniel Coxe, who, it is claimed in some quarters, sent Colonel Welch to explore the country, and who, the English maintained, traversed the region from Charleston to the Mississippi river. But it has been doubted on good grounds whether such a journey was made. The rights of Doctor Coxe passed to his son, who, in order to make something of value out of his estate, published a journal which he claimed had been kept by companions of Colonel Welch, and prepared a map of the colony in 1722, showing the route claimed to have been traversed by that officer, and further showing English factories and settlements in the wilderness of modern Alabama and Mississippi. It has been presumed that this map and this journal were prepared, to use a modern phrase, "for advertising purposes." The younger Coxe anxiously wanted settlers for his colony, and made great efforts to secure them. It was claimed that the English sent their vessels, commanded by Colonel Wood, up the Mississippi as early as 1648, and again in 1676, that he spent nearly ten years in exploring the Mississippi and its branches, and that explorers from Virginia crossed the Alleghanies and penetrated the upper Ohio river valley in 1654 and in 1664. It was claimed that in 1670 a vessel commanded by Captain Bolt navigated the Mississippi in the interests of England.* But these claims are usually disregarded by historians. It is not probable that Colonel Welch made the alleged journey to the Mississippi river. It is not likely that he ever saw any portion of the Louisiana Purchase.

When the charter of Hudson's Bay Company was granted in 1670, Charles the II and his minister were themselves uncertain of their boundaries in Canada. As early as 1630 the French Beaver Company secured a portion of the territory afterward claimed by Hudson's Bay Company. Owing to the uncer-

---

*Jeffery's Natural and Civil History of the French Dominions in North and South America. London, 1760.

tainty of their limits, the English ministry, therefore, inserted a proviso in the charter of Hudson's Bay Company, excluding therefrom "all the lands, territories, etc., at that time possessed by any other Christian prince or state." It later became known that long before the English traders had ventured far from Hudson Bay, the French voyageurs and explorers had penetrated as far west as the Saskatchewan river, and were in communication with all the intervening tribes of Indians. The rights of France and England in the vicinity of Hudson Bay were still undefined at the time of the treaty of Ryswick in 1697, as is shown by an article therein which provides that the country occupied there previously by France, but retaken by England, should be restored to the former. "It is not possible to conceive a more distinct and national acknowledgment that those countries did not belong to the crown of England at the time they were taken in the peace preceding the war, nor *a fortiori* at an earlier period." Thus it is clear that the territory granted to Hudson's Bay Company in 1670 could not have included any of the territory rightfully belonging to France. The treaty of Ryswick provided for the appointment of commissioners on both sides "to examine and determine the rights and pretensions which either of the said kings hath to the places situated on Hudson Bay;" but such a commission seems never to have acted. But even upon the supposition that Hudson's Bay Company's charter embraced the territory claimed by the French, the treaty of Ryswick annulled the company's rights in that quarter by ceding to France all the English territory there. In other words "the country granted by Charles II to Hudson's Bay Company was definitely and unreservedly made over to France." From the treaty of Ryswick in 1697 to the treaty of Utrecht in 1713, nearly all of the territory around Hudson Bay remained in the possession of France. At the latter date all of Hudson Bay passed to England for the first time.

But what did the Hudson Bay country include? All the territory draining into that bay, including the basins of the Albany, Souris, Assiniboine and Saskatchewan rivers and Red River of the North. Thus a considerable portion of the modern Minnesota and North Dakota and a small portion of Montana belonged to the basin of Hudson Bay. Inasmuch as that portion of the basin now within the United States could not have been granted, owing to the above reasons, to the Hudson's Bay Company in 1670, the grant made at a later day to Lord Selkirk could not have been valid. In 1811 he was granted a tract of sixteen thousand square miles in the valley of the Red River of the North, and he extended his limits into the present boundaries of the United States. In fact, he selected the most valuable land in the whole northwest. In 1818, when the forty-ninth parallel was established as the boundary between Canada and the United States, England deliberately divided the grant of Hudson's Bay Company to Lord Selkirk, throwing a portion of the same within the boundaries of the United States without consulting that company; nor did the latter make any complaint, nor ask for compensation for the loss. Lord Selkirk was a member of Hudson's Bay Company, and became a strong factor in that organization at certain periods of its distress, taking a large block of its stock. When the Northwest Fur Company appeared on the scene at a later day asking for a division of the spoils, it was bitterly opposed by Hudson's Bay Company; they finally united. Fearing too great an invasion of their territory, the Company from the very start opposed all attempts to discover a "northwest passage." It was publicly charged that Captain Middleton, who was sent in 1740 to find such a passage, received a bribe of $25,000 from Hudson's Bay Company, either to give up the exploration or to conceal what he should find.*

There is no doubt that the beautiful water-courses and velvet plains of the Upper Mississippi valley were visited and admired by French *coureurs* long before an attempt was made to penetrate the swampy mazes and tangled forests of the lower Louisiana country west of the great river. Canada, which had been settled many years before La Salle explored the Mississippi in 1682, sought every means to secure the fur trade of the northwestern tribes. From conditions in which there were immense profits there sprang up the famous *coureurs de bois,* who refused to be governed by the grants of trade privileges of the king and began an irregular traffic, first on the shores of the great lakes, and a little later on the branches of the upper Mississippi. Doubtless, many of these venturesome men, whose names are wholly unknown to history, traversed the country and opened the trade which became so valuable and so sought after by the merchants of Montreal and Quebec. The Indians were eager for guns, powder, lead, hatchets, scalping knives and merchandise, and readily parted with ten—yes, a hundred—times their valuation in furs and robes to these venturesome traveling traders, for

* An Examination of the Charter and Proceedings of the Hudson Bay Company, &c. James Edward Fitzgerald, London, 1849.

such the *coureurs de bois* were. It is well known that this class of bush rangers largely absorbed the northwest fur trade during the period of the earliest explorations and settlement. The king complained, the Company of the West complained, but what could be done when the *coureurs* were sustained by the merchants of Montreal? At first secrecy was enjoined, but when this course was found unnecessary and more or less burdensome, their dealings with the *coureurs* were openly transacted, despite the servants of the king. When such men as Du Lhut (Duluth) and Le Sueur openly placed themselves at the head of roving bands of *coureurs* and invaded the northwest, building palisaded forts here and there, forming their own treaties with the Indians, and obtaining the bulk of the immensely valuable fur trade, and when the merchants of Canada, knowing the power of such leaders and facing ruin if they opposed them, deliberately bid for their custom and openly sustained them, what could the King or the King's officers do but submit? Thus the Upper Mississippi valley came to be explored long before the slow-acting officers of the King had started west of the great lakes to find the Mechasipi or Mississippi, called the "Great River," with the hope that it would lead them to the South Sea.

One of the earliest Frenchmen to visit the Mississippi basin was Jean Nicolet. In 1643 he passed from Montreal to Georgian Bay, thence into Lake Huron, thence to the straits of Mackinac, whence he discovered Lake Michigan, and having coasted along its western shore in a small canoe, he entered Green Bay and there found the Ouinipegous (Winnebagoes), by whom he was well received. He brought with him a robe of gold cloth of some fanciful Chinese pattern, either for the purpose of impressing the Indians, or because he thought he might reach China, in which case he could appear in court costume without extra trouble or expense. Having robed himself in this garment, he astonished and awed his savage beholders. He told them that his object was to secure peace between the Indians and the French, and the savages gave him a royal feast, at which were served one hundred and twenty beavers. He went up the river Fox to the portage, and then down the Wisconsin, until, according to his own story, he was within three days' sail of the sea, as he supposed from the statements of the Indians, but really of the great water, the Mississippi. He thus narrowly missed a fame that would have made his name far more prominent in the annals of American discovery and exploration than the one he attained.

Nicholas Perrot accompanied the expedition under M. St.

Lusson, who took possession of the western country at the Sault Ste. Marie in 1671. In time he attained great influence over the western tribes, particularly over the Foxes, with whom the French had more trouble than with any other tribe, not excepting even the Sioux. The Foxes called him Metamenens, or Little Maize. He accompanied St. Lusson in the capacity of interpreter, and was sent to Green Bay and to the river Wisconsin to secure delegates to the conference at the Sault and to take possession of the western country in the name of France. The Foxes and Mascoutins refused to send delegates to the conference at the Sault. All the others in modern Wisconsin did. But the temper of the other two tribes was mollified by the courageous Perrot. On this visit he reached the headwaters of the Wisconsin river.

In the spring of 1685 Perrot was commissioned to go to Green Bay and was made commandant of the new countries he should discover. Taking twenty Frenchmen with him, representatives of Canadian merchants, he reached that point, and a few days later arrived at the portage between the Fox and the Wisconsin rivers, and there encountered opposition from a small band of the Hurons; but he continued on, reached the Mississippi, where he built a fort which was called St. Nicholas, sent a few Winnebagoes to open friendly communication with the Aiouez (Iowas) to the westward, and ascended the river for the purpose of finding another suitable location for a fort. One was selected on the Wisconsin shore of Lake Pepin, and the stockade was speedily erected and named Fort St. Antoine. The following year the Foxes, Kickapoos, Mascoutins and others to the number of one hundred made an attempt to surprise and destroy the fort, and would have done so if it had not been for the sagacity and courage of Perrot. He had been away and only six men were left in charge of the fort. Returning as the attack was on the point of being made, he deceived them into believing that the fort contained forty men, all well armed; but he would not have been able to accomplish this ruse had it not been for a friendly Mascoutin chief, who informed him of the intentions of the savages. A little later Perrot was ordered on important eastern service, and during his absence the fort was evacuated, owing to the hostility of the Indians, particularly the Sioux. In 1688 he returned, and with him at this time came forty Frenchmen, also representatives of Canadian merchants, all well armed and prepared to invade the territory of the dreaded Sioux. At Green Bay the wily and treacherous Foxes attempted to dissemble, but Perrot refused their feast until they had explained their recent hostile conduct.

Having humbled them, he continued down the Wisconsin and up the Mississippi to Fort St. Antoine. Here he soon made his influence felt, backed as he was by forty Frenchmen armed to the teeth. The Sioux became tamer and finally friendly. In the spring of 1689 they sent for him and escorted him to their villages, where he was received with great enthusiasm, real or affected. He was carried around on a beaver robe, followed by many Indians, all smoking, and was wept over after the custom of the savages by the head chiefs. He was probably now in the region of St. Croix river, the principal land of the Sioux. At this time he visited the Mantantans on St. Peter's river,* and other bands of the Sioux nation on the upper branches of the Mississippi. Descending the river to Fort St. Antoine or Anthony he took formal possession of the country in the name of the king of France, as shown by the following document:

"Nicholas Perrot, commanding for the King at the post of the Nadouesioux, commissioned by the Marquis D'Denonville, governor and lieutenant-general of all New France, to manage the interests of commerce among all the Indian tribes and peoples of the Bay des Puants, Nadouesioux, Mascoutins and other western nations of the Upper Mississippi, and to take possession in the King's name, of all the places where he has hitherto been and whither he will go. We this day, the 8th of May, 1689, do in presence of Father Marest of the Society of Jesus, missionary among the Nadouesioux; of M. D'Borie-Guillot, commanding the French in the neighborhood of Ouiskonche (Wisconsin) of the Mississippi; Augustin Legardeur, Sieur D'Caumont and MM. Le Sueur, Hebert, Lemire and Blein: Declare to all whom it may concern, that having come from the Bay des Puants and to the lake of the Ouiskonches and to the river Mississippi, we did transport ourselves to the country of the Nadouesioux on the border of the river Saint Croix, and at the mouth of the river Saint Peter, on the bank of which were the Mantantans, and farther up into the interior to the northeast of the Mississippi as far as the Menchokatoux, with whom dwell the majority of the Songestokous and other Nadouesioux, who are to the northeast of the Mississippi to take possession for, and in the name of the King, of the countries and rivers inhabited by said tribes and of which they are proprietors. The present act, done in our presence, signed with our hand and subscribed by Father Marest, MM

---

*The river St. Peter was no doubt named in honor of Peter Le Sueur, who later built Fort L'Huillier on one of its branches. He was present when Perrot thus took possession of the country in the name of France.

D'Borie-Guillot and Caumont and the Sieurs Le Sueur, Hebert, Lemire and Blein. Done at the post, St. Anthony, the day and year aforesaid."

About the year 1676 an engineer named Randin, who had assisted in laying out Fort Frontenac, was commissioned by the provincial government to visit the nations of the Ojibways and the Sioux living at the head of Lake Superior, to make them valuable presents for the purpose of gaining their good will. As nothing further is heard of this expedition, it is probable that it was abandoned.*

In September, 1678, Daniel Greysolon du Lhut (Du Luth) was granted the privilege of visiting the Sioux and Assiniboin nations for purposes of trade and discovery. With three French companions he went to Lake Huron, where he wintered, and early in April of the following year reached Sault Ste. Marie. Early in July he arrived at the country of the Issatis, a branch of the Sioux living at this time on Mille Lacs in the modern State of Minnesota, and formally took possession of the country for France. He had no doubt gone up the St. Louis river, thence crossed over to the Mississippi and descended to Sandy lake, then having on its shores the principal villages of this branch of the Sioux. He seems to have remained here a considerable length of time, and had the courage to make a long journey to the country of the Sissetons, another branch of the Sioux living about two hundred and fifty miles to the westward. His companions were MM. Lamonde, La Taupine and Dupuy. The following winter he lived at a rude post on the northern border of Minnesota, trading for all the beaver skins the Indians had, and collecting a large quantity. He and his companions were *coureurs de bois,* and did not scruple to take all the beaver skins offered. No doubt the authorities at Montreal divided the profits with him as a consideration for mutual benefits. In June, 1680, with four French companions and an Indian, he went again to the Sioux (Issatis) country, and while there learned of the presence of two whitemen farther south on another branch of the Mississippi. Thinking they might be Englishmen, bent on invading the territory which he had taken possession of in the name of France, he went down to investigate, and met Father Hennepin and his companion, as elsewhere narrated. Through the instrumentality of Du Luth they were set at liberty, and the Indians were severely rebuked for having treated them so shamefully.

Soon after this date Du Luth returned to Montreal, and later went to France. Upon his return in 1683, he was again licensed to trade with the western Indians and was authorized to hold them in subjection. About the time of his arrival at Keweenaw point of Lake Superior, two French traders there were murdered and plundered by the Indians. He immediately apprehended the murderers, gave them a fair trial and shot them in the presence of four hundred of their friends. By this date there were many French traders with headquarters at Keweenaw point—probably as many as one hundred. In performing this act of retaliation, Du Luth had back of him forty-two of these resolute men.

As early as 1659 Medard Chouard des Groseilliers and Peter Esprit de Radisson, two French runaways, who had assisted the English on Hudson Bay as against the French, were located at St. Esprit Point, or Chequamegon, on Lake Superior, about midway between the modern cities of Ashland and Washburn, Wisconsin. On that date they were engaged in trading with the Indians; and for the protection of their goods against the weather and the Indians, had erected a log fort. They had on hand guns, ammunition, hatchets, kettles, bells, beads, tobacco, etc., to be traded for the furs of the redmen. About this time, or a little later, it is known that they went as far to the northwest as the Mille Lac in Minnesota and Lake Assiniboine in Manitoba, and in doing so very probably passed across the divide to the Mississippi a short distance below the town of La Prairie, Minnesota. They were not alone, but no doubt had a number of French Canadians with them for the purpose of visiting the Indian tribes and trading for their furs. There is some evidence to show that they went to that point in about 1655; and it is claimed by some writers that they went there by the way of the Wisconsin and the Mississippi rivers, but this is not known to be a fact. If it were true, their discovery of the Mississippi would ante-date that of Joliet and Marquette by fifteen to eighteen years. Father René Menard had come to this section about the same time as a missionary among the Tinnontates, the Tobacco band of the Hurons, who had fled west to Lake Superior before the hostile Iroquois. It is claimed that the Tinnontates fled to Green Bay, thence across to the Mississippi via the Wisconsin, thence up the former and either the Chippewa or the St. Croix to Lake Superior, and that Father Menard accompanied them. If so, he may have been the discoverer of the upper Mississippi. But it is not known to be true. It is known, however, that Radisson and Groseilliers met the Tinnontates among the marshes of the upper Chippewa

branches. Here and on Lake Superior this tribe met the Ottawas and formed an alliance with them against the Sioux. They
seem to have located finally on Black river, Wisconsin, where
Father Menard served them until his disappearance in about
1660-1. His hassock and breviary found later among the Sioux
proved what had become of him. In 1660 Radisson and Groseilliers returned to Canada with sixty canoes loaded with valuable
furs and were accompanied and assisted by several hundred
Indians. They had heard of the great river to the westward.

Every attempt made by the French to explore the northwest,
was governed by the particular object of limiting the advances
of the English in that direction. Du Luth, although one of the
most prominent and indefatigable of the *coureurs de bois,* took
upon himself nevertheless the task of preventing the English
from reaching the upper branches of the Mississippi or the southern and western borders of Lake Superior. The dauntless Perrot assumed the same responsibility. In fact the licenses of the
coureurs were granted at Montreal upon the distinct proviso that
the English must be forestalled, as one of the primary objects of
the westward movements of the French traders. But notwithstanding this injunction which was faithfully observed, and notwithstanding the covert approval of the illicit trade of the *coureurs* at
Montreal and the friendship and encouragement of the merchants
there, the former found it decidedly to their advantage to take
their furs to the English settlements along the Atlantic coast.
By doing so they often received double the price for their furs.
It was reported that during the summer of 1679, the trader La
Taupine obtained from the Ottawas in two days' trading about
nine hundred beaver skins. Others were equally lucky, and the
trade went to the English. In 1681 amnesty was granted to the
coureurs, and after that date they were duly licensed, but their
operations would have continued the same, license or no license.
Unquestionably, the presence of Du Luth on the upper branches
of the Mississippi and along the western border of Lake Superior,
prevented the English of Hudson Bay from invading that rich
fur country and fastened the claim of France to that soil.

Father Marquette reached La Pointe de Esprit in September,
1669. The French traders had been there for more than ten
years. He writes, "When the Illinois (Indians from the west
side of the Mississippi, near the mouth of the Des Moines river)
come to La Pointe, they cross a great river, which is nearly a
league in width, flows from north to south and to such a distance
that the Illinois, who do not know what a canoe is, have not yet

heard any mention of its mouth. . . . It is hard to believe
that that great river discharges its waters into Virginia, and we
rather think it has its mouth in California. If the savages who
promise to make me a canoe do not break their word to me, we
shall explore this river as far as we can, with a Frenchman and
this young man (an Illinois Indian), who was given me (to be
his slave) and who knows some of those languages (of the tribes
along the Mississippi), and has a facility for learning the others.
We shall visit the natives dwelling there, in order to open the
passage to such of our Fathers as have been awaiting this good
fortune for so long a time. This discovery will give us full
knowledge either of the South sea or the Western sea." Father
Marquette would have gone to the Mississippi at this time had it
not been for the threats of the Sioux. Through his Indian slave
and otherwise he heard much of the Illinois across the Mississippi
and earnestly desired to open that field to the missionary service.
At this time the Illinois had eight large villages west of the Mississippi near the mouth of the Des Moines, and invited visits
from the missionaries. It was an opportunity, or "good fortune"
as he termed it, which greatly impressed the good Father Marquette. Where so many nations received the Fathers indifferently
or with death, it was an important epoch to be invited to visit
them. He therefore waited impatiently to make the journey to
the Illinois on the Mississippi.

Father Allouez wrote in 1669 of the Wisconsin river that "it
leads to the great river called Messisipi* which is only six days'
sail from here." Father Dablon wrote in 1670 that the Indians
reported the great river to flow over three hundred leagues to the
south and that it was more than a league wide. It was in 1669
that La Salle went down the Ohio river to the falls at Louisville.
The same year two French traders at La Pointe de Esprit, while
out on the lake fishing, were surprised by a sudden and violent
storm and drowned. West of La Pointe about fifty or sixty
leagues were the fierce and unrelenting Sioux, standing as a barrier against the westward advancement of the eastern Indians
or the Frenchmen. But by going in considerable numbers and
well armed, the latter steadily made inroads in their domain.
Good results were anticipated from these visits. Father Claude

---

* Father André, while on Green Bay and Fox river in 1672, learned that Missipissi was the Neptune, or evil Manitou, of the Indians then there—Menomonees,
Pottawattomies and others. At their village of Chouskouebika (probably the
modern Pensaukee), the Indians gave feasts and sacrifices to gain the favor of this
deity. As the name Missipissi is much like Mississippi, and as it signified the
deity of the water or great water, may not this have been the origin of the latter
which signifies great water?

Allouez wrote in 1672, "Thus our holy faith is more and more gaining a foothold among these peoples, and we have good hope that in a short time we shall carry it as far as the famous river named Missisipi and perhaps even to the South Sea."

The zeal of the missionaries for the conversion of the Indians—for the salvation of their souls—led to their visits to the savage villages. As early as 1559 the Dominicans traversed the country from Pensacola to the Mississippi—may have even crossed that river. They felt amply repaid for all their dangers and hardships when they were permitted to baptize dying infants or adults, believing, as they did, that the souls of such were sent thereby to heaven. It was not until 1658 that the Jesuits of Canada determined to visit the country of the Foxes, Illinois, and the tribes on the Mississippi. The missons at Sault Ste. Marie, Green Bay and Mackinac were the first in the West. René Menard went to Keweenaw on Lake Superior in 1660, and Claude Allouez followed him in 1665, going to Chequamegon. He was the first missionary to meet the Sioux and to learn of the existence of the Mississippi. A few years later Marquette was prevented from visiting the Sioux by their hostility, but he likewise learned of the Mississippi and determined to visit the tribes thereon at the first opportunity, for the purpose of carrying the light of the gospel to those heathen. Then came the Kaskaskia mission founded by Marquette and continued by Allouez and Gravier. The Marests, Mermet, Pinet and Bennetau, soon came to the Illinois. With Iberville, came Jesuits to the mouth of the Mississippi, but a mission was not established there until later. In 1698 St. Comé and Davion were sent to Louisiana by the Catholic Seminary at Quebec. Poisson was murdered at Natchez, Souel at Yazoo, Senat burnt at the stake, and Doutreleau wounded at a later date. Aubert was killed while with D'Verendrye in the northwest. Guignas had failed to found a mission among the Sioux. It remained for men like Du Luth to compel the Sioux to treat the missionaries as befitted their efforts and to permit the establishment of missions among them. At no time was the policy of France toward her missionaries as favorable and encouraging as that of Spain toward hers. The latter in almost every instance backed the missions with detachments of soldiers, with colonists, seeds, stock, implements, etc. The former permitted the missions to take care of themselves. If they were destroyed by the Indians, the French government did little or nothing to repair them. The Most Christian King did not prove himself such in the wilds of America. Hence the well-meaning Fathers were derided, starved, burnt and butchered, and yet they immensely assisted in advancing the colonial interests of their country.

Before the nature of the Indians was fully known to Europeans, the policy of Louis XIV was to civilize them, and Frontenac was told to amalgamate them with the whites. His first efforts. were aimed at this object; but his course was not approved by the Jesuits, who were later accused of having at heart a much greater interest in their property than in the usefulness of their missions. In fact, this was one of the charges against them when they were expelled from the colony in 1764. But whatever may be said against them, they cannot be charged with lack of zeal, nor of willingness to face hardships and danger. It is true, however, that their efforts to convert the Indians, likewise the efforts to civilize them, were wholly wasted. The nature of the Indian was hostile to both these prerogatives of the white race.

It was destined that Louis Joliet and Father James Marquette should lay the foundation of French discoveries and claims on the Mississippi river. The former was born in Canada, and educated at the Jesuit college at Quebec, and was afterward in close sympathy with the Jesuit missionary work, though himself engaged in the fur trade. His experience in the western wilderness, familiarity with the Indian tongues, skill in overcoming the hostility of the natves, and hardihood and invincible courage, caused him to be selected by the Provincial Government for the discovery of a route to the South Sea. This expedition was incited by M. Talon, Intendant of Canada, to whom the distinguished credit should be given. He selected Louis Joliet as the fittest man then available in the Province, to conduct the expedition; and further decided that one of the Jesuit priests should accompany him in the capacity of companion and assistant.

At this stage of the proceeding that was destined, undreamed of by the actors, to become so prominent a feature in subsequent French negotiations in America and in the history of the United States, M. Talon, the father of the enterprise, was recalled to France upon his own request, owing to serious disagreements between him and Governor Courcelles, and was thus no longer identified with the expedition. However, he was succeeded luckily by an able and ambitious man, Count Frontenac, who continued his laudable yet daring project of sending out the expedition under Joliet for the primary purpose of discovering the South Sea and incidentally a practicable route to the same. Frontenac charged Joliet with the leadership of the expedition upon the recommendation of Talon, who had described him "as being a man experienced in this kind of discovery, and who had been already very near that river." The object of the expedition was to go to the Mississippi river (then unnamed and unknown, save as called by the Indians, "The Great River," or the Mechisipi, and extravagantly described by them) and explore it with the expectation of finding some water route leading by it, or from it, to the South Sea. Some writers lose sight of the paramount object—the discovery of a route to the South Sea. They presume that the design was to discover the Mississippi, which had been discovered by the Spaniards more than one hundred and fifty years before. Numerous Spanish and Portuguese maps, showing the Mississippi extending up into the heart of the continent, had been published long before and circulated throughout Europe. Unquestionably, copies had reached Paris. Making all due allowances for the imperfect means then existing for the communication of such information, accounts of the expeditions of D'Garay and De Soto had no doubt attained the same wide publicity. In other words, it is reasonable to suppose that France had learned of the existence of the Mississippi from the Spanish accounts and maps. But this, of course, was the lower Mississippi.

The French of Canada learned from the missionaries, who obtained their information from the Indians, of the existence of a "great river" far to the west of Lake Michigan. But it is not unreasonable to suppose that the idea entered the minds of Talon and Frontenac that the "great river" of the Spanish might be the same as the "great river" west of Canada and the lake system; but this surmise is not known to be a fact. The air was full of rumors concerning the mysteries of the western wilderness. The "great river" reputed to lie there might lead southwestward to the South Sea. The "great river" of the Spanish might not extend so far to the north, or might turn to the east or the west. Therefore, there is nothing to show that prior to the expedition of Joliet and Marquette any one had determined the identity of the two "great rivers." The object of the expedition is unmistakably laid bare by the following letter from Frontenac to the French minister of state, Colbert, after the return of the explorers. In the caption and in the text the object is shown to be the discovery of the South Sea. It will be admitted that no one could speak with higher authority on this subject than Frontenac, unless it was Talon:

"Return of Sieur Joliet from His Voyage for the Discovery of the South Sea:

"The Sieur Joliet, whom M. Talon advised me when I arrived from France to send to discover the South Sea, returned here three months ago, and has discovered some admirable countries, and a navigation so easy by the fine rivers, that he found that from Lake Ontario and Fort Frontenac they could go in barques to the Gulf of Mexico, having only to unload once, where Lake Erie falls into Lake Ontario. These are some of the enterprises they could work upon when peace is established, and it shall please the king to push these discoveries. He has been within ten days of the Gulf of Mexico and believes that (through) the rivers, which empty into the great river from the west . . . they will find some communication by these waters which will lead to the Vermillion Sea and that of California. I send you by my secretary the map which he has made and the remarks which he is able to remember, having lost all his memoirs and journals in the shipwreck which he suffered in sight of Montreal, where, after a voyage of twelve hundred leagues, he came near being drowned and lost all his papers and a little Indian that he was bringing back with him. He had left at Lake Superior, with the Fathers at Sault Ste. Marie, copies of his journals, which we cannot obtain until next year; through these you will learn more of the particulars of that discovery in which he acquitted himself very creditably."

"Frontenac."

"Quebec le 14 Novemb., 1674."

The expedition, then, presents two important features: First, a commercial one, represented by Louis Joliet, an experienced fur-trader and explorer, who was charged to find a route to the South Sea, in order that the commerce of Asia and its adjacent islands might find thereby a shorter route to the marts of Europe; and was further charged to find and explore the "great river" with the hope that it would solve the riddle which had thus puzzled Europe for nearly three centuries; Second, a religious one, whereby the powerful and invaluable influences of the Jesuits upon the Indians might contribute to the success of the expedition and open the way to an easier conquest of the country by the crown of France.

The companion and assistant of Joliet was chosen upon the recommendation of the superior general of the Jesuits at Quebec, and proved to be James Marquette, who had spent many years among the various Indian tribes, could speak several of their languages fluently, possessed to a remarkable degree the power to assuage the fiery spirit of the savages, and was endowed by his Creator with one of the most lovable souls ever offered to martyrdom in the American wilds. He had been west as far as Green Bay and the southwestern shore of Lake Superior; but in 1672 was stationed at Sault Ste. Marie, which, with Father Dablon, he had previously founded, engaged in his holy work of instructing the savages in the rites of the Catholic faith. While in the west, he continued to hear of the "great river," which the Indians called variously "Mechisipi," "Mesissipi," etc.,* learned of the fierce and powerful Sioux and other large nations along its banks or in its vicinity, and formed the resolution with all the fervor and piety of his ardent nature to carry to them at the first opportunity the blessings of Christianity. His enthusiasm possessed no touch of commercialism; he was there to save the souls of the heathen, and was ready to brave every danger and hardship to carry the cross to new tribes. As the sequel proved, his selection was eminently wise, because his peaceful demeanor and fine, magnetic presence more than once unquestionably prevented an attack upon the little expedition.

Owing to the loss of Joliet's journal, it has been necessary for historians to rely for details upon the accounts given by Father Marquette. Doubtless, this has led some writers to put him in the first place of importance in the expedition. Without disparaging his eminent services, it is not just to slight, nor omit just recognition of, the heroic Joliet, the official head and commander of the expedition. No doubt the comparative prominence given to the services of Father Marquette has resulted from the publicity given to his account by the Jesuits and by historians. Joliet seems to have set out from Montreal, passing up the lakes to Michillimackinac, where he found Father Marquette at his mission house and chapel at Point St. Ignace. The latter says in his journal: "In 1673, the Count de Frontenac, our governor, and M. Talon, then our intendant, knowing the importance of this discovery, either to seek a passage from here to the China sea by the river which empties into the California or Red sea, or

---

* Many names were applied to the Mississippi, among which are the following: Espiritu Santo; La Plicada and Rio Escondido by the Spaniards; La Conception (Marquette), St. Louis (La Salle), Buade, the family name of Frontenac, Joliet), Colbert by the French; Match-cha-sipi, Malbouchia or Balbouchia, Mirabichi, Chacagua, Messippi, Meschasebi, Oquechiton by the Indians. It is claimed that "Miss" means "great" and "sipi" means "water."

to verify what was afterward said of the two kingdoms of The-
guaio and Quivira, which border on Canada, and where gold
mines are, it is said, abundant, these gentlemen, I say, both at
the same time selected for the enterprise the Sieur Jollyet, whom
they deemed competent for so great a design, wishing to see
Father Marquette accompany him.   They were not mistaken in
their choice of the Sieur Jollyet, for he was a young man, born
in this country, and endowed with every quality that could be
desired in such an enterprise.   .   .   .   The day of the Immac-
ulate Conception of the Blessed Virgin, whom I had always
invoked since I have been in this Ottawa country, to obtain of
God the grace to be able to visit the nations of the river Missisipi,
was identically that on which M. Jollyet arrived with orders of the
Count de Frontenac, our governor, and M. Talon, our intendant,
to make this discovery with me.   I was the more enraptured at
this good news, as I saw my designs on the point of being accomplished, and myself in the happy necessity of exposing my life for
the salvation of all these nations, and particularly for the Illinois,
who had, when I was at La Pointe du St. Esprit, very earnestly
entreated me to carry the word of God to their country.   We
were not long in preparing our outfit, although we were embarked
on a voyage the duration of which we could not foresee.   Indian
corn, with some dried meat, was our whole stock of provisions.
With this we set out in two bark canoes, M. Jollyet, myself, and
five men, firmly resolved to do all and suffer all for so glorious
an enterprise."

From this extract is learned what the object of the expedition was thought by them to be—to seek a passage to China or
to verify the old stories of gold at Quivira, or the "Seven Cities
of Cibola," tales based upon actualities.   No mention is made
that the object was to discover the Mississippi.   The expedition,
consisting of seven men, left St. Ignatius on May 17, 1673, having
been since the previous December engaged in preparing for the
journey.   Marquette says, "As we were going to seek unknown
countries, we took all possible precautions, that, if our enterprise
was hazardous, it should not be foolhardy; for this reason we
gathered all possible information from the Indians who had fre-
quented those parts, and even from their accounts traced a map
of all the new country, marking down the rivers on which we were
to sail, the names of the nations and places through which we
were to pass, the course of the great river, and what direction we
should take when we got to it."

They passed up the Fox river, carried their canoes across the portage, re-embarked on the Wisconsin river, and slowly sailed down that treacherous stream. They were assisted as far as the portage by Indians from Green Bay; there their guides stopped, not daring to go farther, as their nation was at war with the tribes farther down the Wisconsin river. Finally they reached the "great river," which Father Marquette had so earnestly longed to visit; and he says, "After forty leagues on this same route, we reached the mouth of our river, and finding ourselves at 42½ N., we safely entered the Mississippi on the 17th of June, with a joy that I cannot express."*

On sounding, they found ten fathoms of water. They floated down with the current, rowing to assist, and having passed about half a degree, observed that the surrounding woods and mountains had disappeared, and that the "islands are more beautiful, and covered with finer trees." He describes the various animals in detail, and the natural features of the country. "Proceeding south and south-southwest, we find ourselves at 41 north: then at 40 and some minutes, partly by southeast and partly by southwest, after having advanced more than sixty leagues since entering the river, without discovering anything." He meant by the latter clause that they had encountered no human beings. Continuing, "at last, on the 25th of June, we perceived footprints of men by the water side, and a beaten path entering a beautiful prairie. We stopped to examine it, and concluded that it was a path leading to some Indian village, we resolved to go and reconnoitre; we accordingly left our two canoes in charge of our people, cautioning them strictly to beware of a surprise; then M. Jollyet and I undertook this rather hazardous discovery for two single men, who thus put themselves at the discretion of an unknown and barbarous people." This was a remarkable undertaking, and signifies the heroic character of the two explorers. They had been told again and again that the Mississippi tribes would kill them on sight, and for aught they now knew they were approaching their dooms of torture. That knowledge did not deter them in the slightest degree: they had come for the purpose of visiting the tribes along the river and exploring its shores and the surrounding country, and were prepared to meet death at any moment in the discharge of their duty. Although the narrative does not say so, the maps show that this landing was made on the

---

*Joliet named the Mississippi "Buade," the family name of Governor Frontenac.

west side of the Mississippi river; they were, therefore, upon modern Iowa soil, near the mouth of the Des Moines river.*

The narrative continues, "We followed the little path in silence, and having advanced about two leagues (a little more than five miles), we discovered a village on the banks of the river, and two others on a hill half a league from the former." The location of these villages will always be a matter of doubt. From the accompanying map made by Marquette, it will be seen that the three villages are placed on what appears to be an island of a river surely too small to be, as claimed, the Des Moines. But it is now generally conceded that no other river was meant, and that the landing was at or near the modern village of Montrose, a small creek to the west of it forming a curve, and the land beyond appearing like an island. Two of the villages are named by Marquette—Peouarea and Moingwena. The latter is known to have been the modern Des Moines, and the former the modern Peoria, branches of the Illini family.

The narrative continues (after they had caught sight of the Indian villages), "Then, indeed, we recommended ourselves to God, with all our hearts; and having implored his help, we passed on undiscovered, and came so near that we even heard the Indians talking. We then deemed it time to announce ourselves, as we did by a cry, which we raised with all our strength, and then halted without advancing any further. At this cry the Indians rushed out of their cabins, and having probably recognized us as French, especially seeing a black gown (Marquette evidently had on his priestly garb), or at least having no reason to distrust us, seeing we were but two and had made known our coming, they deputed four old men to come and speak with us. Two carried tobacco pipes well adorned, and trimmed with many kinds of feathers. They marched slowly, lifting their pipes toward the sun, as if offering them to him to smoke, but yet without uttering a single word. They were a long time coming a little way from the village to us. Having reached us at last, they stopped to consider us attentively."

They immediately made friends with the Frenchmen, and said they were of the Illinois nation, presented their pipes to be smoked, and invited the visitors to the village "where all the tribe awaited us with impatience." At the door of the main cabin, they were received by an old man, who was standing stark naked,

* Along the Des Moines river Joliet places the Illinois, Peorias, Moingwenas, Pawnees, Omahas, Otontantas, Pawlets, and others. He says that the Peorias had 300 cabins.

with his hands raised as if to shield his eyes from the sun, and who delivered this salutation: "How beautiful is the sun, O Frenchmen, when thou comest to visit us! All our town awaits thee, and thou shalt enter all our cabins in peace." There could hardly have been rendered a finer compliment or a more beautiful greeting. The reaction in the feelings of the two Frenchmen from iron to sunny peace, must have afforded them the most intense delight. The whole village was theirs for the asking. Then succeeded a long round of ceremony, of feasting and smoking, of friendly speeches and greetings. "You must not refuse the calumet, unless you would pass for an enemy, or at least for being impolite. It is, however, enough to pretend to smoke. While all the old men smoked after us to honor us, some came to invite us on behalf of the great sachem of all the Illinois to proceed to his town, where he wished to hold a council with us. We went with a good retinue, for all the people who had never seen a Frenchman among them could not tire looking at us; they threw themselves on the grass by the wayside, they ran ahead, then turned and walked back to see us again. All this was done without noise, and with marks of a great respect entertained for us."

At the great sachem's town, they were received by the sachem himself at his cabin door, standing between two old men like himself, all three stark naked, and with their calumets turned toward the sun. The Frenchmen were greeted as usual, and then the designs of the Frenchmen were made known to the following effect, Marquette acting as spokesman: 1st, They were on their journey by this river to the sea; 2d, They came to reveal God to them; 3d, The French chief sent word "that he had spread peace everywhere and had overcome the Iroquois;" 4th, They desired all the information the Indians could give them of the sea and the nations along the river banks to the south. "When I had finished my speech, the sachem rose, and laying his hand on the head of a little slave, whom he was about to give us, spoke thus, 'I thank thee, Blackgown, and thee, Frenchman (Joliet), for taking so much pains to come and visit us; never has the earth been so beautiful nor the sun so bright as today; never has our river been so calm nor so free from rocks, which your canoes have removed as they passed; never has our tobacco had so fine a flavor, nor our corn appeared so beautiful as we behold it today. Here is my son that I give thee, that thou mayst know my heart. I pray thee to take pity on me and all my nation. Thou knowest the Great Spirit who has made us all; thou speakest to him and hearest his word; ask him to give me life and health, and come and dwell with us, that we may know him.' Saying this, he placed the little slave near us and made us a second present, an all-mysterious calumet, which they value more than a slave." How was it possible to prove his friendship in a stronger way? Gave his son to Joliet for a slave; gave away his sacred calumet; offered a free home to Father Marquette; said the earth was more beautiful for their coming. Thus the savages in Iowa greeted the first Frenchmen to visit them—men who were there to fasten the chains of France to their limbs and bring to them an unknown and unappreciated religion.

At the conclusion of this ceremony, a great feast followed consisting of four courses: 1st, Indian meal boiled in water and seasoned with grease; 2d, Fish with the bones removed; 3d, a large dog, which was politely declined by the guests; 4th, a piece of wild ox (probably buffalo), "the fattest portions of which were put into our mouths." In fact, the Frenchmen were fed by the Indians with spoons as little children are. This village was a large one, consisting of "full three hundred cabins." The Frenchmen were made all sorts of presents, and were finally escorted to their boats by nearly six hundred persons. "We take leave of our Illinois (friends) about the end of June, at three o'clock in the afternoon, and embark in sight of all the tribe, who admire our little canoes, having never seen the like. We descend, following the course of the river, toward another called Pekitanoui, which empties into the Missisipi, coming from the northwest, of which I have something considerable to say, after I have related what I have remarked of this river. From the start they used every precaution against surprise. "We advanced constantly, but as we did not know where we were going, having already made more than a hundred leagues (from Wisconsin) without having discovered anything but beasts and birds, we kept well on our guard (written when above the Des Moines). Accordingly, we make only a little fire on the shore at night to prepare our meal and after supper keep as far off from it as possible, passing the night in our canoes, which we anchor in the river pretty far from the bank. Even this did not prevent one of us being always as a sentinel for fear of a surprise."

When they reached the mouth of the Pekitanoui, while rowing in clear water, they suddenly heard a noise like a waterfall, and looking ahead, saw a large mass of trees floating across their course, and threatening to engulf them. "The agitation was so great that the water was all muddy and could not get clear."

He did not know then that the normal condition of the Missouri water was "all muddy." For this was the great Missouri.* "Pekitanoui is a considerable river which coming from very far in the northwest, empties into the Missisipi. Many Indian towns are ranged along this river, and I hope by its means to make the discovery of the Red or California sea. We judged by the direction the Missisipi takes, that if it keeps on the same course it has its mouth in the Gulf of Mexico; it would be very advantageous to find that which leads to the South sea, toward California and this, as I said, I hope to find by Pekitanoui."

Proceeding, they reached the mouth of the Ouaboukigou, or Ohio, above which, evidently on the west side of the river, they "perceived an iron mine, which they deemed very rich; there are many veins and a bed a foot thick. Large masses are found combined with pebbles." Going on, they saw Indians with guns, who proved to be Chicachas, or Chickasaws, and who received them with friendly greetings, and fed them on wild beef, bear's oil and white plums. "They have guns, axes, hoes, knives, beads, and double glass bottles in which they keep their powder. . . . They assured us that it was not more than ten days' journey to the sea; that they bought stuffs and other articles of Europeans on the eastern side; that these Europeans had rosaries and pictures; that they played on instruments. . . . This news roused our courage and made us take up our paddles with renewed ardor. We advanced then, and now begin to see less prairie land, because both sides of the river are lined with lofty woods." They heard wild cattle bellowing. "We had now descended to near 33 degrees north, having almost always gone south, when on the water's edge we perceived a village called Mitchigamea." This was situated on the west side of the river, in modern Arkansas. Here it was that they passed successfully their greatest danger during the journey. The Indians made preparations to attack them both by land and water, but were finally pacified by the sight of the calumet. They remained here all night, but received little information, though they were told that down the river eight or ten leagues they would reach a great village called Akamsea (Arkansas), where they would learn all they desired to know. Arriving at Akamsea (near the mouth of the River Arkansas),† they were well received and feasted for an entire day, evidently to a surfeit, on sagimity, Indian corn whole, pieces

*Joliet omitted to name the Missouri on his map; but he places the Missouris, Kansas, Osages, Pawnees and others along its course.
†Joliet named the Arkansas river "Bazire" after a Quebec merchant.

of dog flesh, etc.   During the night a secret council was held by some of the sachems "on the design to kill us for plunder, but the chief broke up all their schemes, and sending for us, danced the calumet in our presence as a mark of perfect assurance: and then to remove all fears presented it to me."

"M. Jollyet and I held another council to deliberate on what we should do, whether we should push on, or rest satisfied with the discovery that we had made.   After having attentively considered that we were not far from the Gulf of Mexico, the basin of which is 31 degrees, 40 minutes north, and we at 33 degrees and 40 minutes, so that we could not be more than two or three days' journey off; that the Missisipi undoubtedly had its mouth in Florida or the Gulf of Mexico, and not on the east in Viriginia, whose seacoast is 34 degrees north, nor on the western side in California, because that would require a west or west-southwest course, and we had always been going south.   We considered, moreover, that we risked losing the fruit of this voyage, of which we could give no information, if we should throw ourselves into the hands of the Spaniards, who would undoubtedly, at least, hold us as prisoners.   Besides, it was clear, that we were not in a condition to resist Indians allied to Europeans, numerous and expert in the use of firearms, who continually infested the lower part of the river.   Lastly, we had gathered all the information that could be desired from the expedition.   All these reasons induced us to resolve to return: this we announced to the Indians, and after a day's rest prepared for it.   After a month's navigation down the Missisipi from the 42d to below the 34th degree, and after having published the gospel as well as I could to the nations I had met, we left the village of Akamsea on the 7th of July, to retrace our steps.   We accordingly ascended the Missisipi, which gave us great trouble to stem its currents.   We left it indeed, about the 38th degree, to enter another river, which greatly shortened our way, and brought us, with little trouble, to the lake of the Illinois."   Marquette remained in the west, but Joliet continued on to Montreal, to make his report to the Provincial Government.   When within a few miles of that place, and while still on the river St. Lawrence, his boat was upset in the rapids, and the journal of the expedition was lost, together with the little Indian boy, whom the chief of the Peorias had given him in what is now Lee county, Ia.   It is said that Joliet struggled several hours in the water before he succeeded in reaching shore.

The object of the expedition was accomplished in part only—the South sea had not been discovered; neither had the golden

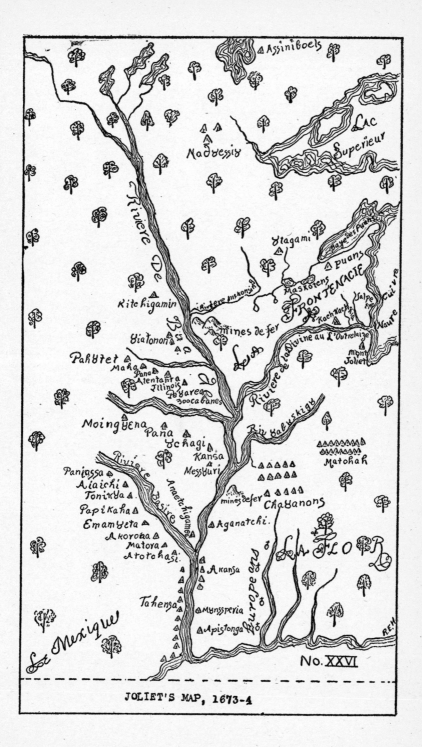

Assiniboels

LAC
Superieur

Nadvessiv

Riviere De

Ytagami
Baye des Puans

Maskotens
FRONTENACIE
Riviere mskonsin

Kitchigamin

mines de fer

Ytatonon

Riviere de la Divine au L'Outrelaize

Mont
Joliet

Pahutet
Maha
Pana
Atentanra
Illinois
Peyarea
3oo cabanes

Riu babuskigu

Moinguena
Pana
Ychagi
Kansa
Messpuri

Matohah

Paniassa
Aiaichi
Tonikya
Papikaha
Emamueta
Akoroba
Matora
Atotchasi

Riviere

Basire

Anaetchigamea

mines de fer
Chayanons

Aganatchi.

LA FLOR

Akansa

Tahensa

Europeans o

Mansspeia

Apistonga

Le Mexique

R.E.H.

No. XXVI

JOLIET'S MAP, 1673-4

land of Quivira, if that had been one of the objects; but the upper Mississippi had been found, explored from the mouth of the Wisconsin to about the mouth of the Arkansas; its identity with the Rio del Espiritu Santo of the Spaniards established; and the fact that it flowed into the Gulf of Mexico instead of the Vermillion sea definitely settled. It was further learned that the Missouri extended far westward, and that via it a way might yet be found to reach the South sea. The great Joliet and his no less great assistant and companion, Marquette, secured at once among Frenchmen the credit to which they were entitled for the results of their hazardous expedition. Joliet was obliged to make his report from memory, but this was sufficient to satisfy the Provincial Government. He had merely carried the route to the South sea one step nearer its destination. Unknown to him, he had also invaded the modern Louisiana Purchase at several points, and had made one of the first maps of its eastern border, of the river course, and of the Indian villages in that section of the province.

As an additional proof that the paramount object of this expedition was the discovery of the South sea and not that of the Mississippi, it may be noted that no action was taken by the Provincial Government to establish settlements in the region thus explored under Joliet—to take advantage of the discovery, which added to France a splendid new empire, which she was not slow to estimate at its true value a few years later. For ten years this land, flowing with milk and honey, went begging for occupancy by the nations of Europe. Had the English at that time established a few settlements on the upper Mississippi, the war of 1755-62 might have been avoided, and European history vastly changed. Had Spain, during this period, sent colonies to the upper and lower Mississippi, she would have secured what she struggled so hard to obtain in subsequent years—the exclusive right to navigate that river, and the establishment of the Gulf of Mexico as a *mare clausem,* or closed sea. However, no matter which nation had profited by this expedition of Louis Joliet, the end would have been the same—the transfer of the river and the country to the United States in spite of all Europe.

It appears strange at first glance to observe that France did not take immediate advantage of this discovery of the Upper Mississippi; but it does not seem so strange when the object of the French is taken into consideration. They were not looking for a country to colonize, nor for the ultimate object of finding the Mississippi; but were in search of a water route to the South sea

I—6

(Pacific ocean). When it was learned that the Mississippi did not lead to the South sea, except perhaps remotely through the Missouri, the object of France was accomplished. This view seems to afford the only reasonable conclusion as to why France did not follow up the discovery with colonies along the Mississippi. Father Marquette, on the other hand, desired to reach the "great river" in order to establish missions among the Indians there—particularly among the Illinois. His object was wholly realized. But the time had not come for France to feel the imperative necessity, in order to forestall Spain and Great Britain, of establishing permanent colonies on the banks of the Mississippi. She therefore waited; and in the meantime other important discoveries were made. The following patent explains itself:

"LOUIS, BY THE GRACE OF GOD, KING OF FRANCE AND NAVARRE: To OUR DEAR AND WELL-BELOVED ROBERT CAVELIER, SIEUR DE LA SALLE, GREETING:

"We have received with favor the very humble petition, which has been presented to us in your name, to permit you to endeavor to discover the western part of New France; and we have consented to this proposal the more willingly, because there is nothing we have more at heart than the discovery of this country, through which it is probable a road may be found to penetrate to Mexico; and because your diligence in clearing lands which we granted to you by the decree of our council of the 13th of May, 1675, and by Letters Patent of the same date, to form habitations upon the said lands, and to put Fort Frontenac in a good state of defense, the seigniory and government whereof we likewise granted to you, affords us every reason to hope that you will succeed to our satisfaction and to the advantage of our subjects of the said country.

"For these reasons, and others thereunto moving us, we have permitted and do hereby permit you by these presents, signed by our hand, to endeavor to discover the western part of New France, and for the execution of this enterprise to construct forts wherever you shall deem it necessary; which it is our will that you shall hold on the same terms and conditions as Fort Frontenac, agreeably and conformably to our said Letters Patent on the 13th of March, 1675, which we have confirmed as far as is needful, and hereby confirm by these presents. And it is our pleasure that they be executed according to their form and tenor.

"To accomplish this and everything above mentioned we give you full powers; on condition, however, that you shall finish this enterprise within five years, in default of which these presents shall be void and of no effect; that you carry on no trade whatever with the savages called Outaouacs and others who bring their beaver skins and other peltries to Montreal; and that the whole shall be done at your expense and that of your company, to which we have granted the privilege of the trade in buffalo skins. And we command the Sieur de Frontenac, our Governor and Lieutenant-General, and the Sieur Duchesne, Intendant, and the other officers who compose the supreme council of the said country, to affix their signatures to these presents; for such is our pleasure. Given at St. Germain en Laye, this 12th day of May, 1678, and of our reign the thirty-fifth.

"(Signed)   Louis."

Inasmuch as the above "letters patent" were the basis and authority for the proceedings of M. de la Salle in his attempt to explore the western country for his king, it may be well to regard it with more than a passing glance. The king acknowledged that he received with favor "the very humble petition" of M. de la Salle to explore for the glory and benefit of his sovereign "the western part of New France" upon the conditions that he should finish the enterprise within five years, that he should carry on no trade with the Indian tribes which brought their beaver and other skins to Montreal, and that the whole expense should be borne by M. de la Salle and his company, their only recompense being "the privilege of the trade in buffalo skins." If La Salle expected any other remuneration for this extraordinary service, he seems to have been left free to get such as he could from the forts he should establish and the savage tribes through which he should pass. After he had already done such good service for his country, which was duly acknowledged by his sovereign, it seems passing strange that the whole expense of this expedition of discovery, from which France was sure to gain such immense benefit in knowledge and territory, should have been coolly placed on the shoulders of this heroic man. But if the King of France was not actuated by noble motives, his "humble" subject, the Sieur de la Salle, most certainly was. He did not hesitate to risk all his property and his life on the explorations which he knew meant so much to the colonial importance and graudeur of France. He was pre-eminently, if not the leader, one of the leaders of the newly developed movement to place the whole of the Mississippi valley under the control and sovereignty of France before any other nation could forestall the attempt. The king's patent shows nothing of all this. The king seems to have had no other or higher motive than to permit M. de la Salle to explore the western part of New France at his own risk and expense. The vast question that was destined soon to shake the world in war—the rightful possession of the Mississippi valley through the sovereignty of that river—had yet found no serious consideration at the Court that was seeking by force of arms to dismember all Europe in order that it might bind the fragments to its emaciated self. The mighty Louis, therefore, in response to the "humble" petition of his faithful subject, M. de la Salle, condescended to permit him under severe restrictions to go among the Western savages, where death was almost certain to be encountered, and make important and valuable discoveries for the enlightenment and benefit of France. He may have known the man to whom he committed this privilege. If so, he knew him to be brave, intelligent, unconquerable by hardships, loyal to his sovereign, patriotic in every beat of his great heart and faithful unto death.

La Salle hoped to secure recompense from the seignory of the forts which he should erect and from certain other privileges; but this was merely a hope, from which nothing was realized. It was necessary for him to abandon all his own pursuits, to suffer serious losses at the outset, to fight against severe sickness and other discouraging misfortunes, to put everything he possessed into the venture, and to borrow extensively from his friends, for people instinctively trusted this uncommon man. He was expected to establish forts in the wilderness, around which should grow up prosperous colonies, yielding him a pleasing revenue. His past was excellent. He had written his name deep in the tomes of the perpetual woods, by the deadly swamp and the roaring river, along the perilous trails where cannibals skulked and prowling wolves waited their repast. His views were correct. The Mississippi flowed into the Gulf; forts established along its course cemented the ownership of France; the marvelous fertility of the great valley was revealed; the establishment of a splendid empire for France in the New World kindled the heart. All this he saw, and it passed with his blood. He fought down ill report; overcame all opposition to his scheme of adding to the crown of France a jewel of dazzling radiance; and willingly placed in the balance the fortunes of himself and his friends and the glorious reputation he had earned with his vital breath on other deadly journeys among the savages.

It would seem that Colbert, the French minister, had in view in thus sending out M. de la Salle, the establishment of forts along the Mississippi for the purpose of hampering the movements of the Spaniards in their mining operations farther to the west. It became known to the French that Spain was receiving immense amounts of gold and silver from her American possessions, and the hearts of the great Louis XIV and Colbert became exceedingly envious. It was a period in the history of human events when the prosperity of one nation was succeeded by the jealous hostility of every other. If one made a lucky find or stroke, others demanded a division, and war followed a refusal, all for the glory of the King and the Holy Church. Thus it was natural and politic that France should want a division of the spoils wrested from the American savages. Incidentally, they may have thought that the possession of the Mississippi valley might be advantageous to French finances and pride. La Salle was just the man to suit their wishes, because he was wholly unselfish, devoted to his country, and an earnest adherent of the Catholic Church. His influence upon the Indians was sure to be beneficial; his power to cement men and hold them to broad ideas of improvement, was all important where organization was everything. He was young, his birth having occurred at Rouen, in Normandy, France, November 22, 1643; he was therefore fuller of vigor and less liable to become dogmatic than an older person would have been. After having performed a number of important services among the savages of America, all with uncommon success, he was now, without suitable compensation, to be sacrificed in the terrible Mississippi country.

In preparing for his expedition La Salle requested that Father Louis Hennepin, the Recollet friar, might accompany him in the capacity of chaplain and misisonary. As it turned out, Hennepin became the chief chronicler of the expedition, but it is not always possible to tell when he is recording history and when sailing on the seas of fancy. Luckily for La Salle, he had a powerful assistant in the redoubtable Henry de Tonty, who could always be depended upon in any emergency, but about whom unfortunately very little is positively known. Though an Italian, he had lost his right hand in battling for the king of France, but this loss was partly remedied or supplied by an iron or a copper one. The expedition journeyed westward by stages, first to Niagara, in the vicinity of which their boat was built, the first of considerable size to navigate the upper lakes. It was begun January 22, 1679, and continued under the immediate supervision of Sieur de Tonty. It was necessary to guard it constantly to prevent its being burned by the Senecas. It was finished and launched above the Falls by the middle of July and towed up the river nearly to Lake Erie, to be rigged before being set adrift on the treacherous waters of the inland lakes. It was a sail-rigged and sea-going schooner, armed with five small cannon and three large muskets. At the bow was rudely carved the armorial bearings of the Count de Frontenac, a griffin, which gave name to the ship. It was of about sixty tons burden, and cost according to Father Hennepin about $12,000, but this estimate was made at the time it was loaded with furs, worth say $2,000.

At length the start was made August 7, 1679, amid the discharge of the cannon and the chanting of the Te Deum. They ascended through Lake St. Clair, Lake Huron, where they weathered a terrible gale, passed through the straits of Michillimackinac, stopping at the chapel at St. Ignace, continued the voyage about the 2d of September, and in due time arrived at Green Bay, on the western shore of Lake Michigan. It was here that La Salle received large quantities of furs, to be sent back to Montreal on the Griffin for his private account. It does not appear to have been a violation of his patent, provided he did not deal in beaver skins. But the vessel after setting forth on her return was never again heard from. Whether she foundered in a gale, was burned by the Indians at some stopping place, or was scuttled by the sailors, after they had first sold the furs for their own gain, will never be known. It has been stated that La Salle himself long entertained the latter notion. He had previously lost so often and so heavily from similar dishonest practices, that this view is not to be wondered at, nor is it probably wrong.

He had committed the Griffin to a pilot and five sailors, which act reduced his forces to fourteen men. On the 19th of September, he proceeded in four canoes along the western shore of Lake Michigan, rounding the southern end and finally landing at the mouth of the St. Joseph river, Michigan. It was now about the first of November. Here they awaited the arrival of Sieur de Tonty with twenty-four men, and in the meantime built a wooden fort eighty feet long and forty feet wide near the mouth of the river, and named the same Fort Miami, after the tribe of Indians in the neighborhood. On December 3, the Tonty party having arrived, the forces now aggregating about thirty-three persons, ascended the St. Joseph river or its branches to the vicinity of South Bend, Ind., thence by portage passed across to the Kankakee, and thence down the same to the Illinois river, which they slowly descended in their boats. During much of this journey, snow mantled the earth, and the cold was severe. Near

Starved Rock they found the principal village of the Illinois Indians, consisting of four hundred and sixty lodges or wigwams. Here La Salle arrived December 25. After securing a quantity of maize from the Indian stores, they continued their journey, the village being deserted. The Indians were away on their annual hunt. In two days they arrived at Lake Peoria or Lac Pimiteoui. They were well received by the village, comprising about eighty lodges, and treated to a feast of buffalo meat. At this point some of his men deserted him. Messengers from the Iroquois prejudiced the Peorias against him. He was poisoned by some of his own men, but an antidote saved him.

Under these and other almost insuperable obstacles, La Salle was at last forced to the conclusion to proceed no farther until the return of spring. The remainder of his men were set to work to build a fort on a hill in what is now the suburb of Peoria. By about the first of March, 1680, it was so near finished that it was occupied by the whites and named Crevecoeur, or Broken Heart, after a fortress of that name in the Netherlands. During this time, also, he put his best mechanics to work on a brigantine to be used in navigating the Illinois and the Mississippi rivers the ensuing year. Finally, leaving the faithful Tonty in charge of the forces and fort, La Salle returned to Canada to procure appliances that were absolutely needed, leaving instructions with Michael Accault to proceed to the Mississippi as soon as the ice should break up and explore the upper course of that river, La Salle promising to send men down the Wisconsin as soon as possible to meet him and assist him in making the exploration. Thus, after the most herculean labors, the expedition was brought to a temporary standstill. Although the Griffin had likely been sent to the bottom; her valuable cargo of furs had probably been sold and the proceeds confiscated by his men; his best forces had deserted him; all had been saved from starvation only by the Indians; some of his men had tried to murder him with poison, and he was ruined financially and his friends ruined with him, this remarkable man did not for an instant falter in the line of duty marked out for him by his king, but resolutely set forth anew to build and equip a brigantine that should yet carry him to success on the waves of the surging Mississippi. Struck by the severest adversity, he showed like flint the fire that was in his adamantine heart. His fort should have been named Coeur de Leon.

He had left with Tonty at Fort Crevecoeur fifteen men, and had taken with himself four and in addition his Mohegan hunter.

They passed up the Illinois river, thence across the portage to Lake Michigan, thence around to Fort Miami on the St. Joseph river, thence across Michigan to Detroit, thence down the lakes, and finally arrived at Fort Frontenac May 6, 1680. Here La Salle found that his affairs had gone from bad to worse, and his creditors were preparing to seize the residue of his estate. While here he learned, also, that the deserters from Fort Crevecœur had captured and destroyed Fort Miami. With a party of men, he waylaid these rascals on their return to Canada, killed two and imprisoned the others at Frontenac. Nothing was heard from the Griffin; it had disappeared forever. A vessel for his relief from France was wrecked in the Gulf of St. Lawrence, and much of the cargo was lost. As a whole, matters could scarcely be worse, and would have taken the heart out of any other person than this iron man.

On the 10th of August, with a new outfit and a company of twenty-five new men, and assisted by a lieutenant named La Forest, he started for Fort Crevecœur and the relief of Tonty. Upon his arrival there he found the fort dismantled, the camp deserted, although his unfinished brigantine was apparently uninjured. He continued on down the Illinois to its mouth, and saw for the first time the mighty stream to which his name was destined to be inseparably linked through all history. Not finding Tonty nor any trace of him, he resolved to turn back, despite the counsel of his associates to go on down the Mississippi. But he well knew that he would need all his forces, especially the invincible and faithful Tonty, and so resolved to find him before continuing the journey. Accordingly, he passed back to Fort Miami on Lake Michigan, arriving in January, 1681.

In the meantime, Tonty had been deserted by all his men but five, and the deserters had dismantled Fort Crevecœur, and gone back to Canada. Under the direction left by his chief, he went up the Illinois and fortified Starved Rock, and afterward repaired partially the dismantled Fort Crevecœur. The five men who remained with him were Francois de Boisrondet, Etienne Renault, Fathers Ribourde and Membre and L'Esperance, the servant of La Salle. Here they would have been found by La Salle on his return, had they not been dispersed by the Iroquois, who came to attack the Illinois. The extraordinary dealings of Tonty with the Iroquois on this occasion—his tact, courage, persistence and generalship—have scarcely ever been surpassed in the history of Indian negotiation. He saved the Illinois tribe from destruction, though they were dispersed and he was finally compelled to start back for Canada. He was several times wounded and a dozen times within an inch of death. On this journey Father Ribourde was murdered by a small band of Kickapoos. After extraordinary hardships, the remainder of the little party reached Green Bay, and were saved from starvation in mid-winter by the friendly Pottawattomies. In the spring they continued on to Mackinac to await the return of La Salle. The latter had made no mistake in selecting the heroic Tonty for his lieutenant.

While La Salle was away from Fort Crevecœur, Michael Accault as instructed took two men and a canoe, rowed down the Illinois to the Mississippi, and thence up that stream on a voyage of discovery. La Salle had told Father Louis Hennepin that he should expect him to accompany the expedition. He gave Accault a calumet of peace and one man to row the canoe and assist him, and commodities to the value of about $200, to be used in making presents to the savages, whom they were sure to encounter. Ten knives, twelve shoemaker's awls, two pounds of colored glass beads, a parcel of needles, were included in the outfit. Thus provided Accault and his two companions set out down the Illinois on the 29th of February, 1680. Hennepin says, "When we had gone fifty leagues down the river, we came to the place where it falls into the Mississippi. . . . The ice which came down stopt us here till the 12th of March." Hennepin claims that the expedition went south to the sea, but it could not possibly have done so in the time he mentions. His story is so irregular, and so manifestly incorrect, that no absolute dependence can be placed in his narrative. It seems, however, that they went up the Mississippi, as they had been told to do, or were taken up, as far as the Falls of St. Anthony, which Hennepin really named; and they were thus apparently the first white men to explore the Mississippi above the mouth of the Wisconsin. They were captured a short distance above the mouth of the Illinois by a large war party of savages (Sioux) on their way down the river and came near being killed through the ardor of the young warriors. "Having thus traveled nineteen days in our canoe by water, we came within six leagues of the fall of St. Anthony, where they held an assembly to consult what they should do with us." (Upon reaching Lake Pepin, Hennepin named it Lake of Tears from the wailing of some of the Indians.) At last they separated and gave us to three of their chiefs, instead of three of their sons which had been killed in the war; then they seized our canoe (when near St. Paul) and took away all our equippage; our canoe they pulled to pieces; their own they hid among the alders, so that though we might have gone conveniently enough quite up to their country by water, yet we were obliged by their conduct to travel no less than sixty leagues afoot."

According to the account of Hennepin, they were taken far to the north, on the Rum or St. Francis river in Minnesota, near Mille Lac, where they were adopted into different bands of the same tribe, after which their treatmnt was about the same as that of the Indians. Hennepin became the son of Aquipaguetin, a sub-chief of the Issati, or Issanti, a division of the great Sioux nation, the terror of all the nations to the south and east. The three whites made themselves useful, and soon gained the good graces of their captors. The principal chief, Ouasicoudé, became their fast friend—was really angry that they had been despoiled of their goods. Finally, they all went on a grand buffalo hunt to the mouth of the St. Francis or Rum river. Here Hennepin prevailed upon the principal chief to permit him to go to the mouth of the Wisconsin, to meet his friends whom La Salle had promised to send there to join him. Michael Accault, who liked the wild Indian life, refused to go with him; but Pickard Du Gay accompanied him. The two were given a small birch canoe, an earthen pot, a gun, a knife and a robe of beaver skin. They soon reached the Falls of St. Anthony and passing round it, continued down the Mississippi, suffering intensely from want of sufficient food, reaching and passing Lake Pepin. They soon after met Aquipaguetin and a party of warriors, who reported that no white traders had yet reached the mouth of the Wisconsin; whereupon, in sheer desperation, they determined to join a large party of Sioux hunters, to save themselves from starvation. Among this band they found Accault. All participated in the grand hunt along the borders of the Mississippi, in the heat of July and amid the wonderful foliage of the upper river. While thus engaged they learned that a party of whitemen from Lake Superior were approaching their vicinity, and soon afterward there arrived Daniel Greysolon du Lhut and four other Frenchmen, all well armed. They were now east of the Mississippi on the Chippeway river. Du Lhut had already become famous as a discoverer in the region of Lake Superior. All being French, and having in view the same general objects, they went back with the Sioux to their villages on Mille Lac. After this, undoubtedly through the influence of Du Lhut, Hennepin and his party were feasted and permitted to do as they pleased. Du Lhut and his party finally determined to accompany Hennepin on his journey to the mouth of the Wisconsin, and thence to Green Bay. It was now autumn, but the journey was made without accident. The men whom La Salle had promised would be sent to the mouth of the Wisconsin were not seen, and the travelers continued on to Green Bay, and thence on to Canada.

The incursion of the Iroquois into the Illinois country, evidently an attempt of the English to extend the Iroquois domain well into the valley of the Mississippi and hence a corresponding extension of their own territory, was estimated at its true import by the observant La Salle. To counteract the attempt, he resolved to try to cement the western tribes against the Iroquois, and to center them around a strong fort which he should erect on the Illinois river. In the spring, La Salle went with a small party from Fort Miami to the Illinois river, and while there learned what had become of Tonty, and also learned that Father Hennepin had passed through the Wisconsin country on his way to Canada. After attempts to cement the friendship of the Miamis and and the Illinois, La Salle returned to Mackinac, and there met Tonty and his little party. Their adventures were recounted and their ready sympathies exchanged. One would think that they were now ready to give up the project of exploring and taking possession of the Mississippi, but not for an instant was this paramount object lost sight of by La Salle and Tonty. It was determined to return to Canada, recruit themselves thoroughly, and try again.

With a force of thirty men and with ten or a dozen heavily-laden canoes, La Salle again finally set forth, passing up Lake Ontario to about the present Toronto, thence across to Georgian bay, thence through the straits and down the eastern side of Lake Michigan to Fort Miami, thence around the lake to the Chicago river, thence up the same and across the portage to the Des Plaines, and thence down the same and the Illinois. It was now January, 1682, and the prairies were covered with snow and the rivers with ice, so that the journey was made mostly by sledge. Some of his men had deserted him at Mackinac, but at Fort Miami he had recruited his forces with French-Canadians and Indians to forty-one men and a number of squaws to do the cooking. Arriving at Peoria Lake, they resolved not to finish the brigantine, but to proceed as they were, and accordingly continued, and on February 6, 1682, reached the Mississippi, which was then filled with floating ice and formed a beautiful but dangerous sight. On February 13, the river having become comparatively clear, they all started down on the swift current. Thus, after the lapse of two years and a half from the date of first setting out, the expedition was afloat on the sweeping Mississippi, a fact all important to the modern inhabitants of the Louisiana Purchase.

"We descended the river and found six leagues below on the right a great river (the Missouri—Ed.), which comes from the west, on which there are numerous nations. We slept at its mouth. The next day we went on to the village of Tamarous, six leagues off on the left. There was no one there, all the people being at their winter quarters in the woods. We made marks to inform the savages that we had passed, and continued our route as far as the river Ouabache (Wabash), which is eighty leagues from that of Illinois. It comes from the east, and is more than 500 leagues in length. It is by this river that the Iroquois advance to make war against the nations of the south. Continuing our voyage about sixty leagues we came to a place which was named Fort Prudhomme (Memphis), because one of our men lost himself there when out hunting and was nine days without food. As they were looking for him they fell in with two Chikasas savages, whose village was three days' journey inland. . . . M. de la Salle sent back one of them with presents to his village, so that if they had taken Prudhomme they might send him back, but we found him on the tenth day, and as the Chikasas (Chickasaws) did not return we continued our route as far as the village of Cappa, fifty leagues off (one hundred and thirty miles below Memphis). We arrived there in foggy weather, and as we heard the sound of the tambor we crossed over to the other (west) side of the river, where in less than half an hour we made a fort. The savages having been informed that we were coming down the river, came in their canoes to look for us. We made them land and sent two Frenchmen as hostages to their village; the chief visited us with the calumet and we went to the savages. They regaled us with the best they had, and after having danced the calumet (dance) to M. de la Salle, they conducted us to their village of Toyengan, eight leagues from Cappa. They received us there in the same manner, and from thence they went with us to Toriman two leagues further on, where we met with the same reception.

"It must be here remarked that these villages, the first of which is Osotonoy, are six leagues to the right descending the river, and are commonly called Akancas (Arkansas). The first three villages are situated on the river (Mississippi). M de la Salle erected the arms of the King there; they have cabins made with the bark of cedar; they have no other worship than the adoration of all sorts of animals. Their country is very beautiful, having abundance of peach, plum and apple trees, and vines flourish there; buffaloes, deer, stags, bears, turkeys are very numerous. They have even domestic fowls. They have very little snow during the winter, and the ice is not thicker than a dollar. They gave us guides to conduct us to their allies, the Taencas, six leagues distant. The first day we began to see and to kill alligators, which are numerous and from fifteen to twenty feet long. When we arrived opposite to the village of the Taencas, M de la Salle desired me to go to it and inform the chief of his arrival. I went with our guides, and we had to carry a bark canoe for ten arpens (nearly two-thirds of a mile), and to launch it on a small lake in which their village was placed. I was surprised to find their cabins made of mud and covered with cane mats. The cabin of the chief was forty feet square, the wall ten feet high, a foot thick, and the roof, which was of a dome shape, about fifteen feet high. I was not less surprised when on entering I saw the chief seated on a camp bed, with three of his wives at his side, surrounded by more than sixty old men, clothed in large white cloaks, which are made by the women out of the bark of the mulberry tree and are tolerably well worked. The women are clothed in the same manner; and every time the chief spoke to them, before answering him, they howled and cried out several times, "O-o-o-o-o-o-o!" to show their respect for him, for their chiefs are held in as much consideration as our kings. . .

"When I was in his cabin, the chief told me with a smiling countenance the pleasure he felt at the arrival of the French. I saw that one of his wives wore a pearl necklace. I presented her with ten yards of blue glass beads in exchange for it. She made some difficulty, but the chief having told her to let me have it, she did so. I carried it to M de la Salle, giving him an account of all that I had seen, and told him that the chief intended to visit him the next day, which he did. He (La Salle) would not have done this for savages, but the hope of obtaining some merchandise induced him to act thus. He came the next day with wooden canoes to the sound of the tambour and the music of the women. The savages of the river use no other boats than these. M de la Salle received him with much politeness and gave him some presents; they gave us in return plenty of provisions and some of their robes. The chiefs returned well satisfied. We stayed during the day, which was the 22d of March. An observation gave thirty-one degrees of latitude. We left on the twenty-second and slept in an island ten leagues off. The next day we saw a canoe, and M. de la Salle ordered me to chase it, which I did, and as I was just on the point of taking it, more than one hundred men appeared on the banks of the river to defend their people. M. de la Salle shouted out to me to come back, which I did. We went on and encamped opposite them. Afterward, M. de la Salle expressing a wish to meet them peaceably, I offered to carry them the calumet, and embarking went to them. At first they joined their hands as a sign that they wished to be friends; I who had but one hand told our men to do the same thing. I made the chief men among them cross over to M. de la Salle, who accompanied them to their village three leagues inland and passed the night there with some of his men. The next day he returned with the chief of the village where he had slept, who was a brother of the great chief of the Natchez; he conducted us to his brother's village, situated on the hillside near the river at six leagues distance. We were well received there. This nation counts more than 300 warriors. Here the men cultivate the ground, hunt and fish, as well as the Taencas, and their manners are the same.

"We departed thence on Good Friday, and after a voyage of twenty leagues, encamped at the mouth of a large river, which runs from the west (Red River). We continued our journey and crossed a great canal, which went toward the sea on the right (probably Atchafalaya river). Thirty leagues further on we saw some fishermen on the bank of the river and sent to reconnoitre them. It was the village of the Quinipissas, who let fly their arrows upon our men, who retired in consequence. As M. de la Salle would not fight against any nation, he made us embark. Twelve leagues from this village, on the left, is that of the Tangibaos. Scarcely eight days before this village had been totally destroyed. Dead bodies were lying on one another and the cabins were burnt. We proceeded on our course, and after sailing forty leagues arrived at the sea on the 7th of April, 1682."*

Concerning the mouth of the Mississippi, or rather the mouths, Tonty wrote as follows: "M. de la Salle sent canoes to inspect the channels; some of them went to the channel on the right hand, some to the left, and M. de la Salle chose the center. In the evening each made his report, that is to say, that the channels were very fine, wide and deep. We encamped on the right bank; we erected the arms of the king, and returned several times to inspect the channels. The same report was made. . . .

---

*Memoir by the Sieur de la Tonty, sent in 1693, on the discovery of the Mississippi and the neighboring nations.

Provisions failing, we were obliged to leave the sea coast sooner than we wished, in order to obtain provisions in the neighboring villages. We did not know how to get anything from the village of the Quinipissas, who had so ill-treated us as we went down the river. We lived on potatoes until six leagues from their village, when we saw smoke." Here the Indians made every pretense of friendship, but the next morning at day break attacked the whites. They were vigorously repulsed, and the journey up the river was continued. When the Natchez nation was reached, again protestations of friendship were made, but the signs of hostility were too numerous. "We went up to their village, and as we saw no women there we had no doubt of their having some evil design. In a moment we were surrounded by 1,500 men. They brought us something to eat, and we ate with our guns in our hands. As they were afraid of fire-arms they did not dare to attack us. The chief begged M. de la Salle to go away, as his young men had not much sense, which we very willingly did— the game not being equal, we having only fifty men, French and savages. We then went on to the Taencas and then to the Akansas, where we were very well received. From thence we came to Fort Prudhomme, where M. de la Salle fell dangerously ill, which obliged him to send me forward on the 6th of May to arrange his affairs at Michillimackinac. In passing near the Ouabache (Wabash meaning the Ohio), I found four Iroquois, who told us that there were one hundred men of their nation coming on after them. This gave us some alarm. There is no pleasure in meeting warriors on one's road, especially when they have been unsuccessful. I left them and at about twenty leagues from Tamaraas we saw smoke. I ordered our people to prepare their arms, and we resolved to advance, expecting to meet the Iroquois. When we were near the smoke, we saw some canoes, which made us think that they could only be Illinois or Tamaraas. They were in fact the latter. As soon as they saw us, they came out of the wood in great numbers to attack us, taking us for Iroquois. I presented the calumet to them; they put down their arms and conducted us to their village without doing us any harm. The chiefs held a council, and taking us for Iroquois, resolved to burn us; and but for some Illinois among us we should have fared ill. They let us proceed. We arrived about the end of June, 1682, at the river Chicagou, and by the middle of July at Michillimackinac. M. de la Salle having recovered, joined us in September."

After reaching the mouth of the Mississippi, they ascended a short distance to a considerable elevation, prepared a column and a cross, and upon the column fastened the arms of France and the following inscription:

LOUIS LE GRAND, ROI DE FRANCE ET DE
NAVARRE, REGNE: LE NOUVIEME
APRIL, 1682.

"The whole party under arms chanted the Te Deum, the Exaudiat, the Domine Salvum fac Regem; and then, after a salute of firearms and cries of Vive le Roi, the column was erected by M. de la Salle, who, standing near it, said with a loud voice, in French: 'In the name of the most high, mighty, invincible, and victorious prince, Louis the Great, by the grace of God, king of France and Navarre, fourteenth of that name, this ninth day of April, one thousand six hundred and eighty-two, I, in virtue of the commission of his Majesty (Louis XIV), which I hold in my hand, and which may be seen by all whom it may concern, have taken, and do now take in the name of his Majesty and of his successors to the crown, possession of this country of Louisiana, the seas, harbors, ports, bays, adjacent straits; and all the nations, people, provinces, cities, towns, villages, mines, minerals, fisheries, streams, and rivers comprised in the extent of Louisiana, from the mouth of the great river St. Louis on the eatsern side, otherwise called Ohio, Alighinsipou (Alleghany), or Chickagoua, and this with the consent of the Chouanons (Shawanoes), Chicachas (Chickasaws), and other people dwelling therein, with whom we have made alliance; as also along the River Colbert or Mississippi, and rivers which discharge themselves therein, from its source; beyond the country of the Kious (Sioux) or Nadouessions, and this with their consent, and with the consent of the Motantees, Illinois, Mesigameas (Metchigamias), Akansas, Natches, and Koroas, which are the most considerable nations dwelling therein, with whom also we have made alliance either by ourselves or by others in our behalf; as far as the mouth at the sea or Gulf of Mexico, about the 27th degree of the elevation of the north pole, and also to the mouth of the river of Palms (Rio de Palmas); upon the assurance which we have received from all these nations that we are the first Europeans who have descended or ascended the River Colbert, hereby protesting against all those who may in future undertake to invade any or all of these countries, people, or lands above described to the prejudice of the right of his Majesty acquired by the consent of the nations herein named, of which and all that can be needed, I hereby take to witness those who hear me, and demand an act of the notary as required by law.'

"To which the whole assembly responded with shouts of Vive le Roi and with salutes of fire-arms. Moreover, the said Sieur de la Salle caused to be buried at the foot of the tree to which the cross was attached a leaden plate, on one side of which were engraved the arms of France and the following Latin inscription:

"LUDOVICUS MAGNUS REGNAT.
NONO APRILIS CIO IOC LXXXII.
ROBERTUS CAVELIER, CUM DOMINO DE TONTY, LEGATO R. P. ZENOBIO MEMBRE, RECOLLECTO, ET VIGINTI GALLIS, PRIMUS HOC FLUMEN, INDE AB ILINEORUM PAGO, ENAVIGAVIT, EJUSQUE OSTIUM FECIT PERVIUM, NONO APRILIS ANNI CIO IOC LXXXII."

"After which the Sieur de la Salle said that his Majesty, as eldest Son of the Church, would annex no country to his crown without making it his chief care to establish the Christian religion therein, and that its symbol must now be planted, which was accordingly done at once by erecting a cross, before which the Vexilla and the Domine Salvum fac Regem were sung, whereupon the ceremony was concluded with cries of Vive le Roi. Of all and every of the above the said Sieur de la Salle having required of us an instrument, we have delivered to him the same signed by us, and by the undersigned witnesses, this ninth day of April, one thousand six hundred and eighty-two."

"De La Salle.
"P. Zenobe, Recollect Missionary.
"Henry De Tonty.
"Francois de Boisrondet.
"Jean Bourdon.
"Sieur D'Autray.
"Jaques Cauchois.

"Pierre You.
"Gilles Meucret.
"Jean Michel, Surgeon.
"Jean Mas.
"Jean Dulignon.
"Nicolas de La Salle."
"La Metairie, Notary."

In a letter to the French minister under date of November 6, 1787, Governor D'Denonville wrote, "The year after, in 1672, the Mississippi river was discovered, as well as the Illinois, Chaounanons (Shawanese) and other tribes unknown to the Europeans, by Sieur Jolliet and the Jesuit Father Marquette, who reached the thirty-second degree, planting the royal arms and taking over in the King's name the newly discovered countries. A few years later, Sieur de la Salle pushed his discoveries further onward as

I—7

tar as the sea, taking possession everywhere by planting the
royal arms."

The following order was issued by the king, pursuant to the
request of La Salle, to be permitted to establish a colony at the
mouth of the Mississippi:

"LOUIS, BY THE GRACE OF GOD, KING OF FRANCE AND NAVARRE,
GREETING:

"Having resolved to cause some expeditions to be undertaken
in North America, to subject to our dominion divers savage
tribes, and to convey to them the light of the faith and of the
Gospel, we have been of the opinion that we could not make a
better choice than of Sieur de la Salle to command in our name
all the Frenchmen and Indians whom we will employ for the
execution of the orders we have entrusted unto him. For these
and other reasons us moving, and being moreover well informed
of his affection and fidelity for our service, we have by these
presents signed by our own hand constituted and ordained, and
do commission and ordain, the said Sieur de la Salle to command
under our authority, as well in the country which will be subject
anew to our dominion in North America, from Fort St. Louis
on the Illinois river unto New Biscay (Durango), as well among
the French and Indians whom he will employ in the expedition
we have entrusted to his care, cause them to live in union and
concord the one with the other; keep the soldiers in good order
and police according to our rules; appoint governors and special
commanders in the places he shall think proper, until it shall be
by us otherwise ordered; maintain trade and traffic and generally
to do and to exercise for us in the said country all that shall apper-
tain to the office of commandant, and enjoy its powers, honors,
authorities, prerogatives, franchises, liberties, wages, rights,
fruits, profits, revenues and emoluments during our pleasure, to
execute which we have given and do give unto you power by these
presents, whereby we command all our said subjects and soldiers
to acknowledge, obey, and hear you in things relating to the
present power. For such is our pleasure. In witness whereof
we have caused our privy seal to be affixed to these presents.
Given at Versailles the 14th of April, 1684."

"(Signed)   "LOUIS."

After his voyage to the mouth of the Mississippi, La Salle
returned to France, made his report and his recommendations,
and was received with such favor that his losses and misfortunes
were, to a great degree, removed and settled. France and Spain

were now at war. La Salle proposed to the French court to establish a fortified colony on the Mississippi, about sixty leagues from its mouth, and make it the principal depot of the trade of the river valley. In order to carry this design into execution he asked for one war vessel of about thirty guns, necessary ordnance for the fort that he should erect, and two hundred men to be recruited in France, to protect the fort and the colony. Should every thing go well with the colony, he further assured the French court that he would have no serious difficulty in raising a large force of Indians for the conquest of New Biscay (Durango) from the Spaniards. These schemes were disclosed by La Salle to Louis XIV in person, who received them with evidences of satisfaction. That monarch was then in the heyday of his ambition and military splendor, and the idea of a vast increase in his American dominions at the expense of the Spanish government met his hearty approbation.

Instead of one vessel, the king offered La Salle four. The little fleet, consisting of the Joly, a frigate of thirty-six guns, the Belle, a small frigate of six guns, the Aimable, a store-ship and the St. Francois, a ketch of two masts, set sail from Rochelle on July 24, 1684. The latter was captured by the Spanish, which was a serious loss, as she was laden with stores and ammunition. After stopping some time at St. Domingo to replenish the losses so far as possible they again set out on the 25th of November, the fleet now reduced to three ships. Rounding the western extremity of Cuba, they steered northward, but through a series of baffling currents and shifting winds were driven far out of their intended course and finally came to anchor in Espiritu Santo Bay on the coast of Texas. After consultation they decided to retrace their steps, and accordingly sailed eastward ten or twelve leagues and anchored in what is now the Bay of St. Bernard, or Matagorda. It had been ordered that Capt. Beaujeu should command the vessels while at sea, and that La Salle should command on shore. This arrangement had already occasioned considerable trouble, but at St. Bernard an unfortunate disagreement arose over the provisions. La Salle, in order to save the provisions designed for the colonists from the sailors resolved to land at this bay, which he accordingly did. It was realized that the vessels had missed the mouth of the Mississippi, but La Salle resolved to make the most of the mistake. He wanted to go to the Mississippi, but as he and Capt. Beaujeu could not agree regarding water and stores, he soon learned that if the object of the expedition was to be accomplished it would be necessary to land at once and begin operations where they were.

Accordingly, he resolved to make a permanent landing where they were. Orders were given to disembark the colonists and troops on the western shore of Matagorda Bay. The Belle was anchored in the bay without accident on the 18th of February; but the Aimable was intentionally run upon the shoals by her captain, D'Aigron, who had formed a dislike for La Salle. There it remained for three weeks or more, and in the meantime all was saved from her that was possible. Finally a storm tore her in pieces and scattered her along the coast. Barring this wholly unnecessary and criminal accident, the landing was effected successfully, including the ordnance, stores, colonists, etc. A total of eight iron cannon was landed for the armament of the fort that should be built. About the middle of March, Captain Beaujeu prepared to return to France, his mission having ceased with the landing of the colonists. Several of the latter, who had become timorous regarding the fate of those who were to remain with La Salle, returned on the vessel with Beaujeu. There had been considerable ill feeling between La Salle and Beaujeu, but at the moment of separation friendly overtures prevailed. It is to be remarked, however, that had it not been for the hostility engendered between them during the voyage, La Salle would not have remained at Matagorda Bay, but would have gone on to the Mississippi as originally intended. Had he done so, the results of the expedition might have been far more successful. As a matter of fact, La Salle should have insisted to be taken to the Mississippi, and to have thrown the responsibility of any other course on the shoulders of Beaujeu. But the nature of La Salle was to make the most of circumstances, without losing sight of his main object. He thought that he could reach the Mississippi from Matagorda Bay without much trouble, or that at the worst could erect a fort where he was, and thus take possession of the coast much farther to the westward, for the benefit of France, than was the mouth of the Mississippi.

Beaujeu was no sooner gone than the colonists set to work to build a fort, largely from the wreck of the ship. The men began to desert—first two and then four or five others; in the meantime La Salle accompanied by about fifty men went up the river at that point to find if it was an arm of the Mississippi, as was suspected by some. He left in the fort about one hundred and thirty persons under the command of Henry Joutel. Strict orders were left to have nothing to do with the natives, who, it had been learned, were not to be trusted. La Salle reported upon his return that the country above was very rich and abounded in all sorts of wild animals; and announced that he had resolved to build his fort higher up the stream in a much better locality. Preparations were made to secure the necessary timbers, which were cast up by the sea. But many days elapsed before the building was at length completed. For want of better designs, La Salle was himself the architect of the building. "He marked out the lengths, the tenons and mortices and made good the defects of the workmen." To complete it, timber was brought up from the coast. "The timber we brought was a mighty help toward carrying on his design, and much fitter than what we had hewed in the wood with so much labor; so that this timber occasioned the raising another structure contiguous to the former. All was covered with planks, and bullocks' hides over them. The apartments were divided, and all of them well covered. The stores had a place apart, and that dwelling had the name of St. Louis given it, as well as the neighboring bay." Several of the men died from one cause or another, and others continued to desert. They named the river on which they erected their fort "La Riviere aux Bœufs," the River of the Bullocks.

Finally, La Salle set out with several men to find the Mississippi, leaving Joutel, as before, in command of the fort. He left in his charge, also, "eight pieces of cannon, two hundred firelocks, as many cutlasses, a hundred barrels of powder, three thousand weight of balls, about three hundred weight of other lead, some bars of iron, twenty packs of iron to make nails, some iron work and tools, as hatchets and the like. As for provisions, all that were left me amounted to twenty casks of meal, one cask and a half of wine, three-quarters of a cask of brandy, and for living creatures some few swine, and a cock and a hen." The settlers had sowed some grain, but for unknown reasons it did not grow. Joutel denied afterward the stories told that he was left well supplied, and concerning the fort he said, "there being nothing but the house I have mentioned, palisaded with some old stakes." Joutel was left in charge of thirty-four persons, men, women, and children. He soon built another little wooden structure, "and in it I lodged the women and maidens by themselves." He says, "We were in about the twenty-seventh degree of north latitude, two leagues up the country (evidently from the sea-coast), near the Bay of St. Louis and the bank of the river aux Boeufs, on a little hillock, whence we discovered vast and beautiful plains, extending very far to the westward, all level and full of greens, which afford pastures to an infinite number of beeves and other creatures. Turning from the west to the southward there appeared other plains adorned with several little woods of various sorts of trees. Towards the south and east were the bay and the plains that hem it in from the east. To the northward was the river running along by a little hill, beyond which there were other large plains."

Finally, La Salle returned about the middle of March, 1686. He had gone far up the river, had discovered several others, but had not found the Mississippi. After fully recovering from the effects of the journey, he resolved to try again to find the Mississippi, or as Joutel calls it, "the fatal Mississippi." He took twenty men with him. While he was gone their only remaining sea-going vessel "Belle" was also run upon the shoals, and in the end proved a loss. Constant encounters were had with the natives. The settlers managed to live pretty comfortably upon buffaloes, fish and wild fowls. La Salle returned some time in August, bringing with him five horses which he had obtained from the Indians. He had traveled over a large portion of what is now northeastern Texas, had made friends with the Cenis Indians and others, but still had not found the Mississippi. Only eight of the twenty men who had gone out with him returned. It seems that at this time La Salle had in view the journey to the Illinois country, and thence to Canada, for the purpose of securing succor for his colony. While others were repining, he was cheerful and took all the misfortunes as a matter to be expected and affably met. Joutel says of him, "The even temper of our chief made all men easy, and he found by his great vivacity of spirit expedients which revived the lowest ebb of hope." Finally, he set out for the Illinois, intending to find the Mississippi on his way there. He left Sieur Barbier in charge of the settlement. Joutel accompanied him, and the start was made January 12, 1687. They left behind about thirty persons, and La Salle took with him the following: M. Cavelier, his brother, Father Anastasius, the priest, MM. Moranget and Cavelier, the nephews of La Salle, the Sieurs Dehaut, the elder L'Arcleveque, Hiens, Liotot the surgeon, young Talon, an Indian, and a footman, Saget, besides enough more to make a total of seventeen persons. Deaths and desertions had reduced the colony to such an extent, that one of the principal objects of the attempt to reach Canada was to secure a fresh ship-load of colonists. They started northeastward, crossing many rivers, large and small and, through the skill and presence of La Salle, appearing upon friendly terms with the

Indian tribes encountered. Finally about the 20th of March, when in the vicinity probably of the present Bryan, Texas, a conspiracy was formed for the death of La Salle on the ground of revenge for alleged wrongs inflicted by him on several of his men. According to Joutel, who was present, the fatal shot that ended the life of La Salle, was fired by Dehaut, who shot him through the head, killing him instantly. The murderers stripped the body and left it in the bushes for the beasts or birds of prey.

Thus died a remarkable man. He possessed exceptional abilities, which would have ranked him high in any walk of life. He was devoted to the cause of France, and his death resulted from the hazardous risks he took to attach the Mississippi valley, in fact all of the Louisiana Purchase, to the colonies of his king. Often to carry his measures through it was necessary for him to call the rough and lawless men under him sharply to account. He thus offended many. If he possessed one fault, it was that of being too irascible, and of thus incurring the ill-will of men who likewise had ideas of their own as to how he should conduct his affairs. But the greatness of his character and the glory of his death in the line of duty shine high over all. He was pure, truthful, loyal; and mainly through his instrumentality the Louisiana Purchase became a colony of France and not one of Spain or Great Britain. He really accomplished in a large degree what he undertook—the occupation of the Mississippi valley by the French.

After the death of La Salle the murderers took charge of his effects. To save themselves from the same fate, the others submitted to their dictation, and all continued on their journey forty leagues farther to the northeast, or until they reached the village of the Cenis in the vicinity of the present Nacogdoches, Texas. They everywhere found evidences of the presence of the Spaniards farther to the west. Among the Cenis were found several Frenchmen, Buter and Grollet, who had deserted from La Salle on his first expedition, and were living naked like the Indians. They were now in northeast Texas. While here a disagreement arose as to the route to be taken. The murderers did not dare to go on to the Mississippi, while the others wished to do so. Hiens, a German by birth, who had been a buccaneer, finally formed a combination against the murderers, and in an altercation shot Dehaut dead. As he and his companions desired to remain with the Indians, the effects were divided, and Fathers Joutel, Anastasius, Cavelier, young Cavelier, Sieur de Marle, Teissier and Bartholomew, with six horses and three Indians for guides, set out alone in a northeast direction for the Mississippi. After a while they reached the allied nation on Red River— Assouis (or Nassouis), Nachitos (Nachitoches), and Cadoda-quois, arriving at the village of the latter sub-tribe near Texarkana. They passed eastward through the present Louisiana, reached the nation of the Cahaynohonas, and learned that the Cappas, for whom they inquired, were on the big river still farther to the eastward. They continued their journey amid great hardships until they finally came to the Arkansas villages on the Mississippi, and there discovered Tonty's post and three of the men he had left there—Coutoure, Charpentier and DeLaunay. Here they left young Bartholomew, but the others continued on to the Illinois country, where they met Tonty, and then on to Canada.

As soon as the Spaniards learned of the building of Fort St. Louis on St. Bernard's Bay, they resolved to destroy it and break up the French settlement there. Accordingly, an army of five hundred men was sent to the nation of the Cenis, where they found the two Frenchmen, James Grollet and John L'Archeveque, and took them prisoners. A few days later another body of two hundred Spaniards arrived, bringing with them Peter Talon and one Mêmier, who had belonged to the La Salle fort, but had been captured by the bloody Clamcoets, the Indians residing in the vicinity of St. Bernard's Bay. A short time after the departure of La Salle, these Indians, partly by means of friendly overtures and partly by strategy and treachery, had overcome the small force at the fort, and massacred all except the three sons of Talon, their sister, a Parisian named Eustace D'Bremen, and one Mêmier, whom they took to their villages and reduced to slavery. All were finally freed and found their way to civilization. The bodies of those killed at the fort were left unburied and were found by the Spaniards who later came there. With the Spanish army above mentioned were several Franciscan friars, sent out to reside among the Cenis and to hold the country against the French. A fort was built and a small garrison left to guard the rights of Spain, and the army, having no occasion to go to St. Bernard Bay, returned to Mexico. The two Frenchmen named above, who were living among the Cenis, were prevailed upon to remain there in the interests of Spain, which they could readily do, being deserters from the French expeditions.

The post which had been established by Tonty seems to have been situated on the east bank of the Arkansas river, but near its mouth. The men in charge had erected a large cross, which was the first object noticed by Fathers Joutel, Cavelier and

Anastasius, as they approached from the west. Seeing across the river that emblem of their faith in the wilderness, they knelt on the sand and thanked God for their great joy. White men came across the river in boats and conveyed them over and made them comfortable during their stay. Joutel writes, "It is hard to express the joy conceived on both sides; ours was unspeakable, for having at last found what we had so earnestly desired, and that the hopes of returning to our dear country were in some measure assured by that happy discovery. The others were pleased to see such persons as might bring them news of that commander, from whom they expected the performance of what he had promised them; but the account we gave them of M. de la Salle's unfortunate death was so afflicting that it drew tears from them, and the dismal history of his troubles and disasters rendered them almost inconsolable. . . . We were informed by them (the men at Tonty's post), that they had been six, sent by M. Tonty, when he returned from the voyage he had made down the Colbert or Mississippi river, pursuant to the orders sent him by the late M. de la Salle, at his departure from France, and that the said Sieur Tonty had commanded them to build the aforesaid house. That having never since received any news from the said M. de la Salle, four of them were gone back to M. Tonty at the fort of the Illinois."

The Arkansas nation consisted of four principal villages: Assotoué or Otsotchove or Osotome (near which was Tonty's post), Torriman, Tongenga and Cappa. The first two were apparently on or near the Arkansas river, but near its mouth, while the second two were on the Mississippi, according to Joutel. Tonty says of the Assotoué that "they lived on a branch of the river coming from the west," evidently on the Arkansas, or one of its lower branches. Joutel, Cavelier and their party left with Coutoure all their horses, for which they had no further use, fifteen pounds of powder, eight hundred balls, three hundred flints, twenty-six knives, ten axes, several pounds of beads, some linen cloth, and other articles not needed. That the village of Assotoué was not situated on the main channel of the Mississippi is shown by the following extract from Joutel's journal: "The remaining part of the day was spent in going with Sieur Coutoure to see the fatal river so much sought after by us, called Colbert when first discovered, and Mississippi or Mechassippi by the natives that were near us. It is a very fine river and deep; the breadth of it about a quarter of a league and the stream very rapid. The Sieur de Coutoure assured us that it has two branches or channels which parted from each other above us, and that we had passed its other branch when we came to the first village of the Arkansas, with which nation we still were." From this statement, it would seem that Assotoué was on a western bend of the Mississippi, and not on the Arkansas, though near it. The early maps show it situated on an island at the mouth of the Arkansas. But it must have been some distance from the main channel of the Mississippi.

In 1686 Sieur de Tonty having learned that La Salle had sailed from France for the mouth of the Mississippi, resolved to join him. He was now at Fort St. Louis (Starved Rock on the Illinois river). He says, "I departed thence on the 16th of February, 1686, with thirty Frenchmen and five Illinois and Chawanons (probably Shawanese, a nation supposed to be the remnant of the Eries, who had been almost totally destroyed by the Iroquois) . for the sea, which I reached in Holy Week. After having passed the above named nations, I was very well received. I sent out two canoes, one towards the coast of Mexico and the other towards Carolina to see if they could discover anything. They each sailed about thirty leagues, but proceeded no farther for want of fresh water. They reported that where they had been the land began to rise. They brought me a porpoise and some oysters. As it would take us five months to reach the French settlements, I proposed to my men that if they would trust to me to follow the coast as far as Manhatte (Manhattan, New York), that by this means they should arrive shortly at Montreal; that we should not lose our time, because we might discover some fine country, and might even take some booty on our way. Part of my men were willing to adopt my plan; but as the rest were opposed to it, I decided to return the way I came. The tide does not rise more than two feet perpendicularly on the sea coast, and the land is very low at the entrance of the river. We encamped in the place where M. de la Salle had erected the arms of the King. As they had been thrown down by the floods, I took them five leagues further up and placed them in a higher situation. I put a silver ecu in the hollow of a tree to serve as a mark of time and place.

"We left this place on Easter Monday. When we came opposite the Quinipissas village the chiefs brought me the calumet, and declared the sorrow they felt at the treachery they had perpetrated against me on our first voyage. I made an alliance with them. Forty leagues higher up, on the right, we discovered a village inland, with the inhabitants of which we also made an alliance. These are the Oumas, the bravest savages of the river. When we were at Arkansas, ten of the Frenchmen who accompanied me asked for a settlement on the river Arkansas, on a seignory that M. de la Salle had given me on our first voyage. I granted the request to some of them. They remained there to build a house surrounded with stakes. The rest accompanied me to Illinois, in order to get what they wanted. I arrived there (Illinois) on St. John's Day (June 24)."

Sieur de Tonty thus failed to find La Salle, but he established the first colony of the French in the Louisiana Purchase about the first of June, 1686. Part of the men who had asked for the settlement remained at their house on the Arkansas, while the others went on to the Illinois to get necessary supplies, tools, etc., and no doubt returned as soon as possible. Later, Tonty says, "On the 7th. of April, 1688, one (Frenchman) named Coutoure brought to me two Akansas, who danced the calumet. They informed me of the death of M. de la Salle, with all the circumstances which they had heard from the lips of M. Cavelier, who had fortunately discovered the house I had built at Arkansas, where the said Coutoure stayed with three Frenchmen. He told me that the fear of not obtaining from me what he desired had made him (M. Cavelier) conceal the death of his brother, but that he had told them of it. M. Cavelier (had) told me that the Cadodaquis had proposed to accompany him if he would go and fight against the Spaniards. He had objected on account of there being only fourteen Frenchmen. They replied that their nation was numerous, that they only wanted a few musqueteers, and that the Spaniards had much money, which they (the French) should take; and as for themselves they only wished to keep the women and children as slaves. Coutoure told me that a young man whom M. Cavelier had left at Arkansas had assured him that this was very true. I would not undertake anything without the consent of the Governor of Canada. I sent the said Coutoure to the French remaining at Nicondiché (Nachitoches) to get all the information he could. He set off, and at one hundred leagues from the fort was wrecked, and having lost everything returned."

In 1688 the Sieur de Tonty, learning that war had been declared by France against Spain, resolved to go to "Nacondiché (Nachitoches) "to execute what M. Cavelier had ventured to undertake and to bring back M. de la Salle's men, who were on the sea-coast not knowing of the misfortune that had befallen him." He embarked five Frenchmen, one Chawanon, and two slaves, and reached the mouth of the Illinois October 17, 1688.

On January 16, he reached the village of the Cappas down the Mississippi, on the 20th reached Tongenga and on the 22d, Torremans (these were the Arkansas villages otherwise spelled by Tonty Toyengan and Toriman). Leaving my crew (at Torremans) I set off the next day for Assotoué, where my commercial house is." This was the house above mentioned which he had ordered built for the ten men of his seignory, below the mouth of the Arkansas river. He refers to it as "the house I had built at Arkansas." This was really a small manor, of which he was the lord. "The savages had not yet seen me, as they lived on a branch of the river coming from the west. They did their best, giving me two women of the Cadodaquis nation, to whom I was going."

From this admission, it is clear that his paramount intention was to join the Cadodaquis in an attack on the Spaniards, as had been suggested to M. Cavelier. From the 22d of January to about the 12th of February, he made his preparations at the villages of Cappa, Torremans, Tongenga, and Assortoue, etc., and finally rendezvoused at a point on what is now the Tensas river. "We set off on the 12th (of February, 1690,) with twelve Taencas, and after a voyage of twelve leagues to the northwest, we left our boat and made twenty leagues portage, and on the 17th of February came to Nachitoches. They made us stay at the place, which is in the midst of the three villages called Nachitoches, Ouasita (Washita), and Capiche." Thus, it appears that Tonty went up the Tensas, or perhaps the Washita river some distance, thence left his boat and journeyed across to Red river and up the same to Nachitoches. He remained here several days and then departed for Yataches (Yattasse). About eighty miles up Red river from Nachitoches he found fifteen cabins of the Natchez, and about one hundred miles farther up reached Yataches, arriving there the 16th of March. Standing there together were three villages—Yataches, Nadas, and Choye. Here he was feasted and given guides to the Cadodaquis, but much against their will. The Cadodaquis nation still higher up Red river was reached on the 28th of March.

He says, "During the time I was there, I learned from them that eighty leagues off were the seven Frenchmen whom M. Cavelier had left. I hoped to finish my troubles by rejoining them, but the Frenchmen who accompanied me would go no further. They were unmanageable persons, over whom I could exercise no authority in this distant country. I was obliged to give way. All that I could do was to engage one of them, with a savage, to accompany me to the village of Naoudiché, where I hoped to find the seven Frenchmen. I told those who abandoned me that to prevent the savages knowing this, it was best to say that I had sent them away to carry back the news of my arrival, so that the savages would not suspect our disunion. The Cadodaquis are united with two other villages called Natchitoches and Nassoui (or Assoui) situated on Red river. All the nations of this tribe speak the same language. Their cabins are covered with straw, and they are not united in villages, but their huts are distant one from the other. Their fields are beautiful. They fish and hunt. There is plenty of game, but few cattle (boeufs). The Cadodaquis possess about thirty horses, which they call cavali (from Spanish caballo, a horse). They call this the Red river, because in fact it deposits a sand which makes the water as red as blood.

"I left this place on the 6th of April, directing our route southwards, with a Frenchman, a Chaganon and a little slave of mine, and five of their savages, whom they gave me as guides to Naouadiché. . . . On our road we found some Naouadichés savages hunting, who assured me that the Frenchmen were staying with them. This gave me great pleasure, hoping to succeed in my object of finding them. On the 23d we slept half a league from the village, and the chiefs came to visit us at night. I asked them about the Frenchmen." The conflicting stories caused Tonty to suspect that the Frenchmen had been killed. "I told them that they had killed the Frenchmen. Directly all the women began to cry, and thus I saw that what I had said was true. I would not, therefore, accept the calumet. I told the chief that I wanted four horses for my return, and having given him seven hatchets and a string of large glass beads, I received the next day four Spanish horses. Horses are very common among them. There is not a cabin which has not four or five. As this nation is sometimes at peace and sometimes at war with the neighboring Spaniards, they take advantage of a war to carry off the horses. We harnessed ours as well as we could, and departed on the 29th, greatly vexed that we could not continue our route as far as M. de la Salle's camp. . . . It was at the distance of three days' journey from thence that M. de la Salle was murdered." Tonty returned to the Cadodaquis nation, arriving May 10th. He then started for the Coroas village on the Mississippi and after incredible hardships arrived there on the 14th of July, 1690.

Henry de Tonty has never been given the credit he deserves for his sacrifices and discoveries. He seems to have been utterly without selfishness. The courage and address shown by him in all his dealings with the Indians proved that he possessed personal forces which few credit to him. He had the highest admiration for La Salle, of whom he wrote, "Such was the end of one of the greatest men of the age. He was a man of wonderful ability and capable of undertaking any discovery." His fidelity was remarkable in this period when few if any men could be trusted. When on the Illinois, he no sooner heard of the sailing of La Salle for the mouth of the Mississippi than he started to join him for the purpose of rendering him any assistance in his power. He did every thing he could to assist in carrying out his designs, knowing they had been sanctioned by the French court. He obeyed orders promptly, with a cheerfulness that always set a good example. He was both truthful and generous, and it may be said that next to La Salle, he did more than any other person to place the Mississippi valley under the flag of France.

CHAPTER III

The Settlements Made by D'Iberville

THE termination of war in Europe by the treaty of Ryswick in 1697, presented the opportunity which Louis XIV had desired of establishing a permanent colony at the mouth of the Mississippi. His haste at this juncture was occasioned as much by his jealousy of both Spain and Great Britain as by his own wish to add to his crown an empire of wilderness in the New World. Spain, after two centuries of opportunity, had continuously turned her back on the Mississippi valley and had fastened her grasp on the islands and mainland farther to the south. Great Britain was directing her energy and attention to the Atlantic coast; but was complacently expecting that, later, she would have an opportunity to despoil France and Spain of the colonies they had established at such an immense sacrifice of blood and treasure. Thus, this was the beginning of a prolonged system of strategy between the leading nations of Europe for colonial supremacy on the American continent.

Accordingly, orders were issued in 1698 by Louis XIV for the despatch of an expedition of colonists to the Mississippi, the command of which was intrusted to Pierre le Moyne (Captain D'Iberville), who had recently distinguished himself in the French naval service. The squadron comprised two frigates, the Marin and Badine, each carrying thirty guns, the former commanded by Compte de Surgéres and the latter by D'Iberville himself, and two smaller vessels bearing nearly two hundred colonists and a company of marines. Among the colonists were women and children, who were destined to see harder times before they again saw France than they dreamed of. They were mostly the families of ex-soldiers, who had been granted extra

liberal inducements to join the expedition. Among the colonists
were agriculturalists and mechanics, and all were well supplied
with provisions and clothing and the necessary articles and implements required in the new settlement.

The expedition set sail from Rochelle on September 24, 1698,
and late in December, was joined by a war ship, the Francois,
carrying fifty guns, commanded by the Marquis de Chateaumo-
rant, while stopping for refreshments at St. Domingo. Doub-
ling the coast of Cuba January 15, 1699, they sighted the Florida
coast on the 24th of January, and soon afterward reached
Apalachicola Bay, where they found a Spanish colony. Continuing westward, they reached Pensacola Bay, where it was found
that another Spanish settlement had been formed within the last
three months. Thus they were apparently none too soon to
secure the mouth of the Mississippi, before the Spaniards located
therein. On the 31st of January, they arrived in Mobile Bay,
but not liking the anchorage, they continued westward about
thirteen or fourteen leagues farther, where they found excellent
anchorage and protection from storms between several islands
and the mainland. Having landed his colonists on Ship island,
some distance from the mainland, and having learned of a large
river to the southwest called by the natives, Malabouchia, and
inferring that it must be the Mississippi, he resolved to leave his
vessels where they were safe and go in search of it.

The frigate, Francois, which had escorted him from St.
Domingo, not being needed, was sent back. With two strong
row-boats, several bark canoes and fifty-three men, Iberville now
started to find the mouth of the Mississippi. "We entered this
river (Colbert or Mississippi) on the night of the 2d of March.
I found it obstructed by rafts of petrified wood of a sufficient
hardness to resist the action of the sea. I found there twelve feet
of water, and anchored two leagues from the mouth of the river,
where the depth is from ten to twelve fathoms, with a breadth of
from four to five hundred yards. On the 3d, the winds prevented
me from making soundings between the rafts and the three out-
lets, which extend some three leagues before entering the sea.
I resolved to go as far up as the Bayagoulas, whom we had met
with at the Bay of Biloxi, and who had given us to understand
that their village was at the distance of eight days' travel in a
canoe from the bay, which would be equal to about sixty leagues.

"As I had already gone thirty leagues, and as it was necessary
that I should ascend the river to become acquainted with its
depth, observe the places proper for establishments, and visit the

various Indian villages, which our Frenchmen said they had seen upon its banks in ascending and descending the river, and as they pretended that the Quinipissas were established at a distance of thirty leagues from the mouth of the Mississippi, I took advantage of a favorable wind from the southwest to continue my route, leaving until my return the work of sounding the passes. On the seventh, at a distance of about thirty-five leagues up the river, I met with some Indians who told me that it was yet three and a half days' travel before I could reach the Bayagoulas, and that theirs was the first village I should reach. I took one of these Indians with me as a guide, as well as for information. On the 14th I reached the village, where I was received with friendly embraces after their manner. By exact observations, I found its position was sixty-four leagues from the mouth of the river. The chief of the Mongoulachas, a nation allied with the Bayagoulas, had on a poitou-cloak of blue serge, which he told me was presented to him by M. de Tonty. I was, moreover, confirmed with regard to his visit, by seeing in their hands axes and knives: but from the sea up to this village I found no other sign of the French having visited this section. I met with none of the Tangipahoes nor Quinipissas mentioned in the narratives of the Jesuits, and concluded they must be false, as well as those writings about Canada, Hudson Bay, and the return of Sieur Cavalier from the Bay of St. Louis. The Bayagoulas told me that the Quinipissas dwelt fifty leagues in the interior and consisted of six villages. They assured me that the river was never obstructed and was navigable very high up. They named all the nations that inhabited its banks above.

"But seeing myself so far up the river without positive proof that this was the Mississippi, and that it might be said in France I was deceived, not having met with any of those tribes mentioned in the narratives, I concluded that I ought to visit the Houmas on the east side of the river, among whom I knew M. de Tonty had been; and believing, moreover, that in the course of at least thirty leagues I must meet with that branch of the river spoken of in the narratives, down which I could send a chaloupe and canoe for the purpose of exploration, and ascertain which of the two rivers would be most suitable for settlements. I was apprehensive the Indians only desired to conceal from me that branch in order to get me to remain upon theirs, as they hoped to reap some advantage thereby. I renewed my journey in company with the chief of the Bayagoulas, who offered to go with me with

I—8

eight of his men, and arrived at the village of the Houmas, distant thirty-five leagues. On the morning of the twentieth, at ten o'clock, I entered the village, which is situated two leagues and a half in the interior, where I was well received; but I could learn nothing more than I had been informed of before. They spoke much of M. de Tonty, who had remained some time among them and made them many presents.

"On the 21st I returned to my boats, much embarrassed as to the course I should pursue, seeing that I was one hundred and thirty leagues from the ships and one hundred from the sea; having procured no other provisions than Indian corn, without meat and without grease, my men were fatigued with stemming the strong currents; and having little hope of finding that branch I was in search of, I thought the Houmas would have the same motives as the Bayagoulas in concealing from me the truth. I told them I knew there was a branch, and desired to descend by it to the sea with a portion of my men; that this branch ought to be near a river coming from the west and falling into the Mala-bouchia (Mississippi). They told me it was the Tassenoeogoula (Red river). Finally I told them I would visit the Natchez or Tpelois, who are their nearest neighbors in ascending the river. They offered to conduct me there, and for this purpose gave me six men and a canoe. I left the Houmas on the 22d and took with me a Tensas, who was acquainted with the country and had traveled over as far as the Arkansas. He spoke to me of the Sablon-iere (Red river), which he called the Tassenoeogoula. He also mentioned the nations dwelling along its banks, and across which M. de Cavalier had passed upon his return from the Bay of St. Louis (St. Bernard, Texas).

"Not doubting but that these Indians as well as the Tensas had an understanding with each other to conceal from me what I was eagerly desirous to know, in the hope that I would go to their village near which I already was, I deemed it prudent to enter into no further engagements. Besides, it was time for me to return and look out for a proper place to make a settlement, which hitherto I had been unable to find. Moreover, the fleet was falling short of provisions. I retraced my steps to the Houmas, after having gone beyond their village three leagues and a half, very much vexed at the Recollet,* whose false narratives had deceived every one and caused our sufferings and total failure of our enterprise by the time consumed in search of things which alone existed

---

* Narrative of Father Louis Hennepin.

in his imagination. On the 24th, I arrived at a small river or stream, about five leagues above the Bayagoulas on the east side of the river, which empties into the sea. This was the only branch of the Malabouchia the Indians pointed out to us. I descended to the sea by this stream (the Manshac) in two bark canoes with four men and sent the chaloupes down the river with orders to sound the passes. I entered this small river, which is not more than eight or ten paces wide and about five feet in depth in low water. It was full of logs, which in places totally obstructed the navigation, so that in many places we were under the necessity of making several portages during its entire length of eight or nine leagues. After a while other rivers fall into it, by which its volume is increased, with a good depth of water at all times, from two to three fathoms in the river and seven to eight in the lakes. It terminates by emptying at the extremity of the Bay of Lago de Lodo, eight leagues west of the place where our ships were anchored. It passes through a fine country. The lake I crossed was about three leagues wide and twenty-five long. Its direction runs parallel with the Mississippi, and in many places they are separated only by a narrow strip of land, from a quarter to half a league wide, for a distance of twenty-five, thirty, forty and forty-eight leagues, as far as the mouth of the Malabouchia. I reached the ships upon the 31st."

Father Douay accompanied D'Iberville on this trip up the Mississippi, because he had been one of La Salle's companions on his last Mississippi expedition. He thought he recognized the great river from its seething waters, but was not certain. The Bayagoulas exhibited many evidences of European visits, among which were cloth stuffs and domestic poultry, which, according to the Indians, had been obtained from the nations farther to the westward, doubtless originally from the Spaniards. The Tangi-pahoes, whom D'Iberville expected to find on the Mississippi, had been exterminated or driven away by the Bayagoulas, who were really the Quinipissas mentioned by La Salle and his lieu-tenant, Tonty. The finding among the Indians by D'Iberville of a letter left by Tonty for La Salle, dated at the village of the Quinipissas April 20, 1685 (meant to be 1686), settled all doubts as to the river they were now on. An old suit of Spanish armour, no doubt left by De Soto's army, found among the Indians, still further identified the river. Probably the highest land they saw on their ascent of the river, was at Baton Rouge. Farther up they noticed the wide detour in the river, which after-ward became Pointe Coupée. Still higher, at the village of the

Houmas, they saw other domestic fowls in considerable numbers. D'Iberville was really in search of the Atchafalaya, which extended from near the mouth of Red river to the Gulf westward of the Mississippi. At this time the Bayagoulas comprised about 350 people and 100 fighting men. The Houmas were more numerous, having more than 300 warriors. D'Bienville, afterward so long the governor of Louisiana, the younger brother of D'Iberville, accompanied this expedition up the Mississippi. He was sent down to the mouth of the main river to sound the passes, while D'Iberville went down the Manshac to rejoin the ships. It seems strange now that they should have had any misgivings as to the identity of the Mississippi. It was so wide, deep and swift that their doubt seems now unaccountable. No doubt their misgivings resulted, as D'Iberville says, from the deceptions of the Recollect missionary, who had drawn so largely upon his very vivid imagination.

It was at once perceived by D'Iberville that the most expeditious route to the Bayagoulas was via the lakes and river Manshac. M. D'Sauvolle accompanied Bienville, to assist in sounding the passes of the Mississippi; but they found this task impracticable, owing to the strong winds blowing at the time. On his way down D'Sauvolle observed at the distance of thirty leagues from the sea a spot sufficiently elevated not to be inundated; also still farther down a similar tract extending back a league or more from the river, which they were unable to examine, owing to the immense growth of canes along the shore. It was observed that the Mississippi was from eighteen to twenty fathoms deep throughout its whole course so fas as they examined. D'Bienville obtained for an ax the letter of Tonty on his trip down the river. In it the faithful Tonty deplored not having met La Salle, and said that the savages greatly feared him since the attack of La Salle upon them. D'Iberville proceeded to build a fort on the Bay of Biloxi, around which were erected many log cabins for the colonists. Here nearly one hundred people were left, while he returned to France. M. D'Sauvolle de la Villantry (Sauvolle), naval ensign, was left in command, with D'Bienville as king's lieutenant; Le Vasseur de Boussouelle, a Canadian, as major; D'Bordenac as chaplain; M. Caré, surgeon, and about eighty men, consisting of two captains, two cannoniers, four sailors, eighteen filibusters, ten mechanics, six masons, thirteen Canadians and twenty sub-officers and soldiers, who comprised the garrison. D'Iberville left on the 3d of May.

It is noteworthy how many erroneous impressions and ideas

prevailed in Europe concerning the American colonies. Rumors of the most ridiculous and extravagant nature were circulated and believed by many men who ought to have known better. Consider for a moment the following instructions to D'Iberville, when he sailed for the mouth of the Mississippi for the purpose of founding a colony: "One of the great objects proposed to the king, when he was urged to discover the mouth of the Micissipi, was to obtain wool from the cattle of that country; and for this purpose these animals must be tamed and parked and calves sent to France. Although the pearls sent to his Majesty are not fine, either in water or shape, they must nevertheless be carefully sought, as others may be found; and his Majesty desires M. D'Iberville to bring all he can, ascertain where the fishery is carried on, and see it in operation." The cattle here referred to were the wild buffaloes which roamed over all the western country. The Indians used the hair of these animals for some of their rude garments; but why any sane and civilized white man should arrive at the conclusion that it was worth a second thought as an article of clothing may be marveled at. Domestic cattle were first introduced into the Illinois country in 1711. In a comparatively short time, beef was as common and as cheap as pork.

Now that D'Iberville had gone, the real metal of the colonists was put to the test. Unfortunately, there were too many among them who cared nothing for agriculture and who from the start set forth on expeditions to obtain gold, jewels and valuable furs from the natives. They were soon nearly out of provisions and in sore straits. But it is not the intention here, nor is it the province of this work, to follow the fate of the colonists, except so far as they were connected with what afterward became Louisiana proper. The French and the missionaries had become well established on the Illinois river by this time. The colonists at Biloxi Bay were not a little pleased early in July to receive two small canoes containing Fathers Davion and Montigny and a few Frenchmen, who had journeyed all the way from the Illinois in those frail vessels down the treacherous current of the mighty Mississippi. They had really come down to establish a mission among the Indians of the lower river, but learning from the Houmas of the presence of the French at Biloxi, they determined to go there before taking other action. After a visit of about ten days they returned up the river as far as the Tonicas, where they founded a mission. There arrived at Mobile in May, 1700, M. Sagan, a traveler from Canada, who showed a memoir from the French minister, Pontchartrain, to the effect that he had

traversed the entire Mississippi valley and had ascertained that
gold mines existed in that country. The minister requested that
M. Sagan be supplied by M. D'Sauvolle with twenty-four
pirogues and one hundred Canadians for the purpose of making
an exploration of the Missouri river and its branches.

After the departure of D'Iberville, the men left behind began
the task of exploring the country, among the first objects being
a careful examination of the Mississippi, with the view of finding
a suitable site for a fort and a village. This soon was seen to
be more difficult than was thought probable at the outset, owing
to the low banks and the evident fact that they were often inundated. D'Bienville commanded one of these expeditions. He it
was who named Massacre Island from the large pile of human
bones found there. Still later, with a body of men, he endeavored
to reach the Mississippi over the route traversed by D'Iberville
on his return from the voyage up the Mississippi. Having
reached the large lake mentioned by the latter, he named it Pontchartrain, from the south shore of which they made preparations
to leave their boats and cross over to the Mississippi. "Having
crossed these canes for a quarter of a league, we arrived on the
borders of the Mississippi, at which we were greatly rejoiced.
We regarded this beautiful river with admiration. . . . We
encamped that night on the river's bank, under the trees, upon
which a vast number of wild turkeys roosted. We killed as many
of them as we wanted, by moonlight, as they were not in the least
disturbed by the firing of our guns. I can truly say that I never
saw turkeys in France so fat and large as these were, as their
net weight was about thirty pounds. The next day we returned
to our boats; and our companions, whom we had left as a guard,
were highly delighted to learn we had slept on the banks of the
mighty river."* This encampment was no doubt on the present
site of New Orleans, probably the first ever there by white men.
Think of the experience—the bright fire of the camp, the multi-
tude of wild turkeys roosting overhead yet unafraid of man, the
rejoicing and feasting Frenchmen, the moonlight sifting down
like golden mist and the gurgling voices of the hurrying waters.
An agreeable introduction it was to the future metropolis of the
great South. Here came messages from the distant Rockies,
from the gnarled Alleghanies and from the sunny summits of the
heights of Minnesota. From a thousand tribes and from the perpetual hills overlooking innumerable velvet vales came swelling

---

* Annals of Louisiana from 1698 to 1722, by M. Penicaut.

tributes on the stentorian tones of the rushing river. The next day they journeyed on, passing through Lake Maurepas, and then for several days continuing to explore the surrounding country without again approaching the Mississippi before returning to the fort at Biloxi. Here their report was made to D'Sauvolle, who was presented with a fine assortment of pearls which had been collected on the expedition.

While on one of these expeditions in the absence of D'Iberville, his brother, D'Bienville, on the 16th of December, 1699, saw at what has since been called the "English Turn," a small English vessel carrying sixteen guns and commanded by Captain Barr. He informed the Englishman that he was on the Mississippi, upon which the French had established settlements, and that therefore he was a trespasser. After satisfying himself to his satisfaction, the Englishman, who had really come prepared to lay claim to the Mississippi and Louisiana, returned down the river to its mouth and rejoined another vessel which had remained there while he made his discoveries. The spot where the English vessel turned about has ever since been called from that circumstance "Detour des Anglais," or Turn of the English. Thus the French were none too soon to prevent the English as well as the Spaniards from settling on the Mississippi. It has even been claimed that D'Bienville deceived the English captain as to the number and extent of the French settlers on the Mississippi. As a matter of fact the French had not a single settlement on the Mississippi at this time, and had the English captain brought with him a load of colonists, which he may have done, he would have been justified in landing them and taking possession. The mere fact that the French under La Salle had taken possession of the banks of the river in their king's name, and had explored the river, was not yet sufficient to fix the claims of the French to the river as against an actual settlement by the English or the Spanish. There may be some truth, therefore, in the statement that D'Bienville hoodwinked the English captain, either by declaring the river not to be the Mississippi, or by making it appear that the French occupancy was too certain and strong to be disputed.

All were anxious for the return of D'Iberville, but it was not till the 6th of January, 1700, that he reappeared at Biloxi. He was in command of the Renommee of fifty guns, and M. de Surgeres in command of the Gironde with forty-six guns. He brought with him sixty Canadian immigrants and a large supply of provisions and stores. "M. de Iberville was received with every possible demonstration of joy; but he only remained a few days at the fort, at the end of which time he selected sixty men to go with him to the Mississippi, among whom were his two brothers, D'Bienville and D'Chateauguay, D'Boisbriant, D'St. Denis, and others" who afterward distinguished themselves one way or another in the new country. D'Sauvolle was left in command of the fort and in charge of the ships. The exploring party departed in three long boats, or chaloupes, as they were called, and in due time reached the mouth of the Mississippi and encamped on the left bank. The next day being the 15th, having ascended ten leagues, they came to a dense forest bordering both sides of the river. "Eight leagues higher up M. D'Iberville observed a spot very convenient for the erection of a fort, which he resolved to construct when he descended the river. Eight leagues beyond is a bend in the river, three leagues around, which is called the English Turn, the reason for which I will give in its proper place. Twenty-four leagues higher up on the left is a river called Chetimachas (Bayou La Forche), and five leagues beyond this is the first Indian nation inhabiting the banks of the river, called the Bayagoulas, where we arrived on the 19th of February." Here they secured a supply of provisions. "M. D'Iberville told the chief that we would depart in the morning, and would like some fowls to take with him. The village was filled with them, and they supplied us bountifully. We took four of this nation as guides, and left with them a young Frenchman to learn their language."

They left the next morning and in five leagues reached the river Manshac and five leagues beyond reached the bluffs (ecores), or as the Indians called the place, Istrouma, which in French was Baton Rouge, or Red Stick. This was the boundary line between the Bayagoulas and the Houmas. Reaching what afterward became called Pointe Coupée, many walked across the portage rather than go the long distance around by the river. Eight leagues higher up was a cross which had been planted by M. D'Iberville on his former visit. Here on a small island was chanted the Vexilla Regis, all on their knees, while the wondering savages looked on. This spot was called Portage de la Croix, from which, two leagues inland, a path led to the main village of the Houmas. The boats made the wide detour, while the officers and guards cut across the portage, visiting the Houma village on the way, and securing a supply of provisions, such as game and poultry. Soon after this they passed the mouth of a large river called Sabloniere (Red river). Sixteen or seventeen leagues farther and they passed Ellis' cliffs, above which they landed to visit the village of the Natchez, "the most civilized of all the nations." With them a treaty of peace was concluded on the 5th of March. Going on they, in turn, passed Petit Gulf and Grand Gulf, journeying from the latter westward four leagues in the interior to visit the Tensas Indians. While here the French witnessed a thrilling sight. The Tensas were sun worshippers, and were allied to the Natchez. "A sudden storm burst upon us. The lightning struck the temple, burned all their idols and reduced the whole to ashes. Quickly the Indians assembled around, making horrible cries, tearing out their hair, elevating their hands to heaven, their tawny visages turned toward the burning temple, invoking their Great Spirit, with the howling of devils possessed, to come down and extinguish the flames. They took up mud with which they besmeared their bodies and faces. The fathers and mothers then brought their children and after having strangled them threw them into the flames. M. D'Iberville was horrified at seeing such a cruel spectacle, and gave orders to stop it by forcibly taking from them the little innocents; but with all our efforts seventeen perished in this manner; and had we not restrained them the number would have been over two hundred." D'Iberville succeeded in inducing the Tensas to remove to the banks of the Mississippi. As the time was fast approaching when he would have to return to France, he now began to descend the river. At Natchez he met Father D' St. Comé, a missionary, who had recently come down from the Illinois country with Father Gabriel Marest, they having left the mouth of the Illinois on December 6, 1699, and having stopped several times on the way. With them had come the ever famous Tonty.

Having reached the spot where he had decided to built his fort, D'Iberville found waiting him a gunboat which had been brought there by D'Bienville, who some time before had been dispatched from the expedition for that purpose. On the vessel was everything necessary for the construction of the fort, except the timber, and that stood ready on the banks. This spot was below the English Turn, and on the left bank of the river. A commencement had been made by D'Bienville in the absence of D'Iberville. The latter at once drew up the plans, showing the measurement and size, and the fort was rapidly completed. D'Bienville was then left in command of the same with a force of twenty-five men, and D'Iberville returned to Biloxi for supplies and cannons. By this time the news had reached the Illinois country that the French had established settlements on the lower Mississippi; and accordingly boat loads of hardy Canadians began to arrive from the upper country. While the French were building 'the fort, five loads arrived; they were taken to Biloxi. From the fact that the Canadians were familiar with the habits of the Indians and with the peculiarities of the country, they were regarded as a most desirable acquisition at any time to the young colony. Many of them who were not *coureurs de bois,* took readily to the cultivation of the soil. In fact it may be truthfully said that the success of the French settlements on the lower Mississippi was as much due to the industrious habits of their French Canadian inhabitants as to any other cause. But the *coureur de bois* were a greater curse than a blessing, and they led many others astray with fanciful tales of the fortunes to be made in the fur trade and with the easy life in the deep woods, under the burning stars, without restriction from church or state.

On the 3d of May, 1700, D'Iberville started on his second return to France, but before doing so, recommended to M. D'Sauvolle, who was left in command at Biloxi, to send twenty men under the direction of Pierre le Sueur, to the copper mines of the Sioux Indians, on the upper Mississippi, in the interests of France, they having been sent down by the Canadian merchants for that purpose. Near the end of April, 1700, Le Sueur set forth with twenty-five men in one long boat, and was soon stemming the terrible current of the mighty river. So strong was the flow at this season of the year, that it took them twenty-four days to reach the Tensas country a little above the mouth of the Arkansas. At the Indian villages above the mouth of the Yazoo river, on the east side, they met a French priest and another Frenchman, both of whom were delighted to see Le Sueur and his party. They passed the Arkansas river, which they called the Tonty, and soon afterward reached the Arkansas nation, where they received a kind reception. Here they found an English fur trader. A little higher up they named a small river on the west side the St. Francis, which it retains to this day. Fifteen leagues above the mouth of the Ohio, on the east side, they passed the Cape of St. Anthony, where the early French settlers came to obtain their mill-stones. In this vicinity, their provisions gave out and they were compelled to wait twenty-two days for a fresh supply. They were forced to go into the woods in the meantime to kill game, gather buds, young leaves and sap on which to live.

"Three of our comrades went on the other side of the Mississippi (the west side) with a' canoe, where, having landed, they fastened it to a tree, and, being separated in the hunt, they killed some bears, which we found excellent eating." They had sent to the Illinois country for provisions by a priest whom they had met in the vicinity of the Prudhomme Bluffs, or Memphis. Finally, a large canoe loaded with "every kind of provision" reached them, in charge of Father Limoges and four Frenchmen, who continued on their way to Biloxi. Continuing their journey, they passed the mouth of the Kaskaskia and about sixty miles farther, at a village of the Illinois Indians, encountered several Canadian traders, who were engaged in purchasing furs and skins. Besides there were four French missionaries and other Frenchmen in the village. Here four of the Frenchmen in the Le Sueur party left but their places were supplied with five others, among whom was Chapougar, an excellent interpreter, "as he spoke nearly all the Indian languages." Going on they reached the mouth of the Missouri about six leagues above the village of the Illinois, and a little farther up the mouth of the Illinois, where they were joined by three Canadian travelers, who bore a letter to Le,Sueur from Father Marest. "Opposite its mouth (the Illinois) commences a series of the most beautiful and most extensive prairies in the world."

Ten leagues higher they reached Boeuf (Buffalo) river, which they ascended half a league and encamped on its banks. Here four of the men killed a buffalo about half a league distant and returned for assistance to convey it to camp. "When it was cooked we ate a good part of it, at the same time emptying several bottles of brandy, which greatly invigorated us." They finally came to the Moingona (Des Moines), and a league higher reached the rapids, where they were obliged to unload and push the boats along near the shore by hand. Thus they continued for seven leagues. "On the left of these rapids (on the west side) are open prairies, extending ten leagues from and along the banks of the Mississippi. The grass upon these prairies is like clover, upon which an infinite number of animals browse." A little higher, on the right, they noticed the lead mines, called Nicholas Perrot. They noticed the mouth of the Wisconsin as they passed. Ten leagues above the Wisconsin they observed Prairie aux Ailes (Winged Prairie) on the east side, and on the west side a beautiful prairie called Paquitanet, but not so large as Winged Prairie. They finally reached Lake Pepin, and on the right saw the fort which had been built by Perrot. Upon reflection, they concluded not to carry their boats around the Falls of St. Anthony; instead, they went up St. Peter river (Minnesota) until they reached

Green (Blue Earth) river, which they ascended. Here was the copper country, it was reasoned, because the soil was tinged green by the large quantity of that mineral prevailing. After traveling up Blue Earth river about a league, M. Le Sueur determined to build a fort. It was now the last of September, and ice often formed during the nights. "The weather had become rough and tempestuous."

It was necessary to build a fort and other house accommodation for the men; because it was impossible to survive the terrible winters without such structures. The men were divided into two parties, and half began to construct the fort and half to hunt and kill buffaloes for the winter's supply. They succeeded in killing four hundred of these animals, which they placed on scaffolds in the fort, after having skinned them and cut them up. Several cabins were built within the enclosure of the fort, for the comfort of the men. The boats were securely taken care of. Soon after the erection of the fort had been commenced, seven French traders from Canada arrived, stating that they had been robbed of all their merchandise and stripped of all their clothing by the Sioux, and asked permission to remain with the Le Sueur party during the winter, which was granted. The fort was named L'Huillier in honor of the leading merchant who had sent out the expedition. Here these men remained all winter—about thirty of them—with nothing to live on during the cold dreary months but buffalo meat and such green messes—buds, bark, etc.—as they could gather from the surrounding woods. No telling how bad the meat became before spring. No telling how earnestly these men longed for a change. There was no alternative—stale buffalo beef or starve. When to this state of affairs is added the other that they had no vegetables, were obliged to endure the stinging cold and eat their rotten buffalo meat without salt, the picture of discomfort and hardship is rendered complete.

On the 3d of April, 1701, the weather having become somewhat settled, twelve of the men and four hunters set out for the reputed copper mine situated about a league from the fort, and there in a comparatively short space of time took out about 30,000 pounds of ore, from which they selected about 4,000 pounds of the purest, carried it to the fort, and later had it transported to France. As nothing further was ever heard from this exportation, it is to be presumed that the chemists pronounced it of no commercial value. The men worked twenty-two days at the mines and then returned to the fort, where the Sioux came to exchange their furs for the merchandise in the possession of the Frenchmen. Le Sueur secured more than four hundred beaver robes, together with many other rare skins. This valuable purchase compensated to some extent for the disappointment over the copper ore. This had been a terrible winter. M. Penicaut, one of the party, declares that the snow lay on the ground to the depth of three feet on the level, and that the smaller streams were frozen to the bottom. In the early part of May, they loaded their ore and peltries in their boats and made preparations to return down the rivers. Before going, Le Sueur held a council with the leading Sioux chiefs—three brothers—and formed what he supposed and hoped would be a permanent treaty of peace with their nations. He then left M. D'Eraque and a dozen men in charge of Fort L'Huillier, made valuable presents to the three great chiefs, and after promising to send up supplies from the Illinois country for the men who remained at the fort, set forth with about a dozen men for the mouth of the Mississippi. Upon reaching the Illinois he secured a boat and loaded it with 2,000 pounds of powder and lead and sent it by three men back to Fort L'Huillier.

Le Sueur and his party succeeded in reaching Fort Iberville, afterward called Fort la Boutaye, near the mouth of the Mississippi commanded by D'Bienville. Here after a while came the three men whom Le Sueur had sent with the boat load of war munitions to Fort L'Huillier, who declared that the boat had broken in pieces and every thing been lost just opposite the mine of Nicholas Perrot on the Mississippi. D'Bienville immediately loaded another boat with military stores and provisions and dispatched it up the rivers to the relief of Fort L'Huillier. In the meantime, M. D'Eraque and his little force of twelve men at Fort L'Huillier ran out of provisions and well nigh out of ammunition, and after waiting as long as possible, and having been attacked by the fierce Sioux and had three of their number killed in the woods, embarked all their merchandise in their boat, abandoned the fort and descended the rivers to the mouth of the Mississippi. On their way down they fell in with Juchereau D'St. Denis, who was conducting from Canada a party of thirty-five Frenchmen to the Illinois country for the purpose of establishing a tannery, which they did at the mouth of the Ohio.

When D'Iberville returned from France to the Mississippi in January, 1700, he brought with him commissions for the officers of the colony. D'Sauvolle was made governor, D'Bienville lieutenant and D'Boisbriant major. Many Frenchmen were now constantly going up and down the Mississippi river and no doubt up the various branches flowing from the west. The country was thoroughly explored by the merchants of Canada with the hope and expectation of finding mines of some valuable mineral, and in the event of failure, to secure all the beaver and other rare furs they could find. The missionaries, too, thronged the Mississippi country; and at all the leading Indian tribes there was soon found one of their representatives. The Louisiana Purchase began to be penetrated in earnest. Its rushing rivers, beautiful plains, vast forests and snowy mountains with their ribs of gold, silver and copper, could not long remain unenvied and undeveloped. The establishment of Fort L'Huillier within its boundaries was followed by a continuous stream of exploration and settlement. In 1700 Father James Gravier and a party of Frenchmen descended the Mississippi from the Illinois, reached Biloxi; but soon after returned to the Illinois where he resumed his missionary labors.

While Pierre le Sueur was engaged in the difficult and dangerous task of establishing a permanent fort in the Sioux country for the purpose of controlling the Indians and opening copper and other mines, the Frenchmen at Fort Iberville were not idle. D'Bienville and D'St. Denis were dispatched up Red river to explore the country and open friendly communication with the Indian tribes residing there. These two able men, accompanied by twenty Canadians and a body of Indians, all well provisioned and armed, set off on the 22d of March, 1700. They passed up Red river until they reached the Ouachita (Washita), then rowed up the latter a considerable distance, and finally struck westward across the country to the Red river, up which they journeyed until they reached the country of the Natchitoches. While here they made careful and prudent inquiries, under their instructions, in regard to the settlements of the Spaniards to the west, it having been reported to the French commander at Biloxi that the white people of Mexico were aiming to poach on the French preserves in the Natchitoches region. They heard of the Spaniards farther to the west, but learned that they had not yet reached the Natchitoches country. While here, they were well entertained by the Indians. They were finally conducted by "White Chief" and ten of his Indians, up the river about one hundred leagues to the country of the Cadodaquis, in what is now Indian Territory, passing on the way the Yatasses, who were related to the Natchitoches and the Cadodaquis. No Spaniards were found among any of these tribes, after learning which important fact, and after making every effort to secure the perpetual friendship of these

Indians and after ascertaining that there were no important mines in the country, the Frenchmen returned down the Red and Mississippi rivers to Fort Iberville.

In July, 1701, Governor D'Sauvolle having died, the command of the colony was placed in the hands of D'Bienville, and about the same time Fort Iberville was intrusted to the command of D'St. Denis. At this time, it seems that the veteran Tonty was often in Louisiana, although he no doubt still was governor of, and retained an interest in, the Illinois colony. He assisted the governor of the Louisiana colony in the expeditions to secure the friendship of the various Indian tribes. Very few of the early explorers possessed greater skill and sagacity in this respect than Tonty, and he was regarded at all times as a valuable acquisition to any party desiring to negotiate a treaty of peace with the savages.

In December, 1701, D'Iberville again returned to the colony from France with a large supply of provisions, arms, merchandise and a number of colonists. So great had been the distress during his absence that sickness had reduced the inhabitants to about one hundred and fifty and the provisions had been reduced to a limited quantity of maize, as they continued to call it. At this time the principal colony was transferred from Biloxi to Mobile, where a large fort had been built. Thus far Fort Iberville on the Mississippi and Fort L'Huillier on the Blue Earth river (in Minnesota) were the only establishments of the French on, or west of, the Mississippi. But the latter had been abandoned, so that Fort Iberville was the only positive claim the French had to the great river. They did not possess a single settlement in what is now the Louisiana Purchase. This vast and beautiful tract of country was still anybody's property. But English traders were along the Mississippi and Spanish colonies were moving eastward from Mexico, though the French still held the lead by a considerable distance in this race for a golden empire.

In June, 1702, D'Iberville again returned to France. A few days after his departure, Tonty came down from the Illinois with a body of Canadian merchants, and all were warmly welcomed by D'Bienville. At this time, it was customary for the Frenchmen to secure permission from the governor to reside among the Indian tribes for the purpose of trade. The Indians desired their arms, ammunition and merchandise in exchange for their furs; and in these exchanges were immense profits to the Frenchmen daring enough to assume the risks. Soon French traders began to go up all the western rivers—the Arkansas, Missouri, Red, Des

Moines, Minnesota and the smaller streams. About this time, the Tensas Indians made war upon the Bayagoulas, defeated them, burned their villages, and the few who escaped death came to Fort Iberville, and besought protection from D'St. Denis. They were given cabins near the fort. In October, 1702, the fort was visited by Father Davion from the Yazoo country and Father Limoges from the Natchez, who reported that the Coroas had killed Father Foucault. In January, 1703, D'St. Denis, commanding at Fort Iberville, received intelligence that Father D'St. Comé and four other Frenchmen had been murdered by the Chetimachas near the Bayagoulas villages; whereupon he transmitted the information to D'Bienville at Mobile, and suggested that the death of these Frenchmen should be avenged. D'Bienville directed that he should come immediately to Mobile for the purpose of holding a council of war. It was decided to attack the Chetimachas in their villages on the Chetimachas river (Bayou Lafourche), and accordingly, ten Frenchmen and two hundred warriors of the Houmas, Chicachas and Bayagoulas nations were assembled at Fort Iberville for that purpose. The party passed up the Mississippi to the Chetimachas river, thence down that stream to the enemies' towns. They surprised the Chetimachas, killed fifteen of them, and captured about forty prisoners, men, women and children. One of the murderers of D'St. Comé was recognized, placed in irons and taken to Mobile, where he was placed upon a wooden horse, his brains beaten out with clubs, his scalp torn off and his body thrown in the river, by the orders of D'Bienville, to serve as an example of French vengeance.

It is known that in 1703 about twenty Canadians attempted to make their way from the Illinois to New Mexico by way of the Missouri river, and that they built some sort of a structure, possibly a stockade, where Fort Orleans was afterward located. Their design was to open trade with the Spaniards of New Mexico, to search the country for mines, and to win the friendship of the tribes on the Missouri and its branches. Their advance westward was no doubt prevented by the Indians.* In 1704 there were more than one hundred Frenchmen scattered in small bands along the Mississippi and the Missouri rivers.† The next year, one Laurain, with a small party, passed up the Missouri, but how far is uncertain. Three years latef, Nicholas D'La Salle proposed

---

* Iberville to ——— 15 Fev. 1703.
† Bienville au Ministre 6 Sep. 1704.

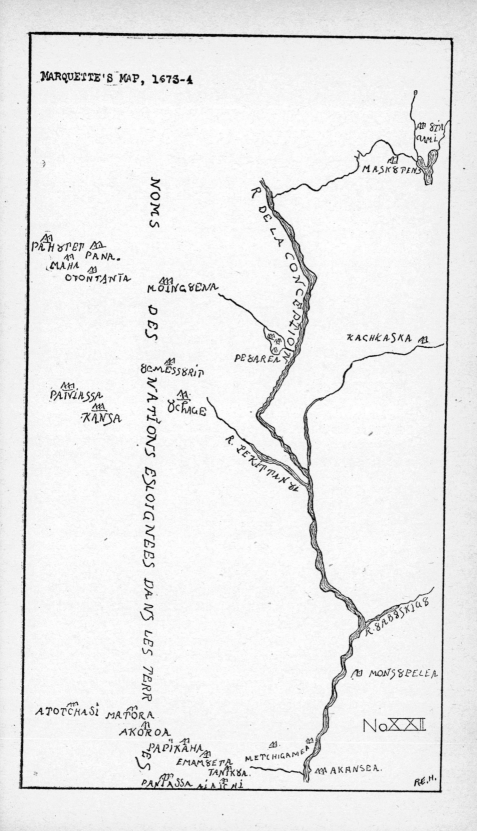

MARQUETTE'S MAP, 1673-4

NOMS DES NATIONS ESLOIGNEES DANS LES TERR ES

PAHЎTEꝉ
PANA.
MAHA
OTONTANTA
MOINGꝠENA
8EMESSꝠRIꝉ
8CHAGE
PAꞮꝠIASSA
KANSA
PESAREA
KACHKASKA
MASK8ƮENS
8TA CAMI
R. DE LA CONCEPꞮꞮON
R. PEKIꞮꞮAN8Ɪ
R. 8AB8SKIG8
MONS8PELEA
ATOTCHASI MAꞮORA
AKOROA
PAPIꞮAHA
EMAM8ETA
TANIꝠA
PAꞮꞮASSA NIAICHI
METCHIGAMEA
AKANSEA.
No XXII
RE.H.

to go up the Missouri with one hundred men; he probably did so, and it may have been the work of this party in the mines of the Osage country, which was still seen extensively by explorers sent out by the United States after 1803.*

It is fairly certain that at this time the French explorers ascended the Missouri as far as the Platte river of Nebraska, but were there prevented from going any higher by the Panis or Pawnees. Governor D'Bienville particularly desired to go far enough up the Missouri and its branches to reach those Indian nations which had large numbers of Spanish horses and which had an established trade with the Spaniards of New Mexico. It was thought by him that the Spaniards would be found among the Pawnees, but when that tribe was reached about the year 1704, it was learned that they were still further to the west or southwest. So much was heard from the Indians of the Spanish mines of copper, silver and gold, that the French were eager to reach the mining country. It was even reported that the Spaniards used pack-mules to carry off the ore. The few Sioux that were seen spoke of a river flowing to the westward. It was the mystery that the French were ever after—the unknown river, mines, riches, so they pushed on until the dream was dissipated in mist.

Soon after this event, D'Bienville sent messengers to the Madeline river (Bayou Teche) to ascertain what tribes resided thereon; and by this means learned that seven nations occupied the course of that stream, among whom were the Attakapas, or man-eaters. In the summer of 1703 M. D'Chateauguay, the brother of D'Iberville and D'Bienville, arrived at Mobile with seventeen Canadian colonists, a goodly supply of provisions and an abundance of agricultural implements, etc. In May, 1704, there arrived at Mobile from France the ship Pelican, mounting fifty guns, and having on board Father D'Lavente engaged in the missionary service, four priests, two grey nuns, and twenty-three poor, but wholly respectable, young women, all of whom or nearly all of whom were afterward married to the single men of the colony. They were under the care of Father Huet, one of the priests. This was the first shipment of unmarried women to Louisiana, but was not the last. The Pelican also brought out two companies of soldiers to reinforce the colonial ranks, which had become sadly depleted by death and other causes. In February, 1703, a boat came down the river with the news that Jucherau D'St. Denis, lieutenant general of Montreal, had

*Beaurain, Journal Historique.

I—9

reached the mouth of the Ouabache (Ohio) river with thirty-four Canadians, and designed to form a settlement there for the purpose of trading with the Indians for buffalo skins, robes, etc. This settlement was actually made, as before stated, and seems to have thrived. M. D'Lambert commanded the settlement for M. D'St. Denis. Late in January, 1705, he arrived at Mobile with all his force, having been scared away by the hostility of the neighboring savages among themselves, and leaving behind 13,000 buffalo skins belonging to his employer. The site of this camp was probably where Cairo, Ill., was afterward located; but this is disputed and is uncertain.

In December, 1704, intelligence was received by D'Bienville that an English armament was fitting out in the Carolinas for the capture of Mobile and the reduction of the French fort on the Mississippi. As France and Great Britain were now at war, and as the report seemed true and the attack imminent, D'Bienville instructed D'St. Denis to abandon Fort Iberville, and to bring all his munitions of war, all his merchandise and all his soldiers to Mobile to assist there should an attack be made. This abandonment left the settlers on the Mississippi in the vicinity of the fort without protection from the Indians as well as from the English; accordingly, the most of them also went to Mobile for security, thus leaving not a single settlement of the French on the mighty Mississippi in what is now the Louisiana Purchase.

In January, 1705, the melancholy news was received in the colony that D'Iberville had died of yellow fever at sea. It was now realized that, owing to the European war, the colony would very probably be left pretty much to its own fate. Thus far the colonists, strange as it may seem, had not become self-sustaining so far as provisions were concerned; they had continued to be dependent on the supplies received from France and brought out by D'Iberville. Now, it was realized, they must depend on themselves; and the outlook was black, indeed, to these poor people, who did not seem to have sense enough to go to work. In their distress they received much assistance from the Spaniards of Florida, for Spain and France were at war with England. In November, 1705, there arrived at Mobile two boats of *coureurs de bois* from the Illinois country, among whom was M. Laurain who claimed to have explored the Missouri river for a long distance. He gave an account of the Indian tribes inhabiting that river and its branches.

In February, 1708, the news was received that M. D'Muys had been appointed to succeed D'Bienville as governor of the colony, and Diron D'Artaguette had been appointed intendant commissary to succeed M. D'La Salle. But M'Muys died on the voyage, and D'Bienville continued to serve as governor. The latter was charged with divers acts of mismanagement and misconduct; and it was concluded that contentions over him in the colony warranted his removal. D'Artaguette was a man of great force of character. He first made inquiries as to the needs of the colonists and was told that they were satisfied with the country and the climate, but wanted horses to work the plantations, which had recently been opened. Many concessions along the Mississippi, on both sides of the river, had been granted to Frenchmen, and the time was now opportune to improve them, so it was thought. D'Artaguette, himself, had a large grant on the west side of the Mississippi at Cannes Bruslés (Burnt Canes). At this time, early in 1708, the colony consisted of fourteen officers, seventy-six soldiers, thirteen sailors, three priests, six mechanics, one Indian interpreter, twenty-four laborers, twenty-eight women, twenty-six children and eighty Indian slaves. All the others had been cut off by death or had returned to France. About this time D'Eraque and six men were sent to the Illinois country with orders to the French there to prevent war being made by the Indians of the upper Mississippi against those of the lower stream. These men visited Kaskaskia and Cahokia, and journeyed a long distance up the Missouri river, having in view particularly the establishment of peace with all the tribes along that river and its branches, especially the Osage river.

The death of D'Iberville was the occasion of an attack on the character of D'Bienville. The only physician in the colony, Barrot, attempted to weaken his influence. D'La Salle, whom the historian Gayarre depicts as a public nuisance, did everything in his power to crush D'Bienville. The latter felt that, owing to the fact that he had so few soldiers, his prestige with the Indians had almost entirely vanished. Two parties arose: One which sustained D'Bienville, and one which bitterly opposed him. At a period in which all should have been united, all were at sword's points, writing violent and more or less false letters to the French court, and doing everything in their power to crush the opposition and rise to the control of affairs. D'Bienville did not take the proper precautions to protect his name with the French minister, and accordingly was dismissed by that individual upon the reiterated requests of his enemies and without having been heard in his own defense. After the death of D'Muys, who was appointed to succeed him, the ministry seems to have gained more light on the subject, because D'Bienville was reappointed and D'LaSalle was recalled. A reaction followed and the administration of D'Bienville was approved. Diron D'Artaguette, who had been appointed to succeed D'La Salle, reported that the accusations against the governor were slanders of the most pronounced character. In the meantime the colony languished, and it is not to be wondered at. The population remained at a standstill, there being not over two hundred and eighty persons of settled habits in the colony. In addition, there were about sixty Canadian traders who constantly shifted their locations. There were about 102 cattle, 1,400 hogs and 2,000 fowls in the colony. This was the state of things in 1708.

Little continued to be done of a self-sustaining nature, and in 1709 the colonists were reduced to a sustenance of acorns. D'Bienville requested that he might be permitted to exchange his Indian slaves for negroes, offering three Indians for two negroes; but his request was not well received by the ministry. He further requested that a few of the colonists who had managed to make some money, and desired to return to France, should be prevented from doing so. It was not long before the old recriminations against D'Bienville broke out with greater violence than ever; but he now was awake to the slanders and retaliated with as much virulence as his enemies. Provisions became so scarce in 1710 that the men in the colony were distributed around among the Indians in order that they might obtain food. In this miserable condition the colony passed to Crozat.

Prior to 1712 military law ruled the Louisiana colony. The military commandant was chief constabulary and chief executive. His word was law, but he was accountable to his king, and was sometimes sharply taken to task. Considering the weakness of the colony and the comparative strength of the British settlements on the Atlantic coast, the wonder grows why the latter did not, during some of the wars between France and England, invade and capture the feeble French establishments on the Mississippi. Had England taken such a course at an early date, she would have been saved the tremendous strain of the Seven Years' War. In 1712 the total population of Canada was about 18,000, while that of the English colonies was fully 400,000. How easy it would have been, with the aid of the Iroquois and the Chickasaws, the latter called "the Iroquois of the South," to have crossed the Alleghanies to the Monongahela, thence sailed down to the mouth of the Ohio, where they could have fortified a powerful post, and prepared for operations both up and down the Mississippi. An army of 5,000 whites and as many Indians could easily have performed this exploit, and within one year have transformed Louisiana into an English dependency. This could have been done by the British Atlantic colonies, without asking the mother country for a dollar or a man. Think of the enormous expenditures of blood and treasure at a later date by the English, and wonder why a conquest that could have been so cheaply bought was not ordered into execution during Queen Anne's War from 1702 to 1713. The only excuse offered for not having done so is that the acquisition of Louisiana was not considered worth the price of its purchase. The genius of Pitt a little later retrieved this oversight.

CHAPTER IV

The Grant to Crozat

NEVER under the sun was there a more promising or a more beautiful land than that which was given to the merchant Crozat. Never was there a man better fitted from personal experience to measure the new country at its true worth. It had been a time for memory and for tears; but now the wonderful fertility of the soil, the balm of the climate, the kisses of the fragrant winds, the cheerful music of the rivers, and the landscapes spread out in hazy enchantment, invited millions from plebeian existence in Europe to the nobility of free and happy homes in the New World. Would the promises of the exhaustless acres and the sweetness of domestic life meet a responsive sound in the breast of the cavalier, who had sprung from an ancestry of gold-worshippers and from a history of chivalric conquest? Did Crozat possess the superb penetration that bases the wealth of a state upon the innumerable products of the soil? Were the bloody lessons of Mexico and Peru destined still to spread a gauzy cobweb of gold over the brain of European merchants and statesmen? It was the duty of Crozat to go to his colony, and give it the light of his personal supervision. It remained for him to crown the achievements of his life with an immediate dissipation of the idle dreams about Louisiana. His opportunity was to visit the colony, learn of its minerals, ascertain the wealth of the soil, publish the truth to the world, and build up an empire from the prodigal gifts of nature. His mission was to eliminate from the bright prospect the restless cavalier, the unprincipled adventurer, the disaffected noble, and to herald on every European breeze the certainty of permanent contentment and abundant means in beautiful Louisiana. An excellent commentary on the times is afforded by an observation of what he did in this splendid opportunity.

On the 17th of March, 1713, the frigate Baron de la Fosse arrived at Mobile with the news that a treaty of peace had recently been concluded at Utrecht between France and England. This intelligence was received with the roar of cannons. It was also learned that the king had granted a monopoly of the colony for a term of years to M. Crozat, who designed to improve the conditions prevailing in Louisiana to the utmost, for his own profit and for the happiness and prosperity of the people. Among the passengers on the above vessels was Antoine de la Motte Cadillac, who had been appointed governor-general of Louisiana, and his family consisting of Mde. de la Motte, their sons and daughter and servants. On the same vessel came twenty-five young women from Brittany, who had volunteered to cast their lots in the new colony under M. Crozat, with the expectation of securing husbands and obtaining respectable homes. Under this new regime M. Duclos became intendant commissary; M. Le Bas, comptroller of finances; M. De Richebourg, M. Dirigoin and La Loire des Ursins, agents and directors of the proprietor, M. Crozat. At the time the colony was thus turned bodily *nolens volens* over to M. Crozat, it comprised about four hundred persons, and by this time twenty negroes had been added to the inhabitants, all the slaves of the whites. There were not to exceed three hundred horned cattle in the colony. The ship that brought over these people also brought an immense supply of arms, ammunition and provisions, all of which was deposited in the magazines and public stores for future distribution. The old colonists were now jubilant, because it was thought their season of trials and dangers was past. Everybody assumed a more cheerful tone, and all began to put their hearts in their work of building up homes in Louisiana. Many grants were made along the Mississippi in what is now Louisiana, on both sides of the river. The proprietor ordered Frenchmen sent westward and eastward to the colonies of the Spaniards in Mexico and Florida, for purposes of trade; and others were ordered sent to the Illinois country to explore for mines of any valuable mineral. MM. Jonquiere and Dirigoin, the latter one of the directors of the proprietor, were sent to Vera Cruz to exchange merchandise for the cattle and horses of the Spaniards, and if possible to establish a free trade between Louisiana and Mexico. The latter request was refused, but the former was partially complied with, whereupon the Frenchmen were ordered to depart from the country. Agents were sent up the

Mississippi with instructions to visit all the Indian tribes and
exchange merchandise for their valuable furs. Every means was
sought by the proprietor to make his patent profitable. His
fortune, as well as his reputation, was at stake. But he did not
understand the country. He made the same mistake they all
made in supposing the land was flowing with gold, silver and
jewels. He also presumed that an immense fortune could be
made from the furs alone, and he was right if he could have had
a cold country and the monopoly of that trade.

The Marquis du Chatel, otherwise known as M'. Crozat, to
whom the king granted Louisiana, September 14, 1712, for the
term of fifteen years, was an able and prominent financier, who
had rendered himself conspicuous during the reign of Louis XIV.
The patent reads as follows:

"Lou's, by the grace of God, King of France and Navarre: To
all who shall see these present Letters, Greeting. The care we
have always had to procure the welfare and advantage of our
subjects have induced us, notwithstanding the almost continual
wars which we have been obliged to support from the beginning
of our reign, to seek for all possible opportunities of enlarging
and extending the trade of our American colonies, we did in the
year 1683 give our orders to undertake a discovery of the countries and lands which are situated in the northern part of America, between New France and New Mexico; and the Sieur de la
Salle, to whom we committed that enterprise having had success
enough to confirm a belief that a communication might be settled
from New France to the Gulf of Mexico by means of large
rivers; this obliged us immediately after the peace of Ryswick to
give orders for the establishing a Colony there, and maintaining
a garrison which has kept and preserved the possession, we had
taken in the very year 1683 of the Lands, Coasts and Islands
which are situated in the Gulf of Mexico between Carolina on
the east and Old and New Mexico on the west. But a new war
having broke out in Europe shortly after, there was no possibility
till now of reaping from that new colony the advantages that
might have been expected from thence, because the private men
who are concerned in the sea trade, were all under engagements
with other colonies, which they have been obliged to follow;
and whereas upon information we have received concerning the
disposition and situation of the said countries known at present
by the name of the Province of Louisiana, we are of opinion that
there may be established therein a considerable commerce, so
much the more advantageous to our kingdom in that there has

hitherto been a necessity of fetching from foreigners the greatest part of the commodities which may be brought from thence, and because in exchange thereof we need carry thither nothing but commodities of the growth and manufacture of our own kingdom: we have resolved to grant the commerce of the country of Louisiana to the Sieur Anthony Crozat our Councillor, Secretary of the Household, Crown and Revenue, to whom we entrust the execution of this project. We are the more readily inclined hereto, because his zeal and the singular knowledge he has acquired in maritime commerce, encouraged us to hope for as good success as he has hitherto had in the divers and sundry enterprises he has gone upon, and which have procured to our kingdom great quantities of gold and silver in such conjunctures as have rendered them very acceptable to us.

"For these reasons being desirous to show our favor to him, and to regulate the conditions upon which we mean to grant him the said commerce, after having deliberated this affair in our Council, of our certain knowledge, full power and royal authority, we by these presents signed by our hand, have appointed and do appoint the said Sieur Crozat solely to carry on a trade in all the lands possessed by us and bounded by New Mexico and by the lands of the English of Carolina, all the establishments, ports, havens, rivers, and principally the port and haven of the Isle of Dauphine, heretofore called Massacre; the river of St. Louis, heretofore called Mississippi, from the edge of the sea as far as the Illinois; together with the river of St. Philip, heretofore called the Missouri; and of St. Jerome, heretofore called Ouabache, with all the countries, territories, lakes within land, and the rivers which fall directly or indirectly into that part of the river of St. Louis.

"I. Our pleasure is, that all the aforesaid Lands, Countries, Streams, Rivers and Islands be and remain under the Government of Louisiana, which shall be dependent upon the General Government of New France, to which it is subordinate; and further, that all the lands which we possess from the Illinois be united, so far as occasion requires, to the General Government of New France, and become part thereof, reserving however to ourselves the liberty of enlarging, as we shall think fit, the extent of the government of the Country of Louisiana.

"II. We grant to the said Sieur Crozat for fifteen successive years, to be reckoned from the day of enrolling these presents, a right and power to transport all sorts of goods and merchandise from France into the said Country of Louisiana, and to traffic thither as he shall think fit. We forbid all and every person and persons, company and companies, of what quality and condition soever, and under any pretence whatever, to trade thither, under penalty of confiscation of goods, ships and other more severe punishments, as occasion shall require; and for this purpose we order our Governors and other officers commanding our troops in the said country forcibly to abet and assist the directors and agents of the said Sieur Crozat."

He was permitted to open all sorts of mines in Louisiana, and was required to turn over one-fifth of the gold, pearls and precious stones discovered, and one-tenth of the product of other mines, to the king. It was stipulated that his proprietary in the mines should be forfeited if they were left unworked for the period of three years. He was granted the exclusive right to vend all sorts of merchandise, including powder and fire-arms to the whites and the Indians; and was likewise granted the exclusive right to buy of the natives or otherwise furs, skins, leather, wool, etc., but was forbidden to deal in castor (beaver). He was given property in all settlements for the culture of silk, indigo, wool, leather, and the working of mines, veins, minerals, mills, etc., and the ownership of lands on which the same should be situated. Three years of neglect worked a forfeiture. The "edicts, ordinances and customs and the usages of the mayoralty and shrievalty of Paris" were prescribed for the laws and customs "in the said country of Louisiana." Crozat was required to send to Louisiana every year two ships laden with "twenty-five tuns of victuals, effects and necessary amunition for the maintenance of the garrison and forts of the Louisiana:" and to carry out the troops destined for the colony. "He shall be furthermore obliged to send on board each ship, which he shall cause to set out for the said country, ten young men or women; at his own election." The king bound himself to furnish Crozat ten thousand pounds of gunpowder each year at actual cost. All wares and merchandise sent out by Crozat to his colonies were exempted from duty; and all exported by him, or re-exported from French ports, were likewise exempted. In case he desired goods, not to be obtained in France, he could procure them by passing them through the government custom-houses. The canoes, feluccas and other vessels owned by the king, then in Louisiana, were ordered turned over to Crozat, upon condition that he should replace them at the end of his charter.

"XIV. If for the cultures and plantations which the said Sieur Crozat is minded to make, he finds it proper to have blacks in the said country of the Louisiana, he may send a ship every year to trade for them directly upon the coast of Guinea, taking permission from the Guinea Company so to do; he may sell those blacks to the inhabitants of the colony of Louisiana, and we forbid all other companies and persons whatsoever, under any pretense whatsoever, to introduce blacks, or traffic for them in the said country, nor shall the said Sieur Crozat carry any blacks elsewhere."

"XV. He shall not send any ships into the said country of Louisiana but directly from France, and he shall cause the said ships to return thither again; the whole under pain of confiscation and forfeiture of the present privilege."

"XVI. The said Sieur Crozat shall be obliged, after the expiration of the first nine years of this grant, to pay the officers and the garrison which shall be in said country during the six last years of the continuance of this present privilege: the said Sieur Crozat may in that time propose and nominate the officers, as vacancies shall fall, and such officers shall be confirmed by us if we approve them."

The terms of the charter to Crozat were as liberal as could be desired. It remained now for that shrewd business man to work success from the deplorable conditions. In the colony were about three hundred persons, besides seventy-five Canadian traders and one hundred soldiers. In addition there were probably twenty negroes and a number of Indian slaves. But Crozat himself did not put in an appearance. He attempted by proxy to succeed in a most difficult undertaking, where tremendous energy, large expenditures and supreme tact and experience were requisite. Crozat so far misunderstood the conditions as to instruct Cadillac to look for mines and seek the far-off and elusive trade of Mexico. Ere long there were again two parties struggling for the mastery and control, as if the mastery was really worth struggling after, with Cadillac the leader of one side, and D'Bienville the leader of the other. Unquestionably, the latter, though only lieutenant governor, was endeavoring to dictate the policy of colonial administration. Cadillac was not the man to receive unsolicited advice with perfect equanimity, much less could he endure dictation; war between the factions therefore resulted. Cadillac refused even to be dictated to by the company. When told to give every encouragement to agriculture, he appeared to take great offense; and instead of doing so continued his search after precious stones. He wrote to the ministry, "Give the colonists as much land as they please. Why stint the measure? The lands are so bad that there is no necessity to care for the number of acres. A copious distribution of them would be cheap liberality." He was not the only man in the colony mentally blind. Expeditions after gold were sent in all directions, and the call of the fertile soil was disregarded.

The effort to open and carry on commercial relations with the Spanish colonies on the west was not easily given up by the proprietor. He determined to send an expedition overland to Mexico for the double purpose of instituting commercial relations and of learning the intentions of the Spaniards as to the colonization of the country which had already become called Texas. For the leaders of this important expedition, he selected Juchereau D'St. Denis, a brave and experienced officer, who accepted the responsibility. He was given five strong canoes loaded with ten thousand livres worth of merchandise, was furnished with the necessary passports to the Spanish governor of Mexico, and was accompanied by twenty experienced men and a number of Natchitoches Indian guides. Thus equipped, the valiant D'St. Denis proceeded up the Mississippi. At or near the river Manshac, they stopped long enough to kill on two successive days twenty-three buffaloes and eight deer. They passed beyond the mouth of the Red river, going up the Mississippi as far as the country of the Tonicas to secure as large a stock of provisions as possible. Here he secured the assistance of the chief of the Tonicas and fifteen warriors upon the agreement to recompense them for their services. He then returned to the mouth of Red river, which he ascended, passing the Ouachita (Washita or Black) river at the distance of eight leagues. Nine leagues father they reached Salt river, and six leagues higher reached the Tassengoula nation (Nation of the Rocks). Nine leagues farther up they reached the falls, around which they were obliged to carry their boats and provisions. A league farther they were compelled to repeat the trying experience. From this point onward they encountered great hardships until they finally reached the principal village of the Natchitoches situated on an island in the middle of Red river. Here an important conference was held with the Indians, who were told that the French desired they should begin to cultivate the soil, and for that purpose he had brought along corn, wheat and other seed for them. Pickaxes, hoes and axes were distributed among them. Here the D'St. Denis party remained six weeks, and in the meantime constructed two strong store-houses in which to house their merchandise and in which to lodge. Having made French interests secure here, D'St. Denis again set forth on the 23d of August, 1713, to explore Spanish territory to the westward, taking with him twelve Frenchmen, fifteen Tonicas and about as many more of the Natchitoches as guides. Under his instructions, he was required to penetrate the Spanish country as far as the Rio del Norte (Rio Grande) and to note all the advanced settlements of the Spaniards in what is now Texas. Ten men were left to care for the stores at Natchitoches, and were strictly enjoined to keep constant watch over both the Indians and the Spaniards. It is claimed that they built Fort Dout, west of the Sabine in 1714, and that the fort was occupied uninterruptedly until the province changed hands. The D'St. Denis party went first by land to the country of the Cenis (or Assinais, as the name is often written), reaching there after twenty-two days' travel. They were now in the vicinity of the modern Waco, Tex., or perhaps a little farther to the west and south. During this march, the daily rations of each man were an ear of corn and a piece of buffalo meat. Here they found evidences that the Spanish had formerly been among these Indians. Continuing again for a month and a half, they finally reached the Rio del Norte and stopped at El Presidio del Norte, a Spanish village on or near that river. D'St. Denis made known his mission to Captain Raymond of the Spanish army, but the latter could do nothing until he had heard from his superior officer in Mexico. After waiting fully six weeks, an officer and twenty-five cavalrymen appeared, with instructions to escort M. D'St. Denis to Gaspardo Anaya, governor of Caouis, in Mexico. Leaving everything behind, D'St. Denis accompanied the Spaniards. After a month of waiting, those left behind received word from him to return at once to Natchitoches, which they accordingly did. D'St. Denis was taken to the city of Mexico, where he arrived on the 25th of June, 1714. Here he was detained on one pretext or another until the year 1715, when he returned without having accomplished his mission. While on the Rio Grande waiting for the reply of the Spanish governor, D'St. Denis was made welcome at the pleasant home of Don Pedro de Villescas, who had two very beautiful daughters, one of whom, Donna Maria, D'St. Denis fell deeply in love with.

D'St. Denis returned via the Presidio del Norte, where he remained a considerable length of time and married the bewitching Donna Maria. After a while, it became necessary for him to return to Mobile, which he did, reporting to Governor Cadillac in detail the results of his visit to the Spanish territory. As soon as possible, he made preparations to undertake a similar journey

to the same country on his own account.   Accordingly, he formed
a business partnership with MM. Le Roy, La Freniere, Graveline,
Derbanne, Freres and Beaulieu, all ow whom were Canadians, and
together they purchased of M. Crozat from the proprietary stores
at Mobile merchandise to the value of sixty thousand livres
($11,100), and with a number of Indians for guides and several
Frenchmen for assistants set forth up Red river.   Their design
was to traverse the same territory D'St. Denis had passed over
on the former trip, and finally to dispose of their merchandise in
New Leon, one of the provinces of Mexico.   They left Mobile
on the 10th of October.   The venture did not prove successful,
owing to the hostile feeling existing between the French of Louisiana and the Spanish of Mexico.   The romantic marriage of D'St.
Denis had interfered with his business judgment.   He was for
the second time imprisoned by the Spanish authorities, and his
merchandise was held; but he succeeded in effecting his escape,
and returned to Louisiana in 1719.   Soon after the abandonment of the post at Natchitoches by the twelve men left there by
D'St. Denis, Cadillac, realizing the importance of holding that
position, sent there a sergeant and a few soldiers, with instructions to take possession of the buildings there and guard French
interests in that quarter.   It was not only an important point
from which to trade with the Indian tribes, but was a notable
strategic center for the preservation of French colonial rights on
the Mexican border.

Early in the year 1716, a post was established among the Tonicas on the Mississippi, or near it, and about two leagues above
the mouth of Red river, on the borders of a small lake.   It was
formed for the purpose of holding the Indians in check and to
secure their provisions.   It was learned by Governor D'Bienville
that, in 1715, the Spanish of New Mexico had sent nine missionaries to the countries of the Adayes, Nacogdoches, Youays,
Assinays, Natchitoches and Nadacoes in the province of Lastikas, the Spaniards claiming that the borders of the province
were along Red river.   When the missionaries were ordered out
of the territory of Red river by the French, they withdrew to
the west of the Sabine, though the Spanish officials in Mexico
did not admit the French contentions.   The Spanish mission on
the Adayes was established on January 29, 1717, by Father
Augustin, Patron de Guzman of the Order of Franciscans, and
was named by him St. Michel-Archange de Lignares.   The
Adayes river was the same as the present Sabine, and thus the

mission was an alleged invasion of French territory. A little later it was broken up by the French.

About this time it was the common practice of the Spanish, French and English traders to go among the nations friendly to themselves and incite them to war against other nations for the purpose of capturing prisoners to be sold as slaves. While negro slaves had been introduced in Louisiana, they were not yet sufficiently numerous to meet the demands, and accordingly Indians were substituted. Particularly, the English incited the tribes of the Carolinas to attack the Mississippi nations, buying from them at good prices all the prisoners they captured. The English of the Carolinas even came to the Mississippi to purchase Indian slaves, to be used on their plantations. Upon the return of the D'St. Denis party, in 1714, they found on the Mississippi among the Natchez three Englishmen from the Carolinas busily engaged in buying all the Indian prisoners they could secure. It was about this time that Cadillac ordered the arrest of an English lord, who apparently was thus engaged among the Natchez. Fearing interference from the French, these Englishmen usually concealed their designs, declaring that they came to buy, or exchange merchandise for, furs and peltries. The English lord made this explanation, but was nevertheless arrested and taken to Mobile. He was finally set at liberty, but a few days later was slain by the Indians. The immense number of negroes brought into the Carolinas soon terminated the traffic in Indians for the purposes of slavery. It was found that the negroes made much better slaves, because they were more tractable and obsequious. It was claimed that a mistake was made in the arrest of the English lord, that he really had with him a considerable quantity of merchandise, and that at the time of his arrest he was engaged in sketching and objected strenuously to the proceedings.

Upon hearing that the French had captured the English lord, the Choctaws immediately put to death all the English traders among them, desiring thus to gain the good will of the French, who were located nearer to them and whose friendship they more earnestly desired. This act led to a general hostile movement of the Mississippi tribes, doubtless at the instigation of the French, against the English of the Carolinas, in which the Choctaws, Cherokees, Alibamos, Abeikas and other nations joined, for a general attack on the English settlements. They burned and pillaged many dwellings, captured a large number of men, women, children and negroes, and brought them to their villages. This was carrying matters farther than the French desired;

whereupon D'Bienville provided with the Indians for the redemption of all the English prisoners. During the latter part of the year 1714, Cadillac passed up the Mississippi and visited the Illinois, and later sent fifty miners to that quarter to commence mining operations. The present Missouri was embraced in the Illinois, and no doubt these men began work in what is now the southeastern portion of that state. Late in 1714, the twelve Frenchmen who had been left at Natchitoches by D'St. Denis in charge of the stores there, grew tired of waiting; and, running short of supplies, returned down the rivers and the Gulf to Mobile, thus completely deserting that important post. It was specially desired that this post should stand to prevent the Spanish of the southwest from encroaching too near the mouth of the Mississippi. But it was now abandoned and all the merchandise removed to Mobile.

Late in December, 1714, several Canadians arrived from the Illinois with specimens of mineral ore from southeastern Missouri. Upon an analysis, under the direction of M. Cadillac, the ore was found to be lead with traces of silver. This seemed so encouraging that Cadillac himself resolved to visit that section for the purpose of ascertaining the extent of the deposit and accordingly set out for that section of Louisiana in January, 1715. It was reported that the mines were located about fourteen leagues to the westward of the Mississippi, and presumably to the westward of Kaskaskia. While there, M. Cadillac found considerable iron ore and a limited quantity of lead ore; but the silver, which he had hoped to find in paying quantities, was not present. However, this westward movement of exploration and mining led soon to the opening of mines higher up the Missouri and the Osage rivers.

During the absence of M. Cadillac to the lead mines of Missouri, D'Bienville received orders from the proprietor of the colony to proceed to Natchez and construct a fort at that point. This was deemed necessary to prevent the murder of French and English traders in that vicinity, to hold the savages in check, and to stimulate trade in furs, peltries and provisions. Several Canadians while descending the river had recently been killed by the Natchez. At this time there was a French trading post among the Tonicas on the west side of the Mississippi above the mouth of Red river and one at the mouth of the Arkansas river. It was about this time also that four Frenchmen who were ascending the Mississippi to the Illinois were treacherously murdered by the Natchez at Petit Gulf. This act hurried the French in the attempt to build a fort among the Natchez. They demanded the heads of the murderers; also that the Natchez should furnish the lumber for the fort to be built in their country, all of which was partially granted. With many Frenchmen and a large number of Indians, D'Bienville rushed the fort to completion, and by the 5th of August, 1716, had it fully enclosed and covered. On the 25th it was dedicated by the French and six hundred Indians with the famous dance of the calumet. Except for short intervals, Fort Iberville on the east side of the Mississippi below New Orleans was occupied regularly by a detachment of French troops. The fort among the Natchez was named Rosalie, and D'Pailloux was appointed by D'Bienville the first commandant. He was left with a squad of soldiers in charge of the fort on the 28th of July, 1716. About this time M. de L'Epinay was appointed governor of the colony to succeed Cadillac, but in the absence of the former D'Bienville continued to rule. De L'Epinay arrived in March, 1717. With him came MM. D'Artaguette, Gouris, Dubreuil, Mossy, Trefontaine, Guenot, Aruths de Bonil and other wealthy and prominent Frenchmen, who were, or had been, granted concessions in the new colony. Various changes had been made in the directory of the proprietary company as time passed. Numerous vessels had arrived from France, loaded with provisions and merchandise, and nearly all brought few or many new colonists.

At this time there was a continuous stream of boats ascending and descending the Mississippi; and every tributary to the westward was thoroughly explored for hundreds of leagues and their important features marked. Governor de L'Epinay brought with him the Cross of St. Louis, which the king of France sent out as a special reward to D'Bienville for his long, faithful and distinguished services in the interest of French ascendency on the Mississippi. An honor of that character was never more worthily bestowed. Despite the statements of enemies, despite the tongue of slander, D'Bienville had ever been the stanch friend of Louisiana, had made immense sacrifices, and had largely shortened his life by the hardships he had endured. While D'Iberville had lived, he had ever been his faithful lieutenant and assistant; and after his death had clung to the colony through good and evil report, determined that it should not be abandoned; and in the darkest hours of starvation, sickness and despair he had fought against the relinquishment of any advantage that had thus been gained at such cost for the glory of France. Though often subordinated through the jealousies and intrigues of rivals, he had

I—10

never for a moment faltered in his devotion to the colony and to the crown of France. It is safe to say that had it not been for his unbending resolution, the colony would have been abandoned soon after the death of D'Iberville. He therefore richly deserved the brilliant Cross of St. Louis.

Repeated attempts were made to reach Mexico by way of the Missouri and its branches. Miners and explorers were sent up that river, but did not succeed in reaching the Spanish. While D'St. Denis and La Harpe were exploring Red river, the French were not idle on the Arkansas and the Missouri. It is reasonably certain that there were fur traders on the Missouri as early as 1703. It was learned that both the Pawnees and the Comanches were in direct communication with the Spanish. Later, Dutisnet, with a small party of Frenchmen and Indians, reached the Pawnee country at what is now Fort Riley, Kansas, in 1719, and there planted the French standard. Attempts were made to find La Hontan's famous Long river, which was reported to extend westward from the Mississippi in the vicinity of Lake Pepin until it reached the great divide between the Mississippi and the Pacific basins. An Indian trail led westward from the extremity of Lake Superior past the Lake of the Woods to the Rocky mountains. This route was recommended as early as 1717 by Vaudreuil and approved by the Regent of France. The following year a party was sent out and two forts were built, one on the Lake of the Woods and the other on Lake Winnipeg, which was at this time thought to be the source of the Mississippi. This movement accomplished what it was designed to do—keep the English from descending into the sources of the Mississippi. Indeed this was one of the principal objects of French colonial policy at this time, and was the cause of many expeditions to the upper branches of the Mississippi and led directly to the re-building of Fort Chartres across the Mississippi below St. Louis.

The very men who disregarded the monopoly granted to Crozat and penetrated the country of the Mississippi and its branches were the ones who erected the barrier that prevented the English from getting a foothold in the Mississippi valley. In other words, it was largely individual enterprise that gave to France that important basin. Under Crozat Louisiana was attached to Canada, but under the Western Company Illinois was attached to Louisiana. The treaty of Utrecht did much to check the western advancement of the English, but it must be said that as a whole Louis XIV did little for the prosperity of his American colonies. Le Grande Roi was too busy with his European conquests and domination. His unconcern in America led to English aggressions in the Ohio valley and in a large measure to the Seven Years War of 1755–62. Governor Spotswood of Virginia early perceived the intentions of the French—to join Canada and Louisiana in the rear of the English settlements and thus be able to fall upon them at any moment. It was through his efforts that many of the English traders sought the Mississippi. As early as 1715, Young, an English fur trader, reached the Mississippi, and may have gone up the Missouri. His principal object was to sound the Indian tribes on the question of a treaty with the English. But he was too late. The rapid settlement of Louisiana under the charter to the Western Company completely blocked the plans of the English colonial authorities. As early as 1716 the government of South Carolina said, "It is obvious how formidable the French will grow there during peace, considering how industrious they are in frequently supplying their settlements with people." If this was true in 1716, how much more was it true in 1720 before Law's bubble had burst. The English soon noticed the large number of colonists that were leaving France for "Luciana in Mississippi, which by the small number of inhabitants in Carolina, the French had the opportunity to begin, and by the present hostilities with the Indians are encouraged to increase." It was about the year 1717 that the Carolina colonists petitioned the Lords of Trade to settle the disputed boundaries in America with France by making the "Meschacebe by them styled Messesipy" the line of demarkation between the two Crowns.

Before the surrender of the charter of M. Crozat, the plan of establishing on the right bank of the Mississippi a city that should become the metropolis of Louisiana was projected, but had not been carried into execution, owing to the lack of the necessary colonial strength. The poor colonists had had all they could do to keep body and soul together, without thinking of immense commercial emporiums on the banks of the mighty river. But the expediency of such a project had long before occurred to them. No sooner had the charter of M. Crozat been surrendered and the Western Company taken the reins of government, than steps were taken to remove the seat of the colony from the unhealthy site at Mobile and Biloxi to the banks of the Mississippi. The new proprietors wisely and promptly appointed D'Bienville governor of the colony, and made preparations on a colossal scale to expand the commercial interests of the inhabitants with the view, of course, of their own aggrandizement. By this time the English had been effectually checked from advancing westward of the Carolinas, so that nothing was to be feared from that source. But it was different on the west. By reason of the construction of Fort St. Louis on the Bay of St. Bernard by La Salle in 1685, the French claimed as far to the westward as that river and its branches. This claim was denied by the Spaniards, who insisted that the relinquishment of that colony, if no other cause existed, had extinguished the rights of France in that quarter. Undoubtedly, this contention of Spain was based upon sound reasoning and justice. This was seen to be so by France, and therefore she never pressed the claim to a finality on these grounds during the long period of negotiation and colonization prior to the cession of Louisiana to the United States. The unsoundness of the French claims to the country westward as far as the Bay of St. Bernard had more to do with the attitude of the United States toward Spain after 1803 than any other consideration. The United States, it was reasoned, succeeded to the claims of France; and if the rights of the latter to that western territory were so fallacious as not to be prudently enforced for nearly a century, the rights of the United States were no better. Therefore, no unbending claim to that territory was set up by the United States. But morals and principles were loose and unestablished in those early days. France then regarded her claim to the country as far west as the Bay of St. Bernard as eminently just; and the Louisiana colony had not the strength and vitality to take possession of the disputed territory by founding colonies therein. It was at first very uncertain whether the parent colony at Biloxi and Mobile would not have to be abandoned. Had the Louisiana colony possessed the necessary strength at this early period, there is no doubt that settlements would have been formed by them in the strip which a little later caused so much contention. As it was, Spain, having greatly the advantage by reason of the proximity of Mexico, proceeded to form missions, posts and settlements in the country as far east as the Sabine—perhaps farther, as she claimed. But the French determined to assert their rights to the Red river country. Accordingly, D'Bienville himself sent up to Natchitoches in 1717 and had constructed a square, palisaded fort, which ever afterward was occupied by a small French garrison.

There is no doubt that if M. Crozat had confined his operations wholly to agriculture and the Indian trade, he would have made money under his charter. But neither he nor his agents could dispossess themselves of the glittering fantasy that the interior of the country contained large quantities of the precious metals. As a matter of fact, nearly all his largest and bulkiest expenditures were made to equip the expeditions sent to all quarters of his grant in search of gold, silver or other valuable minerals. His agents were more to blame than he, because they were on the ground and he was not, and they were in a position to determine the false from the true. He was governed by the reports of his agents, and met their suggestions with enormous expenditures. He sent at great cost elaborate expeditions to the upper Red river, the Washita, the Yazoo, the Coosa, the Cumberland, the Missouri, the Illinois and to interior points away from any considerable stream. All were after valuable minerals and all found nothing. His agents enlarged small findings into vast discoveries, and every ship returning to France was burdened with their golden tales. The only valuable minerals found were the lead and iron of Missouri and Illinois. But the venturesome Crozat realized nothing from them. He lost heavily, but the colony as a whole was benefited by his explorations. The Illinois country, during his short proprietorship, became famous for the valuable minerals which it did not possess, and received large accession to its white inhabitants. Finding no gold or silver, they went to work in most cases. The others established trading posts among the natives and exchanged merchandise, shop-worn and undesirable, for the splendid furs of the northern country. The money of Crozat advertised the colony and filled the land with desirable inhabitants.

One of his pet schemes, as before stated, was to establish an overland commerce with the Spaniards of Mexico; but his overtures were repulsed. The English and the *coureurs du bois* cut his prices and carried on a large and lucrative contraband traffic with the Indians of the Mississippi country. The Canadians invaded his grant on the north, the Spaniards on the southwest and the English and irregular traders everywhere. In the meantime, he was misinformed by his agents, ignorantly of course, but none the less damaging and ruinous; and he pursued their dreams with his wealth and his patriotism. Under the shining stories of golden hills were concealed the real sources of revenue—agriculture and the fur trade. In four years he spent in round numbers about 425,000 livres, and received in return less than 300,000 livres. Finding himself unable to withstand this strain and seeing no chance for improvement, he wisely surrendered his charter and pocketed his losses. It is estimated that at the close of his proprietorship the whole of Louisiana contained about

700 persons, the most of whom were located east of the Mississippi.

The principal markets were St. Domingo and Pensacola. Vegetables, corn and poultry were sent to Pensacola. Sugar, tobacco, cacao and French goods came from St. Domingo. Few engaged in the cultivation of the soil. They traded, hunted, endeavored to defraud the Indians, and dealt in planks, bear, deer and cat skins, and many went to the St. Francis river every winter after bear's grease, buffalo tongues and robes. Not a little profit was made by these illicit traders in dealing in both negro and Indian slaves. The fort at Natchitoches, which had been rebuilt by Sieur Dutisnet about 1714 under the orders of Cadillac, was occupied in January, 1717, by a sergeant and six soldiers. From this important point, a large trade with all the Indians of that region, far out into what is now Texas and up into Indian Territory, was carried on by the intrepid *voyageurs* or *coureurs*. It was learned that tobacco, rice, cotton, indigo, silk, etc., could be raised, but where were the settlers and the workers? Even the trading vessels from the Indies ceased coming when his charter went into effect. All this evasion was the reaction from the monopoly. When the settlers were told that they must not go to Pensacola to trade—must do all such through the agents of the company—they found means to evade the restriction, by reaching the English of Carolina and the French of Canada. Many became smugglers; the present site of New Orleans was largely cleared in 1718 by salt smugglers. It was impossible for Crozat to succeed under the existing conditions.

M. Crozat had just cause of complaint against the government of France. He had a right to demand that his chartered privileges should be protected; but the weakness of France in dealing with the Indians, particularly with those of the lower Mississippi, drew upon the colonists the contempt of the savages; the English were permitted to trade westward to the Mississippi; the illicit trade which was not crushed by France reduced the commerce of Crozat to almost nothing; and the government, by not registering his patent in Louisiana and by otherwise neglecting his chartered privileges, occasioned the open, continued and fatal invasion of his trade and the disfavor of all parties in the colony. Particularly, was the Crozat charter disregarded by the French traders who dealt with the Spanish of Mexico. However, had Crozat himself been present in Louisiana, he could have corrected many of the abuses which crept in through the indifference of the French government. On the other hand, the monopoly of

Crozat was so exclusive, that had it been carried into effect literally, every colonist would have been made a slave of the company.
They must pay what he asked for his goods, and could receive
only what he chose to give for their products. The only relief
from this serfdom was the institution of a clandestine trade. The
success of the Crozat grant depended upon two principal things:
1st, settlers in considerable numbers must be sent to Louisiana;
and 2d, they must consume the goods of the company and dispose of their products likewise; neither of which essential conditions of success was realized.

Under the severe exactions of the company the colonists at last
petitioned that all nations should be permitted to trade with the
colony; that they should have the right to leave the province at
their option; that the monopoly should be restricted to whole-
saling; and that the profits of the company should not exceed
fifty per cent above the cost. Cadillac wrote to the ministry,
"Their petition contains several other demands equally absurd.
In order to cut all these intrigues in the bud, I declared that if
this petition was ever presented to me, I would hang the bearer.
A certain fellow by the name of Miragoin had taken charge of
this precious piece of composition, and had assumed the responsibility of its presentation; but on his being informed of my intentions, he tore it to pieces." Soon after this the first Natchez war
was carried to a successful conclusion by D'Bienville, who had
at his command only a handful of men and had in addition to con-
tend with the enmity of Cadillac, who ordered him on the perilous expedition. In June, 1716, Cadillac wrote, "Decidedly, this
colony is a monster without head or tail and its government is a
shapeless absurdity. * * * Has it not been asserted that
there are mines in Arkansas and elsewhere? It is a deliberate
error. Has not a certain set of novel-writers published that this
country is a paradise, when its beauty or utility is a mere phan-
tasm of the brain?. I protest that, having visited and examined
the whole of it with care, I never saw anything so worthless.
* * * What can I do with a force of forty soldiers, out of
whom five or six are disabled? A pretty army that is, and well
calculated to make me respected by the inhabitants or by the
Indians. * * * Verily, I do not believe that there is in the
whole universe such another government."

There appeared so much independence and lawlessness in the
colony that Cadillac came to imagine that some gigantic conspiracy or sedition was brewing. He therefore issued a proclamation prohibiting all the lower classes from wearing a sword

under a severe penalty and fine and requiring the nobility, those who had the right to wear a sword, to produce their titles and have them registered.   His enemies, and there were many, embraced this opportunity of making sport of his proclamation. Seemingly, every fellow prepared a mock certificate of nobility, and all were referred for examination to Cadillac.   His enemies went still further and either organized, or pretended to organize, a society of nobility and chivalry, and amid great ceremony, elected him its principal officer, with the ludicrous title of "Knight of the Golden Calf," with a humorous reference to his trip to the Illinois in search of that metal.   A humorous song was composed also which compared him with the Knight of the Doleful Countenance.*   In other ways he was ridiculed and derided. About this time he was recalled.

Governor L'Epinay and D'Bienville could not agree.   The former did not know the wants of the colony; the latter did.   Soon the colony was divided into two factions, and the war of recrimination was resumed.   The search for precious metals had failed; so had the attempt to open trade with Mexico; the Indians' fur trade was not large, because the climate was too warm for that industry.   There was no cohesion in the colony.   Trade restrictions could not be enforced upon men who could not be found. Had Crozat been present it might have been different, but he at last perceived impending failure and accordingly asked to be relieved of his charter.

_____

* History of Louisiana by Charles Gayarre.   Vol. I.

CHAPTER V

The Western Company and its Successors

THE treatment of the colonies in America by every European government possessing such, was characterized by gross injustice and the most insupportable oppression. Colonies were usually founded to keep rival nations from occupying the soil and to afford revenues to enhance the splendors of the European courts. Incidentally, they were used as dumping grounds for outcasts, convicts, imbeciles and other undesirable inhabitants. No European nation considered for a moment the proposition of buying the soil of the Indians for any sum approximating in value its actual worth. A few trinkets were deemed amply sufficient, and if not accepted were promptly succeeded and seconded by the musket and the sword. In the case of the Western Company, individuals who had been caught in the net of the stockholders with false tales of gold, ground down in turn upon the colonists to squeeze out flitting and evanescent dividends. The Western Company was an oligarchy, pure and simple, or perhaps pure and compound, because their offenses, perhaps felonies, were compounded. The colonists were worse than serfs, because the latter are supported by their lords and masters. The former were expected to make their own living, and besides return liberal dividends to the company. The colonial system of every European government was wrong, because based upon injustice, tyranny and unbearable exactions. It led in the end to the rebellion and independence of the Spanish and the English American colonies; and would have met the same fate in Louisiana had Napoleon not ceded that province to the United States in 1803. Following is the cudgel held over the colonists by the Western Company:

"LOUIS, BY THE GRACE OF GOD, OF FRANCE AND NAVARRE KING, TO ALL TO WHOM THESE OUR PRESENT LETTERS SHALL COME, GREETING:

"From the time of our accession to the crown, we have been successfully engaged in establishing good order in our finances, and in reforming the abuses which long-protracted wars had caused in them; nor have we paid less attention to the restoration of the trade of our subjects which contributes to their prosperity as much as the good administration of our finances. But having taken cognizance of the state of our colonies situated in the northern parts of America, we have remained satisfied that they were so much the more in need of our protection. M. Anthony Crozat, to whom the late King, our most honored lord and great grandfather, had, by letters patent of the month of September, 1712, granted the privilege of exclusive trade in our government of Louisiana, having humbly prayed that we might allow him to resign it, which we did allow him by the order of our council of the 23d of the present month of August, and the contract made with Messrs. Aubert, Neret and Gayot, on the 10th of May, 1706, for the trade of beaver in Canada, expired at the end of the present year: We have thought fit, for the good of our service and the advantage of both colonies, to establish a company capable of upholding their trade and of undertaking the different species of husbandry and plantations that may be established there: Wherefore, and for other reasons us thereto inducing, by and with the advice of our dearly beloved uncle, the Duke of Orleans Regent, *Petit fils de France,* of our dearly beloved cousin, the Duke of Bourbon, of our dearly beloved cousin, the Prince of Conty, princes of our blood, of our dearly beloved uncle the Duke of Maine, of our dearly-beloved uncle the Count of Toulouse, legitimated princes, and other peers of France, grandees and notable persons of our kingdom and by our certain knowledge and royal authority we have said, determined and ordained, do say, determine and ordain, it is our will and pleasure:

"I. That there be formed, by virtue of these present letters, a trading company by the style of the *Western Company,* in which it shall be allowed to all our subjects, of what ever rank and quality they may be, as well as to all other companies formed or to be formed, and to all bodies and corporations, to take an interest for such sum or sums as they may think fit, and they shall not, on account of the said engagements, be considered as having degraded their title, quality or nobility; our intention being that they may enjoy the benefit expressed in our proclamations of the months of May and August, 1664, August, 1669, and December, 1701, which shall be executed according to their form and tenor.

"II. We grant to the said company, for the space of twenty-five years, beginning from the day of the registration of these present letters, the exclusive right of trading in our province and government of Louisiana, and also the privilege of receiving, to the exclusion of all other persons, in our colony of Canada, from the first of January, 1718, until and including the last day of December, 1742, all the beaver, fat and dry, which the inhabitants of the said colony shall have traded for, whilst we shall regulate, according to the accounts which shall be sent over to us from the said country, the quantities of the different sorts of beaver, that the company shall be bound to receive each year from the said inhabitants of Canada, and the prices they shall be bound to pay for them.

"III. We forbid all our other subjects any sort of trade, within the limits of the government of Louisiana, as long as the charter of the Western Company shall last, upon pain of forfeiture of goods and vessels; not intending, however, by the said prohibition, to put any restraint upon their trading within the said colony, either among themselves or with the savages.

*   *   *   *   *   *   *   *   *   *   *

"V. With a view to give the said Western Company the means of forming a firm establishment, and enable her to execute all the speculations she may undertake, we have given, granted and conceded, do give, grant and concede to her, by these present letters and forever, all the lands, coasts, ports, havens and islands, which compose our province of Louisiana, in the same way and extent as we have granted them to M. Crozat, by our letters patent of 14th September, 1712, to enjoy the same in full property, seigniory and jurisdiction, keeping to ourselves no other rights or duties than the fealty and liege homage the said company shall be bound to pay us and to the kings our successors at every new reign, with a golden crown of the weight of thirty marks.

"VI. The said company shall be free, in the said granted lands, to negotiate and make alliance in our name, with all the nations of the land, except those which are dependent on the other powers of Europe; she may agree with them on such conditions as she may think fit, to settle among them, and trade freely with them, and in case they insult her, she may declare war against them, attack them or defend herself by means of arms, and negotiate with them for peace or a truce."

The company was granted all mines opened by it; was given the right to sell or give away land, or even to grant it in free-hold, but could not dispossess prior holders; was empowered to construct such forts, castles and strongholds, as deemed necessary, and garrison them with soldiers raised in France, under the king's commission; and was authorized to appoint any officers wanted, and could remove them at pleasure and install others.

"XI. We allow all our military officers who are at present in our government of Louisiana and who may wish to remain there, as also those who may wish to go there and serve as captains and subalterns, to serve under the company's commissions, without losing on that account the rank or degree they actually enjoy, either in our fleet or in our army, and it is our will that in consequence of the permission thereto that we shall deliver to them, they may be considered and accounted as still in our service, and we shall take into considerations their service under the said company as if it had been rendered to ourselves.

"XII. The said company shall likewise be free to fit out and arm for war as many ships as she may think fit, for the increase and security of her trade, and to place in them as many guns as she pleases, and to hoist the flag on the hindcastle and the bowsprit, but on no other mast: she shall also be at liberty to cast cannons and mark them with our arms, under which she shall put those we shall grant her hereafter."

Being constituted "Lord of the Manor," the company was empowered to appoint or dismiss any and all subordinate officers, civil and criminal—justices, judges, police magistrates, judges of admiralty, sovereign councillors, all to be commissioned by the king, and to act in conformity to the laws of France, "and more particularly according to the common law of the provosty and viscounty of Paris, which shall be followed in all the contracts the inhabitants shall pass, and no other law shall be allowed to be introduced to avoid variety."

"XVII. We shall grant no letter or respite, supersedeas or certiorari, to any person who shall buy goods of the company, and they shall be compelled to pay their debt by the means and in the way they have engaged to do it.

"XVIII. We promise to protect and defend the said company, and to employ the force of our arms, if it be necessary, in order to maintain her in the full freedom of her trade and navigation; as likewise to see that justice be done to her for all the injury or ill treatment she may suffer from any nation whatever."

The company was prohibited from trading in any but French

vessels with French crews, in French ports, and from trading directly with Guinea, upon pain of forfeiture of their vessels; but the company's vessels might take as prizes any French vessels trading in the company lands contrary to the tenor of the patent.

"XXIII. It is our pleasure that such of our subjects as shall go over to the lands granted to the said company, enjoy the same liberties and immunities as if they had remained living in our kingdom, and that those who shall be born there of French inhabitants of the said lands and even of foreign Europeans, professing the Roman Catholic Religion, who may come to settle there, be considered and reputed as inhabitants of our kingdom, and as such capable of inheriting and receiving gifts, legacies and other advantages without being bound to take letters of free denization."

"XXIV. And in order to favor such of our subjects as shall settle within the said lands, we have declared and declare them, as long as the charter of the company lasts, free of all duties, subsidies and taxes whatever, as well on their persons and those of their slaves as on their merchandise."

It was provided that the goods and merchandise shipped by the company for the lands granted it, and those needed by it for building, outfitting and victualling its vessels, should be free of duty; and the company was declared free of toll, crossing, passage or other taxes levied for the king's profit on the river Seine and Loire, on certain supplies. It was further provided that should the company find it necessary to have certain goods from foreign countries, it could do so by passing them first through the French custom-houses, etc. It was stipulated that the goods imported by the company for its account, from the lands granted to it in the ports of France, should pay during the first ten years of the charter's life, one-half the duty usually required.

"XXIX. If the company construct vessels in the lands granted to her, we consent to pay to her, as a bounty, out of our royal treasury, the first time the said vessels enter into the ports of our kingdom, the sum of six livres per tun, for all vessels not below two hundred tuns burthen, and of nine livres also per tun, for those not below two hundred and fifty tuns, which shall be paid on delivery of certificates of the directors of the company in the said lands, showing that the said vessels have been built there."

Leave was given the company to grant special licenses to French vessels to trade with the colony upon conditions deemed just, but they were not to be discriminated against.

"XXXI. We shall deliver to the said company out of our

magazines every year during the time of her charter, forty thousand pounds of gunpowder, for which we shall charge her no more than the prime cost."

"XXXII. Our intention being that the greatest number possible of our subjects participate in the trade of this company and in the advantages we grant her, and that all sorts of persons may take an interest according to their fortunes; it is our pleasure that the stock of this company be divided in shares of five hundred livres each, the value of which shall be paid in exchequer bills, and the interest be due from the first of January of the present year; and when the directors of the said company shall have declared that a sufficient number of shares have been delivered, we shall close the books of the company."

"XXXIII. The certificates of the said shares shall be made payable to the bearer, signed by the treasurer of the company, and approved by one of the directors. Two sorts of certificates shall be delivered, viz.: Certificates of single shares and certificates of ten shares."

"XXXV. All foreigners may take as many shares as they may think fit, though they should not reside in our kingdom; and we have declared, and do declare, that the shares belonging to the said foreigners shall not be subject to the right of *aubaine,** nor to any confiscation for cause of war or otherwise, it being our pleasure that they enjoy the said shares as fully as our subjects.

"XXXVI. And whereas the profits and losses in trading companies are uncertain and the shares of the said company can be considered in no other light than as merchandise, we permit all our subjects and all foreigners, in company or for their private account, to buy, sell and trade in them as they shall think fit.

"XXXVII. Every shareholder, bearer of fifty shares, shall have a vote in the court of proprietors, and if he is bearer of one hundred shares he shall have two votes and so forth, augmenting the number of votes by one for every fifty shares.

"XXXVIII. The exchequer bills received in payment for the shares shall be converted in a stock bearing four per cent interest, the said interest to begin from the first of January of the present year; and as security for the payment of the said interest, we have pledged and assigned, do pledge and assign our revenues of the comptrol of notaries' deeds, of the small seal and of lay registration, in consequence whereof the commissioners of our council,

---

* The right formerly possessed by the king of France to all the personal property of which an alien died possessed. Abolished in 1819.

that we shall name to that end, shall make in our name and in favor of the said company bonds for a perpetual and inheritable annuity of forty thousand livres, each bond representing the interest of a capital of one million at four per cent, against the finance receipts that shall be delivered by the treasurer of our royal treasury, in office this present year, who shall receive from the said company one million of exchequer bills at each payment until the moneys deposited for shares in the said company shall be exhausted."

It was stipulated that the interest of the annuities should be promptly paid, but the company was prohibited from making use of the interest of future years in advance. Dividends were to be declared annually, and were to be paid in the order of the numbers of the shares, the company not being at liberty to make any change in the order.

"XLIV. Neither the shares of the company, nor her effects, nor the salaries of the directors, officers or agents of the said company, shall be subject to distress by any person or under any pretence whatever, not even for our own moneys and affairs, excepting only that the creditors of the shareholders shall be at liberty to attach in the hands of the treasurer and bookkeeper of the said company the moneys due to the said shareholders, according to the accounts closed by the company, to which the said creditors shall be bound to submit without obliging the said directors to show them the state of the company's effects or render them an account, neither shall the said creditors establish any commissaries or sequestrees of the said effects, and all acts contrary to the present edict shall be void."

"L. We bestow in gift to the said company the forts, warehouses, houses, cannons, arms, gunpowder, brigantines, boats, canoes and all other effects and utensils we possess at present in Louisiana, all of which shall be delivered over to her on our orders, which shall be dispatched by our navy council."

"LI. We bestow likewise in gift to the said company, the vessels, goods and effects which M. Crozat delivered over to us, as explained in the decree of our council on the 23d day of the present month, of whatever nature they may be, and whatever may be their amount, provided that in the course of her charter she carry over to the lands granted to her, no less than six thousand white persons and three thousand negroes."

It was agreed that if, after the lapse of the charter's life, the king did not see fit to prolong the life of the company, the entire grant should pass to it absolutely, with liberty to dispose of the

same as it saw fit. The company was required to instruct the
Indians and the people in the established religion. It was also
permitted "to take for its coat of arms an escutcheon vert, waved
at the base argent, lying thereon a river god proper, leaning on a
cornucopia; or, in chief azure service of fleur de lys, or bearing
upon a closet, or supporters two savages; crest a trefoiled crown;
and we grant it the said arms that it may make use of them on its
seals, and place them on its buildings, vessels, guns and wherever
it may think fit."

"LVI. Whereas it is not our intention that the special protection we grant to the said company be in any respect prejudicial
to our other colonies whom we wish also to favor, we forbid the
said company to take or receive under any pretence whatever, any
inhabitant established in our colonies, and transfer them to
Louisiana, unless they have obtained the necessary permission
in writing of the governors general of our said colonies, authenticated by the Intendants or chiefs of the commissariat." (Signed
August, 1717.)

As under Crozat so under the Western Company, exaggera-
tions and misrepresentations were resorted to by the proprietors
to influence the people of France to immigrate to Louisiana.
The stories of gold were adopted to induce colonization and to
fortify the paper-money scheme of Mr. Law. Louisiana was
used as a cat's-paw to snatch the chestnuts out of the fire of financial disaster and disgrace that might result to the monetary system of France. Law was not at heart a knave, as has been
alleged; but was himself deceived by false principles of money
and credit. The mines of Mississippi were declared by the French
ministry to be sufficient to sustain the paper money emitted
by the bank established by Law. If any deception was practiced upon the people of France, it was by the Regent and not by
Law. They deceived the public only by deceiving themselves.
When the collapse came, the name of Mississippi became mal-
odorous, not through any fault of its own, but by association with
bankruptcy and distress. The faith of Law in his system is
shown by the fact that he kept up an enormous expenditure to
sustain his Arkansas colony to the very last and was beggared by
the collapse. The distresses and calamities in Louisiana were
largely concealed from the people of France; correspondence was
secret; but the true state of affairs was known to clear-headed
French statesmen.

Under both Crozat and the Western Company many of the
worst classes in France were sent to the colony. "The people

who are sent there are miserable wretches driven from France for real or supposed crimes or bad conduct, or persons who have enlisted in the troops or enrolled themselves as emigrants in order to avoid the pursuit of their creditors. Both classes regard the country as a place of exile. Everything there disheartens them; nothing interests them in the progress of a colony of which they are only members in spite of themselves. You are not ignorant of the reasons which led to its being reported that Louisiana possessed in its bosom great treasures, and that its occupation brought us into the neighborhood of the famous mines of St. Barbe and of others still richer, from which we flattered ourselves with the prospect of easily driving away the present possessors."* Du Pratz declares that all the letters sent to France were intercepted, meaning that they were opened and examined and those of an injurious nature withheld or destroyed. The proprietors did not dare let the whole truth become known in France.

When the Company of the Indies took the reins in 1723, there was no reform nor no relief from the distresses in the colony. The monopoly became more grinding and burdensome than ever. The tariffs and exactions drove many out of the colony. The company plunged into debt and ere long mortgaged its capital. Bankruptcies and law-suits resulted. In order "to attach the governor and the intendant to the interests of the Company there was assigned to them an annual gratuity and an allowance on the exports of the staple commodities of France." Under this extreme order of affairs, the governor and the intendant in 1726 were the creditors of Louisiana to the amount of $587,190. The colonists did not dispute this debt, but there was no way to compel them to pay it. They refused the police protection of the troops sent out, and engaged in the fur trade. Soon they were involved in intermittent and diminutive wars with the natives, whom, of course, they cheated and otherwise wronged. The massacre at Natchez was one of the direct results of the lack of control over the colony by the company.

The formation of the Western Company was the signal for an important change in colonial proceedings. The new company determined to make agriculture an important feature in the colony. It was determined to form a permanent settlement on the Mississippi, as near its mouth as the banks would allow and be

* Letter of Charlevoix to the Duchess de les Dignieres, which was kept secret for about twenty-five years, in order that its unfavorable review of Louisiana might not be known to the people of France.

I—11

above overflow. The mistake of the past in retaining the seat of government at Mobile was admitted. It had already been learned that rice, indigo and tobacco could be grown in the fertile soil along the Mississippi. In the autumn of 1717, D'Bienville again prospected-the various sites along that river and finally selected the present position of New Orleans as the most eligible. One of the earliest acts of the new administration was to send laborers and mechanics to lay the foundations of the new town. There were trees to be cut down, ditches to be filled, drains to be dug, brush to be removed, plans to be drawn, and considerations of great moment to be considered concerning the periodical over- flow and the facility of communication by ships with the Gulf. No doubt, the proximity of Lake Pontchartrain, as well as that of the Mississippi, influenced the selection of the present site of New Orleans. From the very start, embankments were thrown up around the town to protect it from the overflows of the Missis- sippi. D'Bienville supplied the name New Orleans.

The great influence of the new company was felt in the arrival of a large number of colonists and in the stimulus given to agri- culture, as well as to the Indian trade. In March, 1718, over five hundred persons arrived and established themselves on their con- cessions. The first important grant was that to Paris du Vernay, who brought over with him his brother, two sisters and twenty- five other persons. He was given a large tract twenty-eight leagues above New Orleans at the old Indian village of the Bay- agoulas and opposite Manshac. Preparations were made to culti- vate the soil, rear silk worms and manufacture silk, plant and raise rice, indigo and tobacco. The second concession was made to M. de Muyes at the old Tensas village. That gentleman sent out his two nephews, MM. D'Loire des Ursins, and two associates, Chastan and Roué, in charge of about eighty persons, all pro- vided with the necessary tools and implements for the cultivation of the soil. Two merchants of the city of Lyons, Brossart brothers, were given a large grant on Red river in the vicinity of Natchitoches. They, likewise, sent over laborers and mechanics. To Benard de la Harpe, of the French town of St. Malo, was granted a large concession one hundred leagues above Natchi- toches among the Cadodaquois on Red river. This was in what is now northeast Texas. He sent over twenty-five persons to form this settlement, so far on the outskirts of the colony. In fact, the country of the Cadodaquois was claimed by the Spaniards for many years after this event. A grant among the Tunicas was given to M. St. Reine, and one at Pointe Coupée to M. Dilleuse.

Diron D'Artaguette received the grant at Baton Rouge; and Marquis D'Artagnac that at Burnt Canes. Concessions were also made at the old Natchez and the old Choupitoulas villages on the east side of the Mississippi. Ere long M. D'Boisbriant was made a knight of the Order of St. Louis and appointed governor of the Illinois, which district then embraced all west of the Mississippi and above the Arkansas. A company of troops destined for the Illinois was placed under the command of Major Pailloux and Captain Diron, brother of M. D'Artaguette.

In October, 1718, M. D'Boisbriant set out for his destination in the Illinois; and at the same time M. de la Harpe, accompanied by about fifty men, started up Red river for his concession among the Cadodaquis. At this time M. Bondel was ordered to Natchitoches to relieve M. Dutisnet, the latter being sent to the Illinois with Governor D'Boisbriant. Lieutenant de L'Boulaye, with thirty men, was sent by Governor D'Bienville, to build a fort among the Yazoos on or near the river of the same name. He erected the fort on the Yazoo, four leagues from the Mississippi. M. Dubuisson, who was in charge of the concession of Du Vernay at the Bayagoulas, complained that there was no safety there so long as the French continued at war with the Chetimachas. Accordingly, a treaty of peace was concluded with the chiefs of that tribe, greatly to their satisfaction, as well as to that of the inhabitants at Bayagoulas. They agreed upon their removal to the banks of the Mississippi about a league above the Vernay concession. Many more colonists came over from France in the spring of 1719. On three vessels came one hundred and thirty. M. D'Montplaisir arrived with thirty persons prepared to establish a tobacco factory; and an Irish gentleman brought over sixty men to form a settlement on his concession on the Ouachita (Washita) river, eight leagues from its mouth. M. D'Serigny, commander of one of the vessels, brought to the colony several hundred workmen and soldiers and about two hundred and fifty negroes, the first large importation of Africans to the colony. After this date, however, they continued to arrive rapidly, because the company was bound by its charter to introduce a considerable number each year.

On the 6th of June, 1719, two ships arrived from the coast of Guinea with five hundred negroes, all of whom were sold to the concessionaries. On the 1st of September, four ships arrived, having on board eight hundred and thirty men, all destined to remain in the colony. In the war which broke out between France and Spain and extended to the Louisiana colony, the concessionaries were called upon for assistance and responded as became faithful subjects of the French crown. No attempt was made by the Spanish vessels to ascend the Mississippi for the purpose of attacking the settlements along its banks. The large number of soldiers sent over served to protect the Mississippi settlements, but the outlying districts suffered. Late in September there arrived from France two hundred and fifty miners and several companies of soldiers, and with them came immense quantities of ammunition, merchandise and stores for the colony. The miners were destined for the Illinois, and boats were at once constructed for their transportation up the Mississippi. Thus, the Western Company had fallen into the dangerous habit of looking after minerals instead of crops of corn, tobacco and rice. In October the news was received that the two companies—Eastern and Western—had been united by an edict of May 12, 1719. At the same time the ship brought several scores of Germans who had been secured from one of the German princes to be used in colonizing Louisiana. They were the first installment of twelve thousand, which had been thus "purchased." At this time, M. Pailloux was appointed major-general; Diron D'Artaguette inspector-general; and D'Chateaugue lieutenant of the king. D'Artaguette was ordered to remove from Dauphine Island to the Mississippi, because the lands there were too sterile to be cultivated.

In August, 1718, there arrived in the colony sixty persons designed for the concession of M. De la Harpe in the country of the Cadodaquis on Red river. When the Eastern and Western Companies were united by the edict of May 12, 1719, the colonists learned that they could procure the merchandise of the new company by paying at New Orleans five per cent above cost, at Natchitoches twenty-five per cent above cost, and in Missouri and Illinois fifty per cent above cost. All articles that were not specified in the official schedule were procurable upon the payment of fifty per cent. above cost. In September, 1720, two hundred and fifty colonists arrived under the direction of MM. Elias and Le Bouteaux for the concession of M. Law on the Arkansas. They were nearly all Germans, and were a most desirable class of immigrants, because they were agriculturists. Many more of the same class for the Law concession arrived in the spring of 1721.

In February, 1720, over five hundred colonists arrived from France, and were distributed among the concessionaries. Every effort was made to make them contented with their lot, in order that favorable intelligence might be sent back to France of life in the colony. M. Hubert, director-general of the province, removed all his possessions from New Orleans to Natchez. With him were sixty laborers and domestics. He sent a large batteaux loaded with merchandise and ammunition up the river to Governor D'Boisbriant in the Illinois. M. De la Harpe, whose concession was in the country of the Cadodaquis, used every argument for the Western Company to colonize the country still farther to the westward than his concession. He showed that it would be immensely to the advantage of the company to open commercial relations as soon as possible with the Spaniards on the southwest. He had himself visited many of the Indian tribes of that region and still farther west, and felt that a large trade could be built up with those nations. .

In January, 1721, about three hundred persons arrived for the concessions of Le Blanc and Count Belleville on the Yazoo, and for others. A little later, sixty colonists arrived for the concession of Marquis D'Ancenis on the Houmas (Washita). About this time Governor Bienville sent an armed vessel to the river Madeline (Bayou Teche), with a considerable body of soldiers and workmen and an abundant supply of provisions and merchandise, prepared to build a fort and make a settlement on that river. This was the stream from which the Chetimachas had previously committed so many attacks on the Bayagoulas along the Mississippi. M. De la Harpe, who commanded this expedition, met with opposition from the start. A large body of natives met him and stated that they desired no change and did not wish to form an alliance with the French. They were made many presents and treated royally, and in the end the French were permitted to build the fort and open a trading post. In February, 1721, three hundred and forty-seven Swiss troops arrived and were distributed to the different posts throughout Louisiana. The same vessel brought a letter to D'Bienville, dated October 31st, 1720, and informing him that "it was with great regret they had heard of a disagreement between him and the director-general of the company, and that the king believed him to be at fault. It was, however, contemplated to appoint another director, which act they hoped would prevent any future disagreement in regard to the government of the province." At this time, also, the colonists of Louisiana heard of the failure and flight of John Law, comptroller-general of finance of France. This failure, so important in the history of France and of all Europe, produced no serious effect in Louisiana. There was some shifting on the concessions, but otherwise there was no serious result. Of course, Law's settlement on the Arkansas, was forced to the wall, and compelled to remove to other portions of the colony. But the loss of one locality was the gain of another.

The famous black code of Louisiana was drafted by D'Bienville under the orders of the Western Company in 1724 and was kept in force with few alterations until 1803. The company had found it absolutely indispensable to introduce Africans to work the fields of the south, and it was necessary that they should be thoroughly controlled. Under this code Jews were expelled from the colony, and all other religion than the Catholic was prohibited. In November, 1721, D'Bienville was informed by M. Renard, of Natchitoches, that Marquis Aguayo, governor of the province of Lastikas, had arrived at the Adayes with thirty thousand dollars in gold, four hundred horsemen, and all the necessary materials to build a strong fort at that point. This visit was actually made, but the fort was not built, owing to the opposition of the French. In the autumn of 1721, M. D'Bourgmont commanded the district of Missouri, and M. D'Laboulay of the Arkansas. The latter by permission of Governor D'Bienville, removed with his troops to White river in order to be handier to the concession of M. Law and to be in a position to receive assistance to better advantage. Canadians from the Illinois, with pirogues loaded with provisions, continued to be murdered by the savages along the Mississippi probably at the instigation of the English. They were rich prizes for the starving Indians, who cannot be blamed, in view of the treatment they had received from the Spanish and the French. So great became the danger to these pirogues that the custom was adopted for many to come at the same time in what were called "convoys," where all the men were armed and often numbered several dozen. Constant watch was kept day and night, and any inquisitive Indians were summarily dealt with. In November, 1721, a hospital was ordered built in New Orleans by the commissioners. It was twenty-one feet wide by seventy feet long, and was constructed of cypress boards. In 1722, a negro who had killed a Frenchman was burned alive in New Orleans.

From the first to the fourth of September, 1722, four ships which arrived at New Orleans discharged provisions and merchandise to the value of nine hundred thousand livres ($166,500). There arrived before this date from France, as before stated, M. D'Bourgmont, a knight of the Order of St. Louis, sent out for the purpose of visiting the country of the Padoucas (Comauches), then the allies of Spain, and located on the headwaters of the Kansas and the Platte rivers, to induce them to form a treaty with France. Thus far those Indians had been an effectual bar to the advancement of the French traders beyond their country. Several expeditions had gone to their villages, but were unable to advance beyond, owing to the influences of the Spaniards on New Mexico, who supplied them with horses, merchandise, arms and ammunition. So many were returning to France from the colony at this time that the commissioners ordered that no further desertions from Louisiana would be permitted without their consent. In September, 1722, a violent hurricane blew down many of the houses in New Orleans, and seriously damaged all the rice, corn and beans of the lower valley. About this time, also, the commissioners were informed by several of the directors of the concessions that they had successfully cultivated indigo during the past season, and requested that a vessel might be dispatched to St. Domingo for a further supply of seed. The request was granted. M. D'Artaguette made three or more voyages up the Mississippi from 1718 to 1722, during which time he noted accurately the many phases and courses of the current for the benefit of all navigators.

Late in 1722 a request was received from the Spaniards of Vera Cruz to permit several of their vessels to visit New Orleans for the purpose of procuring a supply of flour; but after deliberation the council refused permission, it not being deemed prudent to permit them to come up the Mississippi, which was not fortified and could not repel an attack should one be made. The Spaniards were told that they could obtain the flour at Mobile, whither it was sent. It will be observed from this circumstance that New Orleans had already become known as a produce market to the cities of the Gulf. As a matter of fact, large quantities comparatively of flour and pork had already begun to descend the river, mainly from the Illinois country, but considerable from the Missouri, Arkansas and Red rivers. Late in 1722, D'Bienville received word that five hundred persons under the command of the Spanish Marquis D'Guallo, had entered the province of Lastikas to the westward of Natchitoches. It was learned later that the number of persons was much exaggerated, but that many had actually arrived there for settlement.

Among the most serious obstacles to retard the progress of the colony were the hostility of the Indians, the shipment to the colony of convicts and abandoned women, the lack of women of good character, the dissipation and debauchery of the soldiers, the prohibition of any crop in the colony which could be raised in France, the oppressive nature of the company's monopoly, the jealousy and ill-will between the colonial officers, the refusal of the colonists to till the soil, and the lack of enough soldiers to protect the remote inhabitants, scattered as they were from the Illinois to Biloxi. From the 25th of October, 1717, to the 22nd of May, 1721, seven thousand and twenty persons were transported by the company to the colony in forty-three vessels. At the latter date there were remaining in the colony five thousand four hundred and twenty persons, all the others having either died, deserted, or returned to France or gone elsewhere.

In 1720 Louisiana Province was divided into nine civil and military posts or districts: Biloxi, Mobile, Alibamos, Yazos, Natchitoches, New Orleans, Arkansas and Illinois. Over each was placed a military commander and judge, and each was protected by a fort. All were constituted three ecclesiastical districts—the first under the Capuchins extending from the mouth of the Mississippi to the Illinois river; the second under the Carmelites extending from the Mobile to the Alibamos, and the third under the Jesuits extending over the Ohio, Illinois and other tributary streams of the Mississippi. The prosperity in Louisiana under the Law system was unnatural and could not last. A check was therefore cast upon colonization and improvement on the various concessions, which occasioned a re-organization to meet the new conditions of trade and prosperity. The extensive grant to Law himself on the Arkansas river near its mouth, was deserted by his German colonists as soon as the news of his collapse reached Louisiana. However, they had come to stay if they could be made comfortable; and accordingly they were given a large and valuable tract on both sides of the Mississippi at what has since been known as the "German Coast," a short distance above New Orleans. It cannot be said that the desertion of some of the outlying settlements was due to the failure of the Law system. Of course the collapse of the Law scheme removed one of the principal supports of the Western Company; and this lack of support to the latter prevented them from properly sustaining the colonists as they had faithfully promised to do. But it is true that comparatively few people returned to France as a result of the failure of the Mississippi scheme. If some of the outlying settlements were abandoned, the people joined other colonies and remained a source of strength to Louisiana as a whole.

In 1719, there again came down to New Orleans from Canada M. Dutisnet (sometimes written Dutistine and Dutisne), to enter the service of M. Crozat. He exhibited samples of sil-

ver, which he claimed had been found in the Illinois country.
He was given every assistance in the power of Governor D'Bienville, and later with a force of men and a liberal supply of provisions, passed up the Mississippi, thence up the Missouri, or at
least in its valley, to the country of the Osages, thence about a
hundred miles up to the Panis or Pawnees, and thence more than
a hundred miles farther to the prairie country of the Padoucas,
or what is now the Kansas river region of Kansas. In all these
regions M. Dutisnet explored and examined the mineral sections, but found nothing more valuable than lead and rock salt.
He took possession of all the territory visited in the name of the
king of France. In the Padouca country he planted a large column* and carved thereon the *fleur de lis* of his country. This
important expedition was made partly by water and partly by
land. It was noted that the waters of the Missouri were very
muddy, were filled with floating timber and that the current was
strong and uncertain. Much of the country visited was mountainous, particularly in the country of the Osages, where many
lead mines were found. It was observed that the nations far to
the northwest were not stationary, but spent the winters in hunting and following the buffalo herds. They were a vigorous
people, and the men were great warriors and nearly always on
the war path.

Late in November, 1721, the colonial commissioners ordered an
expedition sent up the Arkansas river to learn if that stream was
navigable as far as the villages of the Indians who had visited
De la Harpe in 1719 at Fort St. Louis de Carlorette, probably
about as far up as the mouth of the Canadian branch. M. de la
Harpe was placed in command of this expedition, the following
being his orders and instructions: "We, John Baptist D'Bienville, Chevalier of the order of St. Louis and commanding general of the Province of Louisiana, give orders to M. De la Harpe,
commandant of the Bay of St Bernard, to set out with a detachment of sixteen soldiers to the Arkansas and there remain a sufficient time to collect provisions; and further to take with him
M. D'Franchome to act as second in command. That the said
De la Harpe will ascend the headwaters of the Arkansas, to examine the quality of the land and ascertain what Indian tribes live
there, with whom he can make treaties of alliance, as well as to
do all other things he may judge necessary to be done, keep an
exact journal of his route, mark the courses of the streams, their
currents, and their islands, and ascertain what mines are in the
country; and if by chance the Spaniards wish to make any settle-

ments there, to inform them that all the countries lying on these
rivers are dependencies of France; that when the said Sieur de la
Harpe shall have performed all of these duties in a manner that
requires nothing further to be done, he will return to headquarters, leaving M D'Franchome at his post." (Dated Fort St
Louis, Mobile, December 10, 1721.)

The post was to be established there to supply the colony with
cattle and to protect the new settlements that were about to spring
up in that region. The expedition set forth on the 16th of December, taking along a considerable quantity of merchandise to be
exchanged for the corn and beans of the Indians. He really
took with him eighteen men and provisions for forty-five days.
He advanced up the Mississippi, passing Fort Rosalie, at Natchez,
on January 20, 1722. Near the mouth of the Yazoo river he
passed two pirogues of Canadians, who were taking a cargo of
five thousand pounds of salt meat from the Illinois country to
New Orleans. On the 27th of February he reached the lowest
branch of the Arkansas, which he entered and sailed up, passing
White river, upon which higher up lived the Osages, and which
entered the Arkansas near the villages of the Soutoues, a tribe
of the Arkansas nation. Their principal village at this time
comprised about forty cabins and three hundred and thirty inhabitants. Here he found M. D'Laboulay, who had been sent here
the previous September by Governor D'Bienville to protect from
capture the boat loads of provisions sent down the river from the
Illinois to New Orleans. The Indians seemed adverse to giving
any information, and he was told that five Frenchmen from
Law's concession, who had ascended the Arkansas river to purchase horses, had been killed on its headwaters by the Osages.
It was afterward learned that one of these men, Richards, evaded
the Osages and succeeded in reaching the country discovered in
1719 by De la Harpe, where he was well received. After remaining at Arkansas post until March 10, De la Harpe advanced up
the Arkansas river with his detachment increased to twenty-two
men, including M. D'Franchome, who had been serving as ensign
of this post. He arrived at French Rock on the 9th of April.
"This rock is on the right of the river ascending, and forms three
steep hills of one hundred and sixty feet in height, near to which
are several fine slate quarries." He continued ascending until the
17th of April, when running short of provisions and his men
being attacked by dysentery, he concluded to return. He proceeded by land five or six days' journey and then turned back.
However, he had ascended far enough to feel assured that the

river was navigable as far as the country of the Padoucas. The object of the expedition was not accomplished.

On the 10th of November, 1721, Father Peter F. X. Charlevoix made the descent of the Mississippi from Kaskaskia. He was accompanied by three companions. They passed Cape St. Anthony on the 12th on the left. Before reaching the mouth of the Ohio, they passed a spot where the Cherokees had killed about forty Frenchmen, among whom were sons of M. de Ramezai, governor of Montreal, and Baron de Longueuil, the king's lieutenant of the same city. They passed the country of the Chicachas (Chickasaws), where they saw a monument which had been set up to mark the site of the slaughter of some of the tribe by an expedition of the Illinois. On December 2, they arrived at the first of the Arkansas villages, situated in a beautiful meadow on the west side of the Mississippi. "There are three others in the space of eight leagues and each makes a nation or particular tribe; there is also one of the four which unites two tribes; but they are all comprised under the name of Arkansas. The Western Company have a magazine here which expects some merchandises, and a clerk who fares but poorly in the meantime and who is heartily weary of living here. The river of the Arkansas, which they say comes a great way, runs into the Mississippi by two channels four leagues distant from each other. The first is eight leagues from hence. . . . The separation of its two branches is made at seven leagues above the second, and the smallest of its two mouths but only at two leagues above the first. * * * Two leagues higher (up the Mississippi) are the Torimans and the Tongingas, who make but one village. Two leagues higher as the Sothouis (Assotoue). The Cappas are a little further. . . . Over against their village we see the sad ruins of Mr. Law's grant, of which the company remain the proprietors. It is here that the nine thousand Germans were to be sent which were raised in the Palatinate and 'tis a great pity they never came. . . . But Mr. Law was ill-used, as well as the greatest part of the other grantees." Continuing, they reached the mouth of the Yasous or Yachoux (Yazoo) on the 9th of December, and passing up the same three leagues reached the fort, where M. Bizart, the commanding officer, had just died. He was spoken of very highly as a most exemplary man and officer. "The company has in this post a magazine of expectation, as at the Arkansas; but the fort and the land belong to a society composed of M le Blanc, secretary of state, M le Compte de Belle-Isle, M le Marquis D'Asfeld, and M le Mlond, brigadier

engineer. . . . On the 15th we arrived at Natchez. This
canton, the finest, most fertile and the most populous of all Louisiana, is forty leagues distant from the Yasous and on the same
hand." On the top of the hill was a small redoubt, enclosed with
palisades. "The late M. D'Iberville, who was the first that entered
the Mississippi by its mouth, being come as high as the Natchez,
found this country so charming and so advantageously situated
that he thought he could find no better situation for the metropolis of the new colony. He traced out the plan of it and intended
to call it Rosalie, which was the name of Madam de Pontchartrain."

On January 10, 1722, Charlevoix writes, "I am at length
arrived in this famous city, which they have called *la Nouvelle
Orleans*. Those who have given it this name thought that
Orleans was of the feminine gender; but what signifies that?
Custom has established it, and that is above the rules of grammar.
This city is the first, which one of the greatest rivers in the world
has seen raised on its banks. The eight hundred fine houses
and the five parishes, which the newspapers gave it some two
years ago, are reduced at present to a hundred barracks, placed
at no very great order; to a great storehouse built of wood; to
two or three houses, which would be no ornament to a village in
France; and to the half of a sorry storehouse, which they agreed
to lend to the lord of the place, and which he had no sooner taken
possession of, but they turned him out to dwell under a tent. .
. . Two leagues lower than the river of the Tonicas, we leave
on the right hand the Red River or Rio Colorado. . . .
There are several grants situated here, which in all appearance
will not grow very rich. The motive of this settlement is the
neighborhood of the Spaniards, which at all times has been a fatal
enticement to this colony. In hopes of trading with them, they
leave the best lands in the world uncultivated. The Natchitoches
are settled on Red River, and we have judged it convenient to
build a fort among them, to hinder the Spaniards from settling
nearer us." Passing the famous cut-off just below the mouth
of Red river, they came to the grant called St. Reyne, at the head
of which were Messrs. Coetlogon and Kolli. "We went a league
further and came to the grant of Madam de Mezieres." At both
of these settlements they were in sore need of men, because the
residents were not inclined to labor, but preferred to wander and
explore.

On New Year's day they went to say mass three leagues from
Madam de Mezieres, in a grant very well situated and which

belonged to M. Diron D'Artaguette, inspector-general of the troops of Louisiana. "We staid all the day in this grant, which is not much forwarder than the rest, and which they call la Baton Rouge (The Red Stick). The next day we made eleven leagues and encamped a little below the Bayagoulas, which we had left on the right hand, after having visited here the ruins of the ancient village. It was very populous about twenty years since. The smallpox has destroyed a part of its inhabitants, the rest are gone away and dispersed. They have not so much as even heard any news of them for several years, and it is a doubt whether there is a single family remaining. The land they possess is very rich. Messrs. Paris have a grant here, where they have planted in rows a great number of white mulberry trees, and they make very fine silk here already. They also begin to cultivate here, with much success, indigo and tobacco." A little later they passed the night on the fine spot where they had "settled the grant of M le Marquis D'Ancenis, at present Duke de Bethune, which by a fire happening in the great magazine and by several other accidents, one after another is reduced to nothing. The Colapissas had here formed a little village, which did not subsist long. On the 4th of January we arrived at the great village of the Colapissas. It is the finest village of Louisiana, yet they reckon in it but two hundred warriors." Five leagues farther down was Cannes Brulees (or Brunt Reeds), where was located the grant to M. le Comte D'Artaguiere. This was on the east side of the river. On the west side, between the Colapissas and the Cannes Brulees was the site of the old Taensas village; here M. de Meuse had a grant, where was a director, but no men nor merchandise. At the distance of three leagues of New Orleans was Choupitoulas, where considerable improvements had been made. Here were Sieur du Breuil and three Canadian brothers named Chauvins. "I have nothing to add to what I have said in the beginning of the former letter concerning the present state of New Orleans. The truest idea you can form of it, is to represent to yourself two hundred persons that are sent to build a city, and who are encamped on the side of a great river, where they have thought on nothing but to shelter themselves from the injuries of the air, whilst they wait for a plan, and have built themselves houses. M de Pauger, whom I have still the honor to accompany, has just now showed me one of his drawing. It is very fine and very regular, but it will not be so easy to execute it as it was to trace it on paper. Between New Orleans and the sea there are no grants; they would have too little depth; there are only some small private habitations and some magazines for the great grants."

In 1719 the Western Company fixed the prices at which the products of the colonists would be received by them. Deer skins ranged from fifteen to twenty-five cents each, dressed thirty cents; hides (buffalo) eight cents per pound; the best tobacco five dollars per hundred; extra flour three dollars; rice four dollars; wheat two dollars; barley and oats ninety cents; silk from one dollar and a half to two dollars per pound. The only market for the colonists living in the modern Louisiana Purchase was at New Orleans. The settlement had no sooner been formed at Biloxi than the Illinois country began to send down flour, pork and hides. This was the beginning of a trade down the Mississippi which long afterward would have caused war had not the differences been adjusted by Spain and the United States in 1795 and again in 1802–3. It is well known that nearly all the remote Indian tribes of the west, from the time of the earliest settlement of Louisiana, were visited by white traders, who boldly went among them for the purpose of obtaining their various commodities and to exchange therefor the goods of the French people. But Spain had preceded France in securing the trade of the far western tribes; and for many years it was the paramount object of Crozat and the Western Company to divert this trade down the water courses to New Orleans; hence expeditions were sent up Red and Arkansas rivers to form treaties with those tribes. The Spaniards had settled Santa Fé as early as about 1582–3; and by the time the French established Biloxi they were numerously located in the upper valley of the Rio Grande and had already monoplized the Indian trade of all the far western tribes. But the French expeditions failed to alienate the western tribes from the Spanish, and finally the latter determined to retaliate by an attack on the French of the Illinois. An expedition was sent out, of which the following is an account:

"In 1720 the Spaniards formed the design of settling at the Missouris, who are near the Illinois, in order to confine us (the French) more on the eastward; the Missouris are far distant from New Mexico, which is the most northerly province the Spaniards have. They believed that in order to put their colony in safety, it was necessary they should entirely destroy the Missouris; but concluding that it would be impossible to subdue them with their own forces alone, they resolved to make an alliance with the Osages, a people who were the neighbors of the Missouris and at the same time their mortal enemies. With that view they formed a cavaran at Santa Fé, consisting of men, women and soldiers, having a Jacobin (Dominican) priest for their chaplain and an engineer captain for their chief and conductor, with the horses and cattle necessary for a permanent settlement. The caravan being set out mistook its road and arrived at the Missouris, taking them to be the Osages. Immediately the conductor of the caravan ordered his interpreter to speak to the chief of the Missouris, as if he had been that of the Osages, and telling that they were come to make an alliance with him, in order to destroy together their enemies; the Missouris. The great chief of the Missouris concealed his thoughts upon this expedition, showed the Spaniards signs of great joy and promised to execute a design with them which gave him much pleasure. To that purpose he invited them to rest for a few days after their tiresome journey till he had assembled his warriors and held council with the old men; but the result of that council was that they should entertain their guests very well and affect the sincerest friendship for them. They agreed together to set out in three days. The Spanish captain immediately distributed fifteen (five) hundred muskets, with an equal number of pistols, sabres and hatchets; but the very morning after this agreement the Missouris came by break of day into the Spanish camp and killed them all except the Jacobin priest, whose singular dress did not seem to belong to a warrior. All these transactions the Missouris themselves related, when they brought the ornaments of the chapel hither (to Fort Chartres on the Mississippi). These people, not knowing the respect due the sacred utensils, hung the chalice to a horse's neck, as if it had been a bell. They were dressed out in these ornaments, the chief having on the naked skin the chasuble, with the paten suspended from his neck. The Missouris told him (D'Boisbriant) that the Spaniards intended to have destroyed them; that they had brought him all these things as being of no use to them, and that if he would he might give them such goods in return as were more to their liking. Accordingly, he gave them some goods, and sent the ornaments to M D'Bienville, who was then the governor of the Province of Louisiana. It has been claimed that D'Boisbriant planned the destruction of this Spanish army. As the Indians had got a great number of Spanish horses from the caravan, the chief of the Missouris gave the finest of them to M D'Boisbriant. They had likewise brought with them the map which had conducted them so ill."*

*Nouveau Voyages aux Indies Occidentales, par M. Bossu, captaine dans les troupes de la marine. English edition, London, 1771.

It is well known that some time prior to 1705, a number of Frenchmen ascended the Missouri river and built a rude post among the Missouris. It is told that one of the leaders, Dubois, long afterward married the chief's daughter, took her and other Indians to Europe with him, where she was received by royalty and thus signally honored; that he finally returned with her to the tribe via New Orleans and was entertained by the company; and that the Frenchmen, including Dubois, were all finally massacred by the bride's people at her suggestion and perhaps instigation. It is also related that long before the French occupancy, an Indian, probably of the Yazoos, ascended the Mississippi and the Missouri rivers, thence crossed the Rocky mountains and passed down the Columbia river to the Pacific ocean. Finally, after years of wandering, he returned to his people on the banks of the Mississippi and lived to tell the tale, when an old man, to the first Frenchmen to visit the West. His name was Moncachtabi. This tale is wrapped in doubt.

Fort Chartres, built on the Mississippi river, a short distance above Kaskaskia by D'Boisbriant in 1720, was for a long time the headquarters of the traders who ascended the Missouri to carry on traffic with the natives. The construction of this fort was followed by the extension of the Illinois settlements to the banks of the Mississippi, and soon led to the establishment of trading posts on the Missouri. Prairie du Rocher, St. Philippe and Cahokia were built in Illinois in the vicinity of the fort. The Sulpitians erected a water mill for grinding corn and for sawing lumber at Cahokia; and a large warehouse of the Western Company was built at Fort Chartres. Soon the lead and the pelts and furs obtained from the Missouri country began flowing down the muddy current of the river. It was under the governments of Crozat and the Western Company that the colonists began to demand titles to their plantations or farms. The French king was lord paramount of the soil; but armed with authority from him the proprietors granted tracts to the colonists, which were later to be confirmed by the French government. When it was found by the various adventurers that the expected gold and silver was not in the country, they were forced to do something else for a livelihood, and accordingly many of them accepted plantation grants and began to till the soil and form substantial and permanent homes. D'Boisbriant executed the first of these grants in the Missouri country soon after the establishment of Fort Chartres. Whether all the conditions were complied with or not, the more or less permanent occupation of the grants per-

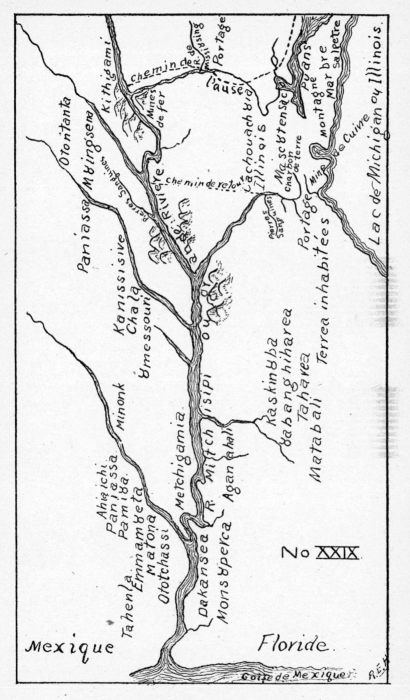

Mississippi Valley, 1672-3
After a Jesuit Map, Parkman

fected the titles in most cases. These primitive grants are the bases of many of the titles to land in Missouri, Arkansas and Louisiana.

In 1723 the Royal Indian Company succeeded to the rights of the Western Company so far as Louisiana was concerned. The changes and depression caused by the failure of Law, the great cost of the Indian wars, the absence of the expected precious minerals, the rupture of the monopoly of the company by the irregular trade of the *coureurs de bois* and by the invasion of the Spaniards on the west and the English to the Mississippi, and the many desertions from the colony, induced the company finally to petition for the relinquishment of its charter, and the surrender was granted. The proclamation of the king on April 10, 1732, transferred the control of Louisiana Province to the French government. Prior to 1711 the scattered French settlements on the upper and lower Mississippi, the Illinois, the Arkansas and the Red rivers, were obscure dependencies of New France or Canada and were without organization as a whole, though each had its specific name, as Illinois, Arkansas, Natchitoches, Biloxi, etc. But in 1711 all the tract of country from the Alleghanies to the Rockies and from the Gulf to Minnesota was constituted Louisiana Province, with a government subordinate to Canada. The Province was ruled by a governor, a commandant general and various subordinate officers, with headquarters at Mobile. Owing to the death of D'Muys, the first appointive governor, Diron D'Artaguette, served as provisional governor, until the arrival of Antoine D'Lamothe Cadillac, who had been appointed in place of D'Muys. The latter served until March, 1717, when he was succeeded by M. D'Epinay. The governorship passed to D'Bienville in February, 1718, and remained with him until 1725, when, owing to the jealousy of his subordinates, he was recalled. D'Perier succeeded, the interim being filled by D'Boisbriant.

In the autumn of 1723, it is known that the Missouri river and its various branches, up probably as far as the mouth of the Platte river in Nebraska, were thoroughly explored by the French miners under Phillip Francois D'Renault. He came with two hundred Frenchmen and three hundred slaves to Fort Chartres, whence they spread out over the west as far as they could do so in safety, and opened many lead and other mines in the present State of Missouri. Not finding the precious metals expected, they finally dispersed, and D'Renault was compensated with six grants of

I—12

land and many of his companions engaged in agriculture. When, in 1725, D'Bienville was deposed from the governorship of the colony, D'Boisbriant was sent to New Orleans from Fort Chartres to serve as such until the arrival of M. D'Perier, his successor, who reached New Orleans in August, 1726.

In order to gain the friendship of the western Indians, particularly of Padoucas or Pawnees living in the present States of Kansas and Nebraska, and thereby, through them, be enabled to open commercial communication with the Spaniards of New Mexico, the governor of Louisiana, with the approval of the Royal India Company and the government of France, dispatched M. D'Bourgmont (who had previously gone up the Missouri several times, but without important results) up the Mississippi and the Missouri rivers in the spring of 1724, with instructions to organize a sufficient force on the Missouri river near the present Jefferson City, to enable him to reach the country of the Pawnees. Accompanied by a small body of Frenchmen, M. D'Bourgmont duly reached the mouth of the Osage river near which, upon an island in the Missouri, he built a fort which he named Fort Orleans, and soon afterward began preparations for the journey. He secured the assistance of about one hundred and sixty Indians of the Missouri and Osage tribes, who were commanded by their great chiefs; and, being well supplied with provisions and merchandise to be presented to the upper tribes, set forth up the Missouri on the 3d of July. They did not go by water, but journeyed by land, with horses and Indians to carry the goods and supplies. On the seventh they reached the outposts of the Kansas tribe, and on the following day crossed the Missouri, swimming their horses, and a few hours later arrived at the first villages of that tribe, situated not far from the mouth of Kansas river. They had come up on the north side of the river, but had crossed over, and late on the 8th arrived at the principal Kansas towns. They were well received, and determined, before going farther, to secure a rendezvous of as many of the western tribes as possible at this point. Messengers were sent to the various tribes; and in the meantime, a firm coalition was established with the Kansas nation. In two days representatives of the Othouez (Otoes) arrived and pledged their friendship and assistance. A large body of them agreed to hunt for him and keep him supplied with fresh meat. Envoys came from several other nations, but were not authorized to conclude terms of peace. A number of Pawnees present promised the friendship of their tribe.

Here D'Bourgmont remained until the 24th, when he set out

with about three hundred warriors of four or more tribes, with their head chiefs in command, accompanied by about three hundred women, five hundred young people "and at least three hundred dogs," the women and the dogs being assigned to the distinguished (?) service of carrying the goods, supplies and baggage. Following the trail to the Pawnee villages, they seem to have left both the Missouri and the Kansas rivers, and directed their course in a northwesterly direction through northeast Kansas, because the narrative of the commander speaks of crossing the headwaters of many small streams which unite and fall into the Kansas river. On the 30th, D'Bourgmont became so ill that he was obliged to return to Fort Orleans, but sent on to the Pawnees several messengers under one Gaillard to announce his coming as soon as he could again travel. With Gaillard were two Pawnee slaves whom D'Bourgmont had set free and sent on in order to gain the good will of that nation. On the 25th of August, Gaillard arrived at the Pawnee villages and was well received. He showed the French flag and told them the object of the expedition, and was assured of the friendship of the tribe. Upon his return, the head chief sent back with Gaillard twenty of his leading warriors, to cement a permanent friendship with the Kansas nation. D'Bourgmont having recovered, the expedition again started on September 20th from Fort Orleans, with the same large following of Indians and dogs. Marching rapidly, they reached the Kansas villages on the 27th. Gaillard and his companions arrived at this point on the 2d of October. Here were gathered representatives of the Missouris, Osages, Otoes, Iowas, Pawnees, and perhaps others. D'Bourgmont assembled them around a large fire in front of his tent, where their presents had been spread out; and there with much ceremony made them a dignified speech, stating the object of the expedition—to cement a permanent friendship between the several tribes and between the tribes and the French. He asked all to smoke the peace calumet, which was done with the rude but dignified ceremonials of the Indians. On the 6th, all joined in the peace dance, which concluded the treaty at this point. Three large lots of goods were presented to the Otoes, Iowas and Panimahas who had just arrived.

The start for the Pawnees was made on October 8th, but the company was greatly reduced, and all the goods, supplies, etc., were carried on horses. MM. Gaillard and Quenel and two Pawnees were sent ahead to announce the coming of the expedition. The main body continued on the south side of Kansas river until the 11th, when they waded that stream, there being but three feet of water. They then took a northwest direction, passing over the headwaters of the streams flowing into Kansas river, and noting the beautiful meadows and the immense herds of buffaloes and elks. Advancing rapidly, they came to an abandoned camp of the Padoucas on the 17th, and here set fire to the prairie in order to signal their arrival. It was answered a long way in advance, and the march was resumed. On the 18th they passed another abandoned camp of the tribe and answered a fire signal as before. Late this day they were met by a large troop of Pawnees on horses, who conducted them to their villages, the Frenchmen marching under arms on the Pawnee horses with as great a show of force as possible. On the afternoon of the 18th they reached the principal villages and encamped at the distance of a gunshot. Since leaving the villages of the Kansas, they had marched ten days, and had covered about two hundred miles, or about twenty miles a day, and were now probably in the southern part of the present Nebraska near the center of the State, east and west, or in the northern part of modern Kansas.

The next day, having assembled the tribe, and having placed their presents in full view, D'Bourgmont addressed them as he had those at the towns of the Kansas, informed them of the objects of the visit and asked them to smoke the calumet of peace. Speeches were delivered by the leading chiefs and assurances given of perpetual peace with the French government. After the peace pipe had been passed around, the presents were distributed, consisting of red and blue Limburgs, shirts, fusils, sabres, gunpowder, balls, musket-flints, gunscrews, mattocks, hatchets, looking-glasses, Flemish knives, wood-cutters' knives, axes, clasp-knives, scissors, combs, bells, awls, needles, drinking glasses, brass wire, rings, etc. The Indians appeared highly pleased with the gifts, and of course promised everything asked for by D'Bourgmont. They readily agreed to live at peace with the Kansas, Omahas, Otoes, Iowas, Missouris, Osages, and Illinois, and accepted the French flag offered them by D'Bourgmont. They asked that French traders might be sent among them, and stated that the Spanish were distant to the westward about twelve days' journey. The head chief said, "You may command all my warriors; I can furnish you with upwards of two thousand."

The expedition started on its return on October 22d, and on the 31st arrived at the villages of the Kansas. The next day they arrived at the mouth of Kansas river, and in due time reached Fort Orleans. Here D'Bourgmont remained some time, but finally descended to New Orleans, leaving a small detachment of soldiers to guard the fort. How it came about will never be known, but in a short time the garrison was murdered by the Indians, not a soul being left alive to tell the tale. Whether the massacre resulted from the outrages of the Frenchmen or from the treachery of the Indians will never be known. But another detachment was soon sent to this important post, and communication was kept up with the Pawnees.

During the continuance of the proprietary government of the Western Company, the western branches of the Mississippi were explored to a great distance. M. De la Harpe, whose concession lay on Red river in the nation of the Cadodaquis, or in what is now northeast Texas, went about eighty leagues up the river to the villages of the Nassonites, and having secured their friendship and permission, he had built a strong log block-house, which he had named Fort St. Louis de Carlorette, for protection against them in case of an outbreak, and to serve as a store-house for the security of his goods, etc. From this far-outlying point, which he employed as a basis for his operations, he sent expeditions, it is claimed, up the river as far as the base of the Rocky mountains. He formed alliances with the Indian tribes living in that region in accordance with the policy of the French, and endeavored to open traffic with the Spaniards of New Mexico, but without avail.

At this time M. Blondel commanded the fort at Natchitoches, while Father Manuel represented French and church interests at a mission which had been established at the Adayes, some distance west of Natchitoches. While at the latter place De la Harpe learned of the visit to Natchitoches of Don Martin de Alarconne, the Spanish commander of the province of Lastekas. He claimed to have established on Matagorda Bay (called by the Spaniards, Espiritu Santo Bay) a military post for Spain in the vicinity of the Guadalupe and St. Mark rivers. As it was reported that this Spanish official had gone on to the country of the Cadodaquis likewise to establish a post for Spain, De la Harpe started for the country of the Nassonites on the 6th of February, 1719, and after a harassing journey arrived at the villages of the latter people on the 21st of April, having traveled one hundred and fifty leagues northwest of Natchitoches. The Assonites (Nassonites), Natsooes, Natchitoches, Yatassees and Cadodaquis were closely related tribes and all dwelt along Red river, often on both sides of the channel. Here De la Harpe was royally received and feasted on buffalo meat and smoked fish. He learned that the Spanish officer had not yet arrived. He was informed by the Indians that they had recently suffered severely from the attacks of the Chicachas (Chickasaws) living far to the eastward.

Making searching inquiries, De la Harpe ascertained that the Spaniards had formed settlements to the southwest about fifty leagues, probably among the Cenis; and also that at the distance of about sixty leagues up Red river, on the right of the stream ascending, they had established themselves—had constructed a small fort or block-house. They were in the country occupied by the Panis, or Pawnees. Attempts were made to build a fort on a branch of the Red river in the country of the Natsooes about ten miles from the Nassonites; but the desertion of his Indian workmen prevented De la Harpe from effecting this object. They had agreed not only to assist him in the work, but had also agreed to supply him with provisions. At this time the Cadodaquis lived about ten leagues above the Nassonites and the Natsooes and Natchitoches about three leagues above the Cadodaquis on the right of the river ascending. They had considerably changed their location, and were now scattered over the plains the better to hunt; but they had become decimated by the attacks of hostile tribes by reason of being thus dispersed. They were scattered through what is now the southwest part of Arkansas. M. De la Harpe established his concession on the lands of the Nassonites, on the right bank of the river in ascending, and in latitude thirty-three degrees fifty-five minutes north latitude. In December, 1718, De la Harpe, having received a letter addressed to Don Martin D'Alarconne by D'Bienville, forwarded it to him at the Assinays villages in the province of Lastikas (northeast Texas). At the same time, De la Harpe wrote the following letter to the same individual: "I am charged with a letter from M. D'Bienville, commanding general of the Province of Louisiana, which I have the honor of sending you. In confiding to me the post of the Nassonites, he has requested me to render all the services in my power to the Spanish nation. I can assure you, sir, nothing can give me more pleasure than to execute his orders on every occasion in which they may be needed." Under the instructions of the Western Company, he likewise opened communication with Father Marcillo, superior of the missions at the Spanish province of Lastikas. He wrote, "Inform your friends of New Mexico and Boca de Leon that they can procure at the Nassonites or Natchitoches all the goods they may need at a moderate price, upon which I will allow you a commission of two or three per cent on all sales that may be made, and thus you may have it in your power to establish your mission upon a solid basis.

In May, 1719, having learned from a Nassonite chief of the existence of metallic ores in the mountains thirty or forty leagues to the northward, De la Harpe, accompanied by nine soldiers and several Indian guides, set forth to find the treasure. As the country above was filled with hostile Indians, the guides deserted him after three days' marching, having seen smoke a long way in advance. On the way back, De la Harpe and party came near being captured by the hostile Osages. The soldiers made salt at a spring about ten leagues northeast of the post. Under date of May 20, 1719, D'Alarconne replied to De la Harpe, in part as follows: "I am compelled to say that your arrival at the Nassonite village surprises me very much. Your governor could not be ignorant that the post you now occupy belongs to my government, and that all the lands west of the Nassonites are dependencies of New Mexico. I counsel you to give advice of this to M. D'Bienville, or you will force me to oblige you to abandon lands that the French have no right to occupy."

An opportunity to answer this letter did not occur until the 8th of July, when De la Harpe forwarded the following missive, dated at Nassonite: "The orders from His Catholic Majesty (the King of Spain) to maintain a good understanding with the French of Louisiana, and the kind intentions you have yourself expressed towards them, accords but little with your proceedings. Permit me to inform you that M. D'Bienville is perfectly informed of the limits of his government, and is very certain that the post of Nassonite is not a dependency of His Catholic Majesty. He knows also that the Province of Lastikas, of which you say you are governor, is a part of Louisiana. M. de la Salle took possession of it in 1685, in the name of His Most Christian Majesty (the King of France); and since the above epoch possession has been renewed from time to time. Respecting the post of Nassonite, I cannot comprehend by what right you pretend that it forms a part of New Mexico. I beg leave to represent to you that Don Antoine du Morior, who discovered New Mexico in 1683, never penetrated east of that province or the Rio Bravo (Rio Grande). It was the French who first made alliances with the savage tribes of this region; and it is natural to conclude that a river that flows into the Mississippi and the lands it waters, belong to the King, my master. If you will do me the pleasure to come into this quarter, I will convince you that I hold a post I know how to defend."

While at this station, De la Harpe endeavored to form alliances with all the neighboring Indian tribes. They came to his post from the banks of the far Arkansas. On the 24th of July, 1719, he received intelligence that war had been declared between France and Spain. As this possibly meant trouble with both the Indians and the Spanish, the soldiers at the post strengthened it in every possible way and otherwise made preparations to receive any enemy after the bloody fashion of war. A few days later, information was received that the Spanish were at work, on the headwaters of Red river, digging for gold or other valuable minerals. Soon after this, the news arrived that M. Blondel, commander at Natchitoches, had driven away the Franciscan fathers from the Adayes and pillaged their missions there. The Spanish had thus formed a settlement east of the Sabine (sometimes called the Adayes) river. News was also received that the Spaniards had all departed from the Trinity (river), or the country of the Assinays (Cenis), whence D'Alarconne had written his warlike letters. This being true, De la Harpe had nothing to fear from the Spaniards.

He now resolved to explore the country much farther to the northwest than he had yet done. "For this purpose he took with him an escort of two officers, three soldiers, two negroes and several Indians who spoke the language of the country, and set out on the 11th of August. By the 21st he had traveled forty-nine leagues through a fine country, with sloping hills and prairies abounding in game. He met a party of Natsooe Indians who had been on a hunting expedition and had killed forty-six buffaloes. On the 22d he passed several prairies and a little river which empties into Red river. He then entered into an extensive prairie surrounded by mountains. By the 26th he had gone eighteen leagues farther, when he met with a party of Osage Indians, who seemed disposed to attack him, but yet suffered him to pass on. On the 27th he traveled six leagues farther, over a beautiful prairie country filled with deer and buffalo, and entered the mountains, where he found a number of Indian huts. Traveling six leagues farther he met a party of Kansas, who were encamped on the banks of the Ouachita with forty farriors, and were in pursuit of the Tancaros. On the 28th he passed a beautiful prairie, interspersed with hills, and a large herd of buffaloes followed by a pack of wolves as large as those of France. On the 29th he traveled six leagues farther to a branch of the Ouachita river, which had about two feet of water in it. Near its banks he met a party of Nacogdoches, who were occupied in smoking meat. On the 31st he reached a branch of the Arkansas, and on September 2d came to several lead mines. Farther on he met six chiefs who had come to meet him from a village called Imaham, and to assure him of their friendship. De la Harpe told them that the great chief of his nation had sent him to assure them of his protection against their enemies; and his desire was that they be at peace with each other. These chiefs had brought Indian bread and smoked beef, with which they regaled the party. . . . They belonged to the Tancaros, Adayes, Ouachitas, Ositas, Assinays and Tayas. They number about four thousand people who live in tents and are the allies of the Panis (Pawnees), a nation living about forty leagues to the north. The Panis are at peace with the Osages, a nation who are continually at war with the Kansas, the Padoucas, the Arickarees and other tribes.

"The old chiefs told M. De la Harpe that a white people (the Spaniards of New Mexico) traded for metals with the Padoucas, fifteen days' journey off, in a northwest direction, where the mountains furnish rock-salt. On the 4th of September, more than five thousand Indians assembled to chant the calumet of peace. The old chiefs of the Arkansas and Tayas performed this ceremony and made speeches. Late at night De la Harpe retired to sleep, and in the morning the chiefs came to wake him up. They washed his head and feet, painted his face blue and red, and placed a cap of eagle feathers upon his head. They also threw buffalo robes and other presents at his feet and presented him with a Kansas slave of about eight years of age, who had escaped out of seventeen prisoners, which they had eaten at a public feast. De la Harpe thanked them for their favors, and regretted it had not been in his power to save these unfortunate victims of their vengeance. He concluded to leave three of his men in this country, until the governor of Louisiana decided whether it was expedient to establish a post here; but afterward changed his mind, as he was informed that the Indians abandoned their villages in the autumn to hunt buffaloes, and in the following spring they returned to sow Indian corn, beans and other seed. . . . On the 8th he was invited by the chiefs of the Canicons to feast at his village about two leagues from the Tancaros, where he met a great many chiefs who professed a great deal of friendship for him. This tribe consists of a few families who live in a very fertile country. . . . On the 10th he erected a cross there and planted a post near it, on which he carved the arms of the King. On the 13th he set out to return to the Nassonites. . . . On the 1st of October, he was surprised by a party of

Kansas Indians, and had only time to make his escape by leaving his baggage behind. He was obliged to make his way back over mountains without any compass to the village of the Nadacos, where he arrived on the 13th of October. On the 21st he reached the portage of the Natchitoches, where he fell sick. He sent several Frenchmen from this place to the Adayes for provisions, and remained here until the 4th of December to recruit his health. On the 10th he reached Natchitoches, and on the 26th arrived at New Orleans."

It is not too much to say that the services of M. De la Harpe prevented the Spaniards from gaining permanent foothold on the Upper Red river and effectually established the rights of France to that important region of country. Had it not been for his courageous and emphatic opposition to Spanish settlement there, all the Upper Red river country, or what is now much of Indian and Oklahoma Territories, would have been left outside of what afterward became the Louisiana Purchase. How well his services were estimated is shown by the following certificate from Governor D'Bienville, dated Biloxi, July 1, 1720:

"I John Baptist D'Bienville, Knight of the Military Order of St. Louis, and Commanding General of the Province of Louisiana, CERTIFY, that the M Bernard De la Harpe, commander of the troops sent to the Cadodaquis, Natsooes, Natchitoches and Nassonites, Indian nations on Red River, and on the confines of the Province of Lastikas, has, during a residence of eighteen months among them, conducted himself with great prudence and wisdom; that he has discovered other tribes of Indians on the Red and Arkansas rivers, adjoining nations to the Spaniards of New Mexico, and made alliances with them in the name of the King: In faith of which I have signed this certificate and affixed the King's seal."

France continued to claim the territory as far to the westward as the Bay of St. Bernard, or Matagorda, and the policy of sending a colony to that point was often urged by the Western Company's officials; but no action had been taken by the Council of Louisiana. Early in August, 1721, Captain Beranger was sent there to make a reconnoissance, but returned without having accomplished much of importance. In 1721, now that the Louisiana colony had acquired great comparative strength, it was deemed opportune to commence the colonization of the country beyond the Sabine. It was realized that such a course would doubtless be succeeded by war not only with the Spaniards, but with the Indian tribes inhabiting that territory. Did the company, then, wish to risk the chances and results of such wars, in order to win the territory and the consequent important trade? It was finally determined to take the risk. In August, 1721, after due deliberation and after the return of the reconnoissance, it was determined to send M. De la Harpe in charge of the first expedition to Matagorda Bay. Accordingly, the following official order was issued:

"We, Jean Baptiste D'Bienville, chevalier of the military order of St. Louis, and commandant-general for the King in the Province of Louisiana: It is hereby decreed that M. De la Harpe, commandant of the Bay of St. Bernard, shall embark in the packet 'Subtile,' commanded by Beranger, with a detachment of twenty soldiers under D'Belisle, and shall proceed forthwith to the Bay of St. Bernard belonging to this province and take possession in the name of the King and the Western Company; shall plant the arms of the King in the ground and build a fort upon whatsoever spot appears most advantageous for the defence of the place. If the Spaniards or any other nation have taken possession, M. De la Harpe will signify to them that they have no right to the country, it being known that possession was taken in 1685 by M. de la Salle in the name of the King of France, etc."

August 10, 1721. B-I-E-N-V-I-L-L-E.

The ship was provisioned with fifteen quarters of flour, fifteen of meat and a quantity of French brandy, and had on board, besides the crew, a force of twenty soldiers, who were under the command of the famous D'Belisle, who recently had seen such severe hardships in the vicinity of St. Bernard Bay. M. De la Harpe was constituted commandant of the colony that should be established there. He was instructed that "if the Spaniards or any other nation has already taken possession of it, M De la Harpe will inform them that they have no right to this country, as it was taken possession of by M de la Salle in the name of the King of France. And in case they make any opposition, M De la Harpe will take possession of it by force in conformity with the orders of the King, dated 16th November, 1718." The ship set sail on the 16th of August, 1721, and on the 27th reached what was presumed to be the bay sought. Owing to the large number of Indians that assembled and opposed his landing and the proposed settlement, De la Harpe and his companions deemed it imprudent to attempt to form a colony at that time, and accordingly sailed back to Mobile, where they arrived in October. They learned that although the Spaniards had been there, they had departed without making attempt at settlement.

A French ship, the Marechal D'Estres, mounting thirty-six guns, and commanded by M. de la Godelle, was lost in 1718 off the coast of Texas. She was loaded with troops and convicts for the colony of Louisiana. It was afterward ascertained from survivors that she had mistaken her course and had arrived at a large bay west of the Mississippi, probably the Bay of St. Bernard, where a dreadful epidemic broke out among the convicts on board. Here a number of the men resolved to land and take their chances in the wilderness among the Indians rather than with the sickness on board. Accordingly MM. D'Belisle, Legendre, Allard, Ducloss and Corbett took arms and eight days' provisions and went ashore. The ship was never heard from afterward. After more than two months of wandering in southern Texas, all five had died except Semiars D'Belisle. He finally fell in with three Indians, who stripped him and took him to their nation where he lived for eighteen months. A tin box in which he kept his papers finally fell into the hands of the Assinays and still later reached D'St. Denis, the French commandant at Natchitoches, who effected his rescue. He was a knight of the Military Order of St. Louis, and in the end proved to be one of the bravest and most capable officers sent by France to the Louisiana colony. He served in many capacities with signal distinction.

The earliest forts built west of the Mississippi by the French were those of St. Louis erected on the Bay of St. Bernard or Matagorda, by La Salle, in 1685, and Fort Arkansas erected the same year by Tonty on the Arkansas river about three leagues from its mouth. The former was abandoned within two or three years; because the French left there by La Salle were driven off by the Spaniards, or were massacred by the Indians. Fort Arkansas, as built by Tonty, was very rude, but was afterward made strong and secure by the French governor of Louisiana. It was built of stockades in the form of a polygon, the interior of each side measuring about one hundred and eighty feet, and a half dozen or more of cannon were mounted to command the approaches. The fort at Natchitoches was founded in 1713–14, and Fort Dout was built west of it a little later. Fort Chartres on the east bank of the Mississippi, about twenty-five miles above Kaskaskia, was the strongest erected by the French in the Mississippi basin. It was built in 1720, and served as a base for all the expeditions which ascended the Missouri and the upper Mississippi and its higher branches. Fort Orleans was built on the Missouri near Jefferson City in 1724. The fort built at Pointé Coupée about the year 1720 was a quadrangle having four bastions and mounted several cannon. It was constructed of stockades and stood on the west bank of the river. Fort Rosalie, at Natchez, was one of the most important in the valley.

Fort St. Louis de Carlorette was built on the south bank of Red river by Bernard De la Harpe in 1719, under the orders of D'Bienville, for the purpose of securing the rights of the French to the country of the Upper Red river, as against the Spanish, who had already visited the head-waters of Red river and worked on the lead mines there. It was located in latitude thirty-three degrees fifty-five minutes north, and stood in northeast Texas. Fort Balize, at the mouth of the Mississippi, was erected in 1699, as a protection against any foreign ships that might try to ascend the Mississippi. However, it was not always garrisoned during the early history of the Louisiana colony. New Orleans was early fortified after the manner, it is said, of Vauban. A ditch was dug around the city, about eighteen feet wide, with ramparts of earth and palisades about six feet high extending along the interior. Strong bastions and redoubts were erected at regular and commanding intervals. All the features of a strong fort were present, including many large cannon—in fact the entire city was thus enclosed and embraced in the end several forts. Two, St. Charles and Condé, were standing when Louisiana was ceded to the United States in 1803. The fort at the present Natchitoches, La., was built in 1713 by D'Bienville and D'St Denis under the orders of France in order to hold the Spaniards in check and to secure the friendship of the Indian tribes of that region. It at first consisted of two strong log houses enclosed with palisades, but was afterward greatly strengthened, and except for very short intervals was always garrisoned by the French, who well realized its importance. It was the key to the southwest, and was later reinforced by Fort St. Louis de Carlorette still higher up Red river. Some time after this date, probably about 1714–15, the French establish posts on the Sabine and at Nacogdoches for the purpose of preventing the Spaniards from advancing beyond the Sabine; and maintained them for several years. Fort Iberville on the east bank of the Mississippi was built in 1700, and was an important shield against the Indians during the first few years of the colony.

Early in 1728 there arrived a vessel containing a number of young girls who afterward became known as the "fillies a la cassette," or the casket girls, owing to the fact that each was possessed of a small casket in which were her clothes. From the fact that these girls were highly respectable, though poor, and from the fact that many of the other girls sent out had been taken from the houses of correction, the proud descendants of later years were always eager to have it known that they were the descendants of one of the casket girls rather than of the others. Governor D'Perier gave great encouragement to agriculture, and under his direction slave labor became well governed. In 1728 it was decreed that those who had not properly improved their concessions should surrender them to the company. A tax was levied for the building of churches and hospitals. The colonial expense for the year 1728 was $89,919.

In 1726 Father Poisson wrote as follows concerning the Law grant on the Arkansas river: "The French settlement of the Arkansas would be an important one had Monsieur Laws continued four or five years. His grant was here on a boundless prairie, the entrance of which is two gunshots from the house in which I am. The Company of the Indies had granted him a tract sixteen leagues square; that makes, I think, fully a hundred leagues in circuit. His intention was to found a city here, to establish manufactures, to have numbers of vessels and troops, and to found a Duchy. He began the work only a year before his fall. The property which he then sent into this country amounted to more than 1,500,000 livres ($277,500). Among other things he meant to arm and superbly equip two hundred cavalrymen. He had also bought three hundred negroes. The Frenchmen engaged for this grant were men of all sorts of trades. The directors and subalterns with one hundred men ascended the river in five boats in order to come here to begin the settlement; they must at the start procure provisions that they might be ready to receive those people whom they had left down the river. The chaplain died on the way and was buried in one of the sandbanks of the Mississippi. Twelve thousand Germans were engaged for this grant. This was not a bad beginning for the first year, but Monsier Laws was disgraced; of the three or four thousand Germans who had already left their country, a large number died in the East, nearly all on landing in the country; the others were recalled. The Company of the Indies took back the grant and shortly after abandoned it; the entire enterprise has, therefore, fallen to pieces. About thirty Frenchmen have remained here; only the excellence of the climate and of the soil has kept them, for in other respects they have received no assistance. My arrival here has pleased them, because they now think that the Company of the Indies has no intention of abandoning this district, as they had supposed it would, inasmuch as they have sent a missionary here. I cannot tell you with what joy these good people received me. I found them in great need of all things."*

The financial scheme of John Law only incidentally affected Louisiana. There were probably not to exceed 2,000 people in all of Louisiana while this experiment was being tried in France, and they were distributed at a score of settlements along the Mississippi and its branches. Very little money or credit was needed here, because traffic was carried on mainly by the primitive system of exchanges—the trader gave his merchandise for the furs of the Indian. The latter did not want his money—had no use for it; so the trader immediately converted his money into merchandise again and repeated the exchange, pocketing his profits. There was very little use for money, and consequently very little was in circulation. Nor was there any credit, because all were strangers, shifting hither and thither, and it would have been folly to extend credit to any man.

But while Law's scheme wonderfully stimulated the financial system of France, and no doubt affected somewhat the rudimentary monetary operations at the centers of settlement in Louisiana, it cannot be shown, never has been shown, that any serious shock was occasioned here by the bursting of the Mississippi bubble. The failure of Crozat to find gold and silver in Louisiana had largely undeceived France concerning the reputed riches of this colony. But Law and his associates, and particularly the Western Company, took advantage of the marvelous advance of credits in France still farther to strengthen their system by reviving the attractive tales of gold and silver in Louisiana. Ingots of gold and silver were falsely exhibited in Paris as the products of Louisiana; the object being to show the wealth and resources underlying the Law monetary and credit system, which had been adopted by the French government. To transfer all the furor and excitement to the wilderness of Louisiana is ridiculous in the extreme—worse, because there is no truth in the statement that the excitement in France seriously affected in any important way the finances of this colony. While the Mississippi people were made a medium to bolster the insecure and tottering system over which all of France and half of Europe had gone mad, the failure of the system did not strike Louisiana a hard blow, mainly because there was nothing here for it to hit, or next to nothing. Of course, it is popular and customary to

---

* R. G. Thwaites's reissue of the Jesuit Relations and other Documents. Tome VI.

envelop the Louisiana wilderness in a shifting tornado of financial excitement and eventual paralysis, but this is a perversion of facts and of history.

That Law should employ the supposed gold and silver and the undoubted fur trade of the Mississippi valley as a basis to strengthen his bank, did not produce any appreciable effect in the poverty-stricken and miserable hamlets of Louisiana. It is improbable that any considerable quantity of the bank's bills were at any time held in the Mississippi colony. In adopting the Louisiana colony as one of the bases of his system, Law was absolutely safe, because in doing so he dealt in futures—was selling short for present prosperity and strength and taking his chances of covering at some hoped-to-be distant day. Thus, the Mississippi scheme was only one of the alleged sources of revenue of the French crown to sustain the Law system of finance. Except as it incidentally affected the operations of the Western Company, the scheme had little bearing and no consequential existence on the banks of the Mississippi. As a matter of fact, however, it must be conceded that the identification of the Western Company with the Law financial system immensely benefited Louisiana, because the stimulus thus kindled was used as a means to induce a large number of wealthy and prominent people to secure concessions therein, send out agents, laborers, implements, etc., and endeavor to build up rich and prosperous plantations. If there was any resultant flurry in Louisiana, therefore, when the Law system collapsed, it fell only upon the conditions which that system had originated and fostered.

The buying and selling of stocks, which occasioned the wild speculation and gambling so conspicuous in France at that time, saw no counterpart whatever in the Louisiana colony. The Mississippi scheme was developed, because Louisiana was unknown, mysterious, supposedly filled with gold, and could therefore be exploited without danger that the sham would soon be unveiled. But the few and scattered people here, struggling to eke out an existence little better than that of the savages, were comparatively unaffected by the disaster which finally sent credit to the bottom of the financial pit in France. Therefore it must be admitted that incidentally the adoption of the Western Company by Law and his associates as one of the means to invigorate his system, was an enormous advantage to Louisiana. Thousands of colonists—men, women and children—were sent out, and vast sums of money were spent. It is even said that the streets and prisons of Paris and other large cities were emptied of their mendicants and vagabonds to swell the colonial stream. These were the laborers sent to work the various concessions in Louisiana. It will thus be seen that the Law system was really an advantage to Louisiana; that it occasioned no harm to the colony as a whole, and that the speculation in stocks was not present here. In the spring of 1720 the system collapsed, having lasted about four years, estimating from the establishment of the Law bank in May, 1716. Louisiana felt the existence of the system, if at all, for only about two and a half years.

The concession to John Law on the Arkansas was one of great extent and great value. It was in the heart of the famous Indian country—the territory of the Arkansas nation, and the lands had been mostly cultivated for a period of centuries by that tribe. Here was grown much of the maize that had sustained the army of De Soto for months when he was engaged in planning the destruction of this faithful people. The tract was twelve miles square,* and located about thirty miles above the mouth of the river. Here the German settlers whom it is alleged he had "bought," were sent—many of them; and here was established the post which was intended to protect them from the savages, and the store-house where they were enabled to obtain their supplies of tools, provisions and merchandise—for the cash or for valuable furs. Upon the failure of the concessionaire, the settlement was abandoned, though the post was occupied for many years by the soldiers from New Orleans. The tract was situated on the right of the river ascending. In March, 1722, M. de la Harpe found here forty-seven persons of both sexes. They had sown wheat, and had commenced other agricultural operations. Thus at this time the concession was nearly abandoned. It was deemed unwise by the colonial commissioners, owing to the great improvements already made there, to permit the Law concession to be abandoned. They accordingly appointed M. Dufresne director of that colony with a salary of 2,000 livres per annum, and directed him to make arrangements for all persons who desired to cultivate the soil and secure permanent homes in that quarter.

What crushed the Western Company more than any other cause were the various Indian wars—against the Natchez, the Alibamos and the Chickasaws. It required an enormous expenditure to equip and sustain an army of from five hundred to a thousand men for several months at a time. When to this depressing

---

*Father Poisson said twelve leagues square.

I—13

expense are added the feverish investments under the Mississippi scheme, there could be no other result than distress until natural commercial conditions had been resumed. These various burdens, at a time when they were most vexatious and hindersome, prevented the Louisiana commissioners from obeying the orders of the king to advance and take possession of the country now called Texas. Spain then made the most of her opportunity and preceded France with settlements in what was called the province of Lastikas, or northeast Texas. It is asserted that France established a permanent post at Nacogdoches about the year 1718, but there is no evidence to show that it was permanent, and very little to show that it was made at all. The Western Company had all it could do at the time to build a fort at Natchitoches and another in the country of the Cadodaquis or what is now Southwest Arkansas, without trying to extend its domain, even under the positive orders of the French monarch. It is known that the orders of the king to this effect remained unacted upon by the commissioners of Louisiana for several years before De la Harpe was finally made governor of the Bay of St. Bernard, and before the expedition was sent there under him for the purpose of forming a permanent colony. The Western Company lacked the strength, and Spain took the lead in the settlement of Texas.

One of the most interesting letters of the missionary era is that of Father Paul du Poisson, dated at the Akensas (Arkansas) in 1726, and addressed to Father Patonillet. The following are extracts from the same: "Here is another anecdote, which shows how generous they are. Day before yesterday I received a visit from a chief and I offered him a pipe; to fail in that would be to fail in politeness. A moment after he went for a mataché (a robe painted in many figures and colors) buckskin, which he had left in the entry of the house in which I live, and put it upon my shoulders; this is their way when they make presents of that sort. I begged a Frenchman to ask him, without appearing to do it for me, what he wished that I should give him. 'I have given without design,' he answered, 'am I trading with my father?' (trading here means paying). Nevertheless, a few moments afterward he said to the same Frenchman that his wife had no salt and his son no powder; his aim was that this Frenchman should repeat it to me. A savage gives nothing for nothing, and we must observe the same rule towards them; otherwise we should be exposed to their contempt."* He further says, "Finally they

---

* R. G. Thwaites's reissue of the Jesuit Relations and other Documents. Tome VI.

returned again to the charge, in order to ask if I would at least
be willing that their young men should come to dance in my village, *without design,* the reconnoitre dance (this is the one they
dance when they send to reconnoitre the enemy). I answered
that it would not trouble me, that their young men could come
to dance, and that I would look at them with pleasure. All the
people of the village, except the women, came the next day at
dawn; we had nothing but dances, songs and harangues until
noon. Their dances, as you may well imagine, are somewhat
odd. . . . I saw well that I must not send them away without giving them a great kettle (feast); I borrowed from a
Frenchman a kettle similar to those which are in the kitchen of
the Invalides, and I gave them corn without stint. Everything
went on without confusion; two of their number performed the
office of cooks, dividing the portions with most exact impartiality
and distributing them in like manner; there was heard only the
usual exclamation "Ho!" which each one pronounced when his
portion was given him. I never saw a meal eaten with worse
manners or with better appetite. They went away well satisfied."

Father Poisson and several companion missionaries ascended
the Mississippi in pirogues, leaving New Orleans May 25, 1727.
He says he was taken up by engagés, "the men who are hired
to paddle a pirogue or boat—and, it may be added, to make those
people whom they conduct furious." He noted five concessions
above New Orleans: Dubreuil's, three occupied by three Canadian brothers and one owned by a Parisian, with M. D'Kole in
charge. On each concession were from fifty to sixty negroes,
engaged in cultivating rice, indigo, corn, tobacco, etc. In Paris
during the Law regime, the Louisiana concessions were called
"Counties" and "Marquisates." Concessionaires were the prominent men in France who received grants or concessions. They
were expected to send out vessels with laborers, agents, provisions, etc., for the purpose of putting their concessions on a profit-
paying basis. The vicissitudes of colonization obliged many to
neglect or abandon their vassals, and the latter often took their
pay by helping themselves to the stores of their lord. "Do you
not recognize in this the Frenchman?" asks Father Poisson. "It
is partly this which has prevented this country from being settled
as it should be, after the immense expenditure that has been made
for that purpose."

A small tract upon which a single family located was called a
plantation. The man would clear a few acres, place his house

on piles, cover it with sheets of bark, get a few negro slaves about him, raise corn, rice, tobacco, etc., and soon be independent. Several of such plantations close together became known as a settlement. Young women from the hospitals of Paris and from the Salpêtrière, all of good repute, made the long voyages in the pirogues; and, according to Father Poisson, many of them shunned marriage as too severe a life, and preferred service, or to take their chances in the Illinois country. Here were young men, too, who had been sent to Louisiana "for various reasons" by relatives and by the law, who preferred rowing on the river or other traveling rather than digging in the soil. Here also were the hunters who ascended the river two or three hundred leagues every year to kill the cattle (buffaloes) on St. Francis river and make their *plats côtés,* by which they dried part of the flesh in the sun. They salted the rest; made bear's oil, obtained buffalo robes, and sent all down the river to market in New Orleans. At this time the buffaloes were first found about thirty leagues above the mouth of the Arkansas. Father Poisson states that in 1726, a Frenchman brought down the river to New Orleans four hundred and eighty buffalo tongues, which he and his partner secured during the previous winter—1725-6. At the Cannes Brulees was the D'Artaguette concession, M. D'Benac being in charge. A little higher were les Allemands. "This is the district that has been assigned to the feeble remnant of that German company (Law's) which perished from destitution either at the East or upon arriving in Louisiana." At Oumas was another French settlement, and still another at Bayagoulas, where M. du Buisson was in charge. At Baton Rouge was an abandoned concession. A little higher was the grant to M. Mezieres. Here was a gang of negroes. Above were a few habitations, and a few Frenchmen at the Tonica villages. Father Poisson reached Arkansas July 7. He wrote, "The villages of the Akensas are wrongly placed in the map. The river at its mouth makes a fork; into the upper branch flows a river that the savages call Niska—White water—which is not marked on the map, although it is a large stream. We entered by the lower branch; from the mouth of this branch to the place where the river divides it is seven leagues. Thence it is two leagues to the first village, which contains two tribes, the Tourimans and the Tongingas; from this first village to the second it is two leagues by water and one by land. This is called the Southonis village. The third village is a little higher up on the same side of the river and the inhabitants are called the Cappas; on the other bank and opposite this last village are the French habitations. The three savage villages which contain four tribes that bear different names, make only one tribe under the common name of Akensas, which the French have also given to the river, although the savages call it 'Ni-gitai,' Red water. They speak the same language and number in all about twelve hundred souls."*

Immediately succeeding the Natchez massacre forts were built at Choupitoulas, Cannes Brulees, Les Allemands, Bayagoulas and Pointe Coupée. In 1728 Father Michel Guignas visited the Sioux near the sources of the Mississippi. He established a mission there, at least in part, but was made a prisoner by the Kickapoos and Mascoutins and kept as such for five months, at the end of which time they made preparations to burn him. He was saved by an old Indian who adopted him and finally gave him his liberty.

The Chickasaws were ever the friends of the English and the enemies of the French; consequently, that nation was the principal one to attack the French pirogues as they floated down the Mississippi. They were regarded by the members of that nation as legitimate and most desirable prizes. In spite of all the French could do, the convoys, though armed and strong, occasionally fell before the prowess of that war-like nation. The hostility of the Natchez tribe was incurred, as it was in nearly all other cases, by the rapacity and abuse of the French. They retaliated to the wrongs and oppressions by slaughtering nearly all the French at their post on November 29, 1729, and repeating the massacre a few weeks later at the fort on the Yazoo river. They killed about two hundred and fifty men, and made most of the women and children captives and slaves. The news of this bloody act caused the greatest consternation throughout all of Louisiana. Fort Chartres and every other post was strengthened, and preparations were made to punish the Natchez tribe. The Choctaws joined the French, but the wily foe managed to evade the army sent against them. They fled before the French and located west of the Mississippi, where they established three villages at or near the modern town of Trinity, La. Here they strengthened themselves to the best of their ability, and later were harassed by the Oumas and the Bayagoulas, allies and friends of the French. Believing that the latter had instigated the attacks upon them, they captured the French fort which was being built near, and in which were ten Frenchmen and twenty negroes, only one white

---

* Thwaites's reissue of the Jesuit Relations and other Documents.

man and two negroes escaping. The capture of this post served
to intensify the bitterness of the French against the Natchez tribe.
They must be severely punished. Immediate steps were taken
to raise a large force, but considerable time elapsed, though
finally all was ready.

The army was divided into three battalions, the marines under
D'Salvert on the right, the militia under D'Benac on the left, and
the Louisiana troops, the grenadiers and fusiliers under General
D'Perier in the center, with D'Cresnay and D'Artaguette in subordinate command. The Indians were in a command by themselves, and the negroes were scattered through all the companies.
There were five hundred and fifty whites and negroes, and about
one hundred and fifty Indians. An advance corps of twenty-
four under D'Coulenges and D'Beaulieu, sent to reconnoitre, was
surprised by the Natchez and sixteen were killed or captured,
including both of the commanders. This act roused the French
to desperation. On January 4, 1731, the army reached the mouth
of Red river, and on the 12th that of Black river, up which was
the entrenched camp of the enemy. On the 20th their camp was
reached and immediately attacked. The battle was resumed on
the 21st, with shells from wooden mortars, and during the day
several were killed and wounded on both sides. Both the 22d
and the 23d were repetitions of the 21st. On the 24th the Natchez
raised the white flag, and hostilities ceased. A messenger came
out with the calumet and offered to surrender all the negroes.
Governor D'Perier insisted on talking with the head chief, but this
was evaded during several interviews. Negroes to the number
of nineteen were delivered, but the head chief still held back, with
very good grounds.

D'Perier finally refused to talk longer with messengers, and sent
word that unless the head chief came out that day no quarter
would be shown the savages. The Natchez warriors to a man
objected to the head chief's going out to meet D'Perier. They, of
course, felt that he would be detained, and that was the deliberate
intention of Governor D'Perier. At this point reingorcements with
cannon arrived. Threats to use the cannon at once brought out
St. Comé, the son of the Woman chief and successor to the Sun.
He attempted to dissemble, but D'Perier again insisted on seeing
the Sun himself, and refused any further negotiations until his
demands were complied with. In half an hour out came St.
Comé, the head Sun and the Flour Chief, the latter being the real
author of the Natchez massacre, though St. Comé had tried previously to conceal that fact. The Sun made an apologetic speech

and promised good behavior in future. They were detained and placed under guard; but during the night, while it was raining, all attempted to escape, and the Flour Chief, the biggest rascal of all, succeeded. He was smart enough to see the inevitable, and accordingly, with eight or ten warriors and their wives and children, escaped from the fort the same night down an unguarded ravine. The next day about thirty-five warriors and two hundred women surrendered. The others refused, and during the succeeding night many warriors likewise managed to elude the guards and escape. The captures the next day were swelled to forty men and three hundred and eighty-seven women and children. The same day, the 27th of January, the army left and on the 5th of February reached New Orleans.

But the Flour Chief and other leaders about as renowned as himself, with a force variously estimated at from two hundred to three hundred warriors, were far from being conquered. Professing friendship for the Tonicas and pretending to desire their good offices to form an alliance with the French, they treacherously fell upon them and killed their head chief and about a dozen of his warriors; but were dauntlessly held in check for five days by the war chief of the Tonicas, who remained master of his village. In this desperate encounter thirty-three of the Natchez were killed, and a few days later three who had been captured were burnt at the stake.

At this time Natchitoches was commanded by the brave D'St. Denis, who had at his disposal forty soldiers and twenty settlers. In order to crush him whom they greatly feared, more so than any other officer in the colony, the survivors sent against him a force of one hundred and fifty of their best warriors, among whom was the Flour Chief. They hoped to surprise him; but upon being discovered by his sentinels, they sent a deputation with the calumet and a message to the effect that, having had some trouble with the French below, they desired him to act as mediator to settle the difficulty, announcing that they had with them a French woman whom they desired to set free as an evidence of their good faith. D'St. Denis replied that he would be pleased to comply with their request if they would at once release the white woman under an escort of ten warriors only; but the Natchez refused unless all their numbers were received. D'St. Denis, who knew the Indian tactics thoroughly and had suspected this large force from the start, replied that he was aware of their designs and knew that they meditated treachery, and offered to pay a ransom for the French woman. The answer of the savages was to burn the white woman in sight of the fort, capture a small Natchitoches village near by, and thoroughly intrench themselves against any attack that might be attempted by the French. But in D'St. Denis they had a foe who was more than able to cope with them, either in strategy or in battle. He resolved immediately to attack their camp. Leaving twenty sol- diers in charge of the fort, and taking with him twenty soldiers and twenty picked Natchitoches warriors, he struck their intrench- ments with great fury before daylight one morning, and so daring and unexpected was his attack that he carried all before him. He routed them, killed eighty-two and lost not a man, and many who were wounded were hotly pursued and tomahawked in the depths of the forests. The savage Flour Chief, as well became him, fell fighting with his face to his foe. This was one of the most notable of the victories of the French over the Indians in the annals of the Louisiana colony, and it is doubtful if any other officer than D'St. Denis then in the colony would have had the boldness, hardihood and skill to accomplish so sweeping a victory over such a select and vigilant enemy.

There still remained in Louisiana fully one hundred warriors of the Natchez tribe, living in scattered bands along Red river and its branches. A little later they combined with the Yazoos and the Caraoes, and for a long time continued to harass the French settlements. After many years they were so decimated and reduced by the remorseless vengeance of the French, that the few survivors lost their identity and became merged with other tribes. All who had been captured were sent to St. Domingo and sold into slavery and the proceeds turned into the treasury of the company.

Thus perished the Natchez tribe, the most intelligent and civ- ilized of all the nations living in what is now the United States. They worshipped the great sun—kept a fire forever burning in his honor; indeed their highest ruler was called "The Sun." This alone was the highest form of nature worship, a recogni- tion in the savage heart of the power and glory of the sun. They surrounded their chief with guards, revered him, obeyed his lightest word, and lived in fixed habitations, which they kept scrupulously clean, one of the best evidences of their superior civilization. At first their utmost hospitality was freely tendered to the visiting Frenchmen; but the abuses of the latter soon alien- ated them. It was the old story of the Spaniards repeated—hos- pitality and kindness repaid with impositions and grievous wrongs. The climax came when the French commandant, Chopart, ordered the abandonment of their time-honored village site that it might be occupied by the white people. The sun and his chiefs remonstrated with respectful mien and language, but were cut short by the French bully and given a fixed time in which to comply with his commands. Seeing no escape, and being unwilling to surrender the homes of their fathers, they saw no better course than to destroy all the French in Louisiana, root and branch. The massacre followed. It was the natural and inevitable result of oppression and outrage. Had the Natchez supinely submitted they would not now be renowned in history for their courage and enlightenment. But the French must win—must possess all the land; and therefore the Nachez must be crushed. D'Soto and Coronado robbed the Indians, and slaughtered them when they resented the robbery. After all, was the French treatment any better than that of the Spanish? Both sacrificed the Indians to gain their possessions. It matters little as to the means adopted.

The attitude of D'Bienville toward the Indians was always fair and humane; that of D'Perier was just the reverse. He visited upon them the same atrocities they perpetrated upon the French, going so far on more than one occasion of burning them publicly in New Orleans and elsewhere. This attitude of severity was regarded as unwise by many of the colonists. Beauchamp wrote to the French ministry, "The evil is now without a remedy unless M. D'Bienville could come back. Perhaps he could succeed in changing the state of things, on account of the consideration which the Indians have always had for him, and of the services which he has rendered them, particularly to the Choctaws." Beauchamp complained bitterly of the state of affairs and further said, "You see to what a state of things is reduced this colony, which has so long groaned under a harsh command (D'Perier's). The colonists are in a miserably wretched condition, and are ill-supplied with the provisions and the merchandise they want. When flour is sent here the heads of the colony take hold of it, as they do with all the brandy and cordials which are imported, and they do not part with these articles except at exorbitant prices. It is, after all, what they do for every sort of merchandise." It is not at all improbable that the French commandant at Natchez, Chopart, did nothing more than he was directed to do by D'Perier in demanding that the savages should leave their village to the French, thus inciting the massacre of the whites at that post. Such an order was in accord with the policy of the governor toward the savages, and Chopart would hardly have issued so important an edict on his own responsibility. Beauchamp, commanding at Mobile, further wrote, "Since the departure of D'Bienville all the Indians are spoiled. In spite of the augmentation of merchandise we have to supply them with, and of the reduction in the quantity of furs which they give us back in return, they are not satisfied. On the contrary, they are insolent and less tractable. . . . The Chickasaws had sent three emissaries to the Illinois to urge them to side against us, but these emissaries have been delivered into our hands, and M. D'Perier intends to have them burnt." The writer was emphatic in requesting the return of D'Bienville; but there were other forces at work.

From 1717 to 1731, the company spent "in a profitless attempt to carry its charter into execution" $3,700,000. It had emitted a considerable number of bonds of its own known as *billets de caisse,* which were still in circulation at the latter date. Though such a course caused serious loss to many of the colonists, these bonds were withdrawn from circulation, upon an order of Governor D'Perier, in fifteen days, and a financial crisis was thus occasioned. This step was taken in closing up the affairs of the company, which on the 23d of January, 1731, had asked to have its charter taken up by the king. The request was granted, and two commissioners, Bru and Bruslé, were sent to the colony by the king to settle the accounts between the company and the government. Slowly the affairs were wound up, and the French government assumed the direct management of the colony.

Thus ended the attempts of one of the worst monopolies ever instituted, to govern the colony of Louisiana. The Indians were usually mismanaged and always abused. Almost every murder of a Frenchman by them may be traced directly or indirectly to some outrageous act of the whites. The policy of Perier was extermination—the unjust and deliberate acquisition of the property of the Indians and their slaughter if they showed resentment or opposition. The official corruption and perfidy of the company's agents were recognized by every settler. The exactions of the company under their charter annihilated commerce, and were the despair of the poor people who sought to keep their heads above the waves of destruction. The only ray of light shining through the gloom was the large number of settlers sent out from 1717 to 1721, the most of whom were forced to remain and become *nolens volens* integral parts of the colony. This was the only factor which saved the colony from abandonment and extinction.

CHAPTER VI

Louisiana Under the French Cabinet

THE relinquishment of the charter of the Royal India Company was the signal for the reorganization of affairs in Louisiana Province. The superior council was placed on a new basis by patent bearing date May 7, 1732. Louisiana was made no longer a dependency of New France, or Canada, and to it was attached the Illinois country. D'Perier was made governor, Salmon intendant, D'Artaguette and Loubois the king's lieutenant governors, and Fleuriau attorney general. Attention was paid to ecclesiastical affairs by the appointment of a vicar-general with residence at New Orleans. In order to revive commerce, all duty was removed from merchandise exported from France into the colony and from the produce of Louisiana imported into France. This at last was a step in the right direction, and it met an immediate response from the colonists and from the merchants of France. D'Perier served but one year under the new order, and was succeeded by D'Bienville upon the request of the colonists. The latter expected great relief from the new conditions and were not disappointed, though the many Indian wars hampered commercial transactions in the interior. Better protection from the Indians was afforded to the outlying districts, and the currency circulating in the colony was improved. D'Perier retired with credit, but his departure was not mourned by the inhabitants. His treatment of the Indians could not have been worse, and all felt that a more pacific and conciliatory policy might have prevented many of the misunderstandings with the savages and saved many a French life. Public rejoicing accompanied the reception of Governor D'Bienville. Pierre D'Artaguette, brother of Diron, was appointed major-commandant of the district of Illinois, his headquarters being at Fort Chartres.

In nearly all the wars with the Indians, the negroes were employed to swell the meager ranks of the French soldiers. This would not have been done at all had not dire necessity required it as a measure of safety. But it served to excite and embolden the negroes and in the end led to their insurrection. It became known to them that by turning against the French, they could secure their own liberty among the Indians. It thus came to pass that all the tribes hostile to the French had with them negroes who had gained their freedom owing to this circumstance. Several of the most crafty and bold of the runaway slaves among the Chickasaws secretly went among the negroes of the settlements along the Mississippi and succeeded in inciting the insurrection. At last a night was set, on whch it was determined to make the attempt to capture New Orleans, kill all the men, possess themselves of the arms, ammunition and stores, and thus be enabled to conquer the whole colony. The plan was revealed by a negro woman and the leaders were promptly captured; four of the men were broken on the wheel, their heads fastened on poles or posts at the gates of the city, and one woman was hung. This example, publicly executed, was sufficiently fearful and impressive to prevent any further uprisings.

In August, 1734, it was ordered by the king that two soldiers annually out of every company should be granted a furlough and a tract of land, a portion of which, to be designated by the governor, was to be cleared within three years. As there were in the colony six hundred and fifty soldiers, or thirteen companies, twenty-six grants were thus made annually alone to the soldiers. The Swiss troops were granted the same privilege. This act was the means of making in the end good farmers out of the soldiers, and was a decided advantage to the colony. Annually the governor selected the men thus to become farmers. The scarcity of current money led to the emission of a card currency in 1735 to the amount of about forty thousand dollars, which needed act greatly stimulated commercial exchanges among the colonists. This act was distinctively a Louisiana measure, the cards being signed by the local officials and being a legal tender for all obligations. But oppressive measures were still thought proper. The price of tobacco was arbitrarily fixed for 1733 at 35 livres per hundred pounds; for 1734 and 1735 at 30 livres; for 1736 and 1737 at 27 livres; and for 1738 at 25 livres. But the colonists near the mouth of the Mississippi continued to be in sore straits, while those in the Illinois country had passed the crucial stage, had an abundance of provisions and clothing and were comparatively safe and happy. The most extraordinary fact in connection with the Louisiana colony was that after the lapse of thirty-five years the colonists were not able to support themselves in the most fertile soil in the world, where nature provided in great abundance every necessity. That fact stands as a most fearful arraignment of either the management or the character and habits of the colonists.

It was in 1735 that steps were taken to confirm the titles to the various concessions and grants in the colony. Complaints were made that the colonists were obliged to pay two hundred per cent more for the same articles than the traders; more negroes were called for. It is said that at the mouth of the Mississippi in 1733, the colonists were compelled to live for some time on the seeds and grains of reeds. This is a crushing commentary on somebody—on the management of course, because the poor people did as they must, or were told. At the same time they of the Illinois country were living on corn, wheat, pork, beef, vegetables, and a wonderful profusion of wild game. But very little went down the Mississippi at this time, however, owing to the fierce hostility of the Chickasaws. The old company of the Indies had a hard time to collect the debts due it, because the only tribunal was in the colony and in sympathy with the people and in all cases favored them. The colony cost the crown in 1734 over one hundred and sixty thousand dollars. D'Bienville wrote in 1735 that at Pointe Coupée one hundred thousand pounds of tobacco were made. Cotton began to appear in considerable quantity. Early in 1735 the river was so high that New Orleans was deep under water. The drouth was so severe for four months the succeeding summer that the river fell fifteen feet, "a circumstance which had never been seen before."

The Chickasaws, the terror of the south, had now become so troublesome that D'Bienville determined to try to crush them. They even tried to alienate the Illinois from the French, but were not successful. The project of an invasion of the Chickasaw country by a large army met the approval of the king of France, and preparations were accordingly made. As many Frenchmen as could be spared were sent down the river from Fort Chartres to assist him. In March, 1736, D'Bienville, with an army of about six hundred Frenchmen and negroes (forty-five of the latter) set out from New Orleans for the place of rendezvous, or Fort Mobile. On the Tombigbee river they were joined by about six hundred Choctaws. Arriving at the principal Indian stronghold, at what is now the town of Pontotoc, Mississippi, they found the Chickasaws so well prepared to receive them that they were repulsed with the loss of thirty-two killed and sixty wounded. Greatly humiliated, D'Bienville retreated, leaving in the hands of the savages several prisoners. Previously, D'Artaguette, who had come down from the Illinois to join him, had fallen into the hands of the enemy. He had descended the Mississippi with thirty regular soldiers, one hundred volunteer Frenchmen and two hundred Indians of the Illinois and Missouri nations. At the third Chickasaw Bluff, or Fort Prudhomme, he met Sieur D'Vincennes with twenty Frenchmen and about one hundred and twenty-five Miamis, who had come down from the Wabash to join the army. Another detachment under Sieur D'Moncherval from the Illinois was expected. D'Granpré, commandant at the Arkansas, sent a body of warriors to his assistance. After due deliberation, D'Bienville not having arrived, Major D'Artaguette concluded to attack the Chickasaws in their stronghold, and accordingly set forth. Though partially successful, he was finally defeated, many of the leaders were captured, and the Illinois and Missouris assisting the French were fiercely pursued for more than one hundred miles by the unrelenting Chickasaws. The retreat was conducted by a young man of sixteen years named Voisin, and is said by writers to have been "a masterpiece of skill and bravery." He conducted his small force the whole distance without food, and handled them so well that there was no rout, nor was any of his wounded left in the hands of the enemy. He inflicted as much punishment on the Chickasaws as was imposed upon his force. His name deserves proudly to be told in story and sung in song. The French leaders who were captured were tortured at the stake over slow fires. Thus perished Father Senat, D'Artaguette, St. Ange, D'Vincennes, Courlonges, Dutisnet, D'Esgly, D'Tonty, Courcelas and other brave men distinguished in the early annals of the Louisiana Province.

Dating from the time the French first met them, the Fox nation of Indians proved hostile to the advancement of the whites. They usually refused to send peace envoys to the treaties, and often killed the whitemen who entered their domains, or the domains claimed by them. At last, in 1734, the French of Canada resolved to send an expedition against them. Many friendly Indians, principally the Iroquois, accompanied the expedition to assist in chastising their ancient enemy. Before this date, the Foxes had left their old haunts on the Wisconsin, and taken up their abode in Iowa, principally on the Des Moines river. Under the command of Col. Nicholas D'Noyelle, the expedition marched over seven hundred leagues, starting from Montreal in August. They found the Foxes prepared for their reception, being thoroughly intrenched on or near the river Des Moines. The attack was only partly successful, for though many of the Foxes were killed, their intrenchments were not captured. However, it was a blow from which they did not soon recover, and one which they never forgot. The Sacs assisted the Foxes, and part of the punishment fell upon them. The following year, a treaty of peace was concluded with them, after a continuous war of twenty-five years.*

In 1727, as before stated, a party of Frenchmen under the command of Boucher de la Perrière, marched from Montreal to the Mississippi by way of the Green Bay and Wisconsin route and built Fort Beauharnais at Lake Pepin on the west side of the river. Other buildings were constructed, and it was late in October before all were comfortably housed. A great flood the following spring forced them to abandon the buildings. The Sioux proving unfriendly, the party returned to Canada, but came again in 1731, erected buildings on higher ground, and succeeded in opening trade with the Indians. The post was finally abandoned in 1737 by Legardeur de Saint Pierre, who was then in command. This was an attempt made by a Canadian company to monopolize the fur trade among the Sioux.†

The Chickasaws now became more insolent and dangerous than ever. A second expedition was sent against them. Whether merited or not, the previous disasters had seriously injured D'Bienville's reputation with the French government. Smarting under the combined humiliation and criticism, he resolved to retrieve all the prestige he had lost, and having secured the approval of the colonial minister he began active and elaborate preparations in the spring of 1739. Every settlement in the province was called upon for assistance, and the point of rendezvous was fixed on the St. Francis river near its mouth and near the Mississippi. Here a temporary fort and a number of cabins were built for the protection of the supplies while preparations were under way. In August the army was moved up the river to a point opposite the present city of Memphis; and, having crossed the river, they built Fort Assumption, with strong fortifications, barracks for the soldiers, a small house for D'Aime, the commander, store-houses, ammunition houses, etc. Here the army was reinforced until it aggregated about twelve hundred French-

---

* See Hubbard's "Wisconsin Under the Dominion of France."
† Memoire de Beauharnais, 1738.

men and double that many Indians, together with a few negroes. Two hundred Frenchmen and three hundred Indians under Capt. Alphonse D'Buissoniere came down from the Illinois—from Fort Chartres. Captain D'Celoron arrived from Canada with thirty cadets and many Indians. For some reason not wholly clear, the command of this army had been intrusted to M. D'Noailles D'Aime instead of D'Bienville, which necessarily occasioned jealousy between those two valuable officers. The result might have been anticipated. The army remained at Fort Assumption for six months, doing nothing, yet suffering everything until the men were reduced to horse-flesh for food and were stricken with a terrible sickness which swept so many off, that by March, 1740, there were probably not to exceed three hundred white men fit for active duty. In this extremity, the heroic D'Bienville was in despair. It was seen that not only must the expedition be given up, but Fort Assumption must be abandoned, a step likely to be fraught with serious consequences. At this juncture D'Aime seems to have been superseded in supreme command by D'Bienville. Finally, Capt. D'Celoron, with as large a body of the well men as could be spared, was sent to reconnoitre the Chickasaw camp. Observing his advance, and believing he was followed by the main army, the Indians opened negotiations for peace. As this had been hoped and provided for, terms were soon reached. This finality was much better than had been expected at one time. After the peace treaty had been concluded, D'Bienville dismantled the fortifications at Memphis and on the St. Francis river, sent the volunteers to their homes, and with the regulars sailed down the Mississippi to New Orleans. This second failure to crush the Chickasaws so impaired the reputation of D'Bienville that he was retired and the Marquis D'Vaudreuil-Cavagnal was sent to govern the province in 1742. But the Chickasaws were quieted by this display of force, and the French colonists enjoyed another peaceful breathing spell.

On the upper Mississippi, many years had elapsed and large settlements been made in the Illinois country east of the river, before any strong and permanent colony was formed west of the river. About the year 1735 a few families located across the river opposite Kaskaskia for the purpose of being near the salt works established there, where the men were employed. This little village was located on the bottom lands and was called Misére, because of the annual overflow of the river and the consequent distress. After many years, or about 1785, the village was removed to higher land near, or on, the present site of St. Genevieve, Missouri. As the years flew by the place seemed to absorb the strength of the settlements east of the Mississippi above the mouth of the Kaskaskia; because, while they slowly died, it steadily flourished and ere long became the center of French people of that vicinity. It even yet retains its Gallic characteristics. Descendants are yet living there whose ancestors were among the first to settle in the upper Mississippi valley. French manners and speech, with perennial and Parisian vivacity and freshness, may be observed on the streets of this ancient village.

In 1736 Father Jean Pierre Aulneau was among the Sioux and the Kristinaux or Krees. He had come out with the Verendryes, but was finally slain by the Prairie Sioux, together with a party of about twenty Frenchmen, who seem to have been surprised in the night, as they were not tortured, but all had their heads cut off. This occurred very close to the northern boundary of Minnesota, perhaps south of the boundary.

In 1737 an ordinance was issued by the French government, exempting from duty for ten years the productions exported to the French West Indies and the productions of those island imported into Louisiana. Considerable tar and pitch was made at this time—six or seven thousand barrels. The production of cotton was not very profitable, owing to the difficulty of getting rid of the seed. From thirty to thirty-five thousand pounds of indigo were produced annually. The manufacture of tobacco had increased, but the productions lacked an outlet. In 1741 several very severe hurricanes destroyed nearly all the crops of the lower Mississippi, so that the people there were reduced almost to the point of starvation. In July, Loubois wrote, "There are many families reduced to such a state of destitution that fathers when they rise in the morning do not know where they will get the food required by their children." Flour was not to be had at any price. A cask of common wine sold for nearly one hundred dollars in Spanish money, or one hundred and forty-eight dollars in the currency of the colony. Starvation was avoided by bringing in produce from adjacent districts. The reason why provisions did not come down from the Wabash or the Illinois is shown by the following incident: A party of twenty-four French traders and trappers, accompanied by a woman and a young girl, were attacked by a force of one hundred and fifty Natchez and Chickasaws at or near Point Coupée, and for six hours presented a stern and successful defense. Both women showed great bravery, venturing out and cutting off the powder-horns of those who

I—14

had fallen. They were both finally shot. Sixteen of the men perished, but the others cut their way out and, though some of them were wounded, effected their escape.

The expenses of Louisiana in 1741 amounted to $59,091, and in 1742 to $59,686. At this time there is noticed a steady advance in all the functions of civil and colonial government. Law began to be enforced more than ever before in the colony. Increase of trade occasioned commercial friction, and friction was followed by suits at law. D'Bienville, the "father of Louisiana," sailed back to France, never again to set foot on the soil where so many years of his active life had been spent. Vaudreuil took the reins, but had many difficulties to encounter. Metallic money had wholly disappeared, and card currency had considerably depreciated. Little relief was experienced by the emission of treasury notes and the strengthening of the treasury at New Orleans.

In 1740 Capt. Benoist D'St. Clair became major commandant in place of Captain D'Buissoniere of the post of the Illinois; but was himself succeeded three years later by the Chevalier D'Berthel, who remained in command until 1749. The settlers along the Missouri and its affluents and in the present State of Missouri along the Mississippi were under the jurisdiction of these officers, being a part of the district of Illinois. The settlements in Missouri were built up largely from those along the Illinois river and along the Kaskaskia delta. No doubt some came directly from Canada and from New Orleans. According to Father Louis Vivier, the five French villages of the Kaskaskia delta, or between the Kaskaskia and the Mississippi rivers, contained in 1750 about eleven hundred whites and about three hundred negro slaves and sixty Indian slaves. Sieur D'St. Clair under a reappointment, served as major commandant of the Illinois from 1749 to 1751. He was then succeeded by Major Macarty, who after nine years surrendered the command to Capt. Neyon D'Villiers. In February, 1753, M. D'Kerlerec succeeded D'Vaudreuil as governor of the Province of Louisiana. The latter was appointed governor-general of Canada. The former served until June, 1763, when M. D'Abbadie assumed the reins of government of the Province as director-general.

New Orleans was beginning to have a steady trade with the other Gulf cities and with Europe. Large quantities of food supplies, such as corn, flour, pork, etc., flowed down from the upper Mississippi country; in fact New Orleans could not get along without such shipments. As for the French settlers of the upper country, it may be said that New Orleans was their only market, and was absolutely indispensable. Life in Louisiana at this time was extremely picturesque. Everywhere the soil was cultivated; mining and adventure had been largely given up. Hunting and trading were extensively carried on. Many Spanish horses began to arrive from the West. Large convoys or flotillas descended the Mississippi loaded with the products of the upper country. These voyages down were usually made from December to February; as soon as the cargoes had been sold, such boats as were needed were filled with sugar, tobacco, rice, cotton, tea, coffee, etc., and the tiresome journey up the river was begun. In New Orleans the jaunty and effeminate airs of Parisian society were to be observed at all social functions. Vaudreuil, himself a court favorite, encouraged the introduction of European fashions and social conduct. The English were not only crowding into the Mississippi valley, but were stirring up the Chickasaws to war on the French. Perhaps they also incited the Sioux to threaten so seriously Fort Beauharnais at Lake Pepin on the Mississippi that the French garrison there abandoned the post for a time. About this time the Mississippi between Kaskaskia and New Orleans was actually captured by the Choctaws, and the communication was cut off with the upper country. All this indicated the influences of the English, and was a prelude to the Seven Years' War which began in 1755. But the French were aroused and commenced to fortify all the exposed points. Fort Chartres later became the most powerful post in America, thanks to Governor D'Kerlerec. By 1750 the French had eight intrenched posts in Louisiana outside of New Orleans, among which were those at Natchitoches, Pointe Coupée, on the Mississippi near the mouth of Red river, one at the mouth of the Arkansas, and one at Saint Geneviève, Missouri. Regardless of the claims and protests of the French, the Ohio Company received a grant of 600,000 acres on the south side of the Ohio river. Christopher Gist had penetrated this country for them in 1750. When Captain D'Aubrey evacuated Fort Duquesne (Pittsburg) at the commencement of the Seven Years' War, he retreated down the Ohio to Fort Massac, and thence up the Mississippi to Fort Chartres.

As early as 1724 when Fort Orleans was built in the Missouri country, that portion of the Province began to be called "Missouri," in distinction to the Illinois country proper. Its trade had become very large and valuable, but prior to 1745 had not been subjected to many official annoyances. Beginning on the 1st of January, 1745, Governor Vaudreuil, following the old and pernicious custom of granting monopolies in order to secure revenues for the crown, gave the exclusive right of trading on the Missouri and its branches and all the territory drained by them for the term of a little more than five years to M. D'Rousseau. The grantee was required to build a fort in the Missouri country, supply the garrison with subsistence, pay its chief officer annually $360, maintain peace with the Indians of the district at his own expense, keep on hand enough merchandise to supply the wants of the Indians, and to transport to the fort the supplies needed by its commander. Vaudreuil regarded this monopoly as a wise step, because it would restrict the illicit trading with the natives and force the colonists to cultivate the soil. He even deprecated the introduction of negroes into the Missouri country, believing that their absence would compel the inhabitants to go to work for themselves. He was a believer in the value of the mines of the upper country, and spent considerable crown money uselessly in that direction. The following was the estimated population of the Province in 1744:

	White male inhabitants.	Blacks of both sexes.
At the Balize	Some soldiers	30
New Orleans	800	300
German Coast	100	200
Pointe Coupée	200	400
Natchitoches	60	200
Natchez	8	15
Arkansas	12	10
Illinois	300	600
Petit Ougas	40	5
Missouri	200	10
Pascagoulas	10	60
Mobile	150	200
Totals	1,880	2,030
Women and children estimated	1,500	
Total	3,380	
Troops	800	
Grand Total	4,180	2,030

In 1743 Governor Vaudreuil issued an ordinance requiring all planters along the Mississippi to put their levees in safe condition within a given time upon pain of forfeiting their plantations to the crown. The card currency which had been issued to take the place of the depreciated money of the India Company, became itself so depreciated within ten years that it required three dollars to equal one of coin. In April, 1744, these card promises were ordered retired on the basis of two and a half to one of coin, and the holders were paid in drafts of the treasury of France, suffering again a severe shave or discount.

Owing to the war with England, preparations to defend the mouth of the Mississippi were made by Governor Vaudreuil. He built two forts, one on each side of the river, at English Turn, and at Plaguemine Turn, down the river from New Orleans, "of mud and facines, with epaulments, the shelving sides of which are to be fenced and secured with hurdles, according to the plans and drawings of Deverges. For the construction of these fortifications, I have ordered, jointly with Mr. Lenormant, the inhabitants of New Orleans and of the neighboring country to send in the fifth of their negroes during six weeks. I hope that in ten days there will be a battery of ten eighteen-pounders in each fort." He further said, "With regard to the forces of the colony, I can dispose of four hundred white men, five or six hundred Indians belonging to the small nations, and from two to three hundred negroes who are to be relied upon. But we are wanting in arms and ammunition." As no attack by the British was anticipated on the upper Mississippi country, no attempt to fortify any post there was considered. In 1746 a terrible hurricane destroyed the crops of the lower country to such an extent as to threaten famine for that portion of the colony; it was saved by shipments from the Illinois. Governor Vaudreuil wrote, "We receive from the Illinois flour, corn, bacon, hams both of bear and hog, corned pork, wild beef, myrtle and beeswax, cotton, tallow, leather, tobacco, lead, copper, buffalo, wool, venison, poultry bear's grease, oil, skins, fowls and hides. Their boats come down annually in the latter part of December and return in February." But the settlers of the upper country were forced to come down in convoys in order to withstand the attacks of the alert and savage Chickasaws.

By 1747 the expenses of the colony amounted to $92,582. At this time Chevalier D'Berthel was commander of the Illinois district, which embraced all the Missouri country. All the tribunals of the upper country were subordinate to the superior council at New Orleans. The period of exemption from duty on exports and imports was extended beyond the fixed term of ten years, and was re-extended. A little later the granting to the Ohio Company of an immense tract in the Ohio valley filled all Louisiana with excitement and forebodings. Conflicts began to occur between the French and the English traders, in which the Indian tribes became involved. In 1750 there were at the command of the governor eight hundred and fifty soldiers, divided into seventeen companies. The government agreed to take all the tobacco raised in the colony at $5.50 per hundred. British agents, it was thought, were busily at work among the savages, because at no time in the history of the colony were so many attacks made upon the French settlements from Quebec to the Balize. The Seven Years' War had already commenced in America. Even the tribe of the Illinois was on the point of joining the English against the French. About this date sugar cane was introduced into the colony from Cuba for the first time by the Jesuits, and the first crop was grown by them in the St. Mary suburb of New Orleans. Wax for candles from berries was quite a "fad." Owing to the numerous attacks of the Indians and to the threatened invasion by the English, the colony in 1751 was supplied with better protection than ever before, there being here two thousand regulars, of whom 975 were at New Orleans, 300 in the Illinois, and 50 each at the Arkansas, Natchitoches, Pointe Coupée and the German Coast. The commander at the Arkansas was Ensign Delino. Serious complaints were forwarded to France against the corruption existing in the colony under the administration of Governor Vaudreuil, and the latter was openly accused of dishonorable conduct. In 1751 the last shipment of poor girls to the colony was made, there being sent over sixty, and the most of them were married to soldiers who were honorably discharged, under the rule previously mentioned. Upon their marriage, they were given a start in life by the government. The Illinois district was at this time placed under the command of Lieutenant Macarty, and embraced six villages: Fort Chartres, Kaskaskia, Cahokia, St. Philip, Prairie de Rocher and St. Genevieve. The upper country was in an exceedingly prosperous condition. They raised from three to five times as much produce as they could find a market for. The lower country was also in better condition than ever before.

Probably through British influence the Chickasaws from 1747 to 1752 renewed their attacks on the French settlements and on the fleets of pirogues which descended the Mississippi to New Orleans with the produce of the upper country. Again the situation became unbearable, and again it was resolved to send an expedition against them. In 1752, Governor D'Vaudreuil, with a force of seven hundred Frenchmen and a large number of Choc-taws, advanced up the Mobile and Tombigbee rivers, but the Chickasaws evaded him. Having destroyed many of their vil-lages and improvements and left a detachment of soldiers at Fort Tombigbee to check their marauding expeditions against the Mississippi convoys and the French settlement, he returned and disbanded his army. But they were again subdued and quieted for a term of years.

Much of the trouble between the Iroquois and the western tribes was due to the intrigues and wars between the French and the English. Both countries struggled to secure an alliance with the powerful Six Nations, but the English were successful, owing to their proximity. The French secured the friendship of nearly all the western nations. As a result, all wars between France and England were followed by wars between the Iroquois on one side and the western tribes on the other. The friendship of the Indians was sought for the purpose of obtaining their fur trade, as well as a claim to the soil occupied by them. At a later day, the English, through their treaty with the Iroquois, claimed all the Ohio and Wabash valleys as a part of the Iroquois domain. This contention cut an important figure at a later date—when the all-important time came to draw the lines of demarkation between the two countries in America. The Iroquois claimed, as a matter of fact, the Ohio valley as far as the Mississippi, and persistently permitted the English traders to reach that river through their territory. But the right of the English to any part of the Mis-sissippi bank was emphatically denied by the French, and in real-ity was wholly unfounded. Even on the rights of the Iroquois, their claims were unsound, because that consolidated tribe did not conquer the country to the Mississippi. Through the Iro-quois, the English ever tried to induce the western tribes to break with the French but their efforts were not often successful.

The explorations of Pierre Gaultier Verendrye and his sons in the northwest were very important to the interests of France in that quarter. With a small company of Canadian boatmen and hunters and a Jesuit missionary, he left Montreal in June, 1731, and in due time reached Lake Superior. They went to Pigeon river, now part of the boundary between Canada and Minnesota, ascended the same till they came to Rainy Lake, and there built a fort and passed the winter. This fort was called St. Pierre. The following year they passed on up the rivers and in July built Fort St. Charles on the Lake of the Woods, locating it on the west side. Here they passed the winter of 1732-3.

Their large supply of peltries was sent to Montreal. In 1734 Verendrye sent one of his sons and a number of Frenchmen to Lake Winnipeg where they built Fort Maurepas and from this point they again sent to Canada an immense quantity of peltries. In 1735 one of his sons died at Fort St. Charles on the Lake of the Woods, from wounds inflicted by the Sioux. In 1736 they built Fort Rouge at or near the mouth of Assiniboine river. So bad was the outlook in 1737, that it seemed likely they would be forced to leave the country. Only the forts and the guns of the Frenchmen prevented the massacre of the whole party by the Sioux. The next year they became quieter, whereupon Verendrye went further into the Sioux country and built Fort de la Reine on the water course near Lake Manitoba. During all their stay in this country they had often heard of the Mandans, a nation of very intelligent Indians living far to the southwest. Late in 1738 Verendrye determined to seek them. Taking with him about twenty Frenchmen and about thirty friendly Indians, he pushed westward to what is thought to have been Turtle mountains. On November 28, he reached the Mandan outposts and on the 3d of December entered their villages. He left two men among them, with their consent, to learn their language, took possession of the country in the name of France, and returned to Fort de la Reine, arriving February, 1739. In this year Fort Dauphine was built near Lake Manitoba by a party under the orders of one of the two remaining sons of Verendrye. While here the son went out and explored the Saskatchewan country. In this year, also, Verendrye returned to Canada for a supply of merchandise, but came back in 1741.

The stories which the two men mentioned brought to Verendrye after a year or two, concerning the western country, determined him to make another attempt to reach the mountains. He sent his eldest son Pierre and two other men to the Mandans, but as they could procure there no guides they were forced to return. In 1742 another attempt was made. Pierre and his younger brother, accompanied by two of the bravest and best Canadians in the West, went to the Mandans, and, having procured horses, marched in a westerly direction across the plains. They crossed the Little Missouri, thence marched to the headwaters of Tongue river, and, still advancing westward, reached a spur of the Big Horn mountains. They now turned back, but passed farther to the south, reaching probably the Black Hills, whence they marched almost directly eastward to the villages of the Sioux on the Missouri. They rejoined their companions at Fort La Reine on the 2d of July. The object of finding the great divide between the Missouri basin and the Pacific slope was not accomplished.

The explorations of Verendrye were continued in the northwest by Legardeur D'St. Pierre, who went out in 1750; but after three years he had accomplished nothing more than his predecessor. He sent an expedition to the Saskatchewan under Chevalier D'Niverville, and a fort called La Jonquiere, was built on that river three hundred miles from its mouth; but it was soon abandoned and the party fell back to Fort La Reine. It was in 1745 that the British parliament offered a reward of twenty thousand pounds to the discoverer of a practical northwest passage. It was at this time, also, that England put forth her strongest claims to the Ohio and the Wabash valleys, based principally upon the treaties with the Iroquois many years before and with the Miamis in 1748. In addition it was claimed that the English colonial traders had entered the Wabash valley as early as the year 1723; but this claim made no weight against the French who had been there for many previous years.

While the French explorations in the West under government auspices were ostensibly undertaken for the purpose of discovering a water route to the South Sea, the participants usually lost sight of that object. Father Nau writing to Father Bonin in 1735 said, "The western sea would have been discovered long ago, if people had wished it. Monsieur, the Count D'Maurepas, is right when he says that the officials in Canada are looking not for the western sea, but for the sea of beaver."

The prices of American commodities did not vary greatly from year to year. A silver fox was worth six beavers, twenty sols being the price of one beaver. Marten, otter, and bear cubs were worth the same price as the beaver. A black fox was worth twenty or more beavers. Father Vivier said in 1750: "In former years when eight or ten ships entered the Mississippi, that was considered a great number; this year over forty entered; mostly from Martinique and San Domingo." At this period the largest settlement on the Mississippi above New Orleans was at the German coast. A palisaded fort stood at Pointe Coupeé. In this vicinity were more than sixty residences strung along the river for five or six leagues, according to Father Vivier. At Natchez was a garrison and a fort. Near the mouth of the Arkansas was also a fort and a garrison. This fort was a famous resort of the convoys which descended the river and stopped here to rest and secure fresh provisions. They likewise received protection here from the Chickasaws to the east. In 1748 a large

band of that tribe attacked this post, killed several persons and
carried away thirteen captives. The rest of the whites managed
to get inside of the fort, where there were fourteen soldiers; but
two of the latter were killed. It was afterward discovered that
among the attacking party was a French drummer who had
deserted from the Arkansas garrison itself. At this time nearly
all of the Indian slaves among the Illinois were of the Panis tribe
beyond the Mississippi—this was true to such an extent that the
word "slave" was locally supplanted by that of "Panis," meaning
the same thing. The Panis were the modern Pawnees.

One of the early missionaries, Father Louis Vivier, seems to
have a very high opinion of the Missouri river. Here is what he
wrote in 1750: "Mississippi in the Illinois language means 'The
Great River.' It seems to have usurped that name from the Missouri. Before its junction with that river, the Mississippi is of
no great size. Its current is slight, while the Missouri is wider,
deeper, more rapid, and takes its rise much farther away. Several rivers of considerable size empty into the Mississippi; but the
Missouri alone seems to pour into it more water than all the other
rivers put together. Here is the proof of it; The water of most—
I might say all—of the rivers that fall into the Mississippi is only
passably good, and that of several is positively unwholesome; that
of the Mississippi itself, above its junction with the Missouri, is
none of the best; on the contrary, that of the Missouri is the best
water in the world. Now that of the Mississippi, from its junction with the Missouri to the sea, becomes excellent; the water
of the Missouri must therefore predominate. The first travelers
who came through Canada discovered the Mississippi; that is the
reason why the latter has acquired the name of 'great' at the
expense of the glory of the other."*

In 1752 the expenses of the colony amounted to $172,191.
D'Kerlerec succeeded D'Vaudreuil as governor in 1753, and one
of his first steps was to undertake to alienate the Choctaws from
the English traders, who were claiming and exercising the right
to come to the left bank of the Mississippi and to both banks of
the Wabash and the Ohio. But the Choctaws answered that they
were better treated by the English, who studied their wants and
let them have merchandise at a less price than the French traders.
They said, "Satisfy all our wants and we shall now and forever
renounce the English." To meet this state of affairs, the governor called for larger shipments of merchandise. He offered

* Thwaites's reissue of Jesuit Relations and other Documents.

ransoms for French prisoners among the Indians, and made important changes in the officers of the various posts. His troops were reduced to thirteen hundred and fifty regulars and about five hundred militia. In 1754 D'Kerlerec wrote, "The English are moving everywhere about us, and threaten to interrupt our communications with the Illinois." It was this year that Captain Villiers, with a column of troops from Fort Chartres, went down the Mississippi and up the Ohio to Pennsylvania to assist in repelling the English from the Alleghany valley. The colonial expense of 1754 amounted to $178,177. D'Kerlerec, having propitiated the Choctaws, received the designation from them of "Father of the Choctaws." This year Captain Favrot was sent to the Illinois country with four companies of fifty men each and an abundant supply of provisions and ammunition. The upper country for the first time was thought to be in danger from the British of the Atlantic coast, and was strengthened. Additional forces were sent to Ship Island, and the fortifications at the English Turn were repaired. He appealed to France for five hundred more soldiers, but Louis XV was too indifferent to pay much attention to his wants or his demands. It was at this time that a bitter war for supremacy was waged between the Capuchins and the Jesuits.

By 1757 the English fleets had almost cut off all communication between Louisiana and France; so much so that D'Kerlerec was forced to send to Vera Cruz for gunpowder. English privateers waited like sharks around the mouths of the Mississippi, ready to pounce down on any French vessel that dared make its appearance, going or coming. D'Kerlerec felt his insecurity, as he had to guard the whole line of the Mississippi with a handful of men. The Indians began to be troublesome, when in 1758 a ship-load of supplies arrived just in time to quiet them. The Choctaws and the Alibamons could place in the field seven thousand warriors. "These two nations are the bulwarks of the colony, and they must be conciliated cost what it may," wrote D'Kerlerec.

It was at this time that he formulated his plan of uniting all the tribes of the Mississippi with the object of moving against the English of the Atlantic coast in order to divert them from a concentration upon Canada. The plan was an excellent one, and should have received the assistance and support of the home government. It is not improbable that such an expedition might even have saved Canada by dividing the British force sent to that Province. General Wolfe would hardly have appeared on the Plains of Abraham with so much confidence and prestige, had a force of eight thousand to twelve thousand French and Indians threatened the English colonies in his rear. But Louis XV was asleep in the arms of his courtesans, and his courtiers were steeped in debauchery; they had no time nor inclination to listen to the death wails of the most magnificent colony in all the world. The English, in 1758, suffered a terrible defeat at the hands of the French and Indians under Captain D'Aubrey of Louisiana at Fort Duquesne or what is now Pittsburg. Had that attack been followed up as it should have been by the whole strength of the West, the disastrous results of this war to France might have assumed a different story. The impotence of the French court, not the French people, caused the loss of Canada and all of Louisiana to France. The victory of Captain D'Aubrey was one of the most notable of the war, and opened a path to the heart of the Atlantic settlements of the English. It was accomplished by the men of the Illinois, the Wabash and the Mississippi, men who knew how to fight after the savage or the civilized method. But they were not sustained and in the end were compelled to fall back.

Trouble arose between Governor D'Kerlerec and Intendent Rochemore. The latter without authority called in 1,800,000 livres of paper money circulating in the colony, and replaced it with an equal amount of a new emission in order to distinguish his administration. He was sharply reprimanded for this insane act. He attacked Governor D'Kerlerec, and accused him of carrying on an illegal traffic with the Indians, and announced that the most extravagant expenses were indulged in. The governor retaliated, and in 1759 Rochemore was dismissed from office, together with several others, all of whom were found to have wrongfully put their hands in the public treasury. Their dishonesty was only another evidence to prove that the officials of Louisiana from start to finish had robbed the colony and crushed it in the dust. Could the facts be known of the corruption under the governments of Crozat and the Company of the Indies, history would no doubt assume an altogether different aspect. The annual deficit on Louisiana was considered a great hamper on the struggles of France for life and commercial supremacy; in fact France was tired of the annual losses of the colony, but should not have been, owing to the immense value of the Province, which all statesmen now recognized. Instead of reinforcing the army in Louisiana, the king withdrew thirty-six companies in order to reduce the expense, and in order that they might be used elsewhere. Late in 1760 New Orleans was fortified. In 1761 it was ascertained that over seven million livres of paper money were in circulation in the colony and that it had depreciated from four to five hundred per cent. At this time the Choctaws, who had been neglected, were on the point of taking the warpath against the French, and assistance was asked for, prayed for, but in vain.

At this juncture, late in 1761, France applied to Spain for assistance against England. In order to incite Spain to this course, France stated that she could no longer hold Louisiana against the English, in which case there would no longer be a bulwark between the Spanish and the British colonies. Spain was asked for pecuniary assistance, and due restitution was faithfully promised by the French ambassador. D'Kerlerec, upon the receipt of this news, sent couriers in all directions to acquaint the Indians and the Spanish that France and Spain would unite to crush England. But Spain was slow to act. And in the meantime the Indians were again becoming importunate for their customary supplies. D'Kerlerec was now in despair, and no wonder. The French armies and fleets were melting away before the English onset, and he only too plainly saw that if affairs continued long in the same straits Louisiana would go with the rest to the British crown. His letters show the extremity in which he was placed. To add to his perplexity and indignation, another fierce attack was made upon him by under officers at New Orleans, who were themselves stealing everything they could lay their hands on, and in the meantime were crying loudly "Stop thief." The upper country was comparatively quiet and prosperous. This was the condition of things when all of the Province east of the Mississippi was ceded to the English.

Governor D'Kerlerec was accused of various offenses, among which were unjustifiable assumptions of authority, violations of official duty and the expenditure of ten millions of livres in four years. It was during his term that the new Fort Chartres was built at a cost of about one million dollars, a sum out of all proportion, apparently, to the actual expense. The fort was the strongest and best ever erected in the Mississippi valley, and was in form an irregular quadrangle, with sides four hundred and ninety feet in length. The wall was built of free-stone and was over two feet thick, pierced with loopholes and flanked with powerful bastions. The interior was thoroughly appointed with all the necessary buildings and magazines. It does not appear that D'Kerlerec deserved the opprobrium cast upon him by the government of France. However, upon his arrival in Paris, he was thrown into the Bastile and kept there for many months, and

soon after his release, so intense was his grief over the accusations and the imprisonment, he died of sorrow and humiliation.

An examination of the facts convinces that a great injustice
was done him. There is nothing to show that he pocketed any
of the large sums spent for civic and military improvement; on
the contrary, he is known to have been an earnest advocate of the
importance of strengthening all the French posts on the Mississippi, owing to the threats of the English colonies. Two years
after he took the helm, England and France were convulsed in
the dreadful Seven Years' War, which shook all Europe and
caused many a throne to tremble and many a king to quake.
Under the stipulations of the "family compact," France and
Spain later were allied for the purpose of checking the pretensions of Great Britain to the mastery of the seas and to colonial
supremacy in America. Under the magical leadership of the
elder Pitt, the navy of Great Britain not only swept every fleet
before it, but threatened wholly to destroy the naval power of
France and Spain and capture the maritime commerce of both
nations. Canada was soon in the hands of the victors. The
passes of the Alleghanies were filled with the colonial troops,
among whom was the youthful George Washington, learning his
first lessons of war. New Orleans was threatened from the
gulf; and had the war continued would likewise have fallen to
the prowess of the English fleets. It was a time to make heroic
efforts, even though the cost was an almost limitless expenditure
of money and sacrifice of human blood. D'Kerlerec seems to
have realized not only the imminency of the danger to the Mississippi valley, but the crushing effect of its loss upon the commercial and naval strength of France. He therefore spent
immense sums to fortify and equip every post along the Mississippi. Why not, when such a course was prudent, consistent
and necessary, so far as he could surmise, to maintain French
interests along that river? Fort Chartres was the French outpost
to the north on the Mississippi. Upon it would fall the first blow,
should the English gain the mastery of Canada or succeed in
penetrating westward through the notches of the Alleghanies. It
would seem that a prudent officer, with the glory of France warm
in his heart, could not do otherwise, under the burning impulses
of loyalty, than make every effort to meet his country's foe with
bristling cannon over adamantine walls. Nor could he watch
where all the money went. He must trust subordinates. The
lilies of France—the memorable tides of history, streaming back
a thousand years—could not be weighed in the balance with the

sordid counting of a few miserable livres or the shedding of loyal, volunteer blood. He spent the money necessary to protect his country's honor—reared impregnable walls, mounted with impassioned cannon, and heard thereby the silver voice of his own patriotism in approval. But what did he receive in return? The slander of associates, the calumny of rivals, the ingratitude of his king, the pitiless walls of the Bastile, the ignominious brand of the criminal. No wonder he grieved at the glaring injustice and pined under the displeasure of the French court. Rascals do not feel such stings; the deliberate criminal is proof against both ingratitude and injustice. The honest, the patriotic, are killed by such blows, and thus in all probability died Governor D'Kerlerec.

When the French were driven down the Ohio river from Fort Duquesne (Pittsburg) in 1758, they were commanded by Capt. Charles D'Aubry, who had gone there from the Illinois country with a detachment of French and Indians to assist in repelling the English. Passing down the beautiful Ohio, he stopped about thirty-five miles from its mouth, where, on the north bank, he built Fort Massac, named in honor of the young officer left there in command with one hundred men. D'Aubry continued on down the Ohio, and then up the Mississippi to Fort Chartres, whence he had gone. Under the terms of the treaty of peace in 1763, both forts—Massac and Chartres—were turned over to the British. Maj. Arthur Loftus of the Twenty-second English regiment, was sent up the Mississippi from Pensacola to take military possession of the post of Fort Chartres. He started in February, 1764, with a force of over three hundred men and a considerable number of women and children, all loaded in ten heavy boats and two pirogues; but when opposite Davion Bluff was attacked from both sides of the river by the Indians and about a dozen of his men were killed and wounded. Presuming that the French were responsible for this attack, Major Loftus returned to New Orleans, but was emphatically informed by D'Abbadie that the French were in no way responsible for the outrage. A little later, another attempt made by the English under the command of Captain Pittman to ascend the Mississippi to take possession of the French posts was prudently checked at New Orleans, owing to the threatening aspect of the Indians along the Mississippi. They were still the friends of the French, and could not be so soon reconciled to their new masters. Maj. Robert Farmer, of the Thirty-fourth English regiment, started a little later with the same object in view; but he also stopped owing to the threats of the Indians.

This persistent hostility of the savages along the Mississippi and in the Illinois country at last became unbearable. In December, 1765, a force was again sent up the river under Major Farmer sufficient to withstand any attack from the Indians; but Fort Chartres was already in the possession of the English. In the autumn of 1765, Capt. Thomas Sterling descended the Ohio from Fort Pitt with over one hundred soldiers of the Forty-second regiment, sailed up the Mississippi to Fort Chartres, and took possession of that important stronghold. This possession did not quiet the Indians; whereupon it was resolved to remove all the French officers in the Illinois country and replace them with those of the British army. An expedition sent down the Ohio and up the Mississippi to Kaskaskia under the command of Lieutenant Fraser, was too weak to effect this object, the commander being glad to escape with his life and in disguise down the Mississippi to New Orleans. At this time the famous Ottawa chief, Pontiac, was encamped near Fort Chartres with about four hundred warriors. He called upon St. Ange D'Bellerive, then in command of the fort, and requested an alliance of the French and the Indians against the English, but was prudently evaded by that officer, because peace existed between the two countries. In the spring of 1765, Col. George Croghan sailed down the Ohio from Pittsburg with a small force of Frenchmen and Indians. While at the "Old Shawanee Village," a few miles below the mouth of the Wabash, they were attacked by a body of Mascoutins and Kickapoos and several were killed and the others taken prisoners. They were conveyed to the present Vincennes, and thence to Fort Ouatanon near the present Lafayette, Ind., where Croghan was released through the influences of the French residents there, an act which should have been performed by the French at Vincennes. Without going to Fort Chartres, as he had originally intended, Croghan contented himself with securing the friendship of the Indians in what is now northern Indiana and southern Michigan, among whom was Pontiac. As the conciliation of the savages was the paramount object of these efforts of the English, they were given up when that finality was reached. Captain St. Ange gracefully surrendered Fort Chartres; but not wishing to become an English subject, retired across the river to the present St. Louis, where he still might witness the tri-color of France flying proudly in the air.

It was during 1765 that the exiled Acadians, driven from their homes in Nova Scotia, came to the hospitable lands of Louisiana to begin anew the struggle of life. In that year, prior to the middle of May, there arrived of them about six hundred and fifty men, women and children, in some instances with broken family groups and all poverty stricken and almost helpless. But it was realized that they must be provided for. In their veins flowed the blood of France and in their hearts were the precious memories of ancestral and national pride. The acting governor gave orders that for some weeks they should draw from the military stores the same rations drawn by the soldiers. They were assigned a fine stretch of land along the western bank of the Mississippi in the district of the Attakapas and Opelousas, where the extraordinary fertility of the soil promised abundance to the gardener or other agriculturalist. Here they built their rude houses and formed their vine-clad homes. Early the next year, over two hundred more arrived and joined their friends along the Mississippi. Soon they were all comfortably homed from a point below Baton Rouge upward to Pointe Coupée on a tract which from that day to this has been called the "Acadian Coast." Their thriftiness enabled them soon to forget the distresses of their inhuman exile. They were intelligent, moral, and industrious; and from them have sprung some of the proudest and wealthiest families of the Pelican State.

An account of the western country, written by Le Page du Pratz previous to the Seven Years' War of 1755–62, contains a singularly strong and correct view of the importance of the Kaskaskia region. The account was first published in 1758, before the results of that war had been reached. If the reader will recollect that there were no railways then, and that navigable water courses into the heart of the continent were all important, the force of the following observations will be recognized: "The most important place in this country, and perhaps in all North America, is at the forks of the Mississippi, where the Ohio falls into that river, which like another ocean is the general receptacle of all the rivers that water the interior parts of that vast continent. Here those large and navigable rivers, the Ohio River of the Cherokees (Tennessee), Wabache, Illinois, Missouri and Mississippi, besides many others which spread over the whole continent from the Apalachian mountains to the mountains of New Mexico, upwards of one thousand miles, all meet together at this spot. . . . In short, this place is the center of that vast continent and of all the nations in it, and seems to be intended by nature to command them both; for which reason it ought no

I—15

longer to be neglected by Britain. . . . The Canadians
who are numerous in Louisiana are most of them at the Illinois.
. . . They bring their wives with them or marry the French
or India women. The ladies even venture to make this long and
painful voyage from Canada, in order to end their days in a
country which the Canadians look upon as a terrestrial paradise.
It is this that has made the French undergo so many long and
perilous voyages to North America, upwards of two thousand
miles, . . . in order to get to this settlement of the Illinois,
which is nigh the forks of the Mississippi, the most important
place in all the inland parts of North America, to which these
French will sooner or later remove from Canada and there erect
another Montreal that will be much more dangerous and prejudicial to us than ever the other in Canada was. They will here be
in the midst of all their old friends and allies and much more convenient to carry on a trade with them, to spirit them up against
the English, &c., than ever they were at Montreal. To this settlement, where they likewise are not without good hopes of finding
mines, the French will forever be removing as long as any of
them are left in Canada. . . . The great river Missouri
which runs to the northwest parts of New Mexico, much farther
than we have any good accounts of that continent. . . .
affords the most extensive navigation of any river we know; so
that it may justly be compared to an inland sea, which spreads
over nine-tenths of all the continent of North America; all of
which the French pretend to lay claim to for no other reason but
because they were possessed of a petty settlement at the mouth
of that river (the Mississippi). . . . The hills on the west
side of the Mississippi are generally suspected to contain mines,
as well as the mountains of New Mexico, of which they are a
continuation. But the fertile plains of Louisiana are perhaps
more valuable than all the mines of Mexico, which there would
be no doubt of if they were duly cultivated. They will breed
and maintain ten times as many people and supply them with
many more necessaries and articles of trade and navigation than
the richest mines of Peru."*

This was a remarkably correct view of the importance of the
western country—Louisiana Province. The vast interior from
the Alleghanies to the Rockies, when densely populated, must
send its immense commerce down the Missouri, the upper Mississippi, the Ohio and its branches (the Tennessee, Cumberland and

*Le Page du Pratz.

Wabash), to the central point on the Mississippi from the Missouri to the Ohio. This spot was pre-eminently the commercial heart of the continent; and had not railways arrived on the scene to destroy all calculations, this would have become the most important business point in all the world. Had the genius of man not devised railways, the banks of all the large rivers would now be occupied by continuous towns; and what would now be the extent of the river commerce? Figures are worse than useless—they are confounded. No, the writer above, reasoning from the wisdom of that day, was wholly correct: so was Governor D'Kerlerec, who built Fort Chartres on such a grand scale to withstand the probable attacks of the English, advancing through the notches of the Alleghanies or westward on the blue and billowy waters of the Great Lakes.

It cannot be said that Louis XIV was an enthusiastic advocate of American exploration and discovery. He was willing that such should be carried on, and that France should get the benefit of it, but did not employ heroic measures nor spend any large sums of French revenue to found colonies in the New World. At all times when Louisiana was under the direct rule of the French government, the colonies were permitted to languish, suffer and take care of themselves. The heroic La Salle received little assistance from him. Had it not been for the jealousy of France at the threatened encroachments of the Spanish and the English up and along the Mississippi river, the French government would have placidly permitted individual enterprise alone to colonize the valley of that stream and its affluents. What set a spur in the ribs of his Most Christian Majesty, was the report that an expedition was forming in England to establish a settlement on the Mississippi near its mouth. A fleet was hurriedly prepared under D'Iberville and dispatched, with what result is known to the world. On the 8th of April, 1699, the French Minister of Marine wrote as follows: "The King does not intend at present to form an establishment at the mouth of the Mississippi, but only to complete the discovery in order to hinder the English from taking possession there." He further stated that the king did not think the discoveries of the Canadians in the western parts of America would prove of much value to France, unless gold or silver mines should be discovered. Such mines were soon reported to exist. This information was part of the inducement under which Louis XIV permitted La Salle to make his sacrifices; the other inducements were pearls and buffalo wool.

Perhaps humanity never suffered more than did the unfortunate people who were induced to come to the mouth of the Mississippi with D'Iberville—all for the purpose of cementing the claims of France to that river and keeping the Spanish and the English out. And the trials continued until Crozat made some improvement in 1713–17. The real relief arrived with the ships of the Western Company from 1717 to 1732. Prior to 1713, the real bone and sinew of the Louisiana colony came from Canada—up the Great Lakes and down the rushing Mississippi. La Salle at his own expense and the missionaries at their own risks had settled the Illinois country and made it "a terrestrial paradise." Hundreds of French Canadians, accompanied by their wives and children, risked the hardships of the journey and the dangers from hostile savages, to reach this far-famed land, the fertility and richness of which they had heard so much. Many came down the mighty Mississippi to swell the numbers and the courage of the settlement at the mouth of the river. They knew the country, knew the Indians, knew how to make a living, and taught the green settlers at Biloxi, Mobile and New Orleans how to survive in spite of the neglect of the French government. These Canadians did more than France did to make the colony at the mouth of the river a permanent one. Crozat would have done more for the colonists had he taken personal supervision of affairs. He soon found that government at long range was not practical nor successful. Had he lived in Louisiana he would certainly have seen that, if he had done nothing else for the colony than to sell the ship-load of slaves, which he was permitted to sell annually, he could have easily maintained his colony, and probably saved his own private fortune.

The Western Company firmly established the colony, but after 1732, when the government of France again assumed the reins, affairs were loose and uncertain. But the colony now could take care of itself and did so. Under the teachings principally of the Canadians, they had learned how to live from the resources of the country. The first colonists at Biloxi were ignorant, indolent or wicked enough not to be able to maintain themselves from their gardens, at least in part; but sat down and waited for provisions, while they chewed the cud of discontent and found it contained very little nourishment. If the soil was bad where the fort stood, that structure should have been built a little higher up where the black alluvial land lay, and where a German could have sustained himself the year round on a tract one hundred feet square. After 1732 the settlers found they could live from their gardens, the chase, by traffic, etc. They were now independent of the government so far as a livelihood was concerned, and doubtless the latter was heartily glad of it. But the officials were high-priced, and the expense was wormwood on the honied tongue of the French monarch. The building of Fort Chartres was regarded as a piece of almost criminal uselessness, though an act of the highest wisdom, from the light then shining in the world. The extravagance of the French nobility, and the folly of many of the European wars, had much to do with the charges of defalcation in Louisiana. The views of the French monarch concerning Louisiana seemed like those of the Indians mentioned by Father Poisson, missionary to the Arkansas nation in 1728-9, "They gave nothing for nothing." Louis XV wanted a revenue—wanted it or wanted no further outlay. The prodigality and splendor of his court must not be dimmed by a thought of the necessities and wretchedness in America.

The Jesuits were expelled from Louisiana by the French in 1764, the year all the territory east of the Mississippi passed to the English as a result of the Seven Years' War. All the missionaries were obliged to leave the territory west of the river as well as east of it. Owing to the apathy of both the Indians and the French, Father Carette had left the Illinois country some time before. There was no longer any chapel in the fort (Chartres)—. no place to say mass except in the dining room where the commandant took his meals. There bad language prevailed; nothing was sacred. While an attempt was made to hold service, a domestic chicken flew in and upset the chalice; whereupon an Indian present exclaimed, "Ah! behold the shop of the good God thrown down." So Father Carette became tired of his well-doing and departed from the wicked post. The good fathers at Natchitoches, the Arkansas and New Orleans were compelled to quit the country. The decree of condemnation against the Jesuits was, 1st, that they did not take care of their missions; 2d, that they cared only for their estates; 3d, and that they were usurpers of the vicariate-general for New Orleans. All these charges were afterward disproved. Notwithstanding the injustice of the decree and the unquestionable outrage and manifest persecution of the act, all their church property was taken from them and sold for the benefit of the king. Nay, even the personal property of the Fathers was seized and sold. Slaves, cattle, sacred pictures, furniture, provisions, religious vessels and vestments—all were "unjustly seized, confiscated and sold by the French government *after* the cession of the country to England." Forty-eight negroes belonging to the Jesuits of Kaskaskia and Saint Genevieve were confiscated and shipped down the river to New Orleans for conveyance to France. They set out from Fort Chartres November 24, 1764, and were in charge of a squad of French soldiers. At the same time there went down twenty Englishmen who had been captured in the West by the Indians and the French. At New Orleans the Jesuits were shown scant consideration by the French officials; but the Capuchin Fathers there, be it said to their credit, made their unfortunate rivals as comfortable as possible. The expulsion was an undoubted act of absolute persecution. The good Fathers who had done so much for the cause of France, as well as for the cause of humanity, in the inhospitable wilderness of America through the trying and dangerous years of exploration and discovery, were now wronged, persecuted and exiled. The act savors in inhumanity of the exile of the Acadians, and can have no justification in the light of human advancement and civilization.

After the expulsion of the Jesuits and the arrival of the English garrison at Fort Chartres, the cemetery at Kaskaskia was used as a garden and the chapel as a store-house. They rented them from Jean Baptiste Bauvais, "who under the decree of confiscation and the contract of sale and purchase of the property was obliged to demolish the chapel and leave its site and that of the cemetery uncultivated under the debris." Bauvais claimed that the executor of the decree sold the property to him. "By what right?" asks Father Meurin in 1768. "The presses used for the vestments and sacred vessels are now used in his apartments, as well as the altar-cruets and the floor, etc." Father Meurin ministered to Kaskaskia and Saint Genevieve at this period. Though France, Spain, Portugal and Prussia had expelled the Jesuits, the English had not done so, and hence Father Meurin had come to this post. But the English did not favor the Jesuits; they merely tolerated them. "Since the English have taken possession of this country, there has been as yet no procession of the blessed sacraments (there being on the west side of the Mississippi French, Spanish and English). This year, at the request of the inhabitants, I asked Messieurs, the commandants, to allow the militia to turn out under arms, as is the custom among Roman Catholics, to escort the blessed sacrament. This they refused. The weather was not settled; I was indisposed and fatigued, through having had a procession very early on the other side at Sainte Genevieve. Here I had one only in the church and likewise on the day of the octave."

Concerning Saint Genevieve, Father Francois Philibert Watrin wrote as follows in 1764: "Fifteen years ago, at a league from the old village on the other bank of the Mississippi, there was established a new village under the name Sainte Genevieve. Then the Curé of Cascakias found himself obliged to go there to administer the sacraments, at least to the sick; and when the new inhabitants saw their houses multiplying, they asked to have a church built there. This being granted them, the journeys of the missionary became still more frequent, because he thought that he ought then to yield himself still more to the willingness of his new parishioners and to their needs. However, in order to go to this new church he must cross the Mississippi, which in this place is three-eights of a league wide. He sometimes had to trust himself to a slave who alone guided the canoe: it was necessary in fine to expose himself to the danger of perishing, if in the middle of the river they had been overtaken by a violent storm. None of all these inconveniences ever prevented the Curé of Cascakias from going to Sainte Genevieve when charity called him thither, and he was always charged with this care until means were found to place at Sainte Genevieve a special Curé, which occurred only a few years ago, when the inhabitants of the place built a house for the pastor."*

Father Vivier seemed to have had a very high opinion of the country west of the Mississippi, not merely on account of its natural resources, but as well on account of its strategic advantages. He wrote in 1750, "For the rest, this country (the Illinois) is of far greater importance than is imagined. Through its position alone, it deserves that France should spare nothing to retain it. It is true that it has not enriched the king's coffers and that convoys to and fro are costly; but it is none the less true that the tranquillity of Canada and the safety of the entire lower part of the colony depend upon it. Assuredly, without this post (Fort Chartres) there would be no communication of land between Louisiana and Canada. There is another consideration: Several regions of the same Canada and all those on the lower part of the river would be deprived of the provisions they obtain from the Illinois, which are often a great resource to them. By founding a solid establishment here (in the Illinois country), prepared to meet all these troubles, the king would secure the possession of the most extensive and the finest country in North America." In the light of subsequent events how true was the view of Father

---

* Thwaites's reissue of the Jesuit Relations and other Documents.

Vivier. But he was not the only Frenchman who saw the immense possibilities of the western country. Governor Kerlerac realized the vast importance to France of not only holding but of materially strengthening the Illinois country; he therefore made Fort Chartres the strongest fort in the Mississippi valley, but was disgraced for this most proper and loyal act.

"On the river Marameg on the west side of the Mississippi they found those mines that gave rise to the Mississippi scheme in 1719. In 1742, when John Howard, Sallee and others were sent from Virginia to view those countries, they were made prisoners by the French, who came from a settlement they had on an island in the Mississippi a little above the Ohio, where they made salt, lead, etc., and went from thence to New Orleans in a fleet of boats and canoes guarded by a large armed schooner."*

In 1708 Nicolas de la Salle reported that there were in Louisiana 122 persons at the garrison—men, boys and priests; 77 outside inhabitants, men, women and children; and 80 Indian slaves. It is uncertain whether these included the few at Natchitoches, the Arkansas and the Illinois, but probably not, as the numbers at those places could not have been known to him. In 1712 there were 400 persons and 20 negroes in the colony—reported to be. At the time L'Epinay succeeded Cadillac in March, 1717, there were said to be present 700 persons, including negroes, but not including Indians. In 1721 there were 5,420 persons in all Louisiana, of whom about 600 were colored. According to La Harpe there were in the colony in 1724, 5,000 whites and 3,000 blacks. In 1732 the Company of the Indies reported 5,000 whites and 2,000 blacks in Louisiana. In 1745 they were said to number 6,020, of whom a few less than 4,000 were white. At no time was an exact enumeration made of the inhabitants of the whole colony. Estimates, of course, varied, so that the above figures must be received with some grains of allowance; still, they are no doubt approximately correct. Every ship that arrived or departed, changed the population, because, while numbers came from France, other numbers and their slaves in some cases returned to the mother country. There will be noticed two important periods of growth: During the Crozat administration, and during the early part of the government of the Western Company—before the failure and flight of Mr. Law. From 1721 to 1732 there was an actual decrease.

*Report of the Government of Virginia.

	Est. 1769.	1785.	1788.	1799.
New Orleans	3,190	4,980	5,338	
Bayou St. John and Gentilly	307	678	772	
Balize to the city	570	2,100	2,378	
At the Terre aux Boeufs	...	576	661	
Barataria	...	...	40	
Tchoupitoulas	4,192	7,046	7,589	
Parish of St. Charles	639	1,903	2,381	
St. John the Baptist	544	1,300	1,368	
St. James	...	1,332	1,559	
Lafourche	267	646	1,164	
Lafourche, interior	...	352	1,500	
Iberville	376	673	944	
Pointe Coupée	783	1,521	2,004	
Opelousas	...	1,211	1,985	
Attakapas	409	1,070	2,541	
New Iberia	...	125	190	
Ouachita	110	207	232	
Rapides	47	88	147	
Avoyelles	314	287	209	
Natchitoches	811	756	1,021	
Arkansas	88	196	119	
St. Genevieve	...	594	896	949
St. Louis	891	897	1,197	925
Manshac	...	77	284	
Galveston	...	242	268	
Baton Rouge	...	270	682	
Feliciana	...	...	730	
Natchez	...	1,550	2,679	
Mobile	...	746	1,468	
Carondelet	...	...	...	184
St. Charles	...	...	...	875
St. Fernando	...	...	...	276
Marais des Liards	...	...	...	376
Maramec	...	...	...	115
St. Andrew	...	...	...	393
New Bourbon	...	...	...	560
Cape Girardeau	...	...	...	521
New Madrid	...	...	...	782
Little Meadows	...	...	...	72
Totals	14,238	31,433	42,346	6,028

CHAPTER VII

D'Ulloa and O'Reilly

IN SUCCESSION the golden opportunity of possessing the whole of the Mississippi basin was presented to Spain, France and Great Britain and in turn was lost to each through its own misconduct and blindness. Dazzled with the gold of Peru and Mexico, Spain was unable to descend from her dizzy dreams of wealth to the exacting experiences and expenditures of colonization in a purely agricultural country; and therefore took no steps whatever to settle her subjects along the banks of the "great river." Her daring navigators led the way to the Gulf, exploring the whole of its treacherous coast and ceremoniously took possession of the same and of the lower Mississippi river; but the Spanish government made no effort to acquire permanently this invaluable possession. After the Spanish abandonment the opportunity of securing the wonderful Mississippi basin remained open to any nation for more than a century; or until France, actuated more by international jealousy than by praiseworthy enterprise, permitted her voyageurs and explorers, mainly at their own expense, to re-discover the Mississippi, and thus attach that vast and marvelous basin to the French American possessions.

After thus acquiring the territory, it may even be admitted that France did all that was necessary to do to hold it, and still it may be far from admitting that she did all that she should have done. As in the case of Spain, blindness lost her the Mississippi basin; so in the case of France, indifference lost her the same glorious possession. Louis XIV did, or perhaps permitted his cabinet to do, barely all that was necessary to hold the whole of the Mississippi valley, except possibly the upper Ohio basin; and his boyish successor, Louis XV, or the Regency, endeavored to pursue the same course, and for many years succeeded, more by reason of good luck than by ability and fitness to wage war and resist attack. France was almost bankrupt when Louis XIV passed from the earthly stage of action ; and no wonder little had been done for the poor colonists of Louisiana. The government had been obliged to borrow money at four hundred per cent, was in debt two thousand four hundred millions of livres at the time of his death in 1715, and three thousand millions a few years later, and taxation had become something crushing and frightful. Meanwhile, the splendors of the court of Versailles had dazzled all of Europe, and are even imitated to this day by all civilized countries. The Mississippi Scheme still further burdened the French people with vexation and debt.

When at last Louis XV took the reins, it soon seemed that the devil himself had broken loose in that kingdom. The whims of the young king's mistresses regulated the national and colonial policies. Imbecile courtiers and designing prelates occupied the principal offices and shaped the destinies of the commonwealth. Madam D'Chotearoux, the king's paramour, became the supreme ruler; and was succeeded by Madam D'Pompadour, another wanton, who had no eyes nor ears for the suffering colonists of Louisiana. Under their dictum Fleury and Choiseul were the only prime ministers who accomplished anything of consequence for France or for Louisiana. The galling taxation and the wicked extravagance of the Versailles court were the twin evils that crushed and humiliated France and prevented the much-needed assistance and attention from being extended to Louisiana. Louis XV at first became "the well beloved," because he permitted everything to be ruled by the devil, and he himself appeared to enjoy the society of that mythical individual. Thus it may be said humorously and to some extent literally that Louisiana was between the devil (France) and the deep sea (England). In fact it is not too much to say that Vice became the actual ruler of France, and that the rule was extended to Louisiana. Defeat in war and dishonor in both war and peace, bowed the heads of all right-minded Frenchmen with shame. All resulted from the weakness, profligacy and licentiousness of the king and his butterfly and brilliant court. This ephemeral glitter, extravagance and wickedness were transferred in modified form to the province of Louisiana. The deliberate malfeasance and corruption of the colonial officials led to their continuous and outrageous quarrels to see which should get the lion's share of the spoils. Thus the burden fell like a curse on the colonists of Louisiana; but all was

accompanied with the soft and entrancing manners and the
knightly bearing and radiance of the courtiers and nobles—exotics
that had no proper place in the primitive soil of the colonies,
because the worm of corruption was gnawing industriously at the
roots and contaminating the virgin earth. Even the "family
compact," which was occasioned by the jealousy of France and
Spain for Great Britain, did not avail when the crisis came,
because England obtained all east of the Mississippi and Spain
all west of that river; while France was left to mourn through all
time for the severest loss that ever fell to the lot of that wonderful
people.

It will now be seen how England, influenced by both blindness
and indifference, lost her American colonies—lost the greatest
opportunity ever offered to her political and territorial development. No one doubts that had the English American colonists
been treated on terms of equality with the residents of England
proper, they would have remained faithful and loyal subjects of
King George III, just as Canada, though almost wholly French,
has remained to this day. Under this probability what a vast field
is offered to conjecture and fancy! The stupidity, blindness and
ill-treatment of the English king and his cabinet alone severed
from the royal crown the whole of the present United States;
because those offences led to the insult, oppression and alienation
of the colonists. Had this course not been taken; had the colonists been treated with fairness and honor, and as the equals of
their brothers, the residents of fair Albion's isle; and had such
kind treatment been continued as the toiling years crawled by,
all of North America above Mexico, and perhaps both Mexico
and Central America, would today be willingly and proudly flying
the glittering Cross of St. George. This country would have
become the seat of the English kings and of the British nobility;
and Great Britain, instead of now being a decadent nation, would
be safe in the Western Hemisphere from her ancient and implacable rivals, and would be like Rome was at the summit of her
splendor—the undoubted and undisputed Mistress of the World.
While there may have been some excuse for the blindness of
Spain and the indifference of France, there was none whatever
for the ill-treatment by England under George III. His course
was that of the spendthrift who threw away his patrimony without hope of relief; and was worse than that of the Prodigal Son,
because he had no kind old father to forgive his wrong-doings,
receive him again to his bosom, and kill for him the fatted calf.
The colonies were gone forever.

The colony of Louisiana had been maintained by France with the principal, perhaps the sole, object of keeping the Spanish and the English out of the Mississippi valley. Louis XIV had hurriedly sent D'Iberville there in 1798, and none too soon, in order to forestall the ships of both of the other countries. Only sufficient colonists and means were sent out from time to time to maintain his frail tenure to the soil, because the expense was large and the revenue nothing. Stimulated with the hope of acquiring great wealth, either from the mines or from the Indian and Spanish trade, Crozat took the colony, but lost a fortune and retired from sight. The Western Company and its successor, the Company of the Indies, did no better, but sank 20,000,000 of livres ($3,700,000) in fourteen years in a vain attempt to place the colony on a profit-paying basis. Afterward, the colony was maintained at the expense of the government, but no returns rewarded the outlays. It is safe to say that France alone, from first to last, spent 50,000,000 of livres ($9,250,000) to sustain the colony. The court of Louis XV, plunged as it was in extravagance and licentiousness, had become weary with carrying this load; but realizing its ultimate value, had clung to it, hoping that in time all the outlay would come back with profits added, and hoping also that the ancient enemy, England, would thus be kept confined to the Atlantic coast.

But the Seven Years' War (1755 to 1762) instantly changed this panorama of events. France became deeply indebted to Spain for assistance, and besides had lost all of her American possessions east of the Mississippi to England. The latter now possessed much of what France had wrested from the savages through many years of untold dangers and hardships, and stood on the left bank of the Mississippi with bristling bayonets and tawny cannons. France was in no condition, nor was she likely to be for many years to come, to defend the remainder of the colony—that portion west of the river. Her old, cherished, and warlike scheme of a line of impregnable forts stretching from Canada to New Orleans, was now dissolved in a cloud of mist. The vast empire of the interior, peopled with French subjects and dominated by the French cabinet, was now a dream of the past, never to be realized in actuality. The territory west of the river was certain to become the prey of England at the outbreak of the first war. The colony had always been a burden, and was likely to be so for many years to come. Now was the time to turn it over to Spain to repay her for her losses during the Seven Years' War. France thus had every reason to get rid of the colony, and none whatever under the circumstances to retain it. But there is evidence to prove that Spain was not anxious to take the new Louisiana, either in payment for the French obligations, or upon any terms. She had had her own experiences with expensive and rebellious colonies. She saw the danger from the proximity of the English across the river, but finally consented to take it. It is evident that one of the conditions of transfer was that France should re-acquire the colony, either upon her own demand, or upon the request of Spain. The latter found no occasion to make such a request, but the former did find occasion to make such a demand in 1800.

Prior to the Seven Years' War, the Province of Louisiana east of the Mississippi extended on the Gulf eastward to the river Perdido, and farther north to an indefinite and undetermined distance eastward of the Mississippi. By provisional treaty dated at Fontainebleau, November 3, 1762, all of Louisiana Province east of the Mississippi, except the Island of New Orleans, was ceded by France to England; and at the same time and place all of the territory possessed by Spain east of the Mississippi was likewise ceded to England. These treaties were duly ratified by the three governments, respectively (Spain, France and Great Britain), and hence date from November 3, 1762. On the same day (November 3), by secret treaty and wholly unknown to England, France ceded the remainder of Louisiana Province to Spain, i. e., all of Louisiana west of the Mississippi and the Island of New Orleans east of that river. Neither England nor the colonists knew anything of this secret treaty until about a year afterward.*

Did France cede Louisiana to Spain because she felt herself unable to retain it—because she saw that the whole of it was destined at no distant day to pass to Great Britain, and wished to throw the responsibility of its retention upon Spain; or was it transferred to the latter, as alleged, to recompense her for losses in that war? There can be no doubt that had England followed the advice of Pitt and now pressed France to the utmost, when

---

* Some writers in explaining the provisions of these treaties, insist on placing the cart before the horse—on endeavoring to make it appear that France first, by the secret treaty of November 3, ceded all of French Louisiana (east to the Perdido on the south and far east of the Mississippi on the north), to Spain; and then on the same day ceded the same territory east of the Mississippi to Great Britain. France could not possibly have done this. France and Spain on one side ceded to England all they, or either of them, possessed east of the Mississippi except the Island of New Orleans. This was done openly, within the knowledge of the three governments. Therefore, France could not, on the same day, have secretly ceded to Spain that portion of French Louisiana east of the Mississippi, when Spain already knew that such tract had just been ceded to Great Britain.

the chance of doing so was open, all the remainder of Louisiana could have been acquired by Great Britain. The English colonies alone had ten times the fighting strength of the French colonies. After England should be in possession of all the country east of the Mississippi, it would require only the pretense of another war to secure all the country west of that river to the Rocky mountains or to the Pacific ocean. There is evidence to prove that the French cabinet took this view, and hence that it was determined to alienate Louisiana to Spain before England could take possession of it under any pretext. It would seem that the transfer of Louisiana from France to Spain was not made in good faith, because the latter was under some sort of an agreement to return it to the former upon demand, as was actually done in 1800, when Napoleon required it. Thus it would appear that the transfer was made to escape the clutches of England. But Spain had also just been at war with England, although it was well known to the latter that she had been so because of the requirements of the "family compact." However, the view is generally taken, and is usually allowed, that France made the transfer to Spain to reimburse her for the losses she had sustained in Florida and elsewhere.

It was a bitter experience for the French to give up to England even that portion of Louisiana east of the Mississippi, but they did so upon the orders of the king. Thus the west side of that river received a large influx of settlers—those who came from the east side, when England took possession of that portion of the province. Many of these people made great sacrifices to do this, but they loved the tri-color of France and preferred to make the change, rather than remain within the domain of England. For the first time British vessels now came up the mighty Mississippi, and the redcoats began to be seen at the posts on the east side of the river. This was wormwood to the French, but could not be helped. All who went to the west side of the Mississippi, including the Indian tribes, were given liberal grants of land by the French government. It was in June, 1763, that D'Abbadie arrived to succeed D'Kerlerec as governor of the Province of Louisiana.

From this time forward, the term "Louisiana" was applied to the country west of the Mississippi only, but included the Island of New Orleans on the east side. By agreement between France and Spain, the alienation of Louisiana by the former to the latter was kept from the knowledge of all the world; and the more effectually to carry into effect this agreement, the colony was left under

the government of France for a year before the order was issued
for the transfer of the offices to the representatives of Spain.
As soon as the colonists of that portion of Louisiana east of the
Mississippi became assured that they were irrevocably located
on English soil, all who did not wish to become British subjects
were permitted to sell out and leave, taking their belongings with
them. On the lower Mississippi many thus crossed to the west
side and founded Attakapas, Avoyelles, Natchitoches, and Opelousas; and on the upper course of that river others went to
St. Louis, St. Genevieve and several points that afterward became
large settlements. Soon the territory east of the Mississippi and
south of the thirty-first degree of latitude which had been acquired
by England from Spain, was constituted West Florida, and placed
under Governor George Johnston. Above the thirty-first parallel and east of the Mississippi, the country continued to be called
"Illinois," and was placed under Governor Loftus, a major of the
British army. In taking possession of this territory, England
encountered the hostility of the Indian tribes allied to the
French—were even fired upon and suffered losses of men and
munitions. In fact the Indians who were the friends of the
French, were greatly incensed at the transfer of the country to
Great Britain, and did not become reconciled to the change for
several years.

The new Louisiana, that west of the Mississippi, but including
the island of New Orleans, suffered many little vexations at the
beginning of its career. The French inhabitants east of the
river were required, against the stipulations of the treaty of Paris,
to take the oath of allegiance within three months upon pain of
not having their property protected. They were likewise prohibited from disposing of their lands until their titles thereto had
been verified, registered and approved by the British commander.
This order scared many of the French residents, who, under the
liberal colonial laws of France, had nothing to show for their
lands but their periods of occupancy, which among themselves
were regarded as sufficient titles. The English tried first to reach
the Illinois country via Canada, but the hostility of the Indians
prevented this step. They next tried to reach it by ascending the
Mississippi, but were attacked by the Indians, and hence declared
that these attacks were at the instigation of the French, which
charge was probably not correct. Major Loftus was even driven
back after having started from New Orleans. Loftus' Heights
received its name from this circumstance. About four hundred
Indians of the Taensas and Alibamons tribes passed westward

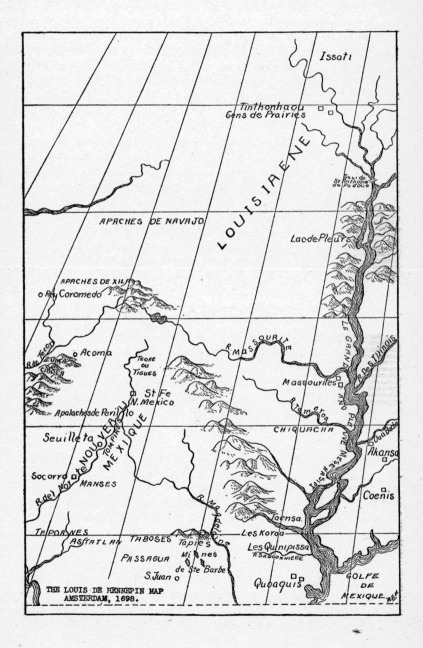

Issati

Tinthonha ou
Gens de Prairies

LOUISIAENE

APACHES DE NAVAJO

Saut de
St Antholne
de Padoue

Lac de Pleurs

APACHES DE XILA

o Rey Coromedo

R. de Tecon
o Acoma
ZUNI
CIBOLA

TEORE
OU
TIGUES

R. MASSOURITE

LE GRAND FLEUVE MISSISSIPI

R. De S. Illinois

Massourites

St Fe
N. Mexico

R. Tamaroa

Apalaches de Perillo

Seuilleta

NOUVEAU
MEXIQUE
TOM PIRES

CHIQUACHA

Oua Bache

Akansa

Socorro

R del Nort
MANSES

Coenis

R. Mo Pedrin

Taensa

TEIPOA NES
ASTATLAN
TABOSES
Tapies
Mines
de Ste Barbe

Les Koroa

Les Quinipissa
R. SABLONNIERE

PASSAGUA

S. Juan o

Quoaquis

GOLFE
DE
MEXIQUE

THE LOUIS DE HENNEPIN MAP
AMSTERDAM, 1698.

across the river, and were assigned lands by the French authorities at Bayou Lafourche.

M. D'Abbadie seems to have been an honest and conscientious man. In June, 1764, he wrote to his government of what he believed to be the causes of the serious troubles which had for many years retarded the progress of the colony. He said, "The disorder existing in the colony, and particularly in its finances, proceeds from the spirit of jobbing which has been prevalent here at all times, and which has engrossed the attention and faculties of the colonists. It began in 1737, not only on the currency of the country, but also on the bills of exchange, on the merchandise in the king's warehouses, and on everything which was susceptible of it. It is to this pursuit that the inhabitants have been addicted in preference to cultivating their lands, and to any other occupation, by which the prosperity of the colony would have been promoted. I have entirely suppressed the abuse existing in connection with the king's warehouses. . . . If the inhabitants of Louisiana had turned their industry to anything else beyond jobbing on the king's paper and merchandise, they would have found great resources in the fertility of the land and the mildness of the climate. But the facility offered by the country to live on its natural productions has created habits of laziness. The immoderate use of taffia (a kind of rum) has stupified the whole population. The vice of drunkenness has even crept into the highest ranks of society, from which, however, it has lately disappeared. Hence the spirit of insubordination and independence which has manifested itself under several administrations. . . . Notwithstanding the present tranquillity the same spirit of sedition does not the less exist in the colony. . . . The uncertainty in which I am with regard to the ultimate fate of the colony, has prevented me from resorting to extreme measures to repress such license; but it will be necessary to come to it at last to re-establish the good order which has been destroyed and to regulate the conduct and morals of the inhabitants. To reach this object, what is first to be done is to make a thorough reform in the composition of the superior council. . . . Three-fourths, at least, of the inhabitants are in a state of insolvency." There is no doubt that this language was too severe, because he called "seditious" and "insubordinate" the act of the merchants of New Orleans in complaining to the king of the wretched condition of the colony, the postponement of the withdrawal from circulation of the depreciated currency, and of the monopoly granted by D'Abbadie to a company to trade with the Indians.

I—16

In a letter dated April 21, 1764, D'Abbadie was informed by the king that Louisiana had been ceded to Spain, and copies of the act of cession and of the various acceptances accompanied the communication. He was told to turn over the Province to the accredited Spanish representatives upon the receipt of the letter, and was advised what should be done to completely carry the transfer into effect. Having fully effected the transfer, D'Abbadie was instructed to return to France to report. All papers and documents, posts or forts, and the town and island of New Orleans were to be delivered to the representatives of Spain, so far as they were necessary to the new management. All property not strictly relating to the colony was to be returned to France. If the division of the Province in 1762-3 had been a severe blow to all persons who loved Louisiana, the alienation to Spain of the remainder in 1764 completely broke their hearts. For a long time after the first rumors to that effect appeared, it could not be believed in the Province that the French government would take such a step. When the official communication was received and proclaimed in October, 1764, the consternation and despair were universal and deep-rooted. It took years to wipe out the effects of the blow—in fact the regret was never wholly assuaged.

But while the French inhabitants welcomed the British goods, they intensely regretted having to become subjects of Spain. Of French extraction and birth, and with the love of their country strong in their hearts, many of them could not become reconciled to the thought of taking the oath of allegiance to the Spanish crown. This discontent finally ripened into action. It was determined to make such representations to the French king of their sentiments of loyalty and devotion as would be likely to cause him to secure an annulment of the cession of Louisiana to Spain. A meeting was called to be held at New Orleans, and every parish in the colony was represented. It was a spontaneous outburst of loyalty to the French crown, and the best elements of the colony were present and outspoken. Here came Lafrénière, Doucet, Jean Milhet, Joseph Milhet, D'Arensbourg, Villeré, St. Lette, Pin, D'Lachaise, St. Maxent, Garic, Marquis, Boisblanc, Grand-Maison, Noyan, Massange, Lalande, Masan, Poupet, Braud, Dessales, Carrère, Kernion, Lesassier, and others, all prominent in the affairs, not only of the colony, but of France as well. Lafréniére the atorney-general, addressed the meeting at length, advocating the preparation of a petition to the French throne, praying that such an arrangement might be made as would not

243

separate the colonists from the government of France. The proposition was warmly received and accepted without a dissenting voice.

Jean Milhet was chosen to lay the petition before the king of France; and upon his arrival in Paris first secured the co-operation of the venerable D'Bienville, who had spent so many years in Louisiana and whose heart was bound up in the success and prosperity of that colony, and together they waited upon the prime minister to formally and feelingly lay their case before him. Milhet's appeal was directed to show the ultimate value of the colony to France, while D'Bienville's took more of the form of a sentimental entreaty. The Duke of Choiseul listened with grave and respectful attention, but stated that he could not change the state of the case. Upon thus hearing the doom of Louisiana pronounced, D'Bienville burst into tears, fell upon his knees, and sobbingly begged the minister "for a reconsideration of the decree against the colony." The latter was greatly moved and embraced the venerable man, now nearly eighty-six years old, and finally said with much emotion, "Gentlemen, I must put an end to this painful scene. I am deeply grieved at not being able to give you any hope. I have no hesitation in telling you that I cannot address the king on this subject, because I, myself, advised the cession of Louisiana. Is it not to your knowledge that the colony cannot continue its precarious existence, except at an enormous expense, of which France is now utterly incapable? Is it not better, then, that Louisiana should be given away to a friend and a faithful ally, than be wrested from us by an hereditary foe? Farewell, you have my best wishes. I can do no more." Thus Choiseul relinquished Louisiana in 1762–3 because he knew that France could not keep it from falling into the hands of England, just as Napoleon relinquished it forty years afterward for precisely the same reason. To maintain it against England meant the expenditure of many millions of dollars to establish powerful forts and maintain a vast army stationed along the west bank of the Mississippi. As Choiseul said, France was "utterly incapable" of this expense, and so reluctantly and tearfully, yet gladly, gave it to her "friend and faithful ally," Spain.

In 1765 Philip Aubry became governor of the colony, D'Abbadie having died in February of that year. One of his first acts was to care for the exiled Acadians who arrived by May to the number of about six hundred and fifty, many of whom were sent to the settlements of Attakapas and Opelousas. The appearance of great numbers of British troops, the many English vessels which passed up and down the river, the evident rapid work of the British commandants in taking possession of the east bank of the river, and their announced design of opening the channel through Bayou Manshac and Lakes Maurepas and Pontchartrain to the sea, were matters of great concern to Governor Aubry. Having ceded Louisiana west of the river to Spain, France, of course, felt under no obligations to strengthen the posts and the army there; nor did Spain do so, because she was not yet in possession. Thus, while the English made themselves strong and secure on the river, the colonists across on the west side realized their weakness, because they were in no way assisted in lines of defense or resistance. At Manshac the English built Fort Bute, and likewise made themselves strong at Natchez and Baton Rouge. The appearance of the English and the opening of the river were the signal for all sorts of smuggling. In fact, the introduction of English goods against the trade laws of France was almost the salvation of Louisiana, because no such relief was extended by either France or Spain to relieve the absolute needs of the suffering colonists. As a matter of fact the new order of affairs gave a great stimulus to Louisiana; it began to thrive and grow as never before. The restrictive and repressive trade laws of France were wholly disregarded, and the smugglers were welcomed.

Notwithstanding the failure of Milhet to secure for Louisiana a revocation of the act of cession to Spain, the inhabitants, owing to the failure of the latter to take possession, were impelled to the thought that for some unknown reason the transfer had been annulled. It was afterward learned that Choiseul had diplomatically prevented Milhet from reaching the ear of the king with his petition, doubtless knowing that he could accomplish nothing in that quarter. But the inhabitants continued to cling to the belief that the colony would not in the end be alienated, the wish, no doubt, being father to the thought or hope. Finally, in the summer of 1765, an official communication was received from Don Antonio D'Ulloa, dated at Havana, announcing that he would soon appear at New Orleans, pursuant to the orders on the Spanish crown, for the purpose of formally taking possession of the Province. So strong had become the belief that the act of cession would be annulled, that the citizens, upon receipt of the announcement from D'Ulloa, showed for the first time a spirit of resistance and independence. It appeared to them that as they had been practically abandoned by France, they ought to be given the privilege of saying what should be their fate and how they should be disposed of. This sentiment was still further strengthened when the entire autumn passed away without bringing D'Ulloa. "Many of the colonists adopted the conviction that the treaty of cession was nothing but a sham instrument, concealing some diplomatic maneuvering.* During the winter of 1765–6 the spirit of independence continued to grow in strength and seemingly was not checked in the least by the conservative advice of a few of the leaders of the colony.

At length D'Ulloa arrived in March, 1766, with two companies of infantry commanded by Piernas, and was given a "cold and sullen" reception. However, instead of assuming the reins at once, he announced that he intended to postpone taking possession until a sufficient force had arrived to protect and defend the inhabitants, and in the meantime visited the various posts of the colony, spending several weeks at Natchitoches and studying in detail the means of defense. Under his direction a census was taken, showing in the colony 1,893 able-bodied men, 1,044 women, 1,375 male children, and 1,240 female children, and about as many negro slaves as there were whites. D'Ulloa was a very amiable and learned man, but wholly unfitted to become the governor of a colony like Louisiana, where both insubordination and destitution were to be encountered and overcome. His salary was fixed at $6,000; that of D'Bienville had been $2,000 and that of Vaudreuil long afterward had been $10,000. He announced that he had no dealings with the supreme council, but was simply authorized to receive from Governor Aubry the colony as it then was. The refusal to recognize the council gave great umbrage to that body, which was sharply shown a little later. Under his instructions he could make no change in the colonial administration. The colony was made independent of the ministry of the Indies, but all relative thereto was required to pass through the ministry of state. Surely, nothing more could be asked.

It cannot be said that D'Ulloa, upon his arrival in New Orleans, encountered an extraordinary state of affairs. In the light of subsequent events, it is clear that the wisest course would have been to take possession positively and firmly of all the affairs of the colony. The chances are that patient, if not quiet, submission would have followed. He seems to have made the mistake of being too kind and conciliatory. No doubt this course had been recommended by the Spanish cabinet. Having received the colony from a friend and ally, Spain had no occasion to resort to

---

* Gayarre.

severe and arbitrary measures. It was presumed that the olive branch would be promptly accepted by the inhabitants. Hence, no doubt, D'Ulloa was following his instructions when he took extreme steps to gain the approval and good will of the Louisianians. But they were in just the state of mind to wholly misunderstand such a pacific policy. They were already on the point of revolting from the authority of Spain. It needed only such a mild policy to fan the fires of independence into the flame of open resistance and rebellion.

The French residents, having expressed their misgivings as to the treatment that would be accorded their discredited currency, D'Ulloa promptly and considerately bought a considerable quantity of it at the French depreciated price of seventy-five cents on the dollar, and tendered it to his soldiers in payment of their wages; but they refused to take it, nor did the act suit the inhabitants, who unreasonably demanded par. The good intentions of D'Ulloa were thus wholly misunderstood and thwarted. Under the agreement with Spain, France ordered her troops then in the colony to continue in the service of the former until the arrival of the forces of the latter; but the order was peremptorily refused by the soldiers, who declared that their time of service had expired. Trouble was also occasioned by the difference in wages paid to the French and the Spanish soldiers respectively; but this was soon adjusted. An examination of the records of Louisiana showed D'Ulloa that the colony since its establishment had been dependent upon France even for its provisions, and at all times was rent with dissensions, disorder and corruption. As this state of things did not accord with the representations of the French cabinet at the time of the cession to Spain, D'Ulloa made careful note of what he discovered. He visited all portions of the province except the Missouri region, conversed freely with the inhabitants, and studied the requirements of the colony.

Later he brought more soldiers, but still refused to take formal possession of the colony. He entered into an alliance with Aubry, under which the latter agreed to execute his orders. The French extremists made fun of this partial surrender of the colony to the representative of Spain, because they had come to believe that, owing to the mild course of D'Ulloa, they could dictate the policy of the colonial administration. They had now apparently lost sight of the great wrong alleged to have been done them in separating them from France, and were bent on something far deeper and more sweeping. Apparently, they had taken the bit in their teeth, determined to gain their independence at the first opportunity, and expected themselves to provide the opportunity. The truth is, they did not know when they were well off, or were determined to try to throw off the yoke of Spain, win their independence and take the consequences of their failure to accomplish that result. D'Ulloa had come to them with the olive branch extended, and they had not only refused to receive it; but had gone so far as to reject every pacific and reasonable proposition. Everywhere the Spaniards were derided and ridiculed. Aubry was hooted for having submitted to the dictation of D'Ulloa. The extremists, under their enthusiastic leaders, regarded the conciliatory policy of D'Ulloa as a manifestation of weakness, not only of that officer, but of the proposed Spanish administration as well. But in spite of this opposition, he went bravely along, doing the best he could under the circumstances, and under the pacific directions of his sovereign. He issued orders for the construction of forts at Bayou Manshac, on the west side of the river near Natchez, and two on Red river below the mouth of the Black. A strong detachment was also sent to Missouri.

As a matter of fact, the French inhabitants were grievously and almost criminally at fault in not promptly accepting the pacific overtures of D'Ulloa, unless they expected to gain their independence. He would have been abundantly justified in resorting to severe, if not heroic, measures to enforce the authority of Spain; but he had undoubtedly been instructed to render the transfer to Spain as agreeable as possible to the inhabitants. All the surroundings show this to have been his instructions. Spain could have had no other object than to gain the confidence and good will of her new subjects. An arbitrary and abusive policy would not only have been the height of folly, but would have been an insult to France, the friend and ally of the crown of Spain, whose subjects the Louisiana people were and had always been. Of course, it is popular in order to condone the mistake of the French residents of New Orleans, to magnify their undoubted loyalty and devotion to France and to dwell on the brutality and savagery of the second Spanish governor. But the truth demands the emphatic statement that the inhabitants were in the first instance openly hostile to Spain, that their insubordination would have been crushed by France herself, and that the failure to welcome the pacific administration of D'Ulloa was an act of blindness or independence that could have had but one outcome under the government of any European country. The wisdom of D'Ulloa's mild measures was wholly lost upon the insubordinate and independent leaders of the revolutionary movement, who should either have wholly thrown off the Spanish yoke, or placed their necks with the best grace possible within the burdensome loop.

Dating from the preliminary treaty of November 3, 1762, France endeavored to cast upon Spain the burden of sustaining Louisiana; but previous to possession being taken by the latter she advanced the amounts necessary, only, however, until 1766, at which time colonial drafts were no longer honored at the treasury of France. In May, 1766, a decree of the Spanish government opened the ports of Louisiana to the commerce of the other Spanish American colonies under severe restrictions, in order to prevent smuggling and other evasions. Corn, lumber, tobacco, rice, etc., upon which an export duty of five per cent was laid, were permitted to pass out of Louisiana in French ships, and flour, wine, fruits, etc., were permitted to pass in. Among the important conditions of the commercial decree was one that no ship should unload until a bill of lading had been signed by D'Ulloa, and until the price at which the commodity was to be sold had been defined and recorded. Merchants were required to accept the currency of the country for their merchandise, and to receive one-third of their return cargo in lumber or other colonial production. Although this order, as a whole, was fair and for the manifest benefit of the colony, it was promptly denounced by the merchants and ship-owners, who had adopted the popular fashion of opposing everything suggested under Spanish auspices. Petitions were prepared both by the merchants and by the ship-owners, remonstrating against the execution of the order; and for a time, to secure their good will, it was partially suspended.

There was never a duty, ordinance, or law laid down that did not restrict some man's business or ambition. It is the order of civilization that the good of the few must yield, if necessary, to the benefit of the many. The consumers of Louisiana were certain to be greatly benefited by these reasonable Spanish requirements; and the merchants and ship-owners could soon have shaped their businesses to the new conditions without serious loss. The temporary suspension of the decree was but another concession to the element that opposed everything Spanish. It cannot be said that the opposition was actuated by the belief that the cession would yet be annulled, because it was known that all of Louisiana east of the river was already in the possession of the British; and the continuance in the colony of D'Ulloa, the promulgation and execution of his many orders, the refusal of France to pay the current expenses of the colony, the opening of trade with the

Spanish Gulf colonies, and the actual construction of various posts and forts by the Spanish soldiers, gave ample proof that the cession was an irrevocable finality. Neither was the exceeding loyalty to France the cause of the hostility to Spain; nor the sale of the colony "like a flock of sheep" so unusual and monstrous as to kindle the fires of defiance and open resistance. In almost every war of ancient or modern times, sections of inhabited country have passed from the vanquished to the victor upon the conclusion of peace, and no agonized cry been raised of "a sale like a flock of sheep."

Almost every order or movement made by D'Ulloa was opposed, derided or thwarted. Bound by his instructions of pacification, he was not authorized to use harsh measures; but he saw that his rule had not been beneficial to the colony nor honorable to Spain. He reported all that had taken place, or had not taken place, in the colony since his arrival, to the Spanish ministry, and in September, 1766, left New Orleans and took up his abode at the Balize, where he remained during the succeeding fall and winter, leaving the colony pretty much to its own devices. Having made his report, he was simply waiting for the next step of his government, and did not care to live longer at New Orleans, where his orders were disobeyed and himself and his country ridiculed and abused. He also went there to meet his lady love, to whom he was there married in the following spring, a performance afterward complained of as of questionable legality under the rules of the Catholic church.

In March, 1767, steps were taken at the Balize by D'Ulloa to assume possession of the Province, but the next day were revoked, the whole of which proceeding kindled the ridicule of the opposition at New Orleans. In the meantime not a Spanish vessel had come to Louisiana with merchandise; all ocean traffic thus far had been done in French ships. Spain was in no hurry "to run after an onerous burden." She had agreed to accept the colony for the same reason that France wanted to get rid of it—"to prevent its being possessed by another nation." It was thought to be in less danger in the hands of Spain than in those of France; and so the latter had agreed to assume the burden of $250,000 to $300,000 per annum in order to save the colony from the clutches of England; but she refused to pay the expenses of the colony previous to the arrival of D'Ulloa.

The arrival of Jean Milhet from France late in 1767, with the final report that his mission to secure the annullment of the cession to Spain had failed, was the occasion of pronounced hostility to every attempt of Spain to govern the colony. "There seemed to be a fixed determination to construe into an offense anything that D'Ulloa could say or do."* The leaders of the opposition had been apprised of the reasons which induced, per-haps compelled, France to cede the colony to Spain, and which obliged the latter, against her will, to accept it. They now learned that the cession was irrevocable. Why then their bitter opposition? Was it because they preferred to become a colony of England rather than one of Spain? Was it because of their determination to attain their independence? Or was it because of a lack of good judgment—just as mobs are led by their enthus-iasm to follow hot-headed and eloquent captains. It would seem the two former, because it afterward became known that they opened communication with the British commander at Pensacola and tendered him the colony if he would take possession and afford them protection. There could have been no object for their course but revolution. In no way had they been oppressed by Spain; the reverse was true. Every change made, though for the general benefit, was turned to sport and mockery. Every act, public and private, of D'Ulloa was burlesqued and caricatured, and his conversations and household customs (for he had returned with his wife to New Orleans) became the object of satire and disrespect, all without the slightest justification.

But D'Ulloa was not without his supporters. All the Spanish officials—Loyola, the commissary and intendant; Navarro, the treasurer; Gayarre, the comptroller; Piernas, the commander of the small Spanish force—stood stanchly by the governor. In addition such men as Aubry, Grandpre, Grandmaison, Bellevue, Roche, St. Protais, Vaugine, D'Vezin, Maxent, D'Lachaise, Reg-gio, Dreux and others gave him their respectful consideration and moral support. By January, 1768, the transfer of possession was an accomplished fact, although Aubry still governed and the for-malities of taking possession were yet to be observed. The Span-ish flag was flying in Missouri, at the Balize, over the post opposite Natchez, and on the bank of the Manshac, at which four places forts had been built and Spanish garrisons placed. But the French flag was also kept flying over all of Louisiana, although many Spanish subjects had come in since 1763. In fact so many Spanish innovations had been introduced that Aubry wrote to France, "When Spain shall take formal possession, I shall feel

---

*Charles Gayarre.

authorized to say to Mr. D'Ulloa that I deliver into his hands a Spanish colony."

But the revolution was vigilant and undying. It assumed the form of a conspiracy to eject everything Spanish from the colony. Among them were the arch-conspirator, "the head and front of the offending," Lafrénière, the attorney-general; Foucoult, the intendant; Masan, a retired captain; Marquis, a captain; Noyan, a captain; Bienville, a lieutenant, and the nephew of Governor Bienville; Doucet, a prominent lawyer; Jean and Joseph Milhet, wealthy merchants; Boisblanc, who had been a member of the Supreme Council; Villere, commander at the German Coast; and Petit, Caresse and Poupet, prominent merchants. Soon the revolutionists met in secret to deliberate and plan their course of action against the Spanish control of the colony, and very probably to consider the question of joining the English colonies, after having first gained their independence. Neither Aubrey nor D'Ulloa knew of the existence of the secret movement until October, 1768. In the meantime the insurrectionary course had spread its roots throughout all of Louisiana. Every settlement, even as far up the river as Missouri, had been tampered with by the agents of the movement, and everywhere adherents were found, by reason mainly of misrepresentations as to the strength of the revolutionists. By pre-arrangement the guns of New Orleans were spiked on the night of October 26; and early the next day a large force of insurgents, at the head of whom was Marquis in supreme command, and Noyan and Villere, subordinates, entered the city and took possession of the public places. Aubry took immediate steps to protect D'Ulloa and Spanish interests generally. In the conference which followed, no conciliation was effected; whereupon, by the advice of Aubry, D'Ulloa and his wife went on board the Spanish frigate for security, while the Spanish officers barricaded houses and prepared to resist to the last. The intense excitement prevailing bewildered everybody. The streets were thronged with citizens crying "Vive la Roi," and attacks upon the barricades seemed imminent, but were diverted by the leaders of both factions.

At a meeting of the so-called Supreme Council, though really of the insurgent leaders, held on the 28th, a petition signed by about six hundred persons was prepared, in which were demanded the restoration of previous rights and privileges and the expulsion from the colony of D'Ulloa and the other Spanish officials. This result was accomplished by the hurried election of extra-superior members of the Council, amid the vigorous and vehement

addresses of the rebellious leaders. It was declared that D'Ulloa
had departed from the instructions of the Spanish crown by issuing orders and decrees which contravened the existing laws and
customs of the colony, though guaranteed to the inhabitants by
the act of cession. Lafrénière took the lead and prescribed the
course that should be taken, and his views were listened to with
enthusiastic attention and approbation. On the 29th about one
thousand armed insurgents, bearing a white flag, congregated on
the public square, prepared to carry into execution the provisions
of the petition which demanded the expulsion of the Spaniards.

The repeated remonstrances of Aubry were unavailing. He
indicated the consequences certain to follow the revolution; but
his remarks fell upon deaf ears, because no ears are so deaf as
those that won't hear. All the violent measures advocated by
Lafrénière were adopted, and D'Ulloa was ordered to leave Louisiana within three days.* The other Spanish officials were permitted to remain long enough to settle their affairs. On the
street it appeared that everybody was wild with enthusiasm.
Many who were perfectly willing to shout "Long live the King,"
were not at all in sympathy with the insurrectionary movement.
Many were led into the maelstrom, because the Supreme Council
apparently headed the rebellion. When so august a body sanctioned the proceedings, what could the mass of the people do but
follow where they led? Rousing acclamations and protracted
festivities crowned these extraordinary proceedings. The colony
was now in the hands of the Supreme Council; the authority even
of Aubry had vanished. The Spanish administration was wholly
uprooted and scattered to the four winds. Both sides now began
to see what was to follow, and their representatives were dispatched to France with voluminous memorials, manifestoes and
what-nots. While D'Ulloa was pained and humiliated, he saw
the coming storm and could afford to be generous. Remarkable
to say, he directed the Spanish commissary to continue to pay the
French troops. To him the revolution was but an episode, somewhat exciting, perhaps dangerous and certainly inconvenient, yet
a knot which the sword of Spain would sever without the slightest
doubt. On November 1, he departed in a French vessel for
Havana.

His expulsion was succeeded by an elaborate manifesto which
attempted to justify the revolution and recapitulated the alleged
grievances of the colonists. Almost every article of this instru-

* Charles Gayarre.

ment seems unsound and untenable. Every complaint made has a pardonable counterpart in the government of every civilized country of the present day. Almost every strike of modern times is based upon sounder justice and broader humanitarianism. The matters complained of were either trifling in the extreme or abundantly excusable from the surroundings. It is evident that the revolution was endeavoring to patch up a truce or divert the approaching hurricane. The manifesto was more of a causeless attack upon the personality of D'Ulloa than an exposition, based upon reason and fairness, of his usurpations and wrong-doings. In other respects, it is a laudatory stump-speech, delivered to the king of France, glorifying his lecherous person and his profligate court. Aubry wrote as follows to the French minister: "I was waiting only for the arrival of the Spanish troops, to deliver up the colony and to return to France to render an account of my conduct, when a general rebellion of the inhabitants of this Province against the Spanish governor and his nation, and which occurred on the 28th and 29th of October, destroyed in a moment the work of four years, and all the dispositions which I have taken on behalf of the crown of Spain. An audacious petition, insulting to the Spanish nation, rebellious against the king of France, whose orders it set at naught, and signed by six hundred planters and other inhabitants, was presented to demand D'Ulloa's expulsion."

The Germans and Acadians were prevailed upon to go to New Orleans partly upon the representation that they would be reimbursed for their Canadian bonds, and upon their arrival arms were placed in their hands, much to their surprise. The merchants of New Orleans were willingly pressed into the revolution on the ground of securing the revocation of the objectionable commercial decree. But nearly all regretted their action as soon as the rebellion had triumphed. Many of the residents were induced through fear to side temporarily with the insurgents. Lafrénière was the unquestioned leader of the revolution. Though unpolished, he possessed much persuasive power and eloquence. He it was who prepared the monster petition addressed to the throne; and he it was who swayed the proceedings of the Supreme Council and the enthusiastic assemblages of the insurrection. Previously, under Governor D'Kerlerec, he had advocated in secret the independence of the colony from France, and his intrigues then had disturbed the tranquillity of the inhabitants at a time when France and England were engaged in war. The spirit of independence breathing through all his utterances is singularly like that which at the same time was appearing in the English American colonies. He continued the same tactics under D'Abbadie, who complained to the French ministry of his revolutionary influences. In his addresses there is shown a spirit of opposition to all governmental restraint—a spirit that could have but one fate under either France or Spain, one which demanded practical independence, while requiring assistance and protection from the home government. Of course, the demands were illogical and inconsistent, because they would have made the Supreme Council superior in authority to the throne of either France or Spain.

Immediately succeeding the expulsion of D'Ulloa, the revolutionists, as before stated, prepared their defense in the form of a manifesto and forwarded it to the king of France; but in the meantime they did not delay to take other steps to complete the work of revolution. They prepared a petition addressed to the Council, now the governing body, soliciting Aubry to "invite the captain of the Spanish frigate, the Volante, to hasten his departure in the interest of public tranquillity." The prayer of the petitioners was granted, and the frigate was required to leave New Orleans. Report of what had happened at New Orleans was sent to the other settlements, and the small squads of Spanish troops agreed quietly to depart from the colony. Aubry summed up the situation admirably in a letter to the French minister: "I find myself under the sad necessity of speaking and of telling all, in spite of my reluctance to do so. The Council behaved badly. The attorney-general, Lafrénière, is one of the principal leaders. Mr. D'Ulloa committed several faults, but never perpetrated crimes, and, setting aside his rank and his character, did not deserve the treatment which he underwent. It is necessary to send here a battalion and a new council. The one to drive out of the country from ten to twelve fire-brands, who rule it as they please and are the causes of all the harm done; the other to administer justice, which is almost entirely set aside. Should this revolution produce no change in the arrangements between France and Spain in relation to this colony, would it not be proper that his Majesty should transmit his orders here as soon as possible and announce his ultimate and irrevocable will on the cession to Spain, promising pardon and oblivion, save to a few who are guilty and whom it is absolutely necessary to punish? Besides, it is probable that the guiltiest will take refuge among the English, when they shall learn of the arrival of troops. . . . Should the province remain to France, its inhabitants would be transported with joy. It would be the most agreeable news they could receive, as they generally have French hearts. But I am certain that at present they would prefer passing under the English domination than the Spanish, unless his Catholic Majesty should be disposed to grant them some privileges and advantages, to induce them to live under his flag." Thus in the opinion of Aubry himself it was "absolutely necessary to punish" some of the leaders of the revolution. He doubtless meant that the spirit of insubordination, of independence, manifested would have to be crushed by the punishment of the leaders. It is to be noted, also, that Aubry was of the opinion that the colonists would rather pass to the English than to the Spanish. This contingency had been taken into consideration by the revolutionists, but had not been carried into effect because they still hoped, if they could not gain their independence, to be retained under the flag of France, as is shown by their fulsome praises of the French king.

D'Ulloa duly reached Havana, and there found eight hundred Spanish troops on their way to New Orleans, under the command of D'Urissa, who had in his possession one million of dollars to be used in paying the expenses of Louisiana. Had this sum of money and this force reached Louisiana before the outburst of rebellion, it is probable there would have been no revolution. It required about forty days for the news to reach Spain; then a cabinet session was promptly called to consider all features of the situation, the meeting being held February 11, 1769. Among the council were men who had been, and were afterward, famous in the diplomatic contortions of Europe. All were given time to consider and were required to make their reports in writing to the minister of state, D'Grimaldi. Their opinions were submitted in March. The Duke of Alba advocated the retention of the colony in order to define the western limits of the English domain; the subjugation of the people by striking all disorders at the root; a complete change in the form of government so that future revolutions would be impossible; a reduction in the inhabited limits so that the cost of maintenance might be as light as possible; "but finally what to my judgment appears to be of more importance than all the rest, is that it be seen throughout the world and particularly in America, that the king knows and is able to repress any attempt whatever derogatory to the respect due to the royal majesty." Jaime D'Lima recommended about the same course, and favored "the most severe and rigorous punishment" for the inhabitants guilty of the revolution. He thought a thorough understanding with France should be arrived at without delay regarding all steps of the cession, and finally said, "The better to provide for the future, I recommend a stipulation by which it should be understood that France shall never cede that province, either to the English or to the colonists themselves, reserving its reversion to us, whenever France shall feel disposed to part with it." This important observation was called out by the consideration of the question whether, on the one hand, England should gain the colony, or, on the other, it should remain with either France or Spain; and if France should retain it what should be the status of Spain.*

Juan D'Arriaga recommended the retention of the province, not because it might become profitable, but because the Mississippi defined the western bounds of the English beyond cavil. He advised a suitable government for the colony, because, as D'Ulloa had said, it was "made up of all sorts of people, without fealty, without law, and without religion." He further recommended that the "most vitiated portion of the population" should be cut off and removed. The Marquis St. Juan D'Piedras Albas joined in advocating the retention of Louisiana. He thought it of "extreme importance" that Spain should keep it; that the "voluntary donation" of tne colony by France imposed upon Spain the duty of maintaining her authority there; and that the insolence of the inhabitants should be suitably resented. Miguel D'Muzquiz favored the abandonment of the colony by Spain. He gave as his reasons the conflicts that were sure to result from the free navigation of the Mississippi; the disagreements probable between the French inhabitants and the Spanish, as shown by the revolution; the enormous expenses of maintaining the colony; the additional burden of sustaining it in case of war; and that if the colony were retained by France, the Spanish province of Texas would be bounded on the east by the domain of an ally and a friend instead of a foe, such as Great Britain was. Juan Gregorio Muniain believed that Spain should take possession of the colony because the Mississippi established a definite boundary; because Louisiana could be used as a barrier to protect the commerce of Mexico; because the cultivation of wheat, etc., was sure to be of great benefit to Havana and the other Spanish Gulf cities; and because the encroachments of France upon Texas, or for that matter of England, would be wholly obviated.

---

* This suggestion may have been the germ of the stipulation, which afterward cut so important a figure, by which both France and Spain agreed never to alienate Louisiana, but which was violated by Napoleon when he ceded the province to the United States in 1803.

The Count D'Aranda, one of the foremost statesmen of Europe, favored the possession of the colony by Spain. He noted the importance of extending the Mexican boundary to the Mississippi and the value of having such a river and such a land barrier between the English colonies and Mexico. Under the supposition that Louisiana might some day become a republic, he drew a strong picture of the probable consequences to Spain and said, "The favorable circumstances in which Louisiana would then be placed, would not only increase her population, but also enlarge her limits, and transform her into a rich, flourishing and free state, in sight of our provinces, which would present the melancholy contrast of exhaustion and of the want of cultivation. From the example under their eyes, the inhabitants of our vast Mexican domains would be led to consider their utter want of commerce, the extortions of their different governors, the little esteem in which they are held, the few offices which they are permitted to fill, and would weigh the great inducement which they would have to hate still more the Spanish domination, and to think that they can brave it with more security, when they shall see that a weak province, compared with their extensive and populous country, can make good her position with impunity and secure her prosperity."

He noted that the possession by France threatened the integrity of Texas and the commerce of both Texas and Mexico; and indicated the startling possibility that should Spain fail to take the gift, Louisiana might be abandoned by France, and thus immediately become independent or fall into the hands of England. France had already signified that she was unable to sustain it, which probably meant her immediate abandonment of what she realized must soon fall into the grasp of England. What would then be the consequences should Louisiana either become independent or fall to the possession of Great Britain? Either finality meant eternal injury to the Spanish–American colonies, because the limits between Louisiana and Texas had never been defined, and England would be sure to stretch them to the utmost. So would the inhabitants of Louisiana should the colony set up a republic. Spain for her own protection should take possession, but should refrain from making the colony strong and prosperous, because to do so would be to invite attack. In other words, Louisiana should be kept weak, inconspicuous, unpopulated and barren to serve as a shield to ward off the attacks of the English on Texas and Mexico. What a prospect for the richest tract of

I—17

the same extent on the face of the globe. And yet such was the subsequent Spanish policy with Louisiana, as shown by the restrictions placed upon her, and by the refusal to permit her people to trade with the citizens of the United States. The Count D'Aranda, with all his sagacity, could not foresee the impossibility of keeping such a wonderful tract of country from being transformed into a populous empire, governed by law and blessed with liberty. He advocated immediate possession, with sufficient force to sustain Spanish authority and honor, and suggested the expulsion of the leaders of the rebellion and the confiscation of their property, the establishment of enough Spanish families there to serve as the root for a new population, the transportation out of the colony of all who were unwilling to abide by Spanish domination, the limitation of colonization, and the establishment of a chain of forts along the Mississippi about every thirty miles to emphasize the authority of Spain.

It now remained for the king himself to decide what should be done with Louisiana. D'Grimaldi, the minister of State, advocated the retention of the colony: in fact it had been chiefly through his advice that it had been accepted at the outset. He saw clearly the wisdom of possessing it, though not upon the basis of subsequent development, and added his recommendations to those of the other statesmen. The recommendations of the Council received the approval of the king, who further considered more seriously the moral effect of the revolution upon the other Spanish American colonies. The seeds of sedition and independence thus sown broadcast could not result otherwise than in a harvest of revolutionary whirlwinds, a probable consequence far more momentous than the puny rebellion itself. The king also decided that practical possession had been taken of the colony, that the inhabitants were, therefore, his subjects, and that it rested with Spain alone to retake possession and punish the heads of the conspiracy. It seemed to him that Spain should show to the world that she was fully capable of protecting her crown and of crushing any rebellion within her borders. "In accordance with these principles, his Majesty has resolved to use force to reduce the rebels to submission, and has ordered that the necessary measures to that effect be taken without delay."*

While waiting to see what would be done with the colony, and what steps would be taken in regard to the rebellion, the inhabi-

*Letter of the Marquis D'Grimaldi to the Count D'Fuentes, Spanish ambassador to the court of France.

tants of Louisiana were tortured with anxiety and misgivings. Hundreds not imbued with the principles of liberty were sorry of the course they had taken. The Spanish officers, Loyola, Gayarre, Navarro and others were shown more favor and consideration than they had reason to expect. Fault began to be found with the course of the revolutionists, but they were not intimidated and boldly advocated their measures of revolution. That they had become weaker in influence was shown when the Supreme Council reissued its decree of expulsion to the Spanish frigate. Aubry succeeded in collecting a force of about four hundred Spanish and French, and declared that the Spanish vessel would depart only at the time set by D'Ulloa. His ability to assemble so large a force and defiantly to carry his point, still further increased the reaction against the rebellion. On the 15th of February, 1769, he wrote as follows to the captain general of Cuba: "I hope that Mr. D'Ulloa does me justice and that he has testified to my good conduct; for no one ever loved and venerated the Spanish nation more than I do. This revolution disgraces the French of Louisiana. Although it has not as yet spent its fury and its frienzied course, yet it seems to me that some of the most obstinate among the insurgents begin to look into the future with some uneasiness and even fear; and if in these circumstances we were favored with the arrival of a battalion and the receipt of some money, coupled with assurances that all that has occurred shall be forgotten or forgiven, tranquillity would soon be restored, after the infliction of the great punishments which they deserve, on a small number of seditious persons, who have usurped all powers in the colony and have done all the harm."

Both sides continued to send to the courts of France and Spain manifestos of all sorts and deputies provided with elaborate documents distorting more or less, while trying to explain, the series of comedies and tragedies which had been enacted on the colonial stage. The currency which D'Ulloa had offered to redeem at seventy-five per cent was ordered converted into five per cent bonds at three-fifths of their face value. The Spanish frigate commanded by Captain D'Acosta was permitted to depart under the orders of D'Ulloa. Even Lafrénière used his influences to restore normal order under the rule of the Supreme Council. The leaders of the revolution, seeing their power waning and wishing to rekindle the revolutionary flame, finally conceived the bold project of forming a republic, the chief officer of which should be termed Protector. As a co-ordinate branch of the proposed government, a council of forty men to be elected by the people was provided for. While the project of forming a republic was not carried into effect, it was seriously considered, and is claimed to have been the first republic to be proposed in the New World. A national bank was likewise planned. Under the revival movement, some went so far as to advise the expulsion of Aubry. It was clear that the serpent of rebellion was not dead but sleeping.

When all the circumstances in the case are considered, it appears that the revolution was due to a variety of causes. Since the establishment of the colony by D'Iberville in 1698, the colonists, being wretchedly poor, few in number and crushed in spirit, were accustomed to do about as they pleased, because they could do no harm by being permitted to live under lax laws, and very few even of them. There had thus grown up an independence of all law, but not a disloyalty to the rightful sovereign. This independence was unquestionably the dominating spirit of the revolutionary movement. The alleged devotion to France was not so pronounced as was the spirit of independence. The hatred of Spain and all things Spanish contributed not a little to the flames of opposition. But the weakness of the administration of D'Ulloa and the accompanying belief that the cession to Spain would be annulled, owing to the unaccountable delay in taking possession, were the immediate causes of the insurrection. Other motives may have contributed. No grave and contributing error was committed by D'Ulloa. The inhabitants were not oppressed more than they had been previously under French administrations. All these claims were merely the pretexts which the revolutionary leaders employed, when the crisis came, to condone their veiled spirit of independence. But neither France, Spain nor England, to whose officer at Pensacola an appeal for help had been made, was in sympathy with a principle so hostile to their forms of government. The independent movement, the first to employ force in America, must stand upon its own bottom; this it could not do, and therefore was crushed under the iron heel of O'Reilly.

It does not appear that Alexander O'Reilly was specially selected to undertake the suppression of the rebellion in Louisiana. He was an inspector and lieutenant-general of the Spanish army, and had been already ordered to Havana for the purpose of reviewing in the Spanish Gulf cities the royal armaments and equipments, and was upon the point of sailing. Not deeming it necessary to make a special appointment for that purpose, the king intrusted the subjugation of the revolutionists to O'Reilly.

It was thought best to conceal the object of his mission so far as Louisiana was concerned: his departure was hastened, and he embarked without forces or equipment, it being well known that he could secure everything necessary at Havana. Upon his arrival in Cuba he was ordered to take whatever he deemed necessary in infantry and ammunition, have all conveyed to New Orleans, there take formal possession of the colony, and have the leaders of the rebellion duly tried and punished after the prescribed forms of law. All others likely to disturb the public tranquillity were to be transported from the colony. He was given large powers—was authorized to provide rules for the administration of finance, justice, commerce; in fact, to frame a new form of government and carry it into execution. He was also authorized to use whatever force was necessary to carry all his orders into effect. "It seemed proper to invest Don Alexandro O'Reilly with these extensive powers on account of the distance at which we are from that country. But as the king, whose character is well known, is always inclined to be mild and clement, he has ordered O'Reilly to be informed that his will is, that a lenient course be pursued in the colony, and that expulsion from it be the only punishment inflicted on those who have deserved a more severe one."*

General O'Reilly was not the sort of man to take half way measures. Abilities of an exactly opposite character had made him one of the foremost military commanders of Europe. Therefore, in coming to a colony which had rebelled against his king, for the purpose of restoring the royal authority and of punishing the rebel leaders, he came as befitted his genius and the dignity and supremacy of the court which he represented. He was aware of the military strength of the revolutionists and made preparations of sufficient amplitude to overawe and overcome any force likely to be trained against him. He embarked about four thousand five hundred selected Spanish soldiers on board of a frigate and twenty-eight transports, and on the 23d of July, 1769, arrived at the mouth of the Mississippi. When the news of the presence of this formidable fleet reached New Orleans early the next morning, the excitement may well be imagined. Of course the whole town was soon on the streets and in an uproar. It is reasonable to suppose that all persons who had taken part in the rebellion were in more or less trepidation, now that the crisis was seen to be at hand. Several of the revolutionary leaders still openly

*Letter of Marquis D'Grimaldi to Count D'Fuentes.

counseled resistance to the landing of the Spanish forces, but the folly of such a course was shown by the size of the approaching fleet and by the fact that the ranks of the opposition had melted away almost to a corporal's guard. In their extremity, the leaders waited upon Aubry, signified their wish to yield to the Spanish authority, and cast themselves upon his mercy and protection. He advised absolute submission, and told them freely that he did not think so kind a king as his Catholic Majesty would resort to extreme measures where the revolution had as yet shed no blood. Having in a measure tranquilized the inhabitants, and having sent messengers to the other settlements near New Orleans to effect the same object, Aubry made preparations to receive the Spanish general and his forces as befitted the solemnity of the occasion.

Late at night on the 24th, a Spanish messenger arrived at New Orleans, bearing dispatches from General O'Reilly, and was received at the landing by all the resident Spanish officers and their friends and sympathizers; in fact, the whole town witnessed his arrival, although long after dark. The messenger Francisco Bouligny immediately inquired for Aubry, and was conducted to the residence of that gentleman, to whom he delivered his dispatches. They announced that General O'Reilly had come to take possession of the colony for Spain, and requested that all steps necessary for such ceremony should be ordered by Aubry. The latter returned answer of his readiness and anxiety to turn the colony over to the Spanish authority. The messenger remained over until the 26th, and was introduced to many of the leading citizens, including the chiefs of the revolution. Aubry took pains to make it clear to Bouligny that the revolution was a thing of the past and that no opposition whatever would be offered to the authority of Governor O'Reilly nor to the landing of the Spanish forces. The reception of the messenger became almost an ovation, so marked was the attention shown him. The resident Spanish officials, who so recently had suffered many threats and insults, were likewise shown every consideration of deference and respect. On the morning of the 26th Aubry announced to the entire town in open air at the public square, the arrival of O'Reilly, stated why a general of such prominence and such a large force had been sent, explained that his arrival was sanctioned by the kings of both France and Spain, and advised all who in any way had supported the revolution to desist and render immediate submission and obedience. He said, "I think that in these delicate circumstances I can assume the responsibility to assure you that if you offer no resistance, General O'Reilly will treat you favorably, and that you will not be deceived in having full reliance on the clemency and tenderness of disposition of his Catholic Majesty."

Succeeding this ceremony, three leaders on the revolution, Lafrénière, Marquis and Joseph Milhet, waited upon Governor Aubry, and announced their intention of visiting General O'Reilly at the Balize, providing Aubry would favor them with a letter of introduction to that officer. The latter willingly complied, and encouraged the revolutionists to take the initiative of submission. Accordingly, when the Spanish messenger returned down the river with Aubry's reply, he was accompanied by those three men. The latter were received ceremoniously by O'Reilly on the deck of the flag-ship, where all the principal officers of the fleet had assembled. On behalf of the revolutionists, Lafrénière delivered an address in which he acknowledged the sovereignty of Spain, signified his perfect submission, declared that it would not be necessary to conquer Louisiana, and explained that the causes of the revolution were the harshness of D'Ulloa and the contravention by him of the ancient privileges of the colonists. O'Reilly gravely and politely informed him that as yet, in the absence of facts and evidences, it was impossible for him to pass judgment on the merits of the insurrection, that he should take pains to learn the whole truth, that his disposition was to "render good services to the colonists," that he was pleased at the submission of Lafrénière and his associates, and that he deprecated the frenzied course which the revolutionists had taken. He concluded as follows: "I will listen to your reasons when the time shall come. Thanks to God, I am free from prejudice, and I know that many things, which at a distance seem as if clothed in the dark garb of guilt, are often decked in the white robes of innocence." He invited them to remain and dine with him, favored them with polite consideration, and from his deference led them to believe that their conduct would, at the worst, receive but a light punishment.

Messengers were sent to New Orleans by O'Reilly to make preparations for the disembarkation of the Spanish forces and for the assignment of their quarters; but this required time and it was not until the 15th of August that Governor Aubry went down the river to confer with O'Reilly and to have a time set for the transfer of possession to the new authority. Finally, on the morning of the 17th of August, the entire fleet arrived and cast anchor before the city or moored at the wharves. By proclamation Aubry had notified all the inhabitants of the town and the surrounding plantations to assemble to witness the ceremony of transfer and to pledge their submission and fidelity to Spain. On the 18th Aubry and his staff visited the Spanish fleet, and Governor O'Reilly returned the courtesy by coming ashore and dining with the retiring Frenchmen. He then returned to the fleet and made preparations to land all his forces. A signal gun at five o'clock announced that the disembarkation had commenced. Aubry and all his troops were drawn up to receive them, and all the citizens were assembled to witness the imposing ceremony. The Spanish soldiers, with great precision, marched down the flying bridges, in solid columns, clad in the glittering paraphernalia of war, with arms blazing in the sun, and with an appearance of strength and invincibility that elicited the admiration of all beholders. Moving on like clock-work, they drew up in battalions, forming the three sides of a square, and were followed by the artillery of more than fifty cannons and mortars, and by about one hundred mounted men. Of course, it was the most imposing scene ever witnessed in New Orleans up to that time. Every flag was flying from the vessels and from the houses, for now everybody seemed loyal to Spain. Every bell in the city was adding its silver notes to the song of thanksgiving that the uncertainties of the wretched past were at an end. There was no mistaking this splendid display of military force. It was meant to crush at the outset the spirit of revolution and of independence. It was now too late to exhibit any other sentiment than servility.

Finally, General O'Reilly came down the bridge of the flagship, preceded by attendants in royal livery, bearing long silver maces, and surrounded with a splendid escort of officers, garbed in the brilliant uniforms of the Spanish army and navy. He advanced to the center of the square, where Governor Aubry stood with his retinue, waiting to receive him, and where from a tall mast still flew the tri-color of France. Here the credentials were exhibited and exchanged, and here the instruments were read which transferred Louisiana to the crown of Spain. As a conclusion of the ceremony, the Flag of France was hauled down and that of Spain run up, amid the flaunting of banners, the strains of martial music and the roar of musketry and artillery. The new sovereignty was hailed with loud acclamations by many who a short time before had anathematized everything Spanish and had invoked every saint in the calendar against the cession of Louisiana. Proceeding to the cathedral, the new authorities were received in stately fashion by the church dignitaries, who signified their willing submission to his Catholic Majesty. The orderly and imposing dismissal of the troops closed the ceremonies. Louisiana was now a Spanish province in name as well as in fact.

Up to this time the bearing of O'Reilly was so free from any exhibition of enmity toward the revolutionists, that they were led to believe that forgiveness for their offenses would be duly bestowed. He had not said so; but his urbanity and politeness gave all the impression that he possessed a kind heart and a forgiving nature. Aubry had previously expressed the belief that, inasmuch as the revolutionists had spilled no blood, they would be leniently dealt with, provided they rendered ready obedience and homage to the new authority. It cannot justly be said, that O'Reilly at any time previous to his taking possession of the province, practiced any deception as to his future course with the offenders. It has been asserted that his excessive suavity and courtesy were used by him as a cloak to conceal the dagger which he expected soon to slip between the ribs of the leading revolutionists. This charge is not probable. There is nothing to show that he was a martinet. Every writer of those memorable occurrences speaks pointedly of his evident fairness and justice. Despite assertions to the contrary, he was no doubt fair-minded and kind-hearted. But having risen to great military prominence in a foreign country (for he was an Irishman) by strict adherence to discipline and by prompt and undeviating obedience of orders, and having received his chief promotions and highest honors by rigorous devotion to an exacting sovereignty, it was beyond his nature and his training to brook the slightest infractions of duty or homage to his king. His excessive politeness was common to every courtier and every court in all the capitals of Europe; for such was the custom of the times under the old monarchies. His conduct thus far in Louisiana was eminently wise and consistent.

Even while the ceremonies of taking possession were in progress, O'Reilly was not idle. He had already set in motion the forces which were destined to search for every scrap of evidence both for and against the revolutionists. The diligence with which he pursued this search, proves his desire to get all the evidence before taking any definite action. The taking of depositions was already in progress. He wrote to Aubry, "I beg you to make me acquainted with all these events and their true causes and to furnish me with the names of the persons who induced the people to commit the offense of presenting themselves with arms in their

hands to enforce the violent expulsion of Don Antonio D'Ulloa
and to renew the same excesses against all the Spanish officers
and troops in the colony. . . It is expedient that you have the
kindness to communicate to me as soon as possible all that you
may know in relation to said revolution, without omitting to
quote literally all the orders, protests and public or secret documents, to which you may have had recourse, in order to reduce to,
and to keep within, the bounds of duty the chief agents of the
conspiracy. . . . It is very essential that I should know
who is the person who wrote, printed and circulated the document having for its title: 'Decree of the Council,' dated October,
1768, and under what authority this was done. I desire the same
information with regard to the other document entitled: 'Memorial of the Inhabitants of Louisiana on the Event of the 29th of
October, 1768,' because all the articles of said documents claim
my special attention. I shall put entire faith in your informa-
tions, and I again beg you not to omit any circumstance relative
to men and things in what concerns said revolution."

About this time Aubry wrote to France as follows: "At the
very moment when all seemed lost, Providence took compassion
on our calamities, and when we were near being submerged by
the storm, sent us a liberator, who by his mere presence and by
his wisdom has in an instant re-established order and tranquillity in a country which for a long time past was in an indescribable
state of disorder and confusion. After having experienced the
most terrible alarms and afflictions in governing a colony, which I
several times saw on the very brink of ruin and destruction, it has
been my good luck, by the grace of God, to deliver it up in its
integrity into the hands of a general, to whose presence, wisdom
and firmness it is now indebted for its tranquillity. Listening
with the greatest kindness to those who have any business to
transact with him, he fills with hope and satisfaction all the inhabitants, who after so many disturbances and disorders see at last
the restoration of peace and justice in the country."* It is well
known that Aubry favored the punishment of the leaders, but
there is nothing to show that he was actuated by any other sentiment than that of justice. To him the treatment of D'Ulloa was
a most outrageous performance, little less atrocious than an attack
on the crown itself would have been. He was actuated not by
revenge, but by justice.

Having secured all the evidence possible, O'Reilly set the

* Charles Gayarre.

wheels of the law in motion. The communication of Aubry was so sweeping and conclusive, so like an indictment by a grand jury, that it served as a basis for the proceedings of the prosecution. In the mind of O'Reilly it warranted the immediate arrest of the leaders and their confinement to await trial. On the 21st of August, on one pretense or another, nearly all of the leaders were attracted to the house of the governor, and when there were informed that they were under arrest. Those thus arrested were Nicolas Chauvin Lafrénière, Joseph Villère, Jean Baptiste D'Noyan, Pierre Marquis, Pierre Caresse, Joseph Milhet, Balthasar D'Masan, Joseph Petit, Pierre Poupet, Hardy D'Boisblanc and Jerome Julien Doucet. They were informed of the nature of their offenses, and were told that O'Reilly had been ordered to bring them to trial according to the laws of the kingdom of Spain. Having expressed the wish that all might be able to prove their innocence, he disarmed them and ordered them into confinement, some on the Spanish ships and some in houses, but all under guard. They were not permitted to communicate with each other nor with their friends. Under the laws of Spain, he ordered all the property of the accused sequestered, and permitted them to appoint an assistant to take the inventory of their estates.

A squad of soldiers having Joseph Villère in charge conveyed him on board of one of the ships. Here within a short time he was killed by his guards with bayonet thrusts, probably in an attempt during an outburst of passion either to resist his captors or to escape. His death and the arrest of the leaders produced the utmost consternation; but a proclamation of O'Reilly to the effect that no others would be brought to trial served to quiet the public mind, although every breath was held in expectancy as to what would be done with the others. By another proclamation, O'Reilly requested all the people to appear at New Orleans on the 26th to take the oath of fealty to the Spanish crown. Subsequent dates were set apart for the more remote settlements to do likewise. Upon further investigations, the arrest of both Foucault and the printer, Braud, was ordered; but the latter upon establishing his innocence, was released, while Foucault was sent to France upon his own demand and was there incarcerated in the bastile. The Acadians and the Germans took the oath of allegiance on the 27th. Messengers were sent to all the distant settlements apprising them of the change in rulers; and the messengers were authorized to see that the French flag was lowered and that of Spain raised. Prompt and energetic measures were taken to put the colony in such a condition of confidence as had never before been

witnessed in Louisiana. The energy of the commander seemed
to be infused into all classes of the population. For almost the
first time in the history of Louisiana, there was present a governor
in fact as well as in name. This is the reason why Aubry wrote
so enthusiastically, as quoted above.

He wrote on another occasion, "After so many disturbances
and disorders, which had so long desolated this colony, it is surprising that the mere presence of one individual should in so
short a time have restored good order, peace and tranquillity.
Had it been the good fortune of this province that General
O'Reilly had arrived sooner, it would never have seen all the
calamities from which it has suffered. With the exception of a
small number of families, which are in a state of consternation
on account of what has so justly befallen some of their members,
who have been arrested, all the rest of the colonists are quiet and
satisfied. They are grateful to his Catholic Majesty for having
sent them a governor, who listens with kindness to those who have
any business with him, and who, although respected and feared,
is not the less loved for his generosity, his magnanimity and his
equity, of which all of us feel the effects. He will make the happiness of this colony."* Can it be possible that Aubry thoroughly mistook the character of the new governor? Even after
the arrest of the leaders, he was still enthusiastic over the qualities of O'Reilly. It cannot be said that he was influenced by fear,
for no smell of sedition was upon his garments. He was influenced solely by his desire to have the guilty leaders brought to
justice. Had he concealed the evidences against the leaders, or
connived at their escape, he would have been guilty as an acces-
sory after the fact. But he has been blamed for furnishing the
evidence in such detail and for refraining or neglecting to recommend the leaders to the clemency of O'Reilly. He thought they
should be punished, and therefore made no recommendations of
the kind.

The trial of the revolutionists is the most momentous event in
the history of Louisiana Province. The bringing to trial for
sedition and high treason of twelve of its most prominent citizens
was an occurrence tragical in the extreme. Besides, they were
related by ties of blood to hundreds of their fellow citizens, and
were arrested while indulging the fond hope that their offenses
would be forgiven. While not given a trial such as is known to
present generations, there is nothing to show that they were not

---

* Translation of Mr. Charles Gayarre.

given every opportunity to answer the charges preferred against them. In fact, their own confessions, coupled with the corroborative evidence of many credible witnesses, left no room for the slightest doubt of their guilt. Any judge of the present day, with the same evidences before him, would be forced to arrive at the same conclusions.

The defense endeavored to show that, as the province had never been taken possession of by D'Ulloa, and, as a corollary, had never been surrendered by France, the charge of sedition or treason could not lie as against Spain. The Spanish prosecutor took the ground that the cession was alone sufficient to pass the title without an act of formal possession. He went farther and contended that practical possession of the province had been taken by Spain. This was shown by the acknowledgment of the French colonial leaders of D'Ulloa as the representative of Spain and the accredited governor of the colony; by the fact that he was tendered more than once complete possession; by his declination solely on the ground that he had not sufficient force to defend the colony; by the surrender of French administrative authority and the assumption of governmental duties by D'Ulloa and the execution of his decrees by Aubry; by the payment of the colonial expenses after March, 1766, from the Spanish treasury; by the recognition of the Spanish orders by the Supreme Council; by the passage of commercial, financial and military control to D'Ulloa; by the payment from Spanish funds of the salaries of Lafrénière, the chief revolutionist, and of others; by passports to the merchants, continuances in office, supplies of provisions sent to famishing colonists, payment of the clergy, granting of privileges of export and of the right to buy negroes—all ordered by D'Ulloa and executed by Aubry. It was shown that for two years, possession was an accomplished fact, and that the formality of taking possession was not necessary when actual possession was abundantly recognized as an actuality. Unquestionably, the revolutionists failed to show sufficient cause to justify their course. The evidence was conclusive that Spain had taken practical possession, and, therefore, the course of the revolutionists was sedition and treason against Spain.

At the conclusion of the evidence and of the addresses of the attorneys, the court, by O'Reilly, president, pronounced judgment to the following effect: That Lafrénière, Marquis, Noyan, Caresse, and Joseph Milhet, the principal authors of the revolution, should be mounted upon asses, each of the condemned with a rope around his neck, should thus be led to the place of execution, and should there be hung by the neck until dead; that Joseph Villère, already dead, but likewise guilty, should be rendered infamous; and that the others should be condemned to imprisonment as follows: Petit for life; Doucet and Masan for ten years; and Poupet, Jean Milhet and Boisblanc for six years. The property of all was sequestered, and the documents, manifestos, etc., of the revolution were gathered into a heap and publicly burned.

As soon as this sweeping sentence became known, the friends of the condemned men made every effort possible to save them, but without avail. Even the ladies made tearful and passionate appeals to O'Reilly, but he would not be swerved from what he considered his duty. However, the impossibility of finding a hangman even among the negroes, finally induced him to commute the sentence to shooting instead of hanging. Accordingly, on the 25th of October, 1769, Lafrénière, Marquis, Caresse, Noyan and Joseph Milhet were shot dead in public by platoons of Spanish grenadiers. Those who had been condemned to imprisonment were pardoned, after having served a short time. Owing to the numerous relatives left by the men who were shot, their trial, condemnation and execution are to this day regarded by many of their descendants as wholly unwarranted. It has been claimed, upon what good authority is not mentioned, that the governments of both France and Spain blamed O'Reilly for having ordered too rigorous a punishment. Even Aubry, whose loyal and consistent course throughout challenges admiration, has not escaped the odium of subsequent, sympathizing generations. But whatever may be said in this connection, the truth is clear that the course of the revolutionists was sedition and treason, for which the legal punishment was death. O'Reilly's barbarity on the one hand, or his devotion to duty on the other, does not alter the nature of the offense against Spain.

Whether O'Reilly was justified in rendering so vigorous a sentence will never cease to be a matter of dispute, because his complete authority has never been published. If D'Grimaldi was right in his letter to Fuentes, O'Reilly exceeded his authority—in fact was prohibited from going beyond a sentence of expulsion from the colony. On the other hand, the almost boundless authority known to have been given to O'Reilly, his high character, his strict obedience of orders and his devotion to duty, lead to the conclusion that, in the face of positive directions to the contrary, he never would have been guilty of an act so grave as to shoot these men, if he had not had ample and definite discretion and authority; indeed, he would not have dared to do so, because it would have been a positive disobedience of his king's commands. It would thus seem that he must have had abundant authority for his rigorous course; but it also seems that he must have had considerable discretion, and could therefore have refrained from ordering the death penalty.

But it must be admitted that the shooting of some of these men and the imprisonment of the others, was the first martyrdom on the altar of liberty in the Western Hemisphere. Why did these men hate Spain? Because she represented the servitude of the common people to a degree far beyond any other nation of that period; her rule in Louisiana meant the serfdom of the colonists. Her plan of crushing Louisiana in the dust for the benefit of Mexico and as a barrier against Great Britain, had become known to the inhabitants. They, therefore, desired to remain with France, or to join the English, or to become independent—anything rather than become the slaves of the Spanish grandees. There was no disloyalty to France. Great effort was made, even the tender of money, to secure the co-operation of the English governor, Elliott, of Pensacola. But independence, the highest boon, was a remote hope, owing to their numerical weakness. There was shown a splendid and memorable love of liberty in both the "Decree of the Council" and the "Memorial of the Inhabitants of Louisiana," the first declaration of independence in the New World. Whether the probable course of Spain was sufficient to justify the revolution, has nothing to do with the spirit of liberty sounding high through all the speeches and manifestos. The commercial decree was declared to be an attack upon the ancient liberties of the merchants. Lafrénière insisted that they were threatened with slavery. He maintained that the subjugation of the Supreme Council by Governor D'Ulloa was a death stroke at the rights of the people; that the cession itself guaranteed the preservation of existing customs and rights; and that "population and commerce are fed by liberty and competition, which are the nursing mothers of the State, of which the spirit of monopoly is the tyrant and step-mother. *Without liberty there are but few virtues.* Despotism breeds pusillanimity and deepens the abyss of vices. Man is deemed as sinning before God, only because he retains his free will. Where is the liberty of our planters, of our merchants, and of all our inhabitants?" That sounds as if it might have been uttered by Patrick Henry a few years later. Lafrénière goes on to specify the various wrongs imposed upon Louisiana, just as the usurpations and injuries of George III are defined in the Declaration of Independence.

However, his cause was clouded, and the spirit of independence
shown was weak. The wrongs complained of were not sufficient
to warrant revolution. The movement was doomed from the
start, because the reasons were too faint and remote to carry all
the people along on the golden tide, and because the revolutionists were not numerically strong enough to conquer success with
the sword. The conquered rebel is a conspirator and traitor;
the successful rebel is a hero and patriot, and becomes the founder
of a State. If the British had conquered George Washington,
he would have been either shot or hung; his success placed his
name high above the glittering titles of kings and conquerors.
What would have been the fame of Lafrénière and his liberty-
loving associates, had they succeeded in achieving their independence? It would have been done had they been strong
enough. It made all the difference in the world whether they
failed or succeeded.

CHAPTER VIII

Louisiana Under the Spanish Cabinet

IMMEDIATELY succeeding the stern measures of O'Reilly in suppressing the revolution and punishing the leaders, steps were taken wholly to reorganize the military, judicial and commercial departments of the province. Although it had been the intention of Spain to retain the established order of affairs in Louisiana, the revolution caused the abandonment of this design and the substitution therefor of a rule wholly in accordance with the Spanish colonial policy. The Supreme Council, which had in reality headed the revolutionary movement, was succeeded by the Cabildo, composed of six perpetual regidors, two ordinary alcaldes, an attorney-general Syndic and a clerk, over which body the provincial governor was authorized wholly to preside. The governor was made subordinate to the captain-general of Cuba, and the intendant controlled the revenues. Many subordinate officers were provided for, and the Spanish language was substituted for that of the French in all proceedings, except the judicial and notarial acts of the commandants. The Cabildo convened in its first session December 1, 1769, with O'Reilly presiding. He had been given "special power to establish in this new part of the king's dominions with regard to the military force, police, administration of justice and finances, such a form of government as might most effectually secure its dependence and subordination, and promote the king's service and the happiness of his subjects." Judge Martin says, "It is oppressive in the highest degree to require that a community should instantaneously submit to a total change in the laws that hitherto governed it, and be compelled to regulate its conduct by rules of which it is

I—18

totally ignorant." While that statement is true, it must also be admitted that, in view of the revolution, the colonists had forfeited their rights to ordinary and proper treatment and had brought upon their own heads repressive measures, which would not have been resorted to under normal conditions. Under his instructions, O'Reilly was authorized to render the province dependent and subordinate, and was given unlimited power for the accomplishment of these ends. The fact that O'Reilly thought it necessary to execute several of the leaders of the revolution, furnishes the reason why he also thought it necessary to change the laws governing the province. It was necessary to root out the spirit of independence prevailing throughout the entire province; hence a complete change of laws and customs was employed to show the power and authority of Spain.

But the change did not produce serious hardship, because the law of Spain, which was substituted for that of France, likewise originated in the Roman Civil Law, and hence its general principles were familiar to the colonists. In several proclamations, O'Reilly made known his will to the people. Every parish was provided with a civil and military commandant, who was required to attend to the observance of law, to examine the passports of travelers, to permit no one to settle within his jurisdiction without a license from the government, to preside in the trial of civil causes where the contention did not exceed twenty dollars, to punish slaves, to arrest and imprison free persons guilty of offenses, to serve as notary public, to attend to the sales of the estates of deceased persons, and to execute the judgments rendered in New Orleans against citizens of his parish. It will thus be seen that the commandant possessed extreme power over the people within his jurisdiction; but as he was sworn to maintain and defend the Catholic faith, he was subordinate to the parish priest in all ecclesiastical matters. In fact, inasmuch as the Catholic church ruled Spain at that date, the will of the church prevailed in all things where a conflict between church and state occurred.

In 1763, when all of Louisiana Province east of the Mississippi passed to Great Britain, there was but one settlement in upper Louisiana west of the river—Ste Genevieve. D'Ulloa had ordered the Spanish flag raised in "the Illinois," and doubtless that ceremony was performed at the little village of Ste Genevieve; also at St. Louis, which was founded as a consequence of the division of the upper country between Spain and Great Britain. The people of the upper colony, though entertaining the same sentiments toward Spain as did their neighbors to the south, resorted to no extreme measures, and hence escaped the rigor of O'Reilly. In fact, St. Ange had communicated his allegiance to Spain soon after the appearance of D'Ulloa at New Orleans, and as a reward for his promptness and adherence had been appointed commandant of Upper Louisiana. Although St. Ange was a Frenchman, it was not found necessary to retire him even under the rigorous policy of O'Reilly. On the contrary, Upper Louisiana was constituted more of an independent province than ever before, though still subordinate to the jurisdiction of the colonial governor. It embraced all of the province north of a line fixed approximately near the present Memphis, and had an estimated population of eight hundred ninety-one. During the Spanish reign, no settlements were formed in Upper Louisiana except in what is now the State of Missouri. But the province as a whole received such an influx of population that many new towns were founded in what is now Louisiana, Arkansas and Missouri.

All new laws went into operation December 1, 1769. They were precisely like those prevailing in the other Spanish American colonies, and hence were the same as those governing the Council of the Indies. As a whole, the province was made a dependency of Cuba. Among other things, O'Reilly instructed the commandant at Natchitoches to terminate the illicit trade between that point and the Mexican provinces and took steps to prevent the future enslavement of the Indians. He issued the following order: "The aforesaid commandants shall take special care that the inhabitants carry on no trade with the English vessels which navigate the Mississippi, nor with any of the settlements situated on the territory of his Britannic Majesty, and that the king's subjects do not go out of the limits of this province without a written permission from the governor general. Those acting in violation of the provisions of this article shall be arrested by said commandants and sent to this town (New Orleans), in order that their case be submitted to the further consideration of the government, but the first proceeding shall be to sequestrate their property." The wisdom of every order issued by O'Reilly is not questioned at this day. The kind treatment of the Indians, charity to the poor, proper respect for the church, consideration for the rights of foreigners on the Mississippi, vigilance in uprooting immorality, the rigid observance of law, and many other sound prnciples were instituted. He issued the following instruction: "The great distance from the capital to the Illinois requires proportionate discretion and prudence in the commandant of that remote district. There are three important objects recommended to his special vigilance and attention. Those are: That the domination and government of his Majesty be loved and respected; that justice be administered with promptitude and impartiality and in conformity to law; and that commerce be protected and extended as much as possible. . . . Should any subject of his Catholic Majesty commit any excess or trespass in the territory of the English, or offer any insult to those of that nation who navigate the Mississippi, the commandant shall do prompt justice, and shall give full and immediate reparation, on the just complaints of the English officer, but without failing to observe the formalities prescribed by law. . . . The commandant shall take care that all the Indians who may come to St. Louis and St. Genevieve be well treated, and be paid an equitable price for the hides they may bring to market, and for whatever other things they may have for sale, and that in the barters or purchases they may make, they be served with good faith. In this way they will derive more benefit from their trade with us; they will provide themselves with what their wants require, without its being at the expense of the king; and the English will not reap all the profits of a commerce which ought to be in our hands. . . . This province wants flour, wine, oil, iron instruments, arms, ammunition, and every sort of manufactured goods for clothing and other domestic purposes. These can only be obtained through the exportation of its productions, which consists of timber, indigo, cotton, furs and a small quantity of corn and rice. . . . By granting to this province, as formerly to Florida, the benefit of a free trade with Spain and with Havana, its inhabitants would find in that very city of Havana a market for all their produce, and would provide themselves with all the articles of which they stand in need. . . . It would also be proper that the vessels belonging to this colony be received in Havana and the ports of Spain on the same condition and footing with Spanish vessels; but with the understanding that no vessels, except they be Spanish or belong to the colony, shall be admitted in this port, or employed in transporting goods, and that this be recommended to the special care of my successor. . . . I found the English in complete possession of the commerce of the colony. They had in this town their merchants and traders with open stores and shops, and I can safely assert that they pocketed nine-tenths of the money spent here. The commerce of France used to receive the productions of the colony in payment of the articles imported into it from the mother country; but the English, selling their goods much cheaper, had the gathering of all the money. I drove off all the English traders and the other individuals of that nation whom I found in this town, and I shall admit here none of their vessels."

The laws and regulations put in force by O'Reilly lowered the colonial expenses to one-half of what they had previously been; but, in accomplishing this reform, he so restricted commerce that, with the large advent of settlers, there succeeded almost a famine from the shortage of provisions, flour advancing to twenty dollars per barrel. At this time a brig load of flour owned by Oliver Pollock was sold in New Orleans for fifteen dollars per barrel. In spite of this extremity, the inhabitants were not permitted to purchase anything from persons navigating the Mississippi or the lakes without a passport. They were permitted to sell fowls and other provisions to boats and other vessels, if delivered on the river bank for cash payment. A violation of this order subjected the offender to a fine of one hundred dollars, to the confiscation of the article thus sold, one-third of the penalty going to the informer.

No change was made in the ecclesiastical organization of the province; the Capuchins remained in absolute control with Father Dagobert in charge of the pastoral functions at New Orleans and in the administration of the southern part of the diocese of Quebec. A Capuchin was placed in charge of the settlements of Upper Louisiana. The Catholic church was aided from the royal treasury in the construction of buildings, grants of land, etc. "The Catholic king, to show his regard for this religious corporation (the Charity Hospital of the Ursuline Nuns in New Orleans), decided that two of the nuns should be maintained at his own expense, for each of whom sixteen dollars was to be paid monthly to the convent out of his royal treasury."

By special proclamation, O'Reilly re-enacted the Black Code that had proved so beneficial for so long a time. Under his orders a body of militia was organized, called the "Regiment of Louisiana," and placed under the command of Col. Don J. Estecheria. The Spanish law of the Indies promptly supplanted the colonial law of France in all parts of the province. That no mistake might be made as to the change, O'Reilly issued an abridgment of the Law of the Indies and of Castile, which was the foundation of all actions during the term of the Spanish domination. All causes begun under French procedure were ordered transferred to the Spanish tribunals instituted in the province. Although it has been disputed there is nothing to show that the acts of O'Reilly were not fully approved by the Spanish king.

In fact, the king's council, "having carefully examined all the documents to which the king had called their attention, could discover in the acts of O'Reilly nothing which did not deserve the most decided approbation, and which was not a striking proof of the extraordinary genius of that general officer."

But Spain gave no encouragement to the education of the masses. It was deemed sufficient for them to obey the laws of church and state provided, without any inquiry on their part. The bible was the word of God; the Pope was the vicegerent of God on earth; and the holy Catholic church was the interpreter of scripture. The king and his counselors prescribed and executed the laws. What more was wanted of the good people but to obey the priest and the king? Both spiritual and temporal wants were fully provided for by the supreme grace of Pope and King. A little later, when settlers were so earnestly wanted, Protestants were permitted to become subjects; but were not permitted to build churches, and the second generation was expected to become Catholic. A school of general learning started in New Orleans, failed totally for want of support. The children grew to manhood and womanhood without learning to read or write. The "Holy Inquisition" endeavored to secure a foothold in the province; but this was too much even for the intolerance of Spain. The Capuchin Father, Antonio de Sedella, became the representative of the Inquisition in Louisiana: but was escorted to Cadiz against his will by Governor Miro. The latter by guaranteeing protection to the Protestants had secured a large accession of them throughout Louisiana. The supremacy of the Inquisition in Louisiana meant the death of every one of them on the charge of heresy. Such an order of affairs meant the destruction of the province and could not be permitted. Strange as it may seem, the course of Governor Miro received the sanction of the king, himself an uncompromising Catholic and the supporter of the Inquisition.

Over Upper Louisiana was placed a lieutenant governor, who was subordinate only to the governor general and the intendent general of the whole province. He was a sub-delegate to the intendent, and superintended all financial operations within his jurisdiction. In this capacity he had charge of Indian affairs, commerce, the sale and grant of lands, the levy and collection of revenue; and next to the governor was at the head of the military department, selecting the commandants and other officers of his province. He likewise had high judicial jurisdiction within his province, and under him the courts became models of promptness and efficiency. It is even stated that the administration of law at St. Louis was so satisfactory that when the American courts were instituted in 1803, with their long and vexatious delays, they were derided by the inhabitants.* With an export duty of only six per cent, the first shipments of the Missouri country—salt and timber—were profitable to the producer. The officials of Upper Louisiana were paid in the bills which they drew on the royal treasury at New Orleans. Prior to the Revolution, the British had monopolized the Indian trade of the Missouri and the upper Mississippi rivers, including the Des Moines and the Minnesota: and St. Louis found it to her interest under both French and Spanish rule to send her furs to Canada and obtain there goods for the Indian trade: but found a better market for lead and provisions at New Orleans, where she purchased the most of her groceries. However, salt, lead, and other commodities were sent to Philadelphia, Baltimore, and Pittsburg near the close of the Spanish domination.

Don Louis de Unzaga succeeded O'Reilly to the governorship of the province in October, 1770. He found commerce at the lowest ebb, owing to the restrictions of O'Reilly and his predecessors. Under D'Ulloa exports had been confined to the Spanish towns of Malaga, Carthagena, Barcelona, Seville, Alicant, and Corunna, and to Spanish bottoms commanded by Spaniards. Some changes had been made in this rule, but others equally oppressive had been substituted in their place, and as a consequence distress and poverty were the portion of the colonists. But Unzaga instituted a revolution in this state of affairs. He almost completely overlooked the commercial and fiscal laws of Spain, and permitted British (American) merchants to trade pretty much as they pleased, with the result that in a short time the trade of the colony was wholly in the hands of foreigners and the condition of the colonists had changed from lethargy and intense distress to activity and prosperity. British vessels navigated the Mississippi in great numbers dealing in all sorts of goods and provisions, even fitting up their boats with counters for the convenience of the people of Louisiana. Ocean-going vessels from Philadelphia, Baltimore, and Boston, keel-boats from up the Mississippi, traders from the interior—all flourished with the connivance of the Spanish officials, though the trade was a direct violation of the laws of the province. Here was a remarkable condition of things: Spain standing back with her

---

* History of Missouri: Carr.

obsolete laws, while her officials winked at an illicit trade that was a god-send to the people of the province. A better commentary on the contradictory policy of that decaying monarchy could scarcely be given.

But complaint arose, owing to the diminution in the revenues of the king. The monopoly of the provincial trade by the British and the consequent prosperity of the colonists, poured the revenue into British pockets instead of into the royal exchequer. The floating stores, the warehouses at Manshac, Baton Rouge, and Natchez, the trading vessels moored in the river near New Orleans, the numerous keel-boats, deprived the Spanish monarch of the means of gratifying his vanity and profligacy. The prosperity of the reign of Unzaga made the colonists partially forget the severity of that of O'Reilly. But as might have been expected, the prosperity led to an enormous extension of credit; so much so that, when the restrictions began again to be enforced, many were obliged to ask for an extension of credit or were forced into involuntary assignment. One important truth is proved by these events: That the removal of the restrictions meant the unbounded prosperity of the province. But the king pressed the thumb-screw on the colonists, as the Inquisition pressed it on the quivering forms of heretics, forcing out the heart's blood in agonizing driblets and rendering the victim pale, weak, and almost lifeless.

The rebellion of the British American colonies was an important event in the history of Louisiana province. With the connivance of the Spanish officials arms and ammunition were sent to Pittsburg for use in the western districts upon the solicitation of Col. George Morgan and others. Unzaga reported fully to the Spanish cabinet on the defenseless condition of Louisiana, pointing out that it was vulnerable on all sides and easy of conquest by a comparatively small force. As no assistance could be expected from Havana, he intimated that in case of attack, he would retire to Mexico after hope of saving the colony had been abandoned. About this time he was relieved of the governorship at his own request, and was succeeded by Don Bernardo de Galvez, colonel of the "Regiment of Louisiana." Under him the trade of the Americans was somewhat restricted in favor of France; but in spite of his rulings American and English vessels in large numbers navigated the lower Mississippi in violation of the Spanish laws. In the spring of 1777, he ordered the seizure of eleven English vessels, and soon afterward no more British boats appeared on the river; Spain and England were at war.

In 1776 a royal schedule reduced the export duty of the province from four per cent to two per cent. In addition, the king agreed to buy for the present all the tobacco the colonists could raise: evidently the price had advanced in the European markets. In fact, tobacco was the staple used by the rebellious Americans to buy munitions of war from France. The king agreed to give seven livres per pound for leaf tobacco and ten livres per pound for the weed in carots. The distinct object of this agreement was to assist in populating Louisiana, and was ordered at the suggestion of Unzaga. The revolution of the British American colonies had been followed by a large accession to the population on the left bank of the Mississippi. Tories, cowards and many others, who felt under no obligation to assist the rebels and who desired to avoid the danger and distress farther to the east, gathered there, but refrained from crossing until they had learned how they were likely to be received on the other shore. In the end, Louisiana was thus benefited, though many persons located at Natchez.

The suggestion of Col. George Morgan to Governor Galvez that the rebels be permitted to descend the Ohio and Mississippi rivers with a large force for the purpose of attacking the British posts of Mobile and Pensacola, was properly refused by that able official and astute strategist. He had other important designs, as was soon shown. Already had the Americans secured too much of a foothold in Louisiana. Should they be allowed to conquer West Florida, they would have possession of the left bank of the Mississippi and have the right to navigate that river. It meant nothing less than the invasion of Louisiana by them and the creation of New Orleans as a free port. In self defense, Louisiana must prevent the aggressions of the rebels as well as of the British. Luckily for Louisiana and the cause of Spain generally, Governor Galvez, though still in his twenties, possessed by nature military genius of a high order. He realized that war between Spain and Great Britain was likely to be followed by the invasion of Louisiana up the Mississippi by the British fleets. He therefore waited only until war had been actually declared by Spain before he began operations for the reduction of the British forts on the Mississippi. He determined to strike, although opposed by all his legal advisors.

He accordingly built four large boats, each carrying either a 24-pounder or an 18-pounder, and provided with both oars and sails, so that quick action in either shoal water or during calms was assured. He knew that he would thus have the advantage of a British fleet, which could advance neither in shallow water nor without wind. Before striking, he sent spies to Pensacola and Mobile to learn the British strength; he also ascertained that the Creeks, Choctaws and Chickasaws were the firm friends of the British. He began operations none too soon, because the Americans under Col. George R. Clark had conquered the British Illinois country, and a movement by them down the Mississippi was contemplated. Others had also crossed the mountains and taken possession of portions of what is now East Tennessee, claiming at the same time an extension to the Mississippi. Further than this, Captain Willing, an American, with a small force of about fifty men, picked up from any quarter, openly attacked the British settlements on the lower Mississippi, burning farm-houses and capturing slaves and other property of British subjects, much to the regret of Governor Galvez, who as soon as possible terminated the movement. The wisdom on the part of Spain of striking at once thus became apparent. The course of Captain Willing was both without the sanction of Galvez and against the designs of Spain. That country had determined to secure both banks of the Mississippi, in order to monopolize the commerce of the Gulf; and accordingly, Galvez was empowered to effect the reduction of the British posts along the Mississippi and, if possible, along the Gulf in West Florida.

Although Galvez had assisted the Americans to the extent of about seventy thousand dollars' worth of arms and ammunition, there was nothing to prevent him from carrying into effect the designs of Spain as to the conquest of West Florida from Great Britain. Spain, unwilling to accede to the terms of the Americans as to the navigation of the Mississippi, refused to enter into an alliance with them, as France had done, and determined to strike Great Britain, the common enemy, and if possible effect for her own benefit the conquest of the Floridas. She now saw that her interest was likely to conflict with that of the Americans, who, when they should secure their independence, might prove a dangerous neighbor. In order to assist the colonists, Spain removed the restrictions on trade between Louisiana and the West Indies, but placed such operations under the control of commissioners. About this time, also, Galvez made New Orleans practically a free port to France and the Americans; and the king, in October, 1778, extended the exports of Louisiana to any port of Spain to which the commerce of the Indies was open. Aided from the royal treasury, several ship loads of new colonists arrived from the

Canary Islands and settled in Louisiana. In fact, Spain granted the annual sum of forty thousand dollars "to facilitate the establishment of the new colonists who may come to Louisiana." Settlements were thus formed at New Iberia, Terre aux Bœufs, on the river Amite, Bayou Lafourche and elsewhere.

No doubt the inhabitants of the Missouri country assisted Governor Galvez in the conquest of West Florida. They likewise assisted Colonel Clark to reduce the British posts of Kaskaskia, Vincennes, etc. After war between Spain and Great Britain had been declared, they drove the English traders from the upper Mississippi, the Missouri, the Des Moines, but left them in possession of their posts in what is now Minnesota. Partly in retaliation for this hostile course, and partly to aid a general movement of the British against the claims of the Spaniards on the Mississippi, an expedition of tories and Indians was organized in Canada in 1780 to attack and reduce St. Louis and to effect the conquest of Upper Louisiana. About one hundred forty Canadians and Englishmen and fifteen hundred Indians rendezvoused at Michillimackinac, and, while the Spanish and the English on the Gulf were struggling for the mastery, marched across the country and attacked St. Louis, but found it too strong to be taken with the force at their disposal. Having killed sixty persons and captured thirty, hearing that Colonel Clark was likely to attack them with a large force of Americans, and being deserted by many of their Indian allies, the British abandoned their designs and returned hurriedly to Canada. Though there is much dispute over the results of this expedition, the facts seem substantially as above narrated. The expedition of Capt. Eugenio Pierre in 1780, with a force of Spaniards from St. Louis across the country in the dead of winter to what is now St. Joseph, Michigan, a British post, resulting in its capture, did much to establish the subsequent claims of Spain to the British territory north of the Ohio and east of the Mississippi. It was an important counter movement which checked any further attempt of the British to capture St. Louis or any other post on the Upper Mississippi.

War was declared by Spain against Great Britain on the 8th of May, 1779; and as soon as the news reached Galvez he prepared to act. He adroitly compelled the people of New Orleans to agree to assist him, by refusing to accept the commission as governor, which arrived with the news of the declaration of war, unless they complied with his wishes and demands. With a force of about 1,400 Spaniards, Americans and Indians and an armament of ten pieces of cannon, he advanced up the river in September, 1779, captured Fort Manshac with an English force of twenty-three men, reduced and captured the strong fort at Baton Rouge with five hundred men, including Lieut.-Col. Dickson, the British commander on the Mississippi, and thirteen pieces of heavy artillery, and at the same time obtained the surrender at discretion of Fort Panmure at Natchez with about eighty men. In the meantime, Captain Grandpré had captured the two small British posts on the Amite and on Thompson's creek. In the end, the Spaniards captured eight vessels, three forts and two posts, five hundred fifty regulars and many militiamen and free blacks. It was a splendid accomplishment, against great opposition at New Orleans, and in spite of many obstacles, and reflected the highest credit on the courage, sagacity and genius of the young commander.

But he had now only well begun. He planned the conquest of all of West Florida, and in the spring of 1780 moved with a force of about two thousand upon Fort Charlotte, at Mobile, and having invested it and made a breach in its walls, received its surrender on the 14th of March. The British General Campbell, who arrived before Mobile a few days later with a considerable force, was chagrined to find the place, not only in possession of the Spaniards, but too strong to be retaken, and was therefore compelled to return to Pensacola. Galvez now determined to attack Pensacola, providing he could secure assistance from Havana. He solicited reinforcements, which were promised, but not sent. Still determined, he himself went to Havana, and succeeded in assembling a satisfactory fleet and force, all of which a little later was scattered and dispersed by a fearful storm on the Gulf. But he persevered, and in February, 1781, had at his command a larger and stronger force than before, and a formidable fleet under the command of Admiral Irazabal. Arriving in front of Pensacola early in March, he prepared to attack; but was opposed by the admiral, owing to some trifling considerations of navigation. Receiving reinforcements from Mobile under Captain D'Espeleta and from New Orleans under Captain Miro, Galvez determined, with the assistance of the small naval force at his command, to attempt the reduction of Fort George. Assuming all responsibility, and acting independently of Irazabal, he ordered the advance of his little fleet, and amid a severe fire from the English, successfully passed the fort and joined his land forces beyond, greatly to their delight. Irazabal now perceived that he must either co-operate or run the risk of being dishonored before the enemy, and accordingly, the next day, he passed the fort as Galvez had done, amid a severe fire. The gallant feat of Galvez, in advancing in an open boat amid shots that fell all around him, to meet the fleet of the admiral, aroused the admiration even of the enemy. The fort and the marine redoubt near it, were immediately invested, the English commander having refused to surrender as had been demanded of him. Early in April, the attack was begun with all the force at the command of the Spaniards, but was met by a continuous and heavy fire from the English. The latter were well supplied with ammunition and provisions, were aware that their works could not be carried by assault; and thus accordingly held out for about a month. Early in May, a shell having set fire to the magazine in one of the English redoubts, a terrific explosion made a breach in the walls, through which the Spaniards poured, taking possession and turning the guns on the English. This decided the contest. Terms of capitulation were agreed on, and over eight hundred men were surrendered prisoners of war. In fact, Governor Chester, of West Florida, being among the prisoners, surrendered without further ado the whole of West Florida. This magnificent victory completed the heroic work of the gallant young Galvez. He was appointed a lieutenant-general, was made a count, was commissioned captain-general of the provinces of Louisiana and Florida, and was decorated with the cross of knight pensioner of the Royal and Distinguished Order of Charles III. In the meantime, an English force under General Lyman had retaken Fort Panmure, at Natchez, but now abandoned it upon learning of the capture of Pensacola and the surrender of West Florida. Thus the conquest of that province was complete, solely through the determination, daring and generalship of Galvez. That the army of Galvez contained men from Upper Louisiana cannot be doubted, though how many seems never to have been recorded.

The importance of this conquest to Spain can scarcely be overestimated and is often overlooked. At the conclusion of peace in 1783, by which the British-American colonies gained their independence and all the territory on the left bank of the Mississippi north of the thirty-first degree of latitude, Spain also, by reason of the conquest of Galvez, secured all of West Florida south of that line, and at the same time was ceded East Florida as well. Had Galvez permitted the Americans to make this conquest, as they desired to do, or had he not effected it himself, the conclusion of the peace of 1783 would doubtless have been followed by the transfer of West Florida to the triumphant rebels. Owing to

the determination of the Americans at a later day to possess West
Florida in any event, the result made little difference either to
Spain or to the United States. However, judging by ordinary
standards, the conquest of Galvez was not only brilliant, but a
measure of extreme wisdom.

The movements of the armies on the lower Mississippi caused
an almost complete abandonment of commerce; to such an extent
in fact that as early as January, 1780, provisions in New Orleans
were very scarce, and commanded almost fabulous prices. In
this emergency all restrictions were abandoned, and even the
king came to the relief of the colonists with liberal measures.
But as time passed the situation became graver instead of better.
Galvez recommended free trade with all countries, but, not being
in harmony with Spanish policy, his suggestions were not adopted.
The peace of 1783 was followed by the greatest prosperity Louisiana ever enjoyed. An immense trade sprung up at New Orleans,
and was largely in the hands of the Americans. Soon the old
trouble arose—complaint of the encroachments of the Americans;
and the restrictions, which had never been repealed, were again
enforced to check their advance from all commercial quarters.
As a bar to the advancement of the Americans, Spain, at great
expense, concluded a permanent treaty of friendship and alliance
with the Talabouches, Creeks, Apalaches, Choctaws, Chickasaws,
and Alibamous, and took care that those powerful nations were
afterward hostile to the Americans. The half-breed chief,
McGillivray, was promptly granted a pension of six hundred dollars per annum by Spain, owing to his strong influence over all
the southern tribes. Strange as it may seem, he even hinted
as early as January 1, 1784, at the separation of the western territory from the United States, his language being, "This
expedient (the levying of duties and taxes by the United
States) has produced so unfavorable an impression, that a good
many of their citizens, in order to escape from the burden of taxation, have abandoned their dwellings for the woods, and have
marched toward the Mississippi, in order to unite with a certain
number of disbanded soldiers, who are anxious to possess themselves of a considerable portion of the territory watered by this
river; and they propose establishing what they call *The Western
Independence,* and throwing aside the authority of the American
Congress. The emigrants are so numerous that, in a short time,
it is possible that they may find themselves strong enough to carry
into execution their scheme of separation; and, if they once form
settlements on the Mississippi, it will require much time, trouble

and expense to dislodge them." This was remarkable language and remarkable prevision for a half-breed savage. He ended by suggesting that the best way to avoid the advances of the Americans was to unite the Indians and the Spaniards. His advice was adopted, and the suggested union was consummated.

In September, 1784, the exclusion of all foreign trading vessels from the Mississippi, and the depreciation of the colonial paper money to about one-half its face value, brought on the old commercial distress. In the resulting extremity, the people even regretted the absence of the British trading boats on the Mississippi. But in spite of all this suffering, both upper and lower Louisiana began to fill up with aggressive Americans, and boat loads of provisions from Kentucky and the Ohio and Illinois regions began to appear at New Orleans. Don Estevan Miro succeeded Galvez as governor in 1785; he at once granted every commercial privilege possible and winked at the violation of many of the iron-clad restrictions, suspended like the sword of Damocles over the heads of the colonists. In April, 1786, there were seen at one time on the river at New Orleans forty vessels engaged mostly in an illicit trade with the inhabitants. In addition, large numbers of keel-boats loaded with flour, pork, corn, tallow, lard, hides and other provisions were there to be exchanged for groceries and other necessaries. Again the colonists were prosperous, but the trade was almost wholly monopolized by the Americans through violations of the Spanish laws. The sword was still suspended over the people. At this time the annual trade of New Orleans with Mobile and Pensacola amounted to about one hundred thousand dollars; with Texas, six thousand dollars; with Arkansas not over half so much; and with the Missouri country about as much as with Texas. The trade of the latter was largely monopolized by the English traders from Michilli-mackinac. The trade of the upper Mississippi, including that of the River Des Moines, was also in the hands of the English of Canada, with the Americans making steady inroads on their profits.

Spain claimed the Natchez district and as far north as the mouth of the Yazoo river by right of her conquest of West Florida. The United States claimed as far south as the thirty-first degree of latitude by virtue of the treaty of peace with Great Britain in 1783. Under the latter claim, Georgia, in 1785, sent commissioners to New Orleans to demand the territory as far south as the thirty-first degree, and of course was met with the statement that the territory demanded belonged to Spain. The policy of alternately violating and enforcing the commercial restrictions at New Orleans, subjected not only the colonists to the whims of the colonial officials, but all the western people of the United States as well. A uniform policy, even if exacting and oppressive, would not have been violently objected to by the western people. What they did object to was to be thrown at any time wholly out of the New Orleans market and to have their goods confiscated at the caprice of the colonial officials.

But Spain rightly thought more of her own revenues and of the perpetuation of her ancient policy of commercial exclusion than she did of the happiness of the people in the western part of the United States. She was under no obligation to make any sacrifice for their gratification or prosperity. If they were unfortunately situated, it was not her fault or concern. She had the undoubted right to exclude the American merchants from New Orleans if she saw fit. She had no right to prevent their navigating the Mississippi, nor did she try to do so at any time. Her only objects were to save the profits of trade to her own subjects, and to turn the revenues arising from her commercial policy over to her king. But the western people complained as if she were at fault, and refused to be comforted until she supinely surrendered her rights and revenues that they might wax rich and fat. There can be no question that, from this time forward, the western people in their extremity and the United States as a whole, were determined to trade with New Orleans, regardless of Spanish laws, rights and customs. The course of the colonial officials, until the province passed from the control of Spain, was one of mingled trepidation, resistance, concession and humiliation. Without the power of prevention, Spain saw her ancient policy crumbling in ruin before the commercial and independent assaults of the Americans.

The necessity of populating Louisiana in order to resist the encroachments of the Americans, caused Governor Miro to relax from the strict observance of the provincial laws of Spain. The Indian nations were deemed a sufficient barrier between the Floridas and the Americans. But the Mississippi could be easily crossed; and so long as the Western people possessed the right to navigate that river, constant infringements of the immemorial customs of Spain might be expected. It was, therefore, necessary to populate Louisiana with a large body of colonists, devoted to Spain and hostile to every advancement of the Americans. Thus, at the worst, the colony, though contaminated somewhat with republican principles, would serve as an effectual barrier

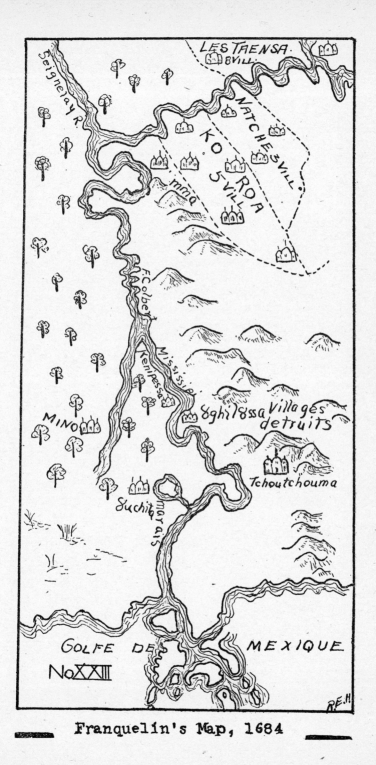

Franquelin's Map, 1684

against the march of the Americans on the provinces of Mexico. Thus, the first steps of Spain were to retain both banks of the Mississippi. When that failed, she endeavored to prove her right to the Natchez district, with a northern extension to the mouth of the Yazoo river, the latitude of which formed the northern boundary of West Florida under the British. Spain consistently maintained this claim until, by the treaty of 1795, she surrendered the left bank of the Mississippi as far south as the thirty-first parallel of latitude. This surrender was deemed advisable to gain the good will of the Americans, and was not the result of a change in the opinion of Spain as to her right to the territory.

The ordinance of 1787, which excluded slavery from the territory northwest of the River Ohio, caused many slaveholders to cross the Mississippi and settle in Louisiana province. The Missouri country received a large accession, as did Louisiana and Arkansas. In order to please the Americans east of the river as well as to benefit the Louisianians, both Governor Miro and Don Diego de Gardoqui, the Spanish minister near the United States, permitted almost a free trade between the western people and the provincials. Finally, Gardoqui, influenced by some whim most probably, called the intendant, Navarro, sharply to account for permitting such a contraband trade; whereupon the latter, in February, 1787, forwarded to Spain a lengthy memorial, showing the necessity of such a course. Among other things he said, "The powerful enemies we have to fear in this province are not the English, but the Americans, whom we must oppose by active and efficient measures. It is not enough to have granted Louisiana a restricted commerce for ten years; it is indispensable to use other resources. . . . This toleration contributes to the daily increase of the white and black population of this colony, extends commerce, quickens industry, spreads the domain of agriculture, and gives rise to a state of things, which, in a few years, will be productive of considerable sums to the king. Without this toleration, and without the commercial franchises granted by the royal schedule of the 22d of January, 1782, this country would have been a desert, when it is calculated to become one of the most important portions of America. There is no time to be lost. Mexico is on the other side of the Mississippi, in the vicinity of the already formidable establishments of the Americans. The only way to check them is with a proportionate population, and it is not by imposing commercial restrictions that this population is to be acquired, but by granting a prudent extension and freedom of trade." But the restrictions instigated by Gardoqui

I—19

caused the complete stagnation of commerce and proved a bar to the continued settlement of the province. By December, 1787, all business was at a standstill. Spain should either have thrown open the ports to the world, or have closed them absolutely to every trader, and have taken the consequences in either case.

It was at this time that Spain entered actively into the scheme of separating the western sections from the rest of the United States and attaching them to Louisiana. It was realized that the dissatisfaction of the western people might lead to a concerted attack on New Orleans; but if they should be attached to Louisiana, not only would that trouble be removed, but they would prove a barrier between Louisiana and the United States. Unwilling to concede the demands of the western people, Spain early perceived the wisdom of encouraging their designs to separate from the United States, and held out the hope of free trade with New Orleans and of the protection of Spain. Thus, Gen. James Wilkinson was favored, because he seemingly represented the western people and was the most prominent man west of the Alleghanies. If his influence and efforts could be gained to aid the scheme of separation, what mattered that his boat-loads of provisions were entered free of duty at New Orleans? It is well known that Governor Miro carefully weighed the chances of being deceived by the general. He even states that it would be better thus to be deceived than to run the risk of offending the Americans by opposing their scheme of separation and their probable attachment to Louisiana. Wilkinson was accordingly received with great distinction. Even if he did not favor the scheme of separation, he no doubt took advantage of the offers of the Spaniards to transport the products of Kentucky to New Orleans free of duty. Whether he favored the scheme of separation, or merely employed it to fill his pocket and those of his neighbors in Kentucky with Spanish gold, will always remain a matter of dispute. The provincial officials showed him the favors, paid him the gold and took their chances.

Gardoqui so far receded from his restrictive orders late in 1787, that he granted to Col. George Morgan a large tract of land on the right bank of the Mississippi a short distance below the mouth of the Ohio, provided he would conduct there, as he agreed to do, a large number of emigrants. Morgan partly complied with his agreement by founding the town of New Madrid. It is well known that Wilkinson counseled the Louisiana officials to grant no concessions to the Americans, in order to force the western people to separate themselves from the rest of the United States and to sue for attachment to Louisiana. He pointed out that if they were given free trade with New Orleans, the inducements of separation would be removed. By shutting that port absolutely against them, Spain would compel them for their own protection to unite with Louisiana, providing the United States did not come to their relief. Every thing possible, short of giving the United States cause for war, was done by Spain to encourage the western people to divide the Union. Within certain limitations, they were promised the right to practice the Protestant religion—a great concession from Catholic Spain.

In the spring of 1788 upon the retirement of Navarro, Miro became intendant, as he was also governor. One of the last official acts of Navarro was to caution Spain against the aggressions of the Americans. He predicted that the United States would not be satisfied until its domain was extended to the Pacific. He declared that the only way to thwart these pretensions was to separate the East from the West and unite the latter with Louisiana, As a means to effect this object, he advised Spain to "grant every sort of commercial privileges to the masses in the western region, and shower pensions and honors on their leaders." It will thus be seen that his recommendation differed materially from that of General Wilkinson, who advised against granting any concessions whatever to the western people. As it came to pass, Wilkinson was right and Navarro wrong, because the western people had no desire to separate from the rest of the Union, unless it was necessary to do so in order to obtain a market for their products. Miro, Gardoqui and Florida Blanca did all in their power to dismember the American Union. They sent spies to every part of the United States to effect this object. Much more would have been accomplished had they not issued conflicting directions to subordinates.

The separation of Kentucky from Virginia in 1788 was thought to be an opportune time for its attachment to Louisiana; but the government of the United States had become so much stronger that its promises of relief deterred the western people from resorting to extreme measures. The anxiety of Spain to divide the Union, caused her officials in Louisiana to permit almost unrestricted trade, and so long as that state of things continued the western people wanted no change. The adoption of the federal constitution in 1789 and the inauguration of George Washington as first president of the United States, gave every indication of a government strong enough, not only to take care of the western settlers, but to prevent with force, if necessary, their separation from the Union. These indications were not lost upon the Spanish leaders. They realized that not a moment was to be lost, if a separation was to be effected. Large sums of money were sent to Wilkinson and others to be employed in accomplishing the design of Spain. A boat load of eatables was sent to Kentucky from New Orleans and ordered sold at the same price they commanded in that city. The delegate of Kentucky to Congress, a man named Brown, opposed the incorporation of that State into the Union, on the grounds that the prosperity of the people demanded their separation. But the incorporation of Kentucky into the Union and the vigorous course of President Washington in asserting the pre-eminent authority of the government, completely checkmated the designs of General Wilkinson (if such were his designs) and those of Spain. The western people were given positive assurance that their requirements would receive proper attention in due time. Wilkinson accordingly informed Governor Miro of this change in the sentiments and opinions of the western people.

Immediately succeeding these important events, others equally important came to light. The British of Canada made an attempt to induce the settlers in the western part of the United States to join them in a movement to disposses Spain of Louisiana. The British agent, Colonel Connolly, visited General Wilkinson in Kentucky, and, in order to gain his approval and assistance, laid bare all the plans of the leaders. Connolly informed Wilkinson that Lord Dorchester would arm and equip ten thousand men, if the Kentuckians would undertake the enterprise. Wilkinson was offered almost any position and emolument he might desire to lead the movement. He was promised the assistance of a fleet, which would move up the Mississippi and co-operate with his land operations. But Connolly seems to have received no encouragement from Wilkinson. The latter was too bright not to see that any attempt to separate the West from the East would be promptly suppressed by President Washington. No sooner had Connolly informed Wilkinson of the designs of the British of Canada to unite with the western people to deprive Spain of Louisiana, than he transmitted the intelligence with his comments to Miro. This act of Wilkinson was rewarded by his appointment as the agent of Spain and by the payment to him of a large sum of money. It was in 1788, also, that Col. John Sevier, as the representative of the State of Frankland, announced to the Louisiana officials that his people desired to form an alliance with Spain and to place themselves under her protection.

So earnest were the people on the Cumberland river in this movement, they named one of their districts Miro in honor of the Spanish governor. The Spanish duty of fifteen per cent. on American products shipped into Louisiana was declared by Miro to be unsound policy, because it removed the necessity of the western people to join Louisiana.

In order to retain the good will of General Wilkinson, Miro, on behalf of the Spanish government, bought of him in April, 1789, tobacco to the amount of two hundred and thirty-five thousand pounds. If Wilkinson was not now the friend of Spain he was making his pretense of being so a very profitable venture for himself and his Kentucky neighbors. The two districts of Frankland and Miro, known formerly as Cumberland, desired to join Spain. James White, a member of congress from the Miro district (now Memphis), communicated this desire to both Gardoqui and Miro. But when the conditions of annexation were announced by the latter, it was found that the Americans were not willing to accept them. They were reasonable and highly proper in every particular; but the Americans wanted to remain practically independent and at the same time to be protected by Spain. The terms granted by Gardoqui to Colonel Morgan were disapproved by Miro, who "called the attention of the cabinet of Madrid to the danger of thus having an *imperium in imperio,* a government within a government." Miro informed Spain that had he agreed to the Morgan grant, an independent republic would have been organized in Louisiana and the states would have been depopulated to settle all of Louisiana upon similar terms. In order to check this independent movement, Miro sent a squad of about thirty-five soldiers under the command of Lieut. Pierre Foucher to build a fort at or near New Madrid, and commissioned that officer civil and military commandant of that district. He was instructed to be extremely friendly to the Americans.

As an indication of the course the United States intended to pursue in regard to the land of the Natchez district, it is sufficient to observe that the State of Georgia sold to the South Carolina Company in 1789 a tract of 52,900 square miles on the left bank of the Mississippi and extending from the mouth of the Yazoo river down to a short distance above Natchez. The company endeavored to secure the co-operation of Wilkinson, but were only partly successful. Of course, the movement encountered the prompt and emphatic opposition of the Spanish officials at New Orleans. Miro wrote to Wilkinson, "Spain is in possession of all that she conquered from Great Britain in the last war, and consequently of the territory which these gentlemen have obtained from the State of Georgia, and therefore so long as the question of limits shall not be settled, every attempt to seize on any portion of the land to which we have a previous right of possession, will be an act of hostility which we must resist." Colonel Morgan, in order to retain the good graces of Spain, was forced to countenance the plans of the provincial administration. His town of New Madrid (L'Anse a la Graisse) did not fulfill his expectations. The settlers there, in a memorial prepared by them, found fault with the exactions of their leader and complained of the lawlessness of their surroundings. An intimation by Wilkinson to Miro that a body of Americans would be pleased to form a settlement at Walnut Hills (Vicksburg) was discountenanced by the latter.

It was the design of Miro to people the Natchez district with Spanish subjects. This he accomplished, but they were mostly Americans, with a decided predilection to revolution and independence. West of the Mississippi the inhabitants were submissive and usually opposed to the inroads of the Americans. The pretensions of the Virginia Company to a large tract on the left bank of the Mississippi above the mouth of the Yazoo were denied by Miro; but he did not oppose, though he did not countenance, the claims of the Tennessee Company to a tract on the Tennessee river near its mouth. In August, 1789, he wrote as follows to the Spanish cabinet: "This leads me to renew the propositions which I have made, to declare New Orleans a free port for all the European nations, and even for the United States of America, and to clothe me with the power, either to restrain, or to stop altogether, as I may deem it opportune, the commerce of Kentucky and the other settlements on the Ohio. You will then see Louisiana densely populated in a few years. . . . I believe that I am not in error when I affirm, that to confine Louisiana to trade with our nation (Spain), would be to ruin her. . . . I have recommended them (the Indians) to remain quiet, and told them, if these people (the Americans) presented themselves with a view to settle on their lands, then to make no concessions and to warn them off; but to attack them in case they refused to withdraw; and I have promised that I would supply them with powder and ball, to defend their legitimate rights." All attempts by the Americans to gain the favor of the Indians under McGillivray were fruitless.

The royal schedule of May, 1789, concerning the education and

occupation of slaves, was so strongly objected to that the Cabildo
forwarded a remonstrance to the Spanish cabinet. In 1790, war
with Great Britain over the Nootka Sound controversy seemed
imminent, and again rumors of a military movement down the
Mississippi were circulated. The fears of the Louisianians were
finally dispelled by the announcement from Philadelphia that the
British would not be permitted to cross the territory of the United
States to attack Louisiana. But the United States took advantage
of this circumstance to press its claims to the right of navigating
the Mississippi. The entire revenue of the province in 1790
amounted to sixty-six thousand one hundred and sixty-three
dollars. The revolution in St. Domingo in 1791 sent many new
settlers to Louisiana. In December of this year, the Baron de
Carondelet succeeded Miro as governor and intendant of
Louisiana and West Florida. His *bando de buen gobierno,* or
proclamation of orders to the inhabitants, inaugurated many
innovations. He wrote to the Spanish cabinet that an expenditure
of two hundred and fifty thousand dollars would be necessary to
put Louisiana in a proper state of defense. The French revolution was raging, and trouble might be expected. In fact war
between Spain and Great Britain seemed likely at this date.

In June, 1793, a royal schedule granted improved commercial
regulations to the Louisianians. Even the Spanish cabinet
"winked at" violations of the trade restrictions, and, as a consequence, the people were prosperous and happy. A large trade
was carried on between New Orleans and Philadelphia. News
was received this year that Louis XVI had perished on the scaf-
fold and that Spain had declared war against the French republic.
So many of the Louisianians favored the French revolution that
there was little mourning over the death of the king; but the war
between France and Spain was an important matter. However,
sympathizers with the French revolution were held totally in
check by Governor Carondelet. He fortified New Orleans and
other points, and wrote to the Spanish cabinet that had it not been
for this fact, and for his strict measures of repression, a revolution
would have taken place in Louisiana. He recommended the abandonment of Fort Panmure at Natchez for the occupation of Fort
Nogales at Walnut Hills. The war declared in 1793 between
France and Great Britain gave him so much concern that, considering the limitation of his means, he put the colony in an excellent state of defense. About this time the Indian slaves applied
for the freedom that had been promised them as far back as the
administration of O'Reilly. On this subject, he reported adversely

to the Spanish cabinet.   In 1794, the first newspaper published in the province, *Le Moniteur de la Louisiane,* was issued at New Orleans.

In 1794, the Jacobins of Louisiana, led by a society of French revolutionists in Philadelphia, attempted to inaugurate a rebellion at New Orleans.   At first public meetings were held, and fiery pamphlets were circulated among the people.   But Carondelet promptly prohibited such assemblages, suppressed the circulars, and transported six of the leaders to Cuba.   The attempts of the French minister near the United States, Genet, to organize an expedition among the western people of the United States for the purpose of descending the Mississippi to attack New Orleans, greatly alarmed the Louisianians; but the course of the government at Philadelphia in promptly demanding the recall of Genet, and in suppressing the whisky insurrection in western Pennsylvania, largely removed the apprehensions of Carondelet.   However, he put all the men—soldiers and militia—at his command, in all about six thousand, in readiness to repel any movement of that character.   At this time he diplomatically removed more of the trade restrictions, in order to appease the western people; but as soon as the danger was past he ordered the restoration of the restrictions.

The first successful manufacture of sugar on an extensive scale in Louisiana was effected in 1795 by Etienne D'Boré.   His crop sold for twelve thousand dollars, a large sum in those days.   It is related that many persons interested in the success of the experiment gathered to witness the sugar granulate, and that, when they saw that it did without a doubt, a great shout of joy arose, and Boré was overwhelmed with congratulations.   By 1800 there were sixty sugar plantations in Louisiana, with an annual product of four million pounds of sugar.

The treaty of 1795 between Spain and the United States, by which the latter was conceded the ownership of the Natchez district, the right to navigate the Mississippi, and the privilege of deposit at New Orleans for three years, did much to quiet the western people and to advance their prosperity and that of the Louisianians.   By 1795 the population of the province had become so large that it was found necessary to appoint six additional regidors.   So strict were the rules adopted, that almost every subject was constituted a spy in the interest of the Spanish government.   Carondelet evidently believed, and he certainly practiced, that "eternal vigilance is the price of safety."

The revolution of France drove many royalists to Louisiana,

among others being Marquis de Maison Rouge, Baron de Bastrop and Jacques Céran de Lassus de St. Vrain. Maison Rouge was granted thirty thousand acres, St. Vrain ten thousand square arpens (nearly five-sixths of an English acre), and De Bastrop twelve square leagues on the Ouichita in Louisiana. But the conditions under which the grants were made were never complied with, and hence a full title did not pass to the grantees. These grants were accompanied by terms of great liberality to individual families. In 1796 still greater inducements were offered. Families were given farms at little more than the cost of the office fees and the surveys. Farms of eight hundred acres were obtained for about forty-one dollars. The object of this liberality was hurriedly to furnish Louisiana, particularly the Missouri region, with a sufficient population, loyal to Spain, to resist any probable attack of the Canadians or the Americans. The Spanish fort opposite the mouth of the Ohio, built by D'Lemos, was made a port of entry, at which all American vessels were required to land to declare their cargoes. This step was taken to prevent the entrance of contraband into Louisiana. The fort was also established to serve as an outpost to check any movement of the British down the river.

In 1795 a conspiracy of the blacks to massacre the white inhabitants at New Orleans and vicinity, was crushed, and twenty-three of them were hung along the Mississippi from Pointe Coupée to New Orleans and thirty-one were severely whipped. The next year Carondelet renewed the Spanish attempts to separate the western people from the rest of the United States; and, in order that no time might be lost, he retained the forts in the Natchez district, upon the order of the Spanish cabinet, regardless of the fact that such a step was a violation of the treaty of 1795. He rightly reasoned that, if Louisiana was to be attacked either by the Canadians, or by the Americans, the possession of those forts would give him an immense advantage at the commencement of hostilities. Elaborate plans were laid by Carondelet and the western people, at the head of whom was Wilkinson again, to divide the Union and attach the western portion to Louisiana. Thus everything was thought to be ready when Spain declared war against Great Britain on the 7th of October, 1796. Carondelet still held the forts of the Natchez district, employed every resource to gain the adherence of the western people, put his fighting strength in the best possible condition, and grimly waited for the advance of the Canadians gathered on the St. Lawrence, or for the appearance of a British fleet at the mouth of the

Mississippi. He knew that one hostile act by the United States would annul the treaty of 1795 and justify Spain in retaining possession of the forts of the Natchez district. But the United States neither countenanced a hostile act of its own against Spain, nor permitted the Canadians to march across its territory to attack Louisiana; and hence, in 1798, the forts at Natchez, Walnut Hills and Chickasaw Bluffs were evacuated. The only other important event prior to the cession of the province to the United States was the interdiction of the deposits at New Orleans in 1802, under the orders, probably, of the French Republic, designed to test the spirit of the western people. The design was fully accomplished.

The reign of Louisiana by Spain was unwise and without foresight. Had the ports freely been opened to all countries, though with some disadvantages to the Americans, and had the Protestants been permitted to practice their religion without serious opposition, the province would have been so densely populated by 1790, that no fear whatever need have been felt by the Spanish officials from either the United States or Great Britain. The only precaution necessary would have been to hold a large standing army in readiness throughout the province to check at its incipiency any manifestation of independence. But the inherent blindness of Spain, and her extraordinary religious intolerance, caused her to lose this invaluable possession.

The policy of commercial exclusion, to which Spain adhered so rigidly, was deemed unwise by her own statesmen, but was insisted on by her "Council of the Indies." At the date of the treaty of Utrecht, M. Mesnager, then one of the greatest statesmen in Europe, favored the free trade of the Spanish-American colonies. He said, "It would be advantageous even to the interests of that monarchy (Spain), to secure to all the nations of Europe the commerce of the New World." It seems also that the King of Spain was not averse to such a policy.* But this project was overruled by the Royal and Supreme Council of the Indies, which recognized no colonial prosperity not founded upon an exclusive monopoly. There can be no doubt that the restrictions placed upon the trade of Louisiana Province by both France and Spain, had much to do with the misery of the colonists and the lack of prosperity of the colony for so many years. The moment the restrictions relaxed, the colony bounded forward to a surprising degree, only again to be repressed by the exactions of the monopoly. "From 1778, a royal ordinance had allowed a trade

---

* Negotiations for the Succession of Spain: By M. Colbert de Torcy.

between the colonies and the principal ports and places of the
mother country. The success of this experiment surpassed every
one's expectation, and yet the eyes of the Spanish ministers were
not opened. Intercourse with the colonies was more rigorously
than ever forbidden to foreigners. The severity had degenerated
into an absolute despotism, when, in 1785, internal commotions
announced dispositions tending to a general insurrection of the
aborigines and even of the colonists." † The rebellion which
was crushed by O'Reilly in 1769 was the first step to cast off the
yoke of commercial despotism.

It was the Royal Council of the Indies that thwarted the designs
of Count D'Aranda to form three great Spanish-American states ;
that body would thereby have lost its powers and its influence.
D'Aranda had foreseen from the commencement of the American
revolution the probability of the spread of independent principles
to the possessions of Spain in America ; and it was largely through
his advice and instrumentality that Spain evaded the persistent
requests of the American revolutionists to join them against
Great Britain. The rising of the Mexican Indians against Spain
in 1778 was an imitation of the example of the American revolutionists. It was clear to the leading statesmen of both France
and Spain that every concession to their American colonists meant
aid and encouragement to revolution. Every enactment for the
prosperity of the Spanish-American colonies weakened Spain and
strengthened independent principles. This was well known,
and furnishes the reason for the tenacity with which Spain clung
to her policy of restriction and exclusion. She thus made extravagant claims to territory at the close of the revolution. She even
demanded in 1788, as a consideration of the grant to the free
navigation of the Mississippi, "that it should only take effect in
case they (the western people) determined to form an empire
distinct from that of the Atlantic States. This overture, in
which the intention of destroying the federal union so indiscreetly
appeared, was not even taken into consideration (by the United
States)."†

There is no doubt that, in the first instance, France attempted
to avail herself of the revolution of the British American colonies
to regain her former possessions in the St. Lawrence and the Mississippi basins. Previous to the treaty between the colonies and
France, the Count de Vergennes, in 1778, attempted to re-establish the claims of France in America on the grounds of priority
of discovery, and suggested in a *projet* to the English court a

---

† History of Louisiana : Marbois.

"practicable means to reconcile the pretensions of the English and French as to the limits of their North American possessions," requiring the renunciation by England of Canada and every portion of ancient Louisiana. But Great Britain refused to agree to the *projet* for two reasons: 1. She expected to conquer the colonies and thus retain both Canada and that portion of Louisiana east of the Mississippi; and 2. She would rather see the colonies independent than see them fall into the hands of her ancient enemy—France. Thus, unable to regain her American colonies by intrigue, France, incensed still more by this refusal and realizing that the battle of Saratoga rendered it fairly certain that the colonies would succeed, agreed to the treaty of mutual hostility against England.*

---

* History of Louisiana: Marbois.

CHAPTER IX

The Expedition of Lewis and Clark

STRANGE as it may seem, the expedition of Lewis and Clark up the Missouri river, across the Rocky mountains, and down the valley of the Columbia river to the Pacific, was projected before the territory west of the Mississippi was ceded to the United States, but not before it was known to President Jefferson that the expedition would be permitted to proceed. The schedule of instructions to Captain Lewis was prepared in April, 1803; while the cession to the United States was not signed by Bonaparte until the last day of the same month and year, and could not, therefore, have been known to Jefferson, who wrote the instructions. They were signed by the President June 20, 1803, about ten days before he learned that the cession to the United States had been signed at Paris.

The instructions recite that "the object of your mission is to explore the Missouri river, and such principal streams of it as, by its course and communication with the waters of the Pacific ocean, whether the Columbia, Oregon, Colorado, or any other river, may offer the most direct and practicable water communication across the continent, for the purpose of commerce." Owing to the fact that Louisiana was not in possession of the United States at the time the instructions were drafted, it became necessary to procure passports for the party from the rightful sovereignty, France, and from both Spain and Great Britain to insure proper reception by their agents and traders scattered throughout the territory. Jefferson became aware of the cession about the 1st of July, and five days later Capt. Meriwether Lewis, whom the President had selected to command the expedition, left Washington for Pittsburg, where a portion of the men were to be secured and suitable equipment was to be provided. Various delays occurred, until the season was so far advanced as to render it inadvisable to start before the spring of 1804.

It was determined by the President to associate two commanders of the expedition, and accordingly Capt. William Clark was chosen, and given co-ordinate powers with Captain Lewis. Both men were members of well-known and prominent families of that period. Captain Lewis was a Virginian, and his great uncle had married a sister of George Washington. Captain Clark was the younger brother of George Rogers Clark, who had wrested the western country from Great Britain near the close of the Revolution. Both Lewis and Clark had already distinguished themselves in the army, and a better selection of leaders for such an important expedition could scarcely have been made. To the highest qualities of leadership, they added broad comprehension, unwavering persistence, wonderful endurance, and a dauntless courage that knew no fear nor recognized no failure. Every citizen of the United States became at once intensely interested in the results, and waited anxiously for the return of the expedition. Particularly were the results vitally interesting to the western people, who prayed that a practical water-way to the Pacific might be discovered.

Captain Clark joined the expedition at Louisville, and all arrived in St. Louis in December, 1803. Until the Spanish commandant should receive official intelligence from his government of the cession to the United States, he requested the expedition to remain on the east side of the Mississippi; and therefore winter encampment was chosen at the mouth of Wood river, beyond his jurisdiction. The start was made May 14, 1804, the expedition consisting of nine Kentuckians, two experienced French boatmen, fourteen soldiers, one interpreter, one hunter and a colored servant; and in addition a corporal, six soldiers and nine boatmen, who were instructed to assist the expedition as far as the Mandan country. There was taken along a considerable quantity of clothing, implements, ammunition and Indian presents, such as richly-laced coats and pants, medals, flags, scalping-knives, tomahawks, beads, pigments, handkerchiefs, looking-glasses, etc. They embarked in three boats—one a keel-boat, fifty-five feet long, bearing one large sail and arranged for twenty-two oarsmen, having a deck provided with cabin and forecastle, and protected amidships by lockers and by a breastwork that could be raised in case of attack. In addition there were two pirogues of six and seven oars respectively. Two horses were ridden along the bank, designed to bring in the game killed, upon which it was planned the expedition would largely subsist. Full provision was made for a complete record of all noteworthy discoveries and occurrences.

It should be borne in mind that the principal cause of the intense interest in the expedition was the wish to learn the secrets hidden in the unknown western country. Previous to this time, only fugitive and contradictory accounts of the upper Missouri territory had reached the ears of the Americans. Now, all that country was theirs; and they wished to learn how true were the fabulous tales of lofty mountains, fertile plains, arid deserts, splendid water-courses, wild animals, savage tribes and rich minerals, which had come down to them from the French and Spanish voyageurs, traders and trappers, and which were so shadowy that little dependence had ever been placed in their accuracy. All the vast territory was now at last to be opened to the enterprise of the Americans; and Lewis and Clark were dispatched to take the first step in the primeval darkness of the wilderness.

They reached the town of St. Charles on May 15, passed Osage Woman river on May 23, and on June 1 reached the mouth of the Osage river. On the 10th they arrived at the two Chariton rivers. Everything of note was duly recorded. On the 26th the mouth of Kansas river was reached, and on June 21 they arrived at the Platte of Nebraska. Passing up the Missouri, they encamped at what is now Council Bluffs, where later a council was held with the chiefs of the neighboring tribes. Another council was held farther up the river on August 3, with the Otoes and the Missouris. A council was held with the Omahas on the 18th and 19th. Continuing to ascend, they held a council with the Sioux August 30. Teton river was reached September 24, and the next day a council was held with the most powerful band of the Sioux. At its conclusion they tried to prevent the advance of the expedition, and a bloody conflict was narrowly averted. The expedition continued to ascend. Cheyenne river was reached October 1. Four days later an old, deserted village of the Arickarees was reached. On the 8th Grand river was passed. The next day a council was held with the Arickarees. Unlike almost every other tribe, they refused to drink whisky, and questioned the friendship of the whites who offered it to them. They had never seen a negro until they saw York, the servant of Captain Clark. They examined him with astonishment, and tried to rub out his color with their fingers wet with spit. They considered it a great honor to serve him.

No sooner had the news of the arrival of the Americans been circulated among the Mandans, than the numerous villages for several miles around sent their informal delegations to see and to greet the strangers. Mr. McCracken and another agent of the Northwest Company were among the Mandans to buy buffalo robes, furs and horses. The boats proceeded along the stream, followed by many of the Indians, who trudged along the shore. Camp was finally spread on the west side. The two Captains visited the villages, and were received with lavish protestations of friendship. In return the entire population of the village came with the Americans to their camp, where they were shown the various curiosities, such as the air-gun, an iron corn-mill, etc. At both places the pipe of perpetual peace was smoked. From an adjacent Ahnahaway village came Jesseaume, another French trader, to visit the arrivals.

All were assembled in a general council at the American camp on the 29th—Mandans, Minnetarees and Ahnahaways. In order to impress the savages as much as possible, the soldiers were paraded under arms and the swivel was fired. Under the sail of the boat, which had been spread to ward off the cold wind, the usual speeches were delivered, and afterward the presents were distributed. All promised peace with the Arickarees and obedience to the laws of the United States. Captain Lewis asked the Mandans to return the goods that had recently been taken from the two Frenchmen previously mentioned, and they promised to comply. Of all the presents given on this occasion, the Indians prized the corn-mill highest. The principal chiefs present were Big White, or Sha-ha-ka; Little Raven, or Ka-go-ha-mi; Big Man, or Oh-hee-naw, an adopted Cheyenne; Coal, or Sho-ta-haw-ro-ra; Black Cat, or Po-cap-sa-he; Raven Man Chief, or Ka-go-no-mok-she; White Buffalo Robe Unfolded, or Te-tuck-o-pin-re-ha; Black Moccasin, or Omp-se-ha-ra; Red Shield, or E-a-pa-no-pa; Neighing Horse, or Min-nis-sur-ra-ree; Old Woman at a Distance, or Lo-can-go-ti-ha; Little Fox, or Oh-haw; Big Thief, or Mah-no-tah; Tail of the Calumet Bird, or Mah-se-ras-sa; Two Tailed Calumet Bird, or Wan-ke-ras-sa; Cherry on a Bush, or Cal-tah-co-ta; and Wolf Man Chief, or Ah-rat-tan-a-mock-she. Presents were sent to the chiefs who were absent.

While at this village the Americans witnessed a prairie fire that started, no one knew how, and traveled so fast that several of the Indians were burned to death and their lodges destroyed. Others were dreadfully scorched and had narrow escapes from death: one little savage was saved by his mother, who spread over him a green buffalo robe. It having been determined to pass the winter near the Mandan villages; Captain Clark was sent up the river to locate a suitable site; but soon returned, not finding sufficient timber. A site was finally selected on the east side a short distance below their camp, where there was an abundance of timber and good water. The men were at once set to work cutting down trees and shaping logs for the rude structures. In the meantime the Mandans were visited and their good will was secured. Much of the stolen property of the two Frenchmen was returned to them. The head chief of the Mandans promised to visit his "great father" at Washington, but wanted to be protected from the lower Sioux, with whom they were at war. Large quantities of corn were obtained from the Indians for presents and services. The agents of the Northwest Company were strictly cautioned against stirring the Indians to make war either on each other or on the Americans. The Mandans declared that the Arickarees were the aggressors in the trouble between the two nations. While the log houses were being built, many Indians came to watch the proceedings. As soon as they were ready for occupancy, the traders in the vicinity came to live with the Americans.

By the 8th of November, the log cabins were well advanced toward completion. At this time large flocks of wild geese, brants, ducks and other water fowl passed southward high in the air. On November 13th the boat was unloaded, its contents were placed in one of the cabins, and all day the snow fell heavily, leaving a white mantle of great beauty on the landscape. About this time the Mandans were visited by parties of Assiniboines and Kristenaux (Krees) from the country around Lake Winnipeg. The two Frenchmen mentioned above, caught twenty beavers in one day on the river and its small branches. It had become quite cold, and much ice began to run in the river. Part of the men— the best hunters—were kept out constantly to supply the fort with fresh meat. On November 16th, the log huts, though still unfinished, were occupied by the soldiers. It was observed that in the intercourse between the Indians, the Mandans were treated by the Assiniboines as the Arickarees were treated by the Sioux, i. e., as partly under subjection. The hunters who had been out for several days, returned on the 19th with thirty-two deer, eleven elks, and five buffaloes. The meat was preserved for future use.

The following day the log cabins were fully completed and were wholly occupied, and the place was formally named Fort Mandan. There were two rows of huts or sheds "forming an angle where they joined each other, each row containing four rooms of fourteen square feet and seven feet high, with plank ceilings, and the roof slanting so as to form a loft above the

I—20

rooms, the highest part of which is eighteen feet from the ground; the backs of the huts formed a wall of that height, and opposite the angle the place of the wall was supplied by picketing; in the area were the rooms for stores and provisions." The latitude of the fort was found to be 47 degrees, 21 minutes and 47 seconds, and the distance from the mouth of the Missouri one thousand six hundred miles. At this time the implacable Sioux seemed bent on war with the Mandans: they abused some of the Arickarees for exhibiting friendship for the Mandans and the Americans. Within the fort, Captains Lewis and Clark felt safe from any numbers of Indians likely to be brought against them; but it was realized that the savages might starve them out by driving off the game or by attacking the hunters. In the immediate vicinity of the fort, were five villages of the Mandans, Minnetarees and Ahnahaways. As soon as the Americans were well settled in their new quarters, almost daily conferences were held with the Indians, and every effort was made to gain their permanent good will. But all attempts to secure the friendship of the Sioux were repulsed. Evidently that arrogant tribe needed a sound threshing. On the 27th, seven traders of the Northwest Company arrived from the Assiniboine country. When one of their interpreters covertly circulated among the Indians damaging stories concerning the Americans, they were informed by Captain Clark that a repetition of such conduct would lead to their expulsion from the Mandan country. Among the Mandan chiefs not previously mentioned was Horned Weasel, or Mah-pah-pa-pa-ra-pas-sa-too.

During the last few days of November, snow fell to the depth of thirteen inches on the level, and the mercury dropped to about zero. Mr. Laroche, the leader of the traders from the Assiniboin, was told that under no circumstances should British medals or flags be given to the Indians; whereupon he replied that he had no such intentions. About this time, several of the Mandans having been killed by the Sioux, Captain Clark, with a force of twenty-three soldiers, visited the former, and volunteered to assist them in punishing the latter. This course was adopted to convince the Mandans that the friendship of the Americans had been promised in good faith, as well as to punish the Sioux. The Mandans were greatly pleased at this act, because they had been told by the Arickarees that the Americans intended to join the Sioux against them. The complete confidence of the Mandans was secured, but they pointed to the fact that the cold weather and the deep snow were an effectual bar to a war expedition to the Sioux territory.

Early in December bands of Cheyennes and Pawnees visited the Mandans. Mr. Henderson, of the Hudson's Bay Company, who had come to the Minnetarees, also called upon the American officers. A message was sent to Messrs. Tebeau and Gravelines, who were in the Arickaree villages, to employ their best endeavors to prevent the Sioux from waging war on the Mandans. On December 7, a large herd of buffalo being in the vicinity of the fort, the Indians and the whites engaged in a general hunt. Only five animals were secured by the latter. The next morning the thermometer stood at twelve degrees below zero. On this day eight more buffaloes were secured, but many of the men were frost-bitten. Nine more buffaloes were killed the following day, but the whites were compelled to go so far from the fort that they were forced to spend the night in the deep snow and the intense cold. On the 11th the thermometer showed twenty-one degrees below zero, and the men were not permitted to leave the fort. Early the next morning it showed thirty-eight degrees below zero. On the 17th it stood at forty-five below zero, and the following day at thirty-two below. Large herds of buffalo crossed the river on the ice. During the mild weather several of the men were kept at work completing the stockade. On Christmas day, the American flag was hoisted over the fort for the first time. The best provisions in their possession and a little brandy enabled all to celebrate the day fittingly.

The new year, 1805, was ushered in "by two shots from the swivel and a round of small arms. In the morning we permitted sixteen men with their music to go to the first village, where they delighted the whole tribe with their dances, particularly with the movements of one of the Frenchmen, who danced on his head. In return they presented the dancers with several buffalo robes and quantities of corn. We were desirous of showing this attention to the village, because they had received an impression that we had been wanting in regard for them, and because they had in consequence circulated invidious comparisons between us and the northern traders." About this time war became imminent between the Minnetarees and the Ahnahaways over a girl of the former who had been stolen by the latter; but the maiden was returned and peace was patched up. This is a common expression in the journal: "Po-cap-sa-he visited us today and brought some meat on his wife's back." It was no uncommon sight to see the lordly buck stalking along empty-handed while his faithful squaw staggered by his side bearing a burden weighing one hundred pounds. Among the Americans was a blacksmith, who was regarded as a superior medicine man by the Indians; particularly was his bellows an object of intense veneration. They never tired watching his flaming forge and the coruscating sparks. He was kept busy all winter mending and making all sorts of articles for both whites and reds. The latter purchased repairs with the various grains. The Indians had two warm-weather dances which were unique in the extreme. The description of one of them in the journal was written in Latin. Thus a naked, indelicate and barbarous custom was clothed in the somber and secret garments of a dead language.

The weather became extremely cold again, the thermometer standing at twenty-one degrees below zero on the 9th, forty below on the 10th, thirty-eight below on the 11th, twenty below on the 12th, and thirty-four below on the 13th, after which it began to moderate. From time to time the Indian chiefs were permitted to pass nights at the fort. On the 15th a total eclipse of the moon was observed. A large band of the Minnetarees visited the fort on the 16th; and their friendship was secured—not promised. When the trader, Laroche, asked permission to accompany the expedition to the mouth of the Yellowstone, he was refused by Captain Lewis, who doubted his friendship where his own interests were concerned, and did not care to identify a private enterprise with a public movement. The American captains were greatly impressed with the firmness, intelligence and integrity of the chief, Po-cap-sa-he, who, in their estimation, was the superior of any Indian they had yet met. Strange as it may seem, the horses of this region preferred the bark and twigs of the cottonwood trees to meal bran moistened with water. "These horses are very severely treated; for whole days they are pursuing the buffalo or burdened with the fruits of the chase, during which they scarcely ever taste food, and at night return to a scanty allowance of wood; yet the spirit of this valuable animal sustains him through all these difficulties, and he is rarely deficient either in flesh or vigor."

A hunting party which had been out for several days returned February 13th with forty deer, nineteen elks and three buffaloes; but unfortunately much of the flesh was too lean to be of any use, except to the wolves, ravens and magpies. The party had gone fifty miles from the fort, and had suffered intensely from the severe cold. About this time another small party of hunters were surrounded by a band of Sioux, who cut their traces and stole two of their horses and several knives. For this flagrant act it was determined to pursue and punish them. The Mandans were asked if they wished to assist: as nearly all of the warriors were away on a hunt, only a few could be secured. These few joined the expedition under Captain Lewis, which set out at sunrise on the 15th with over twenty men. The fierce cold and snow-blindness forced several to return. Though the Sioux were followed a long distance, they were not overtaken; in default of which Captain Lewis formed a hunting party and brought in about three thousand pounds of buffalo, deer and elk meat.

It now being the middle of February, preparations were made to ascend the river as soon as the ice should melt and the river become clear. The boats were cut out of the ice and put in good condition; tools and weapons were cleaned and sharpened, and the supplies of clothing, trinkets, ammunition and provisions looked after. Large trees were cut down to be used in making boats to take the place of the large batteaux, which had brought them thus far on their journey. About this time it was learned from the Arickarees that the Sioux had declared they intended to kill all Americans who came to their country. Early in March the weather became quite warm, and the ice on the river began to break. During the winter all knowledge possible of the Rocky mountain region had been obtained from the various Indian and French visitors. A Minnetaree chief who had not yet seen the Americans, visited the fort, and asked particularly to see the negro, York, of whom he had heard extravagant stories from his tribe. He was astonished at the sight of the negro, and having wet his finger with spit he tried to rub out the color of the skin. "Nor was it until the negro uncovered his head and showed his short hair, that the chief could be persuaded that he was not a painted white man."

Just before the departure of the Americans, there was an enormous demand from the Indians for battle-axes made of sheet iron by the blacksmith. Taking advantage of this demand, large quantities of corn were obtained for use in the upper country, when game should grow scarce. All the traders in the vicinity and all the Indian chiefs visited the fort once more before the expedition again started on its historic journey. Despite the influence of the Americans and the traders, the Sioux continued on the war-path, and in self defense the other nations were forced to take up the hatchet. Previous to the departure of the expedition, several war parties of the Minnetarees set out to retaliate on the Sioux. The Mandans were preparing for similar grim action. Thus one of the missions of the expedition at least—to bring about peace between the tribes—was far from accomplishment.

The Sioux were wholly to blame, and needed a trouncing. The misfortune was great that the expedition was not strong enough to give them at this time a practical lesson of the strength of their great father at Washington.

By the middle of March there was every indication of approaching spring. The snow had almost wholly disappeared from the plains, and terrible prairie fires could be seen in every direction racing faster than the swiftest horse. These fires were set by the Indians so that the tender grass would soon draw to the region the vast herds of buffalo, antelope, elk, deer, etc. Countless numbers of wild fowl were observed flying north day and night. The ice in the river began to break, and on it were caught many buffaloes that tried to cross. The river began to rise and the rushing rainstorms swept furiously across the plains. Preparations for the earliest start possible were completed. The barge which was to be sent down the rivers, freighted with articles for President Jefferson, was loaded on the 4th of April; and the following day was spent in preparing those intended for the up journey. Finally, the barge was sent away, carrying a total of fifteen hands, among whom were five traders and several Indian chiefs on their way to Washington.

The party to ascend the river consisted of thirty-two persons: Captains Lewis and Clark; Sergeants John Ordway, Patrick Gass and Nathaniel Pryor; Privates William Bratton, John Collins, John Colter, Peter Cruzatte, Reuben Fields, Joseph Fields, Robert Frazier, George Gibson, Silas Goodrich, Hugh Hall, Thomas P. Howard, Francis Labiche, Baptiste Lapage, Hugh McNeal, John Potts, John Shields, George Shannon, John B. Thompson, William Werner, Joseph Whitehouse, Alexander Willard, Richard Windsor and Peter Wiser. The two interpreters were George Drewyer, a half-breed, and Touissant Chaboneau, a French adventurer and the husband of Sa-ca-ja-we-ah, or Bird Woman, a Shoshone Indian, who, with her little child, accompanied the expedition. She had been born in the Rocky mountain region; but had been captured by the Minnetarees of the prairie when a child; and later had been purchased by Chaboneau, who finally married her. During the winter, while at Fort Mandan, she had given birth to her first child. Both interpreters were adepts at prairie and wood craft, could speak several of the Indian tongues and were well versed in the sign language, by which it was comparatively easy to converse with any tribe. With the expedition was York, the negro servant of Captain Clark. Cruzatte was the fiddler and Shields the blacksmith.

As they ascended, many hunting parties of the various tribes were seen along the banks. The mounds made by the pocket gopher were observed as soon as the frost was out of the ground. "Our old companions, the mosquitoes, have renewed their visit, and gave us much uneasiness." The Little Missouri river was reached the 12th of April. Game was scarce and wild fowl shy. Having passed Chaboneau creek, the Americans were told that no white man had gone much higher. By the 17th, buffalo, elk, deer, antelope, wolves and bears began to be seen, and soon the camp was well supplied with an abundance of fresh meat. The men relished the flesh of the beaver better than that of any other variety of animal. The timber began to be scanty, but every little grove was found to contain the ruins of some recent Indian encampment. In the vicinity of White Earth river, the soil was found in places almost white with some salt. For some reason not learned, the men suffered greatly from sore eyes; they thought it was caused by the sand storms, which sometimes hid the opposite shore of the river from sight.

Upon reaching the Yellowstone river, the expedition halted long enough to enable Captain Lewis to take celestial observations, etc. This river was known to the French as Roche Jaune. The journey was resumed on the 27th, and game was found to be very abundant. At one spot it was noticed that a tree nearly three feet in diameter had been eaten off by beavers. On the 28th, Captain Lewis and a companion killed a grizzly bear. After being wounded, it pursued them, though not so fast as to prevent their loading their guns, when two more shots ended its life. Martha's river was reached the 29th, and Porcupine river May 3d. They had never before seen such a profusion of wild game as now covered the plains and river valleys. Grizzly bears were numerous, and several were killed, though not without great danger to the hunters. It was something new for the party to meet a wild animal that not only refused to retreat, but immediately started in for a fight. This bear was the monarch of the plains and the mountains; every other animal fled before it. Even the Indians gave it a wide berth. It thus had formed the habit of chasing every living thing and investigating every object it saw. When the white hunters appeared, the bears made a bee line for them, with open mouth and at a rate of speed that required a swift horse to place them at a point of safety. It was rare that one of these huge animals was killed at one shot; it often required ten or fifteen before it succumbed. In the meantime, after being wounded, it pursued the hunters, who were thus often placed in extreme peril. Fortunately, none was killed, but several had narrow escapes. More than once the pursued hunter was obliged to jump down steep embankments, or into the river, before the savage animal could be avoided. One killed May 5th weighed over five hundred pounds, had fore-claws nearly five inches long, and was not killed until ten shots had been fired into his body, five of which passed through the lungs. The only single shot that was sufficient to instantly terminate life was through the brain.

Big Dry river was reached May 6th. "The game is in such plenty that it has become a mere amusement to supply the party with provisions." Many bald eagles were observed. Milk river was passed on the 8th. "The water has a peculiar whiteness, such as might be produced by a teaspoonful of milk in a dish of tea." The water of the Missouri had now become much clearer. An Indian dog joined them on the 10th, but could not be induced to remain. It was conjectured that an encampment as Assiniboins was not far away. Another large grizzly was killed on the 11th, and here again the wonderful vitality of the animal caused all to marvel. "We had rather encounter two Indians than meet a single brown bear." The skin of this bear was "sufficient burden for two men, and eight gallons of oil were obtained from the carcass." Near Gibson creek, another was killed after the most intense excitement and danger. Eight balls were fired through his body in different directions without seriously incommoding him; finally a shot through the brain brought him to the ground. By this time, the men of the expedition began to entertain a most profound respect for the courage and vitality of this wonderful animal.

Near Rattlesnake creek it was observed that the channel of the Missouri was much narrower than before. Almost the only timber was a little cottonwood along the streams and small clumps of scrubby pine and cedar on the hills. Soon after this, an unoccupied, yet fortified, Indian encampment was passed. Musselshell river was reached on the 20th. A branch of this river was named for Chaboneau's Indian wife, Sah-ca-ja-we-ah, or Bird Woman. In this region immense quantities of prickly pear covered the ground. The weather was so cold that severe frosts appeared every night: ice was even formed along the margin of the river, "and the water froze on our oars." The remarkable fertility of the soil in several of the valleys was observed. Many of the largest creeks were found wholly dry, apparently serving merely to carry off the surplus water in times of flood. About this time difficult rapids were found in the river; and the value of the water power, the obstructions to navigation, the regularity of the supply, etc., were noted. The game began to grow scarcer as they approached the mountains, because this was the season when it sought the plains for the luxuriant and nourishing grass. The rough country where they now were was a continuation of the Black Hills. By the 26th, they reached the highest point of the hills, where the valleys were reduced to narrow strips. The journal reads: "It was here that, after ascending the highest summits of the hills on the north side of the river, Captain Lewis first caught a distant view of the Rocky mountains, the object of all our hopes and the reward of all our ambition."

From time to time great danger was encountered in the rapids, where often the boats were on the point of being dashed in pieces. The towline was in almost constant use while advancing. Large numbers of beavers and "big horns" were seen. "We came to a handsome stream which discharges itself on the south and which we named Judith river." Near this spot, on the same date, May 29th, was seen an Indian encampment of one hundred and twenty-six lodges, "which appeared to have been deserted about twelve or fifteen days, and on the other side of the Missouri a large encampment, apparently made by the same nation." Near the mouth of Judith river and at the bottom of a high cliff, were heaped the carcasses of at least one hundred buffaloes. The animals had no doubt been chased over the brink by the Indians, as such was a common practice among them. Slaughter river was duly reached and named for this circumstance; and at this time it was observed that the air was "astonishingly pure." The expedition continued to pass many abandoned Indian encampments, thought to be those of the Minnetarees of the Saskatchewan. Some snow fell in the hills as late as June. The wonderful cliff formations, worn by water into shapes resembling rocky castles, with galleries, parapets, minarets and columns, were greatly admired. The snow on the distant mountains, glistening in the summer sun, cheered the hearts of all with the prospect of cool breezes for the hot months.

Early in June two of the hunters had narrow escapes from a grizzly bear, which they finally succeeded in killing. When Maria's river was reached the two captains were in doubt as to which was the main branch of the Missouri and which would lead by the shortest and most practicable route to the navigable waters of the Columbia river. It was realized that, in a large measure, the fate of the expedition depended upon a right selection. Accordingly, detachments of men were sent up each to ascertain so far as possible the upper courses of both, before the expedition was committed to either. The open country was also explored for additional light on the subject. In spite of these investigations, there remained almost as much doubt after their return as before. A much more extensive preliminary exploration was therefore decided upon. Each of the captains, with a small squad of men, set off up the two branches and remained absent several days. It was ascertained that the upper branch, to which they had given the name Maria's river, pursued a course much too far to the north, and that the southern branch was more likely to lead by a short route to the Columbia. During their exploration, Teton river was discovered and named Tansy. Thinking that they might be forced to return, they determined to "cache" the most of their supplies and then ascend the southern branch. When Captain Lewis, who had gone in advance, at last discovered the great falls of the Missouri, it was no longer doubted that they were on the right course.

The marvelous beauty of the country was a great surprise and a constant delight to the men. The broad plains covered with wild animals, the numerous water-courses with their picturesque rapids, the stone castles carved by the ages from the perpetual hills, the myriads of birds in the fragrant groves, and the gleaming mountains in the distance, were a great inspiration to every man in the party. On one plain they saw "infinitely more buffalo than they·had ever before seen at a single view." The entire expedition reached the great falls on the 16th of June. It now became a momentous question how to pass around the falls; but it was finally accomplished after a vast amount of hard work. Here another boat thirty-six feet in length was built for use in shallower water, and the ascent of the river was resumed. Buffaloes, elks, deer, wolves, bears, beavers, wild fowl, rattlesnakes and grasshoppers abounded. Every few days some one of the party had a narrow escape from a grizzly bear. When closely pursued, the hunters often sought safety in the depth of the river. One of these animals was found to have a forefoot which measured nine inches across. They finally became so bold that they entered the camp in the night and kindled consternation. The fury of the mountain storms was a cause of great wonder. The many fine springs of pure and of mineral water, both hot and cold, were greatly enjoyed, after the many months spent in drinking the muddy and insipid water of the Missouri. By the 5th of July, the boat was finished: it consisted of a light framework of wood, covered principally with the hides of elk, deer, buffalo, etc. It was designed to carry four tons, besides the complement of hands necessary for rowing. The launching occurred on the 9th of July, "and it swam perfectly well." Unfortunately, it was found impossible to use it, owing to the lack of material with which to close the seams. All the labor was thus thrown away.

It was then determined to build several canoes to take the place of the large boat. Accordingly, two were made twenty-five and thirty-three feet long respectively, and with them the advance was resumed July 15th. Food was abundant, the mountains would be reached in a short time, and all were happy. They hoped soon to meet the Indians for two reasons: In order to procure horses to carry them 'over the mountains, and in order to be guided over the best route to the Columbia. Dearborn river was reached on the 18th. In the deep valleys, the heat was almost insupportable, while on the hill tops the frost fell nearly every night. High above them like Tantalus were the everlasting snows on the mountain tops. An extraordinary range of rocks was named Gates of the Rocky Mountains. The mosquitoes were so numerous and so fierce, that it was found necessary to use "biers" during the nights as a protection against them. Sa-ca-ja-we-ah, the wife of Chaboneau, herself a Snake or Shoshone Indian, now recognized the country as having been her home when she was a child and before she was captured by the Minnetarees. She announced that the three upper forks of the Missouri were not far distant; and the announcement revived the hopes and flagging energies of the party. Many kinds of edible fruits were found in the groves, while every day members of the party were wounded by the prickly pear. Finally to the relief of all, the three forks were reached on the 27th. Here a long rest was taken and all necessary preparation was made, before the expedition advanced to cross the mountains. The Missouri river was no longer a pilot to their course. They must find other means of guidance, and it was realized that the knowledge of the Indians must be secured and made available.

The three branches were named Madison, Jefferson and Gallatin, and the surrounding country was thoroughly explored. It was near the forks of the river that Sa-ca-ja-we-ah was captured when a child. Many of her tribe were slain at the time, and she among several others was carried into captivity. The captains finally decided to ascend Jefferson river. Philosophy river was reached and named on the 31st of July. The next day Captain Lewis and three others went in advance to find the most practicable route, while the rest of the expedition followed more slowly in their trail. Upon arriving at Beaver Head, Sa-ca-ja-we-ah

said that only a short distance to the westward the upper branches
of the Columbia could be reached. She said that the Shoshones
were encamped on those streams. As the river became narrower
and shallower, the indispensability of horses became apparent.
But horses could not be procured except from the Indians, and
every effort was therefore made to hold communication with the
members of some tribe. Indian signs were wanted. Wisdom
river was finally reached and ascended, and every eye was kept
open. Finally, Captain Lewis and his little party saw far ahead
a single horseman and the glass revealed an Indian. He was
approached with every sign of friendship known to the whites,
but was very suspicious and finally set off at full speed and was
soon out of sight. They followed his trail for a long time, but a
rain storm at last blotted out all traces of his flight, for it was
nothing else. On the 12th of August, Captain Lewis and his two
companions, Drewyer and Shields, reached the remote source of
Wisdom river, or strictly, the Missouri river, where the stream
was so small that one of the men "thanked God that he had lived
to bestride the Missouri." A few hours later "as they went along
their hope of soon seeing the waters of the Columbia arose almost
to painful anxiety; when after four miles from the last abrupt
turn of the river, they reached a small gap formed by the high
mountains which recede on each side, leaving room for the Indian
ford. From the foot of one of the lowest of these mountains,
which rises with a gentle ascent of about half a mile, issues the
remotest water of the Missouri. They had now reached the
hidden sources of that river, which had never yet been seen by
civilized man; and as they quenched their thirst at the chaste and
icy fountain—as they sat down by the brink of that little rivulet,
which yielded its distant and modest tribute to the parent ocean—
they felt themselves rewarded for all their labors and all their
difficulties."

The journal reads, "They left reluctantly this interesting spot,
and pursuing the Indian road through the interval of the hills,
arrived at the top of a ridge, from which they saw high mountains partially covered with snow still to the west of them. The
ridge on which they stood formed the dividing line between the
waters of the Atlantic and Pacific oceans. They followed a
descent much steeper than that on the eastern side, and at the
distance of three-quarters of a mile reached a handsome, bold
creek of cold, clear water running to the westward. They
stopped to taste for the first time the waters of the Columbia."
They passed the succeeding night in this vicinity. The next

morning they resumed the Indian road, which wound "along a waving plain parallel to the valley for about four miles, when they discovered two women, a man and some dogs 'on an eminence at the distance of a mile before them." Seeing the approaching whites, the Indians precipitately fled, apparently in great fear. Knowing from the presence of women that an Indian encampment was near, Captain Lewis and party followed the trail left by the man and women for several miles, until they suddenly came within thirty paces of three females, from whom they had been concealed by a ravine.

The narrative continues, "One of them, a young woman, immediately took to flight; the other two, an elderly woman and a little girl, seeing we were too near for them to escape, sat on the ground, and holding down their heads seemed as if reconciled to the death which they supposed awaited them. . . . Captain Lewis instantly put down his rifle, and advancing toward them, took the woman by the hand, raised her up, and repeated the words 'tabba bone,' at the same time stripping up his shirt sleeve to prove that he was a white man, for his hands and face had become by constant exposure quite as dark as their own. She appeared immediately relieved from her alarm, and Drewyer and Shields now coming up, Captain Lewis gave them some beads, a few awls, pewter mirrors and a little paint, and told Drewyer to request the woman to recall her companion who had escaped to some distance, and by alarming the Indians might cause them to attack him without any time for explanation. She did as she was desired, and the young woman returned almost out of breath; Captain Lewis gave her an equal portion of trinkets, and painted the tawny cheeks of all three of them with vermillion, a ceremony which among the Shoshones is emblematic of peace. After they had become composed, he informed them by signs of his wish to go to their camp in order to see their chiefs and warriors: they readily obeyed, and conducted the party along the same road down the river. In this way they marched two miles, when they met a troop of nearly sixty warriors, mounted on excellent horses, riding at full speed toward them. As they advanced Captain Lewis put down his gun, and went with the flag about fifty paces in advance. The chief, who, with two men, was riding in front of the main body, spoke to the woman, who now explained that the party was composed of white men, and showed exultingly the presents they had received. The three men immediately leaped from their horses, came up to Captain Lewis and embraced him with great cordiality, putting their left arm over his right shoulder and clasping his back; applying at the same time their left cheek to his, and frequently vociferating 'ah hi e! ah hi e!' (I am much pleased, I am much rejoiced). The whole body of warriors now came forward, and our men received the caresses and no small share of the grease and paint of their new friends."

All now seated themselves in a circle, and Captain Lewis lighted a pipe and offered it to them to smoke; but before doing so they all removed their moccasins, "a custom, as we afterward learnt, which indicated a sacred sincerity of their professions when they smoke with a stranger, and which imprecates on themselves the misery of going barefoot forever if they are faithless to their words, a penalty by no means light to those who rove over the thorny plains of their country." The chief, whose name was Ca-me-ah-wait, was told that the visit of the whites was friendly; and he explained the same to his warriors. The whites were then conducted to the Shoshone camp, distant about four miles, where all again smoked the peace pipe, and where Captain Lewis explained more elaborately the objects of the expedition. All the presents they had with them were distributed among the women and children. Captain Lewis was informed that he was on a stream that flowed west to the Pacific; and when he saw salmon flesh among the Indians, he no longer doubted that he had really crossed the divide.

It was now learned that the Indians who had been seen previously had mistaken the whites for a war party of the Minnetarees, and had hurried back to their villages with the news in order that preparations might be made to repel the expected attack. The advance of the sixty warriors was for the purpose of striking the enemy the first blow. Captain Lewis and his party remained at the Indian camp all night, and the next morning, accompanied by many of the Indians, started on their return to meet the remainder of the expedition. As they proceeded, a report was circulated among the Indians that the whites were but an advance of their enemy and were trying to lead them into an ambush; whereupon, in spite of all the endeavors of Captain Lewis, many of the Indians left them, and even the chiefs stopped for further consideration before proceeding. The women began to cry, which was another proof that an attack from an enemy was expected. Captain Lewis and his men did everything in their power to inspire confidence and anxiously hoped for the appearance of the remainder of the expedition, as it was realized that alone would fully remove the fears of the Indians. It was found that the Indians who had started back, were still following in the rear, and that they were advancing on the wings ready to strike an enemy should one appear. Thus several days passed, and the fears of the Indians seemed to increase rather than subside. They used the greatest precautions by sending out scouts in advance and on the flanks, and conducted themselves in every respect as if they were in the presence of their enemy. They even went so far as to place their own headgear and other articles of clothing on the whitemen, so that in case they proved to be members of the enemy they could not be distinguished from the Shoshones. Finally, in order to inspire confidence, if it was possible, Captain Lewis and his companions delivered their rifles to the Indian chiefs and told them to kill them the moment their statements were found untrue. This was an extreme and dangerous proceeding, because any sudden alarm might cause the unwarranted shooting of the three men; but in their dangerous situation they concluded to take desperate chances. In the meantime they looked anxiously for the appearance of the expedition.

While these scenes were passing, the whole party, both whites and reds, were in the direst straits for food. Game was exceedingly shy and scarce and all were forced to live on roots. The Indians were armed with nothing but bows and arrows, and could not, therefore, bring down the larger game except under the most favorable circumstances. Captain Lewis sent his companions out to hunt (before they relinquished their guns), but they were followed closely by their suspicious friends. Finally, one of the Indian spies came running back at full speed, and as soon as the others heard his first words, the whole band, to the astonishment of Captain Lewis, dashed forward as fast as their horses could carry them, and he was borne along for nearly a mile before he learned with great satisfaction that the rush was caused by the spy's announcement that one of the white men had killed a deer. "When they reached the place where Drewyer had thrown out the intestines, they all dismounted in confusion and ran tumbling over each other like famished dogs; each tore away whatever part he could and instantly began to eat it; some had the liver, some the kidneys; in short no part on which we are accustomed to look with disgust escaped them. One of them who had seized about nine feet of the entrails, was chewing at one end, while with his hand he was diligently clearing his way by discharging the contents at the other. It was indeed impossible to see these wretches ravenously feeding on the filth of animals, and the blood streaming from their mouths, without deploring how nearly the condition of the savages approaches that of the brute creation;

yet though suffering with hunger they did not attempt, as they might have done, to take by force the whole deer, but contented themselves with what had been thrown away by the hunter. Captain Lewis now had the deer skinned and after reserving a quarter of it, gave the rest of the animal to the chief to be divided among the Indians, who immediately devoured nearly the whole of it without cooking. They now went forward to the creek, where there was some brushwood to make a fire, and found Drewyer, who had killed a second deer; the same struggle for the entrails was renewed here, and on giving nearly the whole deer to the Indians, they devoured it, even to the soft part of the hoofs. A fire being made, Captain Lewis had his breakfast, during which Drewyer brought in a third deer; this too after reserving one quarter, was given to the Indians, who now seemed completely satisfied and in good humor."

As soon as the march was resumed, the old fear of an ambush was manifested, notwithstanding the friendly act of killing the deer and feeding them to the Indians; and the same precautions were taken as before. Finally, after the lapse of several days, an Indian scout, to the intense relief of Captain Lewis and his two companions, came running back with the announcement that he had seen the rest of the expedition a short distance below. "The Indians were all transported with joy, and the chief in the warmth of his satisfaction renewed his embrace to Captain Lewis, who was quite as much delighted as the Indians themselves." The report of the experience of the main body of the expedition is equally interesting. "On setting out at seven o'clock, Captain Clark, with Chaboneau and his wife, walked on shore; but they had not gone more than a mile before Captain Clark saw Sa-ca-ja-we-ah, who was with her husband one hundred yards ahead, begin to dance and show every mark of the most extravagant joy, turning round him and pointing to several Indians, whom he now saw advancing on horseback, sucking her fingers at the same time to indicate that they were of her native tribe. As they advanced Captain Clark discovered among them Drewyer dressed like an Indian, from whom he learnt the situation of the party. While the boats were performing the circuit he went toward the forks with the Indians, who as they went along sang aloud with the greatest appearance of delight. We soon drew near to the camp, and just as we approached it, a woman made her way through the crowd towards Sa-ca-ja-we-ah, and recognizing each other, they embraced with the most tender affection. The meeting of these two young women had in it something peculiarly touching, not only in the ardent manner in which their feelings were expressed, but from the real interest of their situation. . . . After this the conference was to be opened, and glad of an opportunity of being able to converse more intelligently, Sa-ca-ja-we-ah was sent for; she came into the tent, sat down, and was beginning to interpret, when in the person of Ca-me-ah-wait she recognized her brother; she instantly jumped up and ran and embraced him, throwing over him her blanket and weeping profusely; the chief was himself moved, though not in the same degree. After some conversation between them, she resumed her seat and attempted to interpret for us; but her new situation seemed to overpower her, and she was frequently interrupted by her tears. After the council was finished, the unfortunate woman learnt that all her family were dead except two brothers, one of whom was absent, and a son of her eldest sister, a small boy, who was immediately adopted by her."

The objects of the expedition were fully explained to the chief and the warriors present; and they expressed their gratification at the prospect of being taken care of and protected from their enemies. They showed great regret that they would not be supplied with arms for a year or more. They were requested to furnish horses and a guide over the mountains, and were promised remuneration therefor. All the usual treaty ceremonies were observed—speeches delivered, medals and flags bestowed and presents distributed. During the conference, the whites were careful to learn all possible regarding the western country and the best methods of getting there. A few horses were traded for on the 18th and a few more on the 19th. As game was very scarce, it was thought best to proceed at once, and the advance was resumed on the 18th. Two days later the Indian encampment was passed, and here another council was held and presents were distributed. At last an Indian who professed to know the western country, was engaged to guide the party over the mountains, and assistants to help carry the baggage were secured.

Having advanced far enough to escape the importunities of the Indians, they decided to camp, while scouting parties went on ahead and explored the country through which they expected to pass. Captain Clark, with a small party, undertook to find a practicable route over the mountains. He started and encountered small bands of Shoshones every day. All were astonished, though friendly; they were found to have an abundance of salmon, but little other food. A stream was reached on the 21st, a head branch of the Columbia, which was named Lewis in honor

I—21

of Captain Lewis. But Captain Clark failed utterly to find a satisfactory path down this stream. Everywhere he was confronted with steep mountains, around which the streams wound, with perpendicular banks rising from the water's edge to a great height. The streams themselves were so deep that a passage along their beds was impracticable. At length they were forced to leave their horses in order to make any progress at all; but after several days spent in climbing almost inaccessible acclivities, it was seen that a path in that direction was out of the question, and it was determined to return to the main party, where they arrived on the 26th.

As it was now thought that the crossing of the mountains would be attended with the utmost hardships and difficulties, it was determined to "cache" the bulk of the supplies, in order to lighten the burden of the assistants and the horses and thus facilitate the advance. The only unfriendly act of the Indians thus far was an attempt to steal the gun of one of the white hunters, Drewyer; but owing to his courage and persistence the attempt was unsuccessful. The empty boats were sunk in the river and weighted down, and more horses were obtained through another council. The Indians generally were now leaving the mountains for the plains to be near the wild game. All except Sa-ca-ja-we-ah and Captain Lewis were on foot, and the latter mounted only for the purpose of riding ahead to find the best path. It will thus be observed that although the expedition had really crossed the divide and reached the waters of the Columbia, the route down the streams there could not be followed, owing to the extreme roughness of the country. It was therefore necessary to find another pass.

After a sufficient number of horses was obtained to carry the goods, provisions, etc., of the expedition, and all was apparently ready for a start, it was discovered that the guides and assistants were unwilling to proceed, because they wished to accompany their tribe to the plains. The chief, Ca-me-ah-wait, had promised faithfully to provide assistants for the expedition; but it now transpired that he and other chiefs had counseled their desertion; this fact was learned through Sa-ca-ja-we-ah. Accordingly, the chief was taken to task by Captain Lewis, and hesitatingly admitted the truth of the charge; but excused himself by the statement that members of the tribe were compelled to follow the wild game or starve. An appeal was made to his honor; whereupon he countermanded his directions for desertion, and the guides and assistants again came promptly forward. It was severely cold at this time (August 26th), the ice forming nearly a quarter of an inch thick. "One of the women who had been leading two of our pack horses halted at a rivulet about a mile behind, and sent on the two horses by a female friend; on inquiring of Ca-me-ah-wait the cause of her detention, he answered with great appearance of unconcern that she had just stopped to lie in, but would soon overtake us. In fact we were astonished to see her in about an hour's time come on with her new-born infant and pass us on her way to the camp, apparently in perfect health."

But in spite of all that could be done to prevent it, the Indian assistants continued to desert and join their tribe destined for the buffalo meadows to the eastward, until, when the journey was resumed on the 30th, only the guides remained, "an old Indian, his four sons and another Indian." However, they managed to secure enough horses to raise the number owned by the expedition to about thirty. As they advanced, they could see fires from all quarters in the mountains, signaling the various bands to join the general exodus to the buffalo meadows. Soon they were again in trouble, owing to the fact that they undertook to cross the mountains at another impracticable spot. They succeeded in crossing the divide, but again met the same difficulties encountered by Captain Clark and his party, for everywhere steep mountains, deep streams and other inaccessibilities sternly confronted them. They endeavored to pass down Fish creek on the west side, but were unable to do so. Often they were obliged to cut their way for a considerable distance, only to find themselves confronted by some insurmountable obstacle. Several of the horses were permanently injured by falling down some steep declivity, in one instance one rolling over and over for nearly a hundred yards. In the meantime every member of the expedition was restricted to the most meager allowance of food, as the wild animals had almost wholly fled to the green meadows to the eastward.

At length, by moving northwest, they crossed a very difficult ridge and found themselves on the headwaters of another river, which they later named Clark, in honor of Captain Clark. All their previous operations were in the valleys of the Missouri or the Lewis river; but in the Clark river valley they had no sooner crossed the divide than the country began to descend in milder lines to the northward and the route steadily became easier. On September 4th, a large encampment of the Oot-la-shoot Indians was reached, and a council was immediately held. Eleven more horses were traded for from a herd of about five hundred fine ones owned by this band. The Indians were friendly and supplied the expedition with such articles of food as they possessed. On the 6th, the main channel of Clark river was reached. They were now almost wholly dependent on their hunters for food, having nearly exhausted the supply of flour and pork they had thus far brought with them. They continued down this river almost directly northward, with the snow capped mountains on their left and the river valley on their right, until they at last reached a creek which they named Travelers' Rest. From this point, their guides informed them, a path led over the mountains to the valley of the Lewis river and to the open and level country.

They now made preparations to leave the streams and scale the low mountains to the westward, and were told by their guides that after five days' journey they would reach the Lewis river valley. Travelers' Rest creek was ascended to its source, and then a northwest direction was taken over a very rough country. Their supply of food was now wholly exhausted, and the hunters could find no game. On the 14th they were on Kooskooskee creek, and here they were compelled to slaughter their first colt for supper. They were at last across the divide and in the modern State of Idaho. On the 16th six inches of snow fell; they were compelled to kill another colt for food. The cold was severe and the route extremely rough; but by the 19th they could see far to the westward a broad, level valley. In the meantime they had killed several other horses for food. The western descent was so steep that again several of the horses were disabled by falling down the sides of the mountains. A small stream was reached which was appropriately named Hungry creek.

The level country was at last reached on the 20th of September, to the indescribable joy of every member of the party. Indian villages were seen dotting the banks of Kooskooskee creek, and soon the hunters began as of old to bring fat deer into camp. The Indians were found to be the Pierced Nose, or Cho-pun-nish tribe, the head chief of which was Twisted Hair, who lived some distance farther down stream. After this the expedition had no serious difficulty in reaching the mouth of the Columbia; but as the route was now outside of the boundary of the Louisiana purchase, the leading events only will be mentioned. The horses were finally turned over to the Indians to be kept until the return of the expedition; and canoes were built, in which to float the baggage down the streams. Colter's creek was reached October 8th, and the main channel of the Columbia on the 16th. The great falls were passed about the 1st of November, and late in this month all were delighted with a sight of the mighty Pacific. They remained encamped near the mouth of the Columbia during the winter of 1805–6, and in March set out up the river on their return. On the 5th of May they arrived at the mouth of the Kooskooskee, and on the 8th reached Twister Hair's camp. The horses had become scattered, but about twenty-one were finally assembled; and on the 10th of June preparations were fully completed for the trip across the mountains to Travelers' Rest creek.

They advanced with great trouble up the steep acclivity, and were at length compelled wholly to stop at or near Hungry creek on account of the deep snow. When it had sufficiently melted, they resumed the terrible journey, and in the course of time passed over the divide, down the course of Travelers' Rest creek and encamped at the mouth of that stream. Here it was determined to divide the party for the purpose of more thoroughly exploring the country to the eastward. Captain Lewis and nine men were to proceed on a direct course to the great falls of the Missouri, where three men were to be left to build carriages to carry the baggage around the falls, while Captain Lewis and the other six were to advance northward and explore Maria's river to its source. The remainder of the party were to go to the headwaters of Jefferson river, where the deposits were, and there divide. Sergeant Ordway and nine men were to descend the river with the stores, etc. Captain Clark and ten men were to proceed to the headwaters of the Yellowstone river, taking with them all the horses, and upon their arrival there were to build boats and float down that stream to its mouth, where they were to await the arrival of the other detachments; but in the meantime Sergeant Pryor and two other men were to drive the horses across the country to the Mandan villages on the Missouri, where they were to be left, and Pryor and his companions were then to take a message to the British post on the Assiniboine river in Canada. So far as possible, these designs were carried into execution.

While the expedition was together, it consisted of over thirty experienced riflemen of well-known courage, a force that all the Indian tribes except the Sioux fully respected; but when it was divided into detachments of three or even of nine or ten men danger from roving war parties of Indians might be expected at every encounter. But the dauntless men were willing to take their chances, either with roving bands of Indians or with grizzly bears; in fact, the majority of the men courted stirring and dangerous adventure, because they enjoyed it and because they were willing to take hazardous chances in order to distinguish themselves. The detachments separated July 3d. With Captain Lewis, in addition to nine men, were five Indians. They took an easterly direction, and on the 6th arrived on the divide between the Clark and the Missouri rivers. Two days later Dearborn river was reached, after which they took a course almost directly north to Medicine river. Game was again abundant and the men fared "sumptuously." In one herd it was estimated that there were ten thousand buffaloes within a circuit of two miles. The mouth of Medicine river was reached on the 11th; but it was found that much of the stores "cached" there had spoiled. About this time, McNeal, one of the party, while out hunting on horseback, came suddenly and unexpectedly within a few feet of a large grizzly bear. The horse promptly threw his rider and galloped away. The bear advanced with open mouth upon the hunter, who struck it so violent a blow on the head that the animal was felled to the ground, but the stock of the gun was broken. Before the animal could renew the attack, McNeal sprang into the branches of a willow tree, and thus escaped almost certain death; but was compelled to remain there until late in the afternoon before the bear left the spot.

Leaving Medicine river on the 17th of July, they took a northerly direction, aiming to arrive at Maria's river at a spot above that reached by Captain Lewis in 1805. Indian signs were seen, and the mosquitoes were so thick and fierce as to make the dogs howl. Tansy river was crossed on the 17th, and Maria's river reached on the 18th. They ascended the latter stream nearly to the mountains and until it was seen that it was not navigable beyond the fiftieth parallel of latitude, whereupon they started to return, striking southeast toward the Tansy or Teton river. While yet on one of the branches of Maria's river, they suddenly saw ahead of them at the side of a grove some thirty horses, several of which were saddled, and a few Indians, who apparently were engaged in looking on Drewyer in the valley in advance. As it was seen that an encounter was inevitable, Captain Lewis and his party advanced with friendly signs; but instantly it was observed that the Indian camp was in great confusion. A scout rode rapidly out to examine the whites; but regardless of pacific signs returned to his companions as rapidly as he had come. Finally Captain Lewis went forward alone, and soon a small party of Indians came forward and shook hands with him. Drewyer, who had the peace pipe, was sent for, and upon his arrival all smoked together. As had been feared, they proved to be a band of the Minnetarees of the prairie, notorious thieves and the enemies of nearly all the other tribes. Luckily the band consisted of only eight warriors, of whom Captain Lewis felt no fear, as they had but two guns. They said that at the distance of a journey of a day and a half, a large band of their tribe was encamped. Whites and reds then encamped together and slept side by side; but early the next morning, before the former were aware of it, the latter appropriated several of their guns, and a struggle immediately occurred for possession. Several of the Indians ran off with the guns, but were promptly pursued; and one of them was stabbed to the heart by Robert Fields. Weapons were flourished and several other personal encounters took place, much to the advantage of the whites. The Indian having Captain Lewis' gun was on the point of escaping with it, when the Captain fired and shot him through the bowels; this Indian, who had one of their two guns, returned the fire, and Captain Lewis felt the wind of the ball on his face. The Indians now fled, driving off several of the horses ridden by Captain Lewis and his companions, but leaving more of their own than they took away belonging to the whites. They left, also, considerable of their war outfit.

Concluding that the Indians would make all possible speed to the larger band for reinforcements, the whites now rode very fast, determined to escape any pursuit. After riding eight miles they crossed a stream which they named Battle river, to commemorate their encounter of the morning. Continuing, they rode sixty-three miles without stopping, and then encamped to let the horses feed and to dine themselves. After an hour and a half, they proceeded, but again stopped when they had gone seventeen miles. In two hours they again advanced, though it was after dark, and after riding twenty miles, stopped for the night, having covered exactly one hundred miles since leaving the battleground and now feeling safe from pursuit. The next morning after going twenty miles they met a party of their friends coming down the valley of the Missouri; they proved to be the men under Sergeant Ordway. They had descended without noteworthy incident. The two detachments passed the portage of the great falls, and all moved rapidly down the river. They arrived at the Musselshell August 1st, Milk the 4th and the mouth of the Yellow Stone the 7th, and there found a letter from Captain Clark, who had arrived there before them and gone on down the river. They followed, but did not overhaul his party until the 12th. In the meantime Captain Lewis, while out hunting, was accidentally shot through the left thigh by one of his companions. Though a severe wound he fully recovered from it in about two weeks.

After separating from the Lewis party on Travelers' Rest creek, the party under Captain Clark, consisting of fifteen men, having in charge fifty horses, took a southerly course up Clark river, and on the 6th crossed the divide near the headwaters of Lewis, Clark and Missouri rivers. Sa-ca-ja-we-ah again recognized the country, and pointed out objects she had seen in her childhood on Glade creek, one of the branches of Wisdom river. On the 9th they lost nine horses, which strayed away, but were subsequently recovered. Jefferson river was reached on the 8th, and there the contents of the "caches" were found to be in good condition. Many of the men, who had been without tobacco so long, no sooner came in sight of the spot, than they dropped everything and ran with all their speed to the "caches," where they were soon supplied with a plentiful quantity of "the weed." While doing without it, they had even broken up their pipes into small fragments and chewed them, to satisfy the intense craving. The boats were raised from the bed of the river, and after being repaired were loaded with the baggage. On the 10th the party divided into two detachments, one under Sergeant Ordway, with nine men, going down the river, as before stated, and the other under Captain Clark striking east to the headwaters of the Yellowstone river. With Clark were ten men and the wife and child of Chaboneau and the fifty horses. The Clark party reached the divide between the Gallatin and the Yellowstone river on the 15th, and the same day they named Shields river. Fresh Indian signs were seen here. The Yellowstone was also reached on the 15th, at the place where it issues from the Rocky mountains. About this time twenty-four horses disappeared one night and no doubt were stolen by a band of Indians, whose scouts, it was learned, had shadowed them for several days.

Two canoes were built here, each twenty-eight feet long, and all their supplies were loaded therein. The Clark party now divided, three men under Sergeant Pryor undertaking to drive the horses across the country to the villages of the Mandans, an easy task should they encounter no hostile band of Indians, but otherwise just the reverse. The boats were completed on the 23d, and the down journey was begun the same day. Clark's fork was passed on the 24th, and two days later they reached the mouth of the Big Horn, where they had their last look at the Rocky mountains. Herds of buffaloes literally covered the plain as far as the eye could reach. Several grizzly bears were killed amid scenes of great danger and excitement. On the 29th Lazeka or Tongue river was passed, and the next day they arrived at Field's creek near the mouth of the Yellowstone. Upon reaching the mouth of the latter, being without fresh food and being almost eaten alive by the swarms of mosquitoes, they left a note for Captain Lewis, and continued on down the river, soon passing two American traders from the Illinois, Dickson and Hancock, who had passed the previous winter on the Yellowstone with a French trader named Ceautoin. From the traders it was learned the Mandans and Minnetarees were at war with the Arickarees; and the Assiniboines with the Mandans. About this time they were joined by Sergeant Pryor and party, who reported that their horses had been run off in the night by the Indians, and could not be overtaken. They reported that they had experienced much trouble in driving the horses, which, having had Indian training at hunting the buffaloes, would scatter at the sight of a herd and chase them as if riders were on their backs.

The entire party was reunited on the 12th, and the down journey was begun with great elation. The Minnetaree villages were reached on the 14th, and a council was held by Captain Clark, who was informed that the Sioux had killed eight men of this tribe since the expedition was there before. Two of the Arickarees had been killed by the Minnetarees for attempting to steal horses. In short, war had gone on between the tribes as if the whites had never been there. Large supplies of corn were obtained here, the first they had eaten for a year or more. Big White, the head chief, agreed to go with the party to Washington. Here at the Arickaree villages, Chaboneau and wife left the expedition. They had been extremely serviceable to the party, the husband as a general interpreter and assistant, and the wife as a special interpreter among the Shoshones. They were paid five hundred dollars, and thereafter the faithful wife at least was heard of no more. John Colter, a member of the party, asked leave to remain at the Minnetaree villages, and was permitted to do so. The down journey was resumed the 17th. The Arickarees presented serious complaints against both the Sioux and the Mandans. Near their encampment was a large village of the Cheyennes. On the 22d Captain Lewis began to walk for the first time since the accident. The Teton villages were reached on the 30th; Captain Clark took them severely to task for their many misdeeds, informed them that all their bad conduct would have to be accounted for, ordered them away from the boats, and would have nothing further to do with them.

They were now on the home stretch; and the anxiety to see their friends seemed to double the strength of every man, and the boats fairly flew over the water. On more than one day they rowed over seventy miles. Numerous parties of traders were overtaken or met as they proceeded. James Airs was seen September 3. Augustus Choteau and party, destined for the Upper Missouri, were passed on the 6th. The mouth of the Platte was reached on the 9th. Two parties of traders were met on the 10th, one bound for the Loupe river and the other for the villages of the Mahas. Several parties were met on the 12th, among them being Messrs. McClellan, Gravelines and the elder Durion. Below the old Kansas villages, three parties bound for the Yanktons and the Mahas were passed. On the 16th two parties destined for the Pawnee and the Maha countries were met. Captain McClellan and his soldiers were met on the 17th. Two days later they passed the Osage river, and on the 23d reached St. Louis "where we arrived at twelve o'clock, and having fired a salute, went on shore and received the heartiest and most hospitable welcome from the whole village."

The expedition of Lewis and Clark, which was coeval with those of Lieutenant Pike, was the first to reach the Rocky mountains and the Pacific ocean. The objects were only partially accomplished. Owing to the refusal of the Sioux to accept the overtures of the Americans, the Indian tribes in the two modern Dakotas were not pacified. Their continuance of war with their neighbors forced the latter to defend themselves; and war parties from all the tribes of that region immediately succeeded the sailing westward of the expedition in the spring of 1805. It was different with all the tribes of the Rocky mountain and the Columbia river countries; they were friendly to the Americans and generally at peace among themselves. But from the expedition it was learned what might be expected from the tribes encountered. That information was vastly important; and it was promptly succeeded by the advent of the fur companies and the many private trappers, who boldly penetrated to the heart of the territories occupied by fierce and hostile tribes, in search of the beaver and other fur-bearing animals. Neither can the expedition be said to have discovered a practicable water route across the Rocky mountains for the benefit of commerce; but it did learn that the portage between the headwaters of the Missouri and the Columbia rivers was both long and extremely difficult. That knowledge was also valuable. The most important results of the expedition sprang from the description of the country through which the observant Americans passed. The vast numbers of wild animals, the splendid water-courses, the luxuriant natural meadows, the fertile and beautiful valleys, the wonderful mountains probably containing stores of rich minerals, the astonishing variety of climate—all revealed to the citizens of the United States the marvelous value of their new possession. It was only a question of time until the whole tract would be peopled with millions and glorified with the intricate tracery of modern civilization.

CHAPTER X

The Expeditions of Lieutenant Pike

THE exploration of the Missouri river country, of the Rocky mountains and of the valley of Columbia river, was provided for in the expedition under Captains Lewis and Clark. But other explorations were equally important and necessary. It was imperative to find the remote source of the Mississippi river, in order to settle the dispute over the boundary between the United States and the British possessions on the north. It was likewise vitally necessary, in order to prevent a probable war between the United States and Spain, to find at once the sources of the Arkansas and the Red rivers, the territory drained by which being claimed by both nations. Spain endeavored to secure this immense tract by sending envoys to the various Indian tribes residing on the headwaters of those rivers for the purpose of forming an alliance with them. She likewise undertook, by sending out an army nearly to Natchitoches and nearly to the Missouri river, to impress the Indians with her power and the Americans with the rightfulness of her claims to the country. To thwart these pretensions and extravagant claims, the Pike expedition was sent out. The United States claimed, as she had a right to do, all the country west of the Mississippi drained by its branches. It was, therefore, necessary to find without delay the divide which separated the Mississippi basin from those of the Columbia, the Colorado of the West, the Rio Grande, and the rivers of modern Texas, which flow into the Gulf of Mexico.

Under the orders of Gen. James Wilkinson, of the War Department, then with headquarters at the village of St. Louis, Lieut. Zebulon M. Pike, on the 9th of August, 1805, with a force consisting of one sergeant, two corporals and seventeen privates, and with a keel-boat seventy feet long, well provisioned for four months, set sail up the Mississippi river, intending to visit the Indian tribes on its upper branches, hold peace treaties with them, locate sites for military establishments along the river and elsewhere, inquire into the habits and customs of the white traders, ascertain to what extent British influences stirred up hostilities among the various tribes, locate the source of the Mississippi, and generally to look after the interests of the United States in the upper Mississippi country. On the 11th they passed the mouth of the Illinois river, and on the 14th came upon a small party of Sac Indians engaged in fishing. The men of the expedition caught this day one thousand three hundred and seventy-five fish from the river as they passed along. The next day, opposite Hurricane Island, on the west side in what is now Missouri, they saw a French plantation, with cattle and growing corn. In this vicinity they learned there were fifteen or twenty families. On the 17th they passed three loaded batteaux coming down, and two days later struck a "sawyer," * stove in a plank of their boat and came near sinking, but managed to make shore, where they repaired the break by inserting another plank. While they were thus engaged, three canoes of Indians went by on their way down. On the 20th they reached the "De Moyen" rapids, but had hard work getting through them. They were assisted by William Ewing, a representative of the United States among the Indians, placed there to teach them the art of agriculture, who had with him a French interpreter, and four chiefs and fourteen warriors of the Sacs, all in canoes flying the stars and stripes. They were on their way down to St. Louis, but returned to the Sac village on the Iowa side just above the rapids, where on the opposite side of the river stood the house of Mr. Ewing. Here Pike held a council of the leading chiefs of the Sacs, explained to them how Louisiana had become the territory of the United States, and enjoined upon them the importance of maintaining peace with the Americans and with the neighboring tribes. They all promised peace and obedience, whereupon they were presented with tobacco, knives and whisky.

Continuing up the river, Pike selected a spot about forty miles from the Sac village for the erection of a military post. It was on high ground on the west bank, with plenty of ground back of the river front for gardens, etc. On the 25th they passed the mouth of Iowa river, and encamped at Grant's Prairie. On the 26th there went down three pirogues of Indians, and on the 27th River de Roche (Rock) was passed. Here they met a Scotch-

---

* A concealed tree, log or snag in the river.

man named James Aird, who had a quantity of goods and was on his way to the Indian country to trade. He was very communicative, thoroughly posted on the Indian tribes, and willingly gave Major Pike much valuable information. Here on the east side stood another village of the Sacs. On the 30th they saw Indians in pirogues going down; and on the 31st passed several encampments, one of which stood on a beautiful eminence on the west side, and had the appearance of having been the site of a town for many years. They were now not far from the lead mines; in fact reached them the next day at noon. They were saluted with a field piece from the lead works, and were hospitably received by Monsier Julien Dubuque, who took pleasure in showing them marked attention. The mines were being worked six miles from the river, no nearer.

Under the instructions of the government, Lieutenant Pike asked Monsier Dubuque a series of questions, and he replied as follows: "What is the date of your grant of the mines from the savages? Answer: The copy of the grant is in Mr. Soulard's office at St. Louis. What is the date of the confirmation by the Spaniards. Ans. The same as to first query. What is the extent of your grant? Ans. The same as above. What is the extent of the mines? Ans. Twenty-eight or twenty-seven leagues long and from one to three broad. What the lead made per annum? Ans. From twenty million to forty million pounds. What quantity of lead per cwt. of mineral? Ans. Seventy-five per cent. What quantity of lead in pigs? Ans. All I make, as I neither manufacture bar, sheet-lead nor shot. Is it mixed with any other mineral? Ans. We have seen some copper but having no person sufficiently acquainted with chemistry to make the experiment properly, I cannot say as to the proportion it bears to the lead. Signed at Dubuque, or Lead Mines, September 1, 1805."

From Dubuque it was learned that the Sioux and the Chippewas were at war as usual, that the former had recently killed fifteen of the latter, and the latter had in turn killed ten of the former, at or near the mouth of St. Peter's (Minnesota) river. On September 2d they reached Turkey river, on which, near its mouth, was a Fox village. Everywhere it was found by Pike that the Indians had a great dread of the Americans, whom they regarded as great fighters and very brave men. To a certain degree, this belief had been caused by the French and the Spanish, with whom the Indians had been associated so strong very recently. Thus, whenever the Indians observed the Pike party with the flag of the United States flying, they generally steered clear unless spoken to. Small parties invariably fled before the Americans. It had been, and was yet, to the interest of the French and Spanish traders to influence the Indians against the Americans; and previous to the cession of the province to the United States the Americans had little show of securing the Indian trade, because they were not permitted to cross the Mississippi. But now all was changed. Everywhere the American traders began to root out the others and to gain the savage custom. One of the objects of Pike's expedition was to prove to the savages that the Americans were now their best friends, that the government was ready to assist them with money and provisions, arms and imprements, and to establish posts among them for their benefit. So, from the start, Pike made every effort to secure peace between the tribes, to make them see that the government was their best friend, to open friendly communications with them, and to obtain cessions of land, upon which to build trading or military posts. In this he was very successful.

The mouth of the Wisconsin was reached September 4, and a little later the party arrived at Prairie du Chien. Here was found a strong post of traders. Two sites for military posts were selected near this point. Here a council was held with the Puants or Winnebagoes. At the mouth of the Upper Iowa river a council was held with a band of Sioux. September 16th they reached Lake Pepin, and five days later arrived at the mouth of St. Peter's river. Here a little later a council was held with the Sioux for the purpose of cementing a permanent peace between them and the Chippewas. At this time he succeeded in securing from them two valuable tracts of land. They agreed, provisionally only, to maintain peace with the Chippewas. Late in September, the expedition passed around St. Anthony's falls. On the 13th they arrived at the mouth of Clear river, and here saw their first buffalo signs. It was resolved to build a fort near this spot, in which to pass the winter; this was soon accomplished.

In the meantime, Pike put himself in communication with the traders and the Indian bands of the surrounding country, his object being to regulate the Indian trade, which was here in the hands of British agents. Finally, he left part of his force at the fort in charge of a sergeant, and with the others started to find the source of the Mississippi, to visit several of the British agencies, and to meet the chiefs of the upper tribes. They passed the mouth of Pine river on the 31st of December. A few days later they arrived at the British camp near Red Cedar lake, and soon afterward at Lake de Sable, where stood their principal camp. Pike required the British flag to be hauled down, and exacted from the agents promises to conform to the government requirements. Succeeding in this, they passed up to Leech lake. and at the British post there saw Hugh McGillis, the agent. Here the British flag was also taken down. The British agents were required to take out licenses, were prohibited from selling liquor to the Indians, were forbidden to distribute British medals to the chiefs, and were told to hold no councils with the Indians on political subjects. Here a large council was held with the tribes of Rainy lake, Red Cedar lake, Lake of the Woods, and other distant points—all Chippewas or their relatives. While here, Pike discovered what was supposed to be the source of the Mississippi. Returning down the river he reached his fort early in March. On his way down the Mississippi he held councils with other bands of the Sioux. St. Louis was reached April 30.

While they were at "Prairie des Chiens," they witnessed a game of ball between the Indians, which was thus described by Lieutenant Pike: "This afternoon they had a great game of the cross on the prairie between the Sioux on the one side and the Puants and Reynards on the other. The ball is made of some hard substance and covered with leather, the cross sticks are round and net work, with handles of three feet long. The parties being ready, and bets agreed upon (sometimes to the amount of some thousand dollars), the goals are set up on the prairie at the distance of half a mile. The ball is thrown up in the middle, and each party strives to drive it to the opposite goal; and when either party gains the first rubber, which is driving it quick around the post, the ball is again taken to the center, the ground changed and the contest renewed; and this is continued until one side gains four times, which decides the bet. It is an interesting sight to see two or three hundred naked savages contending on the plain who shall bear off the palm of victory; as he who drives the ball round the goal is much shouted at by his companions. It sometimes happens that one catches the ball in his racket, and depending on his speed, endeavors to carry it to the goal, and when he finds himself too closely pursued, he hurls it with great force and dexterity to an amazing distance, where there are other flankers of both parties ready to receive it. It seldom touches the ground, but is sometimes kept in the air for hours before either party can gain the victory. In the game which I witnessed, the Sioux were victorious, more, I believe, from the superiority of their skill in throwing the ball, than by their swiftness, for I thought the Puants and Reynards the swiftest runners."

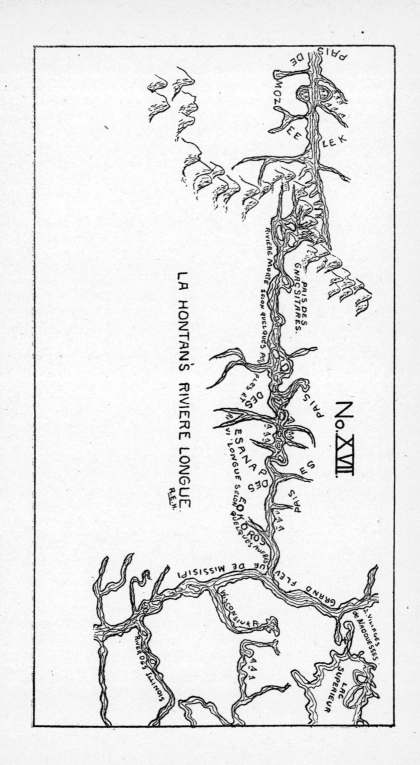

The objects of this expedition, which were to establish peace between the Indian tribes of the Upper Mississippi, to regulate trade with the Indians, to confirm the authority of the United States, to discover more accurately the sources of the Mississippi, to select suitable sites for the construction of military and trading posts, and to shake off the hold of the Spanish, French and English upon the savage nations, had thus been accomplished so far as it was possible to be done. As a whole, the results justified the confidence reposed in (then) Lieutenant Pike, and warranted his promotion and his selection for duties of a similar nature farther to the west. His expedition to the sources of the Mississippi is one of the most interesting and memorable made in the Louisiana Purchase in early times.

Under the orders of the War Department, Lieut. Zebulon M. Pike, with a force consisting of two lieutenants, one surgeon, one sergeant, two corporals, sixteen privates and one interpreter, set out in two boats from Belle Fountaine near St. Louis, on July 15, 1806, for the purpose of "exploring the internal parts of Louisiana." Accompanying him were chiefs and other members of the Osages and the Pawnees, through which nations it was intended the expedition should pass. Many were women and children who were returning to their nations from captivity among the Pottawattomies, having been freed by the United States government. Late on the 16th, the expedition reached St. Charles, where Vasquez, the interpreter, was arrested under a writ of attachment for debt, by Manuel Lisa, one of the leading agents of the Missouri Fur Company. This occasioned a delay, but he was finally released. La Charette was reached on the 21st, and there they found waiting them Lieut. James B. Wilkinson, son of Gen. James Wilkinson, Dr. John H. Robinson, and another interpreter, all of whom had gone on before. Almost from the start it was necessary for them to kill game for their subsistence, and the hunters who accompanied the expedition were kept constantly in the woods. On the 24th they killed three deer, one bear and three turkeys. The next day they reached the mouth of Gasconade river, and on the 28th arrived at the mouth of Osage river, near which a trading post had been established for many years. The Indians of the party had become tired of the slow and tedious advance of the boats, and spent their time on the banks, marching along under the command of Te-to-ba-si, or Big Soldier. Scarcely

I—22

a day passed that did not add to their subsistence deer and other wild animals; on one day they killed as high as nine deer. Wanton cervicide was forbidden by Lieutenant Pike.

Having reached the mouth of the Osage river, they commenced the ascent of that stream, and on August 8, arrived at the Niangua, or as Pike called it, the Yunger river, and on the same day passed Old Man's Rapids. On the 12th they passed Vermillion and Grand rivers, and two days later arrived at the Park, where there were several white traders in the employ of the Chouteaus of St. Louis. While here Pike was informed that a war party of the Little Osages had gone against the Kansas, and that a war party of the Great Osages had gone to attack the whites located on the Arkansas river. On the 18th, the advance expedition under Lieutenant Wilkinson arrived so near the Osage villages that the friends of the Indians returning from captivity came out to meet them. This meeting is thus described by Pike and Wilkinson: "Wives throwing themselves into the arms of their husbands, parents embracing their children and children their parents, brothers and sisters meeting, one from captivity, the others from the towns—they at the same time returning thanks to God for having brought them once more together; in short the *tout ensemble* was such as to make polished society blush, when compared with those savages, in whom the passions of the mind, either joy, grief, fear, anger, or revenge, have their full scope; why can we not correct the baneful passions without weakening the good? Sans Oreille (Big Soldier, or Te-to-ba-si, or Without Ears), made them a speech in which he remarked, 'Osage, you now see your wives, your brothers, your daughters, your sons, redeemed from captivity. Who did this? Was it the Spaniard? No. The French? No. Had either of those people been governors of the country, your relatives might have rotted in captivity, and you never would have seen them; but the Americans stretched forth their hands, and they are returned to you. What can you do for all this goodness? Nothing; all your lives would not suffice to repay their goodness.' This man (Te-to-ba-si) had children in captivity, not one of whom were we able to obtain for him."

The main expedition reached Prairie Hills on August 13th, and passed Sac river above Osceola the 16th. The next day they reached a spot where the Spanish had erected a fort which they called Carondelet, and had fortified it and placed several swivels high enough to command the surroundings. Here about ten families resided, mostly of French origin. Having reached the forks on the 18th, they passed up the left branch, and the next

day, with the assistance of the Indians, who came out with forty
or fifty horses, they carried their baggage across to the vicinity of
the Osage villages and near the trading establishment of Lisa.
While here Pike inquired particularly into the proceedings of the
traders, as had been enjoined upon him by General Wilkinson,
and learned that many abuses existed, which he ordered corrected.
Among them was the disrespect shown the American government
by Lisa and the Chouteaus, who had not yet become reconciled
to the change in their nationality. Neither had they taken out
the licenses and passports required by the government. The
Indians were informed of the change in governments, and presents were made them on behalf of the United States. The expedition was met by practically the whole of each village, and as
all the men were very thirsty, they were given a "stiff drink"
each. The old medals of the Spaniards and the French were
taken up and new ones, representing America, were given in their
places. The Indians were informed that the traders had no
power to make or unmake chiefs. White Hair, or Ca-ha-ga-
ton-ga, and Tutt-a-sug-gy, the Wind, the former of the Great
Osages and the latter of the Little Osages, both head chiefs, were
very friendly to Captain Pike. At least they professed to be, but
when it came to supplying the expedition with horses, it was very
difficult to procure them except at an extravagant price. Pike
wondered at this fact, when they had seven or eight hundred
horses, professed such undying friendship for the whites, and yet
at first would part with only about ten horses. One of the objects
of the expedition was to take along several of the highest chiefs
of the Osages to meet the Pawnees for the purpose of assisting in
establishing permanent peace between the two nations, but the
leading chiefs evaded the request, and several of the under chiefs
who started afterward deserted and returned to their villages.

The villages of the Great and the Little Osages were about six
miles apart. While here they learned that a war party of Pawnees had recently attacked an expedition of Americans on the
Arkansas river, had killed two and wounded two, and had killed
an Osage warrior, who was with them. The camp of the Pike
expedition among the Osages was called Independence. A big
council was held the 22d, with the two villages together, on which
occasion Pike delivered a long and carefully prepared "talk" or
speech, pointing out to the Indians what was necessary for them
to do to retain the good will of the United States and avoid having an army sent against them for their forcible subjection. It
is clear that Pike did not use good judgment at this council,

because he delivered the presents of the government before he made his demands for horses and for chiefs to accompany the expedition to the country of the Pawnees. Had he reversed this course, it is probable he would have obtained all he asked for at the outset.

The act of freeing the captive Osages among the Pottawattomies and sending them to their homes by Captain Pike, was a step taken by the government to convince the savages of the well-wishes of the United States and to gain in return the good will of the Indians. The immediate correction of the many abuses of the traders was another step in the same direction. Preliminary proceedings were taken also to establish military posts in the country of the Osages, so that the interests of the United States and the safety of the traders and the few settlers might be conserved. A careful report on the fauna, flora, topography, etc., was also required. At the council the rights of the Indians and of the United States were severally set forth, and the importance to the savages of permanent peace with the government purposely dwelt upon. The next step was to secure peaceable relations between the Osages and their savage neighbors.

Having sold his batteaux, obtained horses enough to carry his baggage, and engaged a number of sub-chiefs to go to the country of the Pawnees, the expedition, on the 1st of September, prepared to leave. There were now fifteen loaded horses, two lieutenants, one doctor, two sergeants, one corporal, fifteen privates, two interpreters, three Pawnees returning from captivity, and four sub-chiefs of the Great Osages, one being Shen-ga-was-sa, or Beautiful Bird. After having started, it was learned by Captain Pike that Mr. Chouteau of St. Louis had just arrived among the Osages, whereupon he returned, because he desired particularly to have a serious talk with that well known and somewhat famous individual. The many abuses of which the Indians and the government agents complained were pointed out to him and their correction demanded to which Mr. Chouteau acquiesced, apparently without any expectation of complying therewith, because Pike soon afterward learned that after he had gone Chouteau told the Indians that the Americans were "bad men," and that in a short time the country would again pass to Spain, as a war was then in prospect. When an account of this outrageous course was sent to General Wilkinson at St. Louis, he informed Mr. Chouteau that a repetition of such statements would be followed by expulsion from the Indian country, and directed him to correct his unfriendly conduct at once.

The transfer of Louisiana Province to the United States meant the early invasion of all that territory by American settlers, whom both the French and the Spanish residents and traders had been taught to detest and avoid. The old regime of commercial seclusion, it was realized, must give way to the energetic and progressive customs of the American settlers. This meant the decadence of French and Spanish prestige and power among the savages. Thus it was that the Americans at first met with rebuffs, not only from the white residents, but from the Indians who were yet under the influences of the French and the Spanish. Pike early realized this state of affairs, and did all he could to correct it. But it required several years before the savages fully admitted the authority of the United States.

After the expedition had been out a few days, several of the Osages who had agreed to go to the Pawnee villages announced that they "had been dreaming," which meant that they had changed their minds about accompanying Pike any farther. September 5, all but two went back. The next day, the company arrived in the vicinity of what is now Xenia and Harding, Kan., and passed over the divide separating the Osage valley from the Neosho valley. On September 10, they reached the divide between the Neosho and the Verdigris valleys, and on the 11th camped on the latter stream not far from what is now the town of Bazar, Chase county. Every day they killed enough game for their subsistence. The hunters began to bring in cabrie, or antelopes. The beautiful prairies, covered with wild flowers and wild game, kindled the warmest praises of Captain Pike. From the top of a hill, he writes, on September 12, he saw at one view on the beflowered plain below buffalo, elk, deer, antelope and panther. On this day five buffaloes were killed, almost the first. This was the Kaws (Kansas) hunting ground, and the animals began to appear almost without numbers. Pike gave strict injunctions to kill no more than was needed, but no limits were placed on the needs, and the camp was feasted on buffalo hump, tongue, tenderloin, and marrow, with variations of elk, deer, cabrie and wild fowl. On the 14th all day long they journeyed through an unending herd of buffaloes, which simply opened ranks to let the intruders pass, and then closed again as if nothing had happened. The report of guns seemed new to the animals, showing that the Indians had not yet secured those weapons. Pike asserted that one hunter could support two hundred men with his rifle. He forbade unnecessary killing "not because of a scarcity of ammunition, but as I conceived the laws of morality forbid it also." In looking over his report, one is astonished at the quantity of game killed, however. From three to ten animals were slaughtered every day without a thought that a fewer number might have answered just as well. Only the choicest portions of the animals were eaten: the remainder was left to the wolves and panthers.

They passed on the 15th a large unoccupied encampment of the Kansas Indians, and on this day observed in the distance the buffaloes running, which indicated the presence either of Indians or white men. On this day they camped near what is now Tampa, Marion county. Two days later they reached the Smoky hill branch of the Kansas river, and after this game began to grow scarcer. September 21st, Pike learned that the only remaining Osage Indians with him were preparing to take horses and depart from the expedition, fearing, no doubt, the consequences of their meeting the Kansas, with whom they were at war; but when taken to task by Pike and called cowards, they boastingly determined then to remain at all hazards. Pike writes, "Thus were we obliged to keep ourselves on our guard against our own companions and fellow-travelers, men of a nation highly favored by the United States, but whom I believe to be a faithless set of poltroons, incapable of a great or generous action; among them, indeed, there may be some exceptions." Probably among the exceptions was the Indian woman who had informed Captain Pike of the intended desertion of her own people, one of whom was her husband. Or was this because she was not to be taken with them?

Some days previous to this event, Doctor Robinson and a Pawnee hunter had been sent on in advance, so as not to surprise the Pawnee village, but to prepare them for the visit of the American expedition. On the 22d a Pawnee messenger arrived with the intelligence that the Doctor and several chiefs and a band of warriors had come out to meet them, but had passed them far to the north. It was afterward learned that the Osage guides with the expedition, fearing an attack from the Pawnees or the Kansas, had purposely led the expedition much too far to the south and west in order to avoid the enemy as long as possible. The messenger told Pike that the Tetons (or Ietans, or Comanches), had recently killed six of the Kansas and Pawnees and had stolen many of their horses. He also stated that a large body of Spanish cavalry, numbering several hundreds, had lately been to the Pawnee villages for the purpose of gaining the friendship of that tribe. This was somewhat startling news, and set Captain Pike to thinking of the consequence should such an army meet his comparatively small force. There could be no reasonable doubt that the Spaniards had no right thus to invade the probable territory of the United States unless war was already in progress. Of course Pike was aware of the strained relations on the Texas border between the United States and Spain and knew that the boundary had not been established. He realized as a consequence that the invasion of the country by the Spaniards might mean that war had already commenced, and that his own capture might be the result of a meeting between the above-mentioned Spanish force and his own. From this time forward, therefore, he was not without concern at all times regarding what might happen should his little command meet a considerable body of the Spanish troopers.

As the command continued to advance they met members of the Pawnee tribe—several on the 23d and more on the 24th—all of whom were well mounted and well supplied with Spanish mules, horses, bridles and blankets. Some were clothed in Spanish garments, while others not so well favored had on nothing except the usual breech cloth; indeed some had on nothing but a buffalo robe. On the 25th Pike crossed the Spanish trail, and knew from the tracks that there were several hundred of them. Finally, when he arrived within three miles of the Republican Pawnee villages, he was asked to wait until the tribe was ready to receive him fittingly. He was now on the Republican branch of the Kansas river, near the present boundary between Kansas and Nebraska, having just crossed the Great Saline, the Little Saline and Solomon's Fork. All having seated themselves in the open, a large body of Pawnee warriors advanced toward them, all splendidly mounted and armed as if for actual war; indeed the reception had all the realistic features of an attack. Several hundred of them came toward the Americans at full speed, circling out on each side as if to flank the visitors, all brandishing their arms and yelling at the top of their voices. This was a customary ceremony of all the Indian tribes, when wishing to impress visitors with their strength and prowess. In fact they outdid themselves on this occasion, in order to impress the Osages who were present as well as the Americans. Finally, all drew rein, and the chiefs, White Wolf, or Char-ac-ter-ish, and Rich Man, or Is-ka-tap-pe, advanced and extended their hands, after which all mingled in friendship. The pipe of peace was passed and all blew up clouds of smoke, while they were thinking of how to outwit each other.

Succeeding this event, all were escorted to the Pawnee villages, where the whites were feasted on the best the savages had, which is not making a very strong statement. The whites were plentifully supplied with corn, but remained encamped at some distance from the Indians. On September 26, twelve Kansas arrived, and were warmly received by the Pawnees. A big council was called for the 29th, and on that day all the Indians were present, probably because they knew that they were to be given many valuable presents. In reality, the friendship of the Pawnees was one of the principal objects of the expedition, and Pike took extra precautions to impress the savages with the power and good will of the United States. But he encountered an obstacle he had not at first figured on: Namely, the influences of the Spaniards, particularly of their last visit of three or four weeks before. He was not without misgivings as to the effect on the four hundred warriors present of his little force as compared with that of the Spaniards, which numbered nearly four hundred. In the end it transpired that his misgivings were well founded. Having noticed that the Spanish flag was flying over the villages, he inquired why it was permitted in the territory of the United States. He was told that it was because of the recent visit of the Spanish dragoons, the friends of the Pawnees. He asked to have it removed, and dead silence followed. Finally, an old Indian advanced and pulled it down and handed it to Captain Pike, who immediately returned it to him, saying that it was not the act that he condemned, but the outward appearance of hostility to the United States. This act of giving back the Spanish flag was a stroke of excellent policy, which after events fully confirmed; because the Pawnees at once assisted in raising an American flag, and so showed a friendlier attitude. But the act brought sharply to the attention of the observant Pike that the savages might at any moment turn against the Americans; in fact, it was clear that among the younger savages at least, the large body of Spanish dragoons, with their bright uniforms and glittering arms, was regarded much more highly than his own insignificant force. The act of the Pawnees in raising the flag of the United States greatly pleased the Kansas and the Osage Indians present, because it betokend the friendship of their tribes and those of the Pawnees; and hence would result in the accomplishment of the designs of the expedition.

It soon became apparent to Pike that he had not succeeded in removing the favorable opinion of the savages for the Spanish.

When, in the course of the council, he intimated his intention of
going on west as far as the Spanish country, the Indians were
sternly silent and cast down their eyes; and when he reiterated
his intentions, he observed that a hostile spirit was manifested in
the assembly. In this instance, the usually impassive countenances of the savages told only too clearly their thoughts. When
the Spanish flag was pulled down, Pike noted that sorrow was
plainly manifested on many countenances. He therefore thought
quickly of how he might overcome this prejudice in favor of the
Spaniards. The occasion was presented when he returned the
Spanish flag to the Indians after it had been lowered. Pike
merely told the Indians not to raise the Spanish flag during his
stay in their village, which request was strictly complied with.
His course was fully appreciated by the savages, who raised a
great shout of applause. The council was continued several days,
and the savages used all the arguments and arts in their power to
prevail upon the Americans to go no farther; but as this, of
course, could not be accorded, Pike was finally told that the savages would feel called upon to use force to prevent his advance.
This finality was reached by the Indians only after all other means
had been exhausted by them to induce Captain Pike to
return to the states. Char-ac-ter-ish told Pike that the
Spanish had proposed to go much farther to the east, but that he
had persuaded them not to do so. And now for the same reasons,
he would advise the Americans to advance no farther. The chief
went to the extent of saying that he had promised the Spanish
commander not to permit the Americans to pass beyond his
villages.

The position thus taken by the Pawnees, and nearly all seemed
to favor it, sharply defined the pending issue and showed at once
the metal that was in Captain Pike. He spoke at considerable
length in reply to these points, saying that all this region belonged
to the United States, and was not seriously disputed even by the
Spanish themselves; that the Father at Washington had sent him
out to see all the red children in the territory of the United States
in the West; that he had come to make the red children presents
and to tell them to live in peace with one another; that he was
compelled to proceed by the orders of the Father, that if he did
not at this time there would be sent out a large army that would
not be so kind to them, and that he was determined to proceed
as he had been ordered. He said, "I have been sent out by our
Great Father to explore the western country, to visit all his red

children, to make peace between them, and turn them from the shedding of blood; and you may see how I have caused the Osage and Kaws to meet to smoke the pipe of peace together, and take each other by the hands like brothers; that as yet my road has been smooth, and a blue sky over our heads. I have not seen any blood in our paths; but you must know that the young warriors of our Great American Father are not women to be turned back by words, that I shall therefore proceed, and if you think proper to stop me, you can attempt it; but we are men, well armed, and will sell our lives at a dear rate to your nation, and we know our Great Father will send our young warriors there to gather our bones and revenge our deaths on your people; when our spirits will rejoice in hearing our exploits sung in the war songs of our chiefs."

Having thus spoken, Pike "then left the lodge and returned to camp in considerable perturbation of mind." He writes under date of October 2d, "We received advice from our Kansas that the chief had given publicity to his idea of stopping us by force of arms, which gave serious reflections to me, and was productive of many singular expressions from my brave lads, which called for my esteem at the same time that they excited my laughter." Pike was fortunate in having only men with him who would stand by him in any extremity; for all now favored advancing and taking what consequences the Indians might offer. He continued to make preparations, and sought to buy horses, but was unable to do so at first. He noticed a hostile sentiment throughout the villages, and accordingly kept to himself, and strengthened his force at all points, guarding everything securely at night to prevent possible surprise. On October 7, all things being ready, he started, passing around the villages instead of through them, and having everything in readiness to repel an attack. He coolly says that he calculated that his force could kill one hundred savages before they were wholly annihilated. As he passed their village he saw much commotion, and rode up to the lodges to ascertain what was the matter. Having learned that no attack was contemplated, although he saw that many of the warriors had their arms in their hands, he returned to his little army and continued to advance, "feeling immensely relieved." He said, "All the evil I wished the Pawnees was that I might be the instrument in the hands of our government to open their ears and eyes with a strong hand to convince them of our power."

The expedition passed on and was soon far away from the

Pawnee villages; but extra guard was posted for several days, lest the savages should change their minds. There were now two officers, one doctor, eighteen soldiers, one interpreter, three Osages and one woman. On the 8th they came again upon the Spanish trail, and at one of the camps counted fifty-nine fires, which, at six men to a fire, signified a force of three hundred fifty-four troopers. On October 9, the Pawnees put in an appearance, and were guilty of many threatening acts, stealing small articles, and circling fiercely around on the prairie; but they finally withdrew, though they returned again the next day.

Solomon's Fork was again crossed the 9th much farther to the west than on December 23, and here another camp of the Spanish army was found. It was the plan of Pike to follow the Spanish trail, because it would no doubt lead by the most direct route to the mountains where the head of Red river was to be found, the objective now of the expedition. On the 9th Pike says he saw for the first time a buffalo hunt on a grand scale by the Indians armed only with their native weapons. He writes, "The buffalo took back in sight of the Pawnees, who immediately mounted fifty or sixty young men and joined in the pursuit; then for the first time in my life I saw animals slaughtered by the true savages, with their original weapons, bows and arrows: they buried the arrow to the plume in the animal." They reached the Smoky Hill Fork on the 13th, not far from the boundary line of the counties of Russell and Ellsworth, and the following day arrived at the divide between the the Arkansas and the Kansas rivers. Here Pike and a small party became lost on the prairie, and did not turn up for several days: in the meantime the expedition continued to advance to the Arkansas river, where the lost party under Pike overtook it. The river was crossed by all hands on the 19th.

Here an important change had been ordered. The expedition was to be divided, part returning down the Arkansas and part going on up to the mountains for the purpose of discovering the headwaters of Red river, and then of descending that unknown stream—unknown to the Americans. Canoes were made of buffalo and deer hides and wood and were filled with provisions, arms and ammunition. Finally, on the 28th of October, Lieutenant Wilkinson, accompanied by five men and an Indian, started down the river, while the remainder of the force under the command of Captain Pike advanced up the stream. This parting was not without tears on both sides. They had become used to one another, had passed through the same dangers, and slept under the same blankets, and now realizing, as only companions in great dangers can, the sorrows of parting.

The party under Lieutenant Wilkinson soon found that it was impracticable to use their boats, as they soon grounded and were in danger any moment of upsetting and depositing all their provisions and ammunition in the middle of the river. On the 30th the river froze over and obliged them wholly to abandon the boats. The next day they threw away everything they could not carry or did not want to do so, and started ahead on foot. They had but one fear: That some war party of Pawnees might descend upon them. The country was almost wholly barren, scarcely a shrub, and not a tree, being in sight for several days. By the 8th of November, cotton-woods began to line the water courses, and the herds of buffalo began to make their appearance. Lieutenant Wilkinson states that on one day he saw fully nine thousand buffaloes. On the 10th he says he saw a tree that was not a cotton-wood, and felt as if he had met an old friend. By the 12th the buffalo began to disappear, and the deer became more abundant. By the 15th trees large enough to make canoes were found, and it was resolved to try once more to float down instead of walk down. While several began on the canoes, the others went hunting for their winter's supply of meat. Everything being ready by the 24th, they tried again, but as before the boats grounded. But they pushed them along, the men jumping into the icy water bare-legged and bare-footed to put their shoulders to the boats. Finally, on the 28th, one of the canoes upset and deposited all of their provisions and the most of their ammunition in the river, after which they again abandoned them and took to the bank, managing to save enough for present needs.

A band of Osage Indians was encountered the 30th, who brought word that the chief, Wind, was sick on the opposite side of the prairie and desired to see Lieutenant Wilkinson. Accordingly, he went out and found him seriously ill. He complained that, after the departure of Pike's party from the Osage villages, Chouteau had done about all he could to influence the Indians against the Americans, and that because he (Wind) had sustained the Americans, the Frenchman had caused him to be deprived of provisions and goods and had shamefully mistreated him in many other ways, leaving himself and family almost wholly without clothing. Wilkinson furnished the old chief all he needed, and wrote a sharp letter to General Wilkinson concerning the conduct of Chouteau, which in the end brought about the desired reforms.

Their ammunition began to run short, and all were cautioned to waste none. The weather was very cold, and the men had no stockings, and only cotton trousers. Great suffering resulted. December 16 Sabine river was passed, and on the 27th the Verdigris and the Grand. Two days later the mouth of the Illinois was reached, and on January 9 they arrived at Arkansas Post and took a rest from their extremely arduous trials and severe sufferings.

After parting with Lieutenant Wilkinson, the party under Captain Pike advanced rapidly up stream along the valley of the river. On the 29th of October they saw two wild horses feeding among the buffaloes, and tried to catch them by running, but failed, as they were too fast for the horses of the expedition. On the 31st they saw much crystalline salt on the surface of the ground. The country was now covered with snow: they were not far from what is now Kinsley, Edwards county, Kan. On November 1st, a large herd of wild horses observed the intruders, and came rapidly toward them, making the earth tremble with their tread. Among them were animals of all colors—bays, blacks, grays and mixed colors, and several were very fine. An attempt was made to "crease"* a fine black stallion, but the attempt failed. They would advance, paw the earth and whinney, all the time circulating around the strangers with the greatest curiosity. The next day an attempt was made to "noose" some of them. Six men mounted on the best horses were sent out; but although the wild ones came within forty yards of them, it was found impossible to capture one, because no one in the party knew how to lasso them. When they were chased, two of the men, it was found, were so well mounted that they easily came up with the herd, but all efforts to cast the noose over their heads failed. Pike writes, "I have since laughed at our folly; for taking the wild horses in that manner is scarcely ever attempted even with the fleetest horses and most expert ropers." They did not seem to know the meaning of the word "lasso," and certainly did not know how to use it.

It was observed by Pike the 3d, that the wild animals were all heading for the south, occasioned, of course, by the snow and the

---

* To shoot the animal through the neck just above the spinal column, the shot being sufficient to drop the animal in its tracks long enough for the hunters to catch it, without injuring it permanently.

consequent difficulty of finding feed under the white covering. They began to see many salt ponds, and an excellent salt marsh grass was observed. On the 4th they encountered immense herds of buffalo cows and their calves; having previously seen only bulls. They saw three thousand in one herd. Cow buffalo meat was infinitely superior to that of the bulls; in fact Pike avers that it was the best meat in the world, superior to the best beef. He wrote of November 6, "I will not attempt to describe the droves of animals we now saw on our route; suffice it to say, that the face of the prairie was covered with them on each side of the river; their numbers exceed imagination."

By the 9th of November, they were in the vicinity of the present town of Hartland, Kearney county. Here, at one of the Spanish encampments, they counted ninety-six fires, which signified that the force had been augmented to from six hundred to seven hundred troopers. By the 10th their horse feed began to grow scarce and the next day two of the poor animals gave out. The following day they were obliged to leave these animals. They now saw fresh signs of Indians; and being in a hostile country, began to take extra precautions not to be caught napping. On the 15th, for the first time, they perceived in the blue distance the mountains. So glad were they to leave the wearisome plain, the men gave three cheers "for the Mexican mountains." On this day they reached Purgatory river, a branch of the Arkansas. On November 18, the hunters sent out without restrictions killed seventeen buffaloes and wounded twenty more greatly to the mortification of Pike. Another horse died on the 19th. On this day they feasted on one hundred thirty-six marrow bones of the buffaloes killed the day before, and regarded it as one of the most enjoyable feasts they had ever survived. They took on their horses about nine hundred pounds of buffalo meat, notwithstanding that they had one less horse, and all the others were extremely weak. Thus while the men feasted, the poor horses were literally starving. The tracks of two men were crossed about this time, which occasioned fresh words of caution. Hostile Indians or hostile Spaniards might be encountered at any time now, so that everything was kept in condition for resistance.

On the 22d a large war party of Grand Pawnees, who were in pursuit of the Ietans, rode up to the expedition. They were sixty warriors, about half of whom had guns. After the manner of the Indians, when they did not wish to make an open attack, but had no respect for the others, they began to take all sorts of liberties with the expedition—helped themselves to articles of all sorts, a sword, a tomahawk, a broad ax, five canteens, and many other small articles. They even attempted to take the arms of the white men. When they at last began to take liberties with the baggage, it was deemed prudent to stop their nonsense. Pike accordingly ordered his men to their arms, and informed the Indians through his interpreter, that if they touched his baggage, he would open fire upon them; whereupon they immediately drew off. Finding they could gain nothing, they finally departed. Pike wrote as follows: "When I reflected on the subject I felt myself severely mortified that the smallness of my numbers obliged me thus to submit to the insults of a lawless banditti, it being the first time ever a savage took anything from me with the least appearance of force."

What Pike called the third fork was reached November 23. He writes, "As the river appeared to be dividing itself into many small branches and of course must be near its extreme source, I concluded to put the party in a defensible situation; and then ascend the north fork to the high point of the blue mountain, which we conceived would be one day's march, in order to be enabled from its pinnacle to lay down the various branches and positions of the country." The third fork was the St. Charles river, and their encampment was made at what he called the "grand forks," or at the junction of the Fountain river with the Arkansas. The high point he referred to was Pike's peak. The north fork which they determined to ascend was Fountain river. They cut the necessary logs the next day, and erected a strong breastwork, five feet high on three sides, with the other opening on the south bank of the Arkansas. They were now on the present site of Pueblo. Leaving all the others at the fort, Pike, Robinson, Miller and Brown started for the mountains. By the 26th they had ascended so high that they looked down on the clouds rolling across the plain to the east. On the 27th they reached the summit, but had had a very difficult time, being obliged often to wade in snow waist deep. As the soldiers had on only light cotton overalls and were without stockings, and as the weather was severely cold, they suffered intensely. Game was very scarce, but they succeeded in killing two buffaloes on the 28th, and, as Pike says, had the first good meal in three days. On their way back, they noted that the soil was very rich, and that the vallays were full of old deserted Ietan camps. The fort was reached on the 29th, and all there were found well.

It was now December 1st, the snow lay a foot deep, the thermometer hovered around zero, the men were only half clad; but they could not remain idle; the country must be explored; all must keep moving, for self preservation, if for nothing more. The poor horses were forced to subsist on the tops of trees cut down for them. The hungry magpies became so bold, they lighted on the horses' backs and pecked at the wounds made by the packs; they even lighted on the arms of the men to dispute with them the title to the pieces of meat that had just been roasted. Finally, all hands departed, and on the 5th of December they reached the mountains. Having encamped, they tried to find a pass through the mountains, but did not succeed until the 10th, i. e.; through what is now Oil creek. They saw around them abandoned camps both of the Ietans and the Spaniards. They continued to ascend the Arkansas, but made frequent side excursions for purposes of discovery. Their camp was on the main stream at the entrance of Wet mountain. On the 6th, they ascended the river and reached the Royal Gorge; but failed to find the Spanish trace for which they were in search; though the next day they found it north of the Arkansas. On one of their excursions they reached the south branch of the Platte river.

As a precautionary measure, a permanent camp was established on the north bank of the Arkansas, at what is now Cañon City, which served as a rallying point, while the surrounding country was being explored. One of the excursion parties ascended the Arkansas in a northwest direction nearly or quite to its remote source, or until the river was merely a small brook. While thus engaged Pike ascertained that a large party of Spaniards had recently been in this vicinity: he also found an abandoned Indian encampment, where several thousand head of horses had been kept for some time. Having learned, as he thought, that the Spaniards had ascended the river, he writes, December 14, "We determined to pursue them, as the geography of the country had turned out to be so different from our expectations. We were somewhat at a loss what course to pursue." Where they struck the Platte was at the head of Eleven Mile Cañon. In the meantime, Pike and his companions kept wondering where the headwaters of Red river were; their design being to decend that stream. On the 18th, having been to the north of the Arkansas, they marched southwest and again reached that river, although they thought at first it was the Red. Descending the same they finally discovered their mistake. They then began to reason that the sources of the Red must be to the southwest. At one time they nearly starved, but the following day "from being in a starving condition, we had eight beeves in camp."

Christmas was spent together feasting on fresh buffalo meat, without salt or other accompaniment; the men "appeared generally to be content." Thus far Pike had ascertained the sources of the Little Osage and the Neosha rivers; had passed round the head of the Kansas river; and had discovered the headwaters of the South Platte. He was now intent on finding the upper sources of the Red. December 25th, he writes, "Here eight hundred miles from the frontiers of our country, in the most inclement season of the year, not one person clothed for the winter, many without blankets, having been obliged to cut them up for socks, etc., and now lying down at night on the snow or wet ground, one side burning whilst the other was pierced with the cold wind—such was in part the situation of the party, whilst some were endeavoring to make a miserable substitute of raw buffalo hide for shoes, etc. I will not speak of diet, as I conceive that to be beneath the serious consideration of a man on a voyage of such a nature." Soon their horses began to give out, and on January 2, one of them, having fallen and seriously hurt itself, was shot to get it out of its misery. On the 4th of January, they divided into eight small parties, in order the better to make discoveries and kill game. It was on the 7th that Pike learned to his great mortification that they were not on the Red river as they had for some time supposed. All the party reoccupied the camp at Cañon City on the 9th.

Pike wrote under date of January 9th, "The whole party were once more joined together, when we felt comparatively happy, notwithstanding the great mortification I experienced at having been so egregiously deceived as to the Red river. I now felt at considerable loss how to proceed, as any idea of services at that time from my horses was entirely preposterous. After various plans formed and rejected, and the most mature deliberation, I determined to build a small place for defense and deposit; leave part of the baggage, horses, my interpreter and one man; and with the balance, our packs of Indian presents, ammunition, tools, etc., on our backs, cross the mountains on foot, find the Red river, and then send back a party to conduct the horses and baggage by the most eligible route we could discover; by which time the horses would be so recovered as to be able to endure the fatigues of the march. In consequence of this determination, some were

I—23

put to constructing the blockhouse, some to hunting, some to taking care of horses, etc." This blockhouse was built at their encampment on the present site of Cañon City.

The start on their perilous journey was made January 14, each man carrying about seventy pounds. Barony Vasquez, the interpreter, and Patrick Smith were left in charge of the blockhouse. The party advanced up what Pike calls the south fork, but which is now known as Grape creek, and marched in a southerly direction. On the 17th the great Sangre de Cristo range of mountains came in full view around a spur of the Wet mountains. This day it was found that nine of the men had frozen their feet; and within the next few days, no game having been killed, all came near starvation, but by good luck finally brought down a buffalo, which was immediately and hurriedly taken to camp. Pike writes, "We arrived there about twelve o'clock, and when I threw my load down, it was with difficulty I prevented myself from falling: I was attacked with a giddiness of the head, which lasted for some minutes. On the countenances of the men was not a frown, not a desponding eye; all seemed happy to hail their officer and companions, yet not a mouthful had they eaten for four days." As a matter of fact, had it not been for the many buffaloes and deer wintering in the mountains, not a man would have survived to tell the tale. As it was, it must ever stand as a case of remarkable hardihood and endurance, rarely if ever surpassed in the annals of western exploration.

It was found that the feet of two of the men, Thomas Dougherty and John Sparks, were so badly frozen, that they could not proceed. They were accordingly left as comfortable as possible, and the others again set forth. "I furnished the two poor lads who were to remain, with ammunition, made use of every argument in my power to encourage them to have fortitude to resist their fate, and gave them assurance of my sending relief as soon as possible. We parted, but not without tears." On the 24th Pike admits that for the first time he began to feel discouraged. Nearly all the buffaloes had quit the mountains, and the snow lay several feet on the level. On the 27th it was determined to leave one man, Hugh Menaugh, with the most of the goods, while the others made the effort to cross the Sangre de Cristo mountains, believing that by so doing they would reach the sources of Red river. This step was taken. They were now in the extreme southwestern corner of the present Custer county, Col. They set forth through the mountains, and in a short time found themselves on a small stream (Sand creek) running west "which we hailed with fervency as the waters of Red river." Soon the broad San Luis valley opened before them. Ascending a large sand hill, Pike with his glass saw far ahead a large river flowing in a southerly direction; this was believed to be the Red, and all were elated. Around were seen evidences of the late presence of Spaniards or other white men. They marched almost directly southward, and on the evening of January 30th arrived on the bank of the Rio Grande, believed by them to be the long-sought Red river. Not finding any timber, they continued to descend until they arrived at the Conejos, up which they ascended five miles and prepared to build a stockade, to be used as a base, while some of the party returned for the men who had been left behind. They accordingly erected a strong stockade of heavy cotton-wood logs on the north bank of the Conejos, of which Pike writes, "Thus fortified, I should not have had the least hesitation of putting the one hundred Spanish horse (that arrived later) at defiance until the first or second night, and then to have made our escape under cover of the darkness; or made a sally and dispersed them, when resting under a full confidence of our being panic-struck by their numbers and force." By February 15, the fort was practically complete. On the 7th, Corporal Jackson, with four men, was sent back over the mountains to bring up the baggage and the men who had been left behind.

In the meantime, or on February 6, Doctor Robinson, who had volunteered to accompany the expedition, determined to make the attempt from this point to reach Santa Fe, this plan having been determined upon by Robinson and Pike as an excuse to penetrate to that city. Pike had been commissioned to collect a large debt due William Morrison, of Kaskaskia, who had sent out to the Indian country a man named Baptiste La Lande with a valuable supply of goods; but no sooner had La Lande reached the Spanish country, than he converted the goods to his own use, and took up his residence in Santa Fe. To collect this sum and bring the culprit to justice was the ostensible object of Doctor Robinson's visit to that city. He set out on the 7th, and in due time reached Santa Fe.

While out hunting on the 16th, Pike and one of the men discovered two horsemen approaching, and after considerable maneuvering they came near enough for conversation. They told Pike that they had been out four days from Santa Fe, that Doctor Robinson had arrived there, and had been kindly received by Governor Allencaster. Pike satisfied himself that they were spies, and was confirmed when he found that they did not intend to leave at once. They were taken to the fort and remained over night, departing on the 17th. On this day several of the men of the relief expedition returned with the statement that the others would not be out much longer. Dougherty and Sparks were not yet able to come, but sent in bones from their feet, a result of the freezing and the consequent gangrene. The 19th two men, William E. Meek and Theodore Miller, were sent back to bring on Vasquez and Smith, who had been left at the stockade on the Arkansas river, and Dougherty and Sparks, on the horses. "I must here remark," writes Pike, "the effect of habit, discipline and example, in two soldiers soliciting a command of more than one hundred and eighty miles over two great ridges of mountains covered with snow, inhabited by bands of unknown savages, in the interest of a nation with which we were not on the best understanding. To perform this journey each had about ten pounds of venison. Only let me ask, What would our soldiers generally think, on being ordered on such a tour, thus equipped? Yet those men volunteered it with others and were chosen; for which they thought themselves highly honored."

From the fact that Doctor Robinson had no doubt told the Spanish governor of the presence of the white men, and from the visit of the two Spanish emissaries, Pike well knew that he might expect at any time the appearance of the Spaniards at his fort; therefore he issued strict injunctions as to the method of procedure should such an event occur. On the 26th a party of fifty dragoons and fifty mounted militia, under the command of Don Ignatio Saltelo, arrived and a conference was held. They announced that they had been sent to conduct the Americans to Santa Fe, and later to the headwaters of Red river, where they had heard the Americans were aiming. "What," exclaimed Pike, "is not this Red river?" "No, sir," answered Saltelo, "the Rio del Norte." Pike immediately ordered the American flag taken down. The Spanish commander urged the immediate departure of all hands to Santa Fe, but Pike would not listen to such a step without first providing for the others of the expedition away in the mountains. Although told that no force would be employed to compel him to go to Santa Fe, Pike saw that such a step was fully provided for, and realized that compulsory measures of some sort would no doubt in the end be applied. Saltelo was so courteous and mild, that after he had agreed to provide for the safety of the men in the mountains, Pike deemed it best to comply with his request before the leader changed his mind and used force. Five or six men against a hundred could do nothing even in this strong fort. He accordingly left orders with two men who were detailed to remain for the others, and having mounted a horse, with the others of his men, they all set forth for Santa Fe. Late on the 3d of March, that city was reached.

Pike was closely catechised by Governor Allencaster, and though given considerable liberty, felt that he was practically under arrest. All the Americans were well treated. Doctor Robinson was there. After the conference, Pike was informed that it would be necessary for him to go to the commandant general at Chihuahua, who alone was fully empowered to consider the case. They set out under an armed escort, and arrived at Albuquerque March 7, El Paso del Norte March 21, and Chihuahua April 2d. After fully investigating all features of the case, Commandant-general Salcedo determined to conduct all the Americans back to their country at the expense of the United States. This was done. Pike and six others were mounted; and, accompanied by an escort, started back; but returned through the present Texas, reaching San Antonio June 7. There they were received with great cordiality by Governor Cordero and General Herrara. June 24, they arrived at Nacogdoches, and July 1st at Natchitoches. The others of the party were well treated, and in due time returned to the United States.

The schemes of Aaron Burr and the undoubted connection therewith of General Wilkinson, who sent to the West Captain Pike, were not only the cause of arousing the suspicion of Gov. Joachin R. Allencaster and Gen. Nemesio Salcedo against the expedition of Pike, but was also the cause of the subsequent belief by many in the United States that the latter himself might have been knowingly connected with the Burr conspiracy. The Spanish leaders were kept fully posted of the progress of the scheme in the United States; and were also aware of every movement, hostile or otherwise, against their frontier. The expedition of Captain Sparks up Red river became known in Mexico soon after it was projected; and therefore a large force was sent to the Caddoe nation to check its advance, as told elsewhere herein. They were also aware of the movements of the expedition under Captain Pike; but miscalculated the date of his arrival at the Republican Pawnee villages, owing to his delay with the Osages and to his slow movements up the Osage river. Therefore, the Spanish army which had turned back Captain Sparks on Red river, arrived at the Pawnee villages about three weeks too early to encounter Captain Pike. It would have been an excellent stroke of policy for them, had Captain Pike been met by the Spanish army in the presence of the Pawnees and been forced to return: the object lesson with the Pawnees would have been to increase immensely the prestige of Spain with that powerful tribe. This was undoubtedly the object aimed at by Lieutenant Malgares, the commander of the Spanish expedition: even as it was, Pike was almost obliged to use force in order to proceed beyond the Pawnee villages, so favorable had been the reception of the Spanish dragoons by the Indians.

Lieut. Don Faciendo Malgares, though young, was already a distinguished officer in the New World. He was an accomplished courtier; and, while Pike was in New Mexico, showed him and his party every consideration in his power, consistent with his position as an officer of Spain. Pike became greatly attached to him for his gentlemanly qualities and his spontaneous friendship. The army with which he invaded the territory claimed by the United States consisted at first of between three hundred and four hundred dragoons and mounted militia, well armed and otherwise equipped for fast movement and active service. Later reinforcements raised the force to over six hundred men. It has been claimed that the Spanish authorities knew the army was invading the territory of the United States; but such claim has only the color of fact. As will be seen elsewhere herein, the boundary between Spain and the United States was yet indefinite. The United States secured Louisiana with its western boundary undetermined. Spain claimed the sources of the Red and the Arkansas, as did also the United States. The first proposition of Spain for a settlement asked that the boundary be established at the Aroyo Hondo in the present State of Louisiana; thence by a line northwest to the Missouri; thence down the Missouri to the Mississippi; and thence up the latter to its source. The United States first claimed westward to the Rio Grande; and there can be no doubt that, had France retained Louisiana, the western boundary of the same would have been fixed much farther toward Mexico than the Sabine. Thus the territory invaded by Lieutenant Malgares and by Captain Pike was in dispute, and one had as much right to invade it as the other until the dispute was settled. Pike's movements were justified until he entered the valley of the Rio Grande in New Mexico, where the Spanish had been established for more than a hundred years.

It is claimed by some writers that Pike knew he was not on Red river when he built his blockhouse on the Conejos west of the Rio Grande; that his expedition, under the pretense of making explorations on behalf of the United States, penetrated past the Spanish frontier for the purpose of ascertaining the vulnerability of Spain; and that, should the Burr conspiracy succeed, a large tract of the Spanish domain would be wrested from her and made a part of the new republic or empire that was designed to be established with Burr as its supreme ruler. It is well known that Pike himself, having stated in his journal under date of February 7, 1807, that "the demands which Doctor Robinson had on persons in New Mexico, although legitimate, were in some degree spurious *in his hands,*" sanctioned the visit of Doctor Robinson to Santa Fe. Indeed, Pike wrote as follows in the same footnote in explanation of that statement: "In the year 1804 William Morrison, Esq., an enterprising merchant of Kaskaskia, sent a man by the name of Baptiste la Lande, a Creole, to the country up the Missouri and La Platte, directing him, if possible, to push into Santa Fe. He sent Indians to that town, and the Spaniards came out with horses and carried him and his goods into the province. Finding that he sold the goods high, had land offered him and the women kind, he concluded to expatriate himself and convert the property of Morrison to his own benefit. When I (Pike) was about to sail, Morrison, conceiving it was possible I might meet some Spanish factors (merchants) on Red river, intrusted me with the claim, in order, if they were acquainted with La Lande, I might negotiate the thing with some of them. When on the frontiers, the idea suggested itself to us of making this claim a pretext for Robinson to visit Santa Fe. We therefore gave it the proper appearance, and he marched for that place. Our views were to gain a knowledge of the country, the prospect of trade, force, etc., whilst, at the same time, our treaties with Spain guaranteed to him as a citizen of the United States the right of seeking the recovery of all just debts or demands before the legal and authorized tribunals of the country, as a franchised inhabitant of the same, as specified in the 22d article of said treaty."

Thus the claim was placed in Pike's hands for adjustment. "When on the frontiers," in a starving and almost helpless condition, it occurred to Pike and Robinson to use the claim for the double purpose of obtaining assistance for the perishing men, and of entering New Mexico "to gain a knowledge of the country, the prospect of trade, force, etc." According to Pike this idea did not occur to them until they were "on the frontiers." The expression of Pike in the above footnote that the "demands were in some degree spurious *in his* (Robinson's) *hands,*" meant nothing more than that Pike, and not Robinson, had been authorized to adjust the demands of Morrison.

It is argued by some writers that Robinson, at least, was a spy of the Burr conspiracy acting under the orders of General Wilkinson; that his ostensible object of going to Santa Fe to collect a debt had been devised previously to be used if necessary to save his life in case he should be arrested as a spy; and that when he was met by Pike the latter affected not to know him, in order thereby to save him from possible arrest. As a matter of fact, when the expedition reached the mountains, both Pike and Robinson became lost, because, as Pike expressed it, the region was so different from what they expected. Though in search of the head-waters of Red river, they were also instructed to explore the sources of Arkansas river; this they proceeded to do. The reason why both Pike and Robinson sought to find some occupied Spanish camp, was in order to learn where they were and to ascertain the shorest route to Red river. They were aware that any Spaniard could furnish them just the information they wanted. But the Spaniards and the Indians had left that section; and therefore Pike and his freezing and starving comrades wandered in the deep snow for more than a month before they learned that Red river *must* be farther to the south or the southwest. Pike had nothing to fear from the Spaniards because he considered himself within the territory of the United States. The two countries, though disputing over the boundary, were at peace; besides, the army under Malgares had invaded such territory, and, at the worst, Pike had the right to do the same on behalf of the United States.

Doctor Robinson, on his arrival in New Mexico, told Malgares that he was one of Pike's party, and Malgares told Governor Allencaster. But Pike denied it to Allencaster. If both were in the Burr conspiracy, would they thus have contradicted each other? The contradiction proves there was no elaborate concert of action. Doctor Robinson also told of the presence of Pike on the Conejos. Why did he do so when he knew their capture would certainly and speedily follow? Was it not because he thought it better for them to be succored by the Spaniards than to perish from cold and starvation? What reason could either Pike or Robinson have had to desire to be captured by the Spanish, other than to save the expedition or to examine the interior of New Mexico? Would Pike have kept his soldiers in the mountains until they were frozen and almost helpless skeletons, if he had gone out either to attack the Spaniards or to spy upon them? What could he spy with his force that he could not better spy alone or with two or three companions? When once on Spanish soil that had so long been jealously guarded from the sight of Americans, it was natural for them to observe everything possible. Doctor Robinson was not a part of the expedition except in a voluntary capacity, for he was at liberty to leave it when he chose; so that Pike really told the truth when he informed Governor Allencaster that he was not a member of the expedition. But Doctor Robinson also told the truth when he said that he had come as a part of the expedition. This contradiction may have been the principal cause of the suspicion of Governor Allencaster and of his determination to send Pike to General Salcedo, at Chihuahua.

There is no good reason to doubt Pike's statement that he thought he was on Red river. He felt justified in building his blockhouse on a western branch of Red river, because the United States claimed the whole Mississippi basin, of which *all* branches of Red river were a part. The fact that he built at all is alone sufficient proof that he thought he was on Red river; because he never would have had the unmitigated audacity to build beyond the Rio Grande, thus rendering a misunderstanding, likely a conflict, between the two countries possible through his act. Both countries at that time pushed their claims as far as possible by actual occupancy. So Spain crossed the Sabine and went north to the Caddoes and the Pawnees; and the Americans went west of the Sabine and the Red. When Pike became aware that he was west of the Rio Grande, he realized at once that he had gone beyond the widest claims of the United States. He accordingly hauled down his flag; and not fearing anything serious, and desiring to succor his men, reach the sources of Red river, and examine the interior of New Mexico, he wisely yielded and agreed to go to Santa Fe.

But the Spanish governor at Santa Fe at first took an altogether different view. He suspected that Pike was leagued with Burr to detach a portion of Spanish territory. He therefore catechised him closely and examined minutely all his papers, and then not being fully satisfied, and being unwilling to take the responsibility, sent him to Commandant-General Salcedo, at Chihuahua. The latter finding not a scrap to connect him with the Burr conspiracy, treated him and his men as respectable Americans, advanced him one thousand dollars on the credit of the United States for the pressing needs of him and his soldiers, and escorted him safely to Natchitoches, which town was conceded to be within the American domains. But it will be observed that Pike was not permitted to return via Red river, because all the upper course of that stream was claimed by Spain. Had Salcedo permitted him to do so, it would have been tantamount to a recognition that American territory extended to that river. From the above observations it will be seen that, while, in a certain sense, both Pike and Robinson were spies for the United States, though acting on their own violition, they cannot in any particular be connected with the Burr conspiracy. It will also be seen that not all the objects of Pike's second expedition were accomplished.

CHAPTER XI

The Fur Traders, the Santa Fe Commerce, the Pony Express, Etc.

THE United States possesses a chapter of history so unique as not to be matched in many particulars by any other portion of the globe. The settlement of the Great West contains such a wealth and such a blending of remarkable incidents, as to place an account of it in a class of absorbing interest by itself. First, the fur trappers and traders appeared, penetrating to the heart of the hostile Indian country with a fearlessness that seems almost unaccountable. Then came the private trading expeditions, with their goods for the Indians, their hunts of the buffalo, and their privations from thirst and starvation. The opening of the Santa Fe trade opened at the same time another wonderful era in the West—that of the caravans, their herds of horses, cattle and mules, their large stocks of merchandise, their dealings with the crafty Spaniards, and their skirmishes with the Indians. Following immediately, came the post and the express lines, ending with the pony riders, a wonderful exhibiton of what intelligence, pluck and endurance can accomplish. Later, the gold discoveries kindled hope in many despondent hearts; and soon the plains were lined with wagon trains and strewn with broken vehicles, discarded household articles and the skeletons of oxen, mules and men. But all this has vanished. The buffalo, like the Indian, being the product of uncivilized conditions, has almost wholly passed away. The wagon trains are but a thrilling memory. A nobler order of affairs has risen over the ashes of the past, and it seems idle now to count the cost. All of the topics are so filled with surprising incidents, that scores of volumes might be employed in their recital.

The Hudson's Bay Company was organized in 1670, but before that event the Indian trade in furs had become immensely valuable to Canada. Charles Fort had been built by Zachariah Gilliam on Prince Rupert's river; and Medard Chouart and Pierre Esprit Radisson had already distinguished themselves among the Indians. Although it was provided by the treaty of Ryswick that commissioners should be appointed to establish the boundary between France and England in America, it does not appear that they performed their duties, even if they were appointed. The treaty of Utrecht also provided that commissioners should run the line, but they were slow in doing so. Immediately succeeding this treaty, came the designs to discover a northwest passage, the father of which project was Arthur Dobbs, whose real object is said to have been to found a rival organization to Hudson's Bay Company. The two treaties of Ryswick and Utrecht, obliged France to leave Hudson Bay and enter the Lake Superior country. But the re-discovery of the Mississippi river by France did not solve the problem of a northwest passage, though it was thought probable that the Missouri river might lead to the coveted route. Soon after the treaty of Utrecht, Pierre Gaultier Verendrye learned from members of the Assiniboine tribe of the existence of the river of their name and of its many branches, all superior beaver country. This distingushed explorer set out in 1728 and in due time, as elsewhere narrated, built several forts north of the present Minnesota. In 1738, accompanied by over fifty persons, he visited the Mandan villages on the Missouri, made famous later by the visit of Lewis and Clark. Four years later his son and a few companions, not only visited the Mandan villages, but ascended the Missouri by its Yellowstone branch to the first chain of mountains,

General Wolfe had scarcely overthrown the Canada of France in 1759, before the English traders, clerks, agents and wood-rangers began to pierce the western country. Finally, the Montreal merchants in 1783-4 organized the Northwest Company; but were at first handicapped, owing to a division in their ranks, though all differences were adjusted by 1787. By this time the two companies—Hudson's Bay and Northwest—were involved in intense rivalry for the western fur trade. Important stations were established on the Souris and the Assiniboine rivers by both companies. From them nearly all the tribes of Indians living in what is now the States of Wisconsin, Minnesota, North Dakota, South Dakota and Montana were supplied with goods and fire-arms in exchange for their valuable furs. David Thompson, who at first was associated with the Hudson's Bay Company, finally joined the force of the Northwest Company about the year 1796. He was dispatched by the latter to visit the Mandan villages on the Missouri, and was accompanied by René Jussaume and Hugh McCracken, both of whom could speak the Mandan tongue. They took with them a supply of goods for the Indians, several horses, and about thirty dogs to draw the sleds. Thompson learned by this visit that traders of the Hudson's Bay Company had previously made flying trips to the Mandan villages. In February, 1798, with a few companions, he went up Red river of the North, found at Pembina a trading station under Charles Chaboillez, another at Grand Forks under J. Baptiste Cadot; and from this point marched eastward to Red Lake river, thence up the same to Red lake, thence across to Turtle lake, and four days later stood on what he thought was the source of the Mississippi river. He was mistaken. He visited the Northwest Company's forts on Red Cedar lake, Sand lake, St. Louis river and the portage.

It was at this time that the X Y Company began to rival the Northwest Company, and for several years the struggle for the western trade was conducted with great spirit, enterprise and audacity. The union of the two companies in 1805 so strengthened them that they at once became a powerful rival of the Hudson's Bay Company. The junction of the Souris and the Assiniboine soon became the most central and important point of the Indian trade in all the northwest. The sharp rivalry for the furs of the Indians was the cause of the introduction of large quantities of whisky among them. The Indians turned over their furs to the traders who treated them the best—in other words, who gave them the largest supply of spirits. François Antoine Larocque, Charles McKenzie and five others were at the Mandan villages when Lewis and Clark reached there. These traders afterward visited these villages.

Nearly a hundred years before the English race ascended the Missouri river, the French Canadian trappers and voyageurs had gone as far up as the mouth of the Yellowstone, and thence up the latter river to the mountains. The French Canadians feared the English colonists, the Iroquois Indians, who were the friends of the English, and the Canadian government, which would confiscate their furs upon sight, under the laws which granted a monopoly to the Canadian companies. The English interfered with their trade as far west as the Mississippi, but did not go

much beyond that stream, and hence the French Canadian was
for a long time unmolested in his operations in the Missouri valley. This immunity from molestation continued until the cession
of Louisiana Province to the United States in 1803, when all the
western country was thrown open in an instant to the English
colonist, or rather, the American colonist. This proved the death
knell to the prestige of the old French Canadian voyageur so far
as the Missouri country was concerned. Here and there they
continued to linger, and at all times had more influence with the
Indian tribes than the Americans. Nearly all of the interpreters
of the earliest expeditions set on foot by the United States were
French Canadian. Alexander McKenzie, of the Northwest Fur
Company, went westward from Lake Superior and crossed the
Rocky mountains to the Pacific in 1793; this was the first really
important expedition through the western mountain system; but
as it was done under business or private auspices, the details did
not at once become known. Among the most important fur companies organized for private profit were the Mackinaw Fur Company, which operated from the Great Lakes to the Mississippi;
the American Fur Company, which entered the Missouri river
valley and that of the Columbia river; the Missouri Fur Company,
on the Missouri and in the Rocky mountains; the Southwestern
Fur Company, an amalgamation by the Astors of the American
and the Mackinaw companies; and in Canada were Hudson's Bay
Company, the Northwest Company, and the X Y Company.
When all these organizations were in full operation, there were
lively times in the mountains and on the prairie. Their rivalries,
maneuvers, intrigues and battles would fill half a dozen volumes
with incidents of thrilling interest.

In 1739 two brothers named Mallet, accompanied by six companions, set out up the Missouri river, and when at the Arickaree
villages learned that they should have gone west before coming
so far north. They finally retraced their steps, ascended the
Platte, passed the Pawnee villages, continued to the mountainous
country and at last arrived in Santa Fe. They had with them a
small stock of goods—how much is not known. Theirs was the
first commercial enterprise to go from the Mississippi to Santa Fe.
Having disposed of their goods and learned considerable of the
customs of the Spaniards, they started homeward, but divided
into two parties, one returning down the Platte and the other
down the Arkansas. It is known that another party of French
traders took a stock of goods before 1763 to the Rocky mountain
country and tried to sell it partly to the Indians and partly to the

Spanish at Taos and Santa Fe. Before this could be accomplished, they were arrested, their goods confiscated; but the affair was finally settled by the governments of France and Spain, and the men were released and sent to their homes on the Mississippi.

After the treaty of 1762–3, by which the English obtained all the territory east of the Mississippi, all of the country as far west as that river began to be overrun with English explorers, hunters and trappers. Jonathan Carver of Boston, wishing to serve his country, and at the same time gain a competence for himself, secured permission to explore and started for the West. In due time he arrived at Michillimackinac, and on September 18th, was at Green Bay. On the 25th he reached the villages of the Winnebagoes, October 7 arrived at the portage, and October 15 reached the Mississippi. Here he left a number of traders, who had come this far with him, and continued on up the Mississippi with some goods on the 19th. On November 1st, he reached Lake Pepin, and on the 17th arrived at the Falls of St. Anthony. Three days later he reached the St. Francis river, which he ascended to the Sioux villages. Later he descended the rivers to the mouth of St. Peter's river, up which stream he went and arrived at the villages of the Nadissiou on December 7th. These villages were on the headwaters of St. Peter's river, and here Carver passed the winter. Although the Sioux were hostile, he managed to secure their favor and passed the winter without serious event. In April of the following year he started down the streams, and at the mouth of the Wisconsin obtained a supply of Indian goods, which had been sent him by the government, and without which no person then had any business in the Indian country. Carver was in the service of the British government, because these goods were obtained from that source. After securing his goods, he passed up the Chippewa river, trading as he went, and finally crossed over to Lake Superior, and coasted around the entire northern shore of that body of water to Sault Ste. Marie, where stood Cadot's fort. In 1768 he returned to Canada with much valuable information for his government.

It is well known that, while Louisiana was still a province of France, the traders of New Orleans began to penetrate the country beyond the Mississippi for the purpose of trading, not only with the Indian, but with the Spanish of New Mexico, providing they could be reached. After 1763, at which date Spain secured the whole country west of the Mississippi, the trade beyond that river became wholly the possession of Spain; and as the policy of that country was commercial seclusion and exclusion, much of what transpired thereafter is unknown to history. It is clear that, in 1762, Maxent, Laclede & Company were granted the right to the exclusive trade on the Missouri and on the Mississippi as far up as the mouth of the Minnesota, and that they and others under their directions conducted a large business. No doubt their fur trade and that of all others emanating from St. Louis aggregated a total of over one hundred thousand dollars by 1795. But in the meantime, undeterred by the French or the Spanish, the British fur companies of the Lake Superior country, were steadily penetrating the territory as far south as the present states of Iowa and Nebraska. These commercial encroachments were continued by those companies long after the Louisiana Province had passed to the United States. St. Louis, soon after it was founded, became the center of the western fur trade. All her old merchants were thus engaged, sooner or later, and several of their names are famous in history—Chouteau, Lisa, Ashley, Sublette, Campbell and many others. Manuel Lisa arrived at St. Louis about 1790, and ten years later possessed the right to the exclusive trade with the Osages. Finally, when the province passed to the United States in 1803, St. Louis was the most remarkable of the many wonderful towns of the great West. It had a cosmopolitan population of French, Spanish, Dutch, English, French half-breeds, Indians, negroes; and was alive with the peculiar flavor of the plains and the mountains. Everything was ripe for the opening of the province to the aggressiveness of the Americans.

The explorations of Lewis and Clark and of Lieutenant Pike were still unfinished when the trading parties began to stem the rapid current of the turbid Missouri. New partnerships and commercial combinations were formed to take advantage of the opportunity offered by the acquisition of the province. The richness of the territory in valuable furs was already well known to the St. Louis traders. The fur company of Manuel Lisa, Francis M. Benoit, Gregoire Sarpy and Charles Sanguinet was doing business in St. Louis in 1802. Manuel Lisa, who had previously formed a business connection with William Morrison and Pierre Menard of Kaskaskia, passed up in 1807. About the same time Pierre B. Chouteau ascended the river with a large assortment of goods and a considerable force of trappers and hunters. The St. Louis Missouri Fur Company was organized in 1708-9, but is known to history as the Missouri Fur Company. Among the first partners were the following men: Manuel Lisa, Pierre Chouteau, Sr., Benjamin Wilkinson, Auguste Chouteau, Jr., Reuben Lewis, Sylvester Labadie, William Clark, William Morrison, Pierre Menard, Andrew Henry, and Dennis Fitzhugh. This company sent its first expedition up the Missouri in the spring of 1809. The design was to establish several trading posts, and about one hundred and fifty men were sent up to be distributed among them. Under the agreement by which the Missouri Company was formed all the posts, horses, men traps and other accoutrements of the Lisa partnership were turned over to the company. Thus the Lisa post on the Big Horn passed to the new management, and was occupied by members of the first expedition.

In the year 1804 the government agreed to provide the Osage Indians with a trading-house, and the promise was repeated in 1806 to another deputation that had gone to Washington. The promise was not carried out until November, 1808, when Pierre Chouteau, the United States agent for the Osages, held a treaty with them at Fort Clark, and made arrangements for the erection of the post. At this time, it has been claimed, a large tract was obtained from them by fraudulent methods; because they were given no alternative but either to surrender the lands wanted or suffer the enmity of the United States. Of course the chiefs present relinquished the lands wanted, particularly as the demand was accompanied by valuable gifts. Many of the chiefs of the tribe knew nothing of this treaty. The trading-house was kept up until 1813, when the war with Great Britain obliged the government to abandon it. Neither were the annuities agreed upon by the treaty paid by the government according to agreement. But the land was retained.

In the spring of 1807, with Drouillard, one of Lewis and Clark's men, as a guide and interpreter, and with a force of about twenty experienced trappers and a large supply of provisions and Indian presents loaded in a strong keel-boat, Manuel Lisa started up the Missouri from St. Louis on a hunting and trapping expedition. With this party was the afterward famous Bijeau or Bissonette, who deserted at Fort Osage. On the trip up the river, they met John Colter in a small dug-out of his own manufacture, calmly floating down the streams, having come all the way from the mountains. He had been a member of the Lewis and Clark expedition, but had remained behind at his own request, and after hair-breadth escapes from the Indians, was on his way to civilization. This Colter was a remarkable man. Before the Lewis and Clark expedition, he had been up the river among the savages, and after the expedition had returned

I—24

he remained behind to hunt and trap. A trapper named Potts remained with him. One day they were captured by the Blackfeet on the Jefferson fork of the Missouri in southwestern Montana. Potts showed fear, tried to escape and was riddled with arrows. Colter did not flinch, and was given an opportunity to run for his life. He was taken out in front three hundred yards, the word was given, and away he went with six hundred yelling Blackfeet after him. Only one man out of that number gained on him. When within a few yards of Colter, the savage made ready to throw his spear. Colter stopped suddenly, turned and threw up his hands, which so disconcerted the Indian that he tripped and fell, breaking his spear handle. Colter instantly caught up the upper part, and plunged it through the body of the savage, whose only strong qualification seems to have been speed. The white man continued his desperate race, reached the river, plunged in, and succeeded in reaching some brushwood, where he so adroitly concealed himself that the Indians did not find him during the remainder of the day. When night came, he swam cautiously out in the middle of the stream, continued down the river and managed to get away; but had to travel seven days before he reached a fort of the Missouri Fur Company on the Big Horn, and in the meantime subsisted wholly on roots and berries. When he told this story on his return to civilization, the trappers generally discredited it; but historians have generally regarded it as substantially true.

The party under Lisa continued up the Missouri and the Yellowstone to the mouth of the Big Horn, where they built a strong stockade among the Crows and were soon ready for business. In 1808 the keel-boat was sent down the river to St. Louis so heavily loaded with skins, that the astonishment and avarice of every merchant was kindled. The expedition had, in fact, secured the accumulations of the Crows for many previous years. The fort was located in the heart of the Crow country, where few if any trappers had ever before penetrated. The immense profit in this one boat load, stimulated to an intense degree the western fur trade. The Missouri Fur Company at once began very active operations. Their plan at first was to secure the services of all the best and most experienced trappers and Indian interpreters and bind them up with contracts so strong that they could not evade the iron rule of the company. Unscrupulous tactics were resorted to—anything in fact to crush rivals and win the fur trade. At the head of this company were many able men, who pushed the interest of the organization to the utmost. Within

six months after their organization, the company had in their
employ two hundred and fifty experienced trappers, among whom
were fifty trained riflemen, kept for no other purpose than to protect the trappers when at work; but in spite of this precaution
thirty of the men were killed by the Indians during the first two
years; not all, however, from the Lisa party. Other posts had
been established, notably the one at the forks of the Missouri
among the fierce Blackfeet. Drouillard was himself thus killed;
and so venemously was he hated by the savages for having killed
many of their number and so great was their respect for his courage, that when they finally succeeded in killing him, they tore
him in pieces and ate his flesh, in order thereby, as they believed,
to acquire his strength and courage.

The American Fur Company, which also sprang into existence
in 1808, succeeded in securing the interests of the Mackinaw
Company's trade in the United States, and at once became a
powerful rival of the Missouri Company for the northwestern
trade. Many fierce conflicts and elaborate intrigues occurred
between the trapping parties of these companies. Soon the
Northwestern Fur Company was merged in the American Company, and at the head of this strong organization was Mr. Astor.
As elsewhere stated, Lisa did all in his power to prevent Captain
Hunt of the Astor company from getting a foothold in the northwest. His first step was to buy the guides and interpreters as
fast as they were hired by Hunt. But the latter succeeded by
reason of having plenty of money and an abundance of courage
and persistence. The party under Andrew Henry, of the Missouri Company, in the country of the Blackfeet, were really compelled to retreat from the country by the hostility of those
savages; but was reinforced by a party of picked men sent out by
Lisa. The Hudson's Bay Company cut an important figure,
because they crossed into the United States and invaded the preserves of the other companies. They also gave arms, ammunition
and encouragement to hostile bands within the United States,
which, upon being pursued, could find safety by fleeing across
the border into Canada. Fort Douglas and Fort Gibralter, posts
respectively of the Hudson's Bay Company and of the Northwestern Company, were located on or near Lake Winnipeg; and here
was the battle-ground between those two great rivals. When
Lisa died in 1820 there were over three hundred trappers in the
mountains who had been under his supervision. Pilcher, who
succeeded him, never gained the prestige acquired by the redoubtable Lisa. In fact the Missouri Company began to wane with

the death of Lisa, probably, however, not by reason of that event
solely.   More likely, the decadence was due to the active work
of the free trappers, or in other words, to the great number of men
who engaged on their own account in the fur trade.

When the expedition of Lewis and Clark was at the Mandan
villages on the Missouri in the Dakotas, they induced the principal chief, Big White, or Sha-ha-ka, to go to Washington with
them.   At first he declined, because on his return he would be
compelled to pass through the country of the Sioux and would
be certain to be killed.   But he was promised escort back to his
village, and accordingly accepted the invitation.   In the spring
of 1807, twenty men under the command of Capt. Ezekiel Williams started up the Missouri from St. Louis on an expedition of
discovery, having in their company the Mandan chief.   Each
man in the party was well armed, had ammunition for two years,
and carried six traps for operation on the head-waters of the
Platte and elsewhere.   They left the Mandan chief at the mouth
of the Yellowstone, and returned to the Platte, up which they
proceeded to advance.   They marched about twenty-five miles
per day, and at first had plenty to eat and a good time; but when
the timber disappeared and the game became scarce, their real
trials began.   For a time they were obliged to use buffalo chips,
bois de vache, for fuel.   The most of the men were soldiers, who
had seen no experience in the West, and upon whom the hardships fell with crushing force.   Everything was to them a wonder—the treeless plains, the herds of buffalo and elk, the prairie
storms, the fields of deep grass, the wolves and the Indians.   One
day all were invited to hunt the buffalo with the Indians, and
many accepted the invitation; but while the Indians killed several dozen the whites did not "ground" a single animal.   Even
the horses of the whites were inexperienced—several stampeded,
and one in his fright was gored to death by a wounded buffalo
bull.   A little later the expedition narrowly escaped being
crushed to death by a stampede of buffaloes, and would have
been so had it not been for the few leaders, who with all their
force advanced to meet the herd, waving their arms and firing,
which split the line of advancing, frightened and maddened animals.   This occurred far up the river, where the buffaloes roamed
in immense herds.   Near the junction of the North and the South
forks, the expedition crossed the main stream to the south side,
and soon began to meet troublesome bands of Indians.   They
escaped one hostile band of Pawnees by secretly deserting their
camp in the early part of the night and marching westward till

daylight. In fact, this tactic was repeated more than once. Finally the mountains were reached, and here for a time they led an ideal hunter's life, hunting, trapping, exploring and feasting on game of all sorts. At last, one day, ten men engaged in a buffalo hunt, and advanced several miles from camp, and were there surprised by about one hundred Blackfeet, who killed and scalped five of them, the others succeeding in reaching camp. They had been for several days dogged by the Indians, who, down on all fours, and dressed like wolves, had observed all their motions without arousing their suspicions. A little later they encountered the Crows, but they professed friendship. Here one of the experienced men of the expedition left and went to live with the Indians. His name was Rose, and he had previously been a pirate on the Mississippi. He married an Indian girl, and became a chief among the tribe. Of all the men in this expedition, he was the strongest, standing over six feet in height. He led many a successful attack against the Blackfeet, but was finally killed by them. On one occasion he shot one and struck down four others with an Indian war-club. For this act they called him Che-ku-kats, or The Man Who Killed Five.

But the inexperienced men of this expedition were destined to pass through still more trying experiences. The crafty Crows soon revealed their covert hostility. Their chief at this time was Ara-poo-ish, but later he was succeeded by the famous James Beckworth, who soon made the Crows a terror to all the other mountain tribes. The first hostile act of the Crows was to steal the horses of the whites. When they were pursued, they formed an ambush to capture their pursuers; but the seven whites ran and took refuge in a dense thicket, though five of them were killed before this retreat was reached. The camp was roused by the firing, and the remainder of the men came to the rescue, and all barricaded themselves in the timber, and kept up a constant fire on the Indians who were in the open. Nineteen of the Indians were killed of the approximate sixty which were in the party. They were finally repelled, and the ten whites remaining moved away, but were now wholly without horses, and so reduced in numbers that they could be annihilated at the will of any large band. They gathered up all their traps, and having packed and cached their valuables, departed; but were slowly cut away, until Williams and two others were the only ones left to tell the tale. The two tried to reach St. Louis and may have done so; but Williams went to the valley of the Arkansas, where he found succor and managed to save both his hair and his life.

The American Fur Company was organized in New York in 1808, with the following members: John J. Astor, Wallace P. Hunt, Alexander McKay, Duncan McDougal, Donald McKenzie, Ramsay Crooks, Robert McLellan, Joseph Miller, David Stuart, Robert Stuart, and John Clarke. This company immediately formed the design of occupying the Pacific region, particularly the valley of the Columbia river, with the view of monopolizing the fur trade of the whole western coast. Two expeditions were planned: One to go by water around Cape Horn to the mouth of the Columbia; and the other to go overland across the Rocky mountains to the same destination. Mr. Hunt was selected to conduct the overland party. From the start he was strenuously opposed in all his operations by the Missouri Fur Company, in fact by every company of St. Louis. The Missouri Company bought up his guides and interpreters as fast as they were hired. When that course failed, they attached the body of his principal guide, claiming that he owed the company for goods advanced. It is clear that such debts were intentionally permitted to accumulate in order that the trappers and guides might be retained. Such men were absolutely necessary in the upper country for the purpose of holding communication with the Indians and of finding the best beaver fields. However, in October, 1810, he managed to start, but it was too late to reach the mountains before winter set in. He accordingly wintered on the Nodawa river; and during the winter returned to St. Louis still further to complete his party and its equipment. In April, 1811, the party left its winter quarters, sailed up the Missouri, passing the mouth of the Platte on the 28th, the Omaha villages May 10, and arriving at the Arickaree villages about a week and a half later.

In the meantime, Mr. Lisa and a party of about twenty men endeavored to overhaul the Hunt party before it should pass the Sioux and the Arickaree villages. His object seems to have been to secure protection against those hostiles. When well up the river, seeing that he was likely to fail in this object, he sent a messenger by land to ask Hunt to wait until his arrival. Mr. Hunt agreed to do so, but immediately set out up the river regardless of this agreement. However, by going day and night, Lisa managed to catch him near the Sioux villages, from which point they sailed together to the villages of the Arickarees. Hunt seems to have been justified in his failure to meet his agreement by the opposition that had been offered to his expedition by Lisa and his friends, although it was known to the latter that the Hunt party was destined for the mouth of the Columbia, and would not likely interfere with the operations of the Missouri Company.

Hearing of the further hostility of the Blackfeet along the Upper Missouri and the Yellowstone, Hunt determined to abandon his boats and, after procuring horses, to march westward across the open country south of those rivers. After about a month spent in equipping his party, they all set forth on nearly a westward course from the Arickarees, sixty-four men in all, with eighty-two horses, of which seventy-six were loaded with merchandise. On the 30th of August, they were at the foot of the Big Horn mountains, on September 9th at Wind river, and on the 15th crossed the continental divide. Small parties of trappers were left in the mountains to begin operations. Of the party only fifty-four succeeded in reaching Astoria.

In the autumn of 1808, Ramsay Crooks and Robert McLellan, with eighty men and a large stock of merchandise, advanced by the St. Louis merchants to be sold on shares, set sail up the Missouri river, intending to go to the Rocky mountain country to trade for furs, or perhaps to Santa Fe to dispose of the goods to the Spaniards. When well up the river, they met Captain Pryor with bad accounts of the Indians, and turned back, wintering at Council Bluffs. In the spring of 1809, they again proceeded, but were stopped at the Sioux villages by about six hundred warriors. As they had with them at this time only about forty men, open opposition to the demands of the Indians to turn back would have been to invite annihilation. Intrigue was therefore resorted to, and the villages were passed by part of the expedition. But finally all sailed down the river, and abandoned the enterprise. They alleged that the conduct of the Indians was due to the machinations of Mr. Lisa; which allegation was probably true. It is likely that Lisa took this method to thwart the aspirations of business rivals in the Indians' country. Both Crooks and McLellan joined the forces of the American Fur Company and crossed the mountains with the Hunt party.

It was necessary for the government to send back to their homes in safety the Indian chiefs who had gone to Washington in response to their agreement with Lewis and Clark. In May, 1807, Ensign Pryor, with thirteen soldiers, and Lieutenant Kimball, with about twenty-five Sioux, went up from St. Louis to the Mandan villages with the returning chiefs; but were attacked by the Arickarees and after a sharp conflict were driven back. It was alleged that this attack was instigated by English traders, and there is good evidence to support the charge. Previous to the visit of Lewis and Clark to the Mandans and Arickarees, the English had no opposition with those people; they now saw that their trade among these tribes was rapidly drawing to a close. They also saw that by making friends of the Indians, or by instigating them against the Americans, they could prolong their commercial existence in this valuable field.

Manuel Lisa was very active while connected with the Missouri Fur Company. He went up to the Big Horn in 1807, but returned the following year. In the spring of 1809, he again went to the Big Horn, but came down to St. Louis again in October of the same year. The next year he made another round trip. Early in 1811, he started up to learn what had become of Major Henry. With him on this trip were only about twenty men, and this was the occasion when he made such a remarkable spurt to overtake the party under Mr. Hunt. The Missouri Fur Company was reorganized in 1811-12, Lisa becoming still more important and influential under the new order of affairs. He conducted an expedition to the Mandans in the spring of 1812, but returned in June of the following year. While thus engaged, the war with England broke out and the Indians of the upper country became very restless. In this emergency, the government, knowing his influence with the tribes of the upper Missouri, appointed him sub-agent and authorized him to maintain at all hazards the friendship of the Indians as against the representatives of Great Britain. There is no doubt that it was largely due to his efforts and influence that the Missouri tribes refrained from taking up the hatchet against the Americans, notwithstanding that the agents of Great Britain went among them with belts of wampum to incite them to war. The tribes on the upper Mississippi, being as they were more directly under the eye of the English, were almost from the commencement of war hostile to the United States and friendly to Great Britain. Lisa even succeeded in organizing war parties on the Upper Missouri to attack the Chippewas in their homes on the Upper Mississippi. In the spring of 1815 he brought down to St. Louis forty-three chiefs and head men of the Upper Missouri tribes for the purpose of signing treaties with the government. He resigned his subagency in 1817, and about this time became president of his company, but died in 1820.

It was in 1810 that the Missouri Company built a fort about two miles above the confluence of the Jefferson and Madison rivers. In this vicinity a body of trappers under Andrew Henry and Pierre Menard took out three hundred packs of beaver in a comparatively short time, but were finally driven out by the hostility of the Blackfeet. Joshua Pilcher, who succeeded Lisa as president of the company, built Fort Benton in 1821. The following year the company sent a large expedition under Messrs. Jones and Immel to the mountains: the latter sent down the same year about twenty-five thousand dollars worth of furs. In 1823 the same men tried to reach the Blackfoot country, but were finally ambushed by an overwhelming force and seven were killed and four wounded, both Jones and Immel being among the slain. This attack was laid to the instigation of the English. It was afterward learned that the guns, hatchets and ammunition used by the Blackfeet were obtained from British agents on the Assiniboine, and that the furs captured by the Indians were sold to the same agents. At this time the Missouri Company had over three hundred trappers and hunters in the mountains; but the defeat of Henry caused the company to withdraw all to the territory below the mouth of the Platte. Thus the company under Pilcher was not so successful as it had been under Lisa.

Late in the year 1812, it was determined by the Rocky Mountain Fur Company to send a hunting and trapping party up the Platte river to the mountains for the winter, and the following year Gen. William H. Ashley, one of the principal officers of the company, was selected to command this expedition. Under him was placed a force of thirty-four men, the most of whom were experienced hunters and trappers, but several of whom were criminals and refugees. The most distinguished afterward in the party except Ashley, was James Beckworth, a boy in his teens and the future chief of the Crows. After a few days' journey, two Spaniards of the party, who were guilty of an atrocious act, were given the choice of hanging or of one hundred lashes on the bare back: they chose the latter and were accordingly whipped until the blood ran down. They took their revenge the following night by running away with two of the best horses and such articles as they wanted and could carry. For a short time the valley of the Platte seemed wholly deserted by the buffaloes— in fact by game of every sort—and the whites were driven to the last extremity.

Every expedition to cross the plains at that time relied on game for means of subsistence while on the trip. If the game was absent, it meant intense privations, if not absolute starvation. The men were finally reduced to half a pint of flour a day. They were compelled to organize protracted hunts. It is claimed that the boy, Jim Beckworth, saved the expedition from disaster on his first hunt by killing a deer and three elks, and that thereafter he was the hero of the camp.   It was mid-winter, the snow was deep and the cold intense.   When they reached the Pawnee Loup villages, they found an abundance of Buffalo meat.   While there the Indians organized a grand buffalo hunt.   They employed their whole force of several thousand, and surrounded a stretch of country probably ten miles square.   They then began the march toward a common center, making a great noise; and when all the animals were driven to common ground, the slaughter began.   There were killed in this hunt fourteen hundred buffaloes, General Ashley counting the tongues to make certain of the number.   This hunt had been instituted before the arrival of the Ashley party, who were not permitted to proceed until it had terminated.   They were then given all the meat they wanted.   Thus it was with the hunting and trapping parties, first a feast and then a famine, amid the fierce blizzards or burning heats of the plains or the mountains.   Between two thousand and three thousand Indians participated in this circular hunt.   The supply of meat lasted for many days, but again the expedition was reduced to corn and beans, when far out toward the mountains.

At Pilot Butte the Crows stole nearly all of their horses; and soon afterward they were so reduced in means of subsistence that they organized a general hunt.   From the mountain tops, they saw far ahead countless buffaloes in the valley of Green river. All were soon industriously engaged in trapping beaver, divided into parties for greater opportunities for search, but strong enough to make a stubborn defense against the Indians in case of attack, and all within easy reach of each other.   In the spring they made canoes of wood and buffalo hides, and descended Green river, and were at last in Utah mountains.   Here they again divided into parties, scattered in all directions, but under instructions to return to a certain spot July 1st.   In the meantime the bulk of their furs and supplies were cached.   One party on Horse creek took one hundred beaver in a few days. At this time beaver skins of the first class were worth ten dollars per pound in St. Louis, and sixty dried skins made one hundred pounds.   On Le Brache creek another party caught about as many more in a few days.   While here they were attacked by a war party of sixteen Indians and one man, La Brache, was killed, which occurrence gave rise to the name of the stream.   By June the entire party had collected seven or eight packs of sixty skins each of beaver.   While in these mountains they met another party of sixteen trappers, who had been out for two years and had a large number of hides.   Finally the Ashley party returned to their homes with a valuable lot of skins.

In 1812 it became necessary to send important dispatches from Astoria to New York, and accordingly, Robert Stuart was sent overland by the Astor Company. With him were Ben Jones and John Day, both famous in the West, two Canadians, Le Clerc and Vallee, and several others among whom were McClellan and Crooks. The start was made on the 29th of June, and was intrusted to Stuart, because he was experienced, cool-headed, knew the country, could speak nearly all the western Indian tongues, possessed great strength and did not know what fear or hardship meant. John Day soon became demented and was sent back. McClellan was mutinous and gave the leader much concern. When they reached the country of the Snakes and the Crows, they began to experience trouble. They likewise nearly starved to death in the mountains and the desert regions of the mountainous country. Here it was that the nerve of nearly all was exhausted, except that of the dauntless leader. Never for a moment did he falter or think of turning back. He met all the wiles of the Indians with superior wiles and courage. His mutinous men were steadily pressed into the harness and obliged to proceed. He took the brunt of everything and bore the dreadful cold without a murmur. Finally, on October 26, they reached the headwaters of the Platte of Nebraska, where they prepared to pass the winter, because it would never do to try to cross the plains at that time of the year. They selected a suitable location and built a log house eight feet wide, eighteen feet long, with walls six feet high, with buffalo skins for a roof, and with a hole left in the center to let out the smoke. While some were thus engaged, the others went on a grand hunt, and in two days succeeded in killing thirty-two buffaloes, and a little later killed fifteen more, which then gave them sufficient meat to last them all winter.

They now prepared to hunt and trap and "live on the fat of the land" during the remainder of the winter. They killed many deer (twenty-eight in two days) for their skins, with which they made moccasins, mittens, clothing, etc., and had plenty of bear steak from time to time. All would have gone well had they not been discovered by the Indians. One day when all were in their hut, they heard a yell outside, and knew that it meant Indians. No one seemed willing to go out, so Stuart, accompanied by one man, opened the door and stepped out to what was thought death. It was a war party of Arapahoes, out after the Cheyennes and Crows, who they claimed had slaughtered their women and children in their absence. They had followed their enemy so persistently that they had not taken time to hunt for food, and were of consequence almost starved.   There were twenty-three of them and they begged for food.   Stuart saw at once that it would never do to let this many enter the hut; so he told them that he would give them food, but that only the principal chief and one other would be permitted to enter the cabin.   They did so and food was passed to the others outside of the door.   All were armed with bows and arrows, knives, tomahawks and a few guns, but were short of powder.   For two days they gorged themselves like swine with the buffalo meat that Stuart gave them; but then left, being supplied with six days' rations of meat.

After they had gone it became apparent to all that their position was no longer tenable.   The hostile Crows were on one side of them and the Arapahoes and Cheyennes on the other, their presence was now known, because the trail of the visitors would be followed by their enemies, the size of Stuart's party was known, and any considerable band of Indians could at any time, by taking advantage, of which there was abundant opportunity, crush them in a single encounter.   After fully deliberating, they finally determined to brave the awful storms and cold of the plains to the eastward rather than remain and risk the tomahawks of the Indians.   They accordingly packed up everything they could carry (they had one horse), and for fourteen days journeyed eastward down the valley of the Platte.   They now had come about three hundred milés, the snow was fifteen inches deep, and the timber was very small and scant.   They finally concluded to retrace their steps three days to a thick grove, the last they had passed, where there was a suitable camping place.   They turned about on December 27, and on New Year day had one wall of their new cabin up.   They rested and observed the day as well as they could, feasting on buffalo roasts and broils.   On January 6 the cabin was finished, and here they were free from molestation from the Indians and passed the remainder of the winter in comfort, feasting, hunting and swapping stories.   During the winter they made several canoes from the trunks of trees, but as it turned out, they could not use them the next spring, owing to the shallowness of the Platte.   On the 8th of March they started down the river, using their one horse to carry all he could of their outfit.   They were driven back by bad weather, but on the 20th again set forth, and in due time arrived at Le Grande Isle, thus named by French Canadians.   A little later they met two white trappers who told them of the war between the United States and England.   From them they bought boats, floated down to Fort Osage, and on April 30 reached St. Louis.

It was about the year 1822 that the Rocky Mountain Fur Company began active operations, among its leading members at the start being Gen. William H. Ashley, Andrew Henry, William L. Sublette, Milton Sublette, David E. Jackson, Jedediah S. Smith, Robert Campbell, James Bridger, Thomas Fitzpatrick, Etienne Provost, Samuel Tulloch, and James Beckworth. Ashley conducted the following important expeditions to the upper Missouri country: To the Yellowstone in 1822, to the Arickaree villages in 1823, to the Green river valley in 1824, to Great Salt Lake valley in 1825, and to the Rocky mountains in 1826, at which latter time he sold out to the partnership of Smith, Jackson & Sublette, who in turn sold to the Rocky Mountain Fur Company in 1830. Either this was a revival of that company, or General Ashley was operating independently. At a little later date, Fitzpatrick, Sublette & Bridger were active operators in the mountains.

The fight of Ashley with the Arickarees in 1823 is notable for having brought on one of the first encounters between the government and the Indians of the Upper Missouri. With Ashley were about forty men with two or three keel-boats loaded with goods. At daylight on the morning of June 2d, they were attacked by a large force of Arickarees armed with London fusils, and twelve were killed on the spot, two mortally wounded and nine severely wounded, there being twenty-three casualties in all. Their horses and nearly all their other property were captured by the Indians. Under a hot fire, the rest of the force managed to reach a small island below and finally to escape down the river. Ashley promptly called for assistance, and Col. Henry Leavenworth, then at Fort Atkinson, near Council Bluffs, advanced up the river with two hundred and twenty soldiers of the Sixth infantry, two 6-pounders, three small swivels and three keel-boats. Ashley co-operated with the remnant of his force: so did Henry with all his men except twenty, who were left to hold the fort on the Yellowstone. Pilcher assisted with about forty men under Major Henry Vanderburg, a 5½-inch howitzer and a body of Sioux and Yankton warriors numbering from four hundred to five hundred. The total force under Colonel Leavenworth aggregated about one thousand one hundred. Opposed to them were between six hundred and eight hundred warriors at the Arickaree villages. The battle occurred on the 9th and 10th of August, and should have been an overwhelming victory for the allied whites and reds; but instead resulted in a compromise, under which the Arickarees were not subdued and the white traders were not satisfied. Colonel Leavenworth was sharply criticised by Pilcher, Ashley and others, and no doubt deserved censure for his unaccountable clemency. Even the Indian allies deserted him owing to the mildness and inefficiency of his conduct during the battle. It is reasonably clear that the hostility of the Arickarees was caused by the British agents on the Assiniboine.

By 1831 the American Fur Company had practically monopolized the fur trade of the West. Farnam & Davenport operated among the Sacs and Foxes, the Winnebagoes and the Iowas; Mr. Rolette on the Mississippi as high as St. Anthony's Falls and on the Minnesota; Mr. Cabanne on the Missouri as high as Council Bluffs and among the Pawnees; A. P. Chouteau among the Osages; and Messrs. McKenzie, Laidlaw & Lamont, who called themselves the Columbia Fur Company, in the Missouri river country above Council Bluffs. Every spring an immense supply of goods for the western trade was sent on from New York to St. Louis, and thence dispatched up the Missouri in a small steamboat and distributed to the various posts. The furs were brought down to St. Louis, opened, examined, weighed, repacked, and shipped to New Orleans, and thence sent by water to New York, where they were finally assorted, packed in bales and sent to the European markets. Extensive credit was given to the Indians, but at a much higher price than usual to cover probable losses.

By 1831, the mountain country was overrun with hunters and trappers, and furs began to diminish. Rascals of every race and crime infested the camps and posts, and life became cheaper than whisky. A lone man with money or furs or both, need to make haste to get rid of it, because if he did not he would *nolens volens* soon be deprived of his plunder. It was diamond cut diamond among the rough elements of the camps, while the honest trappers froze in the mountains for the furs. Wild men from the South, from New England, from the Mississippi valley, from Canada; deserters from the army, escaped convicts, horse-thieves, pirates from the Gulf, cut-throats from heaven only knew where, bullies, desperadoes and highwaymen, thronged the posts and levied their deadly tributes on the labors of the trappers. After the treaty of 1818 between the United States and Great Britain, the traders of the latter were prohibited from coming south of the forty-ninth parallel, and all of their posts south of that line were bought by the American Fur Company. Kenneth McKenzie had extended a line of posts from Green Bay to the Missouri

river, but had done business in an American's name, as he himself was a Britisher; but when his forts and posts passed to the
American Company, he remained in the service of the latter, and
built a fort at the junction of the Missouri and the Yellowstone.
In that vicinity he afterward became a great power, and he kept
much better order at his post than many of the other company
agents could do. Here he entertained Audubon, the naturalist,
Catlin, the artist, Prince Maximilian, Lord Hamilton, and other
persons famous in the world at that time. It is certain that
McKenzie managed either to outbid or outwit the agents of the
Rocky Mountain Company, because he soon secured nearly all
of the Indian trade in the northwest. The Deschamps made
themselves famous, or rather infamous, at the McKenzie post;
but were finally wiped out of existence by his directions.

In 1832 Captain William Sublette, a member of the Rocky
Mountain Fur Company, passed up the Platte valley with a strong
party of sixty men, among whom was the veteran hunter and
trapper, Robert Campbell. While at Independence, Mo., he had
met a party of about twenty "tenderfeet" under the command of
Nathaniel J. Wyeth, nearly all of whom were from the remote
East and wholly inexperienced in western methods of living—
and dying. For certain considerations Captain Sublette agreed
to permit the Wyeth party to join his, and together they advanced
up the rivers. The green men were very valiant so long as there
was no danger, but after that they were seriously demoralized.
The hardships soon tamed their fiery spirits, but at first the nov-
elty was a delight. The design of Wyeth was to cross the mountains to the Columbia river for the purpose of engaging in the
salmon industry. Although their sufferings were severe in the
valley of the Platte, they finally reached its headwaters without
serious accident. In July, they met a party of fifteen free trappers, who had had excellent success, although opposed by all the
companies and by the Indians incited against them.

About this time eleven of the Wyeth men, while out hunting,
were attacked by a party of Blackfeet, but took refuge in a strip
of thick timber, where they were safe until the arrival of their
comrades, when in turn the Indians were surrounded in a swamp.
The battle lasted several days, but the Blackfeet finally succeeded
in making their escape up the side of the mountain during darkness. Many of the Nez Perces assisted the whites in this engagement, which became called the "Swamp Fight." Five white men
and one half-breed were killed and ten or a dozen wounded, and
the friendly Indians suffered to about the same extent. Twenty

or thirty of the Blackfeet were killed and wounded. This was stern experience to the new men, but they began "to get their mountain clothes on" at last, and were not such weak objects as they had been at first. Several afterward became noted in the West for their courage, skill and hardihood. Soon after the Swamp Fight, six or eight of the Wyeth party resolved to return to the States and not go on to the mouth of the Columbia. They started, but were finally annihilated by the Blackfeet, not one remaining to tell the tale. After securing many beaver skins the Sublette party duly returned to St. Louis.

The famous Fort Laramie was built in 1834 by William Sublette and Robert Campbell, of the American Fur Company, and was at first called Fort William after the former, but later was named Fort John, and finally Fort Laramie after à French Canadian, Joseph Laramie, who had been killed by the Indians near the place. A trading post had been established in 1832 by Louis Vasquez at the mouth of Clear creek, and had been named for him, Fort Vasquez. In 1835 the fort at Laramie was sold to Milton Sublette and James Bridger and others of the American Fur Company; but in 1849 it became a government post. In its busiest times Fort Laramie was not surpassed by any other trading post in the United States. Here it was that all the trappers of the mountains came for their supplies and to dispose of their furs. Here came Kit Carson, Jim Bridger, Jim Baker, Jim Beckworth and a score of others little less noted in border history. The officials of the fur company ruled this section with an iron hand, as it was necessary for them to do among these reckless and lawless men. Here came the criminals from the states to evade the law, and here was dealt out at the end of a pistol or at the noose of a rope sudden death and retribution to many of them. It was seven hundred miles to a spot where the laws of the United States were executed, but here the fur company was a law unto itself.

Quite a large settlement grew up around this spot—wives of the half savage men and their half naked children. Here were the Indian wife and children of many of them, and the gambling fever raged all the time, day and night. Many a trapper, who had worked and frozen in the mountains all the previous winter, came here to drop his pile of money so quickly that he had no time to think of where more was to come from. The trappers of all the eastern slope of the mountains were, with few exceptions, in the power of the fur companies; because the latter took advantage of them when they had gambled away all they possessed by advancing them a fresh outfit upon the condition that the furs they should bring in must go to the company. The wild families assembled here lived almost wholly on dried buffalo meat at first, and not infrequently the hunters had to go fifty miles before the buffaloes were encountered.

James Bridger became a member of Colonel Ashley's expedition in 1826, and in 1843 built Fort Bridger in the mountains of Wyoming, which became an important rendezvous. It consisted of two adjoining log houses, with sod roofs, and surrounded with palisades eight feet high, and was located on an island in the Black fork of Green's river, in the southwestern part of what is now Wyoming. It is famous to this day. Ere long there gathered around this fort a considerable settlement. It seems that Vasquez had an interest in the fort and no doubt assisted in erecting it. Fort Platte was built on the left bank of the North Platte about three-fourths of a mile above the mouth of Laramie river by the American Fur Company, at the head of which was John Jacob Astor. Fort Platte and Fort John (Laramie), being thus close together, there was intense rivalry between them to see which should get the major share of the furs brought in by the trappers. The trappers usually arrived about the same time, and were immediately the targets of the agents of the fur companies. Whisky, though four dollars a pint, flowed like water, and often the season's catch was staked on the turn of a card. The agents resorted to any and every means to get the most furs, even to the extent of winking at crime. Possibly, worse might be said with perfect truth. It is known that occasionally laudanum and arsenic were employed to carry their point; could all the truth be known, stories that would curdle the blood would come to the surface. In 1853 the Mormons scattered the people at Fort Bridger.

In June, 1855, Gen. W. S. Harney assembled six thousand troops at Fort Leavenworth preparatory to their march over the Platte route to Utah as the "Army of Occupation." They took with them an immense supply train, and thousands of cattle. Supply contractors were made rich out of this expedition, and favoritism ran rampant through the army commissary department. In 1857 a train of over one hundred persons from Missouri and Arkansas, with thirty wagons, six hundred cattle, and thirty horses and mules, crossed the plains over the Platte route, but in September of the same year nearly all were slaughtered by the Mormons in what has since become called "The Mountain Meadow Massacre."

I—25

386 THE PROVINCE AND THE STATES.

The expedition of Robert McKnight, James Baird and Samuel Chambers with a stock of goods to Santa Fe in 1812 resulted in failure, the merchandise being confiscated and the men—twelve in number—imprisoned by order of the Spanish authorities. The same penalty was visited on the party under A. P. Chouteau and Julius De Munn in 1815–17; indeed, Chouteau came near being shot by order of the Spanish governor of New Mexico. The policy of Spain opposed all commercial intercourse with the Americans, who were forbidden to enter New Mexico with American goods. All such merchandise was contraband; but in spite of the interdiction considerable quantities were smuggled across the lines to Taos and Santa Fe, and other quantities were taken there by the Indians to whom they were sold in the mountains. It is customary for shallow thinkers to criticise the government for not taking steps to redress the alleged wrongs inflicted on the American traders who thus sought to enter the province of New Mexico with forbidden goods in contravention of the Spanish law; but it cannot be denied that Spain had the right to pass such laws and to enforce them if she saw fit. Those American traders who sought to evade the Spanish law took their chances, and should not have expected the intervention of the government in their behalf, except to see that they received no more than their just deserts. After 1821, when Mexico achieved its independence from Spain, the law was changed, and American traders were permitted under certain restrictions to send their goods to Santa Fe.

The attainment of independence in 1821 rendered possible the immense general trade which set in immediately thereafter between St. Louis and Santa Fe. Not only were large supplies of merchandise sent to Santa Fe, but large herds of Spanish horses and mules were brought back and sold largely to the settlers now rapidly crossing the Mississippi. In order to insure safety, traders found it necessary to unite and cross the plains in large caravans, taking west merchandise of every description, which found its way far down into Mexico and the Central American provinces, and bringing back mainly live stock. While the trans-Mississippi fur trade flourished from 1807 to 1843, the Santa Fe trade did not begin until after 1821. During the above period of forty years, the annual fur trade at St. Louis amounted to between two hundred thousand and three hundred thousand dollars; and after 1821, the general trade with Santa Fe probably amounted to about half as much. After the War of 1812, General Ashley did more than any other person to revive the fur trade on the upper Missouri and to thwart the machinations of the alert representatives of the Canadian fur companies. From first to last the policy of the Americans toward the Indians was clumsy, illogical, unreasonable and unsuccessful. Not so with the British policy, which imitated that of the old Canadian voyageurs.

It is generally conceded that William Becknell of Missouri was the founder of the Santa Fe trail and the father of the Santa Fe trade. No sooner did he learn of the independence of the Mexican provinces, than he prepared to cross the plains to Santa Fe with a large stock of goods. Prior to 1822 all goods taken west had been carried on the backs of horses and mules; but Becknell took out the first train of wagons, besides his pack animals. He passed up the valley of the Arkansas, but finally struck across to the Cimarron, thence to San Miguel, and thence to Santa Fe. The old route led up the Arkansas to the mountains, thence across to Taos, and thence down to Santa Fe. Col. Braxton Cooper also took out a trading expedition, or caravan, to Santa Fe in 1822, and also another the following year; he used wagons mainly, but took along a few pack animals. In 1824 an expedition under A. Le Grand numbered eighty-one men, twenty-five wagons, one hundred and fifty-six horses and thirty thousand dollars' worth of merchandise. This was the first expedition to use wagons exclusively. In 1824 an expedition of twenty-six Spaniards from Santa Fe crossed the plains to Council Bluffs to conclude a treaty with the Pawnees. The Santa Fe trail was greatly aided by Senator Benton, who managed to get an appropriation of ten thousand dollars to mark the route, and twenty thousand dollars to secure the rights of transit from the Indian tribes. In 1825 several large expeditions to Santa Fe were outfitted at Franklin, Mo., one with one hundred and five men, thirty-four wagons and two hundred and forty horses and mules, and another with eighty-one men, two hundred horses and thirty thousand dollars' worth of merchandise. Many caravans crossed the plains in 1826. The following year Ezekiel Williams took out one hundred and five men, fifty-two wagons and a large number of horses and mules. During the same year one caravan brought back over eight hundred head of stock, worth twenty-eight thousand dollars.

In 1827 General Ashley and a party of sixty men with a 4-pounder left Lexington, Mo., crossed the plains in the valley of the Platte, passed over to Great Salt Lake, and returned to Lexington in September; but again left for the same destination, using the same pack animals. In 1828 two parties took to Santa Fe merchandise of the value of one hundred and ninety thousand dollars. With a military escort under the command of Major Bennett Riley, a caravan of seventy men and thirty-five wagons was taken up the Arkansas by Capt. Charles Bent in 1829. The Gregg caravan of 1831 consisted of nearly two hundred persons, one hundred wagons, two small cannon, and two hundred thousand dollars' worth of merchandise; it was prepared at Independence, Mo. In 1831 and 1832, Capt. Charles Bent took up large caravans, the proceeds of the former year being one hundred and ninety thousand dollars and of the latter one hundred thousand dollars in specie. It is said that the town of Franklin on the Missouri "was the cradle of the Santa Fe trade." Under the act of congress, the Santa Fe trail was surveyed by Benjamin Reeves, George C. Sibley and Thomas Mather; but instead of going by San Miguel, they continued up the Arkansas to the mountains and then across to Taos. The caravans followed the former route. They did not escape the bullets and arrows of the Indians. In 1830 Milton G. Sublette conducted probably the first caravan to use wagons over the Oregon trail. His party consisted of eighty-one men mounted on mules, ten wagons loaded with merchandise, and twelve or fifteen head of cattle, taken along to subsist on until they should reach the buffalo country. Almost the first caravan to use ox-wagons was the one conducted west by Captain Bent in 1831. "His party consisted of from thirty to forty men, and if he succeeds with his ox-wagons, the oxen will answer the tripple purpose, 1st, of drawing these wagons; 2d, the Indians will not steal them as they would horses and mules; and 3d, in case of necessity part of the oxen will answer for provisions." Soon after this Spanish merchants from the New Mexico were seen on the streets of Pittsburg, Pa., where they went to buy iron products particularly. They had learned that they could obtain them for a much less price by buying them in Pittsburg and taking them across the plains at their own expense, instead of buying them from the St. Louis merchants put down in Santa Fe. The military expeditions which crossed the plains in the "fifties" reported seeing in New Mexico many wagons that had been manufactured in Pittsburg. The railroads soon annihilated the old order of trade.

The stage lines which threaded the plains and the mountains in early times were marvels of enterprise in regions inhabited only by savages, save at centers of settlement by white people. The one conducted by Russell, Majors & Waddell in the "fifties," had stations ten or twelve miles apart. The horses were driven at a gallop, and no stop was made, day or night, except for meals. Butterfield's was another famous line, extending from the Missouri river to Sacramento. Railways carried the Eastern mail to the Missouri, whence it was conveyed by stages to the Pacific coast. The best time that could thus be made from New York to San Francisco was twenty-two days. The pony express was first tried as an experiment, but proved so successful that it was not only continued, but greatly improved. It reduced the time of the passage of mail from New York to Sacramento to eleven days. There were one hundred and ninety stations from St. Joseph to Sacramento. Five hundred horses were used, and there were in all about eighty riders. Two hundred men were required to guard and take care of the stations; but in the Indian country more than one station was destroyed and the guards were killed and the horses stolen. Each rider rode approximately thirty-three miles on three horses, and returned on three others, each horse being required to go about eleven miles at his best speed. Sometimes the riders were ambushed and killed by the Indians; at others they were fired at from thickets and chased, but being splendidly mounted they usually had no difficulty in distancing the savages. For the dangerous Indian districts, the swiftest horses were selected: to this locality, also, were assigned the most daring riders, those who would not hesitate for any report of hostile bands to make their usual rides. It occasionally happened, owing to the death of the rider of one district, that his nearest neighboring rider would have to cover the dead man's district, in order that the mail might not be delayed. Such riders were sometimes required to travel at full speed nearly two hundred miles, without stopping for a moment and without a mouthful of food. In such cases, the riders were obliged to cross the dangerous Indian country where the other rider had been killed, and not infrequently they, too, were attacked by the same band of savages. Everything carried by each horse was made as light as possible. The riders were small men, with courage at an inverse ratio to their sizes. The saddles were small and light. The heaviest articles were a light rifle and one revolver. The charge for each letter carried the whole route was five dollars, and every letter was required to be written in small compass on tissue paper: all the letters were bound in a single package, thoroughly wrapped from the weather and securely fastened to the saddle. In March, 1861, extra efforts were made to carry

President Lincoln's message through in record-breaking time. It required seven days and seventeen hours to carry it by pony express from St. Joseph to Sacramento. Ere many years a greater wonder, the modern railway, terminated the usefulness of the pony riders.

CHAPTER XII

Explorations by the United States

THE cession of Louisiana by France to the United States in 1803 had scarcely been ratified by congress before the government perceived the necessity of taking immediate steps to circumvent the encroachments of Spain on the southwest border, to explore the various river courses preparatory to settlement and to make friends of all the Indian tribes within the borders of the new territory. Accordingly, late in 1804, an expedition under the command of Dr. John Sibley was sent up Red River of Natchitoches for the purpose of reporting fully on the designs of the Spaniards in that quarter and of locating the Indians in the valley of that stream. With a small party he set out, passed the village of Natchitoches, and in due time arrived at the villages of the Caddoes in what is now southwest Arkansas. He continued to ascend Red river, exactly how far is not known, but certainly as far as the Pawnee villages nearly to the mouth of the North Fork. He learned that there were few, if any, Spaniards, on the river, encountered no serious opposition from the Indians, and finally returned, having added much to the general knowledge of that section.

One of the earliest expeditions sent into the Louisiana Purchase was that under Messrs. Dunbar, Hunter and others, which passed up the Washita of Louisiana and Arkansas in 1804. The party of about a dozen men reached the mouth of Red river on October 17 of that year, and two days later arrived at the mouth of the Washita or Black. At the mouth of the Catahoula, a Frenchman named Hebard had a large plantation. Up a considerable distance stood Fort Miro, that had served the Spanish well against the Indians. At Villemont's prairie was quite a

French settlement, some of the grants there having been made prior to 1762. Here and there scattered along the river in what is now Louisiana, were other French and Spanish settlers, with plantations in all stages of improvement. Post Washita was reached November 6. Near this was the large grant to the Marquis de Maison-Rouge. On the 11th of November, they arrived at the plantation of Baron Bastrop, where there was a settlement of about three hundred people. The baron's grant aggregated about one million French acres. On November 15, they passed the Island of Mallet, just south of the line between the Territories of Orleans and Louisiana, which civil divisions had just been created by the Government of the United States. They passed the mouth of the Little Missouri on the 24th, that of the Cadodoqui on the 30th, and reached the Chuttes on December 3. On December 6, they arrived at Ellis' camp within three leagues of Hot Springs, their objective point. On December 10, the springs were thoroughly explored, and later excursions into the surrounding country were made for purposes of discovery. About the 6th of January, they returned down the Washita, up which they had come. This expedition was the means of sending many settlers into that portion of the Purchase.

In 1806 a force consisting of seventeen privates and five or six commissioned and non-commissioned officers, all under the command of Captain Sparks and Lieutenant Humphrey, left Natchez in several barges and small boats, intending to go to the sources of Red river. They entered Red river on May 3, and sixteen days later arrived at Natchitoches. Here they received intelligence that the Spanish had sent a large force to intercept them and drive them back from the upper branches of Red river. They were accordingly strengthened by a force of twenty men under Lieutenant Deforest. They carried with them a supply of flour sufficient to last nine months and other provisions in proportion. They left Natchitoches June 2, and five days later a message was received from that town saying that a large force had left Nacogdoches to intercept them at the Caddoe villages. When they arrived at a point twenty miles above the great raft of the Red, they learned positively from the Indians that over three hundred Spanish dragoons were encamped at the Caddoe town prepared to prevent their advance any farther in that direction. On July 1st, other messengers arrived and confirmed the former news. They reported that the Spaniards had used every endeavor to make friends with the Caddoes; but that the latter had refused under the pretext that they did not intend to side with either the

Spanish or the Americans, and that both must go elsewhere if they wished to fight; that neither could remain in the country of the Indians. They also reported that the Caddoes were willing for the United States to advance up Red river to its sources for purposes of exploration and discovery, and to visit the Pawnees and other tribes there.

On July 26 word was received that the Spanish forces were one thousand strong and that the American flag which had been flying at the Caddoe villages had been supplanted by that of Spain. The next day they "cached" their extra provisions, papers, baggage, etc., to be in readiness for emergencies and continued to advance. On the 28th the Spanish guns were heard in the distance ahead. On the morning of the 29th they saw they were not far from the Spanish camp, and were kept fully posted by the Caddoe runners. Everything was put in readiness, and they continued to advance as if they did not know of the presence of the Spaniards. An outpost was first encountered which fled to the main camp, and soon afterward a deputation appeared. The Americans camped and prepared for dinner, and in the meantime a conference was arranged for. The Spanish commander and Captain Sparks conferred for over half an hour, the former showing that he had a force ten times as strong as the latter, and insisting that the American must retreat, as he was under orders to prevent at all hazard the advance of the Americans up the valley of the Red. The Americans weighed all the chances, and finally concluded the wisest course was to go back and later return with a much stronger force. They accordingly retreated down the river. This conference took place at a point six hundred and thirty-five miles by water from the mouth of Red river.

As soon as possible after the War of 1812, or in 1816, congress took steps to quiet the Indians in the territory beyond the Mississippi and to check the illicit trading of the Hudson's Bay and Northwest companies. In 1819 Col. Henry Leavenworth, with about a hundred soldiers, went to the mouth of the Minnesota river and established Fort St. Anthony, afterward named Fort Snelling, at the suggestion of General Scott. In December, 1818, a contract was made between the government and Col. James Johnson, of Kentucky, by which the latter agreed to provide two steamboats and transport a large force of soldiers up the Missouri to certain stations to be established at Council Bluffs, the Mandan villages and elsewhere. Colonel Johnson failed to fulfill his agreement, but nevertheless the soldiers to the number of one thousand one hundred and twenty-seven under Col. Henry Atkinson were sent up the river. At Council Bluffs Fort Atkinson was promptly built. Fort Clark was built at the Mandan villages. This was called the Missouri expedition to distinguish it from the Mississippi expedition under Colonel Leavenworth.

An important expedition was sent up the Missouri river in 1819 under Maj. S. H. Long, of the Topographical Engineers, by order of the War Department, for the purpose of thoroughly examining the country, conciliating the Indians and otherwise benefiting the government. A steamboat built near Pittsburg, called the Western Engineer, was well loaded with supplies of provisions and presents for the Indians and dispatched down the Ohio, and about June 1st reached the Mississippi. After reaching St. Louis, where they remained a few days, they started up the Missouri. On July 5 the village of Cote Sans Dessieu was reached, on the 13th Franklin, on July 22d Chariton, and August 1st Fort Osage. A full report was made of the topography, fauna, flora, minerals, soils, climate, timber, wild animals, Indians, settlements, streams, etc. Excursions were occasionally made into the surrounding country, the better to examine the characteristics. At Fort Osage a detachment under Thomas Say, eleven men in all, was sent up the Missouri and the Kansas rivers to examine the country and communicate with the Indians. They made several detours, and left the mouth of the Kansas August 13th. Upon reaching the Kansas villages, below the mouth of Blue Earth river, they were well received after the usual fashion of the Indians. Passing on up the river, they were soon intercepted by a large war party of Pawnees, who robbed them of everything they had—horses, baggage, arms, trinkets, and were thus forced to return. Later the Pawnees guilty of this attack were brought to account and the most of the stolen property was recovered.

On the Western Engineer was Major Benjamin O'Fallon, the Indian agent for the government, on his way up the river to hold peace treaties with the various Indian tribes and punish them for their many misdemeanors of the recent past. On the Missouri a short distance above the mouth of the Kansas, was an encampment of white hunters, a number of whom had fled from the vengeance of the law farther to the east; they were little less wild than the savages themselves, and were shunned by the honest trappers. At this time Fort Osage was the rendezvous for much of the western country. It was situated near the present town of Sibley and had been established in 1808. Colonel

Chambers was the commander. Near Diamond Island about five miles above the mouth of the Little Platte, was the ruin of an old French fortification or stockade. Below Independence river were the old Kansas villages on the west side of the Missouri. At this place they found Captain Martin with three companies of riflemen, who had left St. Louis in September, 1818, had arrived in October at Isle au Vache and had remained there ever since, nearly all the time without provisions, subsisting almost wholly on the game which they killed. In that time they had killed from two thousand to three thousand deer, many bears and turkeys, and a few buffaloes, the latter having migrated farther west. They were given a plentiful supply of provisions from the boat.

It was determined to hold a council here with the various Indian tribes, and accordingly messengers were sent to their villages inviting them to send delegates to the meeting to be held at Isle au Vache on August 24. There came one hundred and sixty-one members of the Kansas tribe and thirteen of the Osage. They were sharply taken to task for their many offenses against the whites by Major O'Fallon, the Indian agent; but they promised in the most abject manner possible to be "good Indians" ever afterward, and thereupon were given valuable presents of cloth, tools, trinkets, weapons and ammunition. They returned to their villages doubtless rejoicing, ready for another attack upon the white settlers and trappers; for they knew that thus attention would be called to them again, and another supply of presents would speedily follow.

As the steamboat was short of men, they took on here Lieutenant Fields and fifteen men to assist them in going up the stream. On the 1st of September they were near the mouth of Wolf river. Here they were overtaken by the party under Say, which had been driven back by the Pawnees as before related. On September 15 they reached the mouth of the famous Platte river of Nebraska. At this time traders were in almost every Indian village near the Missouri river and on many of its branches. Several were at the mouth of the Papillion, where they were established to trade with the Otoes, Missouris, etc. Two days later the steamboat reached the trading post of the Missouri Fur Company, called Fort Lisa and named for the Spanish trapper and hunter, Manuel Lisa. While here they selected the spot for their winter's encampment about half a mile above Fort Lisa on the west side of the Missouri, and about five miles below Council Bluffs. There they stopped on the 19th, and began to cut timber for the houses and to quarry stone for the foundations.

Inasmuch as the Pawnees had recently been guilty of several grave offenses, orders were at once issued to stop all traders from going to their villages until they had come in and given an account of themselves. This prohibition was a severe blow to the Indians, as they must have supplies of ammunition or their guns were useless, and the only way to get the ammunition was from the traders. The Pawnees had recently captured a father and son (whites) and made slaves of them, had robbed and severely whipped two white hunters, and had robbed and sent back the party under Thomas Say. The Republican Pawnees were the particular band guilty of these offenses. The winter's encampment was called Engineer Cantonment, and was soon ready for occupancy. Peace was soon patched up between the Otoes and the Kansas, mainly through the influences of John Dougherty, the trapper who accompanied the expedition. On October 3 a council was held with the Otoes and the Iowas, all of whom promised submission to the government and were given valuable presents. Then in succession came councils with the Osages, Kansas, Pawnee Loups, Republican Pawnees, Grand Pawnees, Puncas, Omahas, Sioux, Padoucas, Bald Heads, Ietans or Comanches, Sauks, Foxes and Iowas. The ceremony was usually introduced by the "beggar's dance," where all the Indians gathered around a post and in turn advanced and struck it, at the same time recounting their most notable achievements as warriors. Many historic incidents thus came to light. The Republican Pawnees made proper restitution for their past misdeeds. Among the leading chiefs present at the various councils were Ietan or Sha-mon-e-kusse, Little Soldier or Mi-a-ke-ta, Big Elk or Shon-ga-ton-ga, Crenier, Long Hair or Tar-ra-re-ca-wa-o, White Cow or Ta-so-ne, Hard Heart or Wang-e-wa-ha, Broken Arm or Ha-she-ah, and others.

The steamboat was a wonderful sight to the Indians, all of whom desired to go on board and were permitted to do so. They feared the cannon and inquired what was meant when the reports rang out. Major Long had returned to Washington in October, 1819, but the proceedings were conducted by Major O'Fallen. All the chiefs complained of being poor and begged for assistance. The traders took advantage of the peace established by this expedition to promptly invade the Indian country with goods of all sorts. They were forbidden to introduce whisky, but always managed to have some on hand when it was needed to gain the furs or good will of the Indians. The fur companies were likewise forbidden to employ it in their trades, but they also managed always to have some on hand for emergencies. The Missouri Fur Company openly gave the Indians all the goods they wanted on credit, taking their furs when they were ready. Some of the tribes, particularly the Iowas, sometimes evaded their creditors and sold the furs elsewhere. During the winter Mr. Pilcher of the Missouri Company, accompanied by Lieutenant Swift of the expedition, went to the Omaha village one hundred and twenty miles up the Elk Horn river, and in a few days returned with one hundred and thirty beaver skins, besides many others of mink, coon, deer, bear, etc. Messrs. Woods, Zenoni, Immel, and Fontanelle were in the employ of the company at this time. There was intense rivalry between the trading companies and between the companies and the independent trappers. All endeavored to incite the Indians against the others and against tribes favorable to the others. Unquestionably, many of the massacres and murders on the plains resulted from these conditions. Sometimes the traders of one company forcibly took the furs belonging to another, usually under some plausible pretext which they themselves had created.

At Camp Missouri during the winter, nearly one hundred soldiers died of scurvy, out of about three hundred there assembled. This fort stood near Engineer cantonment. On January 2, 1820, a party of hunters returned with twelve buffaloes which they had killed. This was quite an achievement, because these animals had become scarce in that vicinity. Some of the Indians had never seen a negro until they saw the cook of the cantonment, and accordingly regarded him with great curiosity. An Omaha called him Black White Man, and another Little Black Bear or Was-a-pa-gin-ga. Feasts and barbecues of buffalo, deer, or bear meat occurred often throughout the winter, amid scenes of much interest. At this time the permanent villages of the Omahas were situated about one hundred miles up the Missouri river a short distance up Omaha creek, and consisted of dirt lodges and comfortable places for stock. On April 24, Major Long, accompanied by Capt. John R. Bell and others, reached St. Louis on his return trip. Instead of passing by boat up the river, they secured horses and struck across the country for Council Bluffs. They passed south of Field's trace through Iowa and Missouri and reached the Missouri at the mouth of the Platte. They reached Engineer cantonment about the 1st of June. As the dealings with the Grand Pawnees had not been satisfactory, it was finally resolved to send a special expedition to their villages on the Loup branch of the Platte. Accordingly, thirty-four men with seventeen well filled packs passed up the streams to their villages, and were well received by Long Hair, the principal chief, doubtless because the wily chief knew they brought valuable gifts with them. Their good will was completely won, of course. Among them at this time were Messrs. Papan and Semino, two traders, who served as interpreters.

It had been determined by the government that the steamboat should go no farther up the Missouri that season and that expeditions should go west to the mountains to explore the valleys of the Platte, Arkansas and Red rivers. Lieutenant Graham was left in charge of the boat, with instructions to leisurely return down the rivers to St. Louis. Major Long was to command the expedition to the West. Under him were Capt. J. R. Bell, Lieut. W. H. Swift, Thomas Say, zoologist, Edwin James, botanist, geologist and surgeon, John Dougherty, hunter, interpreter and guide. The start was made June 6, and on the 11th the Pawnee villages on the Loup were reached. They did not receive a cordial welcome, because, doubtless, they did not make many valuable presents. Four miles farther up that river they met the Republican Pawnees, who formerly dwelt on the Republican fork of the Kansas river, and hence their name. The principal chief of the Loup Pawnees was Knife Chief or La-til-e-sha, and his son was Pe-tal-e-sha-roo, a magnificent specimen of the race. At this time they had from six thousand to eight thousand horses. The principal guides and interpreters of the expedition were Bijeau and Ledoux, both of whom had been several times to the headwaters of the Platte and the Arkansas. The former attempted to desert at this place, but when told that if he did all the traders would be warned to leave the Indian country, he gave up and resumed his engagement.

Having reached the mouth of the North fork of the Platte on the 22d of June, they crossed the main stream to the south side and continued their march. Here for the first time, immense herds of buffalo were encountered. Thus far the expedition had advanced without important event. Prowling bands of savages had visited them no doubt with the hope of receiving presents, and were usually sent away happy with a supply of tobacco. No ammunition was given them, because it was not known how soon it might be used in an attack on the whites. The treeless plains stretched to the horizon in every direction, and the sun beat down with pitiless fury on the parched grass. But the buffaloes thrived, the gaunt wolves feasted on the worn-out stragglers of the herds, the wild flowers sprang in profusion, and the prairie

birds made music while they raised their little broods. The buffaloes were so tame that they, as well as the wolves, simply opened
their ranks to let the intruders pass and then closed up again,
without having moved to right or left more than two or three
hundred yards. The tameness of the wild animals proved that
this section had not been visited by the Indians. Neither did the
expedition meet Indians here. But after June 29th, the herds
again began to grow thinner and the Indians began to be seen.
Clumps of trees began to appear after this as the mountains were
approached. The Fourth of July was celebrated by the expedition with an extra allowance of corn meal and with a swig of
whisky to each man. By this time every man was tired of the
plains, and eagerly watched for the first sight of the mountains.
The botanist, the zoologist, the geologist and the mineralogist had
observed everything and had classified many new varieties. To
them the great plains were a rich treasure house stored with
nature's choicest gifts.

Soon the rich verdure of the mountain valleys, the deep shade
of the heavy woods, the sparkling, rushing streams, the snow-
capped mountains and the refreshing springs of pure water from
endless snows, greeted the tired men and put fresh vigor in their
worn spirits. Bell's Springs were named for Captain Bell of
this expedition, who first discovered them on a short side expedition. James' Peak was named by Major Long for Edwin
James of this expedition, who had the hardihood to ascend to
its wintry summit for scientific discoveries. He was no doubt
the first white man to stand upon its bare crest and see the wonderful panorama spread around—lofty peaks with their crowns
of rock and snow; deep valleys enveloped in almost impenetrable
forests; ranges of lofty mountains far to the north and the south;
the valley to the west shining like emerald in the summer sun;
and the endless plains to the east threaded with silver streams
and intersected with belts of scrubby timber. It was a sight
well worth the labor of making the ascent, but which only a stu-
dent of nature would care to undertake, and for which he alone
would feel amply repaid.

Having pursued his discoveries here as far as his instructions
warranted, Major Long divided his command of about twenty-
five men into two divisions, one of fifteen men under Captain Bell
to descend the Arkansas, and the other of about ten men under
Long himself to go south to Red river and descend that stream.
These were small parties to undertake such hazardous trips, but
nearly all were trained hunters, familiar with the habits of the

Indians and not afraid to meet them in their own way and upon their own ground. Both parties started July 24, 1820, from near Wharf creek, one of the upper branches of the Arkansas. That under Major Long struck nearly due south, expecting to reach he upper branches of the Red before turning to the east, and reached the Canadian Fork of the Arkansas on the 28th, but mistook it for a branch of the Red and therefore turned down the same. They had followed the directions of the Indians, but, in the absence of the guide, Joseph Bijeau (or Bessonet, his real name), who had remained in the mountain country according to arrangement, had been deceived. On August 10th they met a large war party of Keechies, who became insolent and endeavored to take unfriendly liberties with them; but stern resistance and a hostile and steady front checked the savages. From this band they learned that a large war party of Ietans or Comanches was near at hand, but they did not meet it. At first the party found very little game, but as they went on the herds of buffalo became numerous, and finally the animals could not be counted. They were even tamer than they had been on the Platte, and as before simply moved a little to one side until the expedition had passed and then closed up again. Once again the hunters' camp was savory with the tempting odor of roast buffalo rump, steak or tongue. On the 21st of August, they killed a black bear, the first they had seen since leaving the Missouri river.

On the 10th of September, Long's party reached the mouth of the Arkansas, and there for the first time learned that they had descended the Canadian Fork of the Arkansas instead of the Red as they had thought. This caused them great mortification, because they had been directed particularly to descend the Red. But it was now too late to rectify the mistake, so they continued on down to Fort Smith and there found that Captain Bell's party had arrived on the 9th, while Long arrived the 13th of September. Two days after starting, Bell's party had reached a large camp of Kiawas, Keechies, Cheyennes or Padoucas, and Arapahoes. On August 1st, they encountered a war party of four times their number of Cheyennes, who tried to get the advantage of them, but the resolute course of the whites put a stop to their hostile proceedings. On August 2 and 3 they came upon vast herds of buffalo and remarkably large herds of antelopes. On August 12 they encountered a band of about thirty-five Comanches, who endeavored by appearances of friendliness to take their arms, but this course was soon stopped. The whites had a horse which seemed to have an interesting history on the plains. He was known to all the Indians, and each band had some member who claimed him. More than once such an Indian would go to the animal and prepare to take him away, claiming ownership; but they were not permitted to take possession. On the 31st of August, three men—Nolan, Myers and Bernard—deserted from the expedition, taking the three best horses, and many valuable articles, including manuscripts, drawings, Indian presents, etc. They left in the middle of the night, and were pursued, but succeeded in escaping.

After various other stirring experiences from Indians and after suffering severely for want of food, the party under Captain Bell arrived in due time at Fort Smith. . . After they had been joined by that under Major Long a few days later, an expedition was projected to the villages of the Osages. At this time that tribe was divided into three branches: The Chancers under Chief Clermont; the White Hairs under Che-sho-hun-go; and the Little Osages under Ne-zu-mo-me. The first band was on the Verdigris, the second on the Osage, and the third on the Neosho. The expedition left on the 21st of September, and, after visiting these bands, arrived in due season at their predetermined destination—St. Genevieve, Mo. A small party, consisting of Captain Kearney and two other persons, passed by way of Hot Springs, Ark., which they thoroughly examined and reported upon.

In 1820 an expedition under Lewis Cass and Henry Schoolcraft visited the head-waters of the Mississippi and many of the other upper tributaries of that river in search of information of a scientific nature. They ascended the Mississippi to Cass lake, but failed to find the ultimate source of the Mississippi. The year before an expedition of a scientific character, in charge of Thomas Nuttall, passed up the Arkansas, examining every object of interest, and making an elaborate record of their discoveries. In 1823, Maj. S. H. Long, with a scientific corps, thoroughly explored the Minnesota river and several other branches of the Upper Mississippi in the present Minnesota. He marched far enough north to locate the forty-ninth parallel on the north boundary of Minnesota. W. H. Keating was his historian.

The expedition under Col. Hugh Glenn, consisting of about twenty men, thirty horses and mules and a considerable quantity of goods for the Indian trade, left Fort Smith on the Arkansas on September 6, 1821, and started westward up the valley of the Arkansas. On the second night out they were at Bean's saltworks. These wells had been opened in 1820 near the Illinois river on a small creek, under a grant to Messrs. Bean and San-

I—26

ders. They soon reached Fort Gibson, which had just been built. They crossed the Verdigris, on which about four miles from its mouth was an important trading house. This was owned and conducted by Colonel Glenn, the commander of this expedition. Here they remained until September 25, when they again advanced, but were now reduced to fifteen men, five having left. They soon reached the Osage village, but found nearly all the Indians away on their annual buffalo hunt. At this time the prairies were covered with buffaloes and elks, followed stealthily by packs of wolves. On October 1st, they crossed Little Verdigris, and by the 4th were in what is now the Osage reservation of Oklahoma. On the 6th they were at a point south of the present southern boundary of Kansas, not far from Arkansas City, and here they encountered the Osage Indians in great numbers. On October 9, they crossed Walnut creek not far from Arkansas City. Many of the Indians were insolent unless they were well supplied with presents. On the 18th they were near Sterling, Rice county, Kan. On the 20th they crossed Pawnee Fork near Larned, and on the 25th near Dodge City, Ford county. Here the plains were literally covered with herds of buffalo, elk, deer, antelope, wild horses and wolves. On November 3, they were at what is now Hartland, Kearney county. Two days later they were at Hollys, just across the line in Colorado, and on the 12th reached Caddoa. The next day Spanish Peaks were passed, and on the 16th they were near Robinson. They had passed Fort Lyon on the 15th, and were near Catlin on the 20th.

Scarcely a day passed that did not witness the visits to the camp of members of the Kiawas, Padoucas, Ietans (Comanches), Arapahoes, Cheans, Snakes, etc. Many articles were stolen by these pilfering bands, and often collisions were narrowly averted. They were at Boonville on December 25. At this time the party consisted of only thirteen men. A little farther to the westward they passed the winter, being visited often by the Spaniards from New Mexico. Taos was but six days' journey to the westward. It is claimed that Major Jacob Fowler of this party built the first house in Pueblo this winter, a rude log structure. They spent part of the winter in trapping and hunting in this vicinity; but in the meantime Colonel Glenn, with a small party, went across to Santa Fe. Supplies of corn were procured from Spanish traders. With this party was James Beckworth, who afterward became the head chief of the Crow Indians. On the 29th of January, they received word from Colonel Glenn to come on to Santa Fe, and accordingly did so, reaching Taos about February 8th. In April, 1822, they started back via what is now Las Animas and Baca counties, Colo., and after reaching the upper branches of Purgatory river struck straight across the country to Coolidge, Kan. By June 20th they had reached the vicinity of Raymond, Rice county, and in due time returned to civilization without serious accident. The objects of trapping and trading had been accomplished.

Commissioners to treat with the Indian tribes beyond the Mississippi ascended the Missouri in 1825, leaving St. Louis about the 20th of March and reaching Council Bluffs, April 19th. The commissioners were Gen. Henry Atkinson and Major Benjamin O'Fallon, who were accompanied by an escort of one hundred and seventy-six soldiers. They had a large supply of Indian presents and an abundance of provisions. In Fort Atkinson, at Council Bluffs, they remained until May 16th, when, with large reinforcements, they ascended the Missouri in their boats, arriving at the Ponca villages in what is now South Dakota, June 8th. Here a council was held a few days later. Ascending the river, they reached Fort Lookout of the American Fur Company, about twenty miles below the great bend of the Missouri, on the 17th, where a council was held and a treaty effected with the Tetons, Yanktons, Yanktonies and their allies on the 21st and 22d of June. Bad river. A council was held with a band of Sioux at Hidden creek on the 12th of July; and a treaty with the Arickarees was concluded a week later. Late in July the Mandan villages were reached, and here on the 30th a council was held and a treaty effected with the Mandans, Minnetarees and Gros Ventres, and four days later with the Crows. About the middle of August, the mouth of the Yellowstone was reached and here a trapping party of twenty-three men under General Ashley was met coming down that river in hide canoes with a cargo of over one hundred packs of beaver skins. Hoping to meet the Assiniboines, the commissioners sent a detachment up the Missouri over one hundred miles above the mouth of the Yellowstone; but it was obliged to return without effecting its object. On the 27th of August, the expedition, accompanied by the Ashley party, boarded the transports and descended the river, reaching the Mandan villages August 30th, Council Bluffs September 19th, where, on the 26th, a council was held and a treaty concluded with the Otoes, Pawnees and Omahas. Part of the escort remained at Fort Atkinson, but the other part descended the Missouri to St. Louis. The results of this expedition were to cement friendship with the Indians and secure a large tract of territory by treaty. At this time Major O'Fallon was Indian agent on the Missouri.

The expedition of H. B. Schoolcraft and Lieut. J. Allen to the Northwestern Indian tribes and to and beyond the sources of the Mississippi in 1832, was one of the most important made in early years. A large amount of valuable information was the result. With Schoolcraft were twenty of his own *engages* or Canadian *voyageurs,* besides his assistants; and with Allen were about ten soldiers to serve as an escort; in all about thirty-five persons in the expedition. They found the source of the Mississippi river to be Lake Itasca, which they named. They described a large number of unknown lakes and other physical features, found copper ore and agates of wonderful beauty, made valuable additions to the information concerning the origin and habits of the Indian tribes, and made an important contribution to the scientific information of the territory through which they passed. Their explorations were mainly in the present States of Minnesota and Wisconsin. The real source of the Mississippi was unknown until this expedition discovered it to be in Lake Itasca.

In 1832 Capt. B. E. Bonneville, of the Seventh United States Infantry, at his own expense and independent of the orders of the government, left Fort Osage with one hundred and ten men and twenty wagons on a trading and exploring trip to the mountains. The start was made about the first of May, and for a time the journey was monotonous enough indeed; but when the buffalo and Indian country was reached the scene was changed, and such a change! The wagons were drawn by mules and oxen, and a large supply of provisions and Indian presents was taken along. Many of the Indians along the whole route had never seen a wagon before, and regarded them with ever-increasing wonder. On May 24, when far up in the Indian country, a cry was one day raised, "Indians, Indians!" and sure enough there came a mounted band of about sixty Crows at full speed directly toward the wagons, swinging their arms and yelling like demons, and for a while nothing was to be seen whirling around the camp but prancing ponies, yelling savages, streaming hair and feathers, and brandished knives and rifles. All this was intended by the Indians to show their own prowess and their skill in horsemanship and to test the nerve of the whites. After receiving a few presents, they departed at full speed as they had come. On June 2 the party reached the Platte river at a point about twenty-five miles below Grand Island and on the 11th were at the forks where the two branches of the river came together. A little below this point, they crossed to the north side on the usual trail traversed by all the expeditions. On June 25 they were at Scott's

Bluffs, on July 12 at Laramie fork on the Platte, and on July 20 caught their first glimpse of the blue mountains in the distance. They continued, and soon were beyond the present boundaries of the Louisiana Purchase.

Having gone on to the Pacific, they returned and in July, 1833, were again in the mountains of what is now Colorado. This party was so large and so well armed and equipped, that they had little or nothing to fear from the Indians. On their return they found many trappers, free and in the employ of the companies, in the valley of Green river, which at that time was the most noted rendezvous for these hardy and resolute men any where in the West. While here, Bonneville determined to go with a portion of the party to Great Salt Lake. He started in July with twenty-four men, and did not return until the spring of 1835. By this time his party had collected a large supply of skins, and it was determined to return to the States. Accordingly, they advanced down the valley of the Platte, and in August again stood at Fort Osage. Captain Bonneville had gone on this expedition without leave from the War Department, and during his absence had been dropped from the army rolls. He was finally restored to his former rank. This was a private expedition, and many of the incidents were never recorded.

A squadron of dragoons, consisting of thirty-seven men under Captain Ford, forty men under Captain Duncan, and forty men under Captain Lupton, all commanded by Col. Henry Dodge, was sent to the Rocky mountains in 1835 to hold councils with the Indian tribes and to look after the interests of the United States on the (then) Mexican border. A large supply train of wagons was taken along, and in addition two swivels with which to impress the savages. Captain Gantt was guide to the expedition. They left Fort Leavenworth May 29, 1835, accompanied by Major Dougherty, Indian agent to the Pawnees, and marched up the valley of the Missouri, reaching the mouth of the Platte river of Nebraska on the 9th of June. Near this place was held on the 11th a council with the Otoes, of whom Ju-tan, or I-e-tan was head chief. Here, also, the Omahas were brought by messengers, and a council was held with them on the 17th, Big Elk being the principal chief present. At all the councils presents were distributed. The expedition then marched up the Platte to the Pawnee villages about eighty miles distant, where another council was held the 23d, Angry Man being principal chief of the Grand Pawnees, Axe of the Pawnee Loups, Little Chief of the Pawnee Tappeiges and Mole on the Face of the Republican Pawnees.

Departing on the 24th, the expedition reached the lower extremity of Grand Island the following day. When well up the Platte a council was held on July 5th with the Arickarees, the chiefs present being Bloody Hand, Two Bulls and Star or Big Head. This council was held near the falls of the Platte. At this time, immense herds of buffalo surrounded the expedition. On the 15th the Rocky mountains were seen for the first time by the expedition. They were now well up the South Fork. On the 18th they passed the mouth of Cache de la Poudre river, and on the 24th reached the point where the Platte emerges from the mountains. After this date the expedition marched southeast, and on July 26, arrived at the divide between the Platte and the Arkansas. Passing down Boiling Springs creek and the Arkansas, they reached Bent's fort on the 6th of August. Near this noted place, councils were held with the Arapahoes, Cheyennes, Blackfeet, Gros Venres and others. Leaving on the 12th of August, they moved down the Arkansas, holding councils with the Comanches, Kiowas and others, arriving on the 24th at Chouteau's Island. Soon afterward they left the valley of the Arkansas and marched northeast to Fort Leavenworth, where they arrived on the 16th of September, having fully accomplished the object of the journey—to quiet the Indian tribes and ascertain what they were doing and were likely to do in the future.

In 1835-6 an expedition under the command of W. B. Guion, J. D. Webster and others were sent by the government to survey the St. Francis, White and Black rivers in Missouri, Arkansas and Louisiana. Their duties were satisfactorily performed.

The explorations of I. N. Nicollet from 1838 to 1841 were of great value to all subsequent explorers, owing to the thoroughness with which he reported the topographical features of the territory traversed. Lieut. John C. Fremont was one of his assistants, and Louis Freniere one of his guides. The map he made of the Upper Mississippi country, particularly of what is now Minnesota, was so elaborate and so singularly correct, that all subsequent explorers have, in a large measure, been guided by it. During this period, Fremont explored the Des Moines river for him. He had several other assistants, all of whom performed important special duties. The Upper Mississippi, the Missouri well into the Dakotas, the Minnesota, the Des Moines, the Arkansas, the Red, both of the North and of Natchitoches, and many of their smaller branches were examined. His map of the hydrographical basin of the Upper Mississippi is consulted to this day. He likewise reported on the fauna, the flora, the kind of soil, the minerals, the timber supply, the Indians, and other features.

The outposts of the government in 1844 were Fort Jessup on the Red river of Louisiana; Forts Towson and Washita on Red river above Fort Jessup; Forts Smith and Gibson on the navigable waters of Arkansas river; Fort Scott on the southwest frontier of Missouri; Fort Leavenworth on the Missouri; Fort Snelling on the Mississippi, and Fort Wilkins on Lake Superior.

The upper Des Moines river was thoroughly explored in 1814 by an expedition under the command of Capt. J. Allen, of the First Regiment of Dragoons. With fifty, rank and file, of that command, two privates of infantry and a train of wagons loaded with supplies and provisions, the expedition started from Fort Des Moines on the 11th of August, passing first along the "Oregon Trail;" then crossing Beaver river and reaching the Delaware battle-ground, where, three years before, a band of twenty Delawares had been slaughtered by a large war party of Sioux. This event occurred in a deep ravine near the Des Moines river about five miles below the well-known "Iron Banks." The mouth of the West Fork was passed on August 19th. Great trouble was experienced in hauling the wagons through the sloughs, where they often stuck in the black mud. As they neared the northern border of the present Iowa, many small lakes were found, all covered with innumerable water fowl. When in southern Minnesota, the expedition was left at a suitable camp, and Captain Allen, with twenty-five men, started to discover the remote sources of the Des Moines river and of the Blue Earth river of Minnesota. On the 4th of September, they reached the St. Peter's river; and, having passed down the same for several miles, ascended the Blue Earth basin, examining the sources of that stream, finally marching westward to their camp. The source of the West Fork of the Des Moines was found to be a small lake which was named "Lake of the Oaks." Leaving this lake, the expedition took a westerly course, and on the 13th of September arrived at the falls of the Big Sioux river. Previous to their reaching the headwaters of the Des Moines, not an Indian nor a buffalo was seen. Even the small bands of Sioux seen after that time seemed afraid of the expedition and soon disappeared after being encountered. Elks were killed almost every day. "Twenty-five miles west of the source of the Des Moines river we struck the range of the buffalo and continued in it to the Big Sioux and down that river about eighty-six miles. Below that we could not see any recent sign of them. We found antelope

in the same range with the buffalo, but no elk, and very seldom
a common deer. While among the buffalo, we killed as many as
we wanted, and without trouble." A side detachment descended
to the mouth of the Big Sioux, after which the expedition
marched almost on a bee line across the streams to Fort Des
Moines, where it arrived on the 3d of October.

The explorations of John C. Fremont, under an act of congress, were of much importance in placing before the people a
faithful description of the plains and the Rocky mountain region.
His first was made in 1842, with only twenty-one men. He
marched up the Platte valley, but upon reaching the forks, the
main party was sent up the North Fork, while a few men under
Fremont passed up the South Fork to St. Vrain's fort. From
here they marched northward to the North Fork and joined the
main fork at Fort Laramie. Although the Indians were on the
war-path farther up the river, Fremont determined to proceed.
They continued to advance without serious interruption, arrived
at the Sweetwater river, marched through South Pass, and a little later ascended the highest peak of the Wind River mountains.
The return journey down the Platte was made without notable
incident.

His second exploration was made in 1843 with about forty men.
They marched up the Republican fork of Kansas river, and finally divided, the main detachment moving by easy stages to
St. Vrain's Fort on the Platte. Fremont with a party of fifteen
made many detours in order the better to explore the plains.
Upon reaching St. Vrain's Fort, they concluded to remain a considerable length of time in order to explore the surrounding
country. Boiling Spring river was traversed, and the pueblo at
or near its mouth was visited. From Fort St. Vrain, the main
party marched straight to Fort Laramie, while the party under
Fremont passed farther to the west, skirting the mountain, and
carefully examining the country. The two detachments rejoined
on the Sweetwater river, and, having marched through South
Pass, continued on to Fort Bridger, and moved west down the
Bear river valley. Having marched to California and passed a
considerable distance down the coast, they finally returned, reaching Colorado at Brown's Hole. While in Colorado, they
explored the wonderful natural parks there. On their return
they passed down the Arkansas, visiting the "pueblo" and Bent's
Fort. They reached the Missouri river in August, 1844, after
an absence of fourteen months.

The third expedition under Fremont comprised nearly one

hundred men. Many of his old companions joined him, among whom were Carson, Godey, Owens and several experienced Delaware Indians. With him also was his favorite, Basil Lajeunesse, and Lieutenants Abert and Peck. He had a larger force than before, and felt equal to any emergency likely to arise. The plains were crossed without noteworthy incident, except a scare from the Cheyennes, and on the 2d of August Bent's Fort was reached. While here the detachment under Lieutenant Abert was sent to survey the country to the southward, as narrated elsewhere. On the 16th of August, the expedition proper, consisting of about sixty men, mostly picked for their known qualities of courage, hardihood, and faithfulness, left Bent's Fort and started on their journey. On the 20th they encamped at the mouth of Boiling Springs river, and on the 26th at the mouth of the great cañon of the Arkansas river. On the night of September 2d, they reached the remote headwaters of the Arkansas, where to their surprise they found a small herd of fat buffalo, that had discovered a small, rich valley and were living in contentment. They furnished the last buffalo roasts enjoyed by the party for a long time. Two days later Fremont passed across the divide into the valley of the Grand, and camped on Piney river, where a goodly supply of fish was caught. The marvelous beauty of the surroundings were specially noted by the scientists accompanying the party. Continuing westward without noteworthy incident, the party reached Great Salt Lake early in October. After great hardships Sutter's Fort in California was reached in December. The following year Fremont assisted the Californians in gaining their independence.

In the autumn of 1845 Lieut. J. W. Abert was detached with twenty-eight men, four wagons, seven horses and fifty-six mules from the Fremont expedition for the purpose of surveying Purgatory, False Washita and the Upper Canadian rivers. The famous mountaineer, Thomas Fitzpatrick, was his guide. The objects of this side expedition were fully accomplished.

The Army of the West under the command of Gen. S. W. Kearney was ssent by the government in 1846 to operate against New Mexico and California. The war with Mexico was raging, and the conquest of the upper provinces "was a consummation devoutly to be wished." The rendezvous of the army took place at Fort Leavenworth in June of that year. The army was divided into detachments, which were dispatched at different times across the plains. It consisted of two battalions of artillery under Major Clark, three squadrons of the First Dragoons under Major

Sumner, the First Regiment of Missouri Cavalry under Colonel Doniphan, and two companies of infantry under Captain Agney. Although the army crossed the plains in detachments, it again rendezvoused at a camp nine miles below Fort Bent on the Arkansas before advancing to strike Santa Fe. With the army were sent trains of wagons drawn by oxen and mules and loaded with commissary stores. About the 1st of August, the army advanced in a southerly direction from near Fort Bent, mainly up the valley of Purgatory river; thence across the upper branches of the Canadian river; thence southwest to the Pecos river, and thence to Santa Fe. At Bent's fort the army was joined by William Bent, who was placed in charge of a company of scouts or spies. The trail to Santa Fe was lined with dead and dying oxen and mules and broken and abandoned wagons. Several detachments of the army returned over the same route in January and February, 1847, and had narrow escapes from death both by freezing and starvation. They met several expeditions of settlers going to the western country.

As the army proceeded in sections across the plains, several detachments were sent out from the main body to explore branches of the Arkansas and the Red. Col. W. H. Emory commanded one of the detachments, which marched from Fort Leavenworth to San Diego, California, collecting an immense amount of valuable information concerning the route over which he passed. Another detachment under Lieutenant Abert likewise made important discoveries.

It was in 1847 that the Mormons crossed the plains in search of a home where they could live in peace. The advance column, consisting of one hundred and forty-three men, seventy-two wagons, one hundred and seventy-five horses, many mules and oxen, seeds and agricultural implements, and rations for six months, left the Missouri river in September. They marched up the valley of the Platte, ascending the North Fork, but crossing at Fort Laramie. They moved through South Pass, and in July, 1848, reached Salt Lake valley. A week or more later, the main body arrived under the guidance of Brigham Young.

In 1849, Capt. R. B. Marcy conducted a surveying expedition from Fort Smith to Santa Fe. "The expedition had in view the escorting of a number of California emigrants, and at the same time the exploration, survey and construction of a wagon road from that post to Santa Fe by way of the south side of the Canadian river." The escort consisted of twenty-five men of the First Dragoons under Lieut. John Buford, fifty men of the Fifth

Infantry under Lieutenants Montgomery, Harrison and Updegraff, nineteen six-mules wagons, and one six-pound howitzer. The guide was Black Beaver, a Delaware Indian. Lieut. J. H. Simpson accompanied the expedition. A large number of emigrants of the Fort Smith Company under John Dillard was protected by this escort. The expedition struck across the country to the Shawnee Hills, after which it marched much of the time in the valley of the Canadian. They passed Sans Bois creek, Rocky Hills, Edwards' Old Fort, Delaware Mount, Cross Timbers and Old Fort Holmes, near which had stood Chouteau's old trading-house. On May 23d they were near Natural Mound. Their forty-first encampment was at Antelope Hills. They encountered many Indians, and it would have fared hard with the emigrants had it not been for the presence of the troops. Is-sa-kiep, head chief of the Comanches, held a letter of recommendation from Thomas Fitzpatrick, the famous western guide, at this time Government Indian agent for the upper Platte and Arkansas rivers. On June 22d, they saw in the distance the snow-covered peaks of the Rockies. When well up the Canadian, they marched southwest to the river Pecos, thence northwest to the vicinity of Santa Fe. The road thus surveyed was afterward extensively traveled.

In 1849, Capt. L. Sitgreaves was sent with an escort of thirty men, three ox-wagons, one spring wagon for the instrument and five spare horses, to survey and mark the north and west boundaries of the Creek reservation. His party was partly completed at Cincinnati, but mainly at Fort Gibson, where a large party of emigrants waited for the escort of this force. All started July 21st, and from the start encountered much opposition from the Indians; but nevertheless Lieutenant Sitgreaves continued to run the lines as ordered. The emigrants were taken far enough to the west to enable them to reach Santa Fe in safety.

On the 31st of May, 1849, a party consisting of eighteen men, five wagons and forty-six horses and mules, under the command of Capt. Howard Stansbury, of the topographical engineers of the United States army, left Fort Leavenworth to cross the plains for the purpose of exploring the valley of Great Salt Lake. On the 7th of June, they met Mr. Brulet, of the Missouri Fur Company, on his way from Fort Laramie to St. Louis with a large train of wagons loaded with buffalo hides. He stated that he had been forty days thus far on the trip, and during that time had met fully four thousand wagons, averaging four persons to the wagon going to the west for homes or to search for gold. He said that good wagons could be bought a little farther ahead for from ten dollars to fifteen dollars each, and that salt provisions could be had for nothing. On June 9th the graves of six dead emigrants were passed; and on the 10th three of the party's best horses were stolen by a band of Pawnees in the night and were never recovered. This band had evidently watched the train for several days. On the same day there passed them a trading expedition under Bissonet and Badeau from the villages of the Sioux with a goodly supply of furs. On June 11 they passed an emigrant party of seventy or eighty persons bound for California. Immense numbers of killdeer began to be seen, and terrible rain-storms swept across the plains, blowing down every tent, overturning wagons, and playing havoc generally, amid a terrific play of electricity. More Indians began to be seen and accordingly, the cattle and horses at night were "corralled" and guarded. On June 18, a government train crossed their trail, having thirty-one heavy wagons, four hundred oxen and forty men, on their way to establish a new post near Fort Hall within the Rockies. About June 18 they reached the Platte near Grand Island and the next day camped within two miles of Fort Kearney, where they found Colonel Bonneville in command.

Here they remained until the 21st recuperating. On June 27, when over one hundred miles west of Fort Kearney, they killed their first buffalo four or five miles from the trail. On the same day a small herd was seen in the distance. Early the next day three cow buffaloes were killed; and later on this day the first stop was made that all the expedition might enjoy a buffalo hunt: Result, four killed and one wounded. Previous to this, Indian wigwams or lodges had been occasionally seen, which upon being examined were found to contain the dead bodies of Indians raised on poles beyond the reach of wolves. On one occasion the body of a beautiful Indian girl was thus found. It was soon learned that they had died of cholera. On July 2 they were at an estimated distance of one hundred and eighty miles west of Fort Kearney. On the 5th they reached a Sioux encampment of ten lodges, where nearly all were sick with cholera. Here they met Badeau, one of the trappers of the Missouri Fur Company, who had married an Indian girl, and was regarded very highly by the tribe. A few miles farther up was a larger village of the same tribe consisting of about two hundred and fifty persons. On July 12 they reached Fort Laramie, now a government post, where were stationed two companies of infantry and one of mounted riflemen under the command of Major Sanderson. Here they bought many fresh mules to replace their broken-down ones.

The march was resumed on the 18th, and a few days later they added to their train a cow which had been abandoned by some emigrant. As they continued, they began to see abandoned wagons and dead oxen on every mile of the route; and finally the trail was literally strewn with agricultural implements, household articles, furniture, clothing, carpenter's tools, salt meat, stoves, etc., at times almost in heaps. On July 17 they passed seventeen abandoned or broken-down wagons and twenty-seven dead oxen. As they passed the land of alkali and sage-brush, the wrecks became more frequent and melancholy. On July 28 they encountered thirty-one dead oxen, and on August 1st passed about a dozen burnt wagons and nineteen dead oxen. At one alkali pool, ten oxen were found dead in a heap. They were now at "Independence Rock" on the Sweetwater; and here the wrecks became less frequent. The alkali plains along the North Fork and at the crossing of the Sweetwater, had been found literally a charnel house of animals. On August 3, they met Captain Duncan of Fort Laramie, who had been out after five deserters, and had captured them within fifty miles of Fort Bridger. Many sage-hens were now brought into camp. On August 5, the mail from Salt Lake City to the East passed by with about six thousand letters. On August 6th, they entered South Pass, and having gone through the same, encamped at Pacific Springs on Little Sandy Creek. Here they found a grave, well rounded up, with headboard and name thereon; but some time afterward learned that it contained a large supply of whisky, which had been placed there for safe-keeping. The sagacity of the emigrant or trader met its reward, for the grave was not molested, and the whisky was there when he returned for it. On August 9 Green river was reached, and on the 11th they arrived at Fort Bridger, where they again rested and recuperated. Here they met the famous "Jim Bridger," who had been in the mountain country for more than thirty years, and who had the unbounded respect of every passer-by. On August 20 they resumed their march. While on Bear river, they caught many fine trout. In due time they safely reached the famous Salt Lake valley, their objective point.

They remained west of the mountains for the space of thirteen months, surveying the valley and making a number of important excursions; after which they started on their return trip, reaching Fort Bridger September 5, 1850, where they met both Bridger and his partner, Vasquez. North of Fort Bridger were the Shoshones and Crows; east were the Ogallalas and other Sioux; southeast were the Cheyennes and south were the Utahs. While here they received the news that President Taylor had died. Leaving Fort Bridger on September 10, they resolved to find, if possible, a shorter route across the mountains than along the South Pass, through which they had come the year before. Having employed Bridger to act as their guide, they set out and a few days later were charged upon by a war party of Shoshones, who at first mistook them for a band of Utahs, whom they were seeking. They were armed with a few guns, bayonets used as spears, bows and arrows, etc., and were mounted on small, powerful horses. The whites passed along the valleys of Black and Green rivers, and thence up Bitter creek. This valley had been famous in former times for the immense herds of buffalo which came here to winter, owing to the little snow which fell here and to the large tracts of rich grassland. On this account, it became a great resort for the trappers and traders and the scene of many a sharp contest for the furs of the Indians. At this time (1850) there was a scarcity of buffalo to be found here, but their rotting bones lay thick throughout the valley. Having passed up Bitter creek about seventy miles they turned more still to the east, and struck across to the valley of Muddy creek, reaching it about twenty-five miles from its mouth. As this was still the battle ground of several tribes, it was necessary to use great precaution to prevent being surprised by their war parties.

While encamped on this stream, Bridger told the following story: "A partner of his, Henry Frappé, had a party of what in the language of the country are called 'free men,' that is, independent traders, who some nine years before were encamped about two miles from where we then were, with their squaw partners and a party of Indians. Most of the men being absent hunting buffalo, a band of five hundred Sioux, Cheyennes and Arapahoes suddenly charged upon their camp, killed a white man, an Indian, and two women, drove off a hundred and sixty head of cattle, and, chasing the hunters, killed several of them in their flight, the residue escaping only by abandoning their horses and hiding in the bushes. Intelligence of this onslaught reached Major Bridger, then occupied in erecting a trading-post on Green river; he sent Frappé advice to abandon his post at once, for fear of worse consequences. The advice, however, was neglected, when about ten days after, as his party was on their way to join his partner, they were again suddenly attacked by another large party of their savage allies. He had but forty men; but they instantly 'forted' in the correl attached to the trading post and stood on their defense. The assault lasted from noon to sundown, the Indians charging the pickets several times with great bravery; but they were finally repulsed with the loss of forty men. Frappé himself was killed, with seven or eight of his people."*

In his report, Captain Stansbury says, "Before noon we passed a spot where a party of fourteen fur-traders under Mr. Vasquez, had 'forted' and fought forty Ogallala Sioux for four hours, successfully defending themselves and repulsing the Indians. One of our men, a half-breed hunter, had himself been in the fight, and pointed out to me the localities with the most minute particularity of bloody details." This was, in fact, one of the most historic valleys in the whole mountain region, full of reminiscences for the old hunters and trappers. The party continued along Muddy creek until September 20, when they struck east again, and ascended slowly the continental divide, and in a short time stood at the spot where the waters divide, part flowing east to the Mississippi and part west to the Colorado. Far to the east they could see the Platte valley spread out before them like a picture and glistening in the sun. This became called Bridger's Pass.

They had now come about two hundred and seventy miles since leaving Fort Bridger. They continued eastward down a steady and gradual decline until at last, on the 21st, they encamped on the North Fork of the Platte. Here was another famous hunting and trapping ground; and here and there could be seen the ruins of the old Indian stockades, there being in the valley at this time fifteen or twenty of them still standing, silent and deserted. In every direction, also, were the bones of buffalo, scattered, but telling the tale of slaughter. Here the party began to see buffalo for the first time on the return trip. Passing down the Platte, they ascended Medicine Bow river, and on September 25, reached Frappé creek, named for the man mentioned above, who had been robbed at its mouth several years before of sixty horses by a war party of Arickarees. On September 26, they entered Laramie Plains, where, on the open, they were threatened by a party of Indians; but they hastily sought the timber, where they fortified themselves, and sent Bridger out to reconnoiter. There were about thirty whites in the party, and nearly all were expert riflemen and knew no fear. Bridger returned with the report that they were Ogallalas (Sioux), and were friendly. In fact the Indians all came to the camp and became altogether too friendly, for they slyly stole several articles,

* Stansbury's Expedition to the Great Salt Lake.

among which was a valuable gun. They were out after a war party of Crows, with whom they were at war. Bridger knew many of the chiefs personally. They were supplied with tobacco, coffee, flour, sugar and given a square meal: there were several hundred of them. It is a singular fact, yet true, that although Bridger did not know a word of Sioux, nor the Indians understand a word of English, yet he conversed with them for two hours wholly by the sign language, each understanding each other perfectly, the Indians several times bursting out in laughter at the witticisms of the old mountaineer. This language was understood by all the tribes, and by the old hunters and trappers, and was the same everywhere. The whites visited the Ogallala village several miles away, and were entertained at dinner, but did not linger over the meal. Around here were the outliers of the Black Hills, and here the party stopped for some time to take observations and make measurements. The plains at this place were strewn with buffalo carcasses, and the live animals roamed in immense herds. On October 6 they advanced, and reached Fort Laramie on the 12th. Fort Leavenworth was reached on November 6, and Washington, D. C., on December 6.

In the summer of 1849, an expedition under the command of Maj. Samuel Woods was sent to the Red River of the North to ascertain the relations existing there between the Hudson's Bay Company and the Indians south of the British line, and between the latter and the white settlers also south of the boundary. With him went Capt. John Pope, afterward famous in the Civil war, and a company of forty dragoons from Fort Snelling. The expedition, well equipped, marched from Sauk Rapids June 16, passing in succession Sauk lake, Lightning lake, White Bear lake, Pike lake, Elk lake, Potato river, Rabbit river, and when near the latter meeting a train of wagons of the American Fur Company in charge of Mr. Kitson of Pembina. "We were much struck with the primitive appearance of the train of carts, without a particle of iron about them, each drawn by a single ox in the shafts and carrying about one thousand pounds." The expedition crossed Red river a short distance above the mouth of Sioux Wood river, and, keeping out of the valley much of the time, marched northward, crossing Cheyenne, Maple, Rush, Big Salt and other streams, and recrossing Red river several times before Pembina was reached August 1st. They had seen their first buffalo July 22d. At Pembina, it was learned that, while Hudson's Bay Company openly sent whisky across the boundary to the Indians south of the line, the American Company's traders were not permitted to do so, thus seriously reacting on their traffic. It was seen that the abuses of the Indian trade tended to make friends between the British and the Indians at the expense of the Americans. The population was largely half-breeds, who lived almost exclusively on dried buffalo meat. Here was a civilization, or semi-civilization, different from anything the members of the expedition had ever seen. Having accomplished its object in this section of the country, the expedition divided, part under Captain Pope passing up Red river, thence across the divide and down St. Peter's river to the Mississippi, and the other crossing to the Mississippi southeast from Pembina. Much valuable information concerning the Territory of Minnesota was gleaned from this expedition.

An expedition under the command of Thaddeus A. Culbertson was sent across the upper country from Fort Pierre to the Little Missouri river in 1850. He started in April, and by May 10th was on the headwaters of that stream. On his return, he passed across the uplands to the Black Hills, and thence through the Bad Lands, or Mauvaises Terre. The object of the expedition was two-fold: To ascertain what the Indians were doing and to find a new and better trail for wagon and other trains. Immediately succeeding this trip, he passed up the Missouri from Fort Pierre, meeting and endeavoring to make friends of the warring Arickarees and others. On this trip he visited Fort Clark and Fort Buthold, both on the Missouri in what is now North Dakota.

What was called "the Oregon expedition" left Fort Leavenworth in May, 1850, under the command of Colonel Loring, and consisted of an entire regiment, divided into three detachments of two companies each, accompanied by many wagons containing the supplies, and by a large party of emigrants, who availed themselves of this opportunity to secure a safe escort across the plains. It is needless to say that the regiment arrived in Oregon in due season. The divisions marched a few miles apart, so as to be always in readiness to assist one another in case of an attack by the Indians. So many wagon trains crossed the plains at this time that the Indians soon adopted the tactics of stampeding their stock—horses, mules, cattle and sheep—either day or night as seemed best. Indian scouts on horseback could be seen at all stages of the journey watching the emigrants from a safe distance and noting the vulnerability of the trains. When a train was too well guarded to permit this attack, the Indians often approached the wagons under a flag of truce to beg or trade. Many of the chiefs had vouchers, given them by unscrupulous

I—27

traders or travelers for hay, wood, grass, etc., of the country, calling for reimbursement from the government: when this was refused they usually became indignant. It is related that, during the progress of this expedition, the members thereof were always in sight of wagon trains, when in the valley of the Platte. By June 1st, 1850, not counting those who passed along the right bank of the river, over four thousand wagons passed Fort Kearney that year, going westward. Estimating an average of four persons to each wagon, it will be seen that an aggregate of twenty thousand persons had thus gone to the West before that date. There were usually ten or twelve oxen to each wagon, thus aggregating from forty thousand to fifty thousand oxen, to say nothing of the large numbers of cattle, sheep, horses and mules driven along. It was estimated that during the year 1850, fully eight thousand wagons went up the Platte valley alone, representing over thirty thousand persons and nearly one hundred thousand animals. It was estimated that more persons went over the Santa Fe trail than over the Platte trail. When the total is thus estimated, the remarkable westward movement becomes apparent. With the Loring expedition went seven hundred horses and twelve hundred mules, all intended for use in Oregon, where the regiment was to be stationed. But after all, the wonderful westward emigration was natural and is easily accounted for. The marvelous agricultural resources of Oregon and California were just becoming known. That fact was alone sufficient to attract to the coast large numbers of permanent settlers. When to that magnet is added the other of gold in almost every stream and on almost every mountain side, the large emigration may be regarded as natural and reasonable. An incidental result was to open to the gaze of the people, the wonderful possibilities of what was formerly the Louisiana Province.

In 1852 Capt. Randolph B. Marcy, of the Fifth infantry, was detached with fifty-five men of his company to examine the sources of Red river above the mouth of Cache creek. Associated with him as second in command was Capt. George B. McClellan, afterward famous in the Civil war and as a candidate for the presidency. Strange as it may seem, the country thus designed to be explored was, as Marcy termed it, "terra incognita." If it had ever been visited by white men, no record had been kept. Marcy repaired to Fort Smith, and then to Preston, Tex.; and the rendezvous took place by detachments at the mouth of Cache creek. He took with him a supply train of twelve wagons drawn by oxen. The most of his troops were detached from Fort Belknap on the Brazos river in Texas; and all assembled at the mouth of Cache creek on the 13th of May, 1852. The start was made on the 16th, the force ascending the ridge dividing Cache creek from Red river. Indian signs were seen almost every day from the start. Soon buffalo tracks were seen in the prairie sand. On the 17th a panther measuring eight and a half feet from tip to tip was killed. The next day a stray horse was caught. A few days later they turned more to the northward, and on the 23d reached Otter creek. Three days later their first buffalo was killed, and the following day a party of one hundred and fifty Witchita Indians visited the camp to inquire where the expedition was bound. With them were many horses and mules, laden with buffalo meat; also ten wild horses recently captured. The chief was Ca-ne-ja-hex-ee. The object of the expedition was explained; but the Indians used all their arts to dissuade the whites from advancing, stating, among other things, that the country was a desert, destitute of water and animals, and was so barren that even the Indians not only did not live there, but rarely ventured there on any pretext. These stories did not deter Captain Marcy, who determined to proceed. A council was held and presents were distributed. About this time Captain McClellan took a small force and established the one hundredth parallel of west longitude at a point six miles below the mouth of the Dog Town branch of the river. As it afterward turned out, this was much too far to the east, and was partly the cause of a dispute regarding territory between Texas and the United States.

As they advanced, the country, instead of becoming barren, became even better than that through which they had before passed. An excellent grass covered the plains, the water of the streams was good for man and beast, many cool springs bubbled out from the hills or the Washita mountains, the air was delightfully cool and fresh, and the cattle and the mules actually took on flesh instead of losing it. Deer, antelope, buffalo, wild fowl, bear and panther afforded all a chance to prove their prowess as followers of the chase. By the 9th of June they were on Sweetwater creek. Many Indian signs were observed, made both by war parties and by traveling villages of the Kiowas, Comanches, Wacos, Keechies and others. Kiowa creek was reached June 14th. Having arrived at what was thought to be the most northerly point of the North Fork, Captain Marcy determined to march with a small escort across to the Canadian river to examine the country lying between the two streams. This was done from the 17th to the 19th. The Canadian was reached near the mouth of Sandy creek. Returning, they reached the North Fork in what is now Gray county, Tex. The North Fork was now so small that it was thought useless to ascend it any farther, whereupon the expedition marched almost directly southward, and on the 20th reached the stream which they named McClellan creek. Two days later they reached the Salt Fork of the Red and were then in Donley county, Tex. For the last few days, they had seen many of the wonders of the famous Llano Estacado—mirages, streams wholly dry, bare, hot sand, repulsive reptiles, wonderful rock formations, strange gray grass and a brassy sky.

They finally arrived at the Dog Town branch of the river, where they found its bed nine hundred yards wide, but containing very little water. About this time Captains Marcy and McClellan together killed a large panther. They used a deer-bleat to attract a doe, but also attracted a panther, which mistook it for the cry of a fawn and came bounding to the spot. The topography now became very rough and the water so bad that it could scarcely be used. For some time the men were so tortured with thirst that they talked about ice-water during the days and dreamed about it during the nights. One man present said he would give two thousand dollars for a bucket full of pure, cold water. As they ascended this fork the river water became better. They now began to find an occasional spring of fine water, where all thoroughly refreshed themselves before proceeding. By July 1st, the water in the river was good for drinking. The rock formations were wondered at, some being eight hundred feet high, shaped like forts and castles and singularly beautiful. Soon after this they reached the remote headwaters of this fork, in what is now New Mexico. There they found many fine springs and a picturesque country. They were now according to their calculations at the meridian of one hundred three degrees, seven minutes, and eleven seconds of west longitude.

On July 4th, they started to retrace their steps. Mulberry creek was reached on the 6th. Before arriving at the western extremity of the Witchita mountains, they passed the sites of the old Witchita villages, now deserted, but showing where the fields and lodges had formerly stood. By the 19th of July, they were at the eastern end of the mountains, whence they designed to strike across the country to Fort Arbuckle on the Canadian river. They marched northward along the divide between Cache and Beaver creeks, and when they arrived at Rush creek, a branch of the Washita river, they found the two principal villages of the Witchitas and the Wacos. At both places they held councils and distributed presents. To-se-quash was at this time the head chief of the former tribe. On the 23d, Captain Marcy released from captivity a Mexican boy about fifteen years of age, whom the Indians were loth to part with; in fact did not do so until given many presents and threatened that he would be set at liberty in any event. On the 28th, Fort Arbuckle was duly reached, much to the joy of the soldiers. In his report, Captain Marcy recommended the erection of a fort near the mouth of Cache creek, or at the forks of the Red, for the purpose of holding in better subjection the tribes of the remote headwaters of the Red and the Canadian rivers. The objects of the expedition were fully accomplished, and another supposed desert was found to be abundantly fitted for a large population.

By act of March 3, 1853, the Secretary of War was authorized "to employ such portion of the corps of topographical engineers and such other persons as he may deem necessary, to make such explorations and surveys as he may deem advisable, to ascertain the most practicable and economical route for a railroad from the Mississippi river to the Pacific ocean," and the sum of one hundred and fifty thousand dollars was appropriated to defray the expense of such expeditions; later forty thousand dollars more was appropriated to cover deficiencies. Under this act three expeditions were projected: First, westward on a line between the forty-seventh and the forty-ninth parallels of north latitude; second, one between the thirty-seventh and the fortieth parallel; third, one on or near the line of the thirty-fifth parallel.

The first above mentioned was under the command of Hon. Isaac I. Stevens. The design was to locate the most eligible route, for a railroad from St. Paul to Puget Sound, between the above mentioned parallels. A large military escort accompanied the expedition; also many surveyors and engineers. Marching early in June from St. Paul, they reached in succession Sauk Rapids, Sauk Lake, Lightning lake, White Bear lake, Lambert river, Pike lake, Chippewa river, Red River of the North and Cheyenne river July 2d. Soon after this they began to see many herds of buffalo. On the 15th of July, they met a large party of Red river hunters, consisting of about thirteen hundred persons, over eight hundred carts, about twelve hundred horses, mules and cattle, and over one hundred lodges or tents. Vast numbers of buffaloes were slaughtered and the flesh was minced and afterward mixed with tallow and securely packed for future use. The product was used by the fur companies in the far north during the entire seasons and commanded a good price.

Fort Union at the mouth of the Yellowstone was reached August 1st. On the way a large party of Assiniboines were met, but they offered no resistance. About the 1st of September, Fort Benton was reached; and on the 24th they arrived at Dearborn river. Early in October, they crossed the divide by the way of Traveler's Rest Creek, and soon afterward passed across the line into what is now Idaho. The report showed the practicability of the route.

The honor of surveying the second or central route above mentioned fell to Capt. J. W. Gunnison. His party rendezvoused at Westport, near Kansas City, and started in June, 1853. In the party were about sixty persons, all well armed, with a large supply of provisions. They marched up the left bank of Kansas river until they came to the Pawnee or Republican fork, after which they continued farther from the river valley, crossing Solomon and Saline rivers on rafts; and soon afterward passed south across the Smoky Hill fork, and, marching southwest, reached Arkansas river in the vicinity of its Pawnee fork. They then ascended the Arkansas to the mountains, crossed the same and were soon on the soil of the present Utah, where Captain Gunnison and a small party, while out prospecting from the main party, were attacked by a large band of Eutaws, and several were slaughtered, including Captain Gunnison himself, who received eighteen arrow wounds and had his right arm severed at the elbow. This expedition was fortunate in discovering a new route and a better pass through the mountains by way of the Huerfano river. The report shows that this route was practicable for a railroad.

The third route above mentioned was surveyed by Lieut. A. W. Whipple and party. He started from Fort Napoleon at the mouth of the Arkansas river; but finally rendezvoused at Fort Smith in May and June, 1853. His escort, consisting of about fifty soldiers, moved under his command up the valley of the Arkansas until the Canadian fork was reached and then up the right bank of the latter. On the 7th of September, they were at Antelope Hills near the one hundredth meridian of longitude. When near the head of the Canadian river, he turned southwest, crossed the Pecos and entered the valley of the Rio Grande south of Santa Fe. Thence he marched through northern Arizona to California. Of his party were Lieuts. J. C. Ives and D. S. Stanley. A practicable route for a railroad was shown by this report.

Under the act of congress of 1853, Capt. E. F. Beale, the superintendent of Indian affairs in California, who had been on a visit to the East, started from Westport, Mo., in May, 1853, with a party of twelve riflemen, intending to return to his work in the West.   Under the act he was instructed to locate certain Indian reservations in California, and to provide for the subsistence, protection and colonization of the Indians thereon.   The party went first to Council Grove distant from Westport one hundred and twenty-two miles, thence to Fort Atkinson on the Arkansas river two hundred and thirty-nine miles, thence to the mouth of Huerfano river two hundred and forty-seven miles, thence to Fort Massachusetts eighty-five miles, and so on to the coast.   He encountered no serious opposition from the Indians.

The "Sioux Expedition" of 1855, under the command of Gen. W. S. Harney, performed as well important duties of surveying. A detachment under Lieut. G. K. Warren marched across the open country from St. Pierre to Fort Kearney, thence up the Platte to Fort Laramie, thence across a wild tract of territory to Fort Pierre, thence down to the mouth of the Big Sioux, and thence northeast through Minnesota, passing first up the Big Sioux.   It was in 1856 that a wagon road was surveyed from Fort Ridgley in Minnesota to South Pass in the Rockies by Col. W. H. Nobles: fifty thousand dollars had been appropriated by the government to defray the expenses of this survey.   From 1858 to 1862 a military road from Wally Wally to Fort Benton was explored and surveyed by Capt. John Mullan.

An expedition commanded by Gen. William F. Raynolds explored the Yellowstone and other branches of the Upper Missouri river in 1859.   They rendezvoused at Fort Leavenworth and St. Joseph and arrived at Fort Randall June 13, and at Fort Pierre the 18th, where a treaty was concluded with the Sioux and their allies.   From this fort the expedition marched over the plains to the westward in the Bad and Cheyenne river basins, crossing many small creeks, and finally reaching the Black Hills about the middle of July.   With the expedition was James Bridger, the famous hunter, trapper and mountaineer.   Leaving the Black Hills, they marched up the North Fork of the Cheyenne; thence across the divide to the Little Missouri; thence across Powder, Tongue and Rosebud rivers, finally arriving at Fort Sarpy the 19th of August.   This fort was a post of the American Fur Company, with Robert Meldrum in command. During the autumn of 1859 Lieut. H. E. Maynadier was sent with a strong detachment to explore Rosebud, Tongue and Powder rivers.   Passing back to the Powder river, the expedition moved up that stream, and finally across the divide to the North

Fork of the Platte, where winter quarters were secured. During the following winter, many side expeditions thoroughly explored the surrounding country over a radius of nearly a hundred miles. The winter was passed near the big bend of the North Fork of the Platte. The following spring the party marched in a northwest direction, partly east and partly west of the continental divide, explored the valleys of Jefferson, Madison and Gallatin rivers, and on the 14th of July arrived at Fort Benton. Fort Union was reached August 7, Fort Pierre September 7, and Omaha October 4. The expedition accomplished its objects of exploration and Indian pacification.

It was estimated by Capt. Edward F. Beale in 1859, that a railroad from Fort Smith, Ark., to San Filipe, N. M., would cost over twenty-one million dollars. This report was the outcome of an expedition sent by the government under his command across the plains in 1858–9. It passed up the Canadian fork, from the headwaters of which it marched across to the Gallinas, picking out the most practicable route for a wagon road. It finally crossed the Pecos and a few days later entered the valley of the Rio Grande. The road thus surveyed was afterward traveled to a large extent by emigrants and others.

In 1862 Capt. Medorem Crawford conducted a large party of emigrants across the plains from Omaha: he was assisted by Leroy Crawford. The escort consisted of fifty mounted soldiers, with twelve loaded wagons and an ambulance. He started June 16, and by the 28th was opposite Fort Kearney. July 10 he reached Castle Ruins, July 16th Fort Laramie, July 29th Devil's Gate, August 7th Big Sandy creek and August 15th the Smith fork of Bear river near the Idaho line. Wally Wally was reached October 14th. No incident of notable importance occurred on the trip. During the same year, another party of emigrants was conducted across the plains, up the valley of the Platte, by Captain Mackay. He encountered no serious obstacle.

In 1862 Capt. James L. Fisk was sent with a mounted escort of fifty soldiers and the necessary assistants to conduct a large party of emigrants from Fort Abercrombie on Red river of the North to Fort Benton. The country was infested with many hostile bands of Indians; and the government realized that the departure of the emigrants without escort meant their certain annihilation. All being ready, the start was made July 3. Milk river was reached August 19, and Fort Benton September 5. The expedition marched a considerable distance north of the Missouri and then well up Milk river, before passing down

Maria's river to Fort Benton. By so doing, they escaped the Indians lying in wait along the usual route traveled by emigrants. There was little danger from Indians west of Fort Benton.

The next year Captain Fisk conducted another overland expedition from Fort Abercrombie to Fort Benton, his escort rendezvousing at St. Cloud. The principal object of the expedition was to escort a large emigrant train across the plains through a dangerous section of Indian country. The escort consisted of fifty soldiers, a 12-pound howitzer, and wagons containing the necessary supplies. Antoine Frenier was present as the Sioux interpreter, and R. D. Campbell as the Chippewa interpreter. The expedition reached Fort Ripley June 19, at which point many more emigrants were added to the train. Here the equipment was completed, Colonel Rogers being in charge of the garrison. Otter Tail lake was reached on July 8, and here were seen melancholy evidences of the slaughter the year before. On July 11 Dayton was reached, and here again the bloody work of the previous year was visible. At this place a mounted escort from General Sibley's expedition was met. The next day they arrived at the Red River of the North, and on the 13th reached Fort Abercrombie. Squads of hostile Indians surrounded the expedition almost from the start; also packs of prowling wolves. Near this place General Sibley was encamped. Advancing, they crossed the Cheyenne river on the 26th, and two days later encountered one of the famous Red river hunting parties, consisting of over six hundred hunters. Small bands of Sioux hovered about, watching evidently for an opportunity to strike. On the Souris river, immense herds of buffalo were seen: it was estimated that on July 2 one million of those animals were in sight with the aid of a field glass. On the 8th of August, a large war party of Assiniboines was met, the head chief being Is-to-wer-a-han. Though greatly outnumbering the whites, they did not venture to attack. The usual perfunctory peace proceedings—speeches and empty promises—were observed. As a matter of fact, this escort was altogether too small to traverse the plains at that time; because all the Indian tribes were at war with the government, and bands that could easily have overwhelmed the white forces were met every few days. General Sibley should have sent at least one hundred mounted men to the assistance of Captain Fisk. This movement was called "The Northern Overland Expedition for the Protection of Emigrants." Open conflict with bands of hostiles was more than once narrowly averted. Milk river was reached on the 25th of August, and on the same day a band of thirteen Gros Ventres came into camp. The journal of the expedition reads, "Their language is the most extraordinary and uncouth that can be imagined. It is guttural and seems to consist of a cough, a groan, a grunt, a whistle and a tst-tst." The following day, Captain Fisk and Doctor Gibbs together shot a grizzly bear which weighed about nine hundred pounds. On August 31, a party of settlers from Bannock City on their way to Fort St. Charles to procure a quartz mill was met. On September 5, Maria's river was reached. Mr. Dawson of the American Fur Company was in charge of Fort Benton. September 6, Teton river was reached, and on the 20th the summit of the Rocky mountains was crossed. Seven days later Bannock City was reached, and here the expedition was dissolved.

A wagon road from Niobrara to Virginia City was explored and surveyed by Col. James A. Sawyer in 1865. He had an escort of one hundred and forty-three men with twenty-five wagons drawn by six mules each. With the expedition went five emigrant wagons, and a private freight train of thirty-six wagons so coupled together as to be drawn by eighteen teams of six yoke of oxen each. Paul Dorion agreed to guide him, but failed to appear at the last moment; Baptiste Defoud and Benjamin F. Estes took his place. They started on the 13th of June, passing up the Niobrara and reaching Lone Pine creek on the 26th, Snake river on the 30th, Antelope creek July 10, the headwaters of White river on the 13th, on which day they saw the Black Hills for the first time in the far distance. On the 10th, they had crossed the trail made by Lieutenant Warren in 1856, and on the 17th crossed that made by Colonel Harney about the same time. A detachment under Lieutenant Dana was sent to Fort Laramie the 21st: he rejoined the expedition August 1st. While they were near Hat creek on the 22d, a furious hail storm swept across the plain, prostrating the tents and stampeding the animals. Horse creek in the present Wyoming was reached on the 25th and the South Cheyenne three days later, near which their first buffalo was killed by the expedition. The North Cheyenne was reached August 5th, and near this stream was seen a valuable outcropping of bituminous coal. The Indians had begun to be troublesome, and on the 13th they killed one of the party—Hedges. Two days later about five hundred Cheyennes and Sioux attacked the camp at sunrise: but finding they could gain nothing they sued for peace and presents. The next day they tried to stampede the cattle of the expedition, but failed and departed. Had the escort been any considerable degree weaker, the expedition would have been annihilated by the allied Indian enemies. July 24th, they arrived at Fort Connor on Powder river, and a week later at Tongue river, near which they were attacked in desultory fashion by about three hundred Arapahoes, Cheyennes and others, who succeeded in killing several of the men and in running off a few head of stock. Captain Kellogg with twenty-seven men joined him on the 5th of September. General Connor with a large force was in the vicinity, and had whipped the Indians a few days before in a sharp engagement. Two companies under Captain Brown, sent from the command of General Connor, joined the expedition on the 13th; but on the following day they left when on the Big Horn. Immense numbers of buffaloes were seen, followed as usual by packs of ravenous wolves. Pryor's Fork was reached on the 21st, and the Yellowstone the following day. On the 5th of October they arrived at Bozeman City in the Gallatin valley, and a week later reached Virginia City, their destination. They did not succeed in quieting the Indians, as had been expected, or rather hoped. During this period W. W. Brookings conducted an expedition from the western line of Minnesota to Montana, meeting no serious obstacle on the way.

An important survey of the Arkansas river was made in 1869 by Col. John N. Macomb and Lieut. S. T. Abert. A reconnoissance in 1869, under the command of Col. S. B. Holabird, performed important duties in the "Department of the Dakotas." The next year an expedition under the command of Gen. H. D. Washburn left Fort Ellis and explored the Yellowstone river, at the same time executing important duties for the War Department.

CHAPTER XIII

The Indian Tribes

L ONG before the discovery of America by white men, what is now known as the Louisiana Purchase was inhabited by both fixed and roving Indian tribes. Some of them had established villages of dirt and wood; others lived in tents which they removed readily and transported to the proximity of buffaloes and other wild game. De Soto found the Capahas or Pacahas, afterward called Quappas, on the St. Francis river. Lower down he found the Casquins, since known as Kaskaskias. He met the Akansea or Arkansas nation, though they at that time seem to have been known by their local names. They were located on the Arkansas river near its mouth as well as on the Mississippi. In his wanderings he encountered the Cayas or Kansas, the Tensas, the Tonicas, the Natchitoches, the Caddoes, the Adayes and many other tribes whose names, as used by him, can be identified with those of a later date. Joliet and Marquette found on the Des Moines river the Peorias, Moingonas, Odontontas, the Mahas or Omahas, the Panas or Pawnees, the Aiouez or Iowas. They found on the Missouri river the Missouris, the Osages, the Kansas and farther west the Pawnees, the Padoucas or Comanches, and north the Outhouez or Otoes. They found on the Arkansas river the Akanseas, the Kansas and others. La Salle and Tonty encountered the same tribes. Duluth found the Issatis, the Sissetons and the Assiniboines in the present Minnesota, as did also Accault and Hennepin. Nicholas Perrot found in Minnesota the Nadouessioux, from which term, doubtless, came the French name "Sioux." The Indian name of the Sioux was Dakota. D'Iberville found in Louisiana the Houmas, Tangapahoes, Quinipissas, Bayagoulas, Natchez, Chetimachas, Tensas, Coroas, Attakapas and many others. This was about the siutation of the tribes when the province became the property of the United States. The only important change was the appearance of the Chippewas in northern Minnesota. They no doubt invaded the lands of the Sioux, and hence the perpetual war between those two powerful and war-like tribes. The far western tribes—Blackfeet, Arapahoes, Comanches, Kiowas, Apaches and others—became known through later explorations.

As early as 1775, a committee of congress was appointed to devise plans to carry on trade with the Indian tribes; but, of course, this act did not then apply to the territory west of the Mississippi. Little was done under the act; but, in 1786, an ordinance was passed, dividing the Indian department into two districts, a northern and a southern one, with a superintendent and a deputy in charge of each. Under this act the granting of licenses was regulated, all proceedings being controlled by the War Department. Important changes were made in 1790 under the constitution adopted in 1789. The license system was retained, and a suitable bond was required. Nothing was asked for the license, which was issued for two years; but a trader without a license was required to forfeit his goods. "By the treaty of 1794 Great Britain captured the right of trade and intercourse with the Indians residing in our territory; which gave her nearly a monopoly of the trade with the various tribes of the lakes, the Mississippi and the Missouri, and a decided control over all their measures. The effects of this ascendency over them must be remembered and lamented so long as the history of the late war shall be perused. The most distressing occurrences and the greatest disasters of that period may be distinctly traced to it. This right of intercourse and trade with the Indians, which has proved to us so pernicious, terminated in the war, and was not reserved by the treaty of Ghent; and in the year 1816 congress passed a law which authorized the president to prohibit foreigners from trading with the Indians residing within our limits, and instructions have been given under the act to prevent such trade."*

But the act of 1816 did not remedy the evil; however, it was thought that the erection of posts and forts in the Indian country would do so. The act of 1802 so far repealed previous acts, that a fine of one hundred dollars and imprisonment not exceeding thirty days, together with a forfeiture of goods, was made the penalty of trading without a license.

---

*From letter of John C. Calhoun, Secretary of War, to the Congressional Committee on Military Affairs, December, 1819.

The factory system was inaugurated in 1796, but did not supersede the license system of individuals. Congress, under this act, appropriated one hundred and fifty thousand dollars to be used as capital in the Indian trade. In addition the necessary buildings were erected, in which the goods were placed and the factors, agents, clerks, et al., were domiciled. The sum of eight thousand dollars was appropriated per annum to pay such supernumeraries. The factory law was limited to two years; but was re-enacted and continued to 1806, when superintendents of Indian affairs were appointed and the capital was increased to $260,000 and the annual salary of the agents to $13,000. This law was continued in force until 1811, when the capital was still further increased to $300,000 and the annual salaries to $19,500. This act seems to have remained in force until the abolishment of the system in 1822.

The United States had scarcely acquired the province of Louisiana before steps looking to the removal of the Indian tribes east of the Mississippi to the west side were taken. The act of March 6, 1804, by which the province was divided into two territories, provided also for the removal of such Indians as desired to make the change. The plan was to give them acre for acre lands beyond the Mississippi in exchange for their old domains on the east side. As a matter of fact the removal to the west of the Mississippi had begun many years before, while Louisiana was still a province of Spain. In 1793 the Shawaneses and Delawares had been given a tract fifteen miles square west of the Mississippi at St. Genevieve, by Baron de Carondelet, Spanish governor of Louisiana, and the grant had been confirmed and recorded. Many small tribes in Louisiana, who had come from the east side, held tenures of a similar character from the same source. Bands of Choctaws were in Opelousas and on the Ouachita; the Washa swere on Bayou Lafourche; the Tenisas were on Red river near the Pascagoulas; the Choctaws were on Bayou Boeuf; the Pascagoulas were on Red river about sixty miles below Natchitoches; the Tonicas were at Pointe Coupée; the Opelousas were about fifteen miles west of Opelousas church; the Attakapas were about twenty miles west of the Attakapas church, and with them were a few Tonicas and Humas; the Pacanas were located about forty miles southwest of Natchitoches; the Coushattas were on the Sabine about eighty miles south of Natchitoches; the Apalachies were on Bayou Rapide; the Alabamos were on Red river near the Apalachies; the Boluscas were at Avoyelles and on Bayou Rapide; the Natchitoches lived near the town of that name; the Adayes were on Red river about forty miles above Natchitoches; the Yattasses lived on Stony creek near Red river, a short distance above the Adayes; the Caddoes or Cadoques lived about one hundred and twenty miles northwest of Natchitoches; near them were their relatives the Naudakoes, Nabadaches, Ionies or Tackies, Nacogdoches, Keechies, Adayes and others. However, not all of these tribes, or rather small remnants of tribes, had come from east of the Mississippi. Several of them occupied lands which had been theirs from time immemorial. It was necessary for the United States to recognize duly all such tenures. Owing to the fact that there was still an abundance of unsettled land east of the river, the United States was in no hurry, at first, to effect the removal of the tribes to the west sides.

On November 3, 1804, Gen. W. H. Harrison concluded a treaty at St. Louis with the Sacs and Foxes, by which they ceded any claim they might have to a small tract lying along the west side of the Mississippi north of that city. This step was taken more to gain the good will of those tribes than to admit the rightfulness of their claims to such tract. This course was pursued by the United States in the extinguishment of all Indian claims west of the Mississippi, even in case the claims were based upon only a shadow of right.

The expeditions of Lewis and Clark and of Pike revealed in unmistakable characters to the citizens the immense value of the new purchase. It was seen that the friendship of the Indians could be secured with comparative ease, and the settlement of the purchase could be conducted the same as on the east side. Pike secured two tracts in the present Minnesota. In November, 1808, Peter Chouteau, agent for the Osages, and Meriwether Lewis, governor and superintendent of Indian affairs, of Louisiana Territory, concluded a treaty with the Osages at Fort Clark, above the mouth of Osage river, by which the United States acquired all the territory possessed by that tribe between the Arkansas and the Missouri rivers and east of a line running due south to the Arkansas river from Fort Clark. This was the first large cession of lands west of the Mississippi to the United States. The government bound itself to establish and maintain a factory (store of goods) at Fort Clark for the benefit of the tribe, to keep a blacksmith there to mend their arms, implements, etc., to pay an annuity of $1,000 to the Great Osages and one of $500 to the Little Osages, and to reimburse white settlers who had recently been pillaged by the tribe, but not in excess of $5,000.

While this treaty was taken somewhat irregularly, it was duly confirmed by both the Osages and the government at St. Louis in August, 1809.

The step of building Fort Clark and of holding a peace treaty with the Osages was rendered necessary to protect the settlers from the depredations of that tribe. Capt. E. B. Clemson and his company of regulars were accordingly sent up the river in June, 1808, for the purpose of building that fort. Previous to the treaty, the Osages had been forced to peace measures by the act of the War Department in refusing them merchandise, ammunition, etc. Peter Chouteau claimed a tract of thirty thousand arpents on the Missouri at the mouth of Mine river, basing his claim on a grant from the Osages and from the Spanish government. His request to have this claim recognized in the above mentioned treaty with the Osages was refused.

As early as 1805, trading posts under the factory system of the United States were established at Natchitoches, on the Arkansas near its mouth, and at Belle Fontaine near St. Louis. In 1808 trading posts were established at Fort Clark on the Missouri, as before stated, and at Fort Madison, now in Iowa. The factory buildings at Natchitoches cost $2,012; on the Arkansas, $800; and at Fort Clark, $500. In 1808 only the posts of Natchitoches, Arkansas, Fort Clark, and Fort Madison were in operation. The factors were John B. Treat at Arkansas; Thomas M. Linnard at Natchitoches; George C. Sibley at Fort Osage (Clark), and John Johnson at Fort Madison.

Beginning about the year 1807, British agents in the West, doubtless under the direction of the Canadian authorities, commenced systematically to incite the Indians against the Americans. Every tribe on the Mississippi and the Missouri was visited by them. The Indians were told that their old father, the king of England, intended to repossess himself of all the western country. It was mainly through the efforts of Manuel Lisa, who was appointed a sub-agent of the United States for that purpose, that the tribes of the Missouri did not wage a bloody war against the Americans. Large quantities of guns and ammunition were sent by the Canadians to the western Indians long before war with England was declared in 1812. The battle of Tippecanoe in Indiana in 1811 resulted directly from British agencies. As early as 1809, many of the western tribes began petty acts of hostility, and occasionally killed a settler and his family and plundered and burnt their home. One of the first acts was the killing of several Americans at the lead mines on the

Mississippi in January, 1812. The Winnebagoes, or Puants, were particularly hostile. They killed a corporal at Fort Madison, and later shot a sentinel there. They also murdered an American family on the bank of the Mississippi in February, 1812. Even after the battle of Tippecanoe, such hostilities were continued without cessation during the War of 1812.

As soon as possible after the treaty of Ghent in December, 1814, peace treaties were held with all of the tribes that had been hostile to the United States, as well as with many others. William Clark, Ninian Edwards and Auguste Chouteau were the commissioners on the part of the United States to hold many of these treaties. The Kickapoos, Pottawatomies, Sioux of the lakes, Piankeshaws, Sioux of the river St. Peter's (Minnesota), Great and Little Osages, Yanctons, Mahas, Sacs and Foxes, Tetons, Kansas, and others, agreed to maintain peace with the United States. The most of these treaties were held at Portage des Sioux, a short distance above the confluence of the Missouri and Mississippi rivers. Large quantities of goods were distributed to the various tribes. The Sacs and Foxes of Rock river, the Winnebagoes and the Kickapoos were slow to make terms— had been so thoroughly under the influence of the British agents— In fact they were called "the British tribes" long after the war.

Peace had no sooner been concluded, than the British traders, taking advantage of the liberal terms of the treaty, though foreigners were prohibited from trading with the American tribes, came almost in droves to the West with goods of every description and of British manufacture. They promptly monopolized the Western trade. They went so far as to continue the tactics of inciting the Indians against the Americans with the view of keeping out the American traders, and at first were successful. Messengers sent by Governor Clark to Prairie du Chien were not permitted to pass the Sac and Fox villages on Rock river, but were obliged to go by way of Omaha and the St. Peter's river. But a stop was soon put to that state of affairs. At this time (1815) Mr. Boilvin was government agent at Prairie du Chien.

The proposition of removal to the west side of the Mississippi was early broached to the southern Indians, and was revived frequently during many years; but was steadfastly rejected by the majorities of those tribes. However, many small bands accepted the proposition from the start, and were guided by the government to their future home on the west side. Small bands of Cherokees, in particular, took early advantage of the proposition. It was soon learned that, owing to the exodus from the east to the

I—28

west side, many conflicting claims to territory had arisen among the tribes. The Quapaws (the tribe probably known to the early explorers as the Capaha, or Pacaha) claimed both sides of the Arkansas river; but their claims were disputed by the Cherokees on the north and east and by the Osages on the northwest. In fact the limits between no tribes west of the river had been definitely defined. The Arkansas nation had the best right to all this tract of country.

In an open letter, dated January 9, 1809, Thomas Jefferson wrote to the Cherokees, granting permission for such of them as desired to do so to remove to the Arkansas river in what is now Indian territory. Ere long small bands of Cherokees, Chickasaws, Choctaws and other tribes accepted the offer and went West. In 1808 the Cherokees of the lower towns signified their willingness to make the exchange proposed, but the upper towns refused. It was not until 1817 that many of the Cherokees formally made the exchange, and were given a large tract between the Arkansas and White rivers. In time the other tribes followed their example, but it was many years before the last of them were removed. It was at first the policy of the government to let them take their time, when nothing was to be gained by precipitancy. In 1816 the western lines of Missouri and Arkansas territories, as they were first established, were run, beyond which the soil was reserved for the Indians.

The proclamation of the king of Great Britain in October, 1763, prohibited the whites from settling on the Indian lands. This policy was continued by the United States after the Revolution, but circumstances soon demanded a change. The frontier line was too ragged and irregular. Isolated settlements far in the Indian country, and Indian reservations far east of the frontier, afforded the occasion for constant tumult between the two races. The first step was to remove all of the Indians west of the Mississippi, and to restrain the western movements of the whites. The law of 1804 authorized an exchange of western land owned by the government for eastern land occupied by the Indians; but did not provide for the expense of concluding such exchanges. To meet this want, the following resolution, introduced in the United States senate in December, 1816, became a law: "Resolved, That an appropriation be made by law to authorize the President of the United States to negotiate treaties with the Indian tribes, which treaties shall have for their object an exchange of territory owned by any tribe residing east of the Mississippi for other lands west of that river." Many treaties for the removal of the Indians soon succeeded the passage of this law.

The annual general account of debits and credits for the fiscal year ending April 1, 1812, at the government trading posts west of the Mississippi, showed the following result: Des Moines trading-house, debits $33,826, credits $38,112; Osage, debits $35,546, credits $37,476; Natchitoches, debits $35,669; credits $32,035. During the fiscal year ending March 31, 1815, the Des Moines trading-house produced 22,621 pounds of lead. On March 31, 1815, there was on hand at the Osage factory $9,896 worth of merchandise; at the Natchitoches factory $5,386 worth, and at the Des Moines factory $12,301 worth. The Natchitoches factory had on hand furs and peltries worth $8,265. The factor at Fort Osage was George C. Sibley, at Des Moines, John Johnson, and at Natchitoches, Thomas M. Linnard. In 1812 the factory buildings at Fort Madison were burned by the Indians, entailing a loss of sixty packs of peltries valued at $1,800, one hundred and twenty bear skins worth $129, and the buildings which had cost $3,321. The trading-house at Arkansas was either very small, or not conducted at all, before and during the War of 1812. The factor there received for the fiscal year ending March 31, 1815, $2,058 for furs, peltries, etc., sold by him. In a statement made March 31, 1815, it was shown that from 1811 to 1815 the Des Moines trading-house had gained $12,739, the Osage, $14,282, and the Natchitoches, $12,003, while every house east of the Mississippi, except the one at Chickasaw Bluffs, had lost. In 1814 Gov. William Clark, in order to counteract British influence with the tribes of Missouri river Indians, distributed among them presents valued at $11,847.*

In establishing the factory system, the government thought to monopolize traffic with the Indians; but almost from the start, private traders, both American and British, managed to gain the bulk of the trade. This they easily accomplished by going among the Indians with the goods, just as commercial men of the present day go with samples to their customers. The private traders extended large credit to trustworthy Indians, and saved them the trouble of a long journey to the government trading-houses. So individual traders became rich, while those of the government barely held their own. "In the event of the abolition of the factories, the first inquiry that naturally presents itself is, What is to be substituted in place of them? To obtain all these

* American State Papers: Indian Affairs: Vol. II.

furs (of the Upper Missouri and Upper Mississippi rivers and their branches), the government ought to establish at St. Louis a store with a capital of about one hundred thousand dollars, which ought to be augmented according to the augmentation of the trade. That store ought to be furnished with all kinds of goods suited to the Indian trade, well assorted in quality and quantity, and the articles in proportion to the sum. These goods ought to be selected on the notes of a man who understands perfectly well the Indian trade, and who should also know exactly what suits every nation in particular. That store, so established, could equip (without exclusive privilege) for the present about twenty-five or thirty traders for the Missouri, Mississippi and all the rivers that empty in these two. But to enable those traders, so equipped, to enter into competition with the British traders, the government ought, as much as possible, to sell these goods at a very moderate advance, and take their furs and peltries at a reasonable price. By these means the government would employ its capital to the advantage of its citizens, to the annoyance of British traders; and I am bold to say, it is the only means to destroy the British trade; besides which, our two territories would be greatly benefited thereby. Twenty-five or thirty traders would employ about two hundred men. . . I dare give here my decided opinion, which is founded on premises that I believe just, that a company well conducted, which should have the Indian trade (not exclusively) from Cedar Island, above the Poncas, to all the forks of the Missouri, could bring down annually (once well established) from that extent of country, a considerable sum in furs and pelts, which could be estimated at more than two hundred thousand dollars. This sum will appear exaggerated, but I found my opinion on the returns of the Northwest Company of Canada, which, though not well known, on account of the profound silence they have kept on this subject, have been thought, through the observations of knowing men, to be at least two hundred thousand pounds sterling; and this sum is principally got by the trade carried on with those tribes of Indians that reside in the neighborhood of the branches on the left side of the Missouri."*

In 1815 the following special agents were employed west of the Mississippi by the government: Peter Chouteau among the Osages; Nicholas Boilvin among the tribes on the Mississippi

---

* From letter of Gov. Ninian Edwards, dated at Kaskaskia, Illinois Territory, November, 1815, and addressed to Hon. William H. Crawford, Secretary of War Washington, D. C.

above the Illinois, Manuel Lisa among the Missouri river tribes above the Kansas, "has been of great service in preventing British influence the last year by sending large parties to war;"* Maurice Blondeau among the Sacs and Foxes; Peter Menard among the Shawanese, Delawares, Peorias and Piankeshaws on the Mississippi below St. Louis; William Lovely among the Cherokees on the Arkansas; Auguste P. Chouteau special agent among the Osages; and Judge Bullet sub-agent on the Arkansas. The following interpreters were employed by the year: Samuel Solomon, Hypolite Bolon, John A. Cameron (Sioux), Lewis Dorion (Iowas and Sacs), Paul Louis (Osages), Noel Mograine (Osages).

In 1815 the Quapaws were on the Mississippi; the Cherokees (many of them) in what is now Indian territory; the Piankeshaws on St. Francis river; the Shawanese near Cape Girardeau; the Delawares on White and Meramec rivers; the Peorias on St. Francis river; the Osages on the Osage and Arkansas rivers; the Kansas on the Missouri and Kansas rivers; the Iowas on the Missouri and Grand rivers; the Otoes on the Missouri and Platte rivers; the Pawnees on the Missouri and Platte rivers; the Omahas, Poncas, Chehaws and Arickarees on the Missouri; the Sioux on both sides of the Missouri in the present Dakotas; and the Sacs and Foxes on both sides of the Missouri near the present Sioux City, Iowa.

On August 24, 1818, an important treaty with the Arkansas tribe was concluded, by which the United States obtained all of their lands west of the Mississippi, except a reservation in the southeast part of Arkansas territory. In September, 1818, a large cession in what is now Indian territory was obtained from the Osages. From time to time, treaties of peace were held with all the western tribes adjacent to the whites. In 1818 the government, by withholding merchandise, ammunition and annuities, forced a peace between the Osages on one side and the Delawares, Shawanese and Cherokees on the other. A bloody war had been waged between those tribes; and it was afterward renewed in violation of the treaty.

In 1817, during this war, a large body of Cherokees, Delawares, Shawanese and Quapaws, numbering in all about six hundred men, among whom, it is claimed, were eleven Americans, entered the territory of the Osages under pretenses of peace, but with the intention of cutting off Clermont's band on the Verdigris

---

*American State Papers: Indian Affairs.

and slaughtering every person therein. Clermont happened to be away with a large hunting party, but the next chief was called out and promptly butchered. This large force then fell upon the village and slaughtered men, women and children indiscriminately, amid scenes of barbarity and cruelty rarely witnessed. They wound up this atrocious act by destroying all the growing corn and vegetables and burning the village. Many were taken prisoners, to be subjected to slavery or burned at the stake. The Osages retaliated as soon as possible by killing three Cherokee hunters whom they captured and by committing other acts of carnage.

In 1818 Benjamin O'Fallon was sent to Council Bluffs as agent among the Pawnees, of which proceeding a full account will be found elsewhere in this volume. During the same year, at the suggestion of the Shawanese and Delawares near Cape Girardeau, steps were taken to exchange a tract farther west for their lands on the Mississippi, but a long delay occurred. White settlers persisted in crossing the river and locating on their lands in spite of the vigilance of the government agents. In 1819 the Kickapoos exchanged their eastern lands for a tract in the present Kansas. By this time schools had been started among the tribes in the present Indian territory. In 1820 the Choctaws ceded a large tract on the left bank of the Mississippi at the mouth of the Arkansas in exchange for one of equal extent in the present Indian territory. In this year, also, the Omahas ceded a tract fifteen miles square at Council Bluffs. The Weas, upon crossing the river, were at first placed among the Shawanese and Delawares near Cape Girardeau. From this time for many years there was a steady exodus to the west side. By reason of the fact that the government had established the factories under treaty agreements, it became necessary to secure the consent of the Indians to their abandonment before the system could be abolished. This consent was secured from 1820 to 1824 by special treaties.

In 1824 Edward W. Duval was agent among the Cherokees on the Arkansas; George Gray, among the Caddoes at Sulphur Fork near Natchitoches; Benjamin O'Fallon, among the Pawnees and others at Council Bluffs; Richard Graham, a general agent at St. Louis; Lawrence Taliafero, among the Sioux on Minnesota river; Thomas Forsyth, among the Sacs and Foxes at Fort Armstrong, Rock Island: and Nicholas Boilvin, among the Winnebagoes and others at Prairie du Chien.

In 1824 the Iowas and the Sacs and Foxes ceded all their claims to land in northern Missouri, and the Arkansas ceded their large reserve in southeast Arkansas. It was designed to incorporate the Quapaws with the Caddoes. In 1825 several other small tribes gave their consent to removal to the west side. In 1819–20 the trouble over the boundary between Arkansas and the Indian domain to the west occurred. In 1825 the Creeks ceded a large tract east of the Mississippi and were given acre for acre in the present Indian territory. From 1824 to 1826 many treaties for the purpose of definitely fixing the boundaries between the western tribes were held by the commissioners of the government. In 1825 other large cessions were obtained from the Osages and the Kansas. About 1815 the Delawares abandoned their land in southeast Missouri, and went farther west of their own accord. In 1825 the Shawanese were assigned to a tract fifty by one hundred miles in the present Indian territory. In this year treaties of limits were held with the Poncas, Tetons, Yanctons, Yanctonites, Siounes, Ogallalas, Cheyennes, Hunkpapas, Arickarees, Mandans, Minnetarees, Missouris, Otoes, Pawnees, Omahas, and others by Major O'Fallon and General Atkinson.

An important treaty with the Assiniboines was concluded in September, 1825, by Peter Wilson; but as he had no authority to make it, his act was disavowed by the government authorities, though one substantially the same was concluded later. The Quappas, or Quapaws, reached the Caddoe reserve on Red river in March, 1826, but were later removed. Owing to continued hostilities, a second treaty of peace between the Osages on one side and the Shawanese, Delawares, Piankeshaws, Peorias, Weas, Senecas, and Kickapoos on the other, was found necessary to be made in October, 1826. Another important treaty was one held for the purpose of cementing peace between the Sioux and their neighbors: First, between the Sioux and the Chippewas; second, between the Sioux and the confederated Sacs and Foxes; third, between the Sioux and the Iowas, all concluded at Prairie du Chien in August, 1825. War between the Sioux and the Chippewas had continued almost uninterruptedly from time immemorial; the government agents, therefore, regarded this to be one of the most important of the early treaties. By the treaty, the Iowas and the Sacs and Foxes were confined south of a line extending across the present Iowa approximately on the parallel of the Upper Iowa river and the Sioux north of such parallel. The boundary between the Sioux and the Chippewas extended across the present Minnesota a short distance north of St. Paul, except that it passed up the divide between the basins of the Mississippi and the Red river of the North.

In 1825 the Otoes resided on the Platte twenty-five miles west of the Missouri, and consisted of about fourteen hundred persons, of whom about two hundred and seventy-five were warriors. The Grand Pawnees and Pawnee Loups resided on the Platte about one hundred and thirty miles west of the Missouri. The Pawnee Republics lived on the Republican fork of Kansas river. The Grand Pawnees embraced about five thousand five hundred persons; the Pawnee Loups, about three thousand five hundred; and the Pawnee Republics, about twelve hundred and fifty persons. The three tribes could muster about two thousand warriors. The Mahas, or Omahas, lived on Elk Horn river, about eighty miles northwest of Council Bluffs, and embraced about two thousand seven hundred and fifty persons. The Poncas, or Poncars, lived at the mouth of White Paint creek on the Missouri, about three hundred miles by water from Council Bluffs. They consisted of about one thousand people. The Yanctons had no fixed habitation, but wandered over the country north of the Missouri and on the Big Sioux. They numbered about three thousand persons. The Yanctonites were without settled habitation and roamed over the territory on the Upper Jacques and St. Peter's. They consisted of about four thousand persons. The Tetons roamed over the territory south of the great bend of the Missouri, and as far west as the Black Hills. Their general rendezvous was near the Missouri; they numbered about three thousand souls. The Ogallalas occupied the country between the Teton river and the Black Hills. They rendezvoused at the mouth of the Teton, and numbered fifteen hundred persons. The Siounes occupied the country on both sides of the Missouri, between the Teton and the Cheyenne rivers, and embraced about four thousand souls. The Cheyennes, formerly on the Red river of the North, resided along the river Cheyenne from near its mouth to the Black Hills; they numbered about three thousand persons. Their principal rendezvous was near the Black Hills. The Hunkpapas, a branch of the Sioux, numbering about fifteen hundred souls, occupied the country between the Missouri and the headwaters of St. Peter's. The Arickarees, a branch of the Pawnees, had lived near the Mandans for about thirty years; they embraced about twenty-five hundred persons. The Mandans and Minnetarees lived together on Knife river on the Missouri at the mouth of Knife river. They numbered about three thousand people. Fearing the Assiniboines, they hunted mostly south of the Missouri. The Crows occupied the country between the Black Hills and the Rocky mountains, on the Big Horn and other southern branches of the Yellowstone; they numbered several thousand persons. The Kiowas and the Arapahoes occupied the country on the headwaters of the Arkansas and the Platte, and together numbered several thousand souls. The Blackfeet occupied the country between the great falls of the Missouri and the Rockies, and north beyond Maria's river into Canada. They numbered about five thousand warriors. The Assiniboines, a branch of the Sioux, roamed over the country north of the Missouri from Lake Traverse to Milk river. They often descended as far south as the Missouri to attack the Mandans and Minnetarees. They had about two thousand warriors, and were under the influence of Hudson's Bay Company.*

"The events of the last two or three wars, from General Wayne's campaign in 1794, to the end of the operations against the southern tribes in 1818, have entirely changed our position with regard to the Indians. Before those events, the tribes nearest our settlements were a formidable and terrible enemy; since then their power has been broken, their warlike spirit subdued, and themselves sunk into objects of pity and commiseration. While strong and hostile, it has been our obvious policy to weaken them; now that they are weak and harmless, and most of their lands fallen into our hands, justice and humanity require us to cherish and befriend them. To teach them to live in houses, to raise grain and stock, to plant orchards, to set up land marks, to divide their possessions, to establish laws for their government, to get the rudiments of common learning, such as reading, writing and ciphering, are the first steps toward improving their condition. But, to take these steps with effect, it is necessary that previous measures of great magnitude should be accomplished: that is, that the tribes now within the limits of the states and territories should be removed to a country beyond those limits, where they could rest in peace, and enjoy in reality the perpetuity of the lands on which their buildings and improvements would be made. . . . And the country west of Missouri and Arkansas, and west of the Mississippi river, north of Missouri, is the one destined to receive them. . . . In this way a constant tide of Indian emigration is now going on from the States of Ohio, Indiana, and Illinois to the west of the Mississippi. They cross at St. Louis and St. Genevieve under my superintendency."†

"The great object to be accomplished is the removal of these

---

* Report of Gen. Henry Atkinson and Maj. Benjamin O'Fallon to the War Department in November, 1825.

† William Clark, Superintendent of Indian Affairs, March, 1826.

tribes to the territory designated, on conditions which shall be satisfactory to themselves and honorable to the United States. This can be done only by conveying to each tribe a good title to an adequate portion of land, to which it may consent to remove; and by providing for it there a system of internal government, which shall protect their property from invasion, and, by the regular progress of improvement and civilization, prevent that degeneracy which has generally marked the transition from the one to the other state."*

The military movements up the Mississippi and Missouri rivers in 1819 were conducted on a large scale and were later attended with important results. The barracks near Council Bluffs were built large enough to house one thousand soldiers. Several thousand men were sent there, to be distributed to other posts to be established later on the Upper Missouri. A strong body of troops was sent to the mouth of St. Peter's river for the purpose of building a fort and of holding the Sioux in check. At this time various military roads, designed to unite the different posts, were projected. The government built Jefferson barracks in 1826, and the same year built an arsenal in St. Louis. Fort Madison, in the present Iowa, was begun as early as 1809 or 1810. Early in the decade of the twenties Cantonment Jesup, a short distance southwest of Natchitoches, Cantonment Gibson, at the mouth of the Neosho, and Cantonment Towson, near the mouth of the Kimishi, were built by the war department.

The fur traders, thrown in constant contact with the Indians, were the cause of many of the first encounters between the two races. The party under General Ashley, which was defeated and driven back by the Arickarees, no doubt through British influence, was re-enforced by Colonel Leavenworth, and the Indians were partly subdued. This was one of the first large campaigns against them in the Louisiana Purchase. To facilitate the movements of the troops, roads were projected between Natchitoches, Fort Towson, Fort Gibson, Fort Smith, Little Rock, Fort Leavenworth, Council Bluffs, Fort Des Moines, Fort Snelling, St. Louis and Prairie du Chien. More than one million pounds of lead ore were mined in Missouri in 1826.

In the autumn of 1827 a detachment of troops was sent from Jefferson barracks against the Winnebagoes along the Mississippi. That tribe, still under British influence, had continued to commit many petty acts of hostility against the United States.

*Communication of James Monroe to the United States Senate, January, 1825.

The detachment punished them severely, captured several of the leading hostiles, and restored tranquillity. In 1829 six companies, commanded by Major Riley, left Jefferson barracks to act as an escort for a large caravan of traders bound for Santa Fe. In the caravan were seventy-nine men and thirty-eight wagons laden with goods. They had several engagements with the Kansas tribes, but easily landed the traders in safety at their destination.

From 1828 to 1832 important treaties concerning the removal of the Choctaws, Chickasaws, Cherokees and Creeks were concluded, and large numbers of those tribes were escorted to their homes in the west. Small scattered bands of Shawanese, Delawares, Kaskaskias, Peorias, and other tribes, were likewise removed.

Despite their treaty to the contrary, the Sacs and Foxes persistently refused to abandon their ancient home at the mouth of Rock river; indeed, many who had been removed to the west side returned, and began repeated and galling acts of hostility against the United States. They fell upon a band of friendly Menomonies near Fort Crawford, killed twenty-six of them and wounded many more. These various acts led to the Black Hawk war in 1832. An army under Generals Gaines and Atkinson was sent against them, and they were finally subdued and removed to the west side.

In 1834 the Arkansas legislature memorialized congress to remove the troops from Fort Gibson to Fort Smith. It was shown that, when the eastern boundary of Arkansas was removed forty miles farther to the west, the troops were moved from Fort Smith to Fort Gibson; but when the line was brought back, the troops were not returned to Fort Smith, thus leaving that point exposed to Indian depredations. The prayer of the memorialists was granted.

In 1834 the expedition of Col. Henry Dodge, consisting of eight companies of regulars, marched from Fort Gibson west to the villages of the Pawnee Picts near the mountains, for the purpose of impressing them with the strength of the United States, of stopping their attacks on the white settlers and the caravans, of escorting a body of traders and settlers across the plains, and of making a stronger peace with that tribe. He met the leaders of the Pawnees, Comanches, Kiowas, Wacos, Arapahoes and others. The expected results were only partly realized. His second expedition, described elsewhere, was made in 1835.

Under the provision of the constitution which gives congress power to dispose of United States territory, the Indians were granted their lands west of the Mississippi in perpetuity. It was presumed by congress that the Indians thus sent west to lead hunters' lives would remain uncivilized, and that those who remained east of the river would speedily adopt the customs of the whites; but just the contrary state of things occurred. Those who went west put themselves from the start under the direction of the Indian department of bureau, and made rapid strides in the ways of the whites. In 1824 a bureau of Indian affairs was organized by the secretary of war as an adjunct of the war department; but in 1832 the bureau of Indian affairs, with a commissioner in charge, was created. Previous to this time small squads of soldiers, sufficient in number to hold the Indians in check, had been stationed at the various western posts. General Macomb stated in 1830 that nothing more was needed except to mount eight companies of these troops.

As early as December 16, 1824, the committee of Indian affairs of the house of representatives was instructed to "inquire into the expediency of organizing all the territory of the United States west of the State of Missouri and the territories of Arkansas and Michigan into a separate territory to be occupied exclusively by the Indians," and was also required to report on the expediency of authorizing the President to remove the various eastern tribes to such territory. The treaty of May 6, 1828, first formally recognized the policy of removal afterward adhered to by the government. It was improved in May, 1830, and, in 1834, the policy was fully developed and put into execution.

The most notable fact in connection with the law of 1834 is that the faith of the Nation was pledged under the most solemn guaranties that the Indians would never be deprived of their right to the new lands or of their right of self government. Neither were they ever to be constituted a territory or a state of the United States. They could not transcend the laws of the United States, and their affairs were managed by a governor and a general council.

In 1833 it was proposed that all the territory west of the Mississippi and north of the Osage reservations, the Santa Fe trail to where it crosses the Arkansas river, and from the latter river to the mountains, should be constituted a separate Indian district, with headquarters at St. Louis, where the superintendent was required to reside. All west of the river and south of that line, extending to the Mexican possessions, was to be constituted Western territory, of which Francis W. Armstrong was to be made superintendent. These two districts were to be subdivided into agencies and sub-agencies, with a representative of the government in each. This proposition was no sooner broached than it was changed. All the territory of the United States west of the Mississippi not in Missouri, Louisiana or Arkansas, was to be denominated by the general term "Indian country." By thus embracing all the territory in the Indian country, the laws of the United States were extended to the same.

The bill that finally became a law was passed May 20, 1834. It constituted all the territory of the United States west of the Mississippi and south of the Platte, not embraced in Missouri, Louisiana or Arkansas, as the Western territory, with many subdivisions called agencies or sub-agencies. Previous to the passage of this act, no definite steps had been taken for the government of the Indians removed west of the Mississippi. Part of the Cherokees had gone in 1808, and many of the rest in 1817. Many of the Choctaws had gone in 1820. In 1825 and 1826 the passage of a law for their government was pressed in congress, but failed. The law of May 6, 1828, as before stated, was the first to provide definitely for their removal and care. It was amended and improved by the act of May 30, 1830, by the Choctaw treaty of September 27, 1830, and by the Creek treaty of March 24, 1832. The two most important points guaranteed to the Indians were security in the possession of their land and the right of self-government. The territory was bounded east by Arkansas and Missouri, north by the Platte river, and west and south by the Mexican possessions. It did not embrace what afterward became the Platte purchase of Missouri. It was calculated to contain over one hundred and thirty-two million acres.

"This territory is to be dedicated to the use of the Indian tribes forever by a guaranty the most sacred known among civilized communities—*the faith of the nation.* The committee are aware that this guaranty, *the faith of the nation,* has not been illustrated by the history of the past in a manner satisfactory to the Indian tribes. They are not surprised that they should now ask, 'What new security can you give us to the lands in the West that you did not in times past give us to our lands in the East? It is admitted that we have given them guaranties which we have not fulfilled, pledges which we have not redeemed; not because we desired not to fulfill them, but because it was believed by the government that we had no right originally to give them, and therefore had no power to redeem them. The Indians, however, will do us the justice to say that we never had ourselves absolved from the obligations of indemnifying them, and of acknowledging that these very cessions of lands at the West are a portion of the indemnity. Our inability to perform our treaty guaranties arose from the conflicts between the rights of the states and of the United States. Nor is it surprising that questions arising out of such a conflict, which have bewildered wiser heads, should not be readily comprehended or appreciated by the unlettered Indians."*

By November, 1837, the following Indians had been removed to the west side:

Chickasaws	549
Chippewas, Ottawas and Pottawatomies	2,191
Choctaws	15,000
Quapaws	476
Creeks	20,437
Seminoles	407
Apalachicolas	265
Cherokees	7,911
Kickapoos	588
Delawares	826
Shawanese	1,272
Ottawas	374
Weas	222
Piankeshaws	162
Peorias and Kaskaskias	132
Pottawatomies of Indiana	53
Senecas	251
Senecas and Shawanese	211
Total	51,327

In the summer of 1836, owing to a threatened attack from the Indians, four companies were raised in Ray and Clay counties, Mo., for defensive purposes. The two from Ray were commanded by Captains Pollard and Sconce, and the two from Clay by Captains Atchison and Crawford. Col. H. G. Parks commanded the two companies from Ray. They were paid for eighteen days service by the government.

In 1837 William Armstrong, acting superintendent of Western territory, reported a total of 600 Indian scholars within the borders of the territory. In 1838 Joshua Pilcher, Indian agent, reported that the Blackfeet consisted of five distinct bands:

* Report of House Committee on Indian Affairs, May, 1834.

Blackfeet proper, Blood Indians, Searcies, Piegans, and Gros Ventres, the latter speaking an entirely different language from the others.

In 1839 serious trouble arose in the Cherokee nation between the old settlers and the new emigrants resulting in the death of John Ridge, Maj. John Ridge and Elias Boudinot. It was occasioned by jealousy, conflicting claims, and the desire to rule, the John Ross party triumphing. No doubt grievous wrong was committed.

In November, 1837, the following indigenous tribes were within striking distance of the Western frontier,* of which tribes, it was estimated that about one-fifth were warriors able to fight:

Sioux	21,600
Iowas	1,500
Sacs	4,800
Foxes	1,600
Sacs of Missouri	500
Osages	5,120
Kansas	1,606
Omahas	1,600
Otoes and Missouris	1,000
Pawnees	12,500
Comanches	19,200
Kiowas	1,800
Mandans	3,200
Quapaws	450
Minnetarees	2,000
Piegans	30,000
Assiniboines	15,000
Apaches	20,280
Krees	3,000
Arapahoes	3,000
Gros Ventres	16,800
Eutaws	19,200
Crows	7,200
Caddoes	2,000
Poncas	900
Arickarees	2,750
Cheyennes	3,200
Blackfeet	30,000
Total	231,806

*Report of C. A. Harris, Commissioner of Indian Affairs, to the Secretary of War, November 22, 1837.

Generally, during the decade of the thirties and forties, the Indians of the West were quiet, there occurring no general movement against the authority of the United States. During much of the time William Armstrong remained acting superintendent of Western territory. What is now Indian territory and Oklahoma territory soon became Southwestern territory.

Tribes.†	Lodges.	Men.	Persons.	
Poncas	80	250	800	Living on south side of Missouri, at the mouth of L'eau-quo-com.
Yanctons	250	750	2,500	Lower band of Sioux, living near Vermillion river.
Tetons	320	950	3,000	Lower band of Sioux, south side of Missouri.
Ogallalas	150	500	1,500	Sioux; dialect a little different, same river.
Souans	1,150	4,000	12,000	Sioux on rivers Cheyenne and Platte.
Yanctonies	600	1,800	6,000	Upper band of Sioux near Mandans.
Mandans*	30	120	300	Live in dirt lodges on the Missouri.
Arickarees	150	450	1,200	Occupy the same village with the Mandans.
Gros Ventres*	75	300	800	Live in dirt villages eight miles above the Mandans.
Assiniboines	800	2,500	7,000	Wandering tribe between the Missouri and Red River of the North.
Krees	100	300	800	Language same as Chippewas; country Assiniboine.
Crows	500	1,200	2,000	Rascals on the headwaters of the Yellowstone.
Cheyennes	250	500	2,000	Wandering tribe on Platte; language remarkable.
Blackfeet	1,500	4,500	13,000	Wanderers near the falls of the Missouri; both sides.
Arapahoes	300	650	2,500	Prairie tribe between the Platte and the Arkansas.
Gros Ventres, Prairie	400	900	2,500	Wanderers between the Missouri and the Saskatchewan.
Snakes	200	450	1,000	Poor tribe in the Rocky mountains.
Flatheads*	80	250	800	In the mountains; tribe mostly on the Columbia.

† From the Annual Report of D. D. Mitchell, Superintendent of Indian Affairs; St. Louis, September 12, 1842.

* All are wanderers except those marked with an *.

Names of tribes.*	Number of each tribe indigenous to the country west of the Mississippi.	Number of each tribe wholly or partially removed west.	Present western population of each tribe, wholly or partly removed.
Assiniboines	7,000		
Apaches	20,280		
Arapahoes	2,500		
Arickarees	1,200		
Blackfeet	13,000		
Creeks		24,594	24,594
Cherokees		25,911	25,911
Choctaws		16,359	13,592
Chickasaws		5,090	4,211
Chippewas, Ottawas and Pottawatomies, and Pottawatomies of Indiana		5,779	4,298
Chippewas of Swan Creek and Black River		62	62
Chippewas of the Mississippi and Lake Superior			7,605
Caddoes	2,000		
Comanches	19,200		
Crows	4,000		
Cheyennes	2,000		
Krees	800		
Delawares		826	1,039
Eutaws	19,200		
Seminoles		3,824	3,136
Flatheads	800		
Gros Ventres	2,500		
Iowas	470		
Kickapoos		588	516
Kansas	1,607		
Kiowas	1,800		
Miamis			650
Menomonies			2,508
Mandans	300		
Minnetarees	2,000		
New York Indians			3,293
Ottawas and Chippewas of Michigan			7,055
Osages	4,102		
Omahas	1,301		
Ottoes and Missouris	931		
Oneidas of Green Bay			720
Pawnees	12,500		
Peorias and Kaskaskias		132	150
Piankeshaws		162	98
Pottawatomies of Huron			100
Poncas	777		
Piegans	30,000		
Quapaws	247		
Stockbridges, Munsees and Delawares mixed		180	268
Sioux	25,000		
Sacs and Foxes of the Mississippi	2,200		
Sacs and Foxes of Missouri	414		
Shawanese		1,272	927
Senecas and Shawanese		211	241
Senecas from Sandusky		251	153
Snakes	1,000		
Weas		225	176
Winnebagoes		4,500	2,183
Wyandots of Ohio		664	555
Total	179,129	90,630	124,041

* Report of the Commissioners of Indian Affairs, covering several years ending with 1845, and in many instances based on close estimates only.

In 1847 Lieutenant Love, with an escort of dragoons in charge of government funds, left Fort Leavenworth for Santa Fe. At the Pawnee fork of the Arkansas, they overtook two large trains of commissary stores bound for the same place. A few days before, these trains had been attacked by a large party of Indians, and one man had been wounded. Love's party also met a return train of empty wagons, which had suffered the loss of all their cattle thus having over twenty wagons unable to proceed. Through the stubbornness of one man, Love's train lost the cattle of thirty wagons from a similar attack of the Indians. However, the thirty wagons were taken along by dividing the other teams. To prevent such attacks, Thomas Fitzpatrick, Indian agent for the Upper Platte and the Arkansas, recommended the organization of a force of two hundred and fifty mounted riflemen, one hundred dragoons, one hundred Mexicans mounted on their native horses, and two or three mountain howitzers. The force, he said, should consist wholly of western men, who were familiar with the methods of the Indians. He insisted that the regulars of the United States were useless against the Indians. The war with Mexico and the appearance of many soldiers had roused the fighting spirit of the Kiowas, Comanches, Cheyennes, Wichitas, Keechies, and others. In 1848 there were practically two tracts of territory set apart for the Indians: One in what is now Indian territory and one in Minnesota territory, the latter then extending west to the Missouri river and White Earth creek. Alexander Ramsey, governor of Minnesota territory, was ex-officio superintendent of Indian affairs within its border.

In 1848 a party of Iowas attacked a party of Pawnees and killed and scalped twelve of them. The Indian department forced the former to pay the latter eight hundred dollars of their annuities. On the Upper Platte the Sioux attacked and killed twenty-eight Pawnees and twenty-six Otoes; they were also forced to make reparation. The government at this time was making heroic efforts to police the entire west along the leading trails, but found it a difficult task, owing to the cunning and alertness of the Indians. On the Arkansas river, alone, in 1848, were stationed five hundred soldiers. Along the Platte were six hundred soldiers. The method of the Indians was, by a sudden dash on horseback, amid a great noise, to stampede the cattle and horses of the military trains and of the emigrants. The Indians were cunning enough to stampede often the horses or cattle even of the army detachments. It is recorded as a fact that, during the years 1846—50, they thus obtained so much plunder, they for a time stopped the attacks of their own accord. Fitzpatrick warned the government that, owing to the great emigration to the newly acquired lands of New Mexico, California and Oregon, numerous attacks might be expected from all the tribes along the various trails. He declared that nothing would stop the attacks except a large military force. Hundreds of small attacks continued to be reported from all parts of the overland trails. This meant in part that the Indians resented the expeditions of the whites through their country as a violation of existing treaties. They had been taught to believe that the timber, grass, water, buffalo, deer, etc., were their property; and accordingly demanded compensation therefor from the emigrant trains, and caused trouble if it was not forthcoming.

In 1849, upon the creation of the department of the interior, the bureau of Indian affairs was incorporated therewith, supervisory and appellate powers being lodged with the secretary of war. The commissioner of Indian affairs had reported adversely to this step, upon the following grounds: 1. The duties were too great to be assumed by the secretary of war; 2. The step would necessitate a large standing army; 3. It meant perpetual war with the Indians; 4. Already after seventeen years of trial, the war department had failed to control the Indians; 5. It meant the destruction of the Indians; 6. The war department and the Indians were incompatible; 7. The transfer was offensive to the ndians and injurious to the whites; 8. The cost would be greatly increased.

Upon assuming the governorship of Minnesota territory, Mr. Ramsey made an elaborate report on the tribes living there. The Sioux and the Chippewas and their relatives were the leading, and almost the only, tribes. They were constantly at war and one of the principal objects of Governor Ramsey's administration was to establish peace between them. Here, as in the Indian territory, large reservations were set apart for the Sioux and the Chippewas and guaranteed to them in perpetuity much the same as was done with other tribes in the Indian territory. Minnesota thus came to have almost an Indian territory of its own.

The usual objects sought at the Indian treaties were the following: 1. An acknowledgment of the sovereignty of the United States; 2. The right of the government to establish roads and military posts in the Indian country; 3. Peace between the various tribes and between the tribes and the United States;

4. The restoration of captives and of all stolen property; 5. A liberal supply of presents for the grass, timber, buffaloes, etc., on the Indian lands; 6. The cession of additional tracts of land; 7. The settlement on the tribes of fixed annuities; 8. Defining the boundaries between the various tribes and between them and the United States. Of this character was the famous treaty of 1851 at Fort Laramie with the Cheyennes, Arapahoes, Crows, Assiniboines, Gros Ventres, Mandans, Arickarees, and others. It was particularly agreed that the whites should have the right to cross the Indian lands.

In 1852 it was estimated by the Commissioner of Indian Affairs that there were five thousand white people wrongfully on the Sioux lands west of the Mississippi: they refused to obey the orders of the commissioner to vacate, expecting an early purchase by the government. Such an occupancy was almost invariably followed sooner or later by an Indian war, at an enormous expense to the government. The pioneers actually shaped the Indian policy of the country. When they were murdered for their unlawful acts, the government crushed the Indians, and then forced from them the tract desired by the lawbreakers. Such a policy, if it can properly be called by so dignified a name, was unworthy of this great country, and cannot be read without shame.

In 1854 the killing of a stray Mormon cow near Fort Laramie by a band of Sioux, and the refusal of the Indians to surrender the man who killed her, led to a conflict between about thirty soldiers under Lieutenant Grattan and the Indians, during which the entire party of whites was overwhelmed and butchered. This was really the start of a long and bloody Indian war. A government keel-boat loaded with supplies for the Crows, was attacked by the Blackfeet on the Teregue river and several persons were killed. The annihilation of Grattan's party seemed to fire all the tribes with the desire to shed blood. When Vaughan, agent to the Sioux, went to their villages with presents, Red Leaf, a chief, cut open in a rage the bags of presents and scattered the contents over the ground. Even the life of the agent was in danger. The Blackfeet refused to receive their annuities, and began the steady commission of hostile acts. The Cheyennes were very independent and insolent, one of their chiefs going so far as to demand one thousand white women as wives for the warriors of his tribe. J. W. Whitfield, agent at Fort Laramie, was in the storm center of the rising cyclone. The presence of the troops to guard the emigrant trains, the utter disregard for the

Indians' rights, and the construction of posts and roads, seemed to rouse the fighting instincts of the savages. Earnest efforts to secure peace, particularly by the Stevens expedition, met with almost total failure. The Sioux were especially active in these hostilities, among other deeds killing a mail carrier. It was high time something was done to end the reign of terror in the West.

Finally, an army under Gen. W. S. Harney was sent in 1855 to crush the hostile bands. He advanced rapidly and surprised Little Thunder's camp on Blue Water creek. They were thought to be the same band that had slaughtered Lieutenant Grattan's party and killed the mail-carrier. With nine companies, General Harney struck the camp, killing eighty-six, wounding five, and capturing about seventy women and children, together with a large quantity of equippage and fifty ponies. Harney's loss was four killed and seven wounded. A few side expeditions and skirmishes closed the campaign. The operations of General Harney and his associates were succeeded by quiet in the West, all the agents concurring in the opinion that the Sioux and other hostiles had been taught a memorable lesson. At this time the northern superintendency embraced Minnesota and part of Wisconsin; the central the country from the Arkansas river north to the forty-ninth parallel; and the southwestern, the territory from the Arkansas south to Red river. As each territory was afterward created, it was constituted a separate superintendency. Dakota and Colorado superintendencies were established in 1861.

In 1857 occurred the Sioux outrages at Spirit Lake, Iowa. Inkpaduta's band killed and wounded over forty persons and took several women prisoners. Major Williams, sent against them in the dead of winter with three companies of thirty-seven men each, failed to overhaul them. Captain Bee, with fifty regulars, also failed to catch them. All that could be done was to collect and bury the mutilated dead and care for the few survivors. Strange as it may seem, this Sioux band was never fittingly punished by the government.

In 1859 the Sioux of the Mississippi were engaged in almost open war among themselves. It was a contest between the "improvement" and the "blanket" divisions of the tribe; or between incipient civilization and persistent savagery. It was necessary to send troops there to establish order. The "improvement" Indians were those who were endeavoring to adopt the manners and occupations of the whites. They were bitterly opposed by the "blanket" Indians, who desired them to resume the savage customs. It was, therefore, an indirect attack upon the attempts of the government to civilize the tribe. The treaty of Fort Wise in February, 1861, secured to the United States from the Sioux and other tribes vast tracts of territory in the West.

Naturally, the Civil War stirred up all the Indian tribes. Envoys of both the North and the South went among them for the purpose of enlisting their services. Confederate envoys reached the Northwestern Indians from the British possessions, and were undoubtedly largely responsible for the Sioux outbreak in Minnesota in 1862. They likewise incited large factions of the five civilized tribes in Indian Territory to take up arms against the government. Settlers throughout the West were warned by the Indian agents to be on their guard. A sudden uprising of the Sioux in Minnesota was thought hardly possible. The commissioner of Indian affairs said, "After a careful examination of all the data which the Indian Bureau has been able to obtain, bearing upon the causes which produced the immediate outbreak, I am satisfied that the chief cause is to be found in the insurrection of the Southern States." Immediately after the Mason and Slidell affair, the northwestern Indians began their hostilities. Wampum was sent among them by Confederate and British emissaries. The Confederate authorities in paroling Union soldiers, required them to pledge not to take up arms against the Indians. The early disasters to the Federal arms were duly reported and embellished to the various tribes not only of Indian territory, but of all the West. The danger was realized, even in Minnesota, where the Sioux tribe, by levying upon the Missouri bands, could place fully ten thousand warriors in the field. The Confederate authorities well knew that a general outbreak along the whole northern and western border would necessitate the withdrawal of a large force from their immediate front for the purpose of holding the savages in check. This had been the tactics of the British during the War of 1812 and was now adopted by the Confederates, aided by the Canadians.

In Minnesota the first indications of Indian hostility were the acts of certain Sioux chiefs, who visited and harangued the various branches, advising war against the government. These chiefs had undoubtedly been bought or won over to the Confederate cause by emissaries sent among them, and they even visited other tribes, so that mainly through their influence a general attack was finally planned. At this time so apparent and imminent was the danger, that the agent of the Overland Mail Company in the northwest telegraphed that war with the Indians east of the Missouri river was close at hand. Finally the imps broke loose, as is fully narrated elsewhere. The promptness of Governor Ramsey and of General Sibley saved the state from still greater disaster.

But many of the savages were not conquered. They retreated into what is now the Dakotas and found lodgment among their kindred. Out of the uprising, however, grew one very important result: The whites of Minnesota demanded the permanent removal of the Sioux from the state, and included in the demand the Winnebagoes, who, as a tribe, had little to do with the out-break. So general and emphatic was this demand, that the government complied, upon the ground that, as the Sioux had violated the stipulations of the treaties by going to war, the United States was absolved from fulfilling its agreements to guar-antee the Indians their permanent reservation in Minnesota. Both the Sioux and the Winnebagoes, therefore, were assigned reservations in the present Dakotas. There is no doubt that, had the outbreak of the Sioux not been precipitated—had it been left to take its own course and fully to develop, many other tribes would have participated, and all the white settlements of the northwest would have been broken up, with a still more shocking display of indignity and destruction. The people would not trust the Sioux again, and demanded their removal.

The situation on Red river of the North was for a long time wholly dominated by the savages, who committed many hostile acts. The Chippewas committed many petty depredations, those of Chief Hole-in-the-Day being particularly menacing. The set-tlers of Kansas demanded the removal of the hostiles living there to Indian territory. Commissioner of Indian Affairs W. B. Dole recommended the diversion of the Sioux annuities to pay for the losses suffered by the Minnesota settlers. The government now realized the unwisdom of not having placed greater barriers between the Indians and the frontiers; but it was too late to rectify the omission.

The Federal authorities were not behind the Confederates in efforts to secure the friendship and assistance of the Indians. Out of two hundred and one Delaware warriors, one hundred and seventy enlisted in the Union army. Many other smaller tribes of the West did almost as well. A full regiment of Cherokees, though at first listening to Confederate promises and blandish-ments, finally joined the Union forces in a body. At first the Confederates had the best of the argument with the tribes of Indian territory. Their country was mainly south of Mason and

Dixon's line, and their location and pursuits united their interests with those of the South rather than of the North. In addition, and this was perhaps the strongest argument with them, they were told that the success of the Federal arms meant freedom to all the slaves held by the Indians, and they were many. Accordingly, probably at first a majority of the five civilized tribes (Cherokees, Choctaws, Chickasaws, Creeks, and Seminoles) became adherents of the Confederate cause. The result was internecine war throughout the Indian territory, amid scenes of arson, pillage, murder and ferocity unknown to any other section of the Union, except to Minnesota in 1862. Nearly all who remained loyal to the government suffered the total loss of their personal property and were driven from their burning homes across the border into Kansas under circumstances of intense cruelty. Several bloody battles between the two factions—Federal and Confederate—occurred. The former were defeated three successive times, and from six thousand to eight thousand of them, at the head of whom was the Creek chief O-poth-le-yo-ho-lo retreated in midwinter to the southern border of Kansas, where for a long time they were fed from government rations by General Hunter. An attempt to return them, made by the government with two regiments of soldiers and about two thousand armed Indians, was defeated. Later in the war, when the tide turned in favor of the Federal arms, they were returned to their ruined homes and desolate farms.

"A careful perusal of these reports (of the Indian superintendents and agents) and those made during the existence of the present rebellion will, I think, demonstrate that no portions of our people have suffered greater calamities, have met with more overwhelming disasters, or have more heroically battled for the common interests of the country, than have the loyal Indians within its limits."*

Particularly was this true of the Indian territory. The conflicts there between the Federal and Confederate factions were succeeded by a veritable reign of terror. Neither property nor life was safe. Unscrupulous white men invaded the territory and drove off all the stock they could find. The commissioner of Indian affairs estimated that in four years the five civilized tribes lost three hundred thousand head of cattle; that the Cherokees alone suffered the loss of stock to the value of two million dollars, and that all the tribes lost stock worth four million dol-

---

* From the report of W. P. Dole, Commissioner of Indian Affairs, 1863.

lars. At the close of the war, the whole territory was a scene of almost unparalleled desolation, from which it required many years to recover.

When the war ended the most important question arose as to what should be done with the Indians who had joined the rebellion, fought against the government, and violated the treaties by which they held tenures to their lands. It was shown that, at first and for a long time John Ross and others had counseled neutrality on the part of the Indians; but had been practically forced to take up arms against the government by the pressure, proximity and persistence of the Confederate envoys. It was argued that, as the Indians, by fighting against the government, had forfeited their rights under the various treaties, it was right and proper to dispossess them of their lands. Great pressure was brought to bear by home-seekers with this argument as a bludgeon. A new territory of the United States was projected from the Indian country. But congress refused to take the step demanded. In accordance with a generous and pacific policy the Indians were merely required, 1st, to enter into new treaties; 2d, to bear thereafter more of the responsibility of government; 3d, to abandon slavery forever; 4th, to cede part of their lands for the use of other tribes; 5th, to submit to consolidation under one government. They were promised protection from the encroachments of the whites.

The Sioux of the Upper Missouri were not associated with the Sioux of Minnesota in the massacre of 1862, but nevertheless were insolent and defiant. They complained that the protection promised them by General Harney in 1855 had not been given, in consequence of which they had suffered severely from the depredations of other tribes. So bitter were they against the government, that they refused to accept the presents set to them, and even murdered Chief Bears Rib for siding with the government agent. The hostile majority forced the friendly minority to join their ranks. They scattered and were guilty of many barbarous acts against the western settlers. It was estimated that fully one-fourth of the whites living in what is now Dakota fled beyond the borders of the territory. They expected to see in the spring of 1863 a repetition of the horrors of 1862 in Minnesota. General Sully was once more sent against them, and although he managed to save the state from a general massacre, he was unable to crush the savages owing to the rapidity of their movements and the skill with which they conducted their marches. Acting Governor Hutchinson urgently requested that the whole force under General Sully should be stationed in Dakota territory during the winter of 1863–4. He pointed out that the unconquered hostiles from Minnesota had fled into Dakota, where already from twenty-five thousand to forty thousand of their realtives were on the point of a general outbreak, and that thus far the savages of the northwest had not yet been fittingly chastised. The expedition of General Sibley in 1863, in pursuit of the Sioux, did not accomplish as much as had been hoped; because the savages scattered and could not concentrate for a general engagement, though they were defeated in several smaller movements.

"I believe the battles recently fought by General Sibley and General Sully to be but the beginning of the war with the Indians of the Northwest. I believe an expedition against the Indians next year (1864) will be required and even more necessary than the one this year. These hostile tribes must be conquered and must be compelled to make new treaties before there will be any safety to the white men within this superintendency."*

In the summer of 1865 General Sully conducted an army against the Indians north and east of the Missouri river. They scattered and avoided him. He learned that one of the leading chiefs of the hostiles was Sitting Bull, who became famous, or rather infamous, a few years later. General Sully marched to the vicinity of Devil's lake, Mouse river, Fort Berthold and other points, but did not accomplish as much as had been hoped. He learned that the hostiles within fifty miles of Fort Berthold could put in the field ten thousand armed warriors. It was necessary, therefore, to consider with great care the probable results of an encounter with such a formidable force.

In the Colorado superintendency, the Cheyennes, Arapahoes, Comanches, Kiowas, Utahs, Utes and others took up the hatchet and committed many bloody deeds. The guilty bands were small, moved quickly, and concealed themselves in the mountain fastnesses. The emigrant trails for two hundred miles were the scenes of numerous massacres, and the Indian villages reveled in the plunder captured. It was estimated that two or three million dollars' worth of personal property was thus captured by the hostiles. In the summer of 1864, the savages broke loose with redoubled ferocity, whereupon Governor Evans called for and raised a regiment of volunteers, which he divided and sent to many exposed points. After the bands had been cut in pieces a few times, the chiefs sued for peace, but were turned over to the

* Communication of Acting Governor Hutchinson, Yankton, September 23, 1863.

military authorities by the governor. General Curtis thought they should be given greater punishment.

The tribes of the central superintendency—Pawnees, Omahas, Otoes, Missouris, Iowas, Sacs and Foxes of Missouri and Mississippi, Kickapoos, Pottawatomies, Chippewas of the West, Munsees, Kansas, Miamis, Weas, Kaskaskias, Peorias, Piankeshaws, Delawares, Wyandots, and Shawanese, numbering in all about thirteen thousand—remained in the main faithful to the Union and throughout the war were comparatively quiet on their reservations. Many of their warriors enlisted in the Federal service.

The Civil War had no sooner ended that the government sent commissioners to nearly all the western tribes for the purpose of concluding new treaties with them and binding them to peace. Though the commission succeeded beyond their expectations, war was resumed by nearly all of the tribes within a few months after their departure. It was now the custom for large numbers to band together for the avowed purpose of breaking up many of the government posts. This step was caused by the act of the military authorities in taking possession of the Powder river country and in building Forts Phil Kearney, Reno, and C. F. Smith within the Indian country, without their consent, against their protests, and in violation of existing treaties. A bloody war followed, beginning with the slaughter of Fetterman's command in December, 1866. Ninety-six men, sent out to protect a train near Fort Phil Kearney, were ambushed and slain.

In 1865 the Cheyennes strenuously objected to the construction of a military road on Smoky Hill river. Two years later a commission sent to the Indian country by the president to learn the reason of the objections reported that the opening of the road from Fort Laramie to Montana and the passage of emigrants miners, and settlers through the Indian country were the causes of the hostilities. The march of a large body of troops through their country in July, 1866, was regarded by the savages as a declaration of war. It was demanded that the road be abandoned and the soldiers be sent from the Indian country. The Chivington affair, which was partly justified, drove many to join the hostiles. In this emergency General Hancock was sent to the Powder river country in 1866 with a large force of infantry, cavalry, artillery and a pontoon train. Against the protests of the Indian agent, he finally destroyed the large Cheyenne village of Chief Roman Nose, situated about thirty-five miles from Fort Larned. The Cheyennes retaliated by taking the war-path and in the end

killing a total of about three hundred soldiers and citizens and
destroying several million dollars' worth of public and private
property. In 1868 the Cheyennes were guilty of shocking barbarities on Saline and Solomon rivers in Kansas. The expedition against them under Forsyth was only partly successful.
In Montana Major Baker struck a camp of hostile Piegans on
Maria's river and killed one hundred and seventy-three of them,
among whom were many women and children.

It had been realized for many years by the commissioner of
Indian affairs that the reservation system was destined in the
end to prove a total failure. It was seen that surrounding the
reservations with white settlers meant at no distant day the total
destruction of wild game and the constant association of the two
races. The Indians were sure to fall a prey to whisky and the
wiles of sharpers. It had come to be generally thought by the
government authorities that the only remedy was the allotment
in severalty of the Indian lands and the requirement that the
Indians should work for a livelihood. Steps in this direction had
been taken by the government may years before; but had progressed not very far with the Western tribes.

Previous to the Civil War, the government did not have a
well-defined, consistent, comprehensive and harmonious Indian
policy. A usufruct right, or right of occupancy by the Indian
tribes, had been recognized by the highest court ever since the
foundation of the government, and they had been treated as independent sovereignties as well as dependent wards, which extraordinary treatment was the first serious mistake. In spite of their
recognized rights, they had been forced by the pressure of the
home-seekers to surrender from time to time tracts that had been
solemnly guaranteed to them in previous treaties. The incongru-
ity and inefficiency of the government's course became sharply
marked with the passage of time. "From a glance at the history
of our relations with the Indians, it will appear that we have been
governed by the course of events rather than by the adoption of
a well-settled policy."*

"The wonderful influx of population into Colorado and the
subsequent events, indicates the extent of protection afforded.
The white man in his greed for gain robbed them of their homes
and hunting grounds, and when they dared to complain found
justification only in the heartless and brutal maxim, 'An Indian
has no rights which the white man is bound to respect:' a senti-

---

*From the report of the Commissioner of Indian Affairs, April, 1864.

ment in which the government quietly acquiesced. . . . The testimony of some of the highest military officers of the United States is on record to the effect that in our Indian wars, almost without exception, the first aggressions have been made by the white man, and the assertion is supported by every civilian of reputation who has studied the subject. . . . The history of these Indians, since first brought into treaty stipulations with the United States, is one of almost unmitigated wrongs endured. In peace they have been the frequent victims of murderers and marauders and the constant prey of traders and agents. In war their own barbarities have, on some occasions, been more than emulated by their white enemies. . . . The United States first creates the fiction that a few thousand savages stand in the position of equality as to capacity, power and right of negotiation with a great civilized nation. They next proceed to impress upon the savages, with all the forms of treaty and the solemnity of parchment, signatures and seals, the preposterous idea that they are the owners in fee of the fabulous tracts of country over which their nomadic habits have led them or their ancestors to roam. The title becomes thus settled; they purchase and promise payment for a portion of territory, and further bind themselves in the most solemn manner to protect and defend the Indians in the possession of some immense remainder defined by boundaries in the treaty; thus becoming, as it were, *particeps criminis* with the savages in resisting the 'encroachments' of covilization and the progressive movement of the age. Having entered into this last-named impracticable obligation, the first step of its non-performance becomes the occasion of disgraceful and expensive war to subdue their victims to the point of submission to another treaty. And so the tragedy of war and the farce of treaty have been enacted again and again, each time with increasing shame to the nation. . . . Probably all will agree that the rapid development of our western frontiers, by which the Indians have been driven from one reservation to another, and dishonest management and execution of treaties by bad agents, have caused most of our Indian wars."*

The commissioners reported that, 1st, the Indians should be regarded as wards and not as independent sovereignties; 2d, they should all be gathered in Indian territory; 3d, every proceeding should be placed in the hands of honest men; 4th, homes in sev-

* From the report of the special commission to the Indians, appointed by President Grant in 1867, William Welsh, of Philadelphia, being chairman, and Felix Brunot, of Pittsburg, secretary.

eralty should be the ultimate object; 5th, the expense of this course would not exceed one-fifth that of a hostile course. This report became known as "Grant's Indian Policy." It contemplated good treatment for small or peaceable tribes and severe treatment for big or hostile tribes. It was also called the "Peace Policy," with the military department to administer the punishment, not as war, but as discipline. Indians who left their reservations were to be punished, and all were required to live on some reservation.

Owing to the fact that the Sioux claimed and occupied Powder river and Big Horn valleys, the Big Horn Mining Company was not permitted to enter that section, as such a step would be followed by certain war. The construction of the Central Pacific and the Northern Pacific railways was regarded by the Sioux as an infringement of their rights. At this time the Sioux under Red Cloud were mostly south of Fort Laramie. Sitting Bull with a large following separated from the others and went to Montana; he was an avowed hostile. In October, 1870, Colonel Mackenzie severely chastised the Comanches on McClellan creek in Indian territory, killing twenty-three and capturing one hundred and twenty-four.

The many treaties with the Indians concluded from 1867 to 1871 were not ratified by congress. On March 3, 1871, that body declared "that hereafter no Indian nation or tribe within the territory of the United States shall be acknowledged or recognized as an independent nation, tribe, or power, with whom the United States may contract by treaty." This was the doom of the Indian treaty system. Thus were the practices of nearly a hundred years overthrown. It meant a new order of affairs, with many difficult problems to solve. In theory there had been over sixty-five independent nations within the borders of the United States. Now all was changed. "The bounty of the government has pauperized them (the Indians), and in some cases has tended to brutalize more than to civilize." Cash annuities were declared to be wrong, because they went in advance to saloon-keepers and sharpers. The government had never secured the Indians, either in life or in property. The policy had been a utopian dream coupled with unpardonable stupidity.

"It belongs not to a sanguine but to a sober view of the situation, that three years will see the alternative of war eliminated from the Indian question and the most powerful and hostile bands of today thrown in entire helplessness on the mercy of the government. Indeed, the progress of two years more, if not of another summer, on the Northern Pacific railway, will of itself completely solve the great Sioux problem, and leave the ninety thousand Indians ranged between the two transcontinental lines as incapable of resisting the government as are the Indians of New York or Massachusetts. Columns moving north from the Union Pacific and south from the Northern Pacific would crush the Sioux and their confederates as between the upper and nether millstones, while the rapid movement of troops along the northern line would prevent the escape of the savages when hard pressed, into the British possessions, which have heretofore afforded a convenient refuge on the approach of a military expedition.* "Except under extraordinary provocation, or in circumstances not at all to be apprehended, it is not probable that as many as five hundred Indian warriors will ever again be mustered at one point for a fight; and with the conflicting interest of the different tribes and the occupation of the intervening country by advancing settlements, such an event as a general Indian war can never again occur in the United States."†

On the heels of these rosy views, the Sioux were preparing for war on a large scale. The Red Cloud, Spotted Tail and Sitting Bull bands were independent, insolent, and guilty of many depredations in 1873-4. The discovery of gold in the Black Hills, and the flocking there of many miners, despite danger from the Indians, occasioned the intense hostility of the Sioux and their allies. Regardless of consequences, the Sioux, Arapahoes, Cheyennes, Kiowas, Comanches, and others refused to stay on their reservations. The invasion of their country by miners and emigrants roused them to the point of war. When the army of General Custer reconnoitered the Black Hill country in 1874, the indignation of the Indians was complete. Many expeditions of miners were struck by the Indians and turned back. The withdrawal of the army and the checking of the expeditions, served for a time to prevent any general movement of hostility. It became clear, however, that the Black Hills would have to be purchased to meet the demands of miners and settlers, because new discoveries of gold had set all the West aflame. Notwithstanding that soldiers were posted on all the trails approaching the hills, over one thousand miners passed in during the year 1875, and when once there promptly organized for mutual protection.

The peace measures from 1868 to 1875 were productive of

---

* From the report of the Commissioner of Indian Affairs, 1872.
† From the report of the Commissioner of Indian Affairs, 1873.

good results, regardless of the invasion of the Indians' rights;
but during 1874 and 1875 it was necessary to use compulsion to
keep the Indians on their reservations; indeed, these attempts
were only partly successful. Strong Sioux and other bands still
remained out. So great became the pressure of the miners, that
the government ordered a survey of the hills, which was conducted under an armed escort commanded by Colonel Dodge.

"From the first settlement of the country by white men until a
comparatively recent period, the Indians have been constantly
driven westward from the Atlantic. A zigzag, ever-varying line,
more or less definitely marked, extending from Canada to the
Gulf of Mexico, and always slowly moving west, has been known
as the "frontier" or "border." Along this border has been an
almost incessant struggle, the Indians to retain and the whites to
get possession; the war being broken by periods of occasional
and temporary peace, which usually followed treaties whereby
the Indians agreed to surrender large tracts of their lands. This
peace would continue until the lands surrendered had been occupied by whites, when the pressure of emigration would again
break over the border, and the Indians, by force or treaty, be
compelled to surrender another portion of his cherished hunting
grounds. . . . Toward the close of the first half of this
century the tide of emigration and adventure swept even the
frontier away and rushed across the continent. Throughout the
vast regions of the West, the adventurous, grasping Anglo-Saxon
race is dominant and in possession of the fairest and richest portions of the land. Except in the Indian territory and perhaps
Dakota, the white exceeds the Indian population. No new hunt-
ing-ground remains, and the civilization or the utter destruction
of the Indians is inevitable. The next twenty-five years are to
determine the fate of a race. If they cannot be taught, and taught
very soon, to accept the necessity of the situation and begin in
earnest to provide for their own wants by labor in civilized pursuits they are destined to speedy extinction." *

It was now seen that the laws of Indian territory would have
to be changed to meet the demands of better order. The consolidation of reservations and the allotment in severalty of the Indian
lands, became serious questions. Every reservation began to be
threatened with invasion by the irrepressible settler or home-
seeker. Many thousands of whites were permanently established
in the Indian territory upon one pretext or another that could

* From the report of the Commissioner of Indian Affairs, 1876.

not be gainsaid by the government. The ultimate occupation of every reservation by the whites was seen to be inevitable. The only course that would prevent the utter extinction of the Indian was seen to be allotment in severalty and in perpetuity.

The long-threatened Sioux war at last broke forth in the spring of 1876. Armies under Generals Terry, Crook, and Custer invaded the Powder river and Big Horn river basins. General Crook captured and burnt the village of Chief Crazy Horse, a North Cheyenne. Later, he fought another severe battle in the Rosebud valley, but was partly checked by the savages and obliged to send for reinforcements. Then soon followed the complete annihilation of the small army of General Custer on the Little Big Horn. Colonels Miles, Otis, Reno, Gibbons, and others had sharp engagements with small bands. The cause of the war was revealed by the demand of the Indians at all the conferences that the whites should at once leave the Indian country. In October five principal chiefs were surrendered as hostages; this was the beginning of the end. But the crafty Sitting Bull managed to escape. All the Indians at the reservations were disarmed. During the winter of 1876–7 many small engagements occurred. In the spring of 1877, nearly all the bands surrendered and were placed on their reservations.

In 1874 congress appropriated $300,000 to be used in an experiment of enforced civilization among 2,000 or 3,000 Kiowas, Comanches, and Cheyennes who had surrendered; two years later the plan was seen to be impracticable and was abandoned. The rumor in 1876 that the Indian bureau was soon to be transferred to the war department caused great bitterness among the western tribes. In 1877 the commissioner of Indian affairs recommended, 1st, a strong Indian police force; 2d, a code of Indian laws; 3d, allotment in severalty; 4th, common schools; 5th, christian teachers; 6th, economy; 7th, the steady concentration of all Indians on reservations.

The Nez Perces war of 1877 was caused by the encroachments of the whites on the Indian lands in Wyoming and Montana. Chief Joseph headed the war party. Generals Howard, Gibbons and Miles pursued them, fought several battles and finally crushed them. During this year occurred the Cheyenne raid under Chief Dull Knife across Kansas. They murdered over forty women and children, amid appalling barbarities. Major Thornburg severely chastised a band of Utes under Captain Jack in Colorado in 1878, for various depredations, but was himself killed.

I—30

Many important changes succeeded the Sioux war of 1876–7. The Indians were forced to stay on their reservations and were largely disarmed. The loss of the buffalo was a blessing in disguise to the Indians. They were forced to go to work or starve. The new order of affairs was followed by excellent results. Soon many on the reservations were engaged in work. In 1878 the supplies for the reservations were carried by the Indians in wagons furnished by the government. The act of May, 1878, provided for the establishment of Indian police on the reservations; and in 1882 a court of Indian offenses was provided to break up various offensive tribal customs.

Over four million pounds were hauled by the Sioux in 1878–79. By the last of 1879 the Indians had been given one thousand three hundred and sixty-nine wagons and two thousand five hundred sets of double harness. Already many "squawmen," "cattlemen," "lessees" and others were invading every part of Indian Territory. In 1877 Cheyenne and Arapahoe teamsters hauled three hundred thousand pounds, and in 1879, over one million pounds— all in wagons furnished by the government. About the year 1877 the government began to furnish the tribes with stock cattle. From July, 1879, to November, 1880, there were thus distributed ten thousand two hundred and eighty-three head.

It was observed in 1881 that over one million dollars were being spent annually to feed and clothe the Indians where no treaty required such an expenditure. It was determined that this should be stopped, and the Indians be made to work. By November, 1882, there had been furnished the Indians three thousand five hundred and fifty-eight wagons and the necessary sets of double harness to go therewith. By this time the tribal system in Indian territory was fast disappearing. What was called the "Oklahoma Colony" gave the government much trouble from 1881 to 1884. Beginning about 1880–1 the government began an elaborate survey of all the Indian reservations. This necessitated large expenditures by various commissions and escorts, and was the preliminary to ultimate allotment of the Indian lands in severalty. It was seen that a large body of land in Indian territory was yet unassigned to any tribe. It was demanded that this should be thrown into market, and the creation of Oklahoma territory soon followed.

In February, 1887, the general allotment act became a law. This was one of the most momentous steps ever taken in Indian legislation, but had been foreshadowed by the law of 1871. It was preceded by the Indian crimes act of 1885, prior to which an Indian committing offenses against the person or property of another Indian on a reservation could not be punished, because no court held jurisdiction. The intrusion on Indian lands continued, the intruders growing rich at the expense of the simple-minded and unbusinesslike natives. Immense numbers of cattle, including stock furnished by the government, were boldly stolen by unscrupulous whites from the reservations. By private contracts the "cattlemen," as they are called, controlled immense tracts of Indian lands and practically dominated, not only the government agents, but public affairs on the reservations as well.

In 1889 a united district court was established at Muskogee, Indian territory. In 1888-9 the Oklahoma country was cleared of Indian claims by purchase. Many allotments on almost every reservation were in progress after 1887. The new plan embraced the following features: 1st, ownership in severalty; 2d, obliteration of tribal relations; 3d, abandonment of the agency system; 4th, full citizenship; 5th, education; 6th, proper treatment by whites; 7th, christian influences. As early as 1819 congress took steps "to prevent the decline and extinction of the Indian tribes," by appropriating $10,000 annually to be expended by the President in teaching the Indians to read and write. This was the foundation of the Indian educational system in the West. As early as 1817 congress provided that, under proper circumstances, an Indian could became a citizen: this law was improved at later dates. The allotment act of 1887 was followed immediately by the admission of ten thousand one hundred twenty-two Indians to citizenship, as against three thousand seventy-two prior to that date.

In the summer of 1890 the Sioux of the Pine Ridge and Rosebud agencies became greatly excited over what was called "ghost dancing." It was heralded that their Messiah was about to appear on earth to redress their many wrongs. By October an outbreak seemed imminent. The arrest of Sitting Bull and other chiefs was ordered with the hope of stopping the tide of disorder. In November it was learned that the Indians were arming, and trouble was momentarily expected. General Brooke, in command of a strong force, was sent to Pine Ridge and arrived there on November 20. A squad of Indian police, sent to arrest Sitting Bull at his village, encountered resistence, during which that distinguished individual was shot twice and killed. The police were reinforced by Captain Fechet's command. The campaign practically terminated with the bloody engagement at Wounded Knee, where eighty-four Indian men and boys, forty-four squaws, and eighteen children were killed and many were wounded. The troops lost twenty-five killed and thirty-five wounded. The surviving Indians scattered to the four winds. A few sharp skirmishes terminated the campaign.

In 1892 the old method of paying the tribal annuities to the chiefs was changed to that of paying it to the heads of families; the former method had been in vogue since 1847. It had been the old practice to give live cattle to the Indians to be pursued and shot down by them as they were in the habit of shooting the buffaloes. This practice was changed. The custom of issuing rations was also modified. In 1891 the sum of two thousand five hundred dollars was appropriated to pay matrons for teaching Indian women the art of housekeeping. The next year, so promising were the results, five thousand dollars was thus appropriated, and nine tribes were instructed by them.

In recent years much trouble has been experienced from bands which left their reservations and committed various unlawful depredations. The trouble with Colerow's band of Utes in Colorado was due to their refusal to go to Utah and occupy a new reservation. In 1894 Chief Crow Flies High and his band of Gros Ventres left their reservation, but were returned without serious difficulty. In 1895 the Bannock Indians of the Jackson Hole country in Wyoming left their reservation, and many of them were killed before peace was restored.

In late years among the important Indian questions are the following: The leasing of Indian lands to whites; irrigation on reservations; industrial schools; teaching Indian women housekeeping; improvements in agriculture; exhibits of Indian products; Indian homestead rights; allotment in severalty; better laws and courts; extension of the Indian police system; the enrollment of tribal members; surveying lands and incorporating towns; Indians not to be permitted to disburse moneys; enrollment of freedmen; the abandonment of tribal laws, courts, customs, etc.

The act of March, 1893, created a board of Indian commissioners to the five civilized tribes. They were instructed to enter into negotiations with the several nations of Indian Territory for the purpose of carrying into effect more fully the allotment act, "it being the express determination of congress to bring about such changes as would enable the ultimate creation of a Territory of the United States with a view of the admission of the same as a State of the Union." In 1898 is was provided by the Curtis act that, as ownership in common had proved under modern conditions a lamentable failure, congress should undertake formally to administer upon the estate of the five civilized tribes so as to allot them lands in severalty upon a valuation basis. It was observed with great concern that the children among 300,000 white people in Indian territory were wholly without educational facilities. The rations, reservations, blankets, long hair, dances, feasts of dog, etc., are doomed to an early disappearance. The reason is shown by the following pleasing facts: In 1877 the government appropriated $20,000 for the support of Indian schools, and in 1903 appropriated for the same purpose $3,531,220. The interest on the Indian trust fund amounted in 1902 to $1,510,248. The total amount paid them in 1902 including this interest, the gratuities, under treaty agreements, from the proceeds of labor, Indian moneys, etc., was $5,419,106.